A Handbook on the Jewish Roots of the Gospels

Edited by
Craig A. Evans
and David Mishkin

HENDRICKSON
PUBLISHERS

an imprint of Hendrickson Publishing Group

A Handbook on the Jewish Roots of the Gospels

© 2021 by Craig A. Evans and David Mishkin

Published by Hendrickson Publishers
an imprint of Hendrickson Publishing Group
Hendrickson Publishers, LLC
P. O. Box 3473
Peabody, Massachusetts 01961-3473
www.hendricksonpublishinggroup.com

ISBN 978-1-68307-342-0

Olive branch by Malerapaso via Getty Images. Hand painted backdrop by Draganab via Getty Images.

Cover design by Karol Bailey.

Printed in the United States of America

First Printing—January 2022

Contents

Acknowledgments

We are thankful to Hendrickson Publishers for their encouragement regarding this new book. As with our first volume, *A Handbook on the Jewish Roots of the Christian Faith*, this present work was very much a team effort.

It began just as the world was first hearing of the coronavirus—a surprising situation that presented various obstacles for the next year and a half. As a result, several people who had agreed to contribute were not able to complete their articles and some new authors joined late in the game. But the staff at Hendrickson was with us all the way; from Jonathan Kline's enthusiasm for the project, to the hands-on editorial assistance from Patricia Anders and Marco Antunes. Deadlines are often hectic, but this project presented unique challenges that were met with grace and professionalism by the editorial team.

The authors (listed in full on the following pages) of this volume are an international group of scholars, with a core group from Israel College of the Bible in Netanya, Israel. Ultimately, it is these contributors who deserve much of the credit for this book.

Craig A. Evans
Houston Baptist University

David Mishkin
Israel College of the Bible

Contributors

Kyung S. Baek (PhD, University of Manchester), Trinity Western University

Craig L. Blomberg (PhD, University of Aberdeen), Denver Seminary

Darrell L. Bock (PhD, University of Aberdeen), Dallas Theological Seminary

Golan Broshi (DMin, Dallas Theological Seminary), Israel College of the Bible

Michael L. Brown (PhD, New York University), FIRE School of Ministry

Carsten Claussen (ThD, University of Munich), Elstal Theological Seminary

Craig A. Evans (PhD, Claremont Graduate School; DHabil, Karoli Gaspar Reformatus University), Houston Baptist University

Jeffrey Gibbs (PhD, Union Theological Seminary in Virginia), Emeritus, Concordia Seminary

Mitch Glaser (PhD, Fuller Theological Seminary), Chosen People Ministries

Daniel M. Gurtner (PhD, University of St Andrews), Centre for the Study of Judaism and Christianity in Antiquity, St Mary's University (London)

Sheila Gyllenberg (PhD, Bar Ilan University), Israel College of the Bible

Catherine Sider Hamilton (PhD, The University of St. Michael's College in the University of Toronto), Wycliffe College at the University of Toronto

Noam Hendren (ThM, Dallas Theological Seminary), Former Lecturer, Israel College of the Bible

Cristian S. Ile (PhD, Queens University Belfast), Israel College of the Bible

David Instone-Brewer (PhD, University of Cambridge), Tyndale House

Brian J. Kinzel (PhD candidate, Bar Ilan University), Israel College of the Bible

Chris Kugler (PhD, University of St Andrews), Houston Baptist University

Oliver Marjot (PhD candidate, University of Cambridge)

David Mishkin (PhD, University of Pretoria), Israel College of the Bible

Russell Morton (ThD, Lutheran School of Theology at Chicago), adjunct at Ashland Theological Seminary and Asbury Theological Seminary

Hannah E. Pachal (MA, Denver Seminary), Hill City Church, Arvada, Colorado

Seth D. Postell (PhD, Gateway Seminary), Israel College of the Bible

Charles L. Quarles (PhD, Mid-America Baptist Theological Seminary), Southeastern Baptist Theological Seminary

Michael Rydelnik (DMiss, Trinity Evangelical Divinity School), Moody Bible Institute

Eckhard J. Schnabel (PhD, University of Aberdeen), Gordon-Conwell Theological Seminary

Jim R. Sibley (PhD, Southwestern Baptist Theological Seminary), Israel College of the Bible

Sisi Soref (MA, Israel College of the Bible), Israel College of the Bible

Ryan E. Stokes (PhD, Yale University), Carson-Newman University

Mark Strauss (PhD, University of Aberdeen), Bethel Seminary

R. Alan Streett (PhD, University of Wales), Criswell College

Andreas Stutz (PhD in progress, Lancaster Bible College), Israel College of the Bible

David L. Turner (PhD, Hebrew Union College, Cincinnati), Emeritus, Grand Rapids Theological Seminary

Michael J. Wilkins (PhD, Fuller Theological Seminary), Talbot School of Theology, Biola University

Abbreviations

General Abbreviations

ad loc.	*ad locum*, at the place discussed
BCE	before the Common Era
ca.	circa
CE	Common Era
CEB	Common English Bible
cf.	*confer*, compare
ch(s).	chapter(s)
CSB	Christian Standard Bible
d.	died
DSS	Dead Sea Scrolls
e.g.	*exempli gratia*, for example
Eng.	English
esp.	especially
ESV	English Standard Version
et al.	*et alii*, and others
etc.	*et cetera*, and so forth, and the rest
f(f).	and the following one(s)
flor.	*floruit*, flourished
fol(s).	folio(s)
frag.	fragment
Gk.	Greek (referring to lexical forms, not translation)
GNB	Good News Bible
HCSB	Holman Christian Standard Bible
Heb.	Hebrew
i.e.	*id est*, that is
KJV	King James Version
Lat.	Latin
lit.	literally
LXX	Septuagint
MS(S)	manuscript(s)
MT	Masoretic Text
NA^{28}	*Novum Testamentum Graece*, Nestle-Aland, 28th ed.
NET	New English Translation
NIV	New International Version
n.p.	no place; no publisher; no page

NRSV	New Revised Standard Version
NT	New Testament
OT	Old Testament
𝔓	Papyrus
par(r).	parallel(s)
pl.	plural
P. Oxy.	Papyrus Oxyrhynchus
RSV	Revised Standard Version
§	section, paragraph
SBLGNT	The Greek New Testament: SBL Edition
s.v.	*sub verbo*, under the word
UBS⁵	*The Greek New Testament*, United Bible Societies, 5th ed.
v(v).	verse(s)
viz.	*videlicet*, namely
x	times

Journals, Series, and Reference Works

AB	Anchor Bible
ABD	*Anchor Bible Dictionary*
ABR	Anchor Bible Reference Library
ACCS	Ancient Christian Commentary on Scripture
AJEC	Ancient Judaism and Early Christianity
ASJ	*Journal for the Association of Jewish Studies*
AnBib	Analecta Biblica
ANTC	Abingdon New Testament Commentaries
ANTF	Arbeiten zur neutestamentlichen Textforschung
ASMS	American Society of Missiology Series
AYB	Anchor Yale Bible
AYBRL	Anchor Yale Bible Reference Library
BBR	*Bulletin for Biblical Research*
BDAG	Danker, Frederick W., Walter Bauer, William F. Arndt, and F. Wilbur Gingrich. 2000. *Greek-English Lexicon of the New Testament and Other Early Christian Literature*. 3rd ed. Chicago: University of Chicago Press.
BDB	Brown, Francis, S. R. Driver, and Charles A. Briggs. 2003. *A Hebrew and English Lexicon of the Old Testament*. Peabody, MA: Hendrickson [Boston: Houghton Mifflin, 1906].
BDF	Blass, Friedrich, Albert Debrunner, and Robert W. Funk. 1961. *A Greek Grammar of the New Testament and Other Early Christian Literature*. Chicago: University of Chicago Press.
BECNT	Baker Exegetical Commentary on the New Testament
BETL	Bibliotheca Ephemeridum Theologicarum Lovaniensium
BFCT	Beiträge zur Förderung christlicher Theologie
Bib	*Biblica*

BibInt	Biblical Interpretation Series
BibSem	*The Biblical Seminar*
BJRL	Bulletin of the John Rylands University Library of Manchester
BRLJ	The Brill Reference Library of Judaism
BN	*Biblische Notizen*
BTB	*Biblical Theology Bulletin*
BSac	*Bibliotheca Sacra*
BZNW	Beihefte zur Zeitschrift für die neutestamentliche Wissenschaft
CBQ	*Catholic Biblical Quarterly*
CC	Continental Commentaries
CurBR	*Currents in Biblical Research*
ConBNT	Coniectanea Neotestamentica or Coniectanea Biblica: New Testament Series
DCLS	Deuterocanonical and Cognate Literature Studies
DJD	Discoveries in the Judaean Desert
DJG	*Dictionary of Jesus and the Gospels.* 2013. Edited by Joel B. Green, Jeannine K. Brown, and Nicholas Perrin. 2nd ed. Downers Grove, IL: InterVarsity Press.
DNTB	*Dictionary of New Testament Background.* 2000. Edited by Craig A. Evans and Stanley E. Porter. Downers Grove, IL: InterVarsity Press.
DOTHB	*Dictionary of the Old Testament: Historical Books.* 2005. Edited by Bill T. Arnold and H. G. M. Williamson. Downers Grove, IL: InterVarsity Press.
EBC	The Expositor's Bible Commentary
ECL	Early Christianity and Its Literature
EKKNT	Evangelisch-katholischer Kommentar zum Neuen Testament
EJL	Early Judaism and Its Literature
ExpTim	*Expository Times*
FAT	Forschungen zum Alten Testament
HALOT	Koehler, Ludwig, Walter Baumgartner, and Johann J. Stamm. 1994–1999. *The Hebrew and Aramaic Lexicon of the Old Testament.* Translated and edited under the supervision of Mervyn E. J. Richardson. 4 vols. Leiden: Brill.
HBT	*Horizons in Biblical Theology*
HTR	*Harvard Theological Review*
HvTSt	*Hervormde teologiese studies*
ICC	International Critical Commentary
Int	*Interpretation*
ISBE	International Standard Bible Encyclopedia
ISBL	Indiana Studies in Biblical Literature
JASJ	*Journal of the Association of Jewish Studies*
JBL	*Journal of Biblical Literature*
JBLMS	Journal of Biblical Literature Monograph Series
JEPTA	*Journal of the European Pentecostal Association*
JETS	*Journal of the Evangelical Theological Society*

JHS	*Journal of Hebrew Scriptures*
JIBS	*Journal of Inductive Biblical Studies*
JJMJS	*Journal of the Jesus Movement in its Jewish Setting*
JJS	*Journal of Jewish Studies*
JNSL	*Journal of Northwest Semitic Languages*
JSHJ	*Journal for the Study of the Historical Jesus*
JSJSup	Journal for the Study of Judaism Supplement Series
JSNT	*Journal for the Study of the New Testament*
JSNTSup	Journal for the Study of the New Testament Supplement Series
JSOTSup	Journal for the Study of the Old Testament Supplement Series
JSP	*Journal for the Study of the Pseudepigrapha*
JSPSup	Journal for the Study of the Pseudepigrapha Supplement Series
JQR	*Jewish Quarterly Review*
JR	*Journal of Religion*
LCC	Library of Christian Classics
LNTS	The Library of New Testament Studies
MSJ	*The Master's Seminary Journal*
NAC	New American Commentary
NACSBT	New American Commentary Studies in Bible and Theology
NASB	New American Standard Bible
NCBC	New Century Bible Commentary
Neot	*Neotestamentica*
NETS	New English Translation of the Septuagint and the Other Greek Translations Traditionally Included under That Title
NIBC	New International Biblical Commentary
NIDNTT	Colin Brown, ed. 1975–1978. *New International Dictionary of New Testament Theology.* 4 vols. Grand Rapids: Zondervan.
NIDOTTE	Willem A. VanGemeren, ed. 1997. *New International Dictionary of Old Testament Theology and Exegesis.* 5 vols. Grand Rapids: Zondervan.
NICNT	New International Commentary on the New Testament
NICOT	New International Commentary on the Old Testament
NIGTC	New International Greek Testament Commentary
NovT	*Novum Testamentum*
NovTSup	Supplements to Novum Testamentum
NSBT	New Studies in Biblical Theology
NTM	New Testament Message
NTS	*New Testament Studies*
NTTS	New Testament Tools and Studies
NTTSD	New Testament Tools, Studies, and Documents
OBO	Orbis Biblicus et Orientalis
OBT	Overtures to Biblical Theology
PTL	*A Journal for Descriptive Poetics and Theory of Literature*
QD	Quaestiones Disputatae
RB	*Revue biblique*
RTR	*Reformed Theological Review*

SBEC	Studies in the Bible and Early Christianity
SBLRBS	Society of Biblical Literature Resources for Biblical Study
SBT	Studies in Biblical Theology
SHBC	Smyth & Helwys Bible Commentary
SJ	Studia Judaica
SP	Sacra Pagina
SNT	Studien zum Neuen Testament
SNTSMS	Society for New Testament Studies Monograph Series
SNTW	Studies of the New Testament and Its World
SSEJC	Studies in Scripture in Early Judaism and Christianity
TC	*A Journal of Biblical Textual Criticism*
TDNT	*Theological Dictionary of the New Testament.* 1964–1976. Edited by Gerhard Kittel and Gerhard Friedrich. Translated by Geoffrey W. Bromiley. 10 vols. Grand Rapids: Eerdmans.
TDOT	*Theological Dictionary of the Old Testament.* Edited by G. Johannes Botterweck and Helmer Ringgren. 1974–2006. Translated by John T. Willis et al. 8 vols. Grand Rapids: Eerdmans.
ThSt	Theologische Studiën
TJ	*Trinity Journal*
TNTC	Tyndale New Testament Commentaries
TOTC	Tyndale Old Testament Commentaries
TSAJ	Texte und Studien zum antiken Judentum
TynBul	*Tyndale Bulletin*
USQR	*Union Seminary Quarterly Review*
VT	*Vetus Testamentum*
WBC	Word Biblical Commentary
WTJ	*Westminster Theological Journal*
WUNT	Wissenschaftliche Untersuchungen zum Neuen Testament
ZECNT	Zondervan Exegetical Commentary on the New Testament

Ancient Sources

APOSTOLIC FATHERS

ATHANASIUS

Ep. fest.   *Epistulae festales (Festal Letters)*

AUGUSTINE

Quaest. Hept.   *Quaestiones in Heptateuchum (Questions on the Heptateuch)*

CLEMENT OF ALEXANDRIA

Paed.   *Paedagogus (Christ the Educator)*
Strom.   *Stromateis (Miscellanies)*

CLEMENT OF ROME

1 Clem.   1 Clement
2 Clem.   2 Clement

EPIPHANIUS

Pan.   *Panarion (Adversus haereses) (Refutation of All Heresies)*

EUSEBIUS

Hist. eccl.   *Historia ecclesiastica (Ecclesiastical History)*
Vita Const.   *Vita Constantini (Life of Constantine)*

IGNATIUS OF ANTIOCH

Ign. *Eph.*   *(To the Ephesians)*
Ign. *Magn.*   *(To the Magnesians)*
Ign. *Phld.*   *(To the Philadelphians)*
Ign. *Poly.*   *(To Polycarp)*
Ign. *Smyrn.*   *(To the Smyrnaeans)*
Ign. *Trall.*   *(To the Trallians)*

IRENAEUS

Haer.   *Adversus haereses (Elenchos) (Against Heresies)*

JEROME

Comm. Isa.   *Commentariorum in Isaiam libri XVIII*
Comm. Matt.   *Commentariorum in Matthaeum libri IV*
Epist.   *Epistulae*
Vir. ill.   *De viris illustribus (On Illustrious Men)*

JOHN CHRYSOSTOM

Hom. Matt.   *Homiliae in Matthaeum*

JULIUS AFRICANUS

Chron.   *Chronographiae*

JUSTIN MARTYR

1 Apol.   *Apologia i (First Apology)*
Dial.   *Dialogus cum Tryphone (Dialogue with Trypho)*

ORIGEN

Cels.   *Contra Celsum (Against Celsus)*
Comm. Jo.   *Commentarii in evangelium Joannis (Commentary on the Gospel of John)*
Princ.   *De principiis (Peri archōn) (First Principles)*

POLYCARP

Pol. *Phil.*   *(To the Philippians)*

TERTULLIAN

Adv. Jud.   *Adversus Judaeos*
Praescr.   *De praescriptione haereticorum*

THEODORET

Haer. fab.   *Haereticarum fabularum compendium (Compendium of Heretical Falsehoods)*

THEOPHILUS

Autol.   *Ad Autolycum (To Autolycus)*

DEAD SEA SCROLLS

1Q14	Pesher Micah
1Q28a	Rule of the Congregation (appendix a to 1QS)
1Q28b	Rule of the Congregation (appendix b to 1QS)
1Q35	Thanksgiving Hymns[b]
1QapGen ar	Genesis Apocryphon
1QH[a]	Thanksgiving Hymns[a]
1QIsa[a]	Isaiah[a]
1QIsa[b]	Isaiah[b]
1QM	War Scroll
1QpHab	Pesher Habakkuk
1QS	Rule of the Community
4Q17	4QExod-Lev[f]
4Q169	Pesher Nahum
4Q171	Pesher of Psalms 37 and 45
4Q174	Florilegium
4Q242	Prayer of Nabonidus
4Q246	Apocryphon of Daniel
4Q252	Pesher Genesis
4Q255–264	Manual of Discipline[a–j]
4Q265	Miscellaneous Rules
4Q285	Sefer ha-Milḥamah
4Q416	Instruction[b]
4Q418	Instruction[d]
4Q427–432	Thanksgiving Hymns[a–e]
4Q434	BarkhiNafshi[a]
4Q471b	Self-Glorification Hymn / *olim* Prayer of Michael
4Q491–496	War Scrolls[a–f]
4Q510	Songs of the Sage[a]
4Q511	Songs of the Sage[b]
4Q521	Messianic Apocalypse
7Q5	Mark 6:52–53? (disproven)
11Q5	Psalms Scroll
11Q11	Apocryphal Psalms
11Q13	Melchizedek
CD	Cairo Genizah copy of the Damascus Document

JEWISH HISTORY

JOSEPHUS

Ant.	*Jewish Antiquities*
J.W.	*Jewish War*

PHILO

Abr.	*De Abrahamo (On the Life of Abraham)*
Cher.	*De cherubim (On the Cherubim)*

Det.	*Quod deterius potiori insidari soleat (That the Worse Attacks the Better)*
Leg. 1, 2, 3	*Legum allegoriae* I, II, III *(Allegorical Interpretation* 1, 2, 3*)*
Mos. 1, 2	*De vita Mosis* I, II *(On the Life of Moses* 1, 2*)*
Opif.	*De opificio mundi (On the Creation of the World)*
Post.	*De posteritate Caini (On the Posterity of Cain)*
QG	*Quaestiones et solutiones in Genesin (Questions and Answers in Genesis)*
Spec. 1, 2, 3, 4	*De specialibus legibus* I, II, III, IV *(On the Special Laws* 1, 2, 3, 4*)*

DEUTEROCANONICAL WORKS AND PSEUDEPIGRAPHA

4 Ezra	= 2 Esdras
Bar	Baruch
2–4 Bar.	2–4 Baruch
En.	Enoch
Gos. Thom.	Gospel of Thomas
Jub.	Jubilees
Liv. Pro.	Lives of the Prophets
Macc	Maccabees
Pss. Sol.	Psalms of Solomon
Sib. Or.	Sibylline Oracles
Sir	Sirach/Ecclesiasticus
T. Ash.	Testament of Asher
T. Jud.	Testament of Judah
T. Levi	Testament of Levi
T. Sim.	Testament of Simeon
T. Sol.	Testament of Solomon
T. Zeb.	Testament of Zebulun
Tob	Tobit
Wis	Wisdom of Solomon

GRECO-ROMAN

EURIPIDES

Rhes.	*Rhesus*

PETRONIUS

Sat.	*Satyricon*

PLINY THE ELDER

Nat.	*Naturalis historia (Natural History)*

STRABO

Geog.	*Geographica (Geography)*

SUETONIUS

Aug.	*Divus Augustus (Life of Augustus)*

VIRGIL

Aen.	*Aeneid*

MISHNAH, TOSEFTA, AND TALMUDS

'Abod. Zar.	'Abodah Zarah
'Abot R. Nat.	'Abot de Rabbi Nathan
b.	Babylonian Talmud (Bavli)
Bek.	Bekorot
Ber.	Berakot
B. Qam.	Baba Qamma
B. Meṣ.	Baba Meṣi'a
'Ed.	'Eduyyot
'Erub.	'Erubin
Giṭ.	Giṭṭin
Hor.	Horayot
Ḥul.	Ḥullin
m.	Mishnah
Mek.	Mekilta
Mid.	Middot
Midr.	Midrash
Ned.	Nedarim
Nez.	Neziqin
Nid.	Niddah
'Ohal.	'Ohalot
Pesiq. Rab.	Pesiqta Rabbati
Pesiq. Rab. Kah.	Pesiqta de Rab Kahana
Pirqe R. El.	Pirqe Rabbi Eliezer
Qidd.	Qiddušin
Qod.	Qodašim
Rab.	Rabbah
Roš Haš.	Roš Haššanah
Šabb.	Šabbat
Sanh.	Sanhedrin
Šeb.	Šebi'it
Šebu.	Šebu'ot
S. Eli. Zut.	Seder Eliyahu Zuta
Šeqal.	Šeqalim
Soṭ.	Soṭah
t.	Tosefta
Ta'an.	Ta'anit
y.	Jerusalem Talmud (Yerushalmi)
Yal.	Yalquṭ
Yebam.	Yebamot
Yoma	Yoma (= Kippurim)

Introduction

David Mishkin

Is it even possible to say anything new about Jesus of Nazareth? New Testament scholarship has been greatly enhanced by the recognition of the Jewish Jesus. This was the focus of our first volume, *A Handbook on the Jewish Roots of the Christian Faith* (Evans and Mishkin 2019). By "roots," we were referring not only to background information but also to an ongoing interconnectedness that remains relevant today. But, while Jesus is readily accepted as Jewish, the documents that present his life are less often discussed as specifically Jewish literature. This new book, a sequel of sorts, will focus on the four canonical Gospels as not only vehicles that tell a Jewish story (Levine and Brettler 2017; Boyarin 2013), but also as documents which themselves need to be understood as Jewish (Oliver 2013; Blackwell et al. 2018). In this sense, there certainly is something more to learn about Jesus.

According to the Gospels, Jesus was very much a Jewish man of his day and yet unlike anyone who has ever lived. He is both unique and complex. He is described as a sage, storyteller, miracle worker, healer, exorcist, and by such titles as rabbi, Son of man, Son of God, and Messiah. It is the combination of these things, perhaps more than any individual attribute, which is worthy of note to the historian. Yet, he is also distinct within each category. Certainly, there were other individuals in antiquity who were credited with working miracles. But there is a difference. Comparing Jesus with these others, Geza Vermes concluded that "no objective and enlightened student of the Gospels can help but be struck by the incomparable superiority of Jesus" (Vermes 1973, 224).

Another noteworthy factor is the time span of the documentation. The Gospels were written remarkably close to Jesus' life. Historians are hard-pressed to find another ancient figure who is the subject of four major works produced well within the same century in which he lived (and the claim that he was raised from the dead was already documented two decades after his death, see 1 Cor 15). A comparison with other first-century Jewish notables highlights the uniqueness of Jesus. Hillel was one of the most important rabbis in history, although he is not credited with any miracles. He died in the early years of the century, and he is first mentioned in the Mishnah, written two hundred years later (Telushkin 2010). Hanina ben Dosa lived in the Galilee in the later part of the century and is known primarily as a healer and miracle worker. He too is first mentioned in the Mishnah, although it is not until the completion of the Talmud (over five hundred years later) that we learn significantly more of his many deeds (Avery-Peck 2006).

The Gospels themselves are just as unique and complex as Jesus. They were written in the common Greek of the day, they record conversations and teachings that were almost certainly spoken originally in Aramaic, and they often quote or paraphrase verses that were originally in Hebrew. The question might arise: are they Jewish or Christian texts? To most people this sounds paradoxical, as surely the Gospels are the foundational texts of Christianity. However, the word *Christianity* does not appear in the New Testament. The word *Christian* does appear three times (Acts 11:26; 26:28; 1 Pet 4:16), where it simply refers to someone who was a follower of the Messiah. The Jewish origins of the faith were still quite evident.

The split between "Judaism" and "Christianity" was a process and was not finalized until the fourth century. A number of scholars have attempted to trace this trajectory (Becker et al. 2007; Charlesworth et al. 2014). The discussion begins with Jesus, who can only be fully understood within a Jewish context (Sanders 1985; Fruchtenbaum 2017; Hengel and Schwemer 2019). This has been the focus of New Testament scholarship for at least half a century. More recently, the life and letters of Paul have been increasingly seen as Jewish (Blackwell et al. 2015; Nanos 2015). He was bringing a Jewish message to the non-Jewish world, which added a whole new dimension. By the second century, Jewish-Christian polemical literature was already becoming prominent (Nicklas 2014; Robinson 2009). At some point after Paul's letters and yet before the second century, the four canonical Gospels of the New Testament appeared. But where do they fit along this continuum?

There has been much discussion regarding the genre of the Gospels as Greco-Roman biographies (Burridge 2004; Keener 2019). This scholarship has been valuable. It offers a window into ancient literary norms and conventions. Passages in the Gospels that seem perplexing or questionable to modern readers may be quite understandable when seen within this context. However, further questions may be raised if readers do not allow for the complexity of the Gospels. Specifically, are they simply Greco-Roman documents with a few Jewish "proof texts" sprinkled in to add credibility? To what extent are the Gospels examples of Jewish literature? The world of first-century Judaism was vast (Cohen 2014; Tomasino 2003), and exactly what constituted Jewishness at the time (and who got to decide) is a big question. Nevertheless, recognizing Jewish elements within the Gospels is not beyond our reach.

Chapter 1 examines both the early manuscripts of the Gospels and how their content relates to other Jewish texts. These include the Dead Sea Scrolls as well as the Jewish literature that appeared at some point afterwards as recorded by the rabbis. (Note: While there is no specific article here focusing on apocryphal or pseudepigraphic works, a number of the articles below do interact with these texts.) There are points of agreement and disagreement between the Gospels and these other writings, just as there are between all other Jewish groups. Their differences and areas of tension are at times the best evidence that the Gospels should be seen within the diverse and often antagonistic world of first-century Judaism. Discussions about the law or the temple may take a variety of twists and turns, but the topics are undeniably Jewish. This chapter will also survey the influence of the Gospels in the formation of both Judaism and Christianity.

Chapter 2 focuses on how the Gospels make use of the Tanakh (Old Testament). It should first be recognized that the Tanakh is constantly interacting with itself (Schnittjer 2021). There is a running commentary throughout the Scriptures as each author anchors his respective book with an awareness of earlier writings. The Gospels continue this tradition. They contain numerous citations from the Tanakh (Beale 2012). But perhaps more importantly, they are constantly alluding to the Tanakh throughout their narratives (Hays 2017). This adds yet another layer of complexity to the Gospels. Skeptics who dismiss the texts for not meeting contemporary standards of historicity are widely missing the mark. Stories, themes, and references to the Hebrew Scriptures are built into the fabric of the Gospels. Who exactly were these authors, who were not only so well versed in Tanakh but felt these references were foundational to tell their stories, and who also believed that their audience would understand and benefit from such compositions? Indeed, the medium as well as the message must be explored.

Chapter 3 explores the narrative itself: the events in the life of Jesus. The evangelists portray him as a Jew in a Jewish world. There is no getting around this. References to geography are not incidental or coincidental but are vital to the narrative. Even disagreements with Jewish leaders place Jesus firmly within the realm of Judaism (who else would debate so passionately about questions of authority or tradition?). Similarly, as a prophet and as Messiah, he is presented at times as an unexpected but nevertheless Jewish figure. Even events that seem at first to have no Jewish parallels (including the birth narratives and the resurrection narratives) are told within a Jewish framework.

Chapter 4 addresses theological issues. The trend to place Jesus in the world of Second Temple Judaism has also yielded a new appreciation for the Jewish thought and theology of the day. For example, the Jewish understanding of monotheism at the time was much broader and more nuanced than that which would appear by the Middle Ages. This is not to say that other Jewish groups of the first century had a similar view of monotheism as the early followers of Jesus (they did not). But an understanding of this early diversity helps free scholars to examine the claims of the Gospels outside the narrow and purely polemical boundaries of later generations. In this light, both Jewish and Christian scholars have recognized that concepts such as the Trinity and the incarnation are not necessarily at odds with the Tanakh (Newman et al. 1999; Sommer 2011; Wyschograd 1983). The same is true of a number of other theological topics.

Finally, chapter 5 will discuss the intercultural issues that emerge when the Gospels are (or are not) read as Jewish literature. If it is so obvious that Jesus was a Jew who lived in a Jewish world, then why was this truth hidden for most of the last two thousand years? Clearly, something went wrong. Once the New Testament was read apart from its Jewish context, the church lost more than its cultural flavor. The history of "Christian" anti-Semitism runs much deeper than many are prepared to admit, and the problem remains today (Chazan 2016; Brown 2021). For some, this tradition is traced back to the Gospels themselves. This makes the roots of these documents all the more relevant. A fresh examination of the Gospels as Jewish literature challenges long-standing beliefs about how the evangelists viewed the Jewish people and the Jewish tradition. A growing number of scholars (Evans and Hagner 1993; Fredriksen and Reinhartz 2002) are recognizing that the Gospels represent an in-house Jewish debate, rather than an anti-Jewish bias. This has profound implications for biblical studies as well as Jewish-Christian relations.

This book is not solely an argument for the Jewishness of the Gospels. The Jewish roots are indeed valuable, but they are not an end in themselves. Such issues are important insofar as they enhance our understanding of the texts. The articles below are meant to be scholarly yet accessible to students. The contributors are an international group (from Israel, the United States, Canada, England, Germany, Poland, and Romania) comprised of Jewish and Gentile followers of Jesus as Messiah. This book is for all who want to learn more about the Gospels, and how they portray the man from Nazareth within his own historic and cultural setting.

Works Cited

Avery-Peck, Alan J. 2006. "The Galilee Charismatic and Rabbinic Piety: The Holy Man in Talmudic Literature." Pages 149–65 in *The Historical Jesus in Context* (Princeton Readings in Religion). Edited by Amy-Jill Levine, Dale C. Allison, Jr., and John Dominic Crossan. Princeton: Princeton University Press.

Beale, G. K. 2012. *Handbook on the New Testament Use of the Old Testament: Exegesis and Interpretation.* Grand Rapids: Baker Academic.

Becker, Adam H., and Annette Yoshiko Reed. 2007. *The Ways That Never Parted: Jews and Christians in Late Antiquity and the Early Middle Ages.* Minneapolis, MN: Fortress Press.

Blackwell, Ben C., Jason Maston, and John K. Goodrich, eds. 2018. *Reading Mark in Context: Jesus and Second Temple Judaism.* Grand Rapids: Zondervan.

Blackwell, Ben C., Jason Maston, and John K. Goodrich, eds. 2015. *Reading Romans in Context: Paul and Second Temple Judaism.* Grand Rapids: Zondervan.

Boyarin, Daniel. 2013. *The Jewish Gospels: The Story of the Jewish Christ.* New York: The New Press.

Brown, Michael L. 2021. *Christian Antisemitism.* Lake Mary: Charisma House.

Burridge, Richard A. 2004. *What are the Gospels?* 2nd ed. Grand Rapids: Eerdmans.

Charlesworth, James H., Bruce Chilton, and Shaye J.D. Cohen, eds. 2014. *Partings: How Judaism and Christianity Became Two.* Washington, DC: Biblical Archaeology Society.

Chazan, Robert. 2016. *From Anti-Judaism to Anti-Semitism: Ancient and Medieval Christian Constructions of Jewish History.* Cambridge: Cambridge University Press.

Cohen, Shaye. 2014. *From the Maccabees to the Mishnah.* 3rd ed. Louisville, KY: Westminster John Knox.

Evans, Craig A., and Donald A. Hagner. 1993. *Anti-Semitism and Early Christianity: Issues of Polemic and Faith.* Minneapolis, MN: Fortress Press.

Evans, Craig A., and David Mishkin. 2019. *A Handbook on the Jewish Roots of the Christian Faith.* Peabody, MA: Hendrickson.

Fredriksen, Paula, and Adele Reinhartz. 2002. *Jews, Judaism, and Christian Anti-Judaism: Reading the New Testament after the Holocaust.* Louisville, KY: Westminster John Knox.

Fruchtenbaum, Arnold. 2017. *The Life of Messiah from a Messianic Jewish Perspective: The Abridged Version.* San Antonio: Ariel Ministries.

Hays, Richard B. 2017. *Echoes of Scripture in the Gospels*. Waco, TX: Baylor University Press.

Hengel, Martin, and Anna Maria Schwemer. 2019. *Jesus and Judaism*. Baylor-Mohr Siebeck Studies in Early Christianity. Waco, TX: Baylor University Press.

Keener, Craig S. 2019. *Christobiography: Memory, History, and the Reliability of the Gospels*. Grand Rapids: Eerdmans.

Levine, Amy-Jill, and Marc Brettler. 2017. *The Jewish Annotated New Testament*. 2nd ed. Oxford: Oxford University Press.

Nanos, Mark D. 2015. *Paul within Judaism: Restoring the First-Century Context to the Apostle*. Minneapolis, MN: Fortress.

Newman, Carey C., James R. Davila, and Gladys S. Lewis. 1999. *The Jewish Roots of Christological Monotheism: Papers from the Saint Andrews Conference on the Historical Origins of the Worship of Jesus*. Leiden: Brill.

Nicklas, Tobias. 2014. *Jews and Christians?: Second-Century 'Christian' Perspectives on the 'Parting of the Ways'* (Annual Deichmann Lectures 2013). Tübingen: Mohr Siebeck.

Oliver, Isaac W. 2013. *Torah Praxis after 70 CE: Reading Matthew and Luke-Acts as Jewish Texts*. WUNT 2 Reihe. Tübingen: Mohr Siebeck.

Robinson, Thomas A. 2009. *Ignatius of Antioch and the Parting of the Ways: Early Jewish-Christian Relations*. Grand Rapids: Baker Academic.

Sanders. E. P. 1985. *Jesus and Judaism*. Minneapolis, MN: Fortress Press.

Schnittjer, Gary Edward. 2021. *Old Testament Use of Old Testament: A Book-by-Book Guide*. Grand Rapids: Zondervan Academic.

Sommer, Benjamin D. 2011. *The Bodies of God and the World of Ancient Israel*. Cambridge: Cambridge University Press.

Telushkin, Joseph. 2010. *Hillel: If Not Now, When?* Jewish Encounters Series. New York: Schocken.

Tomasino, Anthony J. 2003. *Judaism before Jesus: The Events and Ideas That Shaped the New Testament World*. Downers Grove, IL: InterVarsity Press

Vermes, Geza. 1973. *Jesus the Jew: A Historian's Reading of the Gospel*. London: Collins.

Wyschogrod, Michael. 1983. *The Body of Faith*. New York: Seabury.

CHAPTER 1

Textual Roots

1.1 The Manuscript Traditions of the New Testament Gospels

Daniel M. Gurtner

Matthew, Mark, Luke, and John are attested in earliest canonical lists, attributed to Irenaeus (170–180 CE) and Origen (220–230 CE) and preserved by Eusebius (320–330 CE; *Hist. eccl.* 5.8.2–8 and *Hist. eccl.* 6.25.3–14). By the fourth century, lists of our canonical Gospels were largely solidified and in the traditional order of Matthew, Mark, Luke, and John (Eusebius, *Hist. eccl.* 3.25.1–7; Athanasius, *Ep. fest.* 39; Epiphanius, *Pan.* 76.5; Jerome, *Epist.* 53; McDonald 2007, 446–49). The traditional order, popularized by Eusebius and Jerome, began to see some variations in the fifth century (Metzger 1987, 296–97). At the same time, apocryphal gospels (e.g., Gospel of Peter and Gospel of Thomas) began to be marginalized (see Eusebius, *Hist. eccl.* 3.25.1–7).

The New Testament Gospels were all written in Greek and initially transmitted in that language. The earliest copies of the Gospels were written on papyrus and date from little more than a century after initially composed (see below). If, as seems likely, manuscripts were kept and used in communities for several centuries (Evans 2020, 75–97), then any number of the copies we have from the first few centuries may well have direct access to an original. Regardless, today we are dependent on the task of textual criticism to attempt to reconstruct the early text. There is debate as to whether one may speak of "the original" text or simply the "earliest recoverable" text (Holmes 2013, 637–88). But for most interpreters, the nature of this debate is rather too technical to be of much service for understanding the Gospels. Instead, it is helpful to know something about the manuscripts on which the Gospels are preserved and a few of the distinctive variations found in the respective Gospels. Some of these are interesting but make little difference, while others involve the inclusion or exclusion of large portions of text.

The most important textual witnesses to the Gospels are the so-called Great Codices: primarily, Sinaiticus, Alexandrinus, and Vaticanus (Evans 2020, 34). According to the early Christian historian Eusebius (*Vita Const.* iv.35–37), Emperor Constantine (reigned 306–337 CE) commissioned the production of fifty manuscripts of Bible. Some have conjectured that one or more of these manuscripts derive from that effort. Regardless, they are all extremely valuable to the preservation of the New Testament Gospels to today.

Foremost among these manuscripts is Codex Sinaiticus (א, 01). Though it dates to the fourth century, Sinaiticus first became known to modern scholars when it was discovered by Constantin von Tischendorf in the monastery of St. Catherine at Mount Sinai in 1844 (Metzger and Ehrman 2005, 62–67). The text is written in four even columns on over seven hundred pages, though the Gospels themselves span six folio pages, all originally written by a single scribe, supplemented and at times corrected by two additional scribes (Jongkind 2007, 56–57).

Codex Alexandrinus (A, 02)—long kept in Alexandria, Egypt, until it was brought to Europe in the seventh century—dates from the fifth century and is written in two columns. It contains much of the Gospels, though most of Matthew (Matt 1:1–25:6; 26 leaves) and a portion of John (6:50–8:52; 2 leaves; see below) are missing. The Gospels in Alexandrinus are likely copied by two different scribes (Kenyon 1909, 9–10; Smith 2014, 244).

Finally, Codex Vaticanus (B, 03) is a single codex, the work of two scribes written in three columns per page (O'Neill 1989, 220–21). Many years later, between the ninth and eleventh centuries, another scribe traced over the original ink of every letter or word, except where errors were suspected, seemingly to preserve a fading original (Skeat 1984, 461; Canart and Martini 1965, 8; Payne and Canart 2000, 105). It has been kept at the Biblioteca Apostolica Vaticana (Vat. Gr. 1209) since the fifteenth century and is generally regarded as the most important manuscript witness to the New Testament Gospels (Evans 2020, 36). Nevertheless, there are a number of verses missing from each of the Gospels (Evans 2020, 36n12).

These manuscripts are very important, but there is evidence that they reflect a phenomenon that dates much earlier. Fragments of a manuscript from the late second century may suggest a codex containing all four (canonical) Gospels. These fragments (P^4, P^{64}, and P^{67}) are now recognized as belonging originally to the same ancient manuscript, dating from the late second century CE (Skeat 1997, 1–34). Though it is widely held to at one time to have contained all four Gospels, no fragment from Mark (or John) has survived (Metzger and Ehrman 2005, 53). Nevertheless, it is instructive for the present purposes to focus attention on the early, pre-Constantinian texts, or at least most of those that date up to the time of the great uncials beginning in the fourth century (Head 2012, 108).

The Gospel of Matthew

The earliest manuscript evidence of the Gospel of Matthew is $\mathfrak{P}^{104}$ (P. Oxy. 4404), widely regarded to date from the second century and perhaps as early as 100–125 CE (Comfort 2019, 148). It consists of a single leaf of papyrus written on both sides and contains Matt 21:34–37, 43, and possibly 45, though it notably omits verse 44. Another papyrus, $\mathfrak{P}^{77}$ (P. Oxy. 2683 + P. Oxy. 4405), is comprised of two fragments of a single leaf, containing Matt 23:30–39. It dates from the second or third century. So does $\mathfrak{P}^{103}$ (P. Oxy. 4403), which has fragments on two sides containing Matt 13:55–56; 14:3–5. In total, the Greek witnesses from the mid-fifth century and earlier furnished as principal witnesses cited in the NA[28] for the Gospel of Matthew contains nineteen papyri ($\mathfrak{P}^1$, $\mathfrak{P}^{19}$, $\mathfrak{P}^{21}$, $\mathfrak{P}^{25}$, $\mathfrak{P}^{35}$, $\mathfrak{P}^{37}$, $\mathfrak{P}^{45}$, $\mathfrak{P}^{53}$, $\mathfrak{P}^{62}$, $\mathfrak{P}^{64(+67)}$, $\mathfrak{P}^{70}$, $\mathfrak{P}^{71}$,

$\mathfrak{P}^{77}$, $\mathfrak{P}^{86}$, $\mathfrak{P}^{101}$, $\mathfrak{P}^{102}$, $\mathfrak{P}^{103}$, $\mathfrak{P}^{104}$, $\mathfrak{P}^{110}$). As noted above, the principal uncial manuscripts contain the First Gospel nearly in full in Codices Sinaiticus and Vaticanus (missing Matt 12:47; 16:2b–3; 17:21; 18:11; 23:14) and in part (Matt 25:7–28:20) in Codex Alexandrinus. In total, Matthew is attested in ten uncial manuscripts from the mid-fifth century and earlier (א (01), A (02), B (03), C (04), D (05), 058, 071, 0160, 0171, 0242; NA²⁸, 62).

Careful analysis indicates that the earliest manuscripts of Matthew (to the third/fourth century; $\mathfrak{P}^{1}$, $\mathfrak{P}^{21}$, $\mathfrak{P}^{35}$, $\mathfrak{P}^{37}$, $\mathfrak{P}^{45}$, $\mathfrak{P}^{53}$, $\mathfrak{P}^{64(+67)}$, $\mathfrak{P}^{70}$, $\mathfrak{P}^{77}$, $\mathfrak{P}^{101}$, $\mathfrak{P}^{102}$, $\mathfrak{P}^{103}$, $\mathfrak{P}^{104}$, $\mathfrak{P}^{110}$; 0171) with few minor exceptions, contain a text close to those of the fourth-century uncials (א and B; Min 2005). This is especially the case among the earliest and most important manuscripts for Matthew ($\mathfrak{P}^{1}$, $\mathfrak{P}^{35}$, $\mathfrak{P}^{64(+67)}$, $\mathfrak{P}^{104}$) where one finds several characteristics of controlled production (Wasserman 2012, 83–107), suggesting that at least in some circles consistency in transmission is desirable. Even where some variations do survive where early scribes made mistakes and took some liberties in copying, seldom is there any change in meaning (Wasserman 2012, 83–107).

Matthew's text is largely stable, though there are some noteworthy variations. For example, at Matt 27:49 strong manuscript support from Sinaiticus and Vaticanus, as well as select strands from certain versions, insert a text otherwise found in the Gospel of John. In the passion narratives of both Matthew and Mark, bystanders wait to see if Elijah will come to save Jesus from the crucifixion (Mark 15:36; Matt 27:49). Whereas many manuscripts of Matthew continue to the traditional verse 50 ("And Jesus cried again with a loud voice and yielded up his spirit," RSV), some contain a curious addition: "But another, taking a spear, pierced his side and there came out water and blood" (*allos de labōn lonchēn enyxen autou tēn pleuran kai exēlthen hydōr kai haima*, notably א B). Recent texts (e.g., NA²⁸, UBS⁵, SBLGNT) and most scholars see this as an addition derived from the similar account in John 19:34 (Metzger 1994, 59). This is surely correct, but it does illustrate the fluidity with which readings in the Gospels can be transposed to one another in the course of the manuscript transmission (see Gurtner 2015, 134–50).

A familiar example is found in Matthew's version of the Lord's Prayer (Matt 6:9–13), where the original version ends, "And lead us not into temptation, but deliver us from evil" (Matt 6:13 RSV). This is surely correct, as is attested by a host of manuscripts, notably א B (but also D Z 0170, etc.). Some add a simple "amen" (*amēn* 17 30 288*). But many in the West may be familiar with the addition, "For thine is the kingdom, and the power, and the glory, for ever. Amen" (KJV; *hoti sou estin hē basileia kai hē dynamis kai hē doxa eis tous aiōnas. amēn*). This reading, preserved in the King James Version, is attested in a number of manuscripts (K L W Δ Θ *f*¹³, etc.), and with several minor variations. While it is surely a secondary reading, it is biblical. It derives from a prayer by King David (1 Chr 29:11–13), which contains the familiar statement: "Yours, O LORD, are the greatness, the power, the glory, the victory, and the majesty; for all that is in the heavens and on the earth is yours; yours is the kingdom, O LORD, and you are exalted as head above all" (1 Chr 29:11 NRSV; see Metzger 1994, 14; Delobel 1989, 293–309).

One final matter unique to the early text of Matthew is worth mentioning. According to Eusebius, Papias (ca. 60–130 CE) claims that "Matthew collected the oracles in the Hebrew dialect and each interpreted them as best he could"

(Eusebius, *Hist. eccl.* 3.39.16; Irenaeus, *Haer.* 3.1.1). Although nearly every phrase of this statement is debated, other ancient Christian sources also reference a Hebrew version of Matthew (e.g., Cyril of Jerusalem, *Catechetical Lectures* 14; Epiphanius, *Pan.* 30.3.7; Jerome, *Vir. ill.* 3; *Comm. Matt.* 12:13). This may confuse Matthew with other texts from antiquity, and most scholars agree that the Gospel of Matthew extant today is written in a form of Greek that gives no traces that it was translated from another language. No ancient manuscripts of Matthew survive, but there is a text preserved from the work of a Spanish Jew from around 1400 named Shem-Tob ben Issac ben Shaprut, which some contend is the original Hebrew Matthew (Howard 1995). Though this is largely discounted today, some scholars still favor that a Hebrew version of Matthew did exist at one time, though not represented in Shem-Tob's (Edwards). Another phenomenon in the history of Matthew's text pertains to a fourth-century Coptic text of the First Gospel. This was publicly announced in 2001, known as Codex Schøyen, and was thought by some to be an alternative version of the original Greek. It has since been shown that sufficient attention to the translational nuances of the Coptic text indicate that it is best regarded as a translation reflecting closely with readings found in Vaticanus and Sinaiticus (Leonard 2014).

Manuscripts of Mark

There are several early and reliable manuscripts for Mark, but not as many as for Matthew. Mark is attested in its entirety in all the Great Codices (Sinaiticus, Alexandrinus, and Vaticanus), but in only three early papyri. The earliest manuscript witness to the Gospel of Mark is $\mathfrak{P}^{45}$, a papyrus from the Chester Beatty collection that originally contained about 220 leaves. It dates from the first half of the third century (Kenyon 1933, x). It is among those manuscripts that likely preserved the Gospels in the so-called Western order: Matthew, John, Luke, Mark, Acts (Comfort 2019, 142). Of the surviving thirty leaves, the Gospel of Mark comprises six (fols. 3–8) containing portions of Mark 4:36–40; 5:15–26; 5:38–6:3, 16–25, 36–50; 7:3–15; 7:25–8:1, 10–26; 8:34–9:9, 18–31; 11:27–12:1, 5–8, 13–19, 24–28). The scribe who preserved the text seems to have utilized considerable freedom in copying his exemplar—sometimes harmonizing, smoothing out, paraphrasing, but not, evidently, word for word (Colwell 1969, 114–21). The scribe is also noted for his deliberate pruning, resulting in a readable and precise text (Comfort 2019, 142–43; Royse 2008, 103–97). Otherwise, the manuscript is remarkable for its careful, though sparse, punctuation and for its system of markings to aid the reader found in Mark but not in other Gospels in $\mathfrak{P}^{45}$ (Head 2012, 114).

The other early papyrus in which Mark is preserved is $\mathfrak{P}^{88}$, with four pages of text containing Mark 2:1–26. It dates from the fourth century and resembles the text of Sinaiticus and Vaticanus. Sometimes it shares with Sinaiticus a unique spelling, such as *krabakton* (Mark 2:9, 11–12) or a unique word order (*egeire soi legō*, 2:11; Head 2012, 117). $\mathfrak{P}^{84}$ is also frequently cited in critical editions, containing portions of Mark (2:2–5, 8–9; 6:30–31, 33–34, 36–37, 39–41), but it dates rather late for present considerations (sixth century).

𝔓¹³⁷ (= P. Oxy. 5345) was once thought to come from the first century (see below). It dates from the second or third century and consists of two sides on a single fragment of five lines on each side. It contains Mark 1:7–9, 16–18. It is only the second copy of Mark coming from the Oxyrhynchus cache, the other (069) being a fifth-century parchment codex (Obbink and Colomo 2018, 5). Mark in Codex Vaticanus is most peculiar in its very minor but unique spellings of various words, especially where *ei* is present (Head 2012, 118–19). Head enumerates the many ways in which Sinaiticus preserves unique readings by its many omissions, omitting between one and five words on thirty-eight occasions, for a total of fifty-eight words omitted (Head 2012, 119).

Some have argued that Mark's text is less stable than that of other Gospels (Dewey 2004, 505–06). Yarbro Collins acknowledges that from the third century onward there was some fluidity, but what changes the text of Mark underwent from the time of its composition to the third century is difficult to know (2007, 125). The difficulty in assessing its earliest transmission lies in the ambiguity and ultimate paucity of evidence. To begin with, it is difficult to discern where Mark is cited in the early church, and indisputable citations are difficult to come by. Some authors—such as Clement of Rome (ca. 95 CE), Ignatius, Polycarp, Barnabas, the *Didache*, and the *Martyrdom of Polycarp*—exhibit familiarity with the Synoptic tradition but no certain reference to Mark (Swete 1909, xxix–xxx). Unambiguous references are found in Justin Martyr (*Dial.* 106.3, ca. 150; citing Mark 3:17), Origen (Mark 4:12 in *Princ.* 3.1.7, 16; Mark 10:18 in *Comm. Jo.* 2.7; Yarbro Collins 105), Clement of Alexandria (*Paed.* 1.2 and *Strom.* 6.14 citing Mark 8:36), and Irenaeus (*Haer.* 3.14.3 cites Mark 1:1; see Koester 1983, 37). Regardless of whether Mark was less circulated than the others or widely circulated but presumably supplanted by Matthew and Luke, it seems plausible that Matthew and Luke enjoyed greater popularity than did Mark. Nevertheless, as a text (not in citation), the Gospel of Mark seems to have retained its major elements, except at the beginning and especially the ending (see below) through the duration of its transmission (Yarbro Collins 2007, 125). It is perhaps not surprising that Mark seems to get lost in a sea of Synoptic citations in the early church, since 97.2 percent of the words in Mark have a parallel in Matthew and 88.4 percent have a parallel in Luke (Stein 1987, 48). Why Mark is neglected in earliest Christianity is difficult to say and can only be speculated upon (see Gurtner 2016, 303–25).

A small assortment of Greek papyri fragments from Qumran Cave 7 were once thought to belong to the Gospel of Mark. One of which (7Q5) was identified as Mark 6:52–53 (O'Callaghan 1972, 91–100; Thiede 1992). But the arguments in favor of this understanding are wrought with conjecture, speculations, and emendations that breach credibility and were finally disproven (see Wise 2020, 408–12). Another sensationalist claim was made when an announcement was made at a public lecture regarding the discovery of a first-century copy of the Gospel of Mark. Further research shows that it dates from the second or third century and is among the earliest extant manuscripts of Mark (Obbink and Colomo 2018, 5–6; see above).

Mark has some intriguing variant readings that have attracted considerable discussion among scholars. In the very first verse (Mark 1:1), the original of Sinaiticus (א* also Θ Origen 28ᶜ) omits the words "Son of God" (*hyiou theou*). It is added by the corrector to Sinaiticus (א[1]), as well as Vaticanus (B) and other manuscripts (D L etc. but *tou theou* A *f*[1.13] M). The reading "Son of God" may have simply been overlooked by a copyist (Metzger 1994, 62), but it is difficult to imagine this occurring at the very beginning of a text (Yarbro Collins 2007, 130). Since "Son of God" is elsewhere a strong emphasis of Mark (e.g., 1:11, 34; 3:11; 5:7; 9:7; 14:61; 15:39; cf. 12:6; 13:32), some have argued that a later scribe added it (Head 1991, 621–29; Marcus 2000, 146–47; cf. Yarbro Collins 1995, 111–27).

Later (Mark 1:41), when a leper requests healing from Jesus, some manuscripts say he responded with compassion (*splanchnistheis*, א B L 892 *l* 2211) whereas others say he became angry (*orgistheis*, D a ff[2] r[1*]). The latter is weakly attested and *splanchnistheis* occurs in the Synoptic parallels (Matt 8:3; Luke 5:13). So, it is difficult to see what may have motivated a scribe to insert *orgistheis* (Metzger 1994, 65). Most scholars prefer the "compassion" reading to "angry," but a case has been made for the latter (Ehrman 2003, 77–98).

The most discussed variation occurs at the end of Mark, when after Jesus' disciples discover that the tomb is empty, "they said nothing to anyone, for they were afraid" (NRSV; *ephobounto gar*; 16:8). This is how the earliest and best manuscripts (א and B) end (Elliott 1993, 204; Metzger 1994, 102–07). Yet it strikes many readers, modern and ancient, as an unsatisfactory conclusion, and scholars debate whether there was more to the original written that is now lost (Croy 2003, 45–71, 137–63) or the evangelist intended to write more but did not. There are two additional variations on this ending. But there are also some early and important manuscripts dating from the fifth century (A, C, D, K, etc.) that include an extended ending (Mark 16:9–20) that has been retained in the King James Version. This extended reading contains a resurrection appearance of Jesus (Mark 16:9–14) and something akin to the Matthean Great Commission (Mark 16:15–16; cf. Matt 28:16–20). To the latter is appended a statement attributed to Jesus that promises that his disciples will perform signs, including casting out demons, speaking in new languages, being unharmed by snake bites or poison, and healing the sick (Mark 16:17–18). The narrative concludes with Jesus' ascension (Mark 16:19) and a summary of the disciples' preaching and miracle working (Mark 16:20; see Yarbro Collins 2007, 801–18). Most scholars agree that all the additions beyond verse 8 are later, secondary works, not part of the original Gospel. Yet the lenghtier ending (vv. 9–20) has long been part of Christian tradition since its inclusion in the King James Version, and whether or not the evangelist intended to complete his account at 16:8 remains unresolved.

Manuscripts of Luke

Generally, the text of Luke is stable, though with many small variations (Bovon 2002, 1). It is attested in ten papyri, though some of these date too late for consideration here. 𝔓[82] dates from the fourth or fifth centuries and contains Luke 7:32–34, 37–38. Others date from the sixth or seventh century (𝔓[3], Luke 7:36–45; 10:38–42; 𝔓[97], Luke 14:7–14), or the seventh/eighth century (𝔓[42], Luke 1:54–55; 2:29–32). For the earliest witnesses, then, we consult the principal papyri that date from the fourth century CE or earlier (𝔓[4], 𝔓[7], 𝔓[45], 𝔓[69], 𝔓[75], and 𝔓[111]). All of the papyri in question date from the third century. Though they are all from Egypt, their precise locations of origins differ. And their variations in size, content, and other features exhibit traits that predate the major codices (Hernández 2012, 121).

𝔓⁷ is a small fragment of nine lines that dates from the third or fourth century and contains Luke 4:1–3. There are no unique readings in 𝔓⁷ and it is identical to both 𝔓⁷⁵ and Vaticanus (Hernández 2012, 122). 𝔓¹¹¹ (also known as P. Oxy. 4495) dates from the third century. It is a single leaf with writing on both sides, with Luke 17:11–13 on one side (*verso*; four lines) and 17:21–23 on the other (*recto*; five lines). Divergences are few and minor (e.g., *epithymēsai* at 17:22 with D; *estēsan* with A and ℵ against B at 17:12) and also largely resembles 𝔓⁷⁵ (Hernández 2012, 122).

𝔓⁶⁹ (P. Oxy. 2383) dates to the early third or late second century CE (Comfort and Barrett 2019, 439). It consists of two sides of a single papyrus, with Luke 22:40–48 on the *recto* (fourteen lines) and Luke 22:58–62 on the *verso* (fourteen lines). Its omission of 22:43–44, which recounts Jesus in Gethsemane attended by an angel and his sweat that resembled drops of blood, has generated some interest (Clivaz 2004, 419–40). This reading is generally regarded as a very "free" text with characteristics akin to those of D (Aland and Aland 1995, 100).

There are also three papyri that contain more extensive portions of Luke's text. 𝔓⁴ dates to the second half of the second century (Comfort and Barrett 2019, 31). It was discovered in Coptos, Egypt, in 1889 and contains Luke 1:58–59; 1:62–2:1, 6–7; 3:8–4:2, 29–32, 34–35; 5:3–8; 5:30–6:16. It consists of four fragments written on both sides and two columns per side, with lacuna. Sometimes 𝔓⁴ preserves confusing or confused readings (Luke 3:27; 5:3) or spells a word in a unique way (Luke 1:64) or omits words entirely (e.g., 1:68; 3:9). At other times, its readings harmonize with those of other texts (e.g., 1:65; 5:37; 6:6a, b), make deliberate adjustments based on contextual factors (Luke 5:31) and possibly theological interests (1:76; 3:22; Hernández 2012, 125–26). Overall, it agrees with 𝔓⁷⁵ and B 93 percent (Comfort and Barrett 2019, 31).

𝔓⁴⁵ (discussed above) contains an extensive amount of Luke (6:31–41; 6:45–7:7; 9:26–41; 9:45–10:1, 6–22; 10:26–11:1, 6–25, 28–46; 11:50–12:12, 18–37; 12:42–13:1, 6–24; 13:29–14:10, 17–33). It is generally regarded as one of the best papyri among early Christian texts in terms of orthography and the avoidance of nonsensical readings (Royse 2007, 905). It has been proposed that the manuscript may have been prepared for private use (Charlesworth 2009, 165–66). It contains more omissions (fifty-one words) than additions (thirteen words), meaning a net loss of thirty-eight words in the 𝔓⁴⁵ text of Luke (Hernández 2012, 127). Most of the textual corruption in 𝔓⁴⁵ is derived from harmonization to immediate context or to Matthew (Hernández 2012, 128; Royse 2007, 188–89).

𝔓⁷⁵ dates to the second or third century (ca. 200 CE) and survives in thirty-six folios (72 leaves, 144 pages) approximately 13cm by 26cm in dimension. It contains sections of the Gospel of John (see below) and Luke 3:18–22; 3:33–4:2; 4:34–5:10; 5:37–6:4; 6:10–7:32, 35–39, 41–43; 7:46–9:2; 9:4–17:15; 17:19–18:18; 22:4–24:53 (end). It features text divisions, punctuation and rough breathing, and large script, which suggests to some that it may have been created for public usage, perhaps in worship contexts (Charlesworth 2009, 158–61). 𝔓⁷⁵ is noted for its numerous spelling irregularities (Royse 2007, 647–51) but is nonetheless considered a more accurate copy of Luke than 𝔓⁴⁵ (Hernández 2012, 131). 𝔓⁷⁵ in Luke has more omissions (twenty-eight) than additions (four); some of the omissions are due to harmonization (Royse 2007, 690–98) but also contains grammatical and stylistic changes, as well as orthographic (spelling) adjustments and nonsense readings (Hernández 2012, 131).

Textual Variants in Luke

Variant readings in a number of passages have been the subject of comment (Bovon 2002, 1). Codex Bezae (D) moves Luke 6:5 to after 6:10 and reads at 6:5: "On the same day he saw a man working on the sabbath and said to him, 'Man, if you know what you are doing, you are blessed; but if you do not know, you are accursed and a transgressor of the law.'" In so doing D creates three incidents pertaining to Jesus and the Sabbath in Luke (Metzger 1994, 117). Though not original to Luke, its affinity with other New Testament texts regarding transgression of the law (Rom 2:25, 27; James 2:11; cf. Gos. Thom. 3; 14) suggests to some it may be authentic to Jesus (see Bock 1994, 536).

There is discrepancy among traditions at Luke 10:2 as to whether Jesus sent out seventy disciples (‬א A C L W etc.) or seventy-two (𝔓⁷⁵ B D etc.). The same problem occurs at Luke 10:17, where seventy-two is read by some (𝔓⁴⁵vid, 75 B D etc.) and seventy by others (א A C L W etc.). Either reading would have symbolic value, whether the seventy elders of Moses (Exod 24:1, 9) or the seventy-two nations (Gen 10–11; Bock 1996, 1015). But it is not clear that Luke intended a symbolic meaning, leading some to slightly prefer the reading of seventy-two (Bock 1996, 1015). Yet a scribe may have tried to harmonize with Mark's account of sending the disciples "two-by-two" (Mark 6:7), suggesting seventy is original.

In Luke's account of the Lord's Prayer, some readings support "your holy spirit come upon us and purify us" (Luke 11:2; *elthetō to pneuma sou to hagion eph' hēmas kai katharisatō hēmas* 700; 162). The manuscript support comes from the eleventh century (MS 700) and 1153 (MS 162) and is attested in the writings of Gregory of Nyssa. This is given instead of the familiar "thy kingdom come" (*elthetō/ elthatō hē basileia sou*; see Matt 6:10; 𝔓⁷⁵ א A B C L etc.), the latter of which is the preferred reading. Metzger regards the former as a later liturgical adaptation of the Lord's Prayer, perhaps utilized during baptism or the laying on of hands (Metzger 1994, 131).

In some manuscripts an angel supports Jesus in his agony at Gethsemane (Luke 22:43–44). The full text reads, "Then an angel from heaven appeared to him and gave him strength. In his anguish he prayed more earnestly, and his sweat became like great drops of blood falling down on the ground" (NRSV) and is supported (with minor variations) by א*, 2 D L Δ* Θ Ψ, etc.). Other manuscripts, however, omit it entirely (𝔓⁶⁹vid 𝔓⁷⁵ א¹ A B, etc.). Still others retain verses 43–44 with asterisks or obeli to denote some uncertainty (Δᶜ 0171vid 892c) or transpose it entirely to after Matthew 26:39 (*f*¹³ [13* 828¹ᐟ²]). It is unlikely that the adjustment would be deliberate (Hernández 2012, 137), and reasons for deliberate omission of the addition are not compelling. All this "strongly suggests the addition did not form part of the original text of Luke" (Metzger 1994, 151).

Finally, some manuscripts add "and he was taken up into heaven" (Luke 24:51; 𝔓⁷⁵ א² A B C L W Δ Θ Ψ *f*¹ *f*¹³, etc.) whereas others omit it (א* D itᵃ, b, d, e, ff2 1 syrˢ geo[1]). Many scholars prefer the longer reading, since Luke seems to presume it (Acts 1:2). Yet it does not use the same verb as in Acts 1:2 (*analambanein*) so as to suggest a scribe was influenced by Acts to insert it into Luke 24:51. It is also difficult to account for the origins of the reading if it were an addition as early as 200 CE (𝔓[75]; Metzger 1994, 162–63).

Manuscripts of John

The Gospel of John is the best attested of the Gospels from the second and third centuries. It is attested by a large number of papyri, though some are late for the present purposes, some from the fifth century (𝔓[93]), others the sixth (𝔓[2], 𝔓[63], 𝔓[84], 𝔓[36], 𝔓[76]) or seventh (𝔓[44], 𝔓[55], 𝔓[59], 𝔓[60]). Other early witnesses come from the fourth century (𝔓[6], 𝔓[120], 𝔓[122]), but there are so many that are earlier still that for the present purposes we can examine the fifteen that date from the third century and two from the second, the earliest of which (𝔓[52]) were written perhaps a mere fifty years or less after the composition of the Fourth Gospel. Chapa observes that all the earliest manuscripts of John originate in Egypt (2012, 154), indicating that it is impossible to tell whether the readings they contain are attested in other regions. So, the earliest manuscripts of John typically testify to Alexandrian readings.

The majority of the manuscripts date from the third century. John 10:29–11:11 is the best attested portion of the Gospel in these papyri (𝔓[66], 𝔓[75], 𝔓[45]; Chapa 2012, 143) and the *Pericope Adulterae* (7:53–8:11) is not found in any. Most of these papyri are fragmentary, but one (𝔓[75]) contains about two-thirds of the Gospel (Chapa 2012, 143). Another early manuscript, 𝔓[66], dating to about 200 CE, contains the majority of the Fourth Gospel (John 1:1–6:11; 6:35–14:26, 29–30; 15:2–26; 16:2–4, 6–7; 16:10–20:20, 22–23; 20:25–21:9). It is the latter (𝔓[66]) that is considered the most important manuscript of John (Royse 2007, 399–544).

𝔓[66] is comprised of seventy-five leaves of a codex and the careful work of a competent scribe (Royse 2007, 500–3; Head 2008, 55–74). Even so, it is known for an abundance of corrections, though it is unclear if they are by the same scribe or not (Royse 2007, 409, 414; Fee 1965, 247–57). This suggests a degree of carelessness on the part of the initial scribe (Chapa 144), though its meticulous corrections produced a copy that faithfully transmits its exemplar (Royse 900–01). But it does complicate any determination of the purpose for which it was produced (Chapa 147).

As we have seen above, 𝔓[75] is an important witness to Luke, but it also contains nearly the entire first fifteen chapters of John (John 1:1–11:45, 48–57; 12:3–13:10; 14:8–15:10). It is the work of a professional scribe, with elegant majuscule script that is clear and legible, in which the scribe "intended to be painstaking and faithful in reproducing the text" (Chapa 2012, 147–48). Nevertheless, he created orthographical errors and nonsense readings, often from errors of a letter or two (Royse 2007, 656–59). He tended to omit three times as much as he added (Royse 2007, 630–31; 704). 𝔓[75] and Vaticanus (B) share a very high degree of similarity (92 percent), and it has been suggested that they share a common ancestor, which would date to somewhere in the second century (Porter 1962, 363–76; Royse 2007, 616–19).

𝔓⁴⁵, discussed above, contains only portions of three pages belonging to the Gospel of John (John 4:51, 54; 5:21, 24; 10:7–25; 10:30–11:10, 18–36, 42–57). In full it would have occupied thirty-eight pages of an estimated two hundred twenty-four of 𝔓⁴⁵ that would have contained the four Gospels (Chapa 2012, 150). Chapa regards the scribe of 𝔓⁴⁵ as "undisciplined" (Chapa 2012, 150), and the scribe's affinity for harmonizing, smoothing out, and substituting words causes some to suggest the scribe intended to copy his source phrase-by-phrase rather than word-for-word (Colwell 1969, 117–19; see Royse 2007, 114–18). This results in twenty-nine singular readings found in the papyrus' text of John (Royse 2007, 114–18).

Many other important papyri could be discussed, all of which also date from the third century and contain varying amounts of the Fourth Gospel, as follows:

𝔓⁵, John 1:23–31, 33–40; 16:14–30; 20:11–17, 19–20, 22–25

𝔓²², John 15:25–16:2, 21–32

𝔓²⁸, John 6:8–12, 17–22

𝔓³⁹, John 8:14–22

𝔓⁸⁰, John 3:34

𝔓⁹⁵, John 5:26–29, 36–38

𝔓¹⁰⁶, John 1:29–35; 1:40–46

𝔓¹⁰⁷, John 17:1–2; 17:11

𝔓¹⁰⁹, John 21:18–20; 21:23–25

𝔓¹¹⁹, John 1:21–28, 38–44

𝔓¹⁰⁸, John 17:23–24; 18:1–5

𝔓¹²¹, John 19:17–18, 25–26

Some careful consideration can be given to the earliest papyri representation of John: 𝔓⁵² (P. Rylands 457) is the oldest manuscript of the New Testament, typically dated to the middle or second half of the second century (Nongbri 2005, 23–48; Bagnall 2009, 1–24). It is comprised of a single leaf, 18 cm by 22 cm, with eighteen lines per page and contains John 18:31–34 (*recto*) and 18:37–38 (*verso*). 𝔓⁹⁰ (P. Oxy. 3523) also dates to the second century (Bell and Skeat 1935, 6–7) but is more extensive than 𝔓⁵². It consists of a single leaf, originally 12 cm by 16 cm, with twenty-four lines per page. It contains John 18:36–19:1a (*recto*) and John 19:1b–7 (*verso*). If the date held by most scholars that John was composed somewhere between 85 and 100 CE is accurate, then these manuscripts date within not much more than a single century from the composition of the Fourth Gospel.

Numerous interesting variations could be discussed, but pride of place for the Gospel of John pertains to the well-known account of the woman caught in adultery (John 7:53–8:11). In this passage, Jesus is teaching in the temple when a woman who had been caught in adultery is brought to him and he is asked to give his judgment (John 7:53–8:5). Jesus then writes something on the ground with his finger and announces that anyone who is without sin should be first to stone her (8:6–8). Ultimately, all her accusers abandon the case and the woman departs, forgiven (8:9–11). This moving and memorable story has a long history in the church (Knust and Wasserman 2019). So much so that many are shocked to learn that the manuscript evidence is overwhelming that it is not original to John. Metzger suggests it may nonetheless have some claim to historical veracity, and he claims it belongs to oral traditions circulated in the Western church that were subsequently enveloped into the manuscript at certain places (Metzger 1994, 189). It is absent in some of the earliest and best manuscripts ($\mathfrak{P}^{66}$ ℵ B), as well as in versions such as the oldest form of the Syriac (syr^c) and Coptic (Sahidic). Moreover, the traditions that do retain it place at after 7:52 (D E (F) G H, etc.), after 7:36 (MS 225), after 7:44 (several Georgian manuscripts), after 21:25 (1 565 1076 1570 1582 arm^{mss}), or after Luke 21:38 (f^{13}; Metzger 1994, 188–89). Yet even in many of these, the scribes mark the texts with indications that they questioned the veracity of the reading. Finally, nearly all commentators observe that the Greek style and vocabulary of the passage differs markedly from that of the rest of the Gospel of John.

Beyond Greek Manuscripts of the Gospels

The Gospels find a unique place in their transmission history at the hands of a man named Tatian, who was converted to Christianity by Justin Martyr (ca. 110–165 CE) while in Rome. Recognizing the similar narratives among the four canonical Gospels, he created an interweaving of them into a single, coherent account that generally follows the chronology of the Gospel of John, with Synoptic accounts interwoven. This work is called the *Diatessaron* (*to dia tessarōn*), and though it is said to have been written in Greek and translated by Tatian himself into Syriac around 172 CE, all of this is debated (see Metzger 1977, 30–36). By the fifth century, Theodoret (ca. 423 CE) destroyed perhaps as many as two hundred copies of the *Diatessaron* because of Tatian's eventual condemnation as a heretic (Theodoret, *Haer. fab.* i.20). Aside from some Greek fragments and citations, attestation of the *Diatessaron* is found in the fourth-century commentary on the *Diatessaron* by Ephrem the Syrian. Beyond this special matter unique to the Gospels, the spread of Christianity to regions where other languages were spoken required the production of translations from the Greek original of the entirety of the New Testament. Principal among these languages are Latin, Syriac, and Coptic. These are all important witnesses to the Gospels in terms of reconstructing the text, but they also tell us something more. They testify to the widespread and early dissemination of the Gospels in various forms to different cultural-linguistic localities.

Works Cited

Aland, Kurt, and Barbara Aland. 1995. *The Text of the New Testament.* Revised and enlarged. Translated by Erroll F. Rhodes. Grand Rapids: Eerdmans.

Bagnall, Roger S. 2009. *Early Christian Books in Egypt.* Princeton: Princeton University Press.

Bell, H. I., and T. C. Skeat, eds. 1935. *Fragments of an Unknown Gospel and Other Early Christian Papyri.* London: Oxford University Press for the British Museum.

Bock, Darrell L. 1994, 1996. *Luke.* 2 vols. BECNT. Grand Rapids: Baker.

Bovon, François. 2002. *Luke 1: A Commentary on Luke 1:1–9:50.* Translated by Christine M. Thomas. Hermeneia. Minneapolis, MN: Fortress.

Canart, Paul, and Carlo M. Martini. 1965. *The Holy Bible: The Vatican Greek Codex 1209 (Codex B) Facsimile Reproduction by order of his Holiness Paul VI: The New Testament Introduction.* Vatican City: Vatican.

Chapa, Juan. 2012. "The Early Text of John." Pages 140–56 in *The Early Text of the New Testament.* Edited by Charles E. Hill and Michael J. Kruger. Oxford: Oxford University Press.

Charlesworth, Scott D. 2009. "Public and Private: Second- and Third-Century Gospel Manuscripts." Pages 148–74 in *Jewish and Christian Scriptures as Artifact and Canon.* Edited by Craig A. Evans and H. D. Zacharias. London: T&T Clark.

Clivaz, C. 2005. "The Angel and the Sweat like 'Drops of Blood' Luke 22:43–44: 𝔓⁶⁹ and fʰ¹³." *HTR* 98.4: 419–40.

Colwell, Ernest. 1969. "Method in Evaluating Scribal Habits: A Study in 𝔓45, 𝔓66, 𝔓75." Pages 114–21 in *Studies in Methodology in Textual Criticism of the New Testament.* NTTS 9. Leiden: Brill.

Comfort, Philip Wesley, and David P. Barrett. 2019. *The Text of the Earliest New Testament Greek Manuscripts: Volume 1: Papyri 1–74.* 3rd ed. Grand Rapids: Kregel.

Comfort, Philip Wesley. 2019. *The Text of the Earliest New Testament Greek Manuscripts: Volume 2: Papyri 75–139 and Uncials.* 3rd ed. Grand Rapids: Kregel.

Croy, N. Clayton. 2003. *The Mutilation of Mark's Gospel.* Nashville: Abingdon.

Delobel, Joël. 1989. "The Lord's Prayer in the Textual Tradition." Pages 293–309 in *The New Testament in Early Christianity.* Edited by Jean-Marie Sevrin. BETL 86. Louven: Peeters.

Dewey, J. 2004. "The Survival of Mark's Gospel: A Good Story?" *JBL* 123: 495–507.

Edwards, James R. 2009. *The Hebrew Gospel and the Development of the Synoptic Tradition.* Grand Rapids: Eerdmans.

Ehrman, Bart D. 2003. "A Leper in the Hands of an Angry Jesus." Pages 77–98 in *New Testament Greek and Exegesis: Essays in Honor of Gerald F. Hawthorne.* Edited by Amy M. Donaldson and Timothy B. Sailors. Grand Rapids: Eerdmans.

Elliott, J. K. 1993. "The Text and Language of the Endings to Mark's Gospel." Pages 203–11 in *Language and Style in the Gospel of Mark.* NovTSup 71. Leiden: Brill.

Evans, Craig A. 2020. *Jesus and the Manuscripts: What We Can Learn from the Oldest Texts.* Peabody, MA: Hendrickson.

Fee, Gordon D. 1965. "The Corrections of Papyrus Bodmer II and Early Textual Transmission." *NovT* 7: 247–57.

Gurtner, Daniel M. 2016. "The Gospel of Mark in Syriac Christianity." Pages 303–25 in *Earliest Christianity within the Boundaries of Judaism: Essays in Honor of Bruce Chilton.* Edited by Alan Avery-Peck, Craig A. Evans, and Jacob Neusner. BRLJ 49. Leiden: Brill.

———. 2015. "Water and Blood and Matthew 27:49: A Johannine Reading in the Matthean Passion Narrative?" Pages 134–50 in *Studies on the Text of the New Testament and Early Christianity: Essays in Honor of Michael W. Holmes*. Edited by Daniel M. Gurtner, Juan Hernández Jr., and Paul Foster. NTTSD 50. Leiden: Brill.

Head, Peter M. 2012. "The Early Text of Mark." Pages 108–20 in *The Early Text of the New Testament*. Edited by Charles E. Hill and Michael J. Kruger. Oxford: Oxford University Press.

———. 2008. "Scribal Behaviour and Theological Tendencies in Singular Readings in P. Bodmer II (P⁶⁶)." Pages 55–74 in *Textual Variation: Theological and Social Tendencies?* Edited by H. A. G. Houghton and D. C. Parker. Piscataway: Gorgias Press.

———. 1991. "A Text-Critical Study of Mark 1.1: 'The Beginning of the Gospel of Jesus Christ.'" *NTS* 37: 621–29.

Hernández, Juan Jr. 2012. "The Early Text of Luke." Pages 121–39 in *The Early Text of the New Testament*. Edited by Charles E. Hill and Michael J. Kruger. Oxford: Oxford University Press.

Hill, C. E. 2010. *Who Chose the Gospels? Probing the Great Gospel Conspiracy*. Oxford: Oxford University Press.

Holmes, Michael W. 2013. "From 'Original Text' to 'Initial Text': The Traditional Goal of New Testament Textual Criticism in Contemporary Discussion." Pages 637–88 in *The Text of the New Testament in Contemporary Research: Essays on the Status Quaestionis*. 2nd ed. Edited by Bart D. Ehrman and Michael W. Holmes. NTTSD 42. Leiden: Brill.

Horbury, William. 1999. "The Hebrew Matthew and Hebrew Study." Pages 122–31 in *Hebrew Study from Ezra to Ben-Yehuda*. Edited by William Horbury. Edinburgh: T&T Clark.

Howard, George. 1995. *Hebrew Gospel of Matthew*. Macon: Mercer University Press.

Jongkind, Dirk. 2007. *Scribal Habits of Codex Sinaiticus*. Texts and Studies 3rd ser, vol 5. Piscataway, NJ: Gorgias.

Kenyon, F. G. *The Chester Beatty Biblical Papyri*, ii. *The Gospels and Acts*, 1. London: Emery Walker Limited, 1933.

———., ed. 1909. *The Codex Alexandrinus (Royal MS. 1 D. V–VIII) in Reduced Photographic Facsimile: New Testament and Clementine Epistles*. London: British Museum.

Knust, Jennifer, and Tommy Wasserman. 2019. *To Cast the First Stone: The Transmission of a Gospel Story*. Princeton: Princeton University Press.

Koester, Helmut. 1983. "History and Development of Mark's Gospel (From Mark to Secret Mark to Canonical Mark)." Pages 35–57 in *Colloquy on New Testament Studies: A Time for Reappraisal and Fresh Approaches*. Edited by Bruce Corley. Macon: Mercer University Press.

Leonard, James M. 2014. *Codex Schøyen 2650: A Middle Egyptian Coptic Witness to the Early Greek Text of Matthew's Gospel. A Study in Translation Theory, Indigenous Coptic, and New Testament Textual Criticism*. NTTSD 46. Leiden: Brill.

Lightfoot, R. H. 1950. *The Gospel Message of St. Mark*. Oxford: Clarendon.

Marcus, Joel. 2000. *Mark 1–8*. AB 27. New York: Doubleday.

McDonald, Lee Martin. 2007. *The Biblical Canon: Its Origin, Transmission, and Authority*. 3rd ed. Peabody, MA: Hendrickson.

Metzger, Bruce M. 1987. *The Canon of the New Testament: Its Origin, Development, and Significance*. Oxford: Clarendon Press.

———. 1977. *The Early Versions of the New Testament: Their Origin, Transmission and Limitations*. Oxford: Oxford University Press.

———. 1994. *A Textual Commentary on the Greek New Testament*. 2nd ed. Stuttgart: German Bible Society.

Metzger, Bruce M., and Bart D. Ehrman. 2005. *The Text of the New Testament: Its Transmission, Corruption, and Restoration*. 4th ed. Oxford: Oxford University Press.

Min, Kyoung Shik. 2005. *Die früheste Überlieferung des Matthäusevangeliums*. ANTF 34. Berlin: de Gruyter.

Nongbri, B. 2005. "The Use and Abuse of $\mathfrak{P}^{52}$: Papyrological Pitfalls in the Dating of the Fourth Gospel." *HTR* 98: 23–48.

O'Callaghan, J. 1972. "¿Papiros neotestamentarios en la cueva 7 de Qumrân?" *Bib* 53: 91–100.

O'Neill, John Cochrane. 1989. "The Rules Followed by the Editors of the Text Found in the Codex Vaticanus." *NTS* 35: 219–28.

Obbink, D., and D. Colomo. 2018. "5345. Mark 1:7–9, 16–18." Pages 4–7 in vol. 83 of *The Oxyrhynchus Papyri*. Edited by Peter John Parsons and N. Gonis. London: Egypt Exploration Society.

Payne, Philip B., and Paul Canart. 2000. "The Originality of Text-Critical Symbols in Codex Vaticanus." *NovT* 42: 105–13.

Petersen, W. L. 2009. "The *Vorlage* of Shem-Tob's 'Hebrew Matthew.'" *NTS* 44.4: 490–512.

Porter, C. L. 1962. "Papyrus Bodmer XV (P75) and the Text of Codex Vaticanus." *JBL* 81: 363–76.

Royse, James R. 2007. *Scribal Habits in Early Greek New Testament Papyri*. NTTSD 36. Leiden: Brill.

Skeat, T. C. 1984. "The Codex Vaticanus in the Fifteenth Century." *JTS* 35: 454–65.

———. 1997. "The Oldest Manuscript of the Four Gospels." *NTS* 43: 1–34.

Smith, W. A. 2014. *A Study of the Gospels in Codex Alexandrinus: Codicology, Palaeography, and Scribal Hands*. NTTSD 48. Leiden: Brill.

Stein, Robert. 1987. *The Synoptic Problem: An Introduction*. Grand Rapids: Baker.

Swete, H. B. 1909. *The Gospel according to St. Mark*. 3rd ed. London: Macmillan.

Thiede, C. P. 1992. *The Earliest Gospel Manuscript? The Qumran Papyrus 7Q5 and Its Significance for New Testament Studies*. London: Paternoster.

Wasserman, Tommy. 2012. "The Early Text of Matthew." Pages 83–107 in *The Early Text of the New Testament*. Edited by Charles E. Hill and Michael J. Kruger. Oxford: Oxford University Press.

Wise, Michael Owen. 2020. "Papyri from Qumran Cave 7." Pages 408–11 in vol. 1 of *The T&T Clark Encyclopedia of Second Temple Judaism*. Edited by Daniel M. Gurtner and Loren T. Stuckenbruck. London: T&T Clark.

Yarbro Collins, Adela. 1995. "Establishing the Text: Mark 1:1." Pages 111–27 in *Texts and Contexts: The Function of Biblical Texts in Their Textual and Situational*

Contexts. Edited by Tord Fornberg and David Hellholm. Oslo: Scandinavian University Press.
————. 2007. *Mark: A Commentary.* Hermeneia. Philadelphia: Fortress.

1.2 The Gospels and the Dead Sea Scrolls

Kyung S. Baek

The Dead Sea Scrolls (DSS) and the Gospels share traditions, due to common geographical and temporal factors, despite being two different literary collections with their own literary and historical contexts, and associations with other social movements in the Second Temple period. The scrolls, due to their wealth of information, provide a fuller understanding of the Gospels, though direct influence is almost impossible to prove. A nuanced methodological approach recognizing their distinct literary formation, composition, history, and theology needs to be established before they are placed side by side.

Since their initial discovery in 1946/1947, DSS research has greatly increased our knowledge of Second Temple Judaism. Too often narrowly identified with the literary compositions from the eleven caves near Khirbet Qumran, the scrolls include all the ancient literary remains found in the Judean wilderness surrounding the Dead Sea, from Masada, Nahal Hever, Nahal Ṣeʾelim, Wadi Murabbaʿat, Wadi ed-Daliyah, and Khirbet Mird. Furthermore, the DSS, especially the Cave 4 scrolls, include a wide range of sectarian and nonsectarian texts, compositions depicting variegated perspectives within Second Temple Judaism rather than a particular Jewish sect or movement (i.e., the Essenes). This broader basis of Second Temple thought, including perspectives consistent with the Essene movement, provides a new framework within which to further investigate Gospel studies.

This three-part introductory article offers a general foundation for further research and study. First, it attempts to review the history of research between the Gospels and the DSS. Second, it presents a methodology for comparative examination, avoiding simplistic parallels. Third, it identifies key characteristic features and texts of correspondence and contrast (i.e., terms and phrases) between these two collections.

History of Research

The history of research is often formulated in two ways: general divisions of periods and specific research and proposals. Often divided into four periods, the history of research between the DSS and the Gospels is a cautionary tale oscillating between unsubstantiated conjecture and responsible investigation and publication (Brooke 2005; Frey 2006; Anderson 2011).

Period 1 (ca. 1946/1947–1954), beginning with the discovery of the first scrolls, can be marked by excitement and many unsubstantiated assumptions. As enthusiasm and anticipation spread through media outlets, religious communities, and academic institutions, so did many premature hypotheses. With the promise of a better and fuller understanding of both Jesus and the Gospels, many supposed parallels started emerging between the DSS and the New Testament.

Period 2 (ca. 1955–1979) came with the discovery of more caves and scrolls and an increase in dedicated international researchers. This period is marked by a frenzy of activity, which included: the first volume of *Discoveries in the Judaean Desert* in 1955 by D. Barthélemy and J. T. Milik; both volumes of Millar Burrow's *The Dead Sea Scrolls of St. Mark's Monastery* (Cave 1 scrolls: Great Isaiah Scroll, Habakkuk Commentary, Manual of Discipline) in 1950–1951; *The Complete Dead Sea Scrolls in English* by Geza Vermes in 1962; and *Paul and Palestinian Judaism* by E. P. Sanders in 1977. During this period, DSS and NT studies flourished with many publications, including *John and Qumran* edited by James H. Charlesworth (1972). However, alongside this research, wild speculations and inferences of direct connections between the scrolls and Jesus continued to develop.

Period 3 (ca. 1980–1990), with warnings against "parallelomania" taking hold (Sandmel 1961) and a growing awareness of differences between the scrolls and the Gospels, was a slow time of inactivity for Qumran studies.

Activity improved in Period 4 (ca. 1991–present) as access to the DSS greatly increased including the publication of the texts from Cave 4. As a result, publications of articles and books, symposia, and special collections flourished during this period. Moreover, with social science developments within biblical studies, DSS studies produced more interdisciplinary approaches for examining the scrolls (e.g., Brooke 2013).

An alternative approach to understanding the history of research between the Gospels and the DSS is to present a single strand of research that assumed direct influence (Flint 2013; VanderKam 2010).

- Before the discovery of the scrolls, Karl Bahrdt speculated that Jesus was a secret agent of the Essenes (1780s), and Ernest Renan proposed that Jesus trained as an Essene (1863).

- After the discovery of the DSS, a string of theories emerged assuming a more direct relationship between Jesus and the scrolls.

- In the 1950s, André Dupont-Sommer observed the similarities between Jesus and the "Teacher of Righteousness" of the sectarian texts, but he was careful not to identify them together.

- In 1951, J. L. Teicher claimed the DSS were Christian texts.

- In 1969, Edmund Wilson, a journalist, proposed that Jesus spent his childhood years among the Essenes.

- In 1970s, John Allegro made a direct connection between Jesus and Qumran, proposing and advocating for a Jesus Myth: i.e., early Christianity arose from a fertility cult, and Jesus was invented by early Christians under the drug-induced influence of mushrooms. Based somewhat on pesher Nahum and the Qumran community's worship of a crucified Messiah, he published *The Sacred Mushroom and the Cross* (1970) and *The Dead Sea Scrolls and the Christian Myth* (1979).

- In 1972, José O'Callaghan proposed that a small Greek fragment on papyrus from Cave 7 (7Q5) was a preserved text from Mark 6:52–53.
- In 1981 and 1992, Barbara Thiering suggested that the Gospels were coded Essene writings with two levels of meaning with a cryptic code concealing historical events and persons of two factions of Essenes (i.e., John the Baptist as the "Teacher of Righteousness"; Jesus, John's opponent, as the "Wicked Priest" or the "Man of the Lie").
- In 1997, Robert Eisenman claimed that James, Jesus' brother, was the "Teacher of Righteousness," Ananus the high priest was the "Wicked Priest," and Paul the apostle was the "Man of the Lie."

As these speculations and outrageous assertions have been disproved (i.e., Qumran was the cradle of Christianity; characters in the Gospels are characters in the DSS; or Jesus was a hallucination of a fertility cult experimenting with mushrooms), direct influence and simple comparisons between the Gospels and DSS should be avoided.

Methodology

As noted above, the assumption of direct influence brought about unfounded proposals. However, even with this dubious history, many overlapping themes, beliefs, and practices provide the motivation for comparing parallels. Therefore, without asserting direct influence, similarities—including Jewish reform movements; central teaching figures; communal organization and structure, beliefs of messiah(s) and the "Last Days," practices, and interpretation of Scripture—cannot be overlooked between the Gospels and the DSS (Burrows 1958; Flint 2013).

Acknowledging these challenges, our methodology must incorporate some basic assumptions.

1. The DSS do not mention Jesus or any other character in the NT and the NT does not mention Qumran or Essenes. No parts of any book of the NT are included among the DSS. In other words, the scrolls are Second Temple Jewish compositions and not Christian writings. The overwhelming majority of DSS scholars have concluded that the DSS were written, copied, and owned by Jews who did not acknowledge Jesus of Nazareth as the Messiah. Therefore, only indirect associations should be made between these two collections.

2. There is no textual evidence to postulate a relationship between either the Qumran community or the Essenes and Jesus or the Jesus movement. In some ways, the DSS and the Gospels occupy different worlds with Qumran's emphasis on strict adherence to the entire Torah from its members and the Gospels' accentuation of diversity and inclusion.

3. The DSS and their abundance of nonsectarian texts have greatly enhanced our knowledge of Second Temple and Palestinian Judaism in the two to three centuries before the turn of the era. These writings, with their preservation

of textual pluriformity and religious and thematic plurality, signal a broader diversity of Second Temple Judaism than our previously understood categories derived from the Gospels. However, with the fragmentary nature of most scrolls, only an incomplete knowledge of the past and antiquity can be reconstructed.

Therefore, a nuanced methodology that recognizes these two unique literary collections and considers their different literary forms, features, and compositions; historical contexts and associations; and memories of their significant figures, events, theologies, and practices is essential in evaluating parallels between the Gospels and the DSS. Jörg Frey has called for "an approach based not on vague speculations but on the texts themselves. The similarities and differences between the documents from the Qumran library and the New Testament text must be analyzed with all sophistication" (2006, 438). Today, most scholars have adopted a moderate position and method as they acknowledge their similarities and differences (e.g., their theological vocabulary, religious beliefs, community organization, and ritual practices). Furthermore, as influence is almost impossible to prove, Second Temple Judaism must provide the bridge for shared traditions and overlapping thematic features.

As a way forward, our methodology must be interdisciplinary as it compares the Gospels and the DSS as two separate areas of research with their own unique socio-historical and literary elements. Studies between the Gospels and DSS need to investigate similar areas—history to history, literature to literature, ideology to ideology—without crossing from one to the other. Separate research in each discipline must be the starting point for informed analysis and conclusions before side-by-side comparisons can be made. Then a nuanced correspondence between the Qumran and Jesus movement and their respective literature, the DSS and the Gospels, can be made.

Yes, it is possible that Jesus or early Christians could have met Essenes or encountered their theology and movement, or that some Essenes could have become Christians. However, what is certain is that Jesus and early Christianity emerged out of Second Temple Judaism to formulate and shape its own beliefs and practices. But, as James VanderKam states,

There is no need to go so far as to assert direct influence from scrolls to New Testament authors; rather, the information in some of the Qumran works allow one to interpret a series of New Testament passages in a fuller way with a greater appreciation for them against the backdrop of their time and world. (2012, 120)

Therefore, the DSS within this Second Temple Jewish context enhance our knowledge of Christian origins as they overlap and share many important traditions.

In summary, the consensus view is that the DSS are not Christian texts and not connected with Jesus and the early church. However, due to their geographic and temporal proximity (about twenty miles from Jerusalem on the northwest corner of the Dead Sea and dated from before 250 BCE to 68 CE), the scrolls, in illuminating Second Temple Judaism, are instructive partners for understanding the Gospels, as well as Jesus and Christian origins.

Overview and Intersections

With information provided by the DSS, Craig Evans (2006) declared that all the major themes of the Gospels have close parallels in the DSS, making their Jewish Palestinian provenance certain. Although maybe overly optimistic, the scrolls' discovery and research undeniably affect both Second Temple Judaism and Gospel studies. For example, as parallels confirm the Jewishness of John due to linguistic and religious similarities with the DSS corpus (e.g., dualism and determinism), the context of the Gospel of John has shifted away from a second-century Hellenistic writing to a first-century Jewish composition situated in Palestine (Charlesworth 1992; 2006). The variety of phrases and concepts, as well as the sheer number of similarities, illustrates the correspondence between the Gospels and the DSS and cannot be viewed as anomalies.

The DSS, with its Hebrew, Aramaic, and Greek manuscripts, greatly increase the linguistic landscape of Palestine during the late Second Temple period. Arising from within Second Temple Judaism, the Gospels share with the DSS parallel terms, perspectives, and practices.

Although cautious in their approach to parallels, scholars (Fitzmyer 2000; Struckenbruck 2010; VanderKam 2010; 2012; Flint 2013) observe many general and specific connections (i.e., consider the whole corpus versus particular texts) between the DSS and the Gospels: (1) multiple versions of texts, (2) the use of Scripture and authoritative traditions, (3) thematic associations, and (4) community life.

First, the DSS contain multiple versions of texts, like the Community Rule Scrolls (1QS, 4Q255–264), the Thanksgiving Hymns (1QH^a, 1Q35, 4Q427–432, 4Q471b), and the War Scrolls (1QM, 4Q491–496). These different editions illuminate literary and source critical practices in Second Temple literature, providing evidence for the transmission, editing (which includes additions and omissions), and rewriting of textual traditions. These varieties of textual transmission in ancient sources have provided insight for Gospel origins and transmission (i.e., the Synoptic problem), demonstrating (1) variants within a continuous textual tradition (e.g., 1QIsa^a and 1QIsa^b), (2) the existence of different recensions of the same work (e.g., Daniel), and (3) the existence of common material in two distinguishable works (e.g., Kings and Chronicles). As Struckenbruck confirms, "One may argue that amongst the Dead Sea Scrolls we have the best available and contemporary evidence for how the incremental growth and transformation of written tradition could take place" (2010, 141). Although orality must also be considered in the continuity and fluidity of traditions, the wider literary context of these Second Temple Jewish compositions, with their shared textual traditions (often word for word with minor changes) and rewriting, provide a model regarding the source-critical work on the Synoptic Gospels.

Second, both make a strong emphasis on the knowledge of Scripture or Jewish authoritative traditions. Jesus' Sermon on the Mount and parabolic teaching style (Matt 5–7) is similar to the Qumran movement's instruction to read aloud from the Book, interpreting Scriptures, and praying together (1QS VI, 7–8). The scribal strategy in the Gospels and the DSS for understanding sacred traditions as sources of promises to be appropriated into their contemporary situation is described as fulfillment or prophetic interpretation or pesharim (Brooke 2006; Charlesworth

2006). The *Yahad* use pesharim (continuous, thematic, and isolated pesharim), a hermeneutical strategy that seeks to contemporize Scripture and authoritative traditions by employing ancient prophecies to interpret their current circumstances, recent past, and near future (Berrin 2005). The Gospels also utilize the Old Testament in this way. For example, Krister Stendahl (1968) proposed that pesharim explain Matthew's use of Old Testament fulfilment quotations. Although this was later criticized due to their contrasting structure and style, both pesher and fulfillment quotations are interpretive strategies by authoritative teachers (i.e., "Teacher of Righteousness" and Jesus) that contemporize and actualize ancient traditions into the author's current situations (Fitzmyer 2000; Baek 2017). Regardless, both the DSS and the Gospels use isolated pesharim by referencing previous authoritative traditions to validate their identity, practices, and eschatological expectations (cf. Isa 40:3 in 1QS VIII, 14 [12–16]; Matt 3:3; Mark 1:3; Luke 3:4–6; John 1:23). In sum, the Gospels share with the DSS a similar perspective on the importance of the Scriptures (Jewish authoritative traditions) and the scribal strategy of fulfillment or prophetic interpretation (pesharim).

Third, two key themes in the Gospels correspond with the DSS and provides a fuller understanding of hybridity in Second Temple Judaism as both similar and dissimilar parallels. These are informative: (1) the kingdom of God or heaven and (2) the messiah(s).

1. From the DSS, and more specifically early Jewish apocalyptic literature, the kingdom of God can be understood as the life of the righteous and their existence in the present world order within two overlapping epochs (Struckenbruck 2010). Although the eschatological tension of "already and not yet" or "fulfillment and promise" is widely accepted in Gospel studies, Jewish apocalyptic thought contains the idea of two ages with the domination of evil in the present age. This may explain the Gospels' emphasis on exorcisms and the conflict with Satan (e.g., John 12:31; 14:30; 16:11; cf. Luke 11:24–26). Therefore, Jesus' exorcisms and conflict with evil inaugurate a new age within the framework of the present evil age as is the case in broader Jewish apocalyptic traditions.

2. Both the DSS and the Gospels anticipate the arrival of the messiah(s) in the "Last Days." However, due to its diverse and multifaceted nature in Second Temple Judaism (Collins 2010), expectations of the messiah(s) often brought about religious debate (Mark 8:27–38; 1QS IX, 10–11; 1Q28a II, 11–22; CD XIX, 10–11; XX, 1; cf. Pss. Sol. 17). In the Gospels, messianism is a central theme with its identification of Jesus of Nazareth as the "Messiah" (John 1:41; 4:25); the "Christ" and the "Son of David": e.g., Jesus' genealogy in the line of King David (Matt 1:1–17) and Peter's confession (Matt 16:16). The DSS (particularly the sectarian scrolls) along with the Qumran community expected two messiahs: the messiah of Aaron and the messiah of Israel. The messiah of Aaron is a priestly messiah, while the messiah of Israel is a royal messiah. Although there is some debate concerning the royal nature of the messiah of Israel, his added identification as the "Shoot of David,"

"Branch of David," and the "Prince of the Congregation" seems to confirm his royalty (4Q174 III, 11–13; 4Q252 V, 1–3; 4Q285 VII, 1–4; cf. Gen 49:10). In addition, messianism for the Gospels should incorporate research from 1Q28a, 4Q521, 4Q285, 4Q246 and 4Q169.

- 1Q28a II, 11–22 describes a banquet involving bread and wine where the messiah Aaron and the messiah of Israel are present (cf. Mark 14:22–24; 1QS VI, 4–6).

- 4Q521 frag. II, 2 + IV, 1–15 provide a list of activities by God or his messiah that includes raising the dead (which is not found in Ps 146:7–9; Isa 35:5–6; 61:1–2) echoing Jesus' words and actions in the Gospels (Matt 11:2–5; Luke 7:20–23; cf. Luke 4:16–21; Isa 61:1–2; see Evans 1997; Novakovic 2007).

- 4Q285 VII, 1–4, although debated, contains a piercing (killing) or pierced (dying) messianic figure as the "Branch of David."

- 4Q246 I, 7 – II, 9 contains the phrases "Son of God" and "Son of the Most High" and descriptions of an eternal kingdom.

- 4Q169 IV, 7–8 refers to hanging on a tree as crucifixion.

Fourth, the DSS and the Gospels, and more specifically the Qumran movement and the Jesus movement, have corresponding and contrasting aspects of community life: (1) identify, (2) beliefs and instructions, and (3) practices.

1. Both movements emphasize solidarity and unity. The *Yahad* did so by its very name (which means "community") and demonstrated its importance through their strict membership requirements (1QS V, 1 – VI, 23). Meanwhile, the Gospels call followers of Jesus the *Ekklesia* (Matt 18:15–35; 16:18–19) and Jesus' prayer for his followers calls for radical unity (John 17:20–23). Both are renewed covenant communities (Luke 22:20; Mark 14:24; Matt 26:28; CD VI, 19; VIII, 21; XIX, 33; XX, 12; 1QS II, 10–13, 1Q28b V, 5–23) and display the dualism of light and darkness, often identifying themselves as sons of light and their enemies as the sons of darkness (Luke 16:1–8; John 1:5; 1QM I, 1; 1QS I, 9–11; III, 13; IV, 16–18). Another aspect of community identity and dynamics in 1QS is that true members must love the "sons of light" (everything chosen) and hate the "sons of darkness" (everything that is rejected) (1QS I, 3, 9–11; CD II, 15). This context may help explain what has long been noted by Gospel scholars: the difference in the Synoptic teachings "to love your enemies" (Matt 5:43–45; Luke 6:27, 35) and John's restrictive emphasis "to love one another" (John 13:34; 15:12, 17; 1 John 3:23; cf. Lev 19:18, 34).

2. Rebuking community members, sharing wealth and attitudes toward investing, and keeping the Sabbath are overlapping community instructions between the Gospels and the DSS. Drawing from Lev 19:15–18, Matt 18:15–17 and 1QS V, 24 – VI, 1 (cf. CD VI, 11 – VII, 6) give instructions for rebuking community members; however, the instructions, orders, and purposes

seem to be different (Kampen 2019). While both have similarities, the goal for Matthew seems to be forgiveness and reconciliation (Matt 18:21–22), while 1QS's goal is to keep the Torah and maintain social structures without harboring bitterness (1QS V, 23 – VI, 2).

Additionally, both communities in the Gospels and the DSS have instructions to share wealth and property, to support the poor, the needy, and the alien, and to not accumulate excessive wealth (Matt 6:24; Luke 12:13–21; cf. Acts 2:44–45; CD IV, 16–17; VI, 20–27; 1QS VI, 7–22; 1QH^a XVIII, 31–32). Another aspect of wealth is the instruction to not invest in money that is entrusted to you nor to even touch or take money but to return it or safely deposit it (4Q416 frag. 2 III, 3–5; 4Q418). This opposes Matthew's parable of the talents that advises someone that is entrusted with money to invest it (Matt 25:14–30). It does, however, support Luke's parable of the minas, with its inferences to Archelaus and Rome in 4 BCE, as it does not advocate investing wealth but contrasts two different rulers (Jesus and Archelaus) and their economic strategies (Luke 19:11–27; see Green 1997).

Finally, the instructions around keeping the Sabbath differ between the DSS and the Gospels. Many times, Jesus disagrees with the Pharisees and religious leaders and challenges their interpretation of the Torah. One example is Sabbath observance: Jesus heals a man with a withered hand at a synagogue on the Sabbath (Matt 12:9–14) and uses the illustration of a sheep falling into a pit. In the DSS, if an animal falls into water or a pit, nothing can be done; but if a person falls into water, a garment can be passed to them (4Q265 VI, 5–8) though without doing anything further (CD A XI, 13–14; par. 4Q270 VI, 18; 4Q271 frag. 5 I, 8–9).

3. The community practice of ritual washing at Qumran has been compared with John's baptism; however, John's baptism seems to occur once for repentance, while Qumran's ritual washing happens repeatedly, if not daily, for cleansing (Mark 1:4–8; cf. 1QS III, 4–5, 9). In addition, at Qumran, ritual baths signal the importance of purity, but Jesus' approach to purity is to touch and accept the sick, the disadvantaged (the blind, deaf, mute, and lame), and sinners (Dunn 1993). In contrast to Jesus, the DSS exclude such people from full participation in the worshiping community (1QSa II, 5–8; CD XV, 15–17).

In sum, these four observations, using comparisons that began contextually, give a better picture of the multifaceted and complex overlay between the Gospels and the DSS. Understanding their shared traditions, accompanied by similar or differing responses, is a necessary starting point for identifying commonalities and differences. Consequently, this exploration of perspectives adds to the matrix of Second Temple Judaism: textuality, scribal practice, theology, and religious and social life.

Conclusion

Current Gospel studies cannot ignore the DSS. Four main intersections—multiple versions of texts, scribal strategies, thematic correspondence, and community life—

with similar and contrasting elements reveal this multifaceted association. Although direct influence has produced imaginative assertions and should be avoided, a methodology recognizing the distinct literary compositions and historical associations of the DSS and the Gospels needs to be established before they are compared.

In sum, parallels help us understand and determine the correspondence of various shared traditions. As the scrolls have greatly increased the knowledge of Second Temple Judaism, it provides a bridge with shared traditions and overlapping linguistic and thematic elements for these two collections. Concepts—such as messianism, eschatology, the kingdom of God, dualism, scriptural interpretation and instruction, and communal life—were developed within pre-Christian Palestinian Judaism. Facilitating the recovery of the Jewishness of Jesus and early Christianity, the DSS tether the Gospels in the vibrant diversity of first-century Second Temple Judaism. Therefore, Gospel research arising from this context must incorporate DSS research to validate earlier proposals and formulate fresh perspectives.

Works Cited

Anderson, Paul N. 2011. "John and Qumran: Discovery and Interpretation over Sixty Years." Pages 15–50 in *John, Qumran, and the Dead Sea Scrolls: Sixty Years of Discovery and Debate.* EJL 32. Edited by Mary L. Coloe and Tom Thatcher. Leiden: Brill.

Baek, Kyung S. 2017. "Prophecy and Divination in the Gospel of Matthew." Pages 653–78 in *Reading the Bible in Ancient Traditions and Modern Editions: Studies in Memory of Peter W. Flint.* EJL 47. Edited by Andrew B. Perrin, Kyung S. Baek, and Daniel K. Falk. Atlanta: SBL Press.

Barthélemy, D., and J. T. Milik. 1955. *Qumran Cave 1.* Vol. 1 of *Discoveries in the Judaean Desert.* Oxford: Clarendon Press.

Berrin, Shani. 2005. "Qumran Pesharim." Pages 110–33 in *Biblical Interpretation at Qumran.* Edited by Matthias Henze. Studies in the Dead Sea Scrolls and Related Literature. Grand Rapids: Eerdmans.

Brooke, George J. 2006. "Biblical Interpretation at Qumran." Pages 287–319 in *Scripture and the Scrolls.* Vol. 1 of *The Bible and the Dead Sea Scrolls: The Second Princeton Symposium on Judaism and Christian Origins.* Edited by James H. Charlesworth. Waco, TX: Baylor University Press.

———. 2005. *The Dead Sea Scrolls and the New Testament.* Minneapolis, MN: Fortress Press.

———. 2013. *Reading the Dead Sea Scrolls: Essays in Method.* EJL 39. Atlanta: SBL Press.

Burrows, Millar. 1958. *More Light on the Dead Sea Scrolls and Interpretations with Translation of Important Recent Discoveries.* New York: Viking.

Charlesworth, James H., ed. 1992. *Jesus and the Dead Sea Scrolls.* ABRL. New York: Doubleday.

———., ed. 2006. *The Scrolls and Christian Origins.* Vol. 3 of *The Bible and the Dead Sea Scrolls: The Second Princeton Symposium on Judaism and Christian Origins.* Waco, TX: Baylor University Press.

Collins, John J. 1997. "The Expectation of the End in the Dead Sea Scrolls." Pages 74–90 in *Eschatology, Messianism, and the Dead Sea Scrolls*. Studies in the Dead Sea Scrolls and Related Literature. Edited by Craig A. Evans and Peter W. Flint. Grand Rapids: Eerdmans.

———. 2010. *The Scepter and the Star: Messianism in Light of the Dead Sea Scrolls*. 2nd ed. Grand Rapids: Eerdmans.

Dunn, James D. G. 1992. "Jesus, Table-Fellowship, and Qumran." Pages 254–72 in *Jesus and the Dead Sea Scrolls*. ABRL. Edited by James H. Charlesworth. New York: Doubleday.

Evans, Craig A. 1997. "Jesus and the Dead Sea Scrolls from Qumran Cave 4." Pages 91–100 in *Eschatology, Messianism, and the Dead Sea Scrolls*. Studies in the Dead Sea Scrolls and Related Literature. Edited by Craig A. Evans and Peter W. Flint. Grand Rapids: Eerdmans.

———. 2006. "The Synoptic Gospels and the Dead Sea Scrolls." Pages 75–95 in *The Scrolls and Christian Origins*. Vol. 3 of *The Bible and the Dead Sea Scrolls: The Second Princeton Symposium on Judaism and Christian Origins*. Edited by James H. Charlesworth. Waco, TX: Baylor University Press.

Fitzmyer, Joseph A. 2000. *The Dead Sea Scrolls and Christian Origins*. Grand Rapids: Eerdmans.

Flint, Peter W. 2013. *The Dead Sea Scrolls*. Nashville: Abingdon Press.

Frey, Jörg. 2006. "The Impact of the Dead Sea Scrolls on New Testament Interpretation: Proposals, Problems, and Further Perspectives." Pages 407–61 in *The Scrolls and Christian Origins*. Vol. 3 of *The Bible and the Dead Sea Scrolls: The Second Princeton Symposium on Judaism and Christian Origins*. Edited by James H. Charlesworth. Waco, TX: Baylor University Press.

Green, Joel. 1997. *The Gospel of Luke*. NICNT. Grand Rapids: Eerdmans.

Kampen, John. 2019. *Matthew within Sectarian Judaism*. AYBRL. New Haven: Yale University Press.

Novakovic, Lidija. 2007. "4Q521: The Works of the Messiah or the Signs of Messianic Times." Pages 208–31 in *Qumran Studies: New Approaches, New Questions*. Edited by M. T. Davis and B. A. Strawn: Grand Rapids: Eerdmans.

Sandmel, Samuel. 1962. "Parallelomania." *JBL* 81: 1–13.

Sanders, E. P. 1977. *Paul and Palestinian Judaism*. London: SCM Press.

Stendahl, Krister. *The School of St. Matthew and Its Use of the Old Testament*. 2nd ed. Philadelphia: Fortress, 1968.

Stuckenbruck, Loren T. 2010. "The Dead Sea Scrolls and the New Testament." Pages 131–70 in *Qumran and the Bible: Studying the Jewish and Christian Scriptures in Light of the Dead Sea Scrolls*. Edited by Nóra Dávid and Armin Lange. Leuven: Peeters.

VanderKam, James C. 2010. *The Dead Sea Scrolls Today*. 2nd ed. Grand Rapids: Eerdmans.

———. 2012. *The Dead Sea Scrolls and the Bible*. Grand Rapids: Eerdmans.

Vermes, Geza. 1962. *The Complete Dead Sea Scrolls in English*. London: Penguin.

1.3 Early Reception of Matthew

Russell Morton

Whether or not its designation as "the church's Gospel" is accurate, Matthew held a privileged place among the Gospels in the early church. Twenty-five known patristic writings dealt with Matthew in detail and another forty early writers devoted extensive attention to Matthew. Matthew is the first Gospel mentioned in all the early canonical lists (Williams 2019, xxiii). While it is not possible here to give a detailed account of Matthew's impact on early Christians, the following focuses on the Gospel's impact on writers in the Christian East, among writers in the Western church, and its use in early Christian anti-Jewish polemic.

Syria and Palestine and Asia Minor

Didache

Earlier scholarship held that the *Didache* dates from the second half of the second century (Massaux 1990–1993, 3:145). As a result, similarities with Matthean language were understood as indications of the *Didache*'s dependence on Matthew. Massaux, for example, found numerous instances of direct Matthean influence upon the *Didache*. These passages included: *Didache* 1:2a // Matt 22:37–40; *Didache* 1:2b // Matt 7:12; *Didache* 1:5 // Matt 5:25–26; *Didache* 3:7 // Matt 5:5; and *Didache* 6:2 // Matt 5:48. The similarities between the introduction to the Lord's Prayer and the prayer itself in Matt 6:9–13 and in the *Didache* 8:2 provided further evidence for the *Didache*'s dependence on Matthew (Massaux 1990–1993, 3:145–55). In *Didache* 8.3, the faithful are commanded to repeat the prayer three times a day. Thus from an early date, Christian liturgy employed a Matthean like form of the Lord's Prayer in its liturgy.

More recent scholarship, however, has suggested that the *Didache* and Matthew were likely composed contemporaneously. Therefore, "the Didache does not seem to be dependent upon Matthew itself, but upon certain materials that are known only in Matthew" (Jefford 2005, 45). Determining the *Didache*'s dependence on Matthew is further complicated by the context of proposed parallels in both documents. The greatest convergences between the language of the *Didache* and Matthew occur in *Didache* 1–7: the teaching on the "Two Ways" and Matthew's Sermon on the Mount (Matt 5–7). Both texts reflect traditional two-ways motifs and may be further evidence of dependence on common traditions, especially if both Matthew and the *Didache* were composed in the same Syrian Christian community (Syreeni 2005; Tomson 2005). Yet, even if we cannot determine direct dependence of the *Didache* on Matthew, we can conclude that both emerged from a common Jewish-Christian in Syria-Palestine.

Sayings of Jesus/Gospel of Thomas

As with the *Didache*, the scholarly consensus has been that the Coptic *Gospel of Thomas*, or *Sayings of Jesus* (Gos. Thom.), is generally independent of the canonical Gospels and preserves older forms of Jesus' sayings (Koester 1988, 125). This hypothesis has, however, been challenged by those who note that since Gos. Thom. was most probably written in the second century, it is likely that the author(s) were at least aware of the Synoptic tradition if not directly dependent on one or more of the Synoptic Gospels (Goodacre 2012).

If Gos. Thom. is dependent on Synoptic tradition, is there evidence that its writer(s) utilized Matthew in particular? Parallels between the Matthean parables and the sayings in Gos. Thom. may provide a positive answer to this question. We shall focus on two examples. First, the parable of the dragnet (Matt 13:47–49) is paralleled in Gos. Thom. 8. The saying in Gos. Thom., however, reads like a summary of the Matthean parable and lacks the redactional interpretation of the parable found in Matt 13:49–50. Another possible example of its dependence on Matthew can be found in Gos. Thom. 57, which is a condensed version of Matt 13:24–30, the parable of the weeds in the field. Again, Gos. Thom. lacks the interpretation of the parable found in Matthew 13:36–43. Nevertheless, numerous features of Gos. Thom. 57 indicate that it is an abbreviation of Matt 13:24–30. The account in Gos. Thom. lacks the interaction between the slaves and the master (Matt 13:27–28) as well as the command that the wheat and weeds grow up together. The latter lacunae may reflect a rejection of Matthew's understanding of the church as a mixed community (Hultgren 2000, 295; Snodgrass 2008, 200). Two possible reasons may account for why Gos. Thom. 57 lacks Matthew's interpretation of the parable. One may be that Gos. Thom.'s condensation of the parable left no room for the interpretation. The other possibility is because the ecclesiastical focus of the interpretation ran counter to the interests of Gos. Thom.'s compiler(s). In conclusion, a case can be made for Gos. Thom.'s familiarity, if not dependence, on Matthean traditions.

Matthew in Ignatius of Antioch (d. ca. 118 CE)

While a case can be made that the apparent allusions to Matthew in Ignatius of Antioch derive from use of a common oral tradition (Schoedel 1985, 9), a contrary argument has been made that he was the first early church writer to make extensive use of Matthew. Ignatius was hesitant to quote from large sections of Matthew in his writings. This fact may be because Ignatius did not share Matthew's Jewish perspective (Jefford 2005, 45), as exemplified by Ignatius's vehement opposition to "Judaizers" (Ign. *Phld.* 5.2–9.2). Yet allusions to or quotes from Matthew can be readily discerned. The only other Gospel Ignatius employs as frequently is the Gospel of John. There is no evidence that he utilized either Mark or Luke.

In three passages, Ignatius exhibits familiarity with traditions found only in Matthew. In Ign. *Smyrn.* 1.1, Ignatius states that Jesus was baptized "to fulfill all righteousness" (see Matt 3:14–15). In Ign. *Poly.* 2.2, Ignatius states the necessity to be "prudent as a serpent and . . . always pure as a dove," an exhortation found in the Gospel tradition only in Matt 10:16b. Finally, Ign. *Eph.* 19.2–3 refers to the magi's visit to the Christ child (see Matt 2:1–12; Brown and Meier 1982, 24–25). Further examples of Ignatius's use of Matthew may be found in Ign. *Eph.* 5.2, where Ignatius states that if the prayer of one or two individuals has great force, how much more so the prayers of the whole church (see Matt 18:19–20); Ign. *Eph.* 14.2, where a tree is known by its fruit (see Matt 12:33); Ign. *Trall.* 11.1; and Ign. *Phld* 3.1, where the warning not to eat of the poisoned fruits of false Christian teachers may allude to Matt 15:13 (Massaux 1990–1993, 1:87–89). These brief examples provide evidence that Ignatius uses Matthew's Gospel to defend his own arguments against his opponents (Jefford 2005, 45).

Polycarp of Smyrna (d. after 160 CE)

Polycarp, a younger contemporary of Ignatius, served as bishop of Smyrna until his martyrdom during the reign of Marcus Aurelius. From his *Letter to the Philippians*, it is apparent that Polycarp knew the Gospels of Matthew and Luke as well as the Pauline letters, 1 Peter, John, and possibly Mark. In his Pol. *Phil.* 2.3a, he corrected quotations of Jesus' sayings against judging one's neighbor in 1 Clement 13:2 (see Matt 5:1, 7; 6:14–15; 7:1; Luke 6:37; 1 Clem. 13:2) to correspond with established text used by his church (Massaux 1990–1993, 28–30; Koester 1982, 306). Likewise, in Pol. *Phil.* 7.2, Polycarp conflates Matt 6:13, "lead us not into temptation," with Matt 26:41 // Mark 14:38, "the spirit is willing, but the flesh is weak" (Massaux 1990–1993, 2:31–32).

In the *Martyrdom of Polycarp*, we find few direct allusions to Matthew or any other New Testament writing. *Martyrdom of Polycarp* 1.1, however, expresses the author's intention to compose an account of Polycarp's death that will remind the reader of Christ's passion (Massaux 1990–1993, 2:45). By employing language derived from the four canonical Gospel accounts of Jesus' trial and death to describe Polycarp's own ordeal, the author gives privileged status to Matthew, Mark, Luke, and John. From this usage, we may discern their special status within the church of Asia Minor's incipient canon.

Tatian (Second Century)

Tatian was born of Greek parents who lived in the region of ancient Assyria. They provided him with an education in Greek culture and philosophy. He moved to Rome, where he met Justin Martyr, who converted Tatian to Christianity (Metzger 1987, 114). After Justin's death, Tatian returned to the East where he became founder of the sect of the Encratites, or the "self-controlled." According to Irenaeus, this group, like the Marcionites, denied God's work as creator, as reflected by the Encratites' prohibition of marriage (*Haer.* 1.28.1). Tatian is best known today for his harmony of the Gospels, the *Diatessaron* (see Eusebius, *Hist. eccl.* 4.28–29). Tatian's work combined the four Gospels into a single narrative, generally following the chronology of John. While no complete copy of the *Diatessaron* exists, in 1933 a 9-cm-square fragment was identified. It contains text of Matt 27:26, 57; Mark 15:40; Luke 23:54 (Metzger 1987, 115). From this example, we can see that Matthew, along with the other three canonical Gospels, had already attained a special or possibly incipient canonical status in the churches of the Syria and Asia Minor. The Eastern church's high regard for Matthew would also contribute to its acceptance in the Western church, especially because of the influence of writers such as Justin Martyr and Irenaeus of Lyons.

Theophilus of Antioch "To Autolycus" (ca. 180 CE)

Theophilus was a second-century bishop of Antioch. He received a Greek education but converted to Christianity as an adult (Massaux 1990–1993, 3:134). He was aware of the four canonical Gospels, as well as the letters of Paul. Theophilus's works only survive in Latin translation, so it is difficult to determine if he directly quotes Matthew. There are, however, some hints at his dependence on Matthew. In *Autol.* 3.13, the reader encounters a conflated quotation from Matt 5:28, 32; 19:9: the warning against the wandering eye and the prohibition of divorce. While the prohibition of divorce is also found in Mark 10:11–12 and Luke 16:18, Theophilus includes the exemption clause of Matt 5:32, "except for unchastity." *To Autolycus* 3.14 also reproduces Matthew's longer form of the commandment to love one's enemies (Matt 5:44, 46 // Luke 6:27–28, 32. Finally, *Autol.* 3.14 also reproduces the language of Matt 6:3, which commands almsgivers not to let their right hand know what their left is doing (Massaux 1990–1993, 3:135–38). The scarcity of evidence prevents us from concluding whether Theophilus was quoting from Matthew or a collection of *testimonia*. We can, nevertheless, conclude that Matthew's teachings played an important role in Theophilus's church in Antioch.

Rome and the West

Echoes of Matthew in 1 Clement

Did Clement of Rome (flor. 92–101) make use of Matthew or Matthean traditions in his letter to the Corinthian church? The question is complicated because Clement alludes to rather than quotes from Matthean-like traditions. Determining Clement's direct dependence on Matthew is further complicated by the conflation of various Matthean and Lukan passages. For example, 1 Clem. 13:1b-2 exhorts readers to be humble minded and merciful and to remember that they will be judged to the extent they judge others. This allusion is reminiscent of Matt 5:7; 6:12–15; 7:1–2, 12. It also contains elements of Luke 6:31, 36–39 (Massaux 1990–1993, 1:8–9). Likewise, 1 Clem. 27:5 describes God's faithfulness to divine promises in language similar to Matt 5:18; 24:33; Luke 10:17; 21:33 (Massaux 1990–1993, 1:12–13). Furthermore, 1 Clem. 30:3 exhorts readers to be cautious about speech, to be humble of spirit, and to remember that they will be justified by works rather than words. This passage is reminiscent of common New Testament parenesis, such as that found not only in Matt 7:21 but also in Rom 2:13; 1 Cor 4:20, and Jas 1:22 (Massaux 1990–1993, 1:14–15). In this last instance, a strong case can be made that Clement was paraphrasing from Pauline rather than Matthean tradition.

Clement's use of Matthew or Matthean tradition may also underlie Clement's teaching on the Lord's Supper. In 1 Clem. 46:7–8, Clement alludes to Judas's betrayal of Jesus, noting that it would be better had Judas not been born (Matt 26:24 // Mark 14:21). Dependence here is complicated by Matthew's literary dependence on Mark, reproducing Mark's language. The second half of 1 Clem. 40:8, however, refers to the logia of Matt 18:6 (cf. Mark 9:42 // Luke 17:10): "If any of you put a stumbling block before one of these little ones who believe in me, it would be better for you if a great millstone were fastened around your neck and you were drowned in the depth of the sea" (NRSV). In contrast to Matthew's warning about the offending of "these little ones," 1 Clem. reads, "pervert one of my chosen ones" (Massaux 1990–1993, 1:21). Nevertheless, despite some changes in language, Massaux noted a preponderance of wording common to Matt 18:6, indicating 1 Clem.'s dependence on Matthew (Massaux 1990–1993, 1:23–24).

Despite Massaux's confidence, however, it is safer to conclude that 1 Clem. employs a tradition that uses language common to Matthew. While we cannot rule out the possibility that Clement knew and read Matthew, the extent to which the Roman church was familiar with Matthew's text at such an early stage is open to question, especially since the Gospel's original provenance was Syria-Palestine.

Shepherd of Hermas

Consisting of five visions, twelve mandates, and ten similitudes, the Shepherd of Hermas is a complex document, probably written in Rome or central Italy over a period of time from the end of the first century to the middle of the second century (Osiek 1999, 18–20). Massaux found several instances where Matthean influence was likely. In *Vision* 1.1.18, Hermas is warned that desire for the woman to whom he was sold is a "great sin" (see Matt 5:28). *Mandate* 4.1.1 also warns against carnal desire in terms similar to Matt 5:28. *Mandate* 6.2.4 warns against false teachers, in language Massaux judged as indicating dependence on Matt 7:16 // Luke 6:44. We may also consider *Similitude* 3.3, which Massaux suggested reflected dependence on the parable of the weeds in Matt 13:24–30 (Massaux 1990–1993, 2:111–13, 115–16). The language of *Similitude* 3.3 and Matt 13:24–30, however, is quite different. In Shepherd, the visionary is warned that trees in winter shed their leaves and do not display the life within them, so sinners and saints may look alike. This imagery diverges significantly from that of the parable of the weeds in the field, although both texts exhibit a common understanding of the church as a mixed community containing both the elect and the reprobate.

The parallels that Massaux noted are tenuous at best. One of the best parallels in thought between Matthew and Shepherd is the moral tradition of the Two Ways. This tradition is expressed simply in Matt 7:13–14. The tradition is developed in more detail in *Didache* 1–6. It is described as a conflict between contesting spirits in *Mandate* 5.1–2 and 6.2. The Two Ways are also described as contesting spirits in *Mandate* 12.1–3. In *Similitudes* 9.13.2; 15.2, virtues are spirits personified as women (Osiek 1999, 32). The Two Ways was, however, a common theme in Jewish as well as Greco-Roman moral teaching, and direct dependence on Matthew is questionable.

Thus Osiek has concluded that similarities between Matthew and Shepherd likely reflects dependence on common oral tradition (1999, 26).

Epistle of Barnabas (Second Century)

Composed in Greek, the *Epistle of Barnabas* was highly valued by both Clement of Alexandria and Origen. It purports to have been written by Paul's companion but was likely a second-century composition. The author employs an allegorical interpretation of the Septuagint to engage in an attack on aspects of the Mosaic law, including animal sacrifice, which according to *Barnabas* 9.4 was inspired by an evil angel (Metzger 1987, 56). The anti-Jewish polemic may have also inspired the quotation of Matt 22:14 in *Barnabas* 4.14, "Many are called but few are chosen" (Metzger 1987, 57).

Despite its anti-Jewish perspective, *Barnabas* heavily utilizes the Matthean passion tradition in its apologetic. In *Barnabas* 5.12, for example, the citation of Zech 13:7 mentions the striking of the "shepherd of the flock," which corresponds to Matt 26:31 rather than Mark 14:27, "I will strike the shepherd of the sheep" (Massaux 1990–1993, 1:62). Similarly, *Barnabas* 7.3, 5 mentions how at his crucifixion, Jesus was given vinegar and gall to drink (see Matt 27:34). Metzger, however, notes that the author of *Barnabas* may not have been referring to Matthew but quoting from Ps 79:21 (Metzger 1987, 57). There was, nevertheless, irony in that the most Jewish of the Gospels was read to support an allegorical anti-Jewish reading of the Jewish Bible.

Matthew in Justin Martyr (d. ca. 165 CE)

Although originally from Palestine, Justin immigrated to Rome, where he composed his apologetic works and was eventually martyred. Justin's use of Matthew is concentrated in his *First Apology* and his *Dialogue with Trypho*. One example is found in *1 Apol.* 15.1, where Justin alludes to the second antithesis, noting that whenever a man looks at a woman with desire, he is guilty of adultery (Matt 5:28). On the other hand, determining the extent of Justin's dependence on Matthew is complicated by the apologist's apparent tendency to quote from memory and to conflate quotations from two or three of the Synoptic Gospels or, as Justin referred to them, the "Memoirs of the Apostles." *First Apology* 15.2, for example, where Justin mentions how Jesus commanded those whose eye caused them to sin to pluck out the offending organ, contains elements of three different texts (Matt 5:29; 8:9; Mark 9:47). *First Apology* 15.3, where remarriage after divorce is equated with adultery, is likely a conflation of the four Gospel sayings on the topic found in Matt 5:32; 19:9, Mark 10:11, and Luke 16:18 (Massaux 1990–1993, 3:11–13).

Not only does Justin conflate sayings from different Gospels, he also combines elements from different parts of the same Gospel. For example, in *1 Apol.* 15.12; Matt 16:26, "What does it profit a person to gain the whole world and lose one's soul?" (cf. Mark 8:36–37 // Luke 9:25) is combined with the exhortation to "store up treasures in heaven" (see Matt 6:20 // Luke 12:33). Even more complex is Justin's version of the "Golden Rule" found in *1 Apol.* 15.13, which combines elements of Matt 5:45, 48, Luke 6:36, and Eph 4:32 (Massaux 1990–1993, 3:20–21). Justin's dependence on

Matthean tradition is, nevertheless, further evidenced in *1 Apol.* 33.1, where Justin agrees with Matt 1:22–23 that Isa 7:14 predicted Jesus' virgin birth and that Jesus was to be called Immanuel or "God with us" (Massaux 1990–1993, 3:35).

In *Dial.*, Justin assumes that Trypho is familiar with either Gospel material or some type of Gospel *testimonia* (*Dial.* 10.2; 18.1), Thus it is likely that Gospel material was available to non-Christian readers (Gamble 1995, 103). A few examples will demonstrate Justin's use of Matthew. An instance of Justin's reliance on uniquely Matthean tradition is found in *Dial.* 78.2, which refers again to the visit of the magi (see Matt 2:1–14). Here, Justin precisely utilized the language of Matt 2:11–12 (Massaux 1990–1993, 3:62). An example of conflation of language is found in *Dial.* 17.4, where Justin condemned Jewish "hypocrisy" in language reminiscent of Matt 23:23, 27 // Luke 11:4. In the Gospel texts, Jesus condemns the scribes and Pharisees for tithing mint, rue, and cumin, while neglecting the greater demands of the Torah (Massaux 1990–1993, 3:51). The latter example demonstrates an early tendency of Christian writers employing Matthean language, originally directed at Jesus' opponents, to condemn Judaism as a whole.

The fact that at times Justin quotes language found only in Matthew, while at other times he conflates material from Matthew, Mark, and Luke, raises an important question. Was Justin reading from the canonical Gospels or *testimonia* of Gospel tradition, perhaps like Tatian's *Diatessaron*? Justin did meet with Tatian when the latter visited Rome, where the *Diatessaron* was likely composed (Metzger 1987, 114–15). Whatever his exact source, however, it is indisputable that Justin was acquainted with Matthean tradition.

Second Clement (between 120–170)

Second Clement is not a letter but a homily. It was assigned to Clement by later tradition, and from this evidence the document's Roman provenance has been assumed (Metzger 1987, 68). The author quotes from both Matthew and Luke. Yet at times, 2 Clem. prefers Matthean wording. Second Clement 3:1–2 quotes Matt 10:32–33: "The one who confesses me before humans, I will confess that one before my Father." The use of the first person "I will confess" corresponds with Matthean wording, as opposed to the Lukan phrase, "the Son of Man will confess." Likewise, in 2 Clem. 4:2, "Not everyone who says to me, 'Lord, Lord' will be saved" more closely resembles Matt 7:21, "Not everyone who says to me, 'Lord, Lord,'" than the parallel in Luke 6:46, "Why do you call me Lord, Lord?" (Massaux 1990–1993, 2:6–8). From these examples, we may conclude that 2 Clem. contains some of the best attested evidence of a Western Christian writer utilizing Matthew without some direct dependence on the Eastern church.

Irenaeus (ca. 130–ca. 202 CE)

Irenaeus, although from Smyrna, is best remembered as bishop of Lugdunum in Gaul (modern Lyons in France). It was here (ca. 180 CE) where he composed his apologetic work *Adversus Haereses* (*Against Heresies*). While Book 1 of *Haer.*

is often regarded as primarily a defense of Catholic Christianity against gnosis, or Gnosticism, in fact Irenaeus addressed numerous different groups as diverse as Valentinians, Ebionites, Nicolaitans, Encratites, and other sects not normally considered "gnostic" (Williams 1996, 33–34). In Book 3, Irenaeus presents his "proofs from Scripture" to refute Valentinianism in particular. Irenaeus does not restrict his defense of orthodoxy to exegesis of the Gospels; he also appeals to Acts, the Pauline letters, and the Septuagint.

Irenaeus is famous for defending an incipient New Testament canon, which includes the four canonical Gospels. He argued that it was necessary that the Gospels be no more and no less than four in number, since there are four winds, four zones of the world, and that the church should have four pillars (*Haer.* 3.11.8). Only these Gospels provide apostolic witness to Jesus' life and teaching. By this argument, he sought to refute the additional gospels, such as the *Gospel of Truth*, Marcion's canon (whose gospel witness contained only an abridged Gospel of Luke), the Ebionites' rejection of all Gospels except the Gospel of Matthew, and Tatian's *Diatessaron* (*Haer.* 3.11).

In addition to arguing for the so-called fourfold gospel, Irenaeus also employed the four Gospels to make specific points. He states that there is only one God, who is both the God of Israel and the God of Jesus. John the Baptist makes this point clear in his address to the Pharisees, warning them as "brood of vipers" that "God is able from these stones to raise up children of Abraham" (Matt 3:7–9 NRSV). Thus the ministry of Jesus is connected with God's promise to Abraham. The point is further clarified in Matt 1:1–18 where Jesus' descent from Abraham is described (*Haer.* 3.9.1). At Jesus' baptism, the Spirit of God declares Jesus' divine sonship (Matt 3:16), because as a human Jesus was both a son of Abraham and a son of Jesse. At the same time, as Son of God, the Spirit of God descended on Jesus who fulfilled the promise of the prophets. Irenaeus concluded that for these reasons salvation was through Jesus alone (*Haer.* 3.9.3).

Yet, while Irenaeus affirmed Matthew's portrayal of Jesus as fulfillment of scriptural promise, he also employed Matthew's use of the Septuagint against both Jewish opponents and Ebionite Christians. In particular, Irenaeus argued that since Matt 1:23 quoted Isa 7:14 from the Septuagint, efforts to translate the Hebrew word *'almah* as "young woman," rather than as "virgin" (*parthenos*), were a distortion of Isaiah's message. Since Jesus was the second Adam (see Rom 5:12–21), like Adam Jesus had no earthly father. Hence, Jesus was born of a virgin (*Haer* 3.21.1). Irenaeus, therefore, both further refined Justin's arguments that Isaiah predicted Jesus' virgin birth and cognomen "Immanuel" (*1 Apol.* 33.1) and utilized the passage to intensify an anti-Jewish polemic.

Matthew in Anti-Jewish Polemic

One of the great tragedies of church history has been the use of Matthew in anti-Jewish polemic. This polemic has its origins in the Gospel itself, as it accentuates Mark's representation of Jesus' conflict with Jewish authorities. While Mark 3:6 describes the initial plot against Jesus as being conducted by the Pharisees and the Herodians, in Matt 12:14, the Pharisees alone are portrayed as Jesus' enemies. In contrast to the

Markan Jesus warning the disciples against the "leaven of the Pharisees and Herod" (Mark 8:15), in Matthew the warning is directed against the yeast of the Pharisees and Sadducees (Matt 16:6). Likewise, in Jesus' commission of the disciples in Matt 10:17, the warnings about the persecution of believers by the synagogues and the Sanhedrin are likely a strengthening of the polemic of the Q saying possibly more originally preserved in Luke 12:11.

This tendency was further intensified by early Christian writers. In addition to Justin's and Irenaeus's use of Matt 1:22–23 as both a defense of Jesus' virgin birth and polemic against Judaism, later writers would employ Matthew's harsh language against the Pharisees and Jewish crowds to accuse the Pharisees and Jewish people in particular of hypocrisy and guilt for Christ's death. Our focus will be on Matthew's curses of the Pharisees (Matt 23) and Matthew's accentuation of the people's guilt in the Matthean passion narrative (Matt 27:24–25).

Matthew's Gospel attacks the Pharisees as "hypocrites" in 23:2–3, 13, 15–16, 23, 25, 27, 29. This language may represent common Jewish sectarian polemic against rival groups. At Qumran, for example, the Pharisees are described as "seekers after smooth things" (4Q169 III, 1). In the Jewish context, Jesus would not be criticizing Pharisaic authority (see Matt 23:1–2) but practice (Liebowitz 2014, 61). When Matthew was read outside the context of an intra-Jewish dispute, however, the language of chapter 23 was understood not only as an attack on certain inconsistent practices but as a condemnation of Judaism as a whole. In *Strom.* 6.6, Clement of Alexandria (ca. 150–212) argued that before Christ's advent, the Jews were imprisoned by idolatry and could not, therefore, be reliable teachers of the Mosaic covenant. For that reason, the scribes and Pharisees imposed unnecessary burdens on their adherents, as stated in Matt 23 (Luz 2001–2007, 3:108). Likewise, Origen (185–ca. 254 CE) asserted in his *Commentary on Matthew* that the scribes and Pharisees lacked the insight to interpret the spiritual meaning of Moses' commandments (Simonetti 2001–2003, 2:164–65). The equation of Judaism with hypocrisy would be accentuated throughout church history, especially as expressed in Luther's disparagement of Jews and the almost universally negative portrayal of Judaism by Christian writers in the nineteenth century.

Another text employed in anti-Jewish polemic is Matt 27:25, where the crowd states that Jesus' blood will be upon them and their children. Therefore, it was not uncommon for Christian preachers to hold that the Jewish people bore continued culpability for Jesus' blood. Jerome (ca. 347–420 CE) was one who commented that the guilt of the Jews remained until his own day (Luz 2001–2007, 506–7). While some, such as Leo the Great (ca. 400–461 CE) and John Chrysostom (ca. 347–407 CE), would not be as harsh as Jerome, they still asserted that the only hope for individual Jews was for them to become Christians. For example, in his *Hom. Matt.* 86.2, John Chrysostom condemned the crowd as Jesus' murderers. Yet, John Chrysostom held out hope for individual Jews who converted to Christianity (Simonetti 2001–2003, 2:283). Leo, likewise, was quick to state that Jews could avoid the curse only through conversion to Christianity (Luz 2001–2007, 3:506–7). This harsh interpretation of Matt 27:25 would continue to be the standard view of Christian authors until a more balanced understanding of Judaism emerged in the Enlightenment and the horrors of the Holocaust finally made such an interpretation of the text unacceptable.

Conclusion

From this short summary, certain conclusions may be drawn. First, the earliest attestation to Matthew, or Matthean tradition, comes from Syria-Palestine. It is certain the *Didache* employed tradition that would be found in Matthew, even if it did not utilize Matthew itself. The *Didache* also provides evidence that a form of the Lord's Prayer similar to that of Matt 6:9–13 was employed in early Christian liturgy. Likewise, it is likely that the Coptic Gospel of Thomas contains parables similar to those in Matthew. Ignatius certainly knew Matthew, as did Polycarp.

The cosmopolitan nature of the Roman Empire also provided the means for transmission of Matthew from the Eastern Empire to Rome and the West. Justin's first encounter with Matthew's Gospel likely occurred when he lived in Palestine. He brought his understanding of this "memoir of the apostles" with him to Rome. Likewise, Irenaeus undoubtedly carried Matthew with him to Lugdunum when he assumed his duties as bishop in Gaul. While the extent to which *Shepherd of Hermas* or 1 Clement depended on Matthew or oral tradition may be questioned, 2 Clement certainly had some acquaintance with the Gospel.

The early church's use of Matthew also provides a cautionary tale. Once interpreters forgot the intra-Jewish character of Matthew's disputation scenes, this language was utilized to condemn Judaism as a whole. This unfortunate tradition continued throughout church history, and it was only with the aftermath of the Holocaust that a concerted effort was made to contextualize Matthew's language within its Jewish/Jewish Christian context.

Works Cited

Brown, Raymond E., and John P. Meier. 1982. *Antioch and Rome New Testament Cradles of Catholic Christianity.* New York: Paulist Press.

Gamble, Harry Y. 1995. *Books and Readers in the Early Church.* New Haven: Yale University Press.

Goodacre, Mark. 2012. *Thomas and the Gospels: The Case for Thomas's Familiarity with the Synoptics.* Grand Rapids: Eerdmans.

Hultgren, Arland L. 2000. *The Parable of Jesus: A Commentary.* Grand Rapids: Eerdmans.

Jefford, Clayton N. 2005. "The Milieu of Matthew, the Didache, and Ignatius of Antioch: Agreements and Differences." Pages 35–47 in *Matthew and the Didache: Two Documents from the Same Jewish Milieu?* Edited by Huub van de Sandt. Minneapolis, MN: Fortress Press.

Koester, Helmut. 1988. "Gospel of Thomas, Introduction." Pages 124–26 in *The Nag Hammadi Library in English.* Rev. ed. San Francisco: Harper & Row.

Koester, Helmut. 1982. *History and Literature of Early Christianity.* Vol. 2 of *Introduction to the New Testament.* Hermeneia Foundations and Facets. Philadelphia: Fortress.

Liebowitz, Etka. 2014. "Hypocrites or Pious Scholars?: The Image of the Pharisees in Second Temple Period Texts and Rabbinic Literature." *Melilah* 11:

53–67. https://search-ebscohost-com.proxy.ashland.edu:2648/login.aspx?direct
=true&db=reh&AN=ATLAn3769783&site=ehost-live.

Luz, Ulrich. 2001–2007. *Matthew.* 3 vols. Translated by James E Crouch. Hermeneia.
Minneapolis, MN: Fortress Press.

Massaux, Édouard, 1990–1993. *The Influence of the Gospel of Saint Matthew on
Christian Literature Before Saint Irenaeus.* 3 vols. Translated by Norman J.
Belval and Suzanne Hecht. New Gospel Studies 5: 1–3. Macon, GA: Mercer
University Press.

Metzger, Bruce M. 1987. *The Canon of the New Testament.* Oxford: Clarendon Press.

Osiek, Carolyn. 1999. *Shepherd of Hermas: A Commentary on the Shepherd of Hermas.*
Hermeneia. Minneapolis, MN: Fortress Press.

Schoedel, William R. 1985. *Ignatius of Antioch: A Commentary on the Letters of
Ignatius of Antioch.* Hermeneia. Philadelphia: Fortress.

Simonetti, Manlio, ed. 2001–2003. *Matthew.* ACCS. 2 vols. The Church's Bible.
Downers Grove, IL: InterVarsity Press.

Snodgrass, Klyne. 2008. *Stories with Intent: A Comprehensive Guide to the Parables
of Jesus.* Grand Rapids: Eerdmans.

Syreeni, Kari. 2005. "The Sermon on the Mount and the Two Ways Teaching of the
Didache." Pages 87–103 in *Matthew and the Didache: Two Documents from
the Same Jewish Milieu?* Edited by Huub van de Sandt. Minneapolis, MN:
Fortress Press.

Tomson, Peter J. 2005. "The Halakhic Evidence of Didache 8 and Matthew 6 and
the Didache Community's Relationship to Judaism." Pages 131–41 in *Matthew
and the Didache: Two Documents from the Same Jewish Milieu?* Edited by Huub
van de Sandt. Minneapolis, MN: Fortress Press.

Williams, D. H., trans. and ed. 2019. *Matthew: Interpreted by Early Christian Commentators.* The Church's Bible. Grand Rapids: Eerdmans.

Williams, Michael Allen. 1996. *Rethinking "Gnosticism": An Argument for Dismantling
a Dubious Category.* Princeton: Princeton University Press.

1.4 The Gospels and Rabbinic Literature

David Instone-Brewer

When comparing bodies of literature, it is important to look for differences as well
as similarities, because that is how to discover unique contributions within them.
Material within the Gospels clearly has similarities to rabbinic discussions, parables,
miracle stories, and prayers. These similarities indicate that a relationship existed
between the two worlds, either through personal interaction or literary influence.
Having discovered these similarities, the aim is to examine the differences within
them. Without this later stage, we will uncover the Jewish milieu in which the Gospels are set, but we won't discover why the Jewish world of the time largely rejected
the message attributed to Jesus.

History of Comparisons

Comparison between the Gospels and rabbinic material has a long history. The endeavor began in earnest in the seventeenth century when John Lightfoot aimed to compare the whole New Testament with rabbinic literature. He found that these comparisons were very fruitful in the Synoptic Gospels but much less so in John and Acts and only in isolated passages of the epistles. The lack of parallels in Acts (which appears to be written by Luke) suggests that the cause of these similarities is not due merely to literary influence, but more to the influence of similarities in the source material and a shared culture. That is, the world that Jesus' teachings and life inhabit in the Gospels shared many physical features, intellectual presuppositions, and areas of inquiry with the world later recorded in rabbinic material, in a way that the Roman world of the Acts and epistles did not.

The detailed work of Edersheim and Billerbeck in the nineteenth century confirmed this (Edersheim 1983; Strack and Billerbeck 1922–1928). In his two-volume devotional commentary, *The Life and Times of Jesus the Messiah*, Edersheim retold Gospel material using cultural details from rabbinic material that he had learned as a youth in Jewish schools. Now converted to Christianity, he wrote with an unfortunately anti-Jewish zeal but nevertheless demonstrated a love for the first-century Jewish culture that he convincingly uncovered within the Gospels.

In early twentieth-century Germany, the publishers of Strack-Billerbeck (as the *Kommentar zum Neuen Testament aus Talmud und Midrasch* is usually known) were probably sensible to attribute the work primarily to Hermann Strack rather than acknowledge that Paul Billerbeck (a Jew) was the real author. This is particularly ironic given that Billerbeck demonstrated better than anyone previously that almost every aspect of Jesus' theology could be paralleled in rabbinic literature. When authors such as Jeremias (1967), Vermes (1974), and Charlesworth (1985) explored these similarities in more detail and exactitude, this was no longer surprising. Flusser (1998) arguably succeeded in showing Jewish parallels for all of Jesus' teaching.

These similarities created a new question: Why did the Jews reject someone whose teaching was so similar to their own? Charlesworth pinpointed the disagreement in the act of cleansing the temple. E. P. Sanders believed it was unlikely that Jesus was the only Jewish teacher who spoke of "love, mercy, grace, repentance and forgiveness of sin" or that Pharisees were inclined to "kill people who believed in such things" (1985, 326–27).

Sanders's skepticism was, of course, wholly justified—something that his own extensive work demonstrated (especially in *Paul and Palestinian Judaism*, 1977). First-century Jews believed in God's grace as well as in the importance of keeping the law (this is touched on in "Parables" below), and Jesus did not dismiss the details of Mosaic law. Even when cataloguing Jesus' criticisms of the Pharisees, Matt 23 commences with: "Be careful to do everything they tell you. But do not do what they do." And at the start of a list of Jesus' disputes, we find, "Do not think that I have come to abolish the law or the prophets. . . . [W]hoever practices and teaches these commands will be called great in the kingdom of heaven" (Matt 5:17–20; all Scriptures here are from NIV unless otherwise noted).

However, the Gospels do not show Jesus causing friction on just one occasion or in one matter of disagreement; he stands out from his fellow Jewish teachers as causing dissent in every aspect of engagement. No doubt there were areas where Jesus agreed with his contemporaries, but the Gospel writers choose not to dwell on these.

Teachings and Disputes

Rabbinic Judaism after 70 CE differed in significant ways from that of the early first century. In particular, later Judaism maintained unity by respecting the decision of the majority after a debate, with the threat of excommunication for the occasional individual who refused to accept it. Earlier Judaism is characterized by debates that resulted in factions: the Qumran community (who may be related to Essenes or Therapeutae), Shammaites and their debating partners the Hillelites (whose views are almost identical to those of later rabbis), and other schools such as those of Gamaliel from whom only a handful of distinctive teachings survive.

To say that each rabbi had his own *halakah* (i.e., body of teachings) would be an exaggeration, but only slightly. Although students agreed with and recited the teachings of their rabbi, and rabbis grouped themselves with like-minded fellows, they still reveled in dispute. Significant teachers were remembered by their distinctive decisions, so fame came by individualism. However, in this disputatious climate, some basis for authority was required. This was provided by naming the teacher that one was citing and remaining faithful to the community to which one belonged.

Jesus stood out by not following this convention. The Gospels note the surprise (or complaint) that he did not credit his teachings to any preceding teachers (Matt 7:28–29 // Mark 1:22 // Luke 4:32). He opposed at least some teachings of every Jewish group that we know well, and his teachings do not align exactly with any group that has been recorded elsewhere. In Matt 5, this is deliberately highlighted by collecting significant examples together.

When Jesus opposed those who say "hate your enemies" (Matt 5:43), his most likely target was the Qumran community who referred to their enemy as the children of darkness. Their *Rule of the Community* (1QS) starts: "in order to love all the sons of light . . . detest all the sons of darkness" (García Martínez 1992, 3). Josephus records the same about the Essenes, that they each "take tremendous oaths, that . . . he will always hate the wicked, and be assistant to the righteous" (*J.W.* 2.140).

Before this, Matthew records a summary of Jesus' criticism of mincing oaths (5:33–35; fuller at 23:16–20). As far as we know, all Jewish scholars agreed that someone could circumvent the consequences of an oath by avoiding any direct mention of God or the sacrifices and instead swearing by heaven or the temple. The details were debated for another couple of centuries (m. Ned.1.3; t. Ned.1.2–3; y. Ned.4a-b; b. Ned.10b-13a), and this shows that the basic teaching was generally accepted. Jesus, however, rejected the notion out of hand and thereby set himself against the scholarly establishment.

This followed a summary of Jesus' rejection of the Hillelite divorce for "any cause" (Matt 5:31, 32; fuller at 19:3–9) where Jesus cites the Shammaite phrase "except for indecency" with approval. Here he interacts with a debate that has survived in three apparently reliable records:

The School of Shammai says: A man should not divorce his wife except if he found indecency in her, since it says: For he found in her an indecent matter [*davat 'erwah*, Deut 24:1].

And the School of Hillel said: Even if she spoiled his dish, since it says: [Any] matter [*davar*]. (Sipre Deut 269, also m. Giṭ 9.10; y. Soṭah 1.1, 1a)

The Hillelites had "discovered" in Deut 24:1 a type of no-fault divorce by interpreting the two words (*'erwat davar*) individually. Everyone accepted that *'erwat* referred to divorce for "indecency" (which they understood as adultery), but the Hillelites said that *davar* ("word/cause/matter") was an additional ground for divorce: for "[any] matter." The Shammaites emphasized their assertion that these words were a single phrase by reversing their order to "matter of indecency." Matt 5:32 reflects this Shammaite word order (*logoi porneias*). Matthew also shows Jesus' agreement with the Shammaite interpretation by citing their conclusion that Deut 24:1 refers to nothing "except . . . indecency" (see more details in Instone-Brewer 2002).

To demonstrate that Jesus disagreed even with nonscholars, this catalogue of oppositional teachings starts by condemning "anyone who says . . . 'Raca' or 'You fool!' [*mōros*]. This is the equivalent of criticizing those today who denigrate someone by calling them "empty-headed" or "moron." These terms were used so widely that Matthew doesn't bother to translate *raka* from Aramaic. We find examples of this term throughout rabbinic literature, being used by ordinary people, rabbis, and even by Noah when decrying his detractors (Midr. Eccl. 9.15). Matt 5 is therefore an early warning for the reader that Jesus disagreed with everyone.

Jesus interacted with issues that were important in early first-century Judaism, although some of them decreased in importance after the temple had been destroyed. For example, the issue of impurity was immensely important when everyone ate temple sacrifices such as Passover and voluntary fellowship offerings during festivals. But after the temple was destroyed when these sacrifices could no longer be offered, purity was a minority interest. Thomas Kazen showed that Jesus was discussing the specific impurity issues that concerned other Jews of the time such as Philo, Josephus, and those at Qumran (*Was Jesus indifferent to impurity?*). Jesus, of course, was skeptical about the importance of purity (Matt 15:1–20; 23:25–26; par.), but he nevertheless interacted with issues of the day.

Although Jesus interacted with debates of his time, the Gospels do not aim to show that his teaching fitted in with that of his contemporaries. Indeed, the Gospels appear to deliberately exclude any teaching with which everyone would have agreed. For example, to the consternation of all church youth leaders, Jesus is never recorded as condemning sex before marriage or even rape. One couldn't claim the Gospel writers didn't consider this message worth stating, because it was certainly important in the sexually lax Greek-speaking populations for whom these accounts were written.

Perhaps such teaching was omitted because it did not serve the larger purpose of the Gospel writers, which was to show that Jesus opposed his contemporary Jews. Or, of course, Jesus himself may not have felt it necessary to teach things that were obvious in a Jewish society. However, preachers don't normally avoid stating important teaching simply because their congregation may be familiar with it. If

Jesus really did deliberately avoid teaching anything that was already generally accepted, then this implies that he was as confrontational as the Gospel writers portray him! Either way, he was regarded as being opposed to every other teacher in one way or another.

Parables

Although parables are commonplace in rabbinic writings, there are very few that can be shown to originate in the early first century. Joachim Jeremias (1963), Brad Young (1998), and others have convincingly shown that the later rabbinic parables have similar messages, characters, and images to those used by Jesus. So, even if they can't be shown to originate from the same time, they certainly share the same sources.

One of the two earliest parables preserved in rabbinic works gives a rare insight into Jewish soteriology and, in particular, into their concept of why it was important to obey each commandment. Each day, Jews twice repeated Num 15:40 as part of the *Shema*: "remember and do all my commandments." However, this parable suggests their motivation was not legalistic.

> A certain pious man [*hasid*] forgot a sheaf in the middle of his field. He said to his son, "Go and offer two bullocks on my behalf, for a burnt offering and a peace offering." His son said to him, "Father, why are you more joyful at fulfilling this one commandment than all the other commandments in Torah?" He said to him, "The Lord gave us all the commands in Torah to obey intentionally, but he only gave us this one to obey accidentally." (t. Pe'ah 3.8)

This parable is likely to originate before 70 CE because the outcome is a gift to the temple and not to the local synagogue. We can be sure that if the story were not already well known, the teller would have used it to increase local funds rather than refer to making a sacrifice that was no longer possible.

The heart of this story lies in the fact that obeying this law involved *forgetting* a sheaf (Deut 24:19), so this could not be done deliberately. That means that no one can set out to fulfill this commandment; it has to happen by accident. The man is overjoyed that he has fulfilled this commandment—the offering that he sends to the temple is outrageous in value; it is equivalent to a farmer today giving away his two best tractors. He is thankful not because he has been made righteous, but simply because he has been able to fulfill another command. This does not mean he is pleased by his personal achievement, because this depended on something that could only happen by accident. He has done nothing good by himself and he doesn't regard it as earning him salvation, so his joy must come wholly from the fact that he has pleased God.

Although Jesus would probably have nothing critical to say about this parable or the sentiments behind it, none of his parables expressed anything similar. There were parables about sinners who repented, about those who struggled to do good, about the majority who failed, and about a loving father who welcomes failures. But he told no parables about those who succeeded in obeying God's commands.

This wasn't considered an impossibility because Paul claimed to have done so (Phil 3:5–6), and the Gospels record the rich young ruler making a similar claim without contradiction (Mark 10:20 // Matt 19:20 // Luke 18:21). In a society geared toward living out the Torah in a practical way, it wasn't too difficult for a diligent person to keep every specific commandment.

However, Jesus in the Gospels did warn against smugness among those who managed to obey the commandments. Luke uses a suspiciously Pauline phrase to describe the purpose of the parable of the pharisee and the tax collector who were praying in the temple: he says it was told to those "who were confident of their own righteousness" (Luke 18:9). Perhaps this was added as a later interpretation, but there are similar warnings in other parables such as the jealous non-prodigal son, the early laborers in the vineyard, and the ingratitude of those invited to the feast.

The last of those parables is very similar to one told by Yohanan ben Zakkai. He was a particularly interesting individual because he apparently taught in Galilee for eighteen years during the early first century (m. Šabb. 16.7; 22.3; y. Šabb. 16.7, 15d), which makes it likely that he and Jesus knew each other. It is therefore significant that his most influential saying was his reminder that God said, "I desire mercy, not sacrifice" ('Abot R. Nat. 4.5; cf. Matt 9:13; 12:7). A parable is attributed to him:

> R. Yohanan b. Zakkai said: This may be compared to a king who summoned his servants to a banquet without appointing a time. The wise ones adorned themselves and sat at the door of the palace [because, as] they said: "Is anything lacking in a royal palace?" The fools went about their work, saying: "Can there be a banquet without preparations?" Suddenly the king desired [the presence of] his servants: the wise entered adorned, while the fools entered unwashed. The king rejoiced at the wise but was angry with the fools. "Those who adorned themselves for the banquet," ordered he, "let them sit, eat and drink. But those who did not adorn themselves for the banquet, let them stand and watch." (b. Šabb. 153a, based on the Soncino translation)

There are clear similarities to a group of parables by Jesus: the parable of the banquet (Matt 22:1–14; Luke 14:15–24) in which Matthew includes the man who did not dress appropriately, the foolish virgins who were not waiting outside when the door opened (Matt 25:1–12), and the largely forgotten parable of the guests who arrive too late (Luke 13:25–28). Almost all the elements of Yohanan's parable are reused by Jesus: king, banquet, lack of starting time, doors suddenly open, wise and foolish, inappropriate attire, and the king's angry response as the culmination of the story.

In the light of these similarities, it is unreasonable to assume they are completely independent. Jesus had either heard Yohanan tell this story, or it was well known to both of them. It is unlikely that Yohanan copied Jesus because Jesus included many elements not used by Yohanan, and also because Jews who cited Jesus did not fare well. (Rabbi Eliezer found himself before a court because he had merely listened to and approved of a saying by Jesus; t. Ḥul. 2.24; b. 'Abod. Zar. 17a.)

There are also significant and consistent differences. In Yohanan's version, all those who have been invited are accepted into the banquet hall, although those who weren't ready have to stand and watch the others feast. This doesn't mean they will go hungry, because servants were allowed to eat the leftovers from a banquet and so the listeners would assume that these dishonored guests will also be allowed to do so. They are reprimanded and humiliated, but nevertheless they gain entry to the banquet hall. However, in all of Jesus' versions, the unready or ungrateful invitees are not only excluded or thrown out (Matt 12:10–12; Luke 14:24), but they are even severely punished in hell (Matt 22:13; Luke 13:28).

The reason behind this stark difference lies in the Jews' belief that all Jews will be saved. In the first century, this resulted in a teaching about the "three ways," based on Zech 13:9. This doctrine was shared by both Hillelites and Shammaites, and therefore likely shared by all Pharisees, although they disagreed about the details:

> The School of Shammai says: There are three groups, one for eternal life, one for shame and everlasting contempt (Dan 12:2)—these are those who are completely evil.
>
> An intermediate group go down to Gehenna and scream and come up again and are healed, as it is said: "I will bring the third part through fire and will refine them as silver is refined and will test them as gold is tested, and they shall call on my name and I will be their God." (Zech 13:9)
>
> And the School of Hillel says: "Great in mercy" (Exod 34:6). He inclines the decision toward mercy. (t. Sanh. 13.3; cf. b. Roš Haš. 16b)

First-century Pharisees believed Jews fell into three groups, the perfectly good who deserved heaven, the perfectly evil who deserved hell, and a middle group— presumably the majority. Later traditions made it clear that only seven Jews were irredeemable: Jeroboam, Ahab, Manasseh, Doeg the Edomite, Ahithophel, Balaam, and Gehazi (m. Sanh. 10.2; although more were gradually added to this list). This meant that it was generally accurate to say that all Jews went to heaven. The only thing that Shammaites and Hillelites disagreed about was the extent to which the middle group suffered. The Shammaites thought they went to hell for a short period and the Hillelites did not; they likely believed in some temporary humiliation in heaven such as Yohanan described.

This teaching explains the overwhelming emphasis of Jesus on the "two ways," which is found in one form or another in the majority of his parables: good and bad servants, wise and foolish virgins, wheat and tares, good and rotten fish, ripe and unripe fig trees, wise and foolish builders, properly and improperly dressed guests, sheep and goats, obedient and rebellious sons, lost and found coins, wandering and safe sheep, prodigal and home-abiding sons, and those who are inside or outside as in the previously mentioned parables. There is never a middle or third way. When Jesus' audience heard these parables, we should therefore imagine them being surprised and perhaps disconcerted. Most would have regarded themselves among the third group who were neither totally good nor totally bad, but Jesus taught that this middle option did not exist.

Instead, Jesus replaced this with a reassuring message: repentance brings for-giveness, and everyone is invited to repent. But for those who regarded themselves as righteous because they had nothing to repent of—i.e., those "who were confident of their own righteousness"—the message was uncomfortable.

Miracle Accounts

Geza Vermes (1974) pointed out that there were at least two other miracle workers in Judaism. Honi "the circle-drawer" in the first century BCE, refused to leave a circle he had drawn on the ground until God sent rain—and rain then fell. Hanina ben Dosa, at the start of the second century CE, was a student of Yohanan ben Zakkai who healed the son of Gamaliel II. This particular healing had some similarities to the healing of the centurion's servant: Hanina prayed when the news arrived and then proclaimed that the boy (who was far away) had recovered, and the messengers returned to find he had recovered "at that very moment" (b. Ber. 34b).

The comparison of these miracle accounts with those of Jesus has been some-what weakened by Neusner's conclusions (in his almost numberless works) that biographical stories such as these are never found among the earliest layers of rabbinic tradition, unlike legal material which is more carefully preserved. In other words, wondrous stories about rabbis, like hagiography in the Christian world, tend to be written long after that person's death. While this is generally true, some stories have a greater likelihood of representing what happened, and these two are among them.

This particular story about Hanina is prefaced by "Our Rabbis taught . . . ," which is the formula that introduces a *Baraitha*—i.e., an early account that was not preserved among the earlier traditions in the Mishnah but nevertheless was thought to originate from earlier times. This doesn't ensure that the story was earlier than 200 CE (when the Mishnah was completed), but it still helps to imply an earlier date than for other material in the Talmud. The other miracle stories that grew up around this one, including Hanina's healing of Yohanan's son, need to be treated more cautiously.

The story of Honi praying for rain is unlikely to be a later invention because an important part of the account involves a very highly respected scholar, Simeon b. Shetah, who threatened to excommunicate him. He regarded Honi's prayer as too forceful and disrespectful, because he prayed like a small child nagging his father. However, when the prayer was answered, he relented (m. Ta'an. 3.8). It is unlikely that later fans of Honi or Simeon would have invented these details, because Simeon's accusation remained accurate: Honi did pray like a petulant youth, and Simeon only backed down because God had clearly not been offended by this.

One important insight provided by these two accounts of miracles lies in the fact that they are the *only* two miracles recorded in rabbinic literature that can be attributed to this period of two centuries. The two individuals were also considered to be outsiders by other rabbinic scholars. Honi was criticized, although tolerated in his day. Hanina appears to have been celebrated as an extremely pious man by future generations, partly because his extreme poverty resulted in near starvation (b. Ta'an. 24b). Reading between the lines, however, this means he had no students to support him and little support from his community. This is confirmed by the complete absence of teaching attributed to him.

It is unsafe to conclude from this that miracles were uncommon or, on the other hand, that these miracles actually occurred. However, we can conclude that those who recorded these traditions were not keen on the miraculous and that they did not expect miracles to occur. This is a complete contrast with the Gospels where miracles are interspersed so often throughout the accounts that they appear almost commonplace.

We might conjecture that Jesus' miracles were added due to non-Jewish influence by the Gospel writers or church traditions. However, Eric Eve (2002) has shown that miracles were equally disparaged in the Greco-Roman world where they were regarded as a characteristic of fraudulent religions. The origin of the emphasis on miracles in the Gospels therefore remains a mystery unless one accepts the conclusion by Craig Keener (2011) that these accounts are records of actual events that were too well known to be denied.

Prayers

In later Judaism, liturgical prayers became codified and fixed. According to Joseph Heinemann (1977), this unity originated from diversity. He suggests there was a deliberate policy to preserve early variations within the later fixed prayers.

He points out, for example, that most of the differences in the prayers accompanying the *Shema* in the morning and evening have nothing to do with differences in the occasion. He concludes that wording that became traditional in disparate communities was preserved within these two versions of the same prayer. Similarly, the *Kaddish* (a common prayer that hallows—i.e., glorifies—God's name) occurs frequently in the liturgy, in daily, weekly, and special prayers, in a multitude of slightly different wordings. Some of the variations reflect the occasion (such as for a funeral) but often the differences appear random. He concluded that here, too, local traditions were preserved by being distributed among different versions within the common fixed liturgy.

The wording that is common to most versions of the *Kaddish*, which may therefore represent common elements of great antiquity, includes:

> Magnified and hallowed be his great name, . . .
> May he establish his kingdom, . . .
> May the prayers of all Israel be accepted by their father who is in heaven.

This is, of course, similar to the wording at the start of the Lord's Prayer. The wording of the rest is found in the abstracts of a long prayer called the Eighteen Benedictions.

This prayer was performed twice a day, probably at the time of morning and evening temple offerings, and during the extra Sabbath afternoon offering. These prayer times could occur at inappropriate moments. An actual example that was discussed was praying while you are being attacked by bandits on a journey (b. Ber. 29b)! Therefore, rabbis taught their disciples a short "abstract" of the Eighteen that they could pray instead. A small number of these abstracts have survived. They indicate that different rabbis taught slightly different versions. The version of Eliezer ben Hyrcanus is recorded twice, and even *his* two versions are different.

This illustrates the fact that before 70 CE, variety was permitted or even encouraged in liturgy. Eliezer taught that verbatim repetition indicated a lack of sincerity, so he advocated that prayers should always include at least some slight variations (m. Ber. 4.4). The type of variations that Eliezer advocated can be seen in two versions of his abstract:

In Tosefta Berakot 3.11	In Babylonian Talmud Berakot 29b
Your will **is** done in heaven;	**May** your will be done in heaven **above**;
and grant ease to those who fear you;	and grant ease to those who fear you **on earth below**;
and do what is good in your eyes.	and do what is good in your eyes.
Blessed [is he] who listens to prayer.	Blessed **are you Lord** who listens to prayer.

The small differences set in boldface in these two versions are similar to the differences found in the two versions of the Lord's Prayer recorded at Matt 6:9–13 and Luke 11:2–4. The pair of phrases "in heaven" and "on earth" is contained in only one version of Eliezer's prayer, just as they are found only in Matthew's version of the Lord's Prayer. These and other differences do not change the meaning, so they are likely due to the principle that one should make small changes to a prayer in order to demonstrate one's sincerity.

Other similarities with the Lord's Prayer are also striking. Even the order of the elements is similar: "your will be done" is followed by petitions, which is followed by acceptance of God's will ("what is good in your eyes" or "trials" to be faced). These similarities suggest that Jesus' prayer life was intimately linked with that of his fellow Jews and that he was happy to pass this on to his followers. It is significant that the Gospels made no attempt to harmonize the wording of this prayer between the Gospels or to substitute phrases that might have been more at home in non-Jewish contexts where (for example) there was not the same reverence for the name of a god.

However, the specific wording of the Lord's Prayer also indicates some distinctive concepts that, while being part of the Jewish world, are contrary to Rabbinic Judaism.

Praying to God as Father or in the familiar form of *Abba* is not unique to Jesus (as Joachim Jeremias claimed, 1967). The *Kaddish* prayer shows how common the concept of God's fatherhood is, and although Jewish liturgy never uses the homely child's version "*Abba*," it is likely that Honi used this when he addressed God in a childish way. When he did so, however, he was criticized for it. Addressing God in this way contravened the rabbinic rule that one should never use emotional pressure to gain a request from God. An example they cited was "Your mercy extends to the bird's nest" (m. Ber. 5.3)—e.g., someone might pray: "You grant mercy to a bird (in Deut 22:6–7), so surely you will help me."

Jesus would have been criticized in the same way. Proofs of God's care based on sparrows and lilies (Matt 10:29–31; 6:28–30; par.) and the tradition of using the name *Abba* (Mark 14:36; cf. Rom 8:15; Gal 4:6) imply that Jesus regarded God's fatherly love as a way to encourage prayer, and he did not discourage its emotive use within prayer.

The prayer for "daily bread" stands out as significantly different from normal Jewish prayer terminology. In the full Eighteen Benedictions, Jews give thanks for food from the "Lord, who blesses the years" —i.e., for his annual harvest that they stored in barns or bought in the market. Jesus' followers were encouraged to pray not like farmers but as paupers. Within Jewish social structures, the poor were given weekly supplies of food, although transient beggars were given only daily rations (m. Pe'ah 8.7). It appears from this that Jesus taught his followers the prayer of a beggar. This coheres with other sayings that display his disregard for material planning or ownership: "Foxes have dens" (Matt 8:20), "Why do you worry about clothes?" (Matt 6:28), "hand over your coat as well" (Matt 5:40).

The final phrase of the Lord's Prayer in Matthew is the strangest: "deliver us from the evil [one]." The combination of "deliver" and "evil" (*ryomai* and *ponēros*) could, of course, refer to keeping them from committing wrongs (as in 2 Tim 4:18), but it can also refer to rescue from evil persons (as in 2 Thess 3:2). In the Lord's Prayer, "the evil [one]" is presumably the devil. This latter meaning is likely because the Jesus traditions in all four Gospels are peculiarly full of references to the devil (*ho diabolos*), including the personal names "Satan" and "Beelzebul."

The term "devil" is used mostly by the narrator in the Gospels, but the two personal names are recorded in sayings attributed to Jesus eleven times and seven times, respectively (not counting duplicates in the same verse but counting parallel sayings). For Jesus, the devil was a nemesis that was personified. It is possible that this theme was injected into the Gospels by the early church, which shared an interest in "the evil one" (1 John 2:14) and "Satan" (2 Cor 2:11), which means "the accuser" (as translated at Rev 12:10). But the concentration of this theme is much higher in the Gospels. This corresponds with the excessive number of exorcisms recorded for Jesus (about one-third of all healings) compared to virtual silence on this topic in the rest of the New Testament.

The prevalence of this theme in the Gospels is strange because similar themes are vanishingly rare in rabbinic literature. Even sectarian Jewish literature refers to exorcisms only occasionally. Although "Mastema" and "Belial" are arguably names for a personal devil in the Qumran community, he has no role in testing or tempting; in fact, he asks God to test Abraham (Jub. 17:15–16). By contrast, Jesus faces temptation from the devil after his baptism and before his crucifixion, both of which are warded off by means of prayer; and Peter is warned about similar attacks that he and others will face (Matt 4:1–11 // Mark 1:12–13 // Luke 4:1–13; Matt 26:41 // Mark 14:38 // Luke 22:46; Luke 22:31; John 17:5).

Conclusion

The Gospel traditions demonstrate a striking familiarity with rabbinic forms and topics, and in most aspects agree with Jewish morals and social norms, but within these there are several discordant emphases. Jesus' teaching promoted repentance rather than religious observance and intensified the moral demands of the law in order to prove that everyone needs to repent. His sayings and prayers depart from Rabbinic Judaism by exhibiting a profound sense of God as a loving father, along with a sense of evil spiritual personages that are just as real. Jesus in the Gospels also displays a rejection of the material world, but not like that of mystics who regarded it as a source of evil. Jesus' attitude appears to be indifference, as if material needs and concerns are uninteresting or unimportant.

The similarities outlined here indicate that these materials found in the Gospels came from the same milieu as Rabbinic Judaism and interacted with that same thought-world. The differences, on the other hand, caused most Jews to reject Jesus' teaching. Others, however, concluded that this man was much more than just another Jewish teacher.

Works Cited

Charlesworth, James H. 1985. *Jesus within Judaism*. Minneapolis, MN: Fortress Press.
Edersheim, Alfred. 1983. *The Life and Times of Jesus the Messiah*. Peabody, MA: Hendrickson.
Eve, Eric. 2002. *The Jewish Context of Jesus' Miracles*. Sheffield: Sheffield Academic.
Flusser, David. 1998. *Jesus*. Jerusalem: Magnes.
García Martínez, Florentino. 1992. *The Dead Sea Scrolls Translated*. Leiden: Brill.
Heinemann, Joseph. 1977. *Prayer in the Talmud*. SJ 9. Berlin: de Gruyter.
Instone-Brewer, David. 2002. *Divorce and Remarriage in the Bible*. Grand Rapids: Eerdmans.
Jeremias, Joachim. 1963. *The Parables of Jesus*. London: SCM.
Kazen, Thomas. 2002. *Was Jesus indifferent to impurity?* ConBNT 38. Stockholm: Almqvist & Wiksell.
Keener, Craig. 2011. *Miracles*. Grand Rapids: Baker Academic.
Lightfoot, John. 1658–74 [1859]. *Horae Hebraicae et Talmudicae*. 4 vols. Oxford: Oxford University Press.
Sanders, E. P. 1985. *Jesus and Judaism*. Minneapolis, MN: Fortress Press.
————. *Paul and Palestinian Judaism*. Minneapolis, MN: Fortress Press.
Strack, Hermann, and Paul Billerbeck. 1922–1928 and 1956–1961. *Kommentar zum Neuen Testament aus Talmud und Midrasch*. 6 vols. München: Beck.
Vermes, Geza. 1974. *Jesus the Jew*. New York: Macmillan.
Young, Brad. 1998. *The Parables*. Peabody, MA: Hendrickson.

CHAPTER 2

Intertextual Roots

2.1 Fulfillment in Matthew's Gospel

David L. Turner

Today, Matthew's Jewish setting is accepted by most interpreters (Davies and Allison 1997, 692–704; Konradt 2014; Runesson and Gurtner 2020), not least due
to Matthew's pervasive use of the Old Testament (Blomberg 2007, 1–109; France
1989, 166–205; Gundry 1967; Knowles 2006; Stanton 1992, 346–63; Stendahl 1968;
Turner 2008, 17–25). The prevalence of this intertextuality calls into question
the very notion of an "Old Testament" (OT) in Matthew's theology. Matthew's
Jesus came not to abolish but to fulfill the law and the prophets (Matt 5:17), so it
is doubtful that Matthew conceived of the Jewish Scriptures as "old," at least in
the sense that the OT is an outmoded, albeit quaint, antique. Instead, Matthew
viewed the Torah instructions, the historical patterns, and the prophetic oracles
of the Hebrew Bible as filled with their ultimate significance through the words
and deeds of Jesus.

Hays has provided a helpful taxonomy for understanding biblical intertextuality.
Starting with the notion that the testimony of the Gospels "is the product of a cata-
lytic fusion of Israel's Scripture and the story of Jesus," he categorizes three types of
fusion that range from explicit to implicit: *quotation, allusion,* and *echo* (Hays 2016,
8–11). These three categories help us grasp the material even if they are imprecise
and arguable. *Quotations* are characterized by introductory formulas (e.g., "as it is
written," "that it might be fulfilled") and/or extended verbatim phraseology from
the OT. *Allusions* have neither of these characteristics but utilize multiple words
or mention notable OT persons, places, or events. *Echoes* of the OT may contain
only a single word or short phrase from the OT, but such minimal references occur
in contexts that clearly evoke a precedent or pattern from the OT. Although such
echoes are subjectively determined and easily disputed, they are nonetheless real.
It is estimated that there are around four hundred quotations of the OT in the NT,
with forty-eight in Matthew. I will not even attempt to enumerate the number of
allusions and *echoes.*

Matthew's OT quotations may be categorized in various ways: by introductory
formula ("in order that it might be fulfilled," "for it is written," etc.), or by the source
of the quotation (Jesus, another character in the narrative, or Matthew the narrator).
The table below provides an overview of Matthew's biblical citations as context for
this study of his distinctive theme of biblical fulfillment.

Matthew's Old Testament Quotations

This summary of Mathew's forty-eight OT quotations is based on the table in Aland 2014, 860. In the left column, (J) signifies a quotation by Jesus (32 in number), (M) signifies a quotation by Matthew as narrator (11 in number), and (C) signifies a quotation by one of the characters in the narrative (5 in number). In the middle column, * signifies the introductory formula "as it is written" (8 in number), and ** signifies an introductory formula involving fulfillment (11 in number). In the right column, (U) signifies a unique OT quotation that is found only in Matthew, not in Mark or Luke (24 in number). **The ten fulfillment formula quotations are in bold font.** All the fulfillment formula quotations come from the narrator Matthew, who uses a fulfillment formula nearly every time he quotes the OT. The only exception is Matt 3:3, where Isa 40:3 is quoted to identify John the Baptist with the words, "This is he who was spoken of by the prophet Isaiah."

Old Testament Quotations

Matthew	OT Intertext	Subject
1:22–23 (M)	**Isa 7:14; 8:8, 10 ****	**The virgin will conceive (U)**
2:5–6 (C)	Mic 5:2 *	The Ruler from Bethlehem (U)
2:15 (M)	**Hos 11:1 ****	**God's Son called from Egypt (U)**
2:17–18 (M)	**Jer 31:15 ****	**Wailing for murdered children (U)**
2:23 (M)	**Judg 13:5, 7 or Isa 11:1? ****	**Jesus called a "Nazarene" (U)**
3:3 (M)	Isa 40:3	John a voice in the wilderness
4:4 (J)	Deut 8:3 *	People live by more than bread
4:6 (C)	Ps 91:11–12 *	Angelic protection
4:7 (J)	Deut 6:16 *	Do not test God
4:10 (J)	Deut 6:13 *	God alone to be worshipped
4:14–16 (M)	**Isa 9:1–2 ****	**Galilee sees the light (U)**
5:21 (J)	Exod 20:13 // Deut 5:17	Do not murder (U)
5:27 (J)	Exod 20:14 // Deut 5:18	Do not commit adultery (U)
5:31 (J)	Deut 24:1	Certificate of divorce (U)
5:33 (J)	Lev 19:12 // Num 30:2	Vows must be carried out (U)
5:38 (J)	Exod 21:24 // Lev 24:20 // Deut 19:21	Eye for an eye (U)

5:43 (J)	Lev 19:18	Love your neighbor (U)
8:17 (M)	**Isa 53:4 ****	**He took our sicknesses (U)**
9:13 (J)	Hos 6:6	God wants mercy (U)
10:35–36 (J)	Mic 7:6	Enemies within the household (U)
11:10 (J)	Mal 3:1 *	Messenger prepares the way
12:7 (J)	Hos 6:6	God wants mercy
12:17–21 (M)	**Isa 42:1–4 ****	**The beloved Servant (U)**
12:40 (J)	Jon 1:17	Jonah in the fish's belly (U)
13:14–15 (J)	Isa 6:9–10 **	Hearing without understanding
13:35 (M)	**Ps 78:2 ****	**Mysterious speech in parables (U)**
15:4 (J)	Exod 20:12 // Deut 5:16; Exod 21:17	Honor your father and mother
15:7–9 (J)	Isa 29:13	Hypocritical worship
18:16 (J)	Deut 19:15	Two or three witnesses (U)
19:4–5 (J)	Gen 1:27 // 5:2; Gen 2:24	God made male and female
19:7 (C)	Deut 24:1	Certificate of divorce (U)
19:18–19 (J)	Exod 20:12–16 // Deut 5:16–20; Lev 19:18	Do not murder . . .
21:4–5 (M)	**Isa 62:11 // Zech 9:9 ****	**The king comes on a donkey (U)**
21:9 (C)	Ps 118:25–26	Blessings for the Son of David
21:13 (J)	Isa 56:7 *	A den of thieves
21:16 (J)	Ps 8:3	Praise from children **(U)**
21:42 (J)	Ps 118:22–23	The cornerstone
22:24 (C)	Deut 25:5	A man dies without children (U)
22:31–32 (J)	Exod 3:6, 15	I am the God of Abraham . . .
22:37 (J)	Deut 6:5	Love the Lord your God
22:39 (J)	Lev 19:18	Love your neighbor
22:43–44 (J)	Ps 110:1	Sit at my right hand
23:39 (J)	Ps 118:26	Blessed be the one coming . . .
24:30 (J)	Dan 7:13	The Son of Man arrives
26:31 (J)	Zech 13:7 *	The shepherd struck

26:64 (J)	Ps 110:1; Dan 7:13	Son of Man coming on the clouds
27:9–10 (M)	**Zech 11:12–13 ****	**Thirty pieces of silver (U)**
27:46 (J)	Ps 22:1	Forsaken by God

Matthew's Explicit Fulfillment Texts

Fulfillment Formula Quotations

Matthew's distinctive use of the OT centers in his ten fulfillment formula quotations, highlighted in bold font in the table above. All these formulas use the verb *plēroō*, which is usually glossed in English as "to fulfill" (BDAG 828–29, #4; Silva 2014, 3:784–93). The Septuagint (LXX) often uses *plēroō* to translate various forms of the Hebrew root *mālēʾ*. Such OT texts usually describe spatial or temporal filling, as in a jar being filled up with water or a person's days being completed at death. More to the point here, occasionally *maleʾ/plēroō* marks the fulfillment or accomplishment of the word of the Lord (1 Kgs 2:27; 8:15; 2 Chr 6:14–15; 36:21; cf. Tob. 14:5). Fulfillment formula quotations are especially prominent in Matt 1–2 (Soares-Prabhu 1976).

The element of divine design is primary in all these formulas: they begin with phrases like "in order that" to stress the accomplishment of God's purpose. The expression "what was spoken" is likely a "divine passive," implying that God is the speaker. Be that as it may, two of the formulas explicitly stress the divine origin of the prophecies: they have been spoken *by* the Lord (Matt 1:22; 2:15; cf. 15:4). Each of the formulas stresses the human channel through which the Lord's word came: they have been spoken *through* a prophet who is sometimes named (cf. Matt 15:7; 22:43; 26:56; Acts 1:16; 4:25; 28:25; Rom 1:2; 2 Tim 3:16; 2 Pet 1:19–21). It is noteworthy that Matt 2:23 speaks of the fulfillment of what *plural* prophets have spoken (cf. Matt 26:54–56).

The OT prophets, primarily Isaiah, are the major source of Matthew's fulfillment formula quotations. Isaiah clearly appears in six of the quotations, by name in five of them. Matt 1:23 cites Isa 7:14 without mentioning Isaiah's name. Additionally, in Matt 13:14–15 Jesus refers to Isaiah by name in speaking of the fulfillment (*anaplēroō*) of Isa 6:9–10. Matthew 2:23 may be subtly echoing Isa 11:1, and Matt 21:4 seems to be a composite quotation of Isa 62:11 and Zech 9:9. Matthew 27:9 mentions Jeremiah by name in a composite quotation of Jer 32:6–9 and Zech 11:12–13. Jeremiah is also mentioned by name in Matt 2:15's quotation of Jer 31:15 (cf. Matt 16:14; Knowles 1993). One psalm appears in the fulfillment formula quotations—Matt 13:35 quotes Ps 78:2. Finally, Judg 13:5–7 may be the intended intertext of Matt 2:23.

While each of the fulfillment formula quotations deserves detailed study, only brief remarks can be made here. For additional discussion, see the critical/exegetical commentaries and Blomberg (2007).

- *Isa 7:14 // Matt 1:22–23.* Although many scholars attempt to support a near/far double fulfillment view of this quotation, it seems best to regard it as typological pattern. Isaiah 7:14 is not a straightforward prediction of a future virgin-born Messiah. Rather, it speaks of a sign given to King Ahaz in his own lifetime, and Matthew views it as an event that anticipates the virgin birth of the Messiah, an ultimate sign to the nation of Israel.

- *Hos 11:1 // Matt 2:15.* Hosea 11:1 is not a prediction. It speaks of the historical exodus of Israel from Egypt. Matthew capitalizes on the metaphor of Israel as God's son to speak of a much greater exodus of God's unique son that recapitulates redemptive history.

- *Jer 31:15 // Matt 2:17.* Jeremiah 31:15 personifies the nation of Israel during the Babylonian exile as Rachel weeping for her children who were dead. Another time of weeping for dead children occurred when Herod ordered the slaughter of the babies from the region of Bethlehem. Significantly, the sorrow in Jeremiah's day was mitigated by hope of renewal (Jer 31:31–32). In Matthew's day, that hope was coming to fruition through Jesus, the mediator of the new covenant.

- *Matt 2:23.* Matthew 2:23 speaks of Jesus' move to Nazareth after the death of King Herod as a fulfillment of plural prophets. This fulfillment may be a sort of play on words that connect the place name Nazareth to the OT Nazirite in general and specifically to the angel's promise to Samson's mother in Judg 13:5–7. It is also possible that Matthew has a different pun in mind, one drawn from Isa 11:1. This messianic text speaks of a fruitful *branch* (*netser*) from the root of Jesse. Yet another possibility is that this puzzling text may simply be connecting the prophetic message of the Messiah's humility and dishonor (e.g., Isa 53:1–4) to the obscure, humble village of Nazareth (cf. John 1:46).

- *Isa 9:1–2 // Matt 4:14.* Matthew 4:14 connects the return of Jesus to Galilee to Isa 9:1–2, which speaks of a deliverer who will bring salvation to Galilee after the Assyrian attack and exile. Matthew evidently connected Isa 9:1–2 to Jesus because of the stress on sonship and the throne of David in Isa 9:6–7. Galilee was viewed as a place of Gentile prominence and relative spiritual darkness. Both themes match up well with Matthew's theological emphases.

- *Isa 53:4 // Matt 8:17.* Matthew 8:17 connects Jesus' ministry of healing and exorcism to Isa 53:4, where the servant vicariously removes the infirmities of the nation by bearing them himself. In Matthew's view, the messianic suffering envisioned in Isa 53 brings cosmic *shalom* that heals both physical and spiritual maladies.

- *Isa 42:1–4 // Matt 12:16–21.* This is the longest OT quotation in Matthew. In the context of growing opposition from the Pharisees, Matthew cites Isa 42 to substantiate Jesus' forbidding those whom he had healed from telling who he was. In Isaiah, the Spirit-empowered servant proclaims justice to the Gentiles with mercy and gentleness. In keeping with this model, Jesus in Matthew does not brashly confront his opponents with spectacular miracles. He does not incite a riot. Instead, he opts for strategic withdrawal in his mission of bringing hope to the Gentiles.

- *Ps 78:2 // Matt 13:35*. Here, Matthew connects Jesus' use of parables to the deep sayings of the psalmist. Ps 78 is a historical psalm that recounts God's ongoing faithfulness despite Israel's rebellion. Though no predictions are made in Ps 78:2, Matthew describes the psalmist as "the prophet," indicating that the psalm's recounting of Israel's checkered history informs the situation of Jesus, who is the ultimate revelation of God's faithfulness to Israel.

- *Isa 62:11 // Zech 9:9 // Matt 21:4–5*. Here, Matthew describes Jesus' plans to ride a donkey's colt into Jerusalem as fulfilling what seems to be a composite text drawn from both Isaiah ("say to the daughter of Zion") and Zechariah ("behold, your king comes to you gentle and riding on a donkey"). Matthew sees in these passages support for his presentation of Jesus as a humble Messiah, as in 12:17–21 (cf. Matt 5:5; 11:29). Both OT passages speak of the future deliverance of Jerusalem.

- *Zech 11:12–13 // Matt 27:9*. This quotation is a complicated one due to its attribution and composite nature. The quotation is drawn mainly from Zechariah (with similarities to motifs in Jer 18:2–6; 19:1–13), but Matthew attributes it to the more prominent prophet Jeremiah. In any event, it seems best to view this quotation as Matthew's application of an OT situation to Jesus' betrayal. Matthew does so because of explicit verbal parallels (e.g., betrayal, thirty pieces of silver) and implicit theological parallels (Israel's apostasy and rejection of God's messengers).

Two Programmatic Statements: Matt 3:15; 5:17–48

Jesus' baptism amounts to an endorsement of John's message and an identification with the repentant remnant of Israel. Jesus' admonition to John in Matt 3:15—"Let it be so now; it is proper for us to do this to fulfill all righteousness" (NIV)—explains that his baptism is a representative performance that fulfills the uprightness required of kingdom disciples. At the outset of his messianic ministry, the obedient Son pleases the Father, resulting in his endowment with the Spirit, enabling him to lead in the renewal of Israel. This fulfillment by actualization is explained later when Matt 12:17–21 quotes Isa 42:1–4 regarding the beloved servant who receives the Spirit to proclaim justice to the nations.

In Matthew 5:17, Jesus warns his hearers not to think that he has come to set aside "the Law and the Prophets," an expression that refers to the entire OT (Matt 7:12; 11:13; 22:40; cf. Dan 9:10; Zech 7:12; Luke 22:44; John 1:45; Acts 24:14; Rom 3:21). When Matthew wrote his Gospel, it is likely that non-messianic Jews claimed that followers of Jesus were setting Moses aside. Matthew responds by drawing upon the teaching of Jesus that he had come to fulfill the Torah, not set it aside. But what does fulfillment mean here? Due to a mistaken equation of prophecy and prediction, Christians sometimes think simplistically of fulfillment in terms of an OT prediction coming to pass in a NT event. But fulfillment in Matthew has as much to do with ethical obedience and historical patterns as it does with prophetic promises. This is quite clear in the fulfillment formula quotations of Matt 1–2. Prophetic promise flows from the prophet's revelational foresight of a future event (cf. Matt 2:4–6), but Matthew's fulfillment quotations more often involve christological hindsight in which an OT event serves as the pattern for the NT event it anticipated. Fulfillment is more than mere reaffirmation; Jesus brings ultimate meaning to the ethics and patterns of the OT. Historical events—whether past, present, or future—are viewed as the providential outworking of God's plan (Goppelt 1982). Biblical prophecy is not primarily prediction but covenantal admonition, which utilizes the rehearsal of past events as well as the promise of future events as motivation to effect present covenant loyalty. Fulfillment in Matthew involves ethical and historical matters as well as prophetic promises.

Matthew 5:17 should be understood alongside Matt 3:15 as a statement of Jesus' complete allegiance to and obedience of the law. He has come to actualize the demands as well as the promises of the OT (Delling 1968, 294). His obedient life and authoritative teaching inaugurate God's renewal of Israel. This is stated in general terms in Matt 5:17–20 and illustrated with six examples in 5:21–48. These examples are commonly yet mistakenly viewed as antitheses. In hindsight, Moses was pointing to Jesus all along (Allison 1993). Jesus' teaching does not counter Moses, but the traditional Pharisaic understanding of Moses. Jesus provides six "epitheses" that seem to intensify the Torah, but on further analysis simply expound the original divine intent of the Torah.

Additional Fulfillment Texts

Four additional fulfillment texts presented as the words of Jesus are noteworthy. In the middle of the parabolic discourse in Matt 13:14, Jesus introduces Isa 6:9–10 to explain his use of parables and the recalcitrance of his larger audience. Here the word for fulfillment is *anaplēroō*, a compound form of the verb used in the texts previously considered. Jesus speaks of God's sovereignty and finds the unbelief of his audience to be in keeping with Israel's unbelief during the days of Isaiah (Matt 13:13–15). Unbelief in Isaiah's day was serious, but unbelief in Jesus' day is all the more so (cf. Isa 6:9–10 in John 12:40 and Acts 28:25–27).

Another fulfillment passage presents the legal experts and Pharisees as fulfilling the measure of the sin of their ancestors (23:32). The gist of Matt 23:29–36 is that Jesus' opponents are the culmination of a history of enmity against God's prophetic messengers (cf. 2 Chr 36:15–16; Ezra 9:10; Dan 9:7–11; Matt 5:12; 21:34–39). Just as the prophets anticipate the Messiah, so the prophet's enemies anticipate the Messiah's enemies (Turner 2015). Jesus' ironic imperative in Matt 23:32 is similar to several in the OT, such as Amos 4:4.

Two other references to fulfillment are found in Jesus' words in Gethsemane. In Matt 26:54, Jesus tells Peter not to resist the soldiers who are arresting Jesus. He goes on to say that he has the ability to ask the Father for thousands of angels to defend him. Yet neither response is appropriate because the Scriptures must be fulfilled. Then Jesus turns to the crowd and asks why he is being arrested secretly at night after he has taught openly in the temple. He answers his own question in 26:56— his arrest and the desertion of his disciples fulfills unnamed Scriptures. While no biblical text is introduced here, Jesus probably had in mind Zech 13:7, introduced in 26:31, and perhaps Ps 88:8, 18. The arrest of the shepherd led to the scattering of the sheep. Jesus saw his arrest as the beginning of fulfillment of other biblical passages as well, since he spoke of the prophets in the plural. This text alerts the reader to look for biblical fulfillments in Jesus' trials, crucifixion, and resurrection.

Fulfillment in Allusions and Echoes

Matthew's explicit fulfillment texts may be compared to the proverbial tip of the iceberg. These obvious quotations need to be seen in light of abundant allusions and echoes that are not as obvious, especially to the casual reader. Only three examples can be briefly summarized here.

Matthew's Genealogy

It is clear that Jesus came in fulfillment of the OT at the very outset of the First Gospel. Matthew's presentation of Jesus' genealogy links his identity and mission to the prototypical Israelite Abraham and to the great monarch David (1:1). The three sets of fourteen generations summarize (1) the era of promise from the Abraham to David (1:2–6a); (2) the era of decline from David to the exile (1:6b–11); and (3) the era of fulfillment from the exile to Jesus the Messiah, David's son (1:12–16). The genealogy is intriguing in that David is the fourteenth name mentioned in it, and that assigning numerical value to the Hebrew letters for David results in the number 14. Be that as it may, the genealogy is instructive, showing that Matthew viewed Israel's history as being fulfilled through Jesus, who is Abraham's son by being David's son. Through this Jesus, Israel finds relief from the judgment of the exile as well as renewal of the promises made to the ancestors. Accordingly, the genealogy sets the scene for all of the ensuing Matthean intrabiblical exegesis.

"Haven't You Read?" Texts

Mathew's presentation of Jesus and his ministry as rooted in the OT is also shown by a series of texts where Jesus rhetorically asked his opponents, "Haven't you read the OT?":

- Matt 12:3–5 alludes to 1 Sam 21:1–6 and Num 28:9–10.
- Matt 19:4–5 alludes to Gen 1:27; 2:24.
- Matt 21:16 alludes to Ps 8:2.
- Matt 21:42 alludes to Ps 118:22–23.
- Matt 22:31–32 alludes to Exod 3:6.

These rhetorical questions, tinged with sarcasm, underline the culpability of Jesus' opponents. They *had* read the OT, but sadly they had either forgotten the texts to which Jesus alludes, misunderstood their significance, or refused to accept their testimony to Jesus (cf. John 5:39–47).

Matthew 28:18–20

Matthew's ending is actually a new beginning. The apparent exit of Jesus marks the entrance of the church. This pivotal point in redemptive history is enriched by three OT allusions or echoes. First, Jesus' statement that he has received *all power* (28:18) and his command that his disciples teach *all the nations* both harken back to Dan 7:13–14, where the Son of Man approaches the Ancient of Days and receives universal authority and dominion over all the nations. Second, the command that Jesus' disciples teach the nations *all that he has commanded them* (28:20) alludes to Deut 18:18 and other OT prophetic commissions (e.g., Exod 7:2; Josh 1:7, 16–17; 22:2; Jer 1:7, 9). Jesus is the ultimate prophet like Moses (Deut 18:15, 18; cf. John 1:21, 25, 45; 6:14; 7:40; Acts 3:22; 7:27). He has spoken all that God commanded him, and his original disciples must speak all that Jesus has commanded them, so that additional disciples from all the nations might obey everything Jesus has taught. Third, Jesus' promise to be with his disciples *all the days* until the end of the age echoes many OT promises that God will be with his people (e.g., Gen 26:3 [Isaac]; 28:15; 31:3 [Jacob]; 48:21 [Joseph]; Exod 3:12; 4:12, 15 [Moses and Aaron]; Deut 31:23; Josh 1:5 [Joshua]). Jesus as Immanuel signifies the very presence of God with his people. Matthew 28:20 forms an *inclusio* with Matt 1:23 (citing Isa 7:14) and Matt 18:20. More than that, Matt 28:20 anticipates the last prophetic vision of the entire Bible, a scene where God's presence with his people is finally consummated (Rev 21:3–8). Matthew's final pericope, enriched by these OT allusions, is the crown of the entire Gospel.

Conclusion and Challenge

"The new is in the old concealed; the old is in the new revealed" (*Novum Testamentum in Vetere latet, Vetus Testamentum in Novo patet*). These words of Saint Augustine (*Quaest. Hept.* 2.73) are often quoted, but unfortunately, they are less frequently implemented. Intrabiblical exegesis is a complicated yet rewarding aspect of biblical studies. OT fulfillment in Matthew is multifaceted. It encompasses the whole OT, its ethical instructions, historical narratives, and prophetic oracles. Jesus fulfills the OT by obeying the Torah, recapitulating the narratives, and completing the promises. At times, the actualization of OT ethics is preeminent (3:15; 5:17). At other times, accomplishment of biblical promises is primary (4:14; 8:17; 12:17; 21:4; 26:54, 56). Yet the most prevalent aspect of fulfillment in Matthew concerns the recapitulation of historical patterns (1:22; 2:15, 17, 23; 13:14, 35; 23:32; 27:9). Jesus fills up biblical history with its ultimate, full significance. By "reading backwards" (Hays 2014) in the light of the fourfold Gospel tradition, interpreters can discern God's footprints in the sand, so to speak. The narratives of the OT anticipate many facets of Jesus' ministry, including even his opponents. By recapitulating biblical events, Jesus demonstrates the providence of God in fulfilling his promises to Israel. As indicated in Matthew's genealogy, biblical history is fulfilled by Jesus the Messiah, who is Abraham's son and David's son. All the promises of God are yes and amen in Jesus (2 Cor 1:17–20).

Studying intrabiblical exegesis (how later biblical texts understand and use earlier biblical texts) is not only fascinating, but it also gets to the heart of how the literature we now call "the Bible," with all its diversity, was organically linked from the beginning in the mind of God. If we say we believe the Bible is one book, then we ought to read it that way. Studying intrabiblical exegesis shows us how to do so. It also provides the basic information and structure for the development of biblical theology. If reading this essay whets the appetite for such study, the following steps are recommended (Beale 2012, 41–54; Beale and Carson 2007, xxiv-xxvi; Johnson 1980):

- Study the historical and literary contexts of the OT intertext.

    How do the ancient world and the story of Israel inform the OT intertext?

- Study the OT intertext's relationship to other OT texts.

    Does the OT intertext have its own previous OT intertext(s)?

- Study the historical and literary contexts of the NT text that points to the OT intertext.

    Are there parallels or similarities between the OT and NT contexts?

- Study the details of the text-form of the NT text and compare them to the OT intertext (Menken 2004).

    Do the details of the NT text's form imply anything about the NT author's intent?

- Study the hermeneutic and theological-pastoral intent of the NT author.

    Why did the NT author cite this OT text?

- Articulate the biblical theology found in the intertextual relationship.

    What biblical theme(s) is suggested and what is contributed to that theme?

- Reflect on the contemporary theological and pastoral implications.

    How does this instance of intrabiblical exegesis inform, edify, or warn the church today?

Works Cited

Aland, Barbara, et al., eds. 2014. *The Greek New Testament.* 5th rev. ed. Stuttgart: German Bible Society.

Allison, Dale C., Jr. 1993. *The New Moses: A Matthean Typology.* Minneapolis, MN: Fortress Press.

Beale, G. K. 2012. *Handbook on the New Testament Use of the Old Testament.* Grand Rapids: Baker Academic.

Beale, G. K., and D. A. Carson, eds. 2007. *Commentary on the New Testament Use of the Old Testament*. Grand Rapids: Baker Academic.

Blomberg, Craig L. 2002. "Interpreting Old Testament Prophetic Literature in Matthew: Double Fulfillment." *TJ* 23: 17–33.

———. 2007. "Matthew." Pages 1–109 in *Commentary on the New Testament Use of the Old Testament*. Edited by G. K. Beale and D. A. Carson. Grand Rapids: Baker Academic.

Davies, W. D., and Dale C. Allison, Jr. 1997. *Matthew 19–28*. Vol. 3 of *A Critical and Exegetical Commentary on the Gospel According to Saint Matthew*. ICC. Edinburgh: T&T Clark.

Delling, Gerhard. 1968. "πλήρης." Pages 283–311 in vol. 6 of *TDNT*.

Donaldson, Terrence. 1985. *Jesus on the Mountain: A Study in Matthean Typology*. Sheffield: JSOT Press.

France, R. T. 1971. *Jesus and the Old Testament*. London: Tyndale Press.

———. 1989. *Matthew: Evangelist and Teacher*. Grand Rapids: Zondervan.

Goppelt, Leonhard. 1982. *Typos: The Typological Interpretation of the Old Testament in the New*. Translated by D. H. Madvig. Grand Rapids: Eerdmans.

Gundry, R. H. 1967. *The Use of the Old Testament in St. Matthew's Gospel*. Leiden: Brill.

Hays, Richard B. 2016. *Echoes of Scripture in the Gospels*. Waco, TX: Baylor University Press.

———. 2014. *Reading Backwards: Figural Christology and the Fourfold Gospel Tradition*. Waco, TX: Baylor University Press.

Johnson, S. Lewis. 1980. *The Old Testament in the New: An Argument for Biblical Inspiration*. Grand Rapids: Zondervan.

Knowles, Michael P. 1993. *Jeremiah in Matthew's Gospel*. JSNTSup 68. Sheffield: JSOT Press.

———. 2006. "Scripture, History, Messiah: Scriptural Fulfillment and the Fulness of time in Matthew's Gospel." Pages 59–92 in *Hearing the Old Testament in the New Testament*. Edited by Stanley Porter. Grand Rapids: Eerdmans.

Konradt, Matthias. 2014. *Israel, Church, and the Gentiles in the Gospel of Matthew*. Translated by Kathleen Ess. Waco, TX: Baylor University Press; Tübingen: Mohr Siebeck.

Longenecker, Richard N. 1999. *Biblical Exegesis in the Apostolic Period*. Rev. ed. Grand Rapids: Eerdmans.

Menken, Maarten J. J. 2004. *Matthew's Bible: The Old Testament Text of the Evangelist*. Leuven: Leuven University.

Runesson, Anders, and Daniel M. Gurtner, eds. 2020. *Matthew within Judaism*. Atlanta: SBL Press.

Soares-Prabhu, George M. 1976. *The Formula Quotations in the Infancy Narratives of Saint Matthew's Gospel*. Rome: Biblical Institute Press.

Stanton, Graham. 1992. *A Gospel for a New People*. Edinburgh: T&T Clark.

Stendahl, Krister. 1968. *The School of St. Matthew and Its Use of the Old Testament*. Lund: Gleerup.

Turner, David L. 2015. *Israel's Last Prophet: Jesus and the Jewish Leaders in Matthew 23*. Minneapolis, MN: Fortress Press.

————. 2021. "Israel's Last Prophet: Matthew 23:29–36 and the Intertextual Basis of Matthew's Rejected Prophet Christology." Pages 75–93 of *New Studies in Textual Interplay.* Edited by Craig Evans et al. LNTS 632. London: T&T Clark.

————. 2008. *Matthew.* BECNT. Grand Rapids: Baker Academic.

2.2 The Scriptures in Luke's Gospel

Darrell Bock

The last summary citation of Scripture in Luke-Acts reads, "But God has helped me to this very day; so, I stand here and testify to small and great alike. I am saying nothing beyond what the prophets and Moses said would happen—that the Messiah would suffer and, as the first to rise from the dead, would bring the message of light to his own people and to the Gentiles" (Acts 26:22–23). This is but a variation on Luke 24:43–47, which makes much the same point. What has taken place in Jesus is a realization of what God revealed would happen both for Israel and the nations. In everything Luke does in his Gospel, a key frame is the teaching and promise of Scripture, for Luke's claim is that this seemingly new faith realizes promises of old that God made to his people (Bock 2012).

This citation serves as both an adequate introduction to, and summary of, the Gospel of Luke's use of Scripture. It notes three central themes: (1) the message of the newly emerged Christian teaching spans the full array of scriptural hope from Moses to the prophets; (2) the fact that Scripture is cited shows this movement is part of a long present divine plan, and (3) at the center of that hope is the Christ event, especially his death and resurrection-ascension.

A great disadvantage of a new movement was that it appeared to lack a history and roots spanning the generations. The claim for heritage means being rooted in history and legitimacy, an ancient sociological necessity for obtaining cultural credibility, where what was older and tested was better, especially when making claims about what God had done in history. This chapter examines Luke's scriptural claim for this new Christian movement. One way to make a significant religious claim was to appeal to ancient, sacred writings. The new movement had emerged out of Judaism, so that is where it found its sacred roots. This final summary text, like many others in Luke and Acts, does not reflect taking on the burden of a specific citation, but it presents a broader summary claim appealing to the swath of teaching from the entire corpus of Scripture. The consideration of Luke's broad use of Scripture should show how pervasive his appeal is.

This chapter proceeds in two steps. First, some hermeneutical axioms reveal how Luke saw divine history and thus how he read Scripture. Also treated is a current critical debate over whether Luke appeals to promise and fulfillment. Then we move to the description of Luke's five major scriptural themes that support his claim for the new movement from within his Gospel.

Hermeneutical Axioms Defined

Various themes in Luke's Gospel show his perspective. They set the historical horizon from which he works with Scripture and history. The testimony of Luke's Gospel is crucial in setting the stage for his message. The question is also important, because it shows how Luke sets the table for his claim of fulfillment.

In appealing to hermeneutical axioms, I am presenting the interpretive grid, the lenses that produced these readings (Evans 1993). Luke's take on the meaning of the ancient Hebrew Scriptures is really a claim that the ancient narrative, representing only promise, was incomplete without Jesus' coming and the revelation that accompanied him. Now that he has come, we can understand God's plan more clearly, because the events tied to his coming reveal the priorities and relationships in that ancient plan, in terms of issues like the law, the covenants, and the nations. These events were revelation themselves and set new priorities, witnessed to by the Spirit, but not as a denial of the function of how older elements in revelation prepared for the promise's arrival. In this perspective, the NT writers agree. The enumeration of these axioms is important to understanding the grid through which Luke read Scripture and the events tied to Jesus.

Axiom 1: God's Design and a New Era of Realization

This theme emerges in Luke 1:1. The point surfaces clearly by comparing two recent translations as Luke describes his effort to compose a narrative. The RSV reads 1:1b as "a narrative of the things that have been accomplished among us," while the NRSV reads "an orderly account of the events that have been fulfilled among us" (*peri tōn peplērophorēmenōn en hēmin pragmatōn*). The NRSV is more precise. The key term is *peplērophorēmenōn*, referring to the presence of designed events, acts that stand fulfilled in the midst of Luke's audience. The events of Luke's Gospel are "designed" as part of God's plan, bringing a necessity with them, as Luke 24:43–47 points out, using *dei* ("it must be") while appealing both to events and Scripture.

Two other texts are crucial: Luke 7:28 and 16:16. They show how John the Baptist is, in one sense, the end of an old era. As the greatest man born among women, this forerunner prophet has a unique role in the old era. Until he came, the law and the prophets were at the center of God's plan, always looking forward to the hope of the promise. But now everything is different. The least in the kingdom Jesus brings is greater than the man who was the greatest of the old era. Now the gospel of the kingdom of God is preached. The gospel is the presence of something new and something old. The old era of expectation leads to the new era of realization. That is part of the design. To understand where the story of the new community begins, one must understand that John, as the forerunner whom Malachi promised, is part of a divine design whose roots go back to scriptural hope (Luke 1:14–17; 7:27; Green 1994). The plan's presence is corroborated and declared in Scripture. The movement, new in execution, is old in planning. Event and Scripture are placed side by side. God's plan is what Scripture records. What was revealed and promised long ago has come.

Axiom 2: Christ at the Center

This axiom needs little development, but it is important to place it in proper reference to the more encompassing theme of God's activity and plan. Christology is not the sole goal of Luke's use of Scripture. It is an important port of call on the way to more comprehensive claims about God's plan and the promise's subsequent realization. The literary flow of Luke's use of Scripture reveals that once Jesus' messianic and lordship credentials are established ("He is Lord of all and judge of the living and the dead"), then scriptural attention can concentrate on how Gentiles are included and how Israel must not reject the opportunity to share in the promise. The book of Acts tells that story of inclusion. The plan argues that Jesus is Lord of all, so the gospel can go to all (Bock 1987; Strauss 1995). Israel will miss its blessing if the majority of the nation refuses to share in the call Jesus makes to all humanity. That warning appears in the parable of the tenants in Luke 20:9–19 where Isa 5:1–2 gives the background (Kimball 1994).

Axiom 3: Scripture as an Interpreter of Divine Event and Current Critical Discussion: A Defense of Promise-Fulfillment in Luke

These axioms suggest key elements in Luke's perspective about the relationship between Scripture and events tied to Jesus. God and his plan stand behind the events. These links between events and text show that expectations also existed in Judaism because of God's promises in Scripture. Central to both Christian and Jewish hope was the declaration of the various covenants and the deliverance they anticipated. Most importantly, history was read by both groups in a way that looked for divine patterns of activity that signaled the reemergence of divine design in salvific events.

This feature of pattern is why prophecy is not limited to directly prophetic prediction. Prophecy also includes the noting of a divine pattern or the typological-prophetic reading of the Bible (Bock 2008; for a counterview see Litwak 2005). Promise for the early church included prophetic texts and pattern texts, along with an appeal to covenant hope now freshly realized. The premise behind reading history as involving promise and pattern is divine design and the constancy of God's character as he saves in similar ways at different times. Jewish imagery reused exodus motifs or new creation language; this is how Judaism accepted this cyclical and patterned view of history. Reading history this way also fueled Luke's perspective in seeing divine design in the events tied to Jesus. Understanding this "pattern fulfillment" dynamic is crucial to understanding how Luke reads Scripture.

The center of that hope involved a pivotal figure. Luke's claim is that the events of Jesus' life and ministry began the arrival of that promised era (Luke 11:20; 16:16). Scripture is an interpreter of those events, explaining them and their design. At the same time, the events themselves, as unusual and unique as they are, draw one to Scripture to seek explanation. It would be wrong to view promise and fulfillment as a unidirectional activity, where a repository of texts was simply lined up with events, though that is what some critiques of reading prophecy and fulfillment in Luke have claimed for such a view.

An important critique of approaches that diminish promise-fulfillment, while emphasizing the role of Jesus events as determinative, can be made. It is that in most cases, the texts used by Luke were already regarded as either messianic, prophetic, or eschatological within Judaism before the events tied to Jesus took place. The prophecy was not "discovered" by the event. These texts existed as forming expectation, and Jesus events came to be linked to them. However, there often came with the event a filling out of the text in line with its general theme. Thus, the exact significance of the text was revealed with the event, creating an interactive, two-dimensional impact. To characterize this relationship between text and event as one way by overemphasizing either the text or the event is to fail to appreciate the complexity of the interaction between the two elements.

In some cases, events showed how the texts lined up and how the design worked by connecting the dots. The various strands of christological OT use in Luke reveal functions united in one person that Judaism placed in a variety of eschatological figures. Events tied to Jesus' ministry show the unity of function for which Luke argues when he discusses Jesus as the promise bearer. Most of these points are made in Luke's Gospel, setting the stage for uses of Scripture in Acts. But behind these uses of Scripture stand three fundamental Lukan beliefs: (1) the events surrounding Jesus are divinely designed, (2) he is at the center of God's plan and the arrival of the new era, and (3) Scripture helps to explain what is taking place. The events are recent, and the era is new, but the plan is not. In this way, Luke makes his claim to an ancient, divine heritage for the new movement.

Five Central Scriptural Themes in Luke

Paralleling a list from Craig Evans (1993), this study considers five topics and then discusses their relationship and function: (1) covenant and promise, (2) Christology, (3) ethical direction, (4) commission to the Gentiles, and (5) challenge with warning to Israel.

Covenant and Promise

The theme of covenant and realized promise is fundamental to Luke-Acts since it was raised as early as Luke 1:54–55 (Abrahamic) and 1:68–70 (Davidic). This emphasis continues in Acts, where all the covenants of expectation, or allusions to them, appear in speeches.

The hope of the Spirit is clearly expressed in the OT in new covenant teaching (Jer 31:31–34; Ezek 36:22–32). In Acts 2:16–19, Peter uses another OT text that raises this promise, Joel 2:28–32 (= LXX 3:1–5). He declares the realization of this promise, but he also indicates that "in the last days" this pouring out of the Spirit will come. The remark alludes back to Luke 24:49 and the awaiting of "the promise of my Father," as well as to the instruction to await the Holy Spirit in Acts 1:8. Luke also makes another crucial link. John the Baptist had indicated that the stronger one to come would baptize "with the Holy Spirit and fire," a baptism of purging within humanity. This is how one could recognize that the Christ, the promised coming one, was present (3:15–17). Only Luke among the Synoptic parallels makes the point about how to note who the Christ is as the context for this remark. So, Peter's declaring the Spirit's arrival marks the last days as having arrived and gives decisive evidence of the promised presence of the Christ.

The Spirit's coming is how one can know that God has made Jesus both Lord and Christ and has vindicated him through his resurrection and ascension. The call to share in promise is a call to share in a heritage rooted in Scripture.

Also noted is a tie to Davidic promise. This connection is made in the infancy material as Zechariah praises deliverance coming out of the house of David (Luke 1:67–69) and Mary hears about one born who will rule on the throne of David (Luke 1:31–33). So, Luke appeals to both the new covenant with the remarks about the Spirit and the Davidic Covenant with the remarks about Jesus' regal rule. The promise and the covenant belong together as prophetic Scripture shows.

Connections to Moses also exist. This theme surfaces in Luke 9:35, where the divine voice tells the three disciples present at the transfiguration to hear Jesus, alluding to this same passage from Deuteronomy. Moses and Elijah are present with Moses, likely representing the hope of the law aimed at promise, a theme that Galatians 3 also possesses. Jesus' ministry and the new community's message are not an attempt to break away from Israel, but a claim of the realization of the nation's long-awaited promises rooted in divine covenant commitments.

Christology

Many of the texts in the covenant-and-promise category could also be placed here, but to distinguish the two is helpful since Christology, as the above texts show, often plays a complementary role to additional claims about God's plan. Texts noted here serve a focused christological function.

Most of the christological texts treat activity associated with Jesus' ministry. For example, there is the use of Isa 61 and 58 in Luke 4, in which Isa 61 dominates by stressing proclamation but chapter 58 supports by noting the one who preaches will also bring what is being preached. This synagogue citation summarizes the mission of Jesus, as do the hymns of Luke 1–2, which allude to the Scriptures throughout. The use of a line from Isa 58 is significant. Jesus will do what Israel failed to do in living out the calling of God to serve others. Isaiah 61 is an appeal to servant imagery with the emphasis on the message of the release and cancelling of debt that salvation brings.

Some appeals to the promise of Scripture are generic references to the whole of Scripture. Luke 24:43–47 is a summary citation that says (1) the Christ would suffer, (2) he would be raised from the dead on the third day, and (3) repentance for the forgiveness of sins would be preached to all nations beginning from Jerusalem. Suffering probably comes from Isa 52:13–53:12 and Ps 118:22. Resurrection comes from Pss 16:8–11, 118:22, and 110:1. The preached message is rooted in Gen 12:3 and the promise that in Abraham's seed all the world will be blessed, along with the picture of Messiah's rule over the nations in Ps 2, one that also opens with the rejection of the

Messiah. The themes of the divine necessity of Jesus' suffering and being raised also fit in here, as does the allusion to Isa 53 at the Last Supper and in Jesus' remarks about being numbered among the criminals later in that same scene (Luke 22:37). The Last Supper also alludes to the new covenant that Jesus' death will establish (22:19–22).

Another key activity is the ascension of Jesus and his sitting at God's side. This emphasis appears in the many references to the Messiah or Jesus being seated at God's right hand from Ps 110:1 (Luke 20:41–44; 22:69). Luke prepared for this idea when Jesus asked the question of why the Messiah is called "Lord" by David, his ancestor, and his assertion that "from now on, the Son of Man [i.e., Jesus] will be seated at the right hand of the mighty God" (Luke 22:69). There, Jesus claims direct access to the authority of God by sharing in his ruling authority. He also affirms a divine vindication regardless of what the leaders may do to him. The resurrection was that act of vindication for Luke.

The use of Scripture for Christology describes Jesus' activity in such a way that his suffering, death, resurrection, and ascension are seen not to be surprising for the Messiah. Luke claims that Scripture points to a suffering but raised Messiah. The idea has old roots. Luke also argues through Ps 110:1 that this Savior is Lord, ruling from God's side. Showing this authority allows Luke to use Christology as a basis for claims in other areas later in Acts, especially Gentile inclusion. Since Jesus is Lord of all, the gospel goes to all.

Ethical Direction

Texts pointing to ethics appear in Luke's Gospel as the invocation of the call to love God. Luke 10:27 points to a core ethical value from Deut 6:5, which was also introduced in the picture of John the Baptist's work to turn people to God and to one another in Luke 1:16–17. The description of John's calling appeals to Mal 3:1 and 4:5. Turning people to God or loving God results in a difference in how others are treated and how community unfolds. There is a twofold direction to how turning to God impacts human relationships, as fathers and children are brought together as are the disobedient to the righteous. The result is an ethical triangle where my relationship to God impacts my treatment of others and there is reconciliation across the board. This sets the ethical frame for the people of God whom Jesus gathers. So, we get in the parable of the good Samaritan the idea that everyone is my neighbor; and the call is not to worry who that neighbor is, but to be a good neighbor, recognizing that neighbors can be found in surprising places, as a Samaritan becomes the example.

Commission to the Gentiles

Luke 2:30–32 points to a mission involving the world while alluding to Isa 49:6. Jesus is salvation and light, a revelation for Gentiles and glory for Israel. Though not explicit here, reconciliation is present. Luke 3 cites Isa 40:3–5, while Luke 24:47 makes a generic summary appeal to Scripture as the basis for taking a message of repentance into the whole world.

Gentile inclusion was so innovative from a Jewish point of view, not to mention for the disciples, that God had to force its implementation using vision and radical conversion to make the move stick in Acts 10. In Acts 10, the promise of the Spirit (Luke 24:49) is reintroduced to make sure the point is not missed that the promise of the Spirit indwelling has been realized in the same way as it was for Jewish believers (Acts 11:15–18). When Peter refers to the Spirit's coming on the Gentiles as he did in the beginning, he is alluding to the beginning of the realization of promise that came in Acts 2, which in turn echoes the explanation of Joel 2:28–32 and the distribution of the Spirit, as well as the remarks of John the Baptist in Luke 3:16. This is a major Lukan scriptural thread across his two volumes rooted in ancient Hebrew scriptural promise.

This kind of thematic linkage, which indirectly reintroduces scriptural explanation by echo, reveals how much the issue of Gentile involvement is interwoven with Christology and the divine plan in Luke-Acts. Paul, too, is called to "bring the message of light to his own people and to the Gentiles" (Acts 26:23). The image of Isaiah being a light to the Gentiles speaks not just for Peter's encounter with Cornelius as God's direct leading showed, but for Paul too—even more explicitly as he consistently ministered successfully to them. Such a mission forms the call of the new community (repentance to all the nations, Luke 24:47). To "be light" means to carry out God's call and to fulfill Scripture in taking a message of forgiveness and repentance to all. To be a good Jew is to seek salvation for Gentiles as well. Such an emphasis also shows how false it is to describe Luke as anti-Semitic. He is simply defending what he feels the actual mission of scriptural promise is. In Luke's mind, he is arguing the case for Israel's promise and the hope it extends to people of all nations.

Challenge with Warning to Israel

That the new community is simply carrying out God's long-promised commission puts the nation of Israel in an accountable and vulnerable position where response, not heredity, is imperative.

The texts addressed to Israel take on various emphases, but the note was already struck in Luke 2:34–35, when Simeon said to Mary that Jesus would be the cause of "the falling and rising of many in Israel," an allusion to Isa 8:14. Some passages pick up the theme and explain why Israel is not responding (Ps 2:1–2 in Acts 4:25–26; Isa 6:9–10 in Acts 28:26–27), while others warn the nation of the cost of refusal (Deut 18:19 and Lev 23:29 in Acts 3:22–23; Hab 1:5 in Acts 13:41). Other texts deepen the indictment by chronicling the pattern of the nation's response, treating their current hesitation as part of a history that reflects spiritual disease (Amos 5:25–27 in Acts 7:42–43; Isa 66:1–2 in Acts 7:49–50). Some of these remarks occur in the new community (Acts 4), but most are direct challenges to the nation (Acts 3; 7; 13; 28).

These texts argue that Israel, in any generation, does not have an inalienable right to the promise if the nation refuses to embrace God's grace. Those in the new community do not rejoice at issuing such a warning. These texts are not words seeking vengeance and vindication. Rather, fellow Jews plead with their neighbors not to miss God's work and so risk a dangerous accountability to God (Acts 3:24–26; 7:60).

This observation about the Israel-nations juxtaposition, along with the attention paid to God-fearers in Acts, likely indicates a false dichotomy when some argue that Acts is written primarily to either Gentiles or Jews. More plausible is an explanation that argues for a broad audience. Luke argues to all that Gentiles belong in the new community and need not be Jews to fit. Perhaps he writes with a special eye to God-fearers who left Judaism for Christianity. These Gentiles originally discovered God through a different route than the new community was arguing for through Jesus. Then they were taught about Jesus and embraced him.

Both the amount of appeal to the Hebrew Scriptures and the racial mix in the various passages suggest such a broad audience with a possible God-fearer concern. Imagine the reshuffling of perspective that such an entry into the new Jesus community initially had required. Theophilus may have been a God-fearer who had come to Jesus from Judaism, but he now finds himself wondering if he should go back to his earlier community. He has a fresh set of questions that events and persecution have raised for him and that Luke seeks to address. *Does all the Israelite rejection mean the new community is an object of divine judgment? What am I doing as a Gentile in a movement that was originally Jewish and that many Jews reject? Might my earlier community of the synagogue be where I belong with practices that they have done for so long?* Such questions have raised a sense of doubt for Theophilus. Luke responds and reassures him that God's heritage and promise, as odd as it sounds, rests in the new community (Luke 1:1–4). Even the Jews within the new community understand why Israel refuses to respond. Scripture and Israel's history show that they often have rejected God's way.

Jesus is seen as the prophetic, messianic, martyr sacrifice that is representative of a nation, especially in light of some other clearer texts in Luke-Acts on this theme (Luke 20:19–20; Acts 20:28). Israel's rejection of the community's message about Jesus reflects a serious error in discerning God's plan and is not as surprising as one might think. The pattern of Israel's history and OT texts suggest it was possible and that the nation was responsible for how they responded to the gospel.

Conclusion

The use of Scripture in Luke-Acts serves a variety of roles. Many texts set forth who Jesus is and explain what he is doing in conjunction with the divine plan and covenants. The early church asserted that a faithful response to God would mean: (1) the embracing of Jesus as the promised one, and (2) the inclusion of Gentiles into the community of blessing. Failure to respond has left the nation culpable.

Behind these claims stands the church's understanding of covenant, promise, and Christology. Scripture also allowed the community to appreciate that the church's current suffering was rooted in the way of Jesus, who had traveled a similar road. History taught the sad lesson that people often reject God's way, even in the nation of promise. Circumstances should not deflect the reader of Luke-Acts from seeing that rejection did not evidence God's judgment; rather, it mirrored the path of rejection that Jesus walked. The road they shared was the promised new road, because the new era had arrived with Jesus' coming as the Christ; but paradoxically it was an old road as well, since such rejection was promised by the prophets and practiced earlier by the nation. For Luke, history and the prophetic Scripture show that what was taking place was no surprise.

The new community had every claim of heritage to God's promise in covenant and Christ. They also shared in the suffering that came from those who rejected their message, just as they had earlier rejected the visit of the Sent One. To see that connection between promise and suffering was to understand what being in the light meant as one walked in the midst of a dark world. Believers were under pressure for the hope of God (Acts 26:15–18). Like Paul and the early community before him, the road might not be easy, but what God sought was faithful witness (Acts 1:7–8; 4:24–30; 28:30–31).

Luke's use of Scripture underscores that the message being proclaimed is the realization of a promise that God made long ago. Scripture legitimates the claims of the new community to reside in God's promise, plan, and program. There is a line of continuity between what God had revealed to Israel and what took place in Jesus and the new community. Prophetic word and pattern showed this continuity. The claims attached to the new community are in line with Scripture—even more, with the will of God—and so is the gospel the church preached with Jesus as the center and core of fulfillment.

Works Cited

Bock, Darrell L. 2012. *A Biblical Theology of Luke-Acts.* Grand Rapids: Zondervan.
———. 2008. "Single Meaning, Multiple Contexts and Referents: The New Testament's Legitimate, Accurate, and Multifaceted Use of the Old." Pages 105–51 in *Three Views on the New Testament Use of the Old.* Edited by Kenneth Berding and Jonathan Lunde. Grand Rapids: Zondervan.
———. 1987. *Proclamation from Prophecy and Pattern: Lukan Old Testament Christology.* JSNTSup 12. Sheffield: Sheffield Academic.
Evans, Craig A. 1993. "Prophecy and Polemic: Jews in Luke's Scriptural Apologetic." Pages 171–211 in *Luke and Scripture: The Function of Sacred Tradition in Luke-Acts.* Edited by Craig A. Evans and J. A. Sanders. Minneapolis, MN: Fortress Press.
Green, Joel. 1994. "The Problem of a Beginning: Israel's Scriptures in Luke 1–2." *BBR* 4: 61–85.
Kimball, C. A. 1994. *Jesus' Exposition of the Old Testament in Luke's Gospel.* JSNTSup 94. Sheffield: Sheffield Academic.
Litwak, Kenneth Duncan. 2005. *Echoes of Scripture in Luke-Acts: Telling the History of God's People Intertextually.* JSNTSup 282. London: T&T Clark.
Strauss, Mark L. 1995. *The Davidic Messiah in Luke-Acts: The Promise and Its Fulfillment in Lukan Christology.* JSNTSup 110. Sheffield: Sheffield Academic.

2.3 "Fulfillment" in John's Gospel

Craig A. Evans

The relationship of the Fourth Gospel to the Jewish people and the synagogue has been a major item of interest from the second century to modern times. The polemical expressions in this work have had tragic consequences. In the Fourth Gospel, Jesus is called a sinner and is threatened by his opponents (8:41, 48, 59; 9:16, 24, 31; 10:31). Jesus insults his accusers by asserting that their spiritual father is the devil (8:44). Jesus warns his disciples that they will be cast out of the synagogue for confessing Jesus (16:2; cf. 9:22; 12:42). And yet, as many interpreters today recognize, the Fourth Evangelist is deeply rooted in the Jewish world, embraces Israel's election, and recognizes the authority of Israel's sacred Scriptures. Indeed, the purpose of the Fourth Evangelist is not to drive Jews away but to invite them into the Jesus community (20:30–31). Appeal to Scripture as fulfilled plays a vital role. In many ways, the polemic witnessed in the Fourth Gospel is akin to the polemic seen among rival Jewish groups in the first century.

Fulfillment of Scripture in the Prologue

Nowhere is the Fourth Evangelist's rootedness to the Jewish world more clearly seen than in his appeal to Israel's sacred story, as expressed in the Scriptures. The opening lines of the Fourth Gospel echo the opening lines of the book of Genesis:

> In the beginning was the Word [*logos*], and the Word was with God, and the Word was God. He was in the beginning with God; all things were made through him, and without him was not anything made that was made. In him was life, and the life was the light of humans. The light shines in the darkness, and the darkness has not overcome it. (John 1:1–5 RSV, adapted)

Echoing interpretive traditions related to Genesis and wisdom ideas, the Fourth Evangelist has identified Jesus as the Word (Logos), as will become clear later in the Prologue and elsewhere in the Gospel. But what the evangelist says of the Logos in John 1:1 would have hardly been controversial in the first century, given what Philo says of the divine Logos: "For nothing mortal can be made in the likeness of the Most High and Father of the universe but (only) in that of the second God [*ton deuteron theon*], who is his Logos [*logos*]" (*QG* 2.62 [on Gen 9:6]; cf. *Leg.* 2.86 "But the most universal of all things is God [*ho theos*]; and in the second place the word of God [*ho theou logos*]"). Philo calls the Logos the "second God"! In reaction to Christianity, later rabbis rejected such language, but did Jewish teachers in the first century? There is no evidence that they did. One thinks, too, of what Wisdom (*sophia*) says of herself: "I came forth from the mouth of the Most High. . . . From eternity, in the beginning, he created me" (Sir 24:3, 9); or of personified Wisdom who claims that she was with God "in the beginning" before creation (Prov 8:22–23)—indeed, sitting next to God and taking part in creation (8:30). What Wisdom says of herself is very similar to what the Prologue of John says about the Logos.

In the Melchizedek Scroll from Qumran (11Q13), the mysterious figure Melchizedek, to whom Abraham had offered a tithe (Gen 14:18–20), acts in some way as God himself. According to this scroll, Melchizedek defeats Satan, liberates Israel, and forgives Israel's sins. The prophet Isaiah speaks of this figure, according to the scroll, when he announces "the year of Melchizedek's favor." The allusion to Isa 61:2 is obvious, but the original text reads "the year of the LORD's favor." In some sense, Melchizedek takes the place of Yahweh, or perhaps he is Yahweh. What Philo and the Fourth Evangelist say about the divine Logos is not much different.

The last five verses of the Johannine Prologue appeal to Israel's tradition of the tabernacle, when it was completed and filled by the glory of God (Exod 40), and the stunning demonstration of divine grace in forgiving Israel's egregious sin in making the golden calf (Exod 34):

> And the Word became flesh and dwelt among us, full of grace and truth; we have beheld his glory, glory as of the only Son from the Father. . . . And from his fulness have we all received, grace upon grace. For the law was given through Moses; grace and truth came through Jesus Christ. No one has ever seen God; the only Son, who is in the bosom of the Father, he has made him known. (John 1:14–18 RSV)

These verses reflect Exodus 33–34, where God graciously gives sinful Israel a second chance after the people had foolishly fashioned a golden calf. Moses asks if he may see God's glory, but he is told, "You cannot see my face; for man shall not see me and live" (Exod 33:20). In contrast to Moses, who was granted a glimpse of God's back (33:21–23), the Logos resided from the beginning "in the bosom of the Father." This relationship uniquely qualified the Logos, which "became flesh" (John 1:14), to make the Father known. This is why later Jesus can say to his disciples, "if you had known me, you would have known my Father" (14:7); and "He who has seen me has seen the Father" (14:9). When God passed before Moses, he said, "The LORD, the LORD, a God merciful and gracious . . . full of grace and truth" (Exod 34:6 RSV, modified). This is echoed in John 1:14, when we are told that the Logos is "full of grace and truth."

The first five verses of the Prologue link the Logos to creation, and the last five verses of the Prologue link the Logos to the divine presence in the tabernacle. In doing the latter, the Fourth Evangelist has identified the Logos, which has become flesh and taken up residence in a tabernacle made of human flesh—as opposed to the old tabernacle made of animal skin. The human tabernacle is none other than Jesus, who is the Messiah, the Son of God (20:30–31).

Fulfillment of Scripture in Rejection

In a tract probably written sometime in the early second century, Trypho the Jew acknowledges that he and fellow Jews expect the appearance of the Messiah someday, but they doubt that Jesus of Nazareth fulfilled this expectation. Trypho explains his grounds for this uncertainty: "We doubt whether the Messiah should be crucified with such dishonor, for he that is crucified is said in the law to be cursed, so that with regard to this it is hardly possible that I can be persuaded" (*Dial.* 89.2; cf. Deut 21:23). Trypho goes on to request of the Christian apologist: "Instruct us therefore also out of the Scriptures that we may believe you. For we know that he suffers . . . but prove to us where he must be crucified and die in so disgraceful and dishonorable a fashion" (*Dial.* 90.1).

The objections raised by Trypho at this point probably represent the main reason a majority of Jews in the first century chose not to join the Jesus movement. It was not so much disputes over the interpretation of the law and the question of purity, or how to accommodate the growing Gentile membership—it was the apparent defeat of Jesus and his ignoble execution on a Roman cross. After all, the would-be messiahs in Israel in the first century and early second century all promised to defeat Rome, and some of them drew large and enthusiastic followings. In what sense, then, can Jesus be Israel's Messiah, when the prophecies of sacred Scripture foretell the Messiah's victories and Israel's redemption? How can Jesus be the Son of God, when dying on the cross he cries out, "My God, my God, why have you abandoned me?" If he truly was the Messiah and fulfiller of Scripture, how does he end up hanging on a cross cursed of God?

Justin attempts to answer these and other questions and objections raised by Trypho in his apologetic tract *Dialogue with Trypho the Jew*. On many points Justin does fairly well, but he struggles with the objections just considered. Justin was not the first follower of Jesus to struggle with these Jewish objections; the Fourth Evangelist did too. His apologetic focuses on the fulfillment of Scripture (which is what Trypho demands). The Fourth Evangelist's strategy is remarkable, and it becomes evident not only in the selection of Scriptures to which appeal is made, but also in the formulas used to introduce the quotations of Scripture.

The first half of the Gospel of John (chs. 2–11) is characterized by "signs" (*sēmeia*) that, as we shall see, intentionally allude to the signs that took place in the wilderness under the leadership of Moses. In this part of John, including the first half of chapter 12, several times Scripture is quoted or referenced (sometimes without a specific quotation). They are as follows:

1:23 "he said" (followed by a quotation of Isa 40:3)
1:45 "of whom Moses wrote in the law, and (of whom) the prophets (spoke)"
2:17 "they remembered that it was written" (followed by a quotation of Ps 69:9)
5:46 "for concerning me that one (Moses) wrote"
6:31 "just as it is written" (followed by a quotation of Ps 78:24)
6:45 "it is written in the prophets" (followed by a quotation of Isa 54:13)
7:42 "the Scripture said"
8:17 "and it is written in your law that"
10:34 "it is written in your law that" (followed by a quotation of Ps 82:6)
12:14 "just as it is written" (followed by a quotation of Zech 9:9)
12:16 "they remembered that these things were written of him"

One will observe that not once is Scripture quoted or referenced as "fulfilled." This stands in startling contrast to the way Scripture is cited in the second half of the Gospel of John, in which the emphasis falls on the rejection and suffering of Jesus (Carson 1988, 246–49; Evans 1993, 174–81; Hays 2016, 285–88). In the second half of John, Scripture is introduced and quoted (or referenced with a quotation) as follows:

12:38 "it was that the word spoken by the prophet Isaiah might be fulfilled" (followed by a quotation of Isa 53:1)

12:39 "for Isaiah again said" (followed by a quotation of Isa 6:10 in John 12:40)

13:18 "it is that the Scripture may be fulfilled" (followed by a quotation of Ps 41:9)

15:25 "It is to fulfill the word that is written in their law" (followed by a quotation of Ps 35:19)

17:12 "that the Scripture might be fulfilled"

18:9 "This was to fulfil the word which he had spoken" (with reference to John 6:39)

18:32 "that the word of Jesus, which he spoke, be fulfilled" (with reference to John 3:14; 8:28; 12:33)

19:24 "This was to fulfil the Scripture" (followed by a quotation of Ps 22:18)

19:28 "in order that the Scripture be fulfilled" (followed by a quotation of Ps 69:21)

19:36 "that the Scripture might be fulfilled" (followed by a quotation of Ps 34:20)

19:37 "and again another Scripture says" (followed by a quotation of Zech 12:10)

One will notice that, with the exceptions of the introductory formulas in 12:39 and 19:37, every time Scripture is introduced, we find the words "that it be fulfilled." Even the two apparent exceptions are not exceptions at all, for each is linked to its preceding quotation with "again" (*palin*). In other words, 12:38–40 introduces two passages of Scripture (Isa 53:1 and Isa 6:10) as fulfilled, and 19:36–37 likewise introduces two passages of Scripture (Ps 34:20 and Zech 12:10) as fulfilled. So why was not a single Scripture in the first half of John introduced as fulfilled, in contrast to the second half of John in which *all* Scriptures are introduced as fulfilled?

The best explanation is that the Fourth Evangelist is addressing an objection arising from the synagogue of his day (Martyn 2003), an objection that was probably pretty much the same as the objection Trypho raised, with which a few decades later the Palestinian Christian Justin Martyr grappled. Justin would have been well advised to rely more heavily on the Gospel of John in developing his reply to Trypho (Evans 1993, 178–79).

To appreciate the Fourth Evangelist's strategy, it is necessary to carefully follow the argument in chapter 12. Lazarus, whom Jesus raised from the dead in chapter 11, appears in the first three pericopes in chapter 12. He is at table with Jesus when Jesus is anointed (12:1–8). In the next passage, we are told that the ruling priests wish to kill Lazarus himself on account of his remarkable story that has resulted in "many of the Jews . . . believing in Jesus" (12:9–11). In the entrance narrative, we are told that the reason the crowd greeted Jesus was because of the raising of Lazarus (12:12–19). The true significance of the entrance into Jerusalem and the prophetic text that was fulfilled (i.e., Zech 9:9) was understood by the disciples only "when Jesus was glorified" (v. 16).

The theme of glorification runs throughout the Gospel of John. When the Logos became flesh, the followers of Jesus "beheld his glory" (1:14). Jesus' mysterious reply to his mother, "my hour is not yet come" (2:4), is later understood as a reference to the hour in which his glory will be revealed (2:11; 7:30, 39; 8:40; 12:16, 23, 27–28). This "hour" in which Jesus will be glorified is the hour in which he will "depart out of this world," to return "to the Father" (13:1). Jesus refers to this hour when he tells his disciples: "Now is the Son of man glorified, and in him God is glorified" (13:31). The meaning of all this becomes clear in chapter 12.

It is in chapter 12 that the Fourth Gospel transitions from the signs of chapters 1–11 to the passion of chapters 13–20 (Smith 1976). It is when the Hellenistic Jews (called "Greeks," meaning Greek-speaking Jews) request to see Jesus that he declares, "The hour has come for the Son of man to be glorified" (12:23). This hour of glorification entails death (12:24) by means of being "lifted up" on the cross. This then matches the prophecy of Isa 52:13–53:12, the Suffering Servant Song, in which the servant is said to be "high and lifted up" or, in Greek, "exalted and glorified." Jesus declares that he will not attempt to avoid "this hour." Far from it, the hour of glorification—his being lifted up on the cross—was his goal from the beginning (12:27). So, Jesus prays, "Father, glorify your name" (12:28a). Then, in what Jews would call a *bat qol* (lit. "daughter of a sound"), or a confirming divine word, God speaks from heaven: "I have glorified it and I will glorify it again" (12:28b). The second part of this heavenly declaration, "I will glorify it again," refers to Jesus' exaltation on the cross. The first part, "I have glorified it," probably refers to the incarnation itself, referred to in the Prologue, when the evangelist declares that the Logos "became flesh" and that "we have beheld his glory" (1:14).

The meaning of the "hour" in which Jesus will be glorified becomes clear in the appeals to Isa 52:13–53:12 and Isa 6:1–13. The Fourth Evangelist may have only quoted single verses of these two passages (i.e., 53:1 and 6:10), but he had in mind their entirety. The key part of John 12 is introduced with the concession, "Though he had done so many signs [*sēmeia*] before them, yet they did not believe in him" (John 12:37), followed by the first introduction of Scripture as "fulfilled": "it was that the word spoken by the prophet Isaiah might be fulfilled" (12:38). The Fourth Evangelist has waited until the admission in verse 37 that despite the signs Jesus performed, few believed in him. The admission, however, is not fatal; rather, it introduces the argument for fulfillment that follows.

The language of verse 37 recalls what Moses long ago said to the second generation of Israel shortly before they began their conquest of the promised land: "You have seen all that the Lord did before you . . . the great trials that your eyes saw, the signs [*sēmeia*] and those great wonders. But to this day the Lord God has not given you a heart to know and eyes to see and ears to hear" (LXX Deut 29:1–4). The Fourth Evangelist's allusion to the language of Deut 29 is part of his Moses-Jesus typology. Earlier, Jesus had told Nicodemus, "No one has ascended into heaven but he who descended from heaven, the Son of Man. And as Moses lifted up the serpent in the wilderness, so must the Son of Man be lifted up, that whoever believes in him may have eternal life" (John 3:13–15). The life provided by Moses and the bronze serpent was only temporal; the life that the lifted-up Jesus offers is eternal. Jesus later offers the woman of Samaria "living water" (4:10). The water Jesus gives his followers may be compared to a "a spring of water welling up to eternal life" (4:14). Such water goes well beyond the water that Moses provided in the wilderness. Jesus also offers the people of Israel bread in the wilderness (6:1–14), even as their ancestors were sustained by the manna when they were led by Moses (Exod 16). But the bread that Jesus offers gives eternal life (John 6:47–51). Those who ate the bread Moses offered died.

Many in the crowd confessed that Jesus must be "the prophet who is come into the world" (6:14). Here we have an allusion to the promise of Moses that God would someday raise up a prophet like himself (Deut 18:15). Jesus describes himself as the "good shepherd" (John 10:11), which probably is meant to fulfill not only the prophecies of Isaiah and Ezekiel (cf. Isa 40:11; Ezek 34:11–16) but also to fulfill the petition with which Moses entreated the Lord: "Let the LORD, the God of the spirits of all flesh, appoint a man over the congregation, who shall go out before them and come in before them, who shall lead them out and bring them in; that the congregation of the LORD may not be as sheep which have no shepherd" (Num 27:16–17).

The Moses typology is prominent in John 2–11, that part of the Gospel characterized by signs (sēmeia), which are for the most part similar to the signs that Moses performed in the wilderness. As noted, John 12 concedes that despite the number and quality of these signs, few have responded in faith (Thompson 1991). This minimal response is also part of the Moses typology, for the great lawgiver said the same thing in Deut 29, as has already been mentioned. The failure of the signs to lead to faith results in the fulfillment of Scripture. It is ironic that when Jesus is rejected, that is when Scripture is said to be fulfilled. It is in being rejected (anticipated in the Prologue itself at 1:11) that Jesus will be lifted up on the cross, even as Moses lifted up the bronze serpent (3:14).

The first quotation from Isaiah (53:1) gives expression to unbelief: "Lord, who has believed our report, and to whom has the arm of the Lord been revealed?" (12:38). The "arm of the Lord" refers to God's power, which has been displayed in the mighty signs. The evangelist asserts that the people "could not believe" (12:39) because of something else Isaiah foretold: "He has blinded their eyes and hardened their hearts," etc. (12:40; cf. Isa 6:10). Although Isaiah's prophecy parallels Deut 29:1–4, in Deuteronomy Moses refers to the lack of faith in the past during the sojourn in the wilderness; Isaiah speaks of a lack of faith in the future. Thus the failure to believe despite the signs is more than typology; it is also prophecy.

But the most stunning feature in the Fourth Evangelist's interpretation is the claim that "Isaiah said this"—that is, the words of the Suffering Servant Song, when (or because) "he saw his glory and spoke of him" (John 12:40). The evangelist is speaking of the whole of Isa 6, where in the Hebrew the prophet says, "In the year that King Uzziah died I saw the Lord sitting upon a throne, high and lifted up" (6:1). In the Aramaic paraphrase the verse reads, "I saw the glory of the Lord" (emphasis added). The same paraphrase occurs in 6:5, where the frightened prophet says in the

Hebrew, "My eyes have seen the King," but in the Aramaic he says, "My eyes have seen the *glory* of the Shekinah of the eternal King" (emphasis added). The "glory" of John 12:40, about which Isaiah spoke, is none other than the glory of God, which in the Aramaic paraphrase serves as a circumlocution and perhaps a hypostasis for God himself. The Fourth Evangelist is asserting that when Isaiah saw the Lord "high and lifted up," he uttered his song about the suffering servant, who is described in the Hebrew as "lifted up and very high" (Isa 52:13) but in the Greek as "lifted up and glorified." (The idea that Jesus as the Servant was glorified is not entirely unique to John; cf. Acts 3:13 "The God of Abraham . . . glorified his servant Jesus.")

The Greek words of the LXX are *hypsoun* ("lift up" / "exalt") and *doxazein* ("glorify"), the very verbs used in the Fourth Evangelist's description of Jesus as the Son of Man: "Now is the time for the Son of man to be glorified" (John 12:23) and "when I am lifted up" (12:32). Although it is not emphasized in the Fourth Gospel, the expression "Son of Man" alludes to the human-like figure in Dan 7:9–14 who is presented before God in heaven and receives authority and a kingdom. This is why Jesus describes himself as the Son of Man who has come down from heaven (John 3:13, 31; 6:33, 38, 41–42, 50–51, 58, 62). In being lifted up on the cross, Jesus will return to heaven. It also explains Jesus' response to Pontius Pilate, the Roman prefect of Judea and Samaria, who asks Jesus if he is the "king of the Jews" (18:33). Jesus tells Pilate, "My kingship is not of this world" (18:36). Jesus has received his kingship from heaven; when he is lifted up (literally on the cross, but figuratively he is exalted) and has completed his work, he will return to heaven.

Fulfillment of Scripture in the Passion

After the transition that takes place in John 12, where the rejection of Jesus is said to fulfill the prophecies of Isaiah, every Scripture that is quoted is introduced as *fulfilled*. By using this formula, the evangelist claims that every significant event in the passion of Jesus is in fact a fulfillment of scriptural prophecy. Review of the formulas and quotations will make this clear.

While eating his final meal with his disciples and in anticipation of his betrayal, Jesus says, "I am not speaking of you all; I know whom I have chosen; it is that the Scripture may be fulfilled, 'He who ate my bread has lifted his heel against me'" (13:18). Jesus has quoted Ps 41:9, whose author complains that an intimate friend, who has received food from the author, has committed an act of betrayal. Early critics and skeptics of the Christian movement pointed to the betrayal of Judas Iscariot as evidence that Jesus was no true prophet and certainly not divine, else surely he could have foreseen such treachery (e.g., Origen, *Cels.* 2.11–12, 20). No, says Jesus in the Gospel of John, the betrayal was anticipated and was in fact foretold in Scripture. In the Farewell Discourse, Jesus speaks of those who hate him and his disciples. Their hatred, says Jesus, fulfills what is "written in their law, 'They hate me without a cause'" (John 15:25). Jesus has quoted Ps 35:19, a psalm in which David laments those who fight against him, seek his life, and devise evil against him. In the High Priestly Prayer, Jesus thanks God for preserving his disciples excepting, of course, Judas Iscariot, "the son of perdition, that the Scripture might be fulfilled"

(John 17:12). Jesus quotes no Scripture here, but it is probable that readers and auditors of the Fourth Gospel would have been reminded of the earlier quotations of Ps 41:9 (in John 13:8) and Ps 35:19 (in John 15:25), though the evangelist may also have had in mind Scriptures yet to be cited (Michaels 2010, 870).

In John 18:9 and 18:32, it is noted that things Jesus had said earlier have been fulfilled. The prophetic words of Jesus, now fulfilled, concern his betrayal. In John 19:23–24, the soldiers who crucify Jesus cast lots for his clothing. In doing so, they fulfill Ps 22:18, another lament psalm attributed to David that speaks of those who plot evil against David, gloating over him and dividing his clothes among themselves. When Jesus on the cross says, "I thirst" (John 19:28), he fulfills yet another expression of lament from a psalm attributed to David (Ps 69:21; cf. 22:15). Finally, the manner in which Jesus died—his body pierced but his bones unbroken (John 19:31–37)—is said to fulfill two Scriptures, Ps 34:20 ("He keeps all his bones, not one of them is broken") and Zech 12:10 ("they will look on him whom they have pierced").

The point the Fourth Evangelist is making is that every aspect of Jesus' rejection, suffering, and death fulfills prophetic Scripture. Nothing took Jesus by surprise, and nothing fell outside his mission and the divine plan. But more importantly, the Fourth Evangelist has interpreted the death of Jesus in terms of the slaughter of the Passover lamb, yet another point of Moses typology. Earlier in the Fourth Evangelist's narrative, John the Baptist said of Jesus, "Behold, the Lamb of God, who takes away the sin of the world!" (1:29). The fulfillment of Ps 34:20, in reference to the nonbreakage of Jesus' bones, is not an isolated detail that has been fulfilled, along with other details found in the lament psalms; but it is a reference to the Passover lamb, whose bones were not to be broken (Exod 12:46). Calling Jesus the "Lamb of God" may also allude to the suffering servant, who is led like a lamb to slaughter (Isa 53:7).

The blood of the Passover lamb saved the lives of Israel's firstborn when the death angel struck Egypt (Exod 12:7, 13, 29–30). In the Fourth Gospel, the death of Jesus is understood as the slaughter of the Passover lamb. Even as the blood of the lamb, "placed on the two door posts and the lintel" (Exod 12:7), saved believing Israelites, so the blood of Jesus, the "Lamb of God," will save all who believe in him (John 6:53–56; cf. 19:34). It is true that the slaughter of the Passover lamb was not thought of as providing atonement for sin, but the blood of the Passover lamb does preserve life. This is the mission of Jesus, the mission of him who descended from heaven; it is to give life to the world. Jesus achieves this by giving his blood and his life.

The appeal to the Passover lamb, whose bones are not broken when slaughtered, becomes yet another component in the Fourth Evangelist's Moses-Jesus typology (Evans 1993, 181–84; Grigsby 1995; Porter 2015, 198–224). Of course, this typology is not wholly unique to the Fourth Evangelist, for Paul also appeals to it when he exhorts the Corinthians, who have foolishly and recklessly chosen to ignore egregious sin in their midst, to "clean out the old leaven . . . for Christ, our paschal lamb, has been sacrificed" (1 Cor 5:7). Paul's appeal to Jesus as the sacrificed Passover lamb is found in a context that warns against the spread of sin in the church (seen in the analogy of the spread of leaven throughout a whole lump of dough). So, although there is no specific reference to sin in the Exodus story of the first Passover or in subsequent celebration of the Passover, that the sacrificed lamb of Passover could be understood in some sense as providing atonement for sin is attested in both Paul and the Fourth Gospel.

Summing Up

Fulfillment of Scripture in the Gospel of John is very much focused on Jesus' rejection, suffering, and death by crucifixion. The evangelist's point is that, far from providing evidence that Jesus was a failure and fraud, he was in fact the Son of Man sent from heaven as God's divine Logos, whose mission was to save the world. This is why when Jesus dies on the cross, as depicted in John, he says, "It is finished" (19:30). This concluding remark coheres with the several passages of Scripture that have been quoted and introduced as *fulfilled*. In suffering and dying on the cross, Jesus has fulfilled several important prophetic Scriptures. In going to the cross, Jesus has "finished" his mission and is now ready to return to heaven, his place of origin.

The purpose of fulfillment in the Fourth Gospel is to mount an apologetic intended for a skeptical synagogue, whose members assumed that "the Messiah remains forever" (John 12:34). Being lifted up on a Roman cross surely implies failure, even being "cursed of God," as Deut 21:21–23 teaches. This is the objection that early second-century Trypho raised, and it seems to be the objection that the Fourth Evangelist attempts to answer in his fulfillment apologetic.

Works Cited

Carson, D. A. 1988. "John and the Johannine Epistles." Pages 245–64 in *It is Written: Scripture Citing Scripture. Essays in Honour of Barnabas Lindars*. Edited by D. A. Carson and H. G. M. Williamson. Cambridge: Cambridge University Press.

Evans, Craig A. 1993. *Word and Glory: On the Exegetical and Theological Background of John's Prologue*. JSNTSup 89. Sheffield: JSOT Press.

Grigsby, Bruce H. 1995. "The Cross as an Expiatory Sacrifice in the Fourth Gospel." Pages 69–108 in *The Johannine Writings: A Sheffield Reader*. Edited by Stanley E. Porter and Craig A. Evans. BibSem 32. Sheffield: Sheffield Academic.

Hays, Richard B. 2016. *Echoes of Scripture in the Gospels*. Waco, TX: Baylor University Press.

Martyn, J. Louis. 2003. *History and Theology in the Fourth Gospel*. 3rd ed. Louisville: Westminster John Knox.

Michaels, J. Ramsey. 2010. *The Gospel of John*. NICNT. Grand Rapids: Eerdmans.

Porter, Stanley E. 2015. *John, His Gospel, and Jesus: In Pursuit of the Johannine Voice*. Grand Rapids: Eerdmans.

Smith, D. Moody. 1976. "The Setting and Shape of a Johannine Narrative Source." *JBL* 95: 231–41.

Thompson, Marianne Meye. 1991. "Signs and Faith in the Fourth Gospel." *BBR* 1: 89–108.

2.4 Jesus [Not] as Moses in the Gospel of Matthew

Seth D. Postell

Introduction

Matthew's Gospel has long been considered the Gospel written specifically to the Jewish people (Hagner 1993, lxiv; Harrington 1991, 1; Overman 1994; Turner 2008, 3; Saldarini 1994; Sim 2000). Though there are strategic references to Gentiles in the Gospel (e.g., Matt 1:5–6; 28:19), and a Jewish flavor to all the other Gospels as well, there is something about Matthew's Gospel that "feels" incredibly Jewish. Matthew's very first verse identifies Jesus as the son of Abraham (Matt 1:1). There is an emphasis on the fulfillment of the Old Testament Scriptures and the Torah in particular (Matt 1:22; 2:15; 4:14; 12:17; 21:4; 26:56; see esp. Matt 5:17–19), and Jesus says he was sent to the "lost sheep of the house of Israel." The Jewishness of Matthew's Gospel was a fact well recognized by the early church fathers (Jerome, Irenaeus, Origen) and affirmed in Eusebius's famous quote about the original audience of the Gospel:

> Among the four Gospels, which are the only indisputable ones in the Church of God under heaven, I have learned by tradition that the first was written by Matthew, who was once a publican, but afterwards as apostle of Jesus Christ, and it was prepared for the converts from Judaism, and published in the Hebrew language. (*Hist. eccl.* 6.25.3; cf. Eusebius 1890, XXV.4)

In an article published more than one hundred years ago, Benjamin W. Bacon posited a structural analogy between the Pentateuch (the Five Books of Moses) and Jesus' five discourses in the Gospel of Matthew (Bacon 1918). More recently, Dale Allison devoted an entire monograph to a study of Moses typology in Matthew (Allison 1993). Allison's monograph provided the most thorough study on the theme of the "prophet like Moses," tracing this theme throughout the Old Testament and extracanonical literature (for a similar work on the "prophet like Moses" theme in John's Gospel, see Meeks 1967).

In this essay, I explore the relationship between the figure of Moses and the structure of Matthew's Gospel. Though I am in general agreement with Allison's work, I would like to offer two clarifying comments. First, Allison's use of the word *typology* is problematic. In the history of Christian interpretation, typology is used as a catch-all phrase for biblical interpretation almost always associated with *sensus plenior* (a fuller meaning). This supposed "fuller meaning" of the Old Testament was revealed to the authors of the New Testament but not grounded in the historical intentions of the Old Testament authors. Allison's work would have been far more valuable to Matthew studies in particular, and to New Testament studies as a whole, had he considered the work of Moshe Garsiel. Garsiel is an Israeli Bible scholar, who focused on narrative analogy as a literary strategy in the books of Samuel (Garsiel 1985). An abundance of literature on narrative analogy in Old Testament studies has followed (Alter 1981; Avioz 2006; Bazak 2006; Berman 2004, 2008, 2013; Grossman 2009, 2015; Kline 2018; Postell 2016, 2020; Sailhamer 1992; Sternberg 1987; Zakovitch 1985, 1995, 2009), showing the extent to which Matthew's presentation of Jesus as a "new Moses" is well rooted in a literary device known to the Jewish people as *"maʿaseh avot, siman labbanim"* ("the deeds of the fathers are a sign for the sons"). I believe the insights on narrative analogy have been largely neglected in New Testament studies, and ought to be considered as a far more appropriate category than typology for understanding the literary intentions and strategies of the New Testament authors.

Second, while acknowledging the importance of Allison's work, I do not think he fully appreciates the magnitude of his insights for our understanding of the structure of Matthew's Gospel. Perhaps in part this is because he has not applied the insights of narrative analogy, a field of studies that was, at the time, still in its infancy.

Narrative Analogy

Before we look at the literary structure of Matthew's Gospel in light of narrative analogy, I would like to offer a definition of narrative analogy as a conscious rejection of typology and also make clear the criteria for identifying one. I concur with Jonathan Grossman, who defines narrative analogy as follows:

> An analogy is an intentional literary device which creates a dialogue between two texts, a figurative device that the author uses to express hidden meanings, and through which the reader is invited to reveal them: In many cases in Scripture, the closeness of motifs (and also in language) is so obvious between the two stories that one cannot escape the conclusion that one of its authors knew the other story and used it as bricks in the building of his story. (Grossman 2015, 339; author's translation of the Hebrew)

Throughout this essay, I will look at passages in Matthew that are demonstrably related to passages in the Torah. We rely on eight of Gil Rosenberg's fifteen criteria for intentional allusion (Rosenberg 2020, 704–7): (1) shared vocabulary (on the importance of shared language in allusion, see also Ben-Porat 1976, 110–11; Grossman 2015, 341; Leonard 2017; Leonard 2008); (2) shared phrases; (3) the similar language is rare or distinctive; (4) the shared language appears in similar contexts (parallel-plot structure); (5) the similar language appears in similar structure (on the importance of establishing links via shared common terms in structurally identical places, see Berman 2008, 38–39); (6) the similarity is textually awkward ("ungrammatical") in the alluding text; (7) the *hypotext* (alluded-to-text) was accessible/available (see Hays 1989, 29) to the author of the *hypertext* (alluding text); and (8) cumulative evidence. Although all of Rosenberg's criteria are not explicitly stated by scholars writing about narrative analogy, these criteria are implicitly acknowledged by those who refer to authorially intended narrative analogy. In every case, shared language and parallel plot structure is essential (Garsiel 1985, 25; Grossman 2009, 396; Kline 2018, 18–19; Postell 2016, 163; Shalom-Guy 2016, 3).

I must make it clear from the outset that I did not write this essay with the intention of proving my case to biblical scholars who read the Bible in the original languages. I intentionally avoid using Biblical Greek and Biblical Hebrew in order to include a wider range of readers. That said, all the arguments in this article are based on a close reading of the original languages. I am convinced that the arguments in this essay will be far more appreciated by those who consider them with the Greek Old and New Testaments in hand.

As I hope to show, the whole of Matthew's Gospel is an extended narrative analogy with Moses, wherein Matthew seeks to compare and contrast Jesus with Moses. By way of contrast, Matthew presents a picture of Jesus that differs radically from Moses yet is analogous with the God of Israel. In the words of Grossman, Matthew creates a "dynamic analogy" whereby "the presentation of a certain character from one narrative . . . parallel[s] more than one character in the other" (Grossman 2009, 395).

Matthew's Threefold Structure

The Body (5:1–26:1): Jesus as Lawgiver

An abundance of articles and monographs testify to the lack of agreement among scholars about the structure of Matthew's Gospel (Bacon 1918; Bauer 1989; Combrink 1982; Combrink 1983; Kingsbury 1973, 1987; Krentz 1964; Milton 1962; Przybylski 1974; Smith 1977; Van Aarde 1982; Weren 2006; Weren 2014). Rather than interact with these works, I would like to cut to the chase by suggesting that the body of the Gospel of Matthew is structured around its five discourses. The end of each discourse and the introduction to the next major section in the body of Matthew's Gospel is marked by a virtually identical conclusion. All biblical citations are from the NASB unless stated otherwise.

These literary seams in the body of Matthew's Gospel are, I propose, intended to draw an analogy between Jesus and Moses, and more specifically between Jesus' *Torah* (instruction) and the Torah of Moses. As in Matthew, there are five references in the Pentateuch (LXX) wherein Moses finishes a work or a discourse (Exod 40:33; Num 7:1; Deut 31:1, 24; 32:45). Three of the five references in Matthew's Gospel (7:28; 19:1; 26:1) are nearly identical to Deut 31:1 (LXX). The purpose of these statements is to emphasize Jesus' role as Israel's teacher and the body of his teachings as authoritative *Torah* (instruction).

This point is supported by a number of passages. First, a comparison is drawn between the authority of the Mosaic Torah and Jesus' *Torah* by the phrase "heaven and earth" in the first and the last discourses (Matt 5:18; 24:35). The choice of wisdom or folly with respect to receiving or rejecting Jesus' *Torah* (Matt 7:24–27), moreover, can easily be seen in light of the choice between life and death (Deut 30:15–20) with respect to receiving or rejecting the Mosaic Torah (Allison 1993, 190–91). Second, Jesus' identification of his teaching as a "yoke" (Matt 11:29) is remarkably similar to the Mishnaic identification of the Mosaic commandments as a "yoke" (m. Ber. 2.2; m. Abot 3.5; see also Pss. Sol. 7:9; 17:30). Third, the Gospel

The Sermon on the Mount (Matt 5–7)	Apostolic Mission to Israel Discourse (Matt 10)	The Parable Discourse (Matt 13)	The Church Discourse (Matt 18)	The Last Day Discourse (Matt 24–25)
When Jesus had finished these words, the crowds were amazed at His teaching; for He was teaching them as one having authority, and not as their scribes. (7:28–29)	When Jesus had finished giving instructions to His twelve disciples, He departed from there to teach and preach in their cities. (11:1)	When Jesus had finished these parables, He departed from there. He came to His hometown and began teaching them in their synagogue, so that they were astonished, and said, "Where did this man get this wisdom and these miraculous powers?" (13:53–54)	When Jesus had finished these words, He departed from Galilee and came into the region of Judea beyond the Jordan; and large crowds followed Him, and He healed them there. (19:1–2)	When Jesus had finished all these words, He said to His disciples, "You know that after two days the Passover is coming, and the Son of Man is to be handed over for crucifixion." (26:1–2)

concludes with an emphasis on teaching the nations Jesus' authoritative commandments (Matt 28:18–20).

The analogy between Jesus as an authoritative teacher like Moses is further strengthened by the parallel foci between Jesus' and Moses' first and last discourses. Jesus' ascent up the mountain to give his disciples his *Torah* (Matt 5:1), and the careful interaction with the Mosaic Torah (Matt 5:17–48), is a likely analogy to Moses' first mountaintop "discourse" to Israel (Exod 19:2–3, 11–14, 16–18, 20, 23; 20:18; 24:4, 12–13, 15–18). Jesus' final mountain discourse (Matt 24:3), moreover, is entirely focused on last day events (Matt 24:3–26:1) even as Moses' final discourse also focuses almost exclusively on the last days (Deut 31:29; see 30:1–14; 31:16–21; 32:1–43). And just as the Mosaic commandments appear within a narrative framework and are given in separate codes and/or collections throughout the Torah's narrative, so Jesus' five discourses appear within a larger narrative context.

The Introduction (1:1–4:25): Jesus as Redeemer

The easily identifiable body of Jesus' authoritative instruction vis-à-vis the fivefold summary statements further suggest that we identify Matt 1:1–4:25 and Matt 26:1–28:20 as the introduction and the conclusion, respectively. The arrangement of the first four chapters of Matthew's Gospel is particularly crucial for Matthew's compositional strategy. A nearly verbatim allusion to the account of Moses' return to Egypt suggests that Matthew seeks to present Jesus as the redeemer like Moses. The translation of the LXX below is my own.

But when Herod died, behold, an angel of the Lord appeared in a dream to Joseph in Egypt, and said, "Get up, take the Child and His mother, and go into the land of Israel; for those who sought the Child's life are dead." So, Joseph got up, took the Child and His mother, and came into the land of Israel.	Now after many days, the king of Egypt died. And the Lord said to Moses in Midian, "Go, depart to Egypt. For all those who sought your life are dead." So, taking *his* wife and *his* children, he mounted them upon the donkeys and returned to Egypt.
(Matt 2:19–21)	(LXX Exod 4:19–20a)

The comparison between Jesus and Moses portrays Jesus as a redeemer like Moses who has returned to Israel to save his people from their sins (Matt 1:21).

The structural pattern created by a series of allusions to the Pentateuch in the introduction reinforces this thesis. The Gospel of Matthew begins with the "record of the genealogy" (*biblos geneseōs*; Matt 1:1), a phrase not found elsewhere in the New Testament. It does appear, however, twice in the beginning of the Greek translation of the Pentateuch (Gen 2:5; 5:1) and is the phrase from which the book's title derives its Greek name, Genesis (see Philo, *Opif.* 1.129; *Leg.* 1.19; *Det.* 1.139; *Post.* 1.65; *Abr.* 1.9, 11). The use of this unique phrase is likely Matthew's way of signaling a direct connection between Jesus' genealogy with the story of the chosen line in Genesis.

Matthew 2 contains a number of allusions to the story of Moses and the exodus. As noted, Jesus' return to Israel evokes the story of Moses' return to save his people from Egypt (compare Matt 2:19–21 with Exod 4:19–20a). Other parallels highlight the analogy: King Herod's murder of the Hebrew boys in response to being tricked by the magi (Matt 2:16) is analogous to Pharoah's murder of the Hebrew boys in response to being tricked by the midwives (Exod 1:18–22). Thus Matthew specifically compares Jesus' birth narrative to the story of Moses. Moreover, Jesus' departure from Egypt creates a strong identification between Jesus and the people of Israel (compare Matt 2:15 with Exod 4:22–23; see also Hos 11:1).

It is likely not fortuitous that Matthew places the narrative of Jesus' baptism after his "exodus from Egypt." Matthew refers to the place of Jesus' baptism as the "Jordan River" (Matt 3:6), a phrase used only one other time in the NT (Mark 1:5), and twice in the LXX, in the account of Joshua's miraculous crossing of the Jordan River (Josh 4:7; 5:1), a place specifically associated with the coming of the prophet like Moses in the Second Temple period (see Josephus, *Ant.* 20.97).

The Temptation Narrative follows immediately after Jesus' exit from the waters of baptism.

After being baptized, Jesus came up immediately from the water. . . . Then Jesus was led up by the Spirit into the wilderness to be tempted by the devil. And after He had fasted forty days and forty nights, He then became hungry.	Then Moyses removed the sons of Israel from the Red Sea and led them into the wilderness of Sour. And they were journeying for three days in the wilderness and were not finding water to drink.
(Matt 3:16a; 4:1–2)	(LXX Exod 15:22 NETS)

The shared language in a virtually identical sequence of narrative events bolsters the likelihood that Jesus' baptism is intended to evoke the Red Sea crossing and the trials of Israel in the wilderness. There are a number of allusions to Israel's wilderness temptations in general (compare Matt 4:4 with Deut 8:3; Matt 4:7 with Deut 6:16), but these allusions set the stage for very particular links with Moses. Like Moses, Jesus fasts for forty days and forty nights (compare Matt 4:2 with Exod 34:28; Deut 9:9; see also 1 Kgs 10:8). Matthew's citation of Ps 91:11–12 (Matt 4:6) also draws on a group of psalms (90–92) with numerous associations with Moses (Gundersen 2015, 91–145). The final temptation wherein Jesus is shown all the kingdoms of the world from a mountaintop is remarkably similar to Moses' mountaintop view of the promised land (compare Matt 4:8 with Deut 3:27; 34:1–4).

Let us also take a bird's-eye view of Matthew's compositional string of narrative events:

Matt 1	Matt 2	Matt 3	Matt 4
And the book of Genesis	The birth of the new Moses and the exodus from Egypt	The new Moses and the Red Sea crossing	The new Moses in the wilderness

It is difficult to ascribe to chance this order of events, particularly when we consider how these events serve as the introduction to the body of Matthew's Gospel and the first of Jesus' fivefold *Torah*: "When Jesus saw the crowds, He went up on the mountain; and after He sat down, His disciples came to Him" (Matt 5:1; see Exod 24:18). The Sermon on the Mount following this string of Moses-like events looks remarkably like a new Mount Sinai. The introduction, therefore, casts Jesus as the Redeemer like Moses and sets the stage for us to understand Jesus as the lawgiver like Moses.

The Conclusion (26:1–28:20): Jesus as Covenant Mediation

The conclusion of Matthew's Gospel focuses on Jesus' death, resurrection, and the sending of his disciples into the world. As noted above, strategic allusions to the Pentateuch in the introduction and body of Matthew's Gospel help us identify Jesus as the redeemer and lawgiver like Moses. I would like to posit the presence of another allusion in the conclusion of Matthew that helps us grasp its significance in the macrostructure of the Gospel. Having taken his disciples up the mountain in the pattern of Moses to present the first of five installments of his authoritative *Torah* (Matt 5:1–25:46), Jesus now becomes a covenant mediator like Moses (Matt 26:26–29). Matthew's account is a clear allusion to the words of Moses upon the mediation of the Sinai Covenant.

"For this is My blood of the covenant, which is poured out for many for forgiveness of sins."	Then Moyses, taking the blood, scattered it over the people and said, "Look, the blood of the covenant that the Lord made with you concerning all these words."
(Matt 26:28)	(LXX Exod 24:8 NETS)

The mediation of this covenant becomes the grid through which we are to understand the significance of Jesus' sacrifice.

The Jesus-as-Moses analogy not only helps us understand the meaning of the crucifixion, but also the commission of the disciples in the final chapter of the Gospel. Before we look specifically at the Jesus-as-Moses analogy in this commissioning, it is important to consider the manner in which the disciples are also drawn into this analogy. Chapter 28 is actually the second of two commissioning narratives. The first is found in Matt 9:36–10:42. Here, Matthew takes the words of Moses at the commissioning of Joshua and applies them to the inner thought world of Jesus' reasoning for choosing and sending his disciples.

Seeing the people, He felt compassion for them, because they were distressed and dispirited like sheep without a shepherd. . . . Jesus summoned His twelve disciples and gave them authority over unclean spirits, to cast them out, and to heal every kind of disease and every kind of sickness (Matt 9:36; 10:1)	"Who shall go out before them and who shall come in before them and who shall bring them out and who shall bring them in, and the congregation of the Lord shall not be like sheep that have no shepherd." And the Lord spoke to Moyses, saying, "Take to yourself Iesous [Joshua] son of Naue, a person who has a spirit in him, and you shall lay your hands upon him." (LXX Num 27:17–18 NETS)

This analogy between Joshua and the disciples sheds invaluable light on our understanding of the Great Commission in Matt 28:16–20. The Pentateuch concludes with a final mountaintop commission of Joshua to conquer the promised land and a call to follow all the commandments God had given Moses (Deut 34:9). It is difficult not to see the similar ending of Matthew, wherein Jesus commissions the disciples to go to the nations with the commandments of Jesus in hand (Matt 28:16–20).

The structure of Matthew takes shape around a macrostructural narrative analogy with Moses. Without trying to be reductionistic to other aspects of the theology of Matthew, it would seem that the patterns of comparison with Moses in structurally significant locations are part and parcel of the macrostructure and purpose of the Gospel. Jesus comes to the land of Israel as the redeemer like Moses, provides his disciples with an authoritative *Torah* as the lawgiver like Moses, and establishes the new covenant as the covenant mediator like Moses. The Gospel's conclusion calls to mind the final chapter of the Torah, wherein the disciples stand posed, just like Joshua, equipped with the commandments of God, ready to go and accomplish their mission.

Interpreting the Analogy: Similarities and Contrasts

Narrative analogies are intended to attract careful attention to the details of the hypertext and the hypotext. The meaning of the analogy is found in the similarities and, as is often the case, in the differences. In the case of Matthew, recognizing both the similarities and the differences between Jesus and Moses are essential for understanding his theology.

Jesus as the Prophet Like Moses

We are indebted to Allison who gathered an impressive list of narrative analogies with Moses in the Hebrew Bible and in Second Temple literature (Allison 1993, 1–95). Yair Zakovitch is clearly in agreement with Allison when he writes:

> The most significant biblical character is, without a doubt, the figure of Moses, and many are the characters that have been fashioned according to his image; Joshua for example, Jeroboam the son of Nebat, Elijah, and even David in the Book of Chronicles; and outside the boundaries of the Hebrew Bible—Jesus marches in the strength of Moses' footsteps. (2009, 134; translation of the Hebrew my own)

Based on an abundance of allusions to the Exodus narrative in Isa 40–55, Gordon Hugenberger has cogently put forth a case for interpreting Isaiah's "servant of the Lord" as a "new Moses" figure (1995). Hugenberger's work is particularly helpful in demonstrating how Moses' analogies were part and parcel of a robust Old Testament eschatology.

The Jewish people expected the coming of the prophet like Moses, and this expectation existed long before the first century of the common era. It comes as no surprise, therefore, that Matthew intended to identify Jesus as this long-expected prophet. Matthew's macrostructural narrative analogy is not a freshly minted Christian typological interpretation of the Old Testament, but a Jewish reading deeply rooted in the literary design of the Hebrew Bible itself. The Jewish hope for the coming of a "new Moses" is clearly articulated in *Ecclesiastes Rabbah* 1.28 (sixth to eighth century CE; translation of the Hebrew my own):

> What was will be . . . Rabbi Berchiah said in the name of Rabbi Isaac: like the first redeemer, so will be the last redeemer. As it says (Exodus 4) of the first redeemer: "And Moses took his wife and his sons and mounted them on the donkey." So, it is also said of the last redeemer (Zechariah 9): "Lowly and riding upon the donkey." As it says of the first redeemer who brought down manna (Exodus 15), "Behold I will rain down upon you bread from heaven." So also, the last redeemer will bring down manna, as it is written (Psalm 72), "Let there be an abundance of grain in the land." As the first redeemer brought forth a well, so also the last redeemer will bring forth water as it says (Joel 4), "And a spring went out from the house of the Lord and waters the wadi of Shittim."

Jesus as God with Us

In biblical theological terms, Matthew presents Jesus as the fulfillment of a lengthy inner-biblical longing for the prophet like Moses. Matthew's analogy of Jesus, however, is both dynamic and altogether radical. As noted earlier, a dynamic analogy is "the presentation of a certain character from one narrative . . . [that] parallel[s] more than one character in the other" (Grossman 2009, 395). The full scope of Matthew's analogy cannot be appreciated without considering the deity of Jesus as well (Hays 2016, 145).

Richard Hays calls attention to Matthew's *inclusio* of divine identity (2016, 162). Jesus' final promise to be "with his disciples" until the end of the age is an allusion to the Greek translation of Immanuel, "God with us" (compare Matt 1:23; 28:20). Matthew's *inclusio* provides the necessary framework for fully appreciating the remarkable differences between Jesus and Moses in the Matthean analogies. A few examples will suffice.

It is essential to notice in the Matthean analogy that Jesus is not only the mediator of God's *Torah* for the disciples, but the source of the *Torah* as well. Jesus brings the disciples up the mountain like Moses but gives them his *Torah* like God (Matt 5–7). Jesus' *Torah*, like the Torah from Sinai, must be followed, and the hearers are called to consider the two ways: the way of life for those who listen, and the way of death for those who do not. That Jesus' *Torah* bears the same authority of God's *Torah* is clear when we consider the fact that both will outlast heaven and earth (Matt 5:18; 24:35).

Jesus' call to "come to me" in Matt 11:28–30 would clearly be considered blasphemous on the lips of Moses, or on the lips of any other prophet for that matter! In a book laden with allusions to the Pentateuch, Jesus' claim to be the source of rest for his disciples also parallels God's role as the provider of rest (compare Matt 11:29 with Exod 16:23; 23:12; 31:15; 35:2; Lev 16:31; 23:3, 24, 39; 25:4–5, 8; Num 10:33; see also Jer 6:16).

Earlier, we discussed the manner in which the Great Commission portrays the new Moses sending "the new Joshuas" to conquer the world. But the analogy here is obviously dynamic. Jesus' promise to be with his disciples as they carry his commandments not only resonates with the commissioning of Joshua at the end of the Torah (Deut 34:9), but it also echoes the first chapter of Joshua, wherein God likewise promises to be with Joshua and calls him to faithfully follow his commandments.

"Go therefore and make disciples of all the nations, baptizing them in the name of the Father and the Son and the Holy Spirit, teaching them to **observe all that I commanded you**; and lo, **I am with you always**, even to the end of the age." (Matt 28:19–20)	"No person shall stand against you all the days of your life. And just as I was with Moyses, so **I will also be with you**, and I will not forsake you or overlook you. Be strong and manly, for you shall divide for this people the land that I swore to your ancestors to give to them. Be strong, therefore, **and manly, to observe and act as Moyses my servant commanded you**, and you shall not turn aside from them to the right or to the left so that you may be perceptive in everything you do." (LXX Josh 1:5–7 NETS)

The implications of these analogies show forth a Matthean Christology that is clearly on par with John's. Jesus is not only the redeemer like Moses, the lawgiver like Moses, and the covenant mediator like Moses: he is the God of Moses—Immanuel!

Conclusion

In this essay, we considered the importance of narrative analogy in Matthew's compositional strategy. I have argued for a three-part structure of Matthew, each part emphasizing an analogous aspect of Jesus' ministry in the light of the greatest of Old Testament prophets. In the introduction, Matthew presents Jesus as the redeemer like Moses. In the body of the Gospel, Jesus is the lawgiver like Moses who imparts to his disciples an authoritative *Torah*. The conclusion of Matthew presents Jesus as the covenant mediator like Moses who commissions his Joshua-like disciples to take the gospel of the new covenant to all nations and to teach them to obey his *Torah*.

I would like to conclude this essay by sharing a story about a friend of mine named Irving. Irving was raised as an Orthodox Jew. He served as a Torah reader (*Ba'al Qore*) for fifteen years in various synagogues week in and week out. Because of his gifted mind and photographic memory, Irving eventually memorized almost the entire Torah (including the vocalization and cantillation). Irving, in fact, astonished his rabbis at the yeshivah with the amount of Torah he had memorized. They would only need to give a couple of the words at the beginning of any verse in the Torah, and he would complete the verse for them in the Hebrew, all from memory. In addition to his knowledge of the Torah, Irving also came in first place in his yeshivah, with a student body in the hundreds, in Talmud learned *be'al peh* ("by heart").

Little did Irving expect what would happen after a persistent Christian teenager began calling him every week—for a year. The teenager assured Irving he could demonstrate from the Old Testament that Jesus is the Messiah, without any need to open the New Testament. Because of Irving's religious training, however, he was able to refute each Christian interpretation of the Old Testament presented. After a year, Irving heard the nervous voice of his Christian teenage friend on the other end of the line. "Irving, I know I told you we wouldn't look at the New Testament, but I really feel strongly we should read Matt 5–7 together" (the Sermon on the Mount). Irving agreed, and the young man began to read the passage to him over the phone. By the end of the passage, Irving not only realized that Jesus is the Messiah, but he also immediately understood that Jesus was God. Today, Irving serves as a leader of a messianic congregation.

In many ways, Irving approached the Gospel of Matthew as an ideal reader. Well versed in the Torah, he not only recognized the similarities between Jesus and Moses, but he almost immediately recognized through Jesus' teachings that the prophet like Moses was also God. This essay was my attempt to show that Irving's theological conclusions about Jesus in the Gospel of Matthew are absolutely correct.

Works Cited

Allison, Dale C. 1993. *The New Moses: a Matthean Typology*. Minneapolis, MN: Fortress Press.

Alter, Robert. 1981. *The Art of Biblical Narrative*. New York: Basic Books.

Avioz, Michael. 2006. "The Analogies between the David-Bathsheba Affair and the Naboth Narrative." *JNSL* 32.2: 115–28.

Bacon, Benjamin W. 1918. "The Five Books of Moses against the Jews." *Expositor* 15: 56–66.

Bauer, David R. 1989. *The Structure of Matthew's Gospel: A Study in Literary Design.* JSNTSup 31. Sheffield: Almond Press.

Bazak, Amnon. 2006. *Parallels Meet: Literary Parallels in the Book of Samuel* (Hebrew). Alon Shvut: Tvunot.

Ben-Porat, Ziva. 1976. "The Poetics of Literary Allusion." *PTL* 1: 105–28.

Berman, Joshua A. 2013. "'The Deeds of Moses (Exod 2–4) as a Sign for Israel': Moses as a Reflection Story for the People of Israel in the Book of Exodus" (Hebrew). Pages 20–29 in *Zer Rimonim: Studies in Biblical Literature and Jewish Exegesis Presented to Professor Rimon Kasher.* Edited by Rimon Kasher, Michael Avioz, Eliyahu Assis, and Yael Shemesh. Atlanta: SBL Press.

———. 2008. "Establishing Narrative Analogy in Biblical Literature" (Hebrew). *Beit Mikra* 53.1): 31–46.

———. 2004. *Narrative Analogy in the Hebrew Bible: Battle Stories and Their Equivalent Non-Battle Narratives.* VTSup 103. Leiden: Brill.

Combrink, H. J. Bernard. 1982. "The Macrostructure of the Gospel of Matthew." *Neot* 16.1: 1–20.

———. 1983. "The Structure of the Gospel of Matthew as Narrative." *TynBul* 34: 61–90.

Eusebius. 1890. "Eusebius Pamphilus: Church History, Life of Constantine, & Oration in Praise of Constantine." NP. In *Church Fathers (Nicene & Post 2).* Edited by Philip Schaff and Henry Wace. New York: Christian Literature Publishing. Accordance electronic edition, version 3.1. 14 vols.

Garsiel, Moshe. 1985. *The First Book of Samuel: A Literary Study of Comparative Structures, Analogies and Parallels* (Hebrew). Ramat-Gan, Israel: Revivim.

Grossman, Jonathan. 2009. "'Dynamic Analogies' in the Book of Esther." *VT* 59.3 (2009): 394–414.

Grossman, Jonathan. 2015. *Text and Subtext: On Exploring Biblical Narrative Design* (Hebrew). Tel Aviv: HaKibbutz HaMeuchad.

Gundersen, David Alexander. 2015. "Davidic Hope in Book IV of the Psalter." PhD diss., The Southern Baptist Theological Seminary.

Hagner, Donald A. 1993. *Matthew 1–13.* WBC 33A. Grand Rapids: Zondervan.

Harrington, Daniel J. 1991. *The Gospel of Matthew.* SP 1. Collegeville, MN: Liturgical Press.

Hays, Richard B. 2016. *Echoes of Scripture in the Gospels.* Waco, TX: Baylor University Press.

———. 1989. *Echoes of Scripture in the Letters of Paul.* New Haven: Yale University Press.

Hugenberger, Gordon P. 1995. "The Servant of the Lord in the 'Servant Songs' of Isaiah." Pages 105–40 in *The Lord's Anointed: Interpretation of Old Testament Messianic Texts.* Edited by Philip E. Satterthwaite, Richard S. Hess, and Gordon J. Wenham. Grand Rapids: Baker Books.

Kingsbury, Jack Dean. 1987. "The Place, Structure and Meaning of the Sermon on the Mount Within Matthew." *Int* 41.2: 131–43.

———. 1973. "The Structure of Matthew's Gospel and His Concept of Salvation-History." *CBQ* 35.4: 451–74.

Kline, Joanna Greenlee. 2018. "Imitations of Jacob, Judah, and Joseph in the Stories of King David: The Use of Narrative Analogy in 1 Samuel 16–1 Kings 2." PhD diss., Harvard University.

Krentz, Edgar. 1964. "The Extent of Matthew's Prologue: Toward the Structure of the First Gospel." *JBL* 83.4: 409–14.

Leonard, Jeffery M. 2008. "Identifying Inner-Biblical Allusions: Psalm 78 as a Test Case." *JBL* 127: 241–65.

———. 2017. "Inner-Biblical Interpretation and Intertextuality." Pages 97–142 in *Literary Approaches to the Bible*. Edited by Douglas Mangum and Douglas Estes. Bellingham, WA: Lexham.

Meeks, Wayne A. 1967. *The Prophet-King: Moses Traditions and the Johannine Christology*. NovTSup 14. Leiden: Brill.

Milton, Helen. 1962. "The Structure of the Prologue to St. Matthew's Gospel." *JBL* 81.2: 175–81.

Overman, J. Andrew. 1994. *Matthew's Gospel and Formative Judaism*. Minneapolis, MN: Fortress Press.

Postell, Seth D. 2016. "Abram as Israel, Israel as Abram: Literary Analogy as Macro-Structural Strategy in the Torah." *TynBul* 67.2: 161–82.

———. 2020. "Potiphar's Wife in David's Looking Glass: Reading 2 Samuel 11–12 as a Reflection Story of Genesis 39." *TynBul* 71.1: 95–113.

Przybylski, Benno. 1974. "The Role of Mt 3:13–4:11 in the Structure and Theology of the Gospel of Matthew." *BTB* 4.2: 222–35.

Rosenberg, Gil. 2020. "An Allusion Connecting Genesis 18:10, 14 and 2 Kings 4:16–17." *JBL* 139.4: 701–20.

Sailhamer, John H. 1992. *The Pentateuch as Narrative: A Biblical-Theological Commentary*. Grand Rapids: Zondervan.

Saldarini, Anthony J. 1994. *Matthew's Christian-Jewish Community*. Chicago: University of Chicago Press.

Shalom-Guy, Hava. 2016. "Textual Analogies and Their Ramifications for a Diachronic Analysis of 1 Samuel 13:1–14:46 and Judges 6:1–8:35." *JHebS* 16.10: 1–28.

Sim, David C. 2000. *The Gospel of Matthew and Christian Judaism: The History and Social Setting of the Matthean Community*. SNTW. Edinburgh: T&T Clark.

Smith, Christopher R. 1977. "Literary Evidences of a Fivefold Structure in the Gospel of Matthew." *NTS* 43.4: 540–51.

Sternberg, Meir. 1987. *The Poetics of Biblical Narrative: Ideological Literature and the Drama of Reading*. ISBL. Bloomington: Indiana University Press.

Turner, David L. 2008. *Matthew*. BECNT. Grand Rapids: Baker Academic.

Van Aarde, A. G. 1982. "Matthew's Portrayal of the Disciples and the Structure of Matthew 13:53–17:27." *Neot* 16.1: 21–34.

Weren, Wilhelmus Johannes Cornelis. 2006. "The Macrostructure of Matthew's Gospel: A New Proposal." *Bib* 87.2: 171–200.

———. 2014. *Studies in Matthew's Gospel: Literary Design, Intertextuality, and Social Setting*. Boston: Brill.

Zakovitch, Yair. 2009. *Inner-biblical and Extra-biblical Midrash and the Relationship Between Them*. Tel Aviv: Am Oved. Hebrew version.

———. 1985. "Reflection Story: Another Dimension for the Valuation of Characters in Biblical Narrative" (Hebrew). *Tarbiz* 54: 165–76.

———. 1995. *Through the Looking Glass: Reflection Stories in the Bible*. Tel Aviv: HaKibbutz HaMeuhad. Hebrew version.

2.5 Matthew's Use of Isaiah 7:14

Chris Kugler

"Behold, the virgin shall conceive and bear a son, and they shall call his name Immanuel." (Matt 1:23 ESV, quoting Isa 7:14)

The use of Isa 7:14 in Matt 1:23 constitutes one of the most famous biblical quotations in all of the New Testament. Its putative christological import has garnered attention ever since it was written. But this Matthean citation raises a number of challenging questions even as it opens up interpretive and theological vistas on Matthew's Gospel and on the rest of New Testament Christology more generally. In this essay, we are particularly concerned with the following questions:

1. What is the Jewish background and context of Matthew's appropriation of Isa 7:14, both in terms of its original meaning in Isa 7:14 itself and in terms of that text's reception in Second Temple Jewish literature?

2. How does Matthew's use of Isa 7:14 cohere with his use of other biblical texts?

3. What is the christological import of Matthew's use of Isa 7:14 in Matt 1:23 and in the Gospel as a whole?

4. Whence comes this Immanuel Christology into Matthew's Gospel?

5. Where does Matthew's Immanuel Christology fit within New Testament Christology as a whole?

Let us take each question in turn.

1. What is the Jewish background and context of Matthew's appropriation of Isa 7:14, both in terms of its original meaning in Isa 7:14 itself and in terms of that text's reception in Second Temple Jewish literature?

In the context of Isaiah, the prophecy of 7:14 means what it means within the historical context presupposed by chapter 7 as a whole. Ahaz, king of Judah, is deeply troubled by the combined threat of Rezin, king of Aram, and Pekah, king of Israel. But God promises that their machinations will ultimately prove unsuccessful (7:7–9). And the sign of God's favor and presence with Ahaz and with Judah will come in the form of "a young woman (Heb. *haʾalmah*/Gr. *hē parthenos*) [who] shall bear a son, and [she] shall name him Emmanuel (Heb. *ʾimmanuʾel*)" (7:14).

From the immediate and surrounding context, it is not obvious that "young woman" (Heb. *haʾalmah*/Gr. *hē parthenos*) must refer (as it does in Matt 1:23) to a virgin, but rather simply to a postpubescent female (e.g., Yarbro Collins and Collins 2008, 36–39; Wildberger 1991 [1980], 308; and BDB 761). This sign of God being "with Ahaz/Judah" does not exclude God's presence entailing both salvation *and* judgment (esp. Hays 2016, 164). The woman in view could be one of Ahaz's wives who will, according to the prophecy, soon bear a son (Yarbro Collins and Collins 2008, 37; Barthel 1997, 174–77; and Mowinckel 2005 [1956], 114). Finally, the designation Immanuel, "God with us," does not necessarily indicate the divine ontology or identity of the royal child so designated. The epithet could imply only that the birth of the child will be the sign that God has and will keep his promise to be "with" Ahaz and Judah.

All of our manuscripts of the Old Greek version of Isa 7:14 provide Greek *parthenos* for Hebrew *ʾalmah*, whereas the Greek versions of Theodotion and Aquila provide the much more common translation of Greek *neanis* for Hebrew *ʾalmah* (e.g., Yarbro Collins and Collins 2008, 137; and Luz 2001, 96). The Hebrew *ʾalmah* and the Greek *neanis* do not necessarily refer to a literal virgin. While Greek *parthenos* can and usually does refer to a virgin, some interpreters do not think it does in Matt 1:23 (Brown, 1993 [1977], 145–49; and Luz 2001, 96). Of course, the lexical meaning of the word is only part of the story; the cultural meaning is also important. The assumption in the culture of Near Eastern antiquity was that young unmarried women were virgins.

There is little evidence that Isa 7:14 was understood in a messianic sense in Second Temple literature. The Isaianic passage does not appear in Luke's birth narrative (e.g., at 1:13, 27, and 31), nor anywhere else in the New Testament. So why did the evangelist Matthew appeal to Isa 7:14 and apply it as he did?

It is possible that the evangelist read Isa 7:14 in the wider context of the book of Isaiah. In Isa 9:6–7 (Heb. 9:5–6), the anticipated son will be called "Mighty God" and "Prince of Peace." His government will never end. In Isa 11:1–10, the promised "branch" that will emerge from the "stump of Jesse" will possess the Spirit of God. His rule of righteousness and judgment will be unparalleled. He merely speaks and it is done. All the nations will seek him. Isaiah's contemporary Micah assures Bethlehem that a ruler will come forth "whose origin is from of old, from ancient days" (Mic 5:2–3 [Heb. 5:1–2]). In what way can this be said of a mere mortal from the line of David?

Michael Rydelnik (2019) argues that there are two prophecies in Isa 7, a long-term prediction addressed to the house of David (7:13–15) and a short-term prediction addressed to the frightened king Ahaz (7:16–23). In the latter, the king is assured that the alliance that has formed against him will collapse. But in the former, the prophet assures the "house of David" that a maiden (or virgin, for *ʾalmah* can mean "virgin") will give birth to a child, who will be called *ʾimmanuʾel*, or "God is with us." Although the prophecy could be understood as saying that a young woman (who is a virgin) will marry and then conceive and give birth in the conventional manner, the text can also be read to say that a virgin—*as a virgin*—will conceive and give birth. The Evangelist Matthew has apparently understood the Isaianic passage in this sense.

2. How does Matthew's use of Isa 7:14 cohere with his use of other biblical texts?

As is well known to students of Matthew's Gospel in general and to students of Matthew's use of Scripture in particular, this Gospel is concerned emphatically to present the person and work of Jesus as the promised fulfillment of specific prophetic texts and traditions and of the whole biblical narrative (esp. Hays 2016, 105–9). The common Matthean citation formula involving the use of the Greek word *plēroō*, "to fulfill" (Matt 1:22; 2:15, 17; 4:14; 8:17; 12:17; 21:4; 27:9), makes the point.

It has also been observed that Matthew has (at least) five types of christological uses of Scripture (Hays 2016, 105–90): (1) Jesus as Israel's God returning to his people, (2) Jesus as divine wisdom in their midst, (3) Jesus as Israel, (4) Jesus as the new Moses, and (5) Jesus as the Davidic Messiah. Let us take each in turn.

JESUS AS ISRAEL'S GOD RETURNING TO HIS PEOPLE

Picking up on a theme in Mark's Gospel, which Matthew and Luke respectively use as a source for their own accounts, Matthew presents Jesus as YHWH returning to his people after the exile (also Hays 2016, 109–75, following Wright 1996). With the combined quotation of Mal 3:1 and Isa 40:3 at the opening of Mark's account (Mark 1:2–3), which is designed to introduce the prophet John the Baptist as the one crying in the wilderness who "prepares the way of the Lord" (Mark 1:3), Mark thus presents Jesus as "the Lord" whose way is prepared. And the respective contexts of Mal 3:1 and Isa 40:3 clearly concern the return of YHWH to his people after the exile. Israel had broken the covenant and so God had abandoned his people, leaving them vulnerable to Babylonian siege and exile. But one day God would return, so Malachi and Isaiah prophesied, to cleanse his people of their sins, to reestablish the covenant, to be their God, and for them to be his people. Mark thus implies at the opening and throughout his Gospel that this is in fact what is happening in the life and ministry of *Jesus*.

Matthew, too, appropriates this theme, and not just in his reprisal of the same Markan material in Matt 3:1–6 but in his Gospel as a whole. This is, for example, why Matthew's genealogy periodizes history by going straight from Abraham, the father of the Israelites, to David, then to the Babylonian exile, and then straight to the birth of Jesus the Messiah (1:17). The point is that Jesus is the true Israelite and the promised Davidic Messiah who will bring an end to Israel's long exile (Hays 2016, 110–11). This is, moreover, the larger context of Matthew's wisdom Christology as well, to which we will now turn.

JESUS AS DIVINE WISDOM IN THEIR MIDST

It has often been recognized that in certain passages Matthew seems to depict Jesus as divine wisdom (e.g., Witherington 2006, 47; and Hays 2016, 153–59). This tradition reaches back to Prov 8 and Job 28 and makes its way through later Second

Temple texts like Sir 1; 24; and 50; 1 Enoch 42; Wisd 7; Bar 3–4; and many places in Philo's writings. In Prov 8; Job 28; Sir 1; 24; and 50; 1 Enoch 42; and Bar 3–4, "wisdom" (Heb. *khokhmah*; Gr. *sophia*) is simply a metaphorical and conceptual means of talking about God's wise activity within the world without implying that he is not also simultaneously in transcendent sovereignty over that world (Hurtado 2015 [1988], 41–52; and Kugler 2020, 45–46). Wisdom serves something of the same purpose in Wis 7 and Philo's writings, but in these latter two traditions wisdom (and *logos*) has become properly "hypostatic": that is, wisdom has an actual ontological status as an intermediary being both in the closest possible relationship to God and yet distinct from God (esp. Cox 2007, 24–140).

In Sir 24 and Bar 3–4 in particular, it is clear that some Jews thought of divine wisdom as having taken up her residence in Torah. This, then, had the effect of presenting the Torah as the primary means of mediating and accessing God's wisdom.

All of this is important for an appreciation of the wisdom Christology of Matthew, particularly as this is expressed in Matt 11:18–19, 28–30, and 18:20 (for a longer exposition, see Hays 2016, 153–59; Witherington 2006, 229–40; and Luz 2001, 149–50, 169–76). In Matt 11:18–19, Jesus seems explicitly to identify himself with divine wisdom and to present his deeds as hers:

> For John came neither eating nor drinking, and they say, "He has a demon"; the Son of Man came eating and drinking, and they say, "Look, a glutton and a drunkard, a friend of tax collectors and sinners!" Yet wisdom is vindicated by her deeds. (NRSV)

Jesus is himself, then, the wisdom whose deeds will be vindicated. A few verses later, in 11:28–30, Jesus appropriates a wisdom theme from the earlier text of Sir 51:23–26:

> Come to me, all you who are laboring [Gk. *hoi kopiōntes*] and carrying heavy burdens, and I will give you rest [Gk. *Anapausō*]. Take my yoke [Gk. *ton zygon*] upon you, and learn from me; for I am gentle and humble in heart, and you will find rest for your souls [Gk. *heurēsete anapausin tais psychais hymōn*]. For my yoke is easy, and my burden is light.

Most scholars have rightly concluded that this text alludes to Sir 51:23–27:

> (51:23) Draw near to me, you who are uneducated, and lodge in the house of instruction. (51:24) Why do you say you are lacking in these things, and why do you endure such great thirst? (51:25) I opened my mouth and said, Acquire wisdom for yourselves without money. (51:26) Put your neck under her yoke [Gk. *Zygon*], and let your souls receive instruction; it is to be found close by. (51:27) See with your own eyes that I have labored [Gk. *Ekopiasa*] but little and found for myself much rest [Gk. *pollen anapausin*].

The allusion is unmistakable. Jesus himself is the divine wisdom whose "yoke" provides "rest" to those under heavy labor.

But it is in Matt 18:20 that one sees the explicit christological link with the wisdom-Torah tradition: "Wherever two or three are gathered together in my name,

I am there in their midst" (NRSV). Scholars have long noted the strikingly similar passage in the Mishnah: "But if two sit together and the words between them are of Torah, then the *Shekinah* is in their midst" (m. 'Abot 3.2). Though this rabbinic text postdates Matthew's Gospel, it is likely that Matthew's Jesus has deliberately adapted an older tradition very much like it. In this case, Jesus has taken the place of Torah, and the community gathered around him can be assured of the divine presence (e.g., Luz 2001, 458–59; Witherington 2006, 352; and Hays 2016, 168–69).

JESUS AS ISRAEL

Several passages in Matthew depict Jesus as representing the whole people of Israel in his own person, but this dynamic is most explicit in the early chapters of the Gospel (see esp. Hays 2016, 139–43). When Jesus' family, having fled to Egypt to escape harm, is called back to the land of Israel, Matthew interprets this as the fulfillment of Hos 11:1: "Out of Egypt I called my son." However, in Hos 11:1 itself, of course, the prophet is referring to the original exodus in which God had called the whole people of Israel, his "son" (Exod 4:22), out of Egypt. But here in Matthew, Jesus himself, as God's messianic son, becomes the focal point of the new exodus of the people of God. He is in his own person and work, therefore, both embodying and gathering around himself the reestablished people of God after the exile (hence the twelve disciples to represent the twelve tribes). One can also see this theme at a macro-level in Matt 2–7 and the way in which it coalesces with Matthew's Moses typology.

JESUS AS THE NEW MOSES

It has long been noticed that the macro-structure of Matt 2–7, while also involving an Israel typology, features a Moses typology (e.g., Allison 1993; Hays 2016, 143–53). In 2:13–23, we find the themes of (1) Jesus as a young boy in Egypt and (2) under threat of a wicked ruler who kills all young Israelite males; (3) Jesus is, however, kept safe and escapes the land of Egypt. After Jesus escapes the land of Egypt and following his baptism (Matt 3:13–17), he is immediately led into the wilderness to be tempted "for forty days and forty nights" (4:2), a time period designed to allude to the forty years of wilderness wandering. Beyond this is the whole of Matt 5–7, the Sermon on the Mount, most of which is concerned with Jesus' own exposition of Torah faithfulness. All of this together constitutes a clear Moses typology.

JESUS AS THE DAVIDIC MESSIAH

Matthew is also emphatic about Jesus' Davidic Messiahship (see e.g., Jipp 2020, 21–56). Here one only needs to note the messianic conclusion to the genealogy (1:17); the temptation narrative, which prominently features the common messianic epithet "Son of God" (4:3, 6); the declaration of Peter at Caesarea Philippi (16:13–20); all of the explicit messianic resonances of the triumphal entry (21:1–11); Jesus' messianic self-claim before Caiaphas (26:64); and finally, the title "The King of the Jews" above the cross (27:37). For Matthew as for the other Gospels, Jesus' Davidic messiahship was central and thematic.

And it is in relation to Matthew's Christology as a whole and to intertextual dimensions of his Christology in particular that we should appreciate the Immanuel Christology expressed in 1:23 and elsewhere. Here, too, Matthew is presupposing Old Testament and Second Temple narratives and traditions and appropriating them christologically.

3. What is the christological import of Matthew's use of Isa 7:14 in Matt 1:23 and in Matthew as a whole?

Because Matthew uses Isa 7:14 to explicate his virgin birth narrative and consequently to frame the identity of Jesus, the text takes on a significance in Matthew that it may not have had in its original context or in its reception in Second Temple Judaism. Matthew interprets the Old Greek text, with its use of *parthenos*—a Greek word that *can* and usually does refer to a virgin—as a prediction of a virgin birth. This, then, facilitates a much stronger and more literal interpretation of the epithet "Immanuel." Jesus is *literally* understood as the embodied presence of Israel's God "with" his people (*contra*, e.g., Kirk 2016, 359–87). And while this coheres with the other features of Matthew's Christology outlined above, it fits closest with the theme of "Jesus as Israel's God returning to his people." Jesus is Immanuel, in other words, because he is the God of Israel returning to his people after the long years of exile (see esp. Hays 2016, 109–75).

This theme is present, if less explicit, in Mark's Gospel, a source on which Matthew drew extensively. But it is a major step of beyond Mark to use Isa 7:14 in the way that he does to emphasize this theme. Neither is this theme uncommon in Matthew. Rather, it both introduces Matthew's high Christology and rounds it off at the end, where Jesus' last words come: "And, behold, I will be *with you* always and even to the end of the age" (Matt 28:20; e.g., Hays 2016, 162; Witherington 2006, 47; Luz 2001, 96).

Moreover, this christological theme is not simply "read out" of the original context and meaning of Isa 7:14, however much that text's context exerts force on Matthew's appropriation. In other words, it is not obvious that other interpreters—Jewish or Christian—would have necessarily understood Isa 7:14 as predicting a virgin conception and birth. After all, we do not find examples of such interpretation in the Second Temple literature that has survived. The interpretation of Isa 7:14 as describing a literal virgin birth was likely encouraged on other grounds. The Isaianic prophecy then served as confirmation. So, in a sense, we can say that the prophecy both encouraged the idea and confirmed it.

Coordinating Matthew's Immanuel Christology with other features of the Christology of his Gospel is no simple task. On the one hand, Jesus is presented as God incarnate, "God in their midst." But this Jesus is also, of course, a very real first-century human being. Yes, he is, in some sense, also divine wisdom in their midst. But he is also a first-century Jewish prophet, a prophet like Moses, and—according to Matthew and much of the rest of the New Testament—the Davidic Messiah. Jesus is presented as both God incarnate *and* one who prays to God characteristically as "Father" (esp. Matt 6:9). At the end of the Gospel, he encourages his followers: "Go, therefore, and make disciples of all nations, baptizing them in the name of the Father, the Son, and the Holy Spirit" (Matt 28:18 NRSV). How does Matthew's Immanuel Christology relate to the obvious fact that Jesus was a genuine first-century Jewish human being who prayed to God as "Father"? And how does all of this, moreover, relate to the trinitarian formula of 28:18? Matthew makes no systematic attempt to sort all of this out. Rather, the Evangelist, as do many of the writers of the books of the New Testament, simply bequeathed an early understanding of monotheism, in which Jesus finds his place, to the complex debates that will take place in the third, fourth, and fifth centuries of the Christian era.

4. Whence comes this Emmanuel Christology into Matthew's Gospel?

This question is difficult to answer. Though one cannot prove it, I suspect this is what has happened: the high Christology that quickly emerged in the Christian community may have encouraged some authoritative teachers to search Israel's sacred traditions for clarification, as well as proof. This the Matthean Evangelist did, with the result that he found several prophetic texts that clarified events in the life of Jesus and aspects of his own person, including his origin. In due course, the prophecy of Isa 7:14 was recognized as a key text that explained in what way God came to be "with us." That this idea was embraced by Christian teachers besides Matthew is witnessed in the Gospel of Luke, where the conception of Jesus is due to the Holy Spirit—yet no reference is made to Isa 7:14.

5. Where does Matthew's Immanuel Christology fit within New Testament Christology as a whole?

There is a sense in which Matthew's Immanuel Christology is one of the most explicit features of the divine Christology of the Synoptic Gospels (e.g., Hays 2016, 162–63). On the other hand, Mark and Luke's christologies, while less explicit, are no less divine christologies (*contra* Kirk 2016). And John's divine Christology is the most explicit of all of the Gospels.

But this does not mean that Matthew's Immanuel Christology, coming to textual expression likely in the 70s or 80s CE (though an earlier date is possible), represents a major upward "development" in the tradition of early Christology. Already by the time of Paul's letters—written in the 40s and 50s—a divine Christology is presupposed (esp. Bauckham 2008, 19; and Wright 2013, 652). And what is more, Paul presupposes that this divine Christology is shared with the Jerusalem apostles (esp. Hurtado 2003, 155–67). Therefore, as remarkable as Matthew's Immanuel Christology is, and as striking as his appeal to Isa 7:14 is, it does not represent a dramatic elevation of early Christology.

Matthew's Immanuel Christology, and the way in which it intimately coordinates in Matt 1:18–25 with the claim of Jesus' birth from the Virgin Mary, is remarkable. Here, as in Luke's birth narrative, the divine sonship of Jesus is taken so literally that it rules out natural paternity. Jesus is God's Son born of a virgin. He is Immanuel in the flesh, "God with us."

Works Cited

Allison, Dale C., Jr. 1993. *The New Moses: A Matthean Typology*. Eugene, OR: Wipf & Stock.

Barthel, Jörg. 1997. *Prophetenwort und Geschichte: Die Jasajaüberlieferung in Jes 6–8 und 28–31*. FAT 19. Tübingen: Mohr Siebeck.

Bauckham, Richard. 2008. *Jesus and the God of Israel: God Crucified and Other Studies in the New Testament's Christology of Divine Identity*. Grand Rapids: Eerdmans.

Brown, Raymond E. 1993. *The Birth of the Messiah: A Commentary on the Infancy Narratives in the Gospels of Matthew and Luke*. New Haven: Yale University Press.

Cox, Ronald. 2007. *By the Same Word: Creation and Salvation in Hellenistic Judaism and Early Christianity*. BZNW 145. Berlin: de Gruyter.

Hays, Richard B. 2016. *Echoes of Scripture in the Gospels*. Waco, TX: Baylor University Press.

Hurtado, Larry W. 2003. *Lord Jesus Christ: Devotion to Jesus in Earliest Christianity*. Grand Rapids: Eerdmans.

Hurtado, Larry W. 2015. *One God, One Lord: Early Christian Devotion and Ancient Jewish Monotheism*. 3rd ed. New York: T&T Clark.

Jipp, Joshua W. 2020. *The Messianic Theology of the New Testament*. Grand Rapids: Eerdmans.

Kirk, J. R. Daniel. 2016. *A Man Attested by God: The Human Jesus of the Synoptic Gospels*. Grand Rapids: Eerdmans.

Kugler, Chris. 2020. *Paul and the Image of God*. Lanham: Lexington Books/Fortress Academic.

Luz, Ulrich. 2001. *Matthew 1–7: A Commentary on the Gospel of Matthew*. Hermeneia. Minneapolis, MN: Fortress Press.

Mowinckel, Sigmund. 2005. *He That Cometh: The Messiah Concept in the Old Testament and Later Judaism*. Translated by G. W. Anderson. Grand Rapids: Eerdmans.

Rydelnik, Michael. 2019. "Isaiah 7:1–16: The Virgin Birth in Prophecy." Pages 815–30 in *The Moody Handbook of Messianic Prophecy: Studies and Expositions of the Messiah in the Old Testament*. Edited by Michael Rydelnik and Edwin Blum. Chicago: Moody Press.

Wildberger, Hans. 1991. *Isaiah 1–12*. CC. Translated by Thomas H. Trapp. Minneapolis, MN: Fortress Press.

Witherington, Ben III. 2006. *Matthew*. SHBC 19. Macon, GA: Smyth & Helwys.

Wright, N. T. 1996. *Jesus and the Victory of God*. Vol. 2 of *Christian Origins and the Question of God*. Minneapolis, MN: Fortress Press.

———. *Paul and the Faithfulness of God*. 2 vols. Vol. 4 of Christian Origins and the Question of God. Minneapolis, MN: Fortress Press.

Yarbro Collins, Adela, and John J. Collins. 2008. *King and Messiah as Son of God: Divine, Human, and Angelic Messianic Figures in Biblical and Related Literature*. Grand Rapids: Eerdmans.

2.6 Jesus as Israel in Matthew's Gospel

Brian J. Kinzel

Matthew cites and quotes the Scriptures more than the other Gospels to explain Jesus' relationship with his people. Many of these citations emphasize Jesus' identification and solidarity with Israel. What does Matthew mean by claiming that the Messiah is "God with us" (1:23) and the son called out of Egypt (2:15) who carried his people's infirmities (8:17)? Why does Matthew so obviously emphasize Jesus' solidarity with Israel?

In this chapter, I will argue that Matthew's presentation of corporate solidarity between the king and his people emphasizes above all Jesus' role as promised redeemer of the people. Contrary to some interpretations, Matthew does not indicate that Jesus fulfilled or completed Israel's role; instead, Matthew focuses on Jesus' unique role predicted by the prophets. Jesus' role of redeemer and king assumed and even demanded that he identify fully with Israel. For the blessing of Abraham to reach all the nations (Gen 22:18), Abraham's seed, the Messiah (Gal 3:16), had to come from the chosen people. Matthew's Gospel presents Jesus as the rightful and expected Messiah who came to redeem his people. Matthew's use of the OT shows that Jesus did not come to fulfill the role of *the nation of Israel* but instead came to fulfill the role of *messiah, king, and savior* of the nation. Further, this Gospel account does not indicate that Israel lost its identity or ceased to function as a people. Matthew shows that while Jesus indeed boldly denounced those who rejected him as their Messiah, he countered that rejection by calling a believing remnant of his Jewish followers to preach the gospel first of all to their own nation and then to all the nations of the world. That is, "Matthew thus advocates a replacement not of *Israel* but of *the old leadership*" (Konradt 2014, 338, 352–53). Above all, Jesus identified with his people not to set them aside in the plan of God, but so that he might take on their sin and guilt as the Passover lamb, whose blood was "poured out for many for the forgiveness of sins" (Matt 26:28, this and the following citations from ESV). As the NT makes abundantly clear, by his death, Jesus provides substitutionary atonement for which "he had to be made like his brothers" (Heb 2:17; cf. 2 Cor 5:21; 1 Pet 2:24). The king does not replace his people, nor is the status of spotless lamb and guilty sinner interchangeable. The following analysis attempts to show how this logic is born up by Matthew's portrayal of Jesus by answering five questions.

Is Jesus Savior and Successor of the Nation?

The background for this first question is the assertion made over long centuries that Israel forfeited their place as God's people, and their role has been assumed by the church—a view popularly called "supersessionism" (Soulen 1996, 2008; Donaldson 2016). Believing this, the historic Reformed position is that, in the words of an esteemed Dutch theologian, "the people of Israel have been replaced by the church"

(Bavinck 2008, 298; see also 273, 279, 528). In the same line of reasoning, Christian theologians have long argued that Jesus is actually true or new Israel, meaning that he fulfilled and superseded the role of the nation. A more nuanced view within covenant theology sees Israel as a type pointing forward prophetically to Christ, who became the antitype "new Israel" at his advent. Fairbairn provided a thoughtful and influential expression of this idea (Fairbairn 1866; 1900). Writing in the nineteenth century, he grappled with the dilemma of how to explain the plethora of OT prophetic promises of the renewal of national ethnic Israel. He did not believe that these promises (e.g., Israel's return to its ancestral land) could be literally fulfilled. His solution was to explain that Israel was a type of the expected Messiah (Fairbairn 1866, 244–50, 255). Thus the prophetic promises should be interpreted not literally but figuratively and typologically ("spiritually"); these promises are fulfilled by the Messiah and then given to the church. His conclusion flowed from the supposition that the Jewish expectation of physical, literal fulfillment of OT prophecies cannot be true. Fairbairn used Matt 2:15 (among others) to support his conclusion that Israel's function was to foreshadow the Messiah. He believed that the OT indicates that Jesus perfectly fulfilled the role and identity of Israel (Fairbairn 1900, 32–33, 381). According to this argument, once the messianic antitype arrived, the national type lost its purpose (Vlach 2012, 47).

Scholars have recently reasserted the idea that Jesus is the new and true Israel (Parker 2016; see also Taylor 2012 for a helpful summary), calling their positions "New Covenant Theology" and "Progressive Covenantalism." Unlike the classic Reformed tradition, those identifying with these positions studiously avoid the expression that Jesus and the church have "replaced Israel." Instead, they believe that "Jesus is the antitypical fulfillment of Israel and Adam, and in him *all* of God's promises are fulfilled" (Wellum 2020; see also Gentry and Wellum 2018). These authors have shown a commendable willingness to allow biblical exegesis to shape their theological system and have many helpful insights. In particular, I appreciate their affirmations that Jesus fulfilled actual prophecies and that the Scriptures actually predicted events portrayed in the Gospels, often using typology (so also Beale 2020). This means, these authors assert, that the NT does not add new meaning to the OT texts, "reinvent" them, or ignore the original meaning of OT passages cited, for example, in Matthew's Gospel.

However, Matthew's Gospel shows one non sequitur in their understanding of how the NT uses the OT. Namely, it does not follow that because OT citations affirm Jesus' inseparable solidarity with Israel that Jesus now has assumed the role of the people, rendering Israel superfluous in the plan of God. Parker, for example, asserts that "Jesus has completed the role and work of Israel," which "thus rules out the notion of a future national role of Israel in the plan of God" (Parker 2016, 52–53). Like Fairbairn, new covenant theology typically bases this assertion on Matthew's use of the OT, especially his quotation of Hos 11:1 in Matt 2:15. In the same way, Beale claims that Jesus' corporate solidarity with his people proves that he fulfilled what was expected of Israel, and thus Jesus "represents" the new and true Israel (Beale 1989; 2020, 44–45), by which he means that Israel was only a type awaiting its fulfillment in the messianic antitype. Moreover, they also argue that Christians' solidarity with Jesus means that the church receives the promises given to Israel. Others have compellingly critiqued the concept that Jesus supersedes his people (Vlach 2010; 2012; Blaising 2014; 2015; see also Bock 2015; Saucy 2017). This article builds on those studies by examining the Gospel of Matthew to show that though Matthew presents Israel as a type of its Messiah, the king did not end his relationship with his people but remains in solidarity with them.

How Does Matthew Define "Israel"?

A review of lexical data will help answer this important question. Since Jesus lived and ministered nearly exclusively in Israel, it is no surprise that Matthew's Gospel is steeped with references to Jewish culture of that era. Beginning in 1:1, we read a genealogy of Jewish names, starting with Abraham and David. With few exceptions, the names in the account reflect a Jewish milieu (Mary, Joseph, John, Simon, James, Zebedee, etc.). Matthew includes many Hebrew place names (e.g., Judea, Jerusalem, Bethlehem, Ramah, Galilee, Nazareth). Of the four Gospels, only Matthew uses the phrase "the land of Israel" (2:20, 21; cf. 10:23, "towns of Israel"). Matthew mentions many Jewish institutions (chief priests, scribes, Pharisees, Sadducees, elders, synagogues, prophets, the temple, the Sabbath). In addition, to answer the question posed, one must also look in Matthew's Gospel at the terms "Israel" (used 14 times) and "people" (*laos*, used 12 times). These are parallel terms (2:6) that refer to the national ethnic group (e.g., Israel in 2:6 and 8:10; people in 2:4 and 4:16), including the idioms "the house of Israel" (10:6; 15:24), "the twelve tribes of Israel" (19:28), and "the sons of Israel" (22:9). These terms frequently appear in OT citations referring to the Jewish people (2:6; 4:16; 13:15; 15:8; 27:9). Matthew also uses "Israel" in titles ("God of Israel" in 15:31, "king of Israel" in 27:42). He uses "people" to describe Jewish crowds and also to designate national leadership ("scribes of the people" in 2:4, "elders of the people" in 21:23; 26:3, 47; 27:1).

Often, Bauer's lexicon is cited as proof that in the NT "Israel" is also used of "Christians as entitled to the term Israel" (BDAG 481). But that gloss depends on literature outside the NT; the two NT references used to support this idea (Rom 9:6 and Gal 6:16) are hardly incontrovertible. Indeed, after analyzing every place where the terms are used in the NT, Voorwinde categorically states that this meaning in BDAG is wrong; "Israel" describes the ethnic group by that name: "This is the only meaning it carries in the New Testament. It is always ethnic and literal, never metaphorical" (Voorwinde 2008, 90).

Though only a summary, this information is adequate grounds to question the idea that "Israel" and its other referents could mean something other than how Matthew uses them—a national, ethnic entity. Matthew never uses the term "New Israel," which is found neither in the OT nor in the rest of the NT. While such a lexical study is not by itself conclusive, it should at least cause the modern reader to question if the concept of a "New Israel" reflects biblical thought. It is true that important theological concepts may not appear in the biblical text (e.g., "Trinity"), but to claim that "Israel" somehow means something other than how Matthew and other NT authors normally used it demands an explanation more compelling than a theological presupposition.

Does Matthew Indicate in 2:15 That Jesus Is the New (Replacement) Son?

This question is at the heart of this chapter. In answering it, we will see that even when Israel is presented as a type that foreshadows its Messiah, Matthew does so to emphasize the continuing solidarity between Jesus and his people, not a discontinuity of "fulfillment." Matthew 2 describes how Joseph and Mary fled to Egypt to protect Jesus from the infanticidal Herod. The explanation given for fleeing from Israel is that "this was to fulfill what the Lord had spoken by the prophet, 'Out of Egypt I called my son.'" In the original quotation from Hos 11:1, "my son" describes the nation of Israel, while Matthew's citation applies this to Jesus. That is, Hos 11:1 is "not predictive nor is it Messianic" (Evans 2012, 58). Because of this, commentators give a variety of (and often contradictory) explanations as to why Matthew did this. However one might explain Matthew's hermeneutic, clearly he cited Hos 11:1 to show Jesus' affinity with Israel. But what is the meaning of that solidarity? Does Matthew indicate that Jesus supplants the Israel of old by becoming the new Israel? How is this solidarity is functioning in the text? As stated above, Matthew's citation in 2:15 of Hos 11:1 is a standard proof text for the view that Jesus is the new Israel. We want to understand how Matthew uses the statement from Hosea, and what Matthew wants to prove by quoting from it.

Some modern writers think that Matthew used Jewish interpretive methods (midrashic haggadah) in order to give a "deeper meaning" (*sensus plenior*) to the quotation, and in doing so he ignored or at least went beyond the authorial intention of the OT source (Hagner 1993, lvi, 33). In other words, some think Matthew twisted the original meaning of Hos 11:1 for his own Christian purposes. Though very popular, this explanation unnecessarily assumes that Matthew either misunderstood or intentionally changed Hosea's original meaning. This idea has two problems. First, it is beyond credulity that Matthew did not understand Hosea's original meaning (Davies and Allison 1988, 263). Second, this demands a simplistic and flat understanding of the verb "to fulfill" in 2:15 that ignores how Matthew uses the term. In fact, Matthew shows great sensitivity to the original citation and its context. Matthew cites Hos 11:1, but not from the LXX text; instead, he provides a different Greek translation that follows the Hebrew more closely. The LXX has "my children," but Matthew faithfully reproduces the original reading "my son" from the MT. As chapter 2 of the Gospel account shows, Matthew used OT citations not only to prove direct fulfillment of predicted prophecies (see ch. 7 in Rydelnik 2010, 95–111). As many commentators clarify, Matthew uses this citation typologically, a use that "depends on meaningful associations rather than exact correspondence" (France 2007, 78). This means that Matthew connected Jesus' life with the son who was brought "out of Egypt" in other ways than a prediction of one specific event. We can discern at least three ways that Matthew used this citation as the "fulfillment" of Hos 11:1.

1. Above all, the phrase "my son" highlights the corporate solidarity of the people of God, and their calling as the chosen people. With this citation, Matthew draws the reader to the theme of Hos 11: despite Israel's sinful failures, God loves his son too much to reject them completely, but instead will bring them back to himself in the land of Israel. Hosea 11:1 draws directly from Exod

4:22—"Then you shall say to Pharaoh, 'Thus says the LORD, "Israel is My son, My firstborn."'" This is the only place in a divine speech where Israel is called God's son (Dearman 2010, 275). As Hosea shows, Israel's corporate solidarity as God's son is tied to the exodus and their covenant. In fact, "sonship is a metaphor for the covenant itself" (Mays 1969, 153). Hosea's use of "loved" and "called," terms describing God's election, also highlight their connection to the covenant. By his citation of Hosea, Matthew presents Jesus as part of this collective unity and part of God's covenant people. Just as the many of Israel are one son, so also Jesus, as the one Son, is part of the many of Israel.

2. Matthew uses the reference to Egypt and the exodus to highlight Jesus' connection to Israel's land. The modern reader needs to remember that in the first century, residency in *Eretz Yisrael* was not a foregone conclusion for the Jewish people, with their communities located in many places, from Susa to Rome (cf. Acts 2:8–11). By referring to the historical event of the exodus, Matthew points out God's providential care that also brought Jesus to "the land of Israel" (2:20–21 ESV); and he thus indicates that Jesus belonged in the ancestral homeland of the Jewish people. Related to this, the flight from Herod also draws on the theme of Egypt as a place of refuge (Galvin 2011, 164–79). Egypt served as the standard destination for Israelites and others fleeing famine and oppression (e.g., Abram, Gen 12:10; Jeroboam, 2 Kgs 11:40; Ishmael, 2 Kgs 25:25–26). God told Jacob, "I myself will go down with you to Egypt, and I will also bring you up again" (Gen 46:4). In Hos 11:10–11, God promises to not withdraw his love from the people, but to "return them to their homes" in their own land. Like other Israelites, Jesus' family escaped danger by fleeing to Egypt and then returned to their land after the threat had passed. Jesus' "exodus" from Egypt was typological in that it had these same associations.

3. Matthew used this citation to highlight Jesus' role as promised redeemer. By referring back to the exodus, Matthew draws the reader to the theme of God's salvation, of which Jesus is certainly the fulfilment. Matthew draws on the broader idea that "redemption from Egypt often serves as a type for the messianic redemption" (Davies and Allison 1988, 263). Isaiah and Hosea have vivid examples of this leitmotif in which exodus from Egypt serves to parabolically illustrate God's salvation (e.g., Isa 11:11–16; 49:11–12; 62:10; Hos 2:16–17 [Eng. 2:14–15]). Just as the one son represented all of Israel in redemption from slavery, so Jesus, the Son of God, represented all of Israel in redemption from sin.

The Balaam oracles in Num 23 and 24 provide perhaps the best example of how the exodus from Egypt is linked to the theme of God's salvation, and how this emphasizes the corporate solidarity of the people with the coming king. Matthew connected Jesus' experience to the exodus of the nation in these oracles, and Matthew's quote is similar to the Greek text of Num 24:8. In these oracles, we read that God brings both the people and then an individual out of Egypt, just as in Matt 2 (chart adapted from Rydelnik 2010, 110).

Typology of the Balaam Oracles

All Israel	Individual King
Num 23:18–24	*Num 24:7–9*
"God brings **them** out of Egypt" (23:22a ESV)	"God brings **him** out of Egypt" (24:8a)
"and is for **them** like the horns of the wild ox" (23:22b)	"and is for **him** like the horns of the wild ox" (24:8b)
"Behold, **a people**! As a lioness it rises up and as a lion it lifts itself" (23:24a)	"**He** crouched, he lay down like a lion and like a lioness; who will rouse **him** up?" (24:9a)

As this chart shows, the oracles deliberately parallel the "many" of the nation with the "one," of whom I believe that Num 24:17 speaks also, "A star shall come forth from Jacob" (cf. Matt 2:2, 9–10). Rather than distort the original meaning of Hos 11:1, Matthew has drawn from the Torah the idea that Israel is a type of the coming king. This typology is hardly a novel "deeper meaning," since Israel always expected their Messiah to come from the house of David (Gen 49:10; 2 Sam 7:16; Isa 11:1; Jer 23:5–6; Ezek 34:23–24).

These three ideas—Israel's covenant sonship, Israel's promised land, and Israel's promised king—all emphasize the Messiah's solidarity with Israel. Rather than indicate that Jesus has succeeded Israel or fulfilled its role, all the intertextual parallels indicate that Jesus is one with Israel. With this quote, Matthew is in no way proving or even alluding that Jesus is the "new Israel," but instead he is reminding the reader that Jesus identifies with the Israel of old. How does Jesus' deep and organic connection with his people make him their successor or (dare we say) their replacement? It hardly does justice to the context of Hos 11 to say that Jesus has thus fulfilled or assumed the role of the people for whom he came to provide redemption. The typological understanding does not demand that Jesus is now in place of Israel or that he has fulfilled their role. It makes more sense to say that Matthew shows the solidarity of Jesus with his people to indicate his closeness, his care, his full identity with them as a fellow Israelite. By this broad "fulfillment," Matthew shows that Jesus' solidarity with his people includes physical lineage as well as divine calling.

How Does Matthew Describe Isaiah's "Servant of the Lord?"

The background to this question is the identity of the "servant of the Lord" in Isa 40–66, understood alternately as Israel and an individual. Twice, Matthew quotes from the "Servant Songs" of Isaiah, in 8:17 (citing Isa 53) and in 12:17–21 (citing Isa 42). Matthew alludes to Isa 53 on at least two other occasions (20:28; 26:28). By these references, Matthew emphasizes Jesus' role as redeemer; he also underscores Jesus' sympathetic unity with his people, displayed in his healing. The well-known variation between the collective, national identity of the servant and the individual identity emphasizes this connection.

The Servant of the Lord in Isaiah

As popularly explained, there are four "Servant Songs" in Isa 40–66: (1) 42:1–4; (2) 49:1–6; (3) 50:3–10; and (4) 52:13–53:12. However, the servant appears in other places also in these chapters of Isaiah. As Harrison explains, there has been an enormous amount of attention given to the servant songs because "these passages of Scripture make an individual, a corporate, an ideal, and a historical interpretation possible at different times" (1979, 421). Like in the Balaam oracles, both the nation and an individual are designated by the same Hebrew term ('eved). The first oracle, 42:1–4 or 42:1–9, describes an individual, "Behold my servant, whom I uphold, my chosen, in whom my soul delights" (42:1). The servant rules and judges to "bring forth justice" on a global scale (for the nations, in the earth, for the coastlands). Yet in the next chapter, Israel is addressed: "'You [pl.] are my witnesses,' declares the LORD, 'and my servant whom I have chosen'" (43:10). The second "Servant Song" begins with the servant speaking as an individual ("The LORD called me from the womb," 49:1). The identity of the servant fluctuates between Israel and an individual. On the one hand, the Lord declares of the nation, "You are my servant, Israel, in whom I will be glorified" (49:3). But on the other hand, the Lord declares that the individual servant is called to lift up the nation: "It is too light a thing that you should be my servant, to raise up the tribes of Jacob, and to bring back the preserved of Israel?" (49:6). Of course, in 52:13–53:12 (the final Servant Song), the servant is identified as the suffering Messiah. These examples are sufficient to illustrate the fluctuation between the collective and the individual identity. The servant needs redemption (44:6, 21–24) and the servant will "make many to be accounted righteous, and he shall bear their iniquities" (53:11). Though the servant in these songs has various roles, Schultz explains that "he exhibits so many royal traits and duties that his identification with the future Davidic king of Isa 1–39 is justified" (1997, 1193).

The Servant of the Lord in Second Temple Judaism

Jewish writings from around the time of the NT have iterations of the servant, both national and individual (Jeremias 1967). For example, the Aramaic translations for 52:13 read, "Behold, my servant the Messiah will be successful." Yet in this era the variation between the two identities, national and individual nonetheless remain. Brown notes that "there is a significant interpretive strand which sees the Isaianic servant as a collective for Israel (or a remnant of Israel), even in the reception of Isaiah 52:13–53:12, where we might most expect an individual interpretation" (2020, 55).

The Servant in Matthew

With this background, we can now ask, how then does Matthew explain this servant? Unequivocally, Matthew describes Jesus as the individual servant figure. Jesus' individual role and function are clearly differentiated from the nations. Yet Matthew's account presents Jesus in his role of redeemer as showing sympathetic solidarity with his people by healing them and by providing atonement for their sins. In 8:17,

Matthew records how Jesus responded to the sickness of Peter's mother-in-law and healed her. In 12:15–21, the longest OT quotation in the Gospel, Matthew explains Jesus' gentleness and compassion. It is surprising that Matthew cites Isaiah twice to explain Jesus' healing but not his atonement, particularly since one citation is from Isa 53. Rather than as a warrior and conqueror, Matthew describes the servant as a caring and gentle healer for whom servanthood is the essential attribute of spiritual leadership (20:25–28). Compassion characterizes all of Jesus' ministry (Matt 9:36; 14:14; 15:32; 20:34). He condemned the Pharisees because they lacked compassion (9:13; 12:7). By the citations from Isaiah, Matthew shows how Jesus fulfilled the prophetic expectation of a servant leader.

Matthew 20:28 and 26:28 both allude to the final servant song in Isa 53 in which the servant provides atonement for the nation (France 1998, 116–121; Davies and Allison 2004, 95–96; Blomberg 1992, 308). Jesus came "to give his life as a ransom *for many*" (20:28) and whose blood "is poured out *for many* for the forgiveness of sins" (26:28). Because "many" is a key theme in the final servant song (Isa 52:14–15; 53:11–12), Matthew thus alludes to the one who died for the "many." As redeemer, Jesus identified with the nation in order to die in their place as the substitutionary sacrifice. Matthew thus shows that Jesus stood in solidarity with Israel in order to "save his people from their sins" (1:21). In addition, the quotation in 12:15–21 points to the spread of the gospel message to all the nations—"and in his name the Gentiles will hope" (12:21).

Matthew used quotations and allusions to Isaiah's servant songs to explain Jesus' solidarity with and sympathy for his people; these citations of Isaiah also emphasize Jesus' unique role as atoning redeemer. He identifies with Israel out of deep concern—a concern so deep that he takes their sickness and sin on himself to provide forgiveness (Brown 2020, 66). Despite what some claim, the connection between the Messiah and the sinful nation is not one in which Jesus fulfills Israel's identity and calling (in opposition to Parker 2016, 56). Instead, Matthew explains that as the servant, Jesus fulfilled what his people never could.

Did Jesus Reject the Nation When He Appointed New Leaders?

Some claim that because the leadership opposed and killed Jesus that the entire nation of Israel suffered rejection; hence the new people of God "is not Israel" (France 1989, 226, 230). Rather than accept that interpretation, this section argues that Jesus purposefully prepared new leadership from within Israel for the mission first to Israel and then consequently to all the Gentile nations. Instead of rejecting and replacing Israel, Jesus rejected the corrupt leadership—namely, the scribes and Pharisees whom he condemned as hypocrites (Matt 23)—of Israel and consequently replaced them with his twelve apostles. Indeed, the commission of the disciples in chapter 28 constitutes the culmination of the purpose of Israel to be a light and a witness to the nations.

As in the other Gospels, Matthew describes Jesus' escalating conflict with the Jewish leadership, but particularly with the Pharisees. Conflict begins with Herod the Great's attempt to kill the infant Jesus (ch. 2) and culminates in the chief priests' bribe to the soldiers to lie about the resurrection (28:11–15). The Jewish crowds are also implicated for their demand to crucify Jesus, but, as Matthew notes, they were misled: "Now the chief priests and the elders persuaded the crowd to ask for Barabbas and destroy Jesus" (27:20). Jesus singled out the Pharisees and their scribes for censure. Jesus accused them of transgressing the Scripture "for the sake of your tradition" (15:3) and of giving a destructive example of formalism and hypocrisy. The theme of the Sermon on the Mount is "unless your righteousness exceeds that of the scribes and Pharisees, you will never enter the kingdom of heaven" (5:20). Jesus' blistering discourse in chapter 23 served to warn the people about the Pharisees' negative influence. Certainly, Jesus condemned others in the nation also. Jesus minced no words for the masses who did not accept him and denounced the cities in Galilee saying, "It will be more tolerable on the day of judgment for the land of Sodom than for you" (11:24). Yet Jesus' main conflict was with the Jewish leaders and in particular the Pharisees.

Perhaps the strongest denunciation of the Jewish nation's leadership is in 21:43, where Jesus concludes his parable of the wicked tenants by saying, "Therefore I tell you, the kingdom of God will be taken away from you and given to a people producing its fruits." Though some think that by this Jesus meant that the church will henceforth be in place of Israel, it is better to explain that this phrase "speaks of the ending of the role the Jewish religious leaders played in mediating God's authority" (Carson 1984, 454). Willits perceptively notes that the reader is not left to wonder to whom Jesus referred (i.e., Israel or its leaders) because Matthew adds in 21:45, "When the chief priests and the Pharisees heard his parables, they perceived that *he was speaking about them*" (emphasis mine). That is, "Jesus' judgment is not on ethnic Israel but on the inept and corrupt leadership" (Willitts 2016, 127). In other words, Matthew specifically states that with this parable Jesus rejected *the nation's leadership*. Hence, when Matthew writes, "those wretches" (21:41) and "the kingdom of God will be taken away from you" (21:43), these are best understood not expansively as "all Israel" but contextually narrow as "the leaders of Israel." In the same way, the "other vine-growers" (21:41) and the "people producing the fruit" (21:43) are best understood not expansively as another nation or group but contextually narrow as new leaders of Israel.

From the beginning, Jesus began a program of training his disciples (4:18–22). He delivered his Sermon on the Mount as their charter (5:1). Jesus intended for his disciples to proclaim the gospel of the kingdom (9:35). He then named twelve official representatives ("apostles") with obvious reference to the twelve tribes of Israel (10:1–4). He sent them at first only "to the lost sheep of the house of Israel" (10:6), but he prepared them to bear witness before governors, kings, and "the Gentiles" (10:18). It is significant that the new leadership is made up of Israelites. Some think the discourse in chapter 10 shows that since Jesus put new leaders in place, Israel has been rejected. However, that is hard to maintain since a Jewish leader named twelve of his Jewish followers to go to the people of Israel. It better fits the account to say that Jesus designated new leaders "in conscious opposition to the current leadership of Israel, as the new recipients of God's revelation and grace" (Blomberg 1992, 170). Related to that, in 16:13–20, Matthew presents the "church" (*ekklēsia*) as distinct from terms "Israel" and "people." Nowhere does the account describe the church as the new eschatological Israel (Konradt 2014, 332–45).

Very telling, in response to the rich young ruler turning away (19:16–22), Jesus promised his disciples a most remarkable honor: "Truly, I say to you, in the new world, when the Son of Man will sit on his glorious throne, you who have followed me will also sit on twelve thrones, judging the twelve tribes of Israel" (19:29). This thought is taken from Dan 7, where we read that "one like a son of Man" is given authority (7:13–14). Daniel 7:9 mentions multiple thrones, and 7:18 states, "The saints of the Most High shall receive the kingdom and possess the kingdom forever, forever and ever." The reference from Daniel does not support the idea that Israel has been displaced from God's future plans, nor does the citation here assume that Christians in the church will participate in this. Very simply, Jesus' promise to the apostles in 19:29 indicates that "Israel has a future" (Davies and Allison 2004, 74).

The most dramatic statement about the new leadership comes at the climax of the Gospel: the Great Commission. In the phrase "Go therefore and make disciples of *all nations [panta ta ethnē]*," Matthew refers to the Abrahamic promise in Genesis, that "in your offspring shall *all the nations [panta ta ethnē]* of the earth be blessed" (22:18). Matthew shows that "the blessings promised to Abraham and through him to all peoples on earth (Gen 12:3) are now to be fulfilled in Jesus the Messiah" (Carson 1984, 596; so also Evans 2012, 484; Davies and Allison 2004, 683; Bruner 2004, 816–17). Several significant details confirm that the allusion to the Abrahamic promise is intentional. The first three times the exact wording "all the nations" occurs in the LXX, the phrase is part of the promise to Abraham (Gen 18:18; 22:18; 26:4). References to Abraham serve as an *inclusio*, or envelope structure, for the Gospel (Matt 1:1–2; 28:19), drawing attention to the father of the nation of Israel and his blessing. Also, the Abrahamic promise and the Great Commission are thematically related—chosen representatives commissioned as a blessing for all the nations of the earth. Even the structure of the promise to Abraham (commands supported by assurances) is reflected in 28:18–20 (Bruner 2004, 816–17). The Jewish representatives of the Messiah are thus duly charged to take the blessing of Abraham to the Gentiles. This association with the progenitor of the sons of Israel also strongly indicates an ongoing relevance for Israel in the church age.

Conclusion

This chapter has attempted to show that Matthew uses citations from the OT to show that the Messiah shared a common identity with the sons of Israel but fulfilled a very different role. Matthew's quotation from Hos 11:1 does not support the idea that the Son of Man took the place of the son called out of Egypt. Just the opposite: Jesus came to represent the "many" of Israel in redemption. Matthew cites Isaiah to show that Jesus is the compassionate servant who came to bear the sin and sorrows of his people. Matthew began and ended his account with Abraham, the begetter of the Messiah who commissioned his faithful Israelite disciples to take the blessing of Abraham to all the nations. Matthew cited Dan 7 to show that the new leadership of Israel—the apostles—are assured a place in the age to come.

Why do so many explain citations like Matt 2:15 as evidence that Jesus fulfilled and thus rendered obsolete the role of the nation of Israel? I see two general reasons. One explanation is a tendency to conflate Jesus' roles and NT promises about "newness." Jesus inaugurated the new covenant (Matt 26:28), he promises to make all things new (Rev 21:5), and in him believers are new creations (2 Cor 5:17). Jesus is the "new Adam" (Rom 5:14–19). With all this newness, one might think that Jesus is also the new Israel. However, Matthew indicates a solidarity of continuity between Jesus and his people.

A second general reason for misunderstanding is a tendency to conflate different types. As the book of Hebrews shows, the institution of the new covenant (Matt 26:26–29) rendered the Mosaic covenant "obsolete" (Heb 8:13) because the law is "a shadow of the good things to come" (Heb 10:1). Some might assume that because Israel is a type of its Messiah, that once that antitype has appeared, the substance "replaces" the shadow. But Israel's typology is different from that of the law: the chosen people are not a shadow of the Messiah but his source and the object of his redeeming love.

Works Cited

Bavinck, Herman. 2008. *Reformed Dogmatics. Spirit, Church, and New Creation.* Vol. 4. Edited by John Bolt. Translated by John Vriend. Grand Rapids: Baker Academic.

Beale, G. K. 1989. "Did Jesus and his Followers Preach the Right Doctrine from the Wrong Texts?" *Them* 14:89–96.

Beale, G. K. 2020. "Finding Christ in the Old Testament." *JETS* 63: 25–50.

Blaising, Craig A. 2015. "A Critique of Gentry and Wellum's Kingdom through Covenant: A Hermeneutical-Theological Response." *MSJ* 26: 111–27.

———. 2014. "Israel and Hermeneutics." Pages 151–68 in *The People, the Land, and the Future of Israel: Israel and the Jewish People in the Plan of God.* Edited by Darrell L. Bock and Mitch Glaser. Grand Rapids: Kregel.

Blomberg, Craig L. 1992. *Matthew: An Exegetical and Theological Exposition of Holy Scripture.* NAC 22. Nashville: Broadman & Holman.

Bock, Darrell L. 2015. "A Critique of Gentry and Wellum's Kingdom through the Covenant: A New Testament Perspective." *MSJ* 26: 139–45.

Brown, Jeannine K. 2020. "Jesus Messiah as Isaiah's Servant of the Lord: New Testament Explorations." *JETS* 63: 51–69.

Bruner, Frederick Dale. 2004. *Matthew: The Churchbook, Matthew 13–28.* Vol. 2 of *Matthew: A Commentary.* 2nd edition. Grand Rapids: Eerdmans.

Carson, D. A. 1984. "Matthew." Pages 1–599 in vol. 8 of *The Expositor's Bible Commentary.* Edited by Frank E. Gaebelein. Grand Rapids: Zondervan.

Davies, W. D., and Dale C. Allison, Jr. 1988. *Matthew 1–7.* Vol. 1 of *A Critical and Exegetical Commentary on the Gospel According to Saint Matthew.* ICC. Edinburgh: T&T Clark.

———. 2004. *Matthew 19–28.* Vol. 3 of *A Critical and Exegetical Commentary on the Gospel According to Saint Matthew.* ICC. London: T&T Clark.

Dearman, J. Andrew. 2010. *The Book of Hosea.* NICOT. Grand Rapids: Eerdmans.

Donaldson, Terence L. 2016. "Supersessionism and Early Christian Self-Definition." 3: 1–32.

Evans, Craig A. 2012. *Matthew*. New Cambridge Bible Commentary. New York: Cambridge University Press.

Fairbairn, Patrick. 1866. *Prophecy Viewed in Respect to Its Distinctive Nature, Special Function, and Proper Interpretation*. New York: Carlton & Porter. http://archive .org/details/prophecyviewedin00fair.

———. 1900. *The Typology of Scripture: Viewed in Connection with the Whole Series of the Divine Dispensations*. New York: Funk & Wagnalls. http://archive.org /details/typologyofscript01fairiala.

France, R. T. 2007. *The Gospel of Matthew*. NICNT. Grand Rapids: Eerdmans.

———. 1998. *Jesus and the Old Testament: his Application of Old Testament Passages to Himself and his Mission*. Vancouver, BC: Regent College.

———. 1989. *Matthew: Evangelist and Teacher*. New Testament Profiles. Downers Grove, IL: InterVarsity Press.

Galvin, Garrett. 2011. *Egypt as a Place of Refuge*. FAT 51. Tübingen: Mohr Siebeck.

Gentry, Peter J., and Stephen J. Wellum. 2018. *Kingdom through Covenant: A Biblical-Theological Understanding of the Covenants*. 2nd ed. Wheaton, IL: Crossway.

Hagner, Donald A. 1993. *Matthew 1–13*. WBC 33A. Nashville: Nelson.

Harrison, Roland K. 1979. "Servant of the Lord." Pages 421–23 in *International Standard Bible Encyclopedia (Revised)*.

Jeremias, Joachim. 1967. "παῖς θεοῦ." Pages 654–717 in vol. 5 of *TDNT*.

Konradt, Matthias. 2014. *Israel, Church, and the Gentiles in the Gospel of Matthew*. Translated by Kathleen Ess. English ed. Baylor-Mohr Siebeck Studies in Early Christianity. Waco, TX: Baylor University Press.

Mays, James. 1969. *Hosea: A Commentary*. Philadelphia: Westminster.

Morris, Leon. 1992. *The Gospel According to Matthew*. Pillar New Testament Commentary. Grand Rapids: Eerdmans.

Parker, Brent E. 2016. "The Israel-Christ-Church Relationship." Pages 39–68 in *Progressive Covenantalism: Charting a Course between Dispensational and Covenantal Theologies*. Edited by Stephen J. Wellum and Brent E. Parker. Nashville: Broadman & Holman Academic.

Rydelnik, Michael. 2010. *The Messianic Hope: Is the Hebrew Bible Really Messianic?* NAC Studies in Bible & Theology 9. Nashville: Broadman & Holman Academic.

Saucy, Robert L. 2017. "Is Christ the Fulfillment of National Israel's Prophecies?: Yes and No!" *MSJ* 28:17–39.

Schultz, Richard L. 1997. "Servant, Slave." Pages 1180–95 in vol. 4 of *NIDOTTE*.

Soulen, R. Kendall. 1996. *The God of Israel and Christian Theology*. Minneapolis, MN: Fortress Press.

———. 2008. "Supersessionism." Pages 413–14 in *A Dictionary of Jewish-Christian Relations*. Edited by Edward Kessler and Neil Wenborn. Cambridge: Cambridge University Press.

Taylor, Justin. 20 March 2012. "Jesus as the New Israel." *The Gospel Coalition*. https:// www.thegospelcoalition.org/blogs/justin-taylor/jesus-as-the-new-israel/.

Vlach, Michael J. 2010. *Has the Church Replaced Israel?: A Theological Evaluation.* Nashville: Broadman & Holman .

————. "What Does Christ as 'True Israel' Mean for the Nation Israel?: A Critique of the Non-Dispensational Understanding." *MSJ* 23:43–54.

Voorwinde, Stephen. 2008. "How Jewish Is Israel in the New Testament?" *RTR* 67:61–90.

Wellum, Stephen. 13 April 2020. "Progressive Covenantalism and New Covenant Theology." *The Gospel Coalition.* https://www.thegospelcoalition.org/essay/progressive-covenantalism-and-new-covenant-theology/.

Willitts, Joel. 2016. "Zionism in the Gospel of Matthew: Do the People of Israel and the Land of Israel Persist as Abiding Concerns in the Gospel of Matthew?" Pages 107–40 in *The New Christian Zionism: Fresh Perspectives on Israel and the Land.* Edited by Gerald R. McDermott. Downers Grove, IL: IVP Academic.

CHAPTER 3

Narrative Roots

3.1 Geography in the Gospels: A Comparative Approach

Sheila Gyllenberg

Just as each of the four Gospels tells the story of Jesus from a particular perspective, each includes a unique set of information about the locations and geographical settings of Jesus' ministry. The following sections will look at each Gospel and discuss its unique use of geography and topography. Their use of toponyms and place descriptions (or lack of them) fits the background and purposes of each author.

Geography in the Classical World

Writers in the first century CE understood the physical geography of the world from a much different perspective than their twenty-first century counterparts. Maps were rare and were primarily utilized for military campaigns, as the Roman army marched from Spain to the Persian frontier. The emperor Augustus commissioned a huge map that was erected in a colonnade off the Porticus Vipsanius way in Rome. The information for it was culled from an empire-wide mapping project begun by Julius Caesar and continued under Augustus. It was called the Agrippa Map, after Augustus's close adviser and decorated military commander, Marcus Agrippa (Scott 1994, 488–89). This public map may have served as the source for Kapros (probably "Kypros," the wife of the Jewish King Agrippa I, grandson of Herod the Great), when she wove her famous map tapestry and presented it to Emperor Gaius (Caligula), her husband's close friend (Scott 2000, 411–12).

The Greek historian Polybius, who lived in the second century BCE and wrote histories about the early Roman republic, seems to have had access to Roman military maps and descriptions while writing his histories of the Roman Republic (Hengel 1995, 29–30). Similarly, Jason of Cyrene, upon whose work the book of 2 Macc draws, appears to have had access to detailed geographical descriptions of the campaigns of the Maccabees, perhaps from a military source (Hengel 1995, 30). In addition, the first-century historian Josephus, who was the military commander of the Galilee on behalf of the Jewish rebels at the beginning of their revolt against Rome, was presumably able to use Roman military maps and descriptions while writing his histories of the Jewish revolt.

However, these examples are the exceptions. Most classical writers had only very vague notions of the proximity of various geographical landmarks. The famous first-century Greek geographer Strabo wrote that the coast from Egypt continued east until Joppa, where it turns to the north (*Geog.* 16.2.28; Stern 1976, 291). Actually, the coastline turns north about a hundred miles south of Joppa. Strabo also wrote that Joppa was at such a high elevation that it was possible to see Jerusalem from there. He reports that "vessels of burden" sail down the Jordan River (*Geog.* 16.2.16). The Jordan, then and now, is a twisty, shallow stream on which no cargo vessels can travel. The late first-century geographer Pliny the Elder wrote in his *Natural History*: "Beyond Idumaea and Samaria, Judaea stretches long and broad. The part of it near Syria is called Galilee, and that near Arabia and Egypt is Peraea, scattered among rugged mountains and separated from the rest of the Judaeans by the river Jordan" (*Nat.* 5.70; Marshall 1970, 70). Even Jewish writers from the diaspora (such as the second-century BCE writer of the letter of Pseudo-Aristeas and Pseudo-Hecateus) had no accurate knowledge of the layout of Jerusalem (Hengel 1995, 29).

It is therefore unlikely that any of the Gospel writers had ever seen a map of the southern Levant or had access to military descriptions and measurements (Hengel 1995, 31). Nonetheless, each writer includes a scattering of place names and topographical descriptions in his narrative, which are coherent with what we know of the geography of the Jewish community of the first century CE.

Mark

The Gospel of Mark was considered authoritative in the early church because it was believed to be a compilation of traditions its author had heard from the apostle Peter (see discussion in Bauckham 2017, 125, 214–17). According to Papias (Eusebius's second-century source), "Mark" was John Mark, the cousin of Barnabas who had gone on Paul and Barnabas's first missionary journey and later became the traveling companion and "interpreter" for Peter (*Hist. eccl.* 3.29.17; Bauckham 2006, 203, 206n10). After (or according to some sources, just before) Peter's martyrdom in Rome, Mark wrote a life of Jesus to preserve the stories he had heard from Peter. If indeed John Mark was the author, his mother apparently had a house in Jerusalem (Acts 12:12), so that he would be familiar with the geography of Jerusalem, but not necessarily with that of the Galilee. If, as some have suggested, Mark was also the anonymous "boy clothed in a sheet" who avoided arrest by escaping naked (Mark 14:51–52), he would have at least been an eyewitness to the arrest in the Garden of Gethsemane. Although the evidence is not "so compelling as to demand such a conclusion [that John Mark is the author of the gospel]" (Cole 1989, 48), the vibrancy of the details could reflect listener who recorded an eyewitness account he had heard from a master storyteller.

Under this theory, Mark might have heard from Peter multiple times the stories he recorded, but never necessarily in consecutive order. This would explain his decision to simply group his material according to geography: (1) John's ministry and Jesus' baptism in the Jordan and temptation in the wilderness, (2) his ministry in the Galilee and the north, (3) a journey to Jerusalem through Perea and Judea, and (4) events in Jerusalem, including the crucifixion and resurrection. One need not look for theological symbolism in these groupings as some have done (e.g., Conzelmann 1960), but rather as a convenient way to organize the material when a stricter chronological framework was lacking. The lack of sequence is sometimes indicated by phrases such as "in those days" (e.g., Mark 8:1, where it precedes the introduction of the feeding of the four thousand).

Frequently, Mark does not specify the exact location where an incident took place. He rarely maps out complete itineraries for Jesus' travels, and it is usually not explained why Jesus chose certain destinations. Why did he return to Nazareth (Mark 6:1)? Was it just one of the many villages he visited? Why did he retreat with his disciples to the other side of the lake (Mark 4:35)? Presumably, he could get away from the crowds because he was less known there, or there were less Jewish villages there, but we are left to guess. Some have even suggested the trips to "the other side" were to escape the clasp of Herod Antipas (Pixner 1996), who ruled Galilee (west of the lake) and Perea, but not the eastern side of the lake, which was partially controlled by Herod Philip and partially by the cities of the Decapolis.

Other than Jerusalem, there are no references in Mark to most of the large urban centers of his day (Tiberias, Sepphoris, Sebaste, Caesarea Maritima), and even when he mentions cities, it is in the context of their vicinity: "the villages of Caesarea Philippi" in 8:27 or "the region of Tyre" in 7:31 (Freyne 1980, 375). In addition to these two regions, Mark also mentions two areas on the shore of the Sea of Galilee: Gennesaret (Mark 6:53) and the land of the Gerasenes/Gadarenes/Gergesenes—depending on the Greek manuscript consulted (Mark 5:1). Scholars differ on whether to prefer the "land of Gadara" —a Decapolis town a considerable distance from the southeast shore of the lake, which had agriculture land and docks reaching to the lake; or Gergesa—a Jewish town called Gergeshta, on the northeast side of the lake. The latter is known to the church father Origen as "an ancient city . . . by the lake now called Tiberias" (*Comm. Jo. 6:41*). In his day (third century CE), the nearby hill sloping down to the lake was already being shown to Christians who wanted to visualize the fate of the swine. Gergeshta is also known from several sources in rabbinic literature, for example *Shir Hashirim Zuta* 1.4: "from south of the Kidron Valley to Gergeshta on the eastern side of Lake Tiberias" (Rainey and Notley 2006, 360).

In most cases, the places and journeys are "topographically reasonable" (McCown 1941, 3, although see one exception below). The few towns that are mentioned can be identified. Capernaum, also known to us from Josephus and rabbinic literature, is mentioned three times in Mark. Bethsaida, also found in Josephus's writings, is mentioned twice. Nazareth is only named as a reference to the place where Jesus was raised. When Jesus visits Nazareth, it is called simply his "homeland" (*patrida*, Mark 6:1). One unknown toponym, "Dalmanutha," is included (Mark 8:10), which early copyists often corrected to *Magada* or *Megadala or Magdala*, on the basis of Matthew's mention of Magadan instead of Dalmanutha in the same story.

It should be noted that several times during his Galilee accounts, Mark specifically mentioned that Jesus' opponents had come from Jerusalem (scribes in Mark 3:22, and Pharisees and scribes in Mark 7:1). According to Mark, Jesus also had followers who came from Jerusalem, as well as from Idumea (the province south of Judea), from the vicinity of Tyre and Sidon, and from beyond the Jordan (Mark 3:8).

Jesus' journey to the region of Tyre presents some topographic questions. After his encounter with the Syrophoenician woman, "He went out from the region of Tyre, and came through Sidon [north] to the Sea of Galilee, within the region of Decapolis" (Mark 7:31). Notley has suggested Mark is using this rather circuitous itinerary to demonstrate Jesus' literally fulfilment of Isaiah 9:1 [Heb. 8:23]:

> But there will be no more gloom for her who was in anguish; in earlier times He treated the land of Zebulun and the land of Naphtali with contempt, but later on He shall make it glorious, by the way of the sea, on the other side of Jordan, Galilee of the Gentiles.

Notley suggests that the route from the region of Tyre through Sidon would be equivalent to "the way of the sea," which in Isaiah's time would have been the route of the Assyrian conquest from Ijon and Abel Beth Maacah toward the coast (2 Kgs 15:29), the northern part of the "land of Naphtali." The Decapolis would be equivalent to "the other side of Jordan" (Rainey and Notley 2006, 354). The "Decapolis" is not mentioned by either Strabo or Josephus, but the term is known from Pliny the Elder and later writers. It is not certain which ten (*deca*) cities (*polis*) were included in the term (Pliny says he has seen several variant lists), but cities on the east side of the Sea of Galilee and in Transjordan—such as Hippos, Gadara, Gerasa, and Pella—would be included in the group.

Between accounts of events in the Galilee (Mark 3:1–9:50) and the events in Jerusalem (Mark 11:11–16), Mark places an interlude in which he recounts various events that took place on the way between Galilee and Jerusalem, presumably taking the route down the Jordan Valley and up to Jerusalem through the Judean wilderness. He groups these together as "Judea and beyond the Jordan" (Mark 10:1). Again, most of the teachings are recorded without location, while others are given very general settings such as, "As he was setting out on a journey" (Mark 10:17). However, others are more specific, such as, "they were on the road going up to Jerusalem" (Mark 10:32). Even within the section, the stories are not necessarily chronological, insofar as a story of the healing of blind Bartimaeus (Mark 10:46) in Jericho (located on the Jordan river plain) is related after the story that is set "on the road going up to Jerusalem" (presumably the route from Jericho to Jerusalem).

Once the narrative shifts to Jerusalem, the geographical references become much more specific. We are told that Bethany and Bethpage are near the Mount of Olives (Mark 11:1) and that, when coming from Jericho, one comes to these landmarks before reaching Jerusalem. Simon the Leper's home is in Bethany (Mark 14:3). Mark knows that Jesus, like pilgrims we know of from other Jewish sources, spent the nights outside Jerusalem on the Mount of Olives (Mark 11:11, 19), but that they needed to eat the Passover sacrifice within the city (Mark 14:12–13). He knows of a specific place within the temple compound called the "treasury" (Mark 12:41) and that the most impressive of Herod's stones can be seen when going out of the temple compound (Mark 13:1, a fact that has been confirmed by excavations). There is a place called Gethsemane (meaning "the olive oil press") on the Mount of Olives (Mark 14:26, 32) and an execution site called Golgotha near the city (Mark 15:22).

Finally, even though the Gospel ends in Jerusalem at the empty tomb (Mark 16:8)—and the later ending adds Jesus' appearances and ascension at unspecified locations—Mark reports Jesus' promise to meet them in the Galilee after he has been raised (Mark 14:28) and an angel at the empty tomb's reiteration of this promise (Mark 16:7).

In summary, Mark's Gospel organizes his material according to geography (wilderness and Jordan River, Galilee and the north, travel to Jerusalem, in Jerusalem) rather than strict chronology. He does not record (or does not know) many specifics on locations in the Galilee, but what he does record is reasonable. His knowledge of locations in Jerusalem is somewhat more detailed, as we might expect if the author is John Mark, whose mother had a home in Jerusalem.

The "Q" Source

Both Matthew and Luke show familiarity with Mark's Gospel. In addition, they both seem to have a second source of teachings and events not found in Mark, although each uses this source differently and incorporates the material at different points in their overall narrative. This shared material has been called "Q." Scholars have suggested various provenances for the Q material, including that they were traditions known to the church of Antioch or the Jewish-Christian centers in Transjordan (Freyne 1980, 377), or that they were composed in Hebrew or Aramaic by the disciple Matthew.

Luke and Matthew use this material in quite different ways, inserting it into Mark in various contexts. Streeter suggested that Luke had already composed an account based on the material in Q, with other sources he had ("L") before he obtained Mark's account (Morris 1988, 70).

Accounts from the Q source add only a limited number of geographical references to those found in Mark. The location of John's ministry is simply the Jordan in Mark but becomes the "district of the Jordan" in Q (Luke 3:3; Matt 3:5), perhaps influenced by the Hebrew phrase "*kol kikkar hayyarden*" (Gen 13:11), translated in the Septuagint as "*perichōron tou Iordanou*," "the surrounding region of the Jordan" (McCown 1941, 8).

Stories from Q inform us that the centurion with great faith was from Capernaum. In addition to the miracles in the towns of Capernaum and Bethsaida (that appear in Mark), Q also knows that Jesus did many miracles in Chorazin. However, in general, Q is no more interested in pinpointing the locations of events than Mark is.

Matthew

The writer of Matthew, by tradition thought to be the disciple Matthew, uses Mark's geography-based framework, grouping events in Galilee and then events in Jerusalem. He shortens Mark's descriptions, including much of his information about locations. Matthew 4:23–25 tells us only one time that Jesus' fame went through all Galilee, whereas Mark tells us three times that Jesus was teaching throughout Galilee (Mark 1:14, 28, 39) (Freyne 1978, 362). Matthew adds to Galilee "all Syria . . . Decapolis, Jerusalem and Judaea" (Matt 4:24) as locations from which people came to hear Jesus, while Mark gives a list which includes Jerusalem, Judea, Idumea, beyond the Jordan, Tyre, and Sidon (Mark 3:7-8). This may reflect Matthew's aim to emphasize that the ministry of Jesus and the disciples at this time was to the Jews (Matt 10:5-6). Perhaps for the same reason, Matthew omitted the mention of the Decapolis (a primarily Gentile region) in the stories of the demoniac among the tombs and the healing of a deaf and dumb man (cf. Matt 8:35 // Mark 5:20; Matt 15:29 // Mark 7:31).

Matthew's removal of Mark's information about location is seen again in Matt 9:35-37 where Jesus says the crowds are like sheep without a shepherd, while in Mark we are given the geographic context for Jesus' words: he was trying to take his disciples by boat to a secluded place, when he saw all the people running to the place they would land (Mark 6:32-34).

Sometimes Matthew's abbreviations lead to gaps in his geographic sequencing. For example, in Matt 16:5, Jesus and his disciples cross to the other side (of the lake), and in the subsequent story (Matt 16:13), they arrive at Caesarea Philippi (which is not near the lake). Mark's account, in contrast, gives an entire sequence of travels, which have been omitted by Matthew, that eventually continue to Caesarea Philippi. Another example is Matt 13:1, which tells us that Jesus left the house after his family's visit. But only by reading Mark's account of his family's visit (Mark 3:20) would the reader know that Jesus was in a house at the beginning of the story (McCown 1941, 13).

Wherever Matthew is following Mark, there is no new geography that was not already in Mark's account. For example, neither Mark nor Matthew supply a location for the cure of the leper (Matt 8:1-4; Mark 1:40-44[1]). In material for which Matthew is not dependent on Mark, Matthew is equally uninterested in locations. The healing of the man with the withered hand is in a synagogue of unknown location (Matt 12:9). Afterward Jesus "withdrew from there" (Matt 12:15), even though we have never been told where he was.

In one instance, however, Matthew supplies a story at a location that is only suggested in Mark's text. As we saw above, Mark twice states that Jesus promised to meet the disciples in the Galilee after the resurrection, but only Matthew gives us an account of such a meeting (Matt 28:16).

The few place descriptions that Matthew does include he uses for his own purpose of linking events in Jesus' life to Old Testament passages. For example, he stresses that Capernaum was the center of Jesus' ministry in the Galilee, which he then ties to the fulfillment of Isa 9:1 ("he came and settled in Capernaum . . . the land of Naphtali, by way of the sea"; Matt 4:13-16). Matthew henceforth calls Capernaum Jesus' "own city" (Matt 9:1, *tēn idian polin*), while he calls Nazareth Jesus' "homeland" (Matt 13:54, *tēn patrida*). Another example: whereas Mark only mentions in passing that Jesus came from Nazareth (1:9), in Matthew, the fact that

---

1. Luke also knows no location for this miracle: "While he was in one of the cities" (Luke 5:12).

Jesus' parents had taken him to Nazareth is presented as another prophetic fulfillment: "he shall be called a *nazaraios*."[2]

In material that Matthew adds to Mark (but is not shared with the Luke source),
we learn that Jesus was born in Bethlehem and that the magi first go to Herod in
Jerusalem before proceeding to Bethlehem. We learn of the flight to Egypt and the
attempted return to Archelaus's territory,[3] presented in the context of a prophetic
parallel to Israel coming out of Egypt (Matt 2:15; Hos 11:1).

Matthew also adds that several events took place specifically on "the mountain" (*to oros*) near the sea of Galilee, such as the teachings recorded in Matt 5–7
(the Sermon on the Mount). The words *the mountain* has led to the speculation
that Matthew was intentionally drawing a parallel between Jesus' teachings in the
Sermon on the Mount and the teachings given to Moses on Mount Sinai (Exod
21–31) (for a summary, see Allison 1992, 563). However, there are few similarities
between Moses receiving revelation on Mount Sinai and Jesus' teaching revelation
to his disciples on "the mountain," so that other scholars see the reference to "the
mountain" in Matt 5:1 (and 8:1) as only a topographical note, the equivalent to
"into the hills" (France 2007, 112). Similarly, in Hebrew "*hahar*" is a general term
for "the hill country." This Hebrew usage is reflected in the LXX translation of *hahar*
as "*to oros*" (for example, Gen 31:21) "*eis to oros galaad*" (toward the hill country
of Gilead), Jacob pitched his tent, "*en to orei*" (in the hill country), and numerous
other examples (Gen 36:9; Num 13:17, 29; 14:45; Deut 1:7, 19). This general usage
of the term *to oros* is also found in Matthew's feeding of the five thousand (Matt
15:29 // John 6:3) and his account of Jesus' seeking solitude for prayer (Matt 14:23;
where *to oros* is also used in the parallel passages in Mark 6:46 // Luke 6:12), and
the appointing of the Twelve (Mark 3:13). It is therefore unlikely that Matthew
placed the sermon "on the mountain" to draw a parallel to Moses receiving the law
at Mount Sinai.

In contrast, the transfiguration is specified to be on "a high mountain" *eis oros
hypsēlon*, following Mark 9:2, which seems to not only be a geographic description
but also an allusion to Mount Sinai, which was portrayed as being "high" in Second
Temple period Jewish literature (Philo, *Mos.* 2.70; Josephus, *Ant.* 3.76).[4]

---

2. However, since there is no Scripture prophesying that a messiah would come
from Nazareth, Notley has suggested that this last statement might be an adaption of the
Hebrew word "*natzori*" ("the one whom I have kept"), referring to the multiple angelic
warnings that brought Jesus safely through his infancy to the security of Nazareth, in
fulfillment of Isa 42:6: "I will also hold you [God's anointed] by the hand and watch
over you" (Rainey and Notley 2006, 349–50).

3. Archelaus was the son of Herod who had inherited Judea, where Bethlehem
was located, as well as Idumea and Samaria. Nazareth was in the territory ruled by his
brother Antipas.

4. Other elements of this story also parallel Moses on Mount Sinai: Moses went up
the mountain after six days of cloud covering it top (Matt 17:1 and Mark 9:2 "six days
later," versus Luke 9:28's eight days later); the instructions to build the tabernacle in the
Sinai account and Peter's desire to build three tabernacles, etc.

Luke

By tradition, Luke is thought to have been Luke the physician (Col 4:14) who accompanied Paul on some of his journeys, including his imprisonment in Rome (2 Tim 4:11; Phlm 24).[5] Although there is debate whether the "we" passages in Acts (Acts 16:10–17; 20:5–16; 21:1–18; 27:1–28:16) refer to Luke himself coming with Paul to the land of Israel or whether he simply used the diaries of someone who did. Similarity of vocabulary and style in these passages suggests it was Luke himself (Morris 1988, 21). In support of this, Luke's detailed knowledge of the geography of Jerusalem and the route to the coast, which is found in Acts, can be contrasted with Luke's less detailed geography of Galilee (where he may never have travelled). For example, the author of Acts knows that the Mount of Olives is a Sabbath day's journey from Jerusalem (Acts 1:12) and that the field where Judas perished was called Akeldama (Acts 1:19, a transliteration from the Aramaic name). He names the "Beautiful Gate" and "Solomon's colonnade" in the temple (Acts 3:10–11), as well as steps from the Roman barracks (the Antonia?) that led directly down to the temple courts (Acts 21:40). He refers to an official called the "captain of the temple" (Acts 4:1). He describes the road from Jerusalem to Gaza as "the desert road" (perhaps reflecting the Hebrew usage "desert road" = "the road toward the desert"—presumably, the Sinai desert toward Egypt, and thence to Ethiopia). He is aware of a home where local believers meet (to which Peter goes after being released from prison, Acts 12:10–12). Caesarea is a two-day journey[6] from Jerusalem (Acts 23:23, 31–32). A cohort was stationed in Jerusalem (Acts 21:31) and large contingent of troops might be needed to accompany the prisoner Paul through the rebel-filled hill country of Judea, but unnecessary from Antipatris on the edge of the coastal plain to Caesarea where the Roman governor lived.

The compiler of the Gospel of Luke, like Matthew, had access to Mark's account and simplified the geographical details (Hengel 1995, 32). "Golgotha" and "Gethsemane" are not named. Like Matthew, Luke adds a birth narrative that includes Bethlehem and Nazareth, as well as Jesus' parents' *pidyon habben* (redemption of the firstborn) sacrifice in Jerusalem, and his boyhood discussion with the learned men in the temple. Luke, like Matthew, omits Mark's description of the journey to the region of Tyre, Sidon, and the Decapolis (see above)—perhaps because he recognized that the narrative flowed well geographically and chronologically if the section between Mark 6:53 and 8:22 is omitted (they set out from Bethsaida in Mark 6:45 and arrive in Bethsaida in 8:23). Thus in Luke 9:10, Jesus and the disciples set out for Bethsaida, and following the feeding of the five thousand, Jesus asks them, "Who do you say that I am?" Only in Matthew and Mark are we told that this hap-

---

5. This attribution first occurs in the works of the mid-second-century heretic Marcion and in an "anti-Marcion" prologue to Luke, a late-second-century list of New Testaments books (the Muratorian Fragment) and second-century church fathers such as Irenaeus, Tertullian, and Clement of Alexandria (Morris 1988, 21).

6. A reasonable time for a military attachment to march sixty-two miles.

pens in the region/villages of Caesarea Philippi. It would be a logical topographical route to travel there from Bethsaida (as in Luke).[7]

Luke's travel narrative—from the Galilee to Jerusalem—takes up parts of nine chapters (in comparison to Mark's single chapter), with the destination of Jerusalem repeated six times (Luke 9:51, 53; 13:22; 17:11; 18:31; 19:28), and the reason for the destination is stated emphatically:

> "Nevertheless, I must journey on today and tomorrow and the next day; for it cannot be that a prophet would perish outside of Jerusalem. O Jerusalem, Jerusalem, the city that kills the prophets and stones those sent to her! How often I wanted to gather your children together, just as a hen gathers her brood under her wings, and you would not have it! Behold, your house is left to you desolate; and I say to you, you will not see Me until the time comes when you say, 'Blessed is he who comes in the name of the Lord!'" (Luke 13:33–34)

Fittingly, Luke also ends his Gospel in Jerusalem, with no mention of the post-resurrection appearances in the Galilee.[8]

Other than Bethlehem, the only new place name that appears in Luke, which did not appear in either Mark or Q, is the raising of the widow's son at Nain (Luke 7:11). In addition, there is a specific location (Emmaus) for Jesus' appearance to two disciples walking on their way to the country, which appears as a nonspecified destination in the disputed ending of Mark (16:12).

Also unique to Luke is the addition of the territories ruled by the tetrarchs (Luke 3:1). He alone calls the Sea of Galilee "lake" (*limne*), reflecting the freshwater nature of this body of water, which is left ambivalent by the Hebrew term *yam kinneret* (Sea of Chinnereth; Num 34:11; Josh 13:27) and in the Greek of the LXX *thalassēs Chenara* (Sea of Chenara) and in the Aramaic targumim as Sea of Gennesar (Rainey and Notley 2006, 353). Like Josephus (*J.W.* 2.573; 3.56, 463; *Ant.* 18.28, 36), Luke once calls it the "Lake of Genneseret" (Luke 5:1), a phrase also found in Strabo (*Geog.* 16.2.16) and Pliny (Lat. *lacus*; *Nat.* 5.71).[9] Five times, where Luke presumably found *thalassa* in Mark, he corrects it to *limne*.

---

7. Hengel (1995, 33), however, prefers to see the omission of the journey that included Tyre, Sidon, and the Decapolis as part of Luke's purpose to focus on Jesus' ministry to the Jews. However, elsewhere, Luke does show Jesus as interested in reaching the Gentiles; for example, his mention of miracles worked through Elijah and Elisha on behalf of the widow of Zarephath and Naaman the Syria (Luke 4:25–27) and Simeon's prophecy that the infant Jesus will be a light to the Gentiles (Luke 2:32). In addition, Luke records Jesus' commendation of the [Gentile] centurion's faith (Luke 7:9).

8. Morris (1988, 45) points out that Luke mentions Jerusalem thirty-one times, while the other Gospels mention it only thirteen times (Matthew), ten times (Mark), and twelve times (John).

9. Mark's term "Sea of Galilee," which is followed by Matthew, is unique among ancient writers. Notley has suggested that early Christians used this term in order to emphasize the link between Isa 9:1 ("he shall make it glorious . . . by way of the Sea . . . Galilee of the Gentiles") and Jesus' ministry around the lake (Rainey and Notley 2006, 352–54).

Where Mark mentions Jesus and his disciples going by boat to Bethsaida, Luke 9:10 adds the clarification "to the city" of Bethsaida. Bethsaida, which was turned into a true Greek *polis* during the reign of Philip (4 BCE to 39 CE) probably toward the end of his reign, since he named it Julias in honor of Emperor Tiberias's mother (Livia Julia, the second wife of the emperor Augustus).[10] When Luke refers to "*Samareia*" (Luke 17:11, and several times in Acts), he always refers to the territory where the Samaritans lived and not to the Old Testament city of Samaria that had been rebuilt by Herod the Great and renamed Sebaste ("*Augustus*" in Greek). This is also the way in which Josephus uses the word "*Samareia*" (Hengel 1995, 72). Like John, Luke shows more interest in Samaria and Samaritans than either Matthew or Mark (Morris 1988, 71).

Mistakes in topographical references that have sometimes been attributed to Luke include 4:44—"So he kept on preaching in the synagogues of *Judea*"—when the context is clearly Jesus' ministry in the Galilee.[11] However, the word *Judea* is clearly meant to indicate the area where there was Jewish sovereignty—i.e., the total area ruled by Herod the Great before dividing it among three of his sons. Luke uses the word *Judea* in the same way in 7:17 and 23:5 (Freyne 1980, 365).

In summary, the author of Luke/Acts shows good familiarity with Jerusalem and the temple, compatible with an eyewitness who had been to these places. For the Galilee, when Mark or Q is his source, he has no additional knowledge about locations but does accurately use the word *limne* (lake) rather than *thalassa* (sea). His additional sources, on at least two occasions, know of locations unknown in Matthew or Mark.

John

The Gospel of John claims to be an account of an eyewitness (John 21:24) who was one of the disciples but not necessarily one of the Twelve (Bauckham 2017, 412–37). In Bauckham's opinion, based on the second-century Christian writer Papias, the author of the Gospel is the "disciple whom Jesus loved," who is not "John the son of Zebedee" but rather "John the Elder." He may have also been the disciple who "was known to the high priest" who gained access for himself and Peter on the night of Jesus' arrest (John 18:15).

The author of John mentions several locations not included in the Synoptics: Sychar, Cana, Bethany (or Bethabara) beyond the Jordan, Aenon near Selim, and Cana. The latter is mentioned three times—the wedding (John 2:1), the healing of the royal official's son (John 4:46), and the hometown of Nathanael (John 21:2). John is the only Gospel that records Bethsaida as the hometown of Andrew, Peter, and Philip,

---

10. See the discussion regarding for which "Julia" the city was named, in Rainey and Notley 2006, 357.

11. Westcott and Hort list at least eleven manuscripts of Luke where a scribe has corrected this phrase to read "in the synagogues of the *Galilee*," as it appears in Mark 1:39: "And he went into their synagogues throughout all Galilee, preaching and casting out demons."

and the only Gospel to call the Sea of Galilee the Sea of Tiberias. John also mentions people coming in boats from Tiberias to hear Jesus. Thus John's Gospel suggests a good knowledge of locations from an independent, possibly first-hand, source.

Several of his references reflect the political divisions in the late first century CE, rather than those of the time of Jesus. For example, Bethsaida is called Bethsaida *in Galilee*, a designation that would only be true when Agrippa ruled the entire northern part of the country, but not when sovereignty was divided between the sons of Herod—with Antipas ruling on the west side of the lake (Galilee) and Philip ruling over the northeastern districts (Trachonitis, Gaulanities, etc.). Pliny, writing in the late first century, also refers to the entire area as simply Galilee.[12]

The author of John is the only Gospel writer who mentions several sites within Jerusalem, such as the Pool of Bethesda (John 5:2), the Pool of Siloam (John 9:7), and the Brook of the Kidron, which Jesus crossed to take his disciples to a particular (unnamed) place where they often met (John 18:1). John's Jerusalem orientation includes the Jerusalem elite's derogatory references to Galilee as a place of dubious Torah observance: "Surely the Messiah is not going to come from Galilee, is he?" (John 7:41) and "You (Nicodemus) are not also from Galilee" (John 7:51).[13]

Discussion and Summary

Archaeology has uncovered remains typical of the first-century Jewish community (chalk-stone vessels and ritual baths) at more than a dozen sites in the Galilee.[14] In addition, rabbinic literature knows of Galilean Jewish communities in Shiknin, Kefar Hananiah, and Nahf (whose pottery could be trusted as produced by Jews), Arbela, Hittaia, Hukkok, Chorazin (which were known for their wheat fields), and Sepphoris and Tiberias (which where central markets for wheat and wine) (Strange 2000, 394). Josephus mentions several additional Jewish towns that he fortified[15] (*J.W.* 2.573 [2.20.6]). Although Jesus could have visited each of these towns during his ministry, only five towns in the Galilee and less than ten towns in the rest of the country are mentioned in the Gospels.

---

12. As Notley points out, there is no need to posit two Bethsaidas—one on the west side of the lake in Antipas's territory and one on the northeast in Philip's territory (Rainey and Notley 2006, 357). Philip's Bethsaida best fits the mixed Jewish/Greek (Gentile) character of Bethsaida as portrayed in John's Gospel: Andrew and Philip both have Greek names, and Philip speaks to Greeks in Jerusalem (John 12:20). Notley points out that, according to Josephus, Bethsaida contained both Syrians (Greek-speaking Gentiles) and Jewish populations (*J.W.* 3.57)

13. Freyne (1980, 371) also connects the anti-Galilean nuances in the mocking tone used toward the temple guards who spoke admiringly of Jesus' teaching: "You have not also been led astray, have you? No one of the rulers or Pharisees has believed in Him, has he? But this crowd [presumably Jesus' Galilean followers] which does not know the Law is accursed" (John 7:47–49).

14. Kefar Hanania, Capernaum, Yodfat, Ibelin, Kefar Kenna, Sepphoris, Reine, Nazareth, Bethlehem of Galilee, Migdal Ha-Emeq, Magdala, and Tiberias.

15. Tarichaea, Bersabee, Salamis, Capharecche, Sigo, Japha, and Mount Tabor.

The reason for this lack of toponyms in the Gospels can only be speculated: Mark was probably recording the stories of Peter, preached in locations far away from the land of Israel where the place name was not important to the purpose of the story; Matthew and John, who, although they were eyewitnesses themselves, were intent on apologetic and theological messages, and only included minimal place names; Luke, who was attempting to arrange the stories and teachings chronologically from various sources, including Mark, felt no need to research precise place names for his intended audience. However, the little geography that has been preserved in the four Gospels fits well into what we know of the cities, regions, and routes of the land of Israel in the first century CE, and sometimes sheds light onto the purposes and processes of the compilation of each Gospel.

Works Cited

Allison, Dale C., Jr. 1992. "Mountain and Wilderness." Pages 563–66 in *DJG*. Edited by Joel. B Green, Scot McKnight, and I. Howard Marshall. Downers Grove, IL: InterVarsity Press.

Bauckham, Richard. 2017. *Jesus and the Eyewitnesses: The Gospels as Eyewitness Testimony*. 2nd ed. Grand Rapids: Eerdmans.

Cole, R. Alan. 1989. *Mark: An Introduction and Commentary*. TNTC 2. Downers Grove, IL: InterVarsity Press.

Conzelmann, Hans. 1960. *The Theology of St. Luke*. Translated by Geoffrey Buswell. London: Faber.

Davies, W. D. 1974. *The Gospel and the Land: Early Christianity and Jewish Territorial Doctrine*. Berkeley: University of California Press.

France, R. T. 2007. *The Gospel of Matthew*. NICOT. Grand Rapids: Eerdmans.

Freyne, Seán. 1980. *Galilee: From Alexander the Great to Hadrian 323 B.C.E. to 135 C.E.* Notre Dame, IN: University of Notre Dame Press.

Hengel, Martin. 1995. "The Geography of Palestine in Acts." Pages 27–78 in *The Book of Acts in Its Palestinian Setting*. Edited by Richard Bauckham. Vol. 4 in *The Book of Acts in Its First Century Setting*. Edited by Bruce W. Winter. Grand Rapids: Eerdmans.

Marshall, I. Howard. 1970. *Luke: Historian and Theologian*. Milton Keynes: Paternoster.

McCown, Chester C. 1941. "Geography: Fiction, Fact and Truth." *JBL* 60.1: 1–25.

Morris, Leon. 1988. *Luke: An Introduction and Commentary*. 2nd ed. TNTC 3. Downers Grove, IL: InterVarsity Press.

Pixner, Bargil. 1996. *With Jesus through the Galilee according to the Fifth Gospel*. Collegeville, MN: Liturgical Press.

Rainey, Anson, and R. Steven Notley. 2006. *The Sacred Bridge*. Jerusalem: Carta.

Scott, James M. 1994. "Luke's Geographical Horizon." Pages 483–544 in *The Book of Acts in Its Graeco-Roman Setting*. Edited by David W. J. Gill and Conrad Gempf. Grand Rapids: Eerdmans.

———. 2000. "Geographical Perspectives in Late Antiquity." Pages 411–14 in *DNTB*.

Stern, Menahem, ed. 1976. Vol. 1 of *Greek and Latin Authors on Jews and Judaism*. Jerusalem: Israeli Academy of Sciences and Humanities.

Strange, James F. 2000. "Galilee." Pages 391–98 in *DNTB*.

3.2 Matthew's and Luke's Accounts of the Birth of Jesus

R. Alan Streett

When examining the birth narratives in the Gospels of Matthew and Luke, one must give special attention to their historical, social, and literary contexts. These accounts should be read at two levels: (1) the events as they unfolded in the lives of the original participants (ca. 4 BCE), and (2) their significance for the Jewish and Gentile Christ followers (post 70 CE) who live outside Palestine.

The Gospel According to Matthew

Matthew's Gospel opens with the birth of Jesus. First, he traces Jesus' ancestral roots to King David and only then back farther to Father Abraham, the progenitor of the Jewish people (Matt 1:1–17). This genealogical overview "locates Jesus within Israel's history" (Carter and Levine 2013, 25) and enables the author to authenticate Jesus' credentials as the Messiah. Second, Matthew offers a short narrative of events leading up to and including Jesus' birth (1:18–25), which he uses to show that God has fulfilled his covenantal promise to his people. A savior is born who will restore the kingdom to Israel.

Messianic Genealogy

> An account of the genealogy of Jesus the Messiah, the son of David, the son of Abraham (1:1).

Matthew immediately introduces his audience to Jesus, whom he identifies as *Christou*, a regal title translated as "Messiah" or "Anointed One." In its historical context, Matthew uses this moniker to establish Jesus as Israel's legitimate king and not Herod (Matt 2:2; 21:5; 27:11). The author next identifies Jesus as the "son of David" and traces his ancestry back to Israel's greatest king. Jesus is heir to David's throne. Only then does Matthew call Jesus "the son of Abraham." As Abraham's seed, Jesus is heir to God's covenantal promises to form a people through which he will reach out to the nations (Gen 12:3). At first glance, it appears that Abraham is oddly placed after David in the genealogy, when in fact he precedes David by eight hundred years. We discover the purpose for this arrangement at the end of the pericope (1:17–18):

> So all the generations from Abraham to David are fourteen generations; and from David to the deportation to Babylon, fourteen generations; and from the deportation to Babylon to the Messiah, fourteen generations.

While Abraham is the father of God's ancient people, David takes center stage in the genealogy. Matthew informs us he has divided Jesus' family tree (1:2–16) into three periods of fourteen generations each, with each focusing on King David. Verses 2–6a cover the period from Abraham to David, the promised king; verses 6b–11 from David to the Babylonian exile; and verses 12–16 from the return to the birth of the Messiah (the son of David), Israel's ultimate king.

Even a cursory examination of the genealogy reveals that Matthew is not concerned with historical precision. For instance, he links Salmon (the father of Boaz) to Rahab, although she lived at least a century before Salmon (1:5). Matthew also skips over several kings, leaving the genealogy somewhat truncated. The span of time from Abraham to David is approximately eight hundred years; from David to Babylonian exile, four hundred years; and from exile to Jesus, five hundred seventy-five years (Borg and Crossan 2007, 87).

So how does Matthew, using an imprecise genealogy, make his case that Jesus is the legitimate heir to King David's throne? He employs a Jewish literary device known as *gematria* to embed a hidden message in the genealogy. *Gematria* is a practice that assigns numerical values to letters that when added up spell out a secret word, phrase, or sentence. In Hebrew, the numerical value of David's name (d-v-d) is 14. *Dalet* is the fourth letter of the Hebrew alphabet and *vav* is the sixth letter. The sum total of d (4) + v (6) + d (4) equals 14. Thus David is the central figure in each part of Jesus' genealogy and Jesus is the son of David who inherits his eternal throne (2 Sam 7:12–16). Matthew does not strive for historical accuracy. His coded message is accurate. Jesus is the new David, the royal Messiah.

Interestingly, Matthew includes four Gentile women in the genealogy: Tamar and Rahab (Canaanites), Bathsheba (married to Uriah the Hittite), and Ruth (Moabite). All are known for having noteworthy or unusual sexual experiences. With his audience in mind, the author likely includes Gentiles, women, and sinners in the messianic line to show that: (1) Jesus' pedigree is anything but pure, and (2) the Gospel has universal application. Forgiveness is offered to all, even the marginalized.

Mary, a Jewish teenager, likewise becomes pregnant outside of marriage under suspicious circumstances. In a society that operates on honor and shame, a daughter's loss of virginity and pregnancy brings disgrace on her paternal family (Malina and Rohrbaugh 2003, 25). What will the neighbors say upon learning of Jesus' illegitimate birth? His reputation as a bastard child will likely follow him throughout life. On one occasion when Jewish opponents confront Jesus, they sarcastically respond, "We are not born as a result of immorality [*porneias*; i.e., fornication]" (John 8:41 NET). This implies his adversaries believe Jesus was conceived through an illicit affair. Even into the second century CE, this was the prominent position among unbelievers. Celsus, for instance, specifies that Mary had sexual relations with Panthera, a Roman soldier stationed in Sepphoris, which led to the birth of Jesus (Origen, *Cels.* 1.32).

Matthew offers his readers an alternative explanation: the conception of Jesus is a miracle. As the genealogy concludes, Matthew introduces Jesus' parents and identifies Joseph simply as "the husband of Mary" but not as Jesus' biological father. It is Mary alone "of whom Jesus was born, who is called the Messiah" (Matt 1:16).

Messianic Birth

Matthew next gives an account of Jesus' birth by speaking directly to his readers: "Now the birth of Jesus the Messiah took place in this way" (1:18a). This "inside" information was not readily available to those living at the time of Jesus' birth: "When his mother Mary had been engaged to Joseph, but before they lived together, she was found to be with child from the Holy Spirit" (1:18b). Jesus' birth is the product of divine intervention. God takes the initiative "through the Spirit's involvement in the conception of Jesus" to make known his presence and plan (Carter 2016, 103). As the story unfolds, readers are told how Joseph reacts to the news of Mary's pregnancy. Assuming she has violated her betrothal vows, "Joseph, being a righteous man and unwilling to expose her to public disgrace, planned to dismiss her quietly" (1:19). Since Mary is not carrying his child, Joseph desires a quiet divorce. As a "righteous man" (i.e., covenant keeper and an honorable man), a divorce is in order, but he wishes to keep it discreet. Before the next morning, Joseph's plans are changed.

> But just when he had resolved to do this, an angel of the Lord appeared to him in a dream and said, "Joseph, son of David, do not be afraid to take Mary as your wife, for the child conceived in her is from the Holy Spirit. (Matt 1:20)

The unnamed heavenly visitor changes Joseph's mind. He must not fear for his reputation and carry out his wedding plans. To comply will bring dishonor to this most admirable man, for all will assume he is responsible for Mary's pregnancy. The angel then explains that the child's conception is of divine origin and has a divine purpose:

> She will bear a son, and you are to name him Jesus, for he will save his people from their sins. (Matt 1:21)

Joseph has a part in the plan. The angel reveals to Joseph the gender and the name of the yet-to-be-born child who is elected to perform a salvific mission. As the royal Messiah he will fulfill God's covenant plan to rescue Israel from foreign domination and set up God's kingdom. His birth thus foreshadows his passion (deSilva 2010, 223). Matthew adds an editorial comment:

> All this took place to fulfill what had been spoken by the Lord through the prophet: "Look, the virgin shall conceive and bear a son, and they shall name him Immanuel," which means, "God is with us." (Matt 1:22–23)

Matthew here speaks directly to his readers and offers intelligence not given initially to Mary or Joseph. This inside information explains how Mary's pregnancy and Jesus' birth brought to completion an ancient prophecy addressed originally to King Ahaz of Judah (ca. 735 BCE) at a time when he faced the threat of Assyrian invasion and domination. In its original setting, God assures Ahaz that the southern kingdom will be spared destruction if the king trusts God and does not rely on military alliances for survival (Isa 7:1–9). God then commands Ahaz to ask for a sign as proof of the prophecy's reliability (Isa 7:10–13). When he refuses, Isaiah responds,

"Therefore the Lord himself will give you a sign. Look, the young woman (*'almah*, i.e., maiden) is with child and shall bear a son, and they shall name him Immanuel [meaning *God is with us*]" (Isa 7:14).

The sign has nothing to do with the nature of the child's conception but only with the providential timing of the birth. God will stand with Judah at its most vulnerable moment (Brown 1977, 149). The prophecy indeed comes to pass as Isaiah predicts (Isa 7:15–16; 8:4–10; 9:6–7).

In quoting Isa 7:14, Matthew perceives that the ancient prophecy not only had significance in its historical setting but serves a contemporary purpose as well. He lets his audience know that Jesus' miraculous birth was a sign that God has once again sided with his rebellious people.

Since Matthew's receptors are hearing and/or reading his Gospel in the mid-80s CE, they know how Israel's leaders turned against Jesus and killed him (ca. 30 CE). They also know that God vindicated Jesus and raised him from the dead. As Israel's eschatological king, Jesus commissioned his apostolic band of faithful messianic Jews (Matt 21:43) to complete the kingdom restoration project and to make disciples of all nations, and he gave them a promise: "Remember, I am with you always, to the end of the age" (Matt 28:20), harkening back to the Isaianic title "Immanuel" (Isa 7:14; Matt 1:21–22).

EXCURSUS ON ISAIAH 7:14

Unlike many contemporary scholars who use a grammatical-historical approach to interpreting Scriptures, first-century believers employed several hermeneutical methods. This helps explain the way Matthew interprets Isa 7:14 and applies it to the virgin birth.

Gospel writers, along with their Jewish contemporaries, viewed the Hebrew Bible as a divine book, which placed it in a category different from all other literature. As such, it contained not only a human meaning but also a divine one. What the human author intended to convey to his original audience may not be the only significance of the text. God, the divine author and inspirer of the text, occasionally embedded it with a further sense, which in time he would reveal to an entirely different audience. Accordingly, Gospel writers believed the Hebrew Scriptures should be read twice: the first to discover the human meaning, and the second to discern a possible divine meaning, i.e., *sensus plenior* or fuller meaning (Brown 1977, 146n3).

Additionally, Gospel writers used a variety of hermeneutical methods to interpret afresh the Hebrew Scriptures. They were not the first to do so (see 4Q521). Two of the more popular methods were:

1. The *midrash* method that sought to find a deeper than surface meaning to a text through careful observation and prolonged reflection (e.g., Ps 118:22–23 = Luke 20:17–18).

2. The *pesher* method that sought to uncover the eschatological or messianic meaning of the text, which was not necessarily the meaning of the text in

its original historical context (e.g., Isa 61:1–2 = Luke 4:16–20; Isa 7:14 = Matt 1:22–23).

Matthew, believing Jesus to be Messiah, interpreted relevant OT texts christologically (e.g., Isa 7:14; 53:3). Jesus did the same, stating that the Hebrew Scriptures pointed to him (Isa 61:1–2 = Luke 4:18–20; 24:27, 44).

To read the Hebrew Scriptures (e.g., Isa 7:14) solely through a grammatical-historical lens leads to Judaism but misses Jesus (McCartney and Enns 2001, 97–105). Matthew, like many exegetes of his day, searched for the deeper truth of the Scriptures and discovered Christ.

Matthew again returns to his narrative: "When Joseph awoke from sleep, he did as the angel of the Lord commanded him; he took her as his wife, but had no marital relations with her until she had borne a son; and he named him Jesus" (Matt 1:24–25).

Aftermath

The events that follow—the wise men's visit to Herod and their trek to Bethlehem to find and worship Jesus, the family's escape to Egypt, the slaughter of the innocents, and their return to Nazareth—are all part of a *post-birth* narrative (Matt 2). Four things stand out. First, Herod is depicted as a tyrannical madman, more like Pharaoh of old than the king of the Jews. Both plot to kill all newborn Jewish males in an attempt to thwart God's plan for his people. But divinely protected Jesus, like Moses, will deliver his people from bondage.

Second, Jesus "the son of David" is born in Bethlehem, "the city of David" (the birthplace of King David). To emphasize his royal ancestry, Matthew mentions Bethlehem five times (Matt 2:1, 5, 6, 8, 16). In the opening and closing of his Gospel narrative, Matthew presents Jesus as the legitimate king of the Jews (Matt 27:1, 29; 28:18–20).

Third, the visiting magi offer obeisance to the infant Jesus, which may foreshadow the Gentile multitudes who will eventually become Christ followers. For Matthew, "Jesus . . . is the kingly Messiah of Israel in whom Israel's entire history, begun in Abraham, reaches its eschatological culmination" and will include an ingathering of Gentiles (Kingsbury 2001, 164–65).

Fourth, Matthew frames Jesus' infancy in terms of "a new exodus and an end of exile, marking him out further as the true representative of Israel" (Wright and Bird 2019, 590). Following in the same sequential journey as ancient Israel, the newborn Jesus starts in the promised land, travels to Egypt, and is then "called out of Egypt as God's chosen child" (Horsley 1993, 32).

The Gospel According to Luke

Luke 1–2 contains material unique to this Gospel and includes the announcements and births of John the Baptist and Jesus, which the author has gathered from sources unknown or unavailable to Matthew. Luke opens with the story of Elizabeth, the barren wife of a Jewish priest, who unexpectedly gets pregnant. With the shame of her infertility removed, she praises God (Luke 1:5–24). Luke then introduces Mary, an unwed Galilean peasant girl, who becomes pregnant through divine means. This section will focus on the events surrounding Mary's conception and Jesus' subsequent birth.

The Annunciation (1:26–38)

According to the Lukan account, Gabriel, an angel associated with end-time visions, suddenly appears to Mary and announces that she is "highly favored" ("full of grace") and the "Lord is with her" (vv. 26–28). Mary, a poor girl with no social status, is startled and perplexed, and she ponders the significance of this visit and the nature of the greeting (v. 29). Gabriel allays her fears and reassures her of God's blessing (v. 30). Then he drops the bombshell: "And now, you will conceive in your womb and bear a son, and you will name him Jesus" (v. 31).

The threefold prophecy (conception, birth, and naming of the child) is predicated on God's favor and presence (Bovon 2002, 50). Whereas the Gospel of Matthew focuses on Joseph receiving the news of the pregnancy, Luke focuses on the annunciation to Mary. Therefore, the events in Luke's account sequentially precede those in Matthew. Unlike Matthew's account, no mention is made of calling him Immanuel.

Gabriel then offers information about the child yet to be born: "He will be great, and will be called the Son of the Most High, and God will give him the throne of his ancestor David. He will reign over the house of Jacob forever, and of his kingdom there will be no end" (vv. 32–33). This is a possible allusion to Isa 9:6 (LXX) and/or Daniel's night vision of the son of man receiving "an everlasting kingdom" (Dan 7:14). God is the giver of the throne.

These verses echo "the great Davidic covenant of 2 Samuel 7 in which King David is promised that his throne and kingdom would be established forever" (Evans 1990, 25). As Fitzmyer demonstrates, the parallel is obvious (1970, 338):

2 Sam 7:9	"a great name"	Luke 1:32	"he will be great"
13	"the throne of his kingdom"	32	"throne of his father David
14	"he will be my son"	32	"Son of the Most High"
16	"your house and Your house"	32	"king over the house of Jacob forever"

Verses 32–33 possibly allude to Ezekiel's vision of dead bones, which deal with the resurrection of Israel and the reunification of the nation: "Mortal, these bones are the whole house of Israel" (Ezek 38:11); "My servant David shall be king over them" (v. 24); and "my servant David shall be their prince forever" (v. 25). Jesus as David's successor will usher in the eschatological kingdom and fulfill the "everlasting covenant" through which the nations come to know the Lord (vv. 26–28). As "Son of the Most High," his reign will be perpetual and will challenge Rome's claim of being an "empire without end" (Virgil, Aen. 1.279). Luke's readers know already that at his resurrection and ascension, Jesus took possession of David's throne (Acts 2:30; Rom 1:4; Phil 2:6).

Mary must wonder what this means. Does God intend to use her as an instrument to restore the kingdom to Israel? Will she bear Israel's deliverer? The entire episode must seem outlandish, but Luke wants his readers to understand that is God's intent.

When Mary learns of God's plan, she asks for clarification: "How can this be, since I am a virgin?" (v. 34). The angel replies, "The Holy Spirit will come upon you, and the power of the Most High will overshadow you" (v. 35a). Note the parallelism:

> Line 1   "The Holy Spirit will come upon you"
> Line 2   "The power of the Most High will overshadow you"

Any attempt to discern the process by which the conception takes place is misguided. No sexual connotation is implied, and there is no suggestion that the birth will be the result of a sexual encounter between God and Mary as in some of the Roman myths (Suetonius, *Augustus*, 94). Line 1 is reminiscent of the Genesis account where "the Spirit of the Lord moved over the face of the waters" and God spoke things into creation (Gen 1:1–2). The divine Spirit creates life. In a similar manner, the Spirit moves eschatologically to create a new beginning: "therefore the child to be born will be holy; he will be called Son of God" (v. 35b)—i.e., set apart for his messianic mission. The Spirit is God's powerful creative agent and will later overshadow Christ followers and give birth to the church (Acts 1:8; 2:4, 38–39).

As a sign that all will unfold as predicted, Gabriel informs Mary that Elizabeth, her "barren" relative, is also pregnant (v. 36). Both pregnancies are miracles. This may have been designed to embolden Mary and strengthen her faith. Gabriel then proclaims, "For nothing will be impossible with God" (v. 37). The Greek term *rhema*, often translated "word," stands at the end of the sentence in the Greek text. The sentence thus carries the idea that nothing God *says* is without results. His words are accompanied by divine action and are thus self-fulfilling. They do not return void (Isa 55:11).

We glimpse this meaning in Mary's response as she submits to God's will: "Here am I, the servant of the Lord; let it be with me according to your word [*rhema*]" (v. 38). Mary makes herself available for the Lord's use.

The narrator concludes his account of the annunciation with Mary making a hasty trek to Jerusalem to visit Elizabeth (Luke 1:39).

Mary Visits Elizabeth

While Mary's visit to Elizabeth is not directly related to the birth of Jesus, the narrative offers us additional insight into the nature and scope of Jesus' future mission. To that end, we will make a few relevant observations.

This section constitutes an interchange between Mary and Elizabeth and includes two Spirit-inspired odes. First, Elizabeth breaks into song and pronounces Mary to be blessed for having taken God at his word and believing all that the angel prophesied. In this song, popularly called *Ave Maria* (Latin), Elizabeth addresses Mary as "the mother of our Lord" (Luke 1:40–45). This "is the first time 'Lord' is applied to Jesus" in the Gospel of Luke (Garland 2011, 93).

In turn, Mary breaks into praise. In her ode, traditionally called the *Magnificat*, she exalts God's greatness, proclaims his holiness, and announces that he is merciful toward all who fear him (1:46–55). The song begins, "My soul magnifies the Lord, and my spirit rejoices in God my Savior" (vv. 46–47) and closely reflects Hannah's song (1 Sam 2:1–10). After God opened her fruitless womb and gave her a son, Hannah praised him with these words: "My heart exults in the Lord; my strength is exalted in my God" (v. 1). Both Mary's and Hannah's sons were destined to do great things.

In the second stanza, the hymn shifts direction and portrays God as a mighty warrior who will cause a political and social reversal under the reign of the Messiah. Mary intones:

> He has shown strength with his arm;
> > he has scattered the proud in the thoughts of their hearts.
> He has brought down the powerful from their thrones
> > and lifted up the lowly ones;
> he has filled the hungry with good things,
> > and sent the rich away empty.
> He has helped his servant Israel,
> > in remembrance of his mercy,
> according to the promise he made to our ancestors,
> > To Abraham and to his descendants [seed] forever.
>
> (Luke 1:51–55)

Although the lyrics are in the aorist tense, they point to the future rule of Messiah. Green calls this "eschatological anticipation" (Green 1997, 59), which focuses on liberation from oppression.

The theme of stanza two is clearly about liberation and covenant justice. The powerful will be deposed, and the captives set free. Verses 52–53 mention explicitly three ways God will act on behalf of the oppressed. Each verse takes the form of a contrasting or antithetical parallelism. Each describes ways God will be merciful to his people. First, with a strong "arm" he will defend Israel and defeat its enemies. Israel's opponents are no match for him (v. 51). Second, he will dethrone "the powerful" and promote the lowly (v. 52). Mary is one of the latter along with most peasant Jews. Third, he will provide food for the famished and conversely cause "the rich" to scavenge for food (v. 53).

Verse 54 reintroduces the theme of mercy, which was first mentioned in verse 50, and serves to summarize stanza two. God has acted compassionately toward the nation throughout its long and bumpy history. The basis for his mercy is his ongoing covenant faithfulness: "the promise he made to . . . Abraham and to his seed" (v. 55). As long as Abraham's seed survives, the promise remains in effect.

In the end, justice will prevail. Wickedness will be banished. The world will come under the reign of God. Rulers will bow the knee in submission to Christ as Lord. The Lukan community, living under Roman domination, likely sang the lyrics of the Magnificat during worship. Could anything be more subversive? The song acknowledges that the God of Jesus sides with the poor and oppressed. He will bring political strongmen to their knees, upend the social structure, and install a new king to rule on his behalf. Mary's song is, therefore, a musical call for God's people to acknowledge a king other than Caesar.

The Birth of Jesus

Luke gives little information regarding the actual birth of Jesus, other than to say it took place. He opens this section of his narrative by placing Jesus' birth in its sociopolitical context: "In those days a decree went out from Emperor Augustus that all the world should be registered" (Luke 2:1). The registration or census was a vehicle the empire used to count the population and determine the amount of taxes the tributary nations owed Rome. Taxation was a means of exercising power over people, and it enabled a ruler to determine the number of his subjects and the soldiers he needed to keep them subservient. This census was a tool of oppression.

Luke adds, "This was the first registration [census] and was taken while Quirinius was governor of Syria" (v. 2). There is no reference outside the Gospel of Luke to a worldwide census taking place under Caesar Augustus and carried out in Syria in 4 BCE. Josephus dates Quirinius's governorship a decade later (Josephus, *Ant* 18.1–4). While many have sought to explain away the discrepancy, it may be that Luke is simply not concerned with specific dates any more than Matthew is in the accuracy of his genealogy. Possibly, Luke is using the taxation story as a literary device to get the couple to Bethlehem, Joseph's ancestral home (vv. 3–5), where Messiah must be born (Fitzmyer 1981, 393).

> While they were there, the time came for her to deliver her child. And she gave birth to her firstborn son and wrapped him in bands of cloth, and laid him in a manger, because there was no place for them in the inn. (Luke 2:6–7)

"While" conveys the idea that Mary and Joseph are in Bethlehem for a period of time before the birth. With no lodgings available, a stable or possibly a cave becomes the delivery room, and the animal trough serves as the newborn's cradle. The circumstances speak to the economic poverty of the family. The Jewish Messiah lacks status. Unlike Caesar, who was born into the lap of luxury, Jesus is born into poverty in a backwater town on the easternmost edge of the empire. That such a one is destined to rescue Israel from oppression challenges logic and must cause Joseph and Mary to wonder if their angelic visit was not a deceiving spirit.

The Shepherds and the Angels

The shepherds' visit serves a similar purpose as the visit of the magi. Both attest to Jesus' identity as Messiah. Whereas the magi are Gentile foreigners from the East, the sheepherders are Judean locals. The former are men of wealth, while the latter are of little means. People of status and those without status are witnesses to Jesus' kingship.

Prior to their visit, the shepherds are busy at night protecting their flock, possibly in the same fields as David a thousand years before, when an unnamed angel suddenly appears and God's glory shines over the land (vv. 8–9). The angel announces, "Do not be afraid; for see—I am bringing you good news of great joy for all the people: to you is born this day in the city of David a Savior, who is the Messiah, the Lord" (vv. 10–11). This can mean only one thing: God is about to reestablish David's throne and set up his kingdom. The promise made centuries before are being fulfilled "this day" (Garland 2011, 123).

For the shepherds (ca. 4 BCE), as well as for Luke's readers (ca. 80 BCE), the language of "good news" is familiar. Caesar Augustus is the recognized author of good news. He rescued the Republic and transformed it into a thriving and expanding empire. As such, Caesar is lord (*kyrios*) and savior (*sōtēr*). The angelic message challenges Caesar's claim. Another "Savior" and "Lord" has been born. He is the Jewish Messiah.

Gabriel then offers tangible proof to verify his pronouncement: "This will be a sign for you: you will find a child wrapped in bands of cloth [swaddling clothes] and lying in a manger" (v. 12). Newborns were customarily wrapped tightly in swaths of cloth (Pliny, *Nat.* 7.2–3); this alone cannot be the sign. But what if one spotted a baby sleeping in an animal food trough?

Fitzmyer observes that Luke's narrative brings to memory the saying of Isa 1:3 (LXX), "An ox knows its owner and an ass the manger of its lord, but Israel knows me not, and my people do not comprehend" (Fitzmyer 1970, 394). Israel's elitist leaders will miss out on the birth of their Messiah, but lowly shepherds and animals of the stable will be eyewitnesses to the dawning of a new age. Jesus is Messiah of the common people.

> And suddenly there was with the angel a multitude of the heavenly host, praising God and saying, "Glory to God in the highest heaven, and on earth peace among those whom he favors!" (Luke 2:13–14)

The angelic song is a further challenge to Caesar's claims. Roman peace (*pax Romana*) was Caesar's greatest gift to the world. It entailed a promise of peace and security for all living under the protection of Rome. But according to Gabriel, Roman peace is inadequate. It will be supplanted by a new kind of peace (*pax Christi*).

On their travels to and from the site of discovery, the shepherds tell of their incredible encounter with the angels and the eschatological message they brought, "and all who heard it were amazed at what the shepherds told them" (vv. 15–18, 20). The shepherds become the first heralds of the good news of Christ and his kingdom.

Everyone is ecstatic, including Mary, but she is also perplexed. Luke writes that she "treasured" and "pondered" the events of the past nine months and their meaning. She has kept her commitment to God, and the plan is now unfolding before her eyes. What will the future hold?

Conclusion

In their respective birth narratives, Matthew and Luke provide readers with insight into Jesus' identity and his central role in God's eschatological scheme of the ages:

1. Mary, a Jewish teenager, conceives miraculously and gives birth to a son.

2. The child is genealogically connected to Abraham, the father of God's people and to David, its ideal king; thus the child is the "Son of Abraham" and the "Son of David."

3. He is the legitimate heir to the Davidic throne and will liberate Israel, restore its kingdom, and establish God's eternal reign of peace on earth.

4. He vies with Herod and all his successors who claim to be "king of the Jews."

5. He challenges Caesar's claim to be "Lord" and "Savior."

6. His message is good news for the poor, marginal, and disenfranchised. He will reverse their status and misfortunes in the kingdom. Justice will prevail.

7. The Messiah will fulfil the Abrahamic promise and bring Gentiles into the kingdom and give them equal status with Christ-following Jews.

8. The participants and witnesses to Jesus' birth in 4 BCE have no inkling that Jesus will be crucified. They expect him to overthrow Rome and usher in God's earthly kingdom.

9. Matthew's and Luke's readers living in post-70 CE know how the events actually turned out: God raised Jesus from the dead and took him to heaven from which he reigns.

10. The Gospel readers also know that the church is the present locus of the kingdom on earth. Its members practice kingdom ethics and proclaim the good news to others as they wait for Jesus to return from heaven and set up his kingdom on earth when all people will worship the Jewish Messiah.

11. The virgin birth is a necessary and integral part of God's plan for the ages.

For centuries, the church has taken the canonical Gospel accounts of Jesus' birth at face value. Every week, Christ followers from around the world come together to declare faith in Jesus as their Messiah and Lord by reciting these words of the Apostles' Creed:

> I believe in God, the Father Almighty,
> maker of heaven and earth;
>
> And in Jesus Christ his only begotten Son, our Lord;
> who was conceived by the Holy Spirit,
> born of the Virgin Mary.

Works Cited

Borg, Marcus, and John Dominic Crossan. 2007. *The First Christmas: What the Gospels Really Teach about Jesus' Birth*. New York: Harper One.

Bovon, François. 2002. *A Commentary on the Gospel of Luke 1–9:50*. Hermeneia. Minneapolis, MN: Fortress Press.

Brown, Raymond E. 1977. *The Birth of the Messiah: A Commentary on the Infancy Narratives in Matthew and Luke*. New York: Doubleday.

Carter, Warren. 2016. *Telling Tales about Jesus: An Introduction to New Testament Gospels*. Minneapolis, MN: Fortress Press.

Carter, Warren, and Amy-Jill Levine. 2013. *The New Testament: Methods and Meanings*. Nashville: Abingdon.

Davies, W. D., and Dale C. Allison, Jr. 1988. *Matthew 1–7*. Vol. 1 of *A Critical and Exegetical Commentary on the Gospel According to Saint Matthew*. ICC. Edinburgh: T&T Clark.

deSilva, David A. 2018. *An Introduction to the New Testament: Content, Methods, and Ministry Formation*. 2nd ed. Downers Grove, IL: IVP Academic.

Evans, Craig A. 1990. *Luke*. NIBC. Peabody, MA: Hendrickson.

Fitzmyer, Joseph A. 1981. *The Gospel According to Luke I–IX*. AB 28. New York: Doubleday.

Garland, David E. 2011. *Luke*. BECNT. Grand Rapids: Zondervan.

Green, Joel B. 1997. *The Gospel of Luke*. NICNT. Grand Rapids: Eerdmans.

Horsley, Richard A. 1993. *The Liberation of Christmas: The Infancy Narrative in Social Context*. New York: Continuum.

Kingsbury, Jack Dean. 2001. "The Birth Narrative in Matthew." Pages 154–65 in *The Gospel of Matthew in Current Study*. Edited by David E. Aune. Grand Rapids: Eerdmans.

Levine, Amy-Jill, and Ben Witherington III. 2018. *The Gospel of Luke*. New Cambridge Bible Commentary. Cambridge: Cambridge University Press.

McCartney, Dan, and Peter Enns. 2001. "Matthew and Hosea: A Response to John Sailhamer." *WTJ* 63: 97–105

Nolland, John. 1989. *Luke 1:1–9:20*. WBC 35A. Dallas: Word.

Wright, N. T., and Michael Bird. 2019. *The New Testament in Its World*. Grand Rapids: Zondervan.

3.3 Jesus' Jewish Miracles

Craig L. Blomberg
with Hannah E. Pachal

Biblical scholarship at times runs in cycles. The "history of religions" school of thought in New Testament studies peaked in the very early twentieth century. Wilhelm Bousset's *Kyrios Christos* in 1913 became the best-known representative of this movement, arguing that Christianity was more influenced by Hellenism than Judaism as the New Testament accounts of Jesus took their canonical shape. The influence of this approach gradually waned from that point on, with the last half-century clearly emphasizing the Jewish roots of NT faith as far more formative (see esp. Sanders 1985). In quite recent days, however, some voices have been calling for a return to *Religionsgeschichte*, as the Germans called Bousset's method, especially as one looks for parallels and even backgrounds to Jesus' miracles (e.g., Litwa 2014). On closer examination, the most significantly similar accounts and decisive influences are almost all Jewish. This chapter can only scratch the surface of the most important texts and themes from the Hebrew Bible and Second Temple Jewish literature that inform the milieu of Jesus' signs and wonders. It will focus disproportionately on the Gospel of Matthew, primarily because it is widely seen as the most Jewish of the four canonical Gospels. Brief looks at some of the distinctive miracles or distinctive parts of paralleled miracles in Mark, Luke, and John will nevertheless disclose similar backgrounds (cf. esp. Eve 2002).

Miracles in Matthew

Matthew 4:23–24 forms the first report of the widespread nature of Jesus' healing ministry, accompanying his preaching of the arrival of a new stage of God's reign. The first actual miracle stories, however, appear just after the narrative of Jesus' Sermon on the Mount. Matthew 8:1–17 presents a trio of healing miracles that lead Matthew to declare the fulfillment of Isa 53:4, in which the Suffering Servant takes upon himself our infirmities and bears our diseases (Matt 8:1–17). Debates about whether spiritual or physical healing take precedence here perhaps should be resolved in favor of a third option: healing from ritual impurity given that the beneficiaries are a leper, a Gentile servant, and a fever-filled woman (Wilson 2013, 67–68). Jesus' command to the cleansed leper to show himself to a temple priest and offer the requisite sacrificial offerings demonstrates Jesus' desire for him to obey the procedures in Lev 14:1–20. The healing of the centurion's servant at a distance at the exact moment Jesus pronounced the healing (Matt 8:13) strikingly resembles a miracle attributed to Rabbi Hanina ben Dosa, a younger contemporary of Jesus, in which he prayed for the son of R. Gamaliel and knew from the "fluency" of his prayer that the son had been healed at that very moment (b. Ber. 34b). What was particularly striking about Jesus' miracle was that he did it for one of the Gentile "overlords" within the occupying Roman troops. That he could work it from a distance showed that he hadn't needed to touch the man with leprosy either. But what should have made Jesus unclean (touching someone with a defiling skin disease) became instead an occasion for cleansing the unclean.

Jesus' stilling the storm (Matt 8:23–27) calls to mind numerous OT texts. The three most commonly cited are Job 38:8–11, Pss 65:7, and 89:9. The Job passage reminds us that God set limits to how far the seas could extend their boundaries, while the psalms references allude to God stilling the roaring of the raging waves of the sea. In no sense are these messianic predictions but rather statements about Yahweh's creative and providentially sustaining powers. Jesus displays Yahweh's unique power! The sea's sudden calm and the disciples' amazement recalls the sailors' astonishment at a similar storm's end when they threw Jonah overboard (Jonah 1:15–16). Even Jesus' peaceful sleeping in the boat harkens back to Pss 3:5 and 4:8, where the faith-filled Israelite sleeps peacefully despite attacks on every side.

Exorcisms form an interesting subcategory of Jesus' miracles. The Gadarene demoniac Matt 8:28–34) offers the most detailed example, especially in its Markan parallel (Mark 5:1–20). The OT contains no exorcisms, but various accounts appear in Second Temple Judaism, especially in the Testament of Solomon, which functions almost as a manual for learning the skill. Fear of torture reappears in T. Sol. 2:6 and 5:5, while the desire of the demons to remain in the same area matches Tob 8:3. Josephus (Ant. 8.48–49) narrates an exorcism where the demon makes quite a scene when forced to depart. Particularly distinctive of Jesus' practice is that he uses no incantations, spells, or paraphernalia at all. He does not even pray to God, as Jewish exorcists typically did, but commands the demons directly and they are compelled to exit at once. Comments like those in Matt 8:29 have particularly puzzled commentators; why do demons consistently disclose Jesus' identity, and why is that often the catalyst for their expulsion? Graham Twelftree (2010, 83–85) has shown that this is their attempt at exorcising Jesus, as it were. Knowing and speaking an opponent's name or title was often key to successful spiritual warfare, and probably why Mark's version has Jesus asking the demons themselves for their name and then learning it was "Legion" (Mark 5:9). Even the request to be sent into a herd of pigs is telling for a Jewish audience, since swine were so unclean.

The healing of the paralyzed man in Matt 9:1–8 plays off the frequent link between sin and physical malady, especially in Second Temple Judaism (e.g., 4Q242; 4Q510; John 9:2) and beyond (m. 'Abot 2.7; t. Ber. 6.3; Mek. Nez. 18.55–58). But the threat of illness as a punishment for sin goes right back to the establishment of the Deuteronomic covenant (Deut 28:56–61). It is common for Christians to point to this healing by Jesus as a sign of his divinity, especially when his critics reply with outrage and charges of blasphemy that only God can forgive sins (Matt 9:3). But it is not quite this simple. Priests were empowered to announce or declare God's forgiveness of human sin on the basis of their repentance or sacrifice. What makes Jesus' declaration so shocking is that he announces this man's forgiveness of sin *without* having sent him to the temple to make the appropriate offerings (Perrin 2011, 140).

Matthew's next narrated miracles sandwich the healing of the woman with a twelve-year flow of blood (Matt 9:20–22) inside the story of the resurrection of Jairus's daughter (vv. 18–19, 23–26). Resurrections (in the sense of revivification to this life) occurred in the OT as well, in conjunction with the ministries of Elijah (the son of the widow at Zarephath, 1 Kgs 17:17–24) and Elisha (the Shunnamite's son, 2 Kgs 4:32–37). Both recipients of Jesus' beneficence in Matthew would have been ritually unclean—the woman for her intermittent menstrual flow (Lev 15:19–33) and the girl because she was a corpse (Num 19:11–13). As with the man with leprosy, one would have expected Jesus to incur uncleanness when he touched the ill woman and the dead girl, but instead he imparted wholeness to them. Numerous other details also fit a Jewish context—seizing the edge of a cloak as a gesture of entreaty (1 Sam 15:27), the stigma of childlessness (1 En. 98:5), the presence of hired mourners, including flutists, to display grief at a funeral (J.W. 2.6; 3.437), and the use of "sleep" as a euphemism for death (Jub. 23:1; Pss. Sol. 2:31; 4 Ezra 7:31–32).

When we turn to Jesus healing two blind men (Matt 9:27–31), we discover a kind of miracle without parallel in Judaism. But it was one of the signs that was prophesied for the messianic future in Isa 35:5–6. Jesus will allude to this passage in his conversation with John the Baptist's disciples in Matt 11:4–5, and the covenanters of Qumran appealed to it as well (4Q521). That Jesus healed several blind people in several places in the Gospels testifies to the arrival of the messianic age and therefore to Jesus as Messiah. The same is true of his subsequent healing of a man who couldn't speak (Matt 9:32–34; cf. Isa 35:6, "the mute tongue will sing for joy"). The blind men also recognize Jesus as "Son of David" (9:27), a puzzling address to a teacher from whom they desire a miracle until we recall that David's son Solomon was believed in Jewish tradition to have worked miracles as well (Witherington 2006, 174).

We jump to Matt 12 for the next miracle, where Jesus heals a man with a withered hand (vv. 9–14). First Kings reports an episode in which God punishes Jeroboam for trying to seize "a man of God" who has prophesied judgment against him and caused his hand to wither (13:4). When Jeroboam seems to repent and appeals for the hand's restoration, the man of God prays, and the Lord grants the healing (cf. a similar event in T. Sim. 1:13–14). In Matthew, however, nothing is said about the man having been punished for any sin. The issue, rather, is if Jesus will heal on a Sabbath, which he does. At least some of the Pharisees interpret this as unlawful work, though miracles were obviously too rare for anyone to have actually legislated against them. In Rabbinic Judaism, however, the tradition developed that even a miraculous sign could not contravene what was revealed in either the Written or Oral Torah (t. Yebam. 14.6; t. Sanh. 11.4). Was this at least in part a response to the ministry of Jesus and early Christianity? The later Babylonian Talmud would certainly mirror the attitude assumed here when Jesus asks about the importance of rescuing an animal from grave physical danger on the Sabbath (b. Šabb. 128b). Jesus' *qal-wa-homer* ("from the light to the heavy") reasoning is hard to refute: shouldn't it be even more permissible to rescue a man? At Qumran, however, an animal would not be rescued on the Sabbath (CD A IX, 13–14).

Matthew's next miracle is recorded in a single verse (12:22)—the healing of a blind man who couldn't talk. Here the response of certain Pharisees seems uniquely harsh: Jesus gets his power from the prince of demons, Satan himself (v. 24; cf. v. 26). This would become the most common later rabbinic explanation for Jesus' identity; namely, that he "practiced sorcery and enticed and led Israel astray" (Stanton 1994, 167). In Matthew's context, Jesus appeals to his exorcisms and argues that Satan doesn't intentionally destroy his own work (vv. 25–27), as would be the case if he were empowering Jesus to cast demons out of people. Rather, the exorcisms demonstrate that God's kingdom has arrived. It logically follows that the king must have come and that Jesus is the king.

The feeding of the five thousand (Matt 14:13–21) is one of several miracles of Jesus providing large quantities of food or drink for people. God, of course, had supernaturally provided the manna, another kind of bread in the wilderness, for the Israelites in Moses' day (Exod 16:14–18). The tradition arose that the eschatological prophet like Moses whom God would raise up (Deut 18:15–18) would provide something like bread from heaven on an even grander scale (2 Bar. 29:8, Mek. Vayas. 5.69–77; Marcus 2000, 410). So, Jesus' miracle doubtless sent messianic hopes skyrocketing (see John 6:15; cf. also the eschatological banquet of Isa 25:6–8; though there, meat and wine typify the feast, rather than bread and fish). Second Kings 4:42–44 offers an even closer OT parallel, where Elisha miraculously feeds one hundred men with twenty loaves of barley bread. When we realize these were often no more than fist-sized chunks of bread, one-fifth of such a loaf would hardly have filled anyone up, and there would have been no reason for the leftovers that remained (v. 44).

Immediately after narrating this feeding miracle, Matthew appends the story of Jesus (and Peter briefly) walking on water (Matt 14:22–33). OT resonances are heard throughout this story. Yahweh, and he alone, treads on the sea (Job 9:8; Ps 77:10). Peter's stepping out in faith, however temporary, recalls the Israelites stepping into the Jordan River in Joshua's day before the Lord parted the waters to enable everyone to cross safely (Josh 3:8, 13, 15–17). Maybe the most important OT allusion comes when Jesus in Matt 14:27 tells the disciples to take courage because "It is I" (*egō eimi*), the same words used in the LXX for the divine revelation to Moses at the burning bush of the name of the "Lord" (Exod 3:14). As with the storm stilling, we have no messianic activity here per se but a direct parallel to the words and deeds of the Father of Abraham, Isaac, and Jacob.

Additional summary statements about healing appear in Matt 14:34–36 (and will again in 15:29–31), but the next discrete miracle story appears in 15:21–28. The incident with what Matthew calls "a Canaanite woman" (15:21; harkening back to the ancient enemies of Israel, which once occupied Syro-Phoenicia, has perennially perplexed readers). In verse 24, Jesus insists, "I was sent only to the lost sheep of Israel." This verse combines with 10:5–6 in portraying Jesus' ministry with as restricted a mission as anywhere in the NT, even though Matthew progressively prepares the reader for Jesus' charge to the Eleven at the end of his Gospel to make disciples of all nations (28:18–20). Romans 1:16 seems to be the most succinct interpretation of Jesus' intent: he has been sent to the Jew first but then also to the Greek (a synecdoche for the Gentile). Perhaps the best interpretation of Jesus' apparent ethnocentrism and reluctance to heal the woman's daughter is that he knows her spirit and wants to draw out her tenacious faith so that he can praise it and the disciples can learn the lesson not to send such a person away (v. 28; cf. v. 23) (Witherington 2001, 251).

Matthew 15:32–39 (the feeding of the four thousand) has striking similarities to the previous feeding miracle. The differences that remain, coupled with the probable locations of each event, nevertheless suggest that Jesus is demonstrating his provision for both Jews (the five thousand) and Gentiles (the four thousand) (Strauss 2014, 330–31). A very different kind of supernatural event is narrated in 17:1–9. It has come to be called "the Transfiguration," because Jesus' appearance undergoes a metamorphosis and he appears, along with Moses and Elijah, in radiance and glory. One thinks back to the six days of preparation for Moses before the Lord confirmed his covenant with Israel (Exod 24:13–16; is that why verse 1 tells us this happened "after six days"?). Moses himself has a radiant visage after speaking with the Lord when he returns from receiving the second set of tablets with the Ten Commandments, and he would continue to do so each time he was in God's presence in the temple (34:29–35). Are Moses and Elijah with Jesus on the Mount of Transfiguration because they represent the law and the prophets? Or because tradition with Moses and Scripture with Elijah taught that they never died but went directly into God's presence? Whatever the explanation, there is no doubt it resides in thoroughly Jewish backgrounds.

After his mountaintop experience, Jesus descends from the heights only to find the disciples he had left behind unable to cast a demon out of a boy (17:14–16), despite having been given the authority to do so earlier (10:8). Jesus rectifies matters (17:17–18) and explains to the frustrated disciples that they had too little faith (vv. 19–21). Not all Gospel miracles require a certain amount of faith by any means, but some do, and obviously this was one of them. It is hard to know if 17:27 implies that a miracle happened or not. As it stands, it is simply a command to Peter with a promise of what he will find if he obeys, leaves Jesus, and casts a line into the Sea of Galilee. Given Peter's track record of spotty obedience, it would be foolhardy to insist we knew he did it, but if he did, then he caught a fish with a coin in its mouth that would pay the temple tax (Exod 30:13–16) for both Jesus and him (Blomberg 1984, 433–34). Such scavenger fish have often been found in the lake, so this would be a different kind of miracle—one of knowledge or prescience rather than supernatural action.

The only other miracle of destruction in the Gospels besides the exorcisms that led to the drowning of the pigs is the withered fig tree (Matt 21:18–22). Here, Jewish backgrounds do not merely enhance our understanding of Jesus' action; they are downright crucial for making any sense of it at all. The fig tree in the OT often represented Israel, particularly as a place for the faithful Israelite to live in peace and prosperity ("everyone under their own vine and under their own fig tree"; 1 Kgs 4:25; cf. 2 Kgs 18:31; Mic 4:4; Zech 3:10). Israel was frequently represented as a tree or an entire vineyard (Isa 5:1–7; Jer 11:16; 24:8; 29:17; Hos 9:10), while a tree's barrenness could depict judgment on Israel (Joel 1:12; Hab 3:17; Hag 2:19). While rabbinic tradition used the metaphor of "moving mountains" for accomplishing the difficult or impossible ('Abot R. Nat. 6A, 12; b. Ber. 63b; Sanh. 24a), here Jesus speaks of telling "this mountain" (Matt 21:21) to throw itself in the sea and it will happen. Depending on where Jesus and the disciples were between Bethany (v. 17) and the temple (v. 23), he was referring either to the Mount of Olives or Mount Zion (the Temple Mount). Both have eschatological overtones. Zechariah 14:4 predicts that, in the messianic age, the Mount of Olives will break in two, with one side falling into the sea, while Jesus himself predicts the destruction of the temple (Matt 24:2). Either way, the old order of things comes to a violent end (Telford 1980, 238–39).

Additional Miracles in Mark

Were this a study in the distinctive theologies of the Synoptic Gospels, we should have started with Mark and then proceeded to examine Matthew's and Luke's distinctives. Because it is merely a study of key Jewish backgrounds and parallels, we have proceeded in canonical order. This means that all we have left to do in this and the next section is to discuss miracles in Mark or Luke not found in Matthew or key, distinctive details in Mark's or Luke's versions of miracles paralleled in Matthew that illustrate Jewish backgrounds. Not many such items appear.

Mark 1:23–28 does contain a short exorcism story of a demon-possessed man in the Capernaum synagogue not found in Matthew. Most of what we said about the Gadarene demoniac of Matt 8:28–34 applies here too, especially with respect to the demon knowing and declaring Jesus' name or identity as the Holy One of God (v. 24). The particular violence with which the demon leaves is repeated as well (v. 26). Here, though, Jesus shows his absolute sovereignty over the demonic world by not needing to ascertain the impure spirit's name.

Mark's account of Jesus walking on the water has an important detail not found in the parallel accounts: Jesus intended to "pass by" the disciples (Mark 6:48). In English, this can easily sound as if he didn't want them to see him. But the verb is from *parerchomai*, which does not mean "to hide" from someone but to disclose oneself to a person, as when models "pass by" judges on a walkway for review. It is the same verb used in the LXX of Exod 33:19 and 34:6 when the Lord *passes by* Moses to reveal himself as the God of boundless mercy, who nevertheless does not leave the guilty unpunished. In the context of another theophany, Jesus appears to be doing something quite similar (Yarbro Collins 2007, 334).

Mark 7:31–37 offers another unparalleled miracle. Here, Jesus heals a man who was deaf and had great difficulty speaking. The single Greek word for describing this second issue is *mogilalos*—someone who could "hardly talk" (NIV; cf. CEB, a stronger term than merely having a "speech impediment"; ESV; cf. NRSV). The only other place it appears in the entire Greek Bible is in Isa 35:6 LXX, where it translates the Hebrew *'illem* ("mute"). As with healing the blind, we have a distinctive sign of the miracles pertaining to the messianic age. But if the messianic age has arrived, then the Messiah must have arrived in the person of Jesus.

Mark 8:22–26 provides another miracle of healing attested only in this Gospel, this time of a blind man. Isaiah 35:5 must therefore again lurk in the background (cf. also 29:18). This is one of two miracles in the Gospels where Jesus uses his spittle on a person's malfunctioning body part (cf. 7:33), and the only one that involves two stages to the healing process. There are no distinctively Jewish backgrounds to either of these phenomena, but then Jesus is in Bethsaida, just across the Jordan River. While containing a significant Jewish population, Bethsaida is one of Jesus' stops in his "withdrawal from Galilee" (Mark 7:24–8:30 and possibly even to 9:29). The blind man may have been a Gentile, like several other of Jesus' addressees in this section, in which case allusions to the OT or Second Temple Judaism might have been lost on him.

In Mark 10:46–52, we learn that one of the two blind men Matthew introduced to us (Matt 9:27–31) is named Bartimaeus (Mark 10:46). For his Greek-speaking readership, Mark explains this as equivalent to "son of Timaeus" in Aramaic. In Mark 11:13, an item of information not found in Matthew is that Jesus cursed the fig tree when it wasn't even the season for figs! This was almost certainly his way of indicating that the action was symbolic—namely, of the threatened destruction of the current regime in Israel (Carter 2019, 312–13), in keeping with the OT background already discussed in conjunction with Matthew's account (Mark 11:12–14, 20–26).

Additional Miracles in Luke

Six unparalleled miracles appear in Luke, though not all add significantly to what we have already observed. There are no miraculous fish catches in the OT, nor is one promised in the messianic age. So perhaps the most significant feature that fits Jewish backgrounds in Luke 5:1–11 is Peter's reaction in verse 8, as he requests Jesus leave him since he is sinful. Numerous OT passages present protestations of their protagonists of fear or unworthiness to be in the presence of the Lord (Job 42:5; Judg 6:22; 13:22; 1 Kgs 17:18; Isa 6:5).

Only Luke contains the resurrection of the son of the widow of Nain (Luke 7:11–17). Here, the parallelism proves particularly close to the account of 1 Kgs 17:17–24, even to the identical expression in verse 23 that Elijah "gave him back to his mother" (Luke 7:15; 1 Kgs 17:23). In the case of Elisha's resurrection of the Shunammite's son, what is striking is that ancient Shunem, long since destroyed, was situated extremely close to where first-century Nain was located. With these similarities to Elijah and Elisha, no wonder Jesus was acclaimed by the Jewish populace there as a great prophet (Luke 7:16).

Luke 13:10–17 and 14:1–6 present in back-to-back chapters short miracle stories about a woman crippled for eighteen years whom Jesus healed, along with a man suffering with abnormal swelling (probably from dropsy). In each case, Jesus healed on the Sabbath; the subsequent controversy about him working is the focal point of attention. In each case, Jesus appeals to a *qal-wa-homer* argument. Jews untie animals for Sabbath feedings and rescue animals and even humans if they fall into a well on the Sabbath; how much more appropriate is it to rescue humans from the physical bondage of injury or illness? On the idea of an evil spirit causing an infirmity, cf. 1QapGen ar XX, 17, 21–29; for the allowance of knots to be tied and untied on the ropes that bound cattle, and on their need to be watered, see m. Šabb. 5.1–4; 7.2; 15.1–2; 'Erub. 2.1–4.

Luke 17:11–19 uniquely presents the healing of the ten people with leprosy, nine Jewish and one Samaritan. To appreciate Jesus' marveling that only the Samaritan returned to give thanks, one must understand the enmity between the two people groups since the origins of the Samaritans in the unlawful intermarriages between Jew and Gentile from the eighth century BCE onwards. The final miracle features only in the larger narrative about Jesus' arrest, when Peter slashes one ear off the servant of the high priest (Malchus) but Jesus miraculously replaces it (Luke 22:50–51). The attack is mentioned in the other three Gospels, but not the miraculous healing.

Additional Miracles in John

John includes five or six miracles unique to his Gospel. Perhaps the most distinctive is the first: turning water into wine at a wedding in Cana (John 2:1–12). Wine was often seen as the mark of joy and a sign of God's blessing, even the joy of the new age (cf. Isa 25:6–9; Joel 3:18; Hos 2:22; Amos 9:13–14; for wedding celebrations, see Jer 7:34; 33:11; Joel 2:16). In a short account that is so succinct that the miracle itself is never narrated, only its aftermath, it is surprising that John takes a full verse to describe the kinds of containers storing the water that was then turned to wine (John 2:6). The old stone water jars for the Jewish rites of purification now contain wine that could reflect the joy that gladdened human hearts (Ps 104:15). Just as Jesus in Mark 2:22 declared that new wine required new wineskins, here he suggests that the joy of the kingdom age requires the best wine. Jesus facilitates a celebration that goes well beyond a simple human wedding as the miracle points to his divine identity (Blomberg 1986, 335–36). The second sign—the healing of the nobleman's son in John 4:43–54—may be a parallel to Matt 8:5–13 // Luke 7:1–10, but it does not introduce any dramatic new features impinging on this study.

Jesus' healing of the paralyzed man at the pool of Bethesda (5:1–15) resembles the story of Jesus healing the paralyzed man in Capernaum. But this is a different location, and the issue is different also. Here, the focus is not on who can forgive sins and how, but on the controversy provoked by a healing on the Sabbath. It also occurs in what was one of two enormous *mikva'ot* to the north and south of the Jerusalem temple (von Wahlde 2009b). But Jesus' healing does not require the lame man even to get in the pool. Jesus heals him despite the superstitions that the pool had special healing effects. Chapter 9, however, does present a miracle involving the other largest *mikveh*—the pool of Siloam to the south of the temple (von Wahlde 2009a). As elsewhere, Jesus remains in control. He may choose whether to use secondary means, whether to link a healing to a specific location or what the relationship between the miracle and someone's faith needs to be. Jesus' command to the blind man to go and wash in the pool evokes the story of Naaman the Syrian, who was told by Elisha's messenger to go to wash in the river Jordan in order to have his leprosy cured (2 Kgs 5:10–13).

The most dramatic miracle in John, of course, is the resurrection of Lazarus (John 11:38–44), because his body had been entombed for four days. Not only should one have expected irreversible and extensive decay to have set in, but this was also a longer period of time (at least later) than Jewish tradition asserted a person's spirit still hovered somewhere near its corpse (Gen. Rab. 100). Like the other miracles in John, this is a "sign" meant to instill belief. In that sense, one may call attention to 4 Bar. 7:19–20, where a corpse is supposedly resuscitated by God in the days of Jeremiah to provoke belief among the people. The final Johannine miracle is another fish catch, of no less than 153 fish hauled in by nets that had remained empty all night. Afterwards, Jesus recommissions Peter on the shore of the lake over breakfast (John 21:1–17). The similarities with Luke 5:1–11 are telling, and they suggest that because the first of these two miracles accompanied Peter's initial call, the second one prepared for his "recall." Similarly, T. Zeb. 6:3–8 has the patriarch declaring that the Lord blessed his trawling with an abundance of fish, when the family of Jacob moved from Israel to Egypt, because of his generosity in sharing the fish that he caught with the poor. But it is not clear that a miraculous quantity is being described.

Conclusion

There are more than enough details throughout the miracle of Jesus in the New Testament Gospels to suggest that they are thoroughly at home in a first-century Jewish milieu that we need not even begin looking farther afield for backgrounds. Of course, the Gospel writers portray Jesus demonstrating certain unique features, but these are not to align himself with some other religious background. In some instances, Jesus behaves like a new Moses or a new Elijah or Elisha in a prophetic role, but also as "someone greater than" these heroes of OT times. In other cases, he shows that miracles predicted for the messianic age are starting to proliferate, suggesting that the Messiah has arrived. Or in partially parallel terms, since so much of his message was announcing the arrival of the kingdom, one must presume that the king too had arrived. In still other settings, Jesus goes beyond acting in a messianic, Davidic role and demonstrates powers reserved for Yahweh himself. After surveying all his miracles, we realize that only categories of "the divine" can fully account for Jesus' signs and wonders. And, as such, they are intended to bring to faith people who do not yet believe in him, as well as strengthening the faith of those who already do.

Works Cited

Blomberg, Craig L. 1986. "The Miracles as Parables." Pages 327–59 in vol. 6 of *Gospel Perspectives*. Edited by David Wenham and Craig Blomberg. Sheffield: JSOT Press.

———. 1984. "The New Testament Miracles and Higher Criticism: Climbing up the Slippery Slope?" *JETS* 27.4: 425–38.

Bousset, Wilhelm. 2013 [Germ. orig. 1913]. *Kyrios Christos: A History of the Belief in Christ from the Beginnings of Christianity to Irenaeus*. Waco, TX: Baylor University Press.

Carter, Warren. 2019. *Mark*. Collegeville, MN: Liturgical.

Eve, Eric. 2002. *The Jewish Context of Jesus' Miracles*. London: T&T Clark.

Litwa, M. David. 2014. *Iesus Deus: The Early Christian Depiction of Jesus as a Mediterranean God*. Minneapolis, MN: Fortress Press.

Marcus, Joel B. 2000. *Mark 1–8*. AB 27. New York: Doubleday.

Perrin, Nicholas. 2010. *Jesus the Temple*. Grand Rapids: Baker Academic.

Sanders, E. P. 1985. *Jesus and Judaism*. Philadelphia: Fortress.

Stanton, Graham N. 1994. "Jesus of Nazareth: A Magician and a False Prophet Who Deceived God's People?" Pages 164–80 in *Jesus of Nazareth: Lord and Christ—Essays on the Historical Jesus and New Testament Christology*. Edited by Joel B. Green and Max Turner. Grand Rapids: Eerdmans.

Strauss, Mark L. 2014. *Mark*. ZECNT. Grand Rapids: Zondervan.

Telford, William R. 1980. *The Barren Temple and the Withered Tree*. Sheffield: JSOT Press.

Twelftree, Graham H. 1993. *Jesus the Exorcist: A Contribution to the Study of the Historical Jesus*. Tübingen: Mohr Siebeck, 1993.

———. 1999. *Jesus the Miracle Worker: A Historical and Theological Study*. Downers Grove, IL: InterVarsity Press.

von Wahlde, Urban C. 2009. "The Pool of Siloam: The Importance of the New Discoveries for our Understanding of Ritual Immersion in Late Second Temple Judaism and the Gospel of John." Pages 155–73 in vol. 2 of *John, Jesus, and History*. Edited by Paul N. Anderson, Felix Just, and Tom Thatcher. Atlanta: SBL Press.

———. 2009. "The Pool(s) of Bethesda and the Healing in John 5: A Reappraisal of Research and of the Johannine Text." *RB* 116: 111–36.

Wilson, Walter T. 2013. "The Uninvited Healer: Houses, Healings and Prophets in Matthew 8.1–22." *JSNT* 36: 53–72.

Witherington III, Ben. 2001. *The Gospel of Mark: A Socio-Rhetorical Commentary*. Grand Rapids: Eerdmans.

———. 2006. *Matthew*. SHBC 19. Macon, GA: Smyth & Helwys.

Yarbro Collins, Adela. 2007. *Mark: A Commentary*. Hermeneia. Minneapolis, MN: Fortress Press.

3.4 Jesus as Messiah in the Synoptic Gospels

Andreas Stutz

Peter Stuhlmacher famously wrote: "Jesus's public ministry and proclamation were provocative even in his own day, and novel enough to raise questions among friend and foe alike about who this man really was" (2018, 126). This observation is all the truer when considering the prevailing messianic expectations in Second Temple Judaism and comparing them to Jesus' ministry. Thus some assumed he was John the Baptist, Elijah, or another prophet. However, the church identified Jesus to be the long-awaited Messiah. This article will look into the Synoptic Gospels and ask how the evangelists (i.e., the writers of the Gospels) depicted Jesus as Messiah.

The Messiah as the Anointed One

When it comes to the messianic designation, the New Testament writers could have adopted simply the transliteration of the Hebrew term *mashiakh* (cf. *messias* in John 1:41; 4:25). The fact that they used the translation *christos* demonstrates that preserving the term's original meaning was important to them. Furthermore, since *christos* "is never related to persons outside the LXX, the NT, and dependent writings" (Grundmann 1976, 195), the early church was able, when preaching Christ to the nations, to fill the term with the anointing concept of the Old Testament; that is, individuals being anointed when chosen, appointed, and empowered by God to carry out his purposes.

Anointing was usually done with specially prepared oil (cf. Oswalt 1997, 1124). However, there are cases where persons in the Old Testament are called *the anointed one(s)* though they were not actually anointed (cf. e.g., Isa 45:1; Ps 105:15; 1 Chr 16:22). In these cases, the anointing language serves as a metonymy of cause, referring to the effect; namely, to these persons' appointment and empowerment to carry out God's will. Thus Jesus being the eschatological *mashiakh* or *christos* did not necessarily require an anointment with oil. These rather general observations serve as a basis for the following section, which will look individually into each evangelist's depiction of Jesus' messiahship.

Shared Messianic References among the Synoptic Gospels

Looking into messianic references that the Synoptic Gospels share offers two advantages: *First*, it will highlight messianic references that were central to the early church and, thus, indispensable in the evangelists' eyes. *Second*, it will enable a concentrated treatment of these references and avoiding repetition.

The first central messianic reference shared among the Synoptic Gospels is the report of Peter's confession that Jesus is actually the Messiah (cf. Matt 16:13–20; Mark 8:27–30; Luke 9:18–21). In all three Synoptic Gospels, this report is followed by Jesus' command to reveal this to no one and with the first prediction of Jesus' death (Matt 16:21–23; Mark 8:31–33; 9:22). Thus the Synoptic Gospels mutually emphasize that Jesus did not want to be regarded as the Messiah according to the popular understanding, but that he connected his messiahship with his atoning death. (Peter's reaction shows how little he associated suffering with the concept of Messiah.) Jesus' teaching is reflected in Paul's depiction of the ancient church's message (1 Cor 1:23): "we preach Christ crucified."

Another central messianic reference is the discussion regarding the Messiah's Davidic sonship (cf. Matt 22:41–45; Mark 12:35–37; Luke 20:41–44). Here, Jesus demonstrates that the Messiah must be more than merely David's son. To be clear, Jesus does not deny his Davidic lineage but rather shows that this title is somewhat misleading (France 1985, 324). For, as David calls the Messiah (in Ps 110:1) "my Lord," the Messiah must be superior to David.

Jesus' Messiahship in the Individual Gospels

The following subsections are not to present the entire Christology of each Gospel account. This short study could not fulfill such an endeavor. Rather, the goal is to point to a few emphases and highlights. It is important to remember that the Gospels have much more to say than can be considered here.

Jesus as the Messiah in Matthew

The Gospel according to Matthew connects the title *christos* ("Christ" or the "anointed one") to two messianic epithets—"Son of David" (22:42) and "Son of God" (16:16). As these two epithets serve Matthew to describe Jesus' messiahship, the following presentation will concentrate on them and on the relationship between them.

The reader of Matthew encounters the epithet "Son of David" right at the Gospel's beginning (1:1). However, when arriving at 1:16, the reader wonders at the unusual expression, which avoids describing Joseph as Jesus' physical father. Only in 1:18–25 does he understand that Jesus' Davidic lineage is by means of adoption. As Novakovic nicely puts it: "While adoptionist christology asserts that a human person was exalted to be the Son of God by an act of divine adoption, Matt 1:18–25 asserts that the Son of God became the Son of David by an act of human adoption" (1997, 156). Thus, as Joseph is Jesus' legal father, Jesus stands legally in the Davidic line and is indeed a son of David.

Generally speaking, in Matthew's narrative when people address Jesus as the "Son of David," they acknowledge him as the promised Messiah. However, Matthew points toward the more concrete meaning of this epithet. After establishing that Jesus is indeed David's descendant, Matthew reports in 2:6 that he was born as prophesied in Mic 5:2 in David's home village Bethlehem. However, when quoting Micah, Matthew deviates somewhat from the Hebrew wording by replacing "a ruler in Israel" with "shepherding my people Israel." To be sure, this deviation does not change original meaning of Mic 5:2, for "the symbol of the shepherd to represent the duties of a ruler was widely used in the ancient Near East" (Baldwin 1988, 208). Rather, Matthew adapts Mic 5:2 to describe Jesus, the "Son of David," as the messianic shepherd-king. Thus just as David is described as shepherding God's people (2 Sam 5:2; 7:7), Jesus is depicted as shepherding God's people (Matt 2:6), who are like sheep without a shepherd (9:36), and as the one who searches the ones among them lost (15:24). Keeping this in mind, one is not surprised that people address Jesus as the "Son of David" when they need help (cf. 9:27; 15:22; 20:30, 31) and when they celebrate him as the long-awaited king (21:9).

While Jesus accepts the epithet "Son of David," he points in Matt 22:41–46 to the fact that the "Son of David" is in fact David's Lord. Here, the discussion points at the fact that Jesus is actually God's Son, probably even that "the divine sonship of Jesus ['outranks'] his Davidic sonship" (Kingsbury 1976, 596).

Jesus' divine sonship was implied already in the missing generation in the genealogy's third unit (viz., 1:12–16) together with the passive verb egennēthē ("was born"); both point toward the unmentioned father—God (cf. Nolan 1979, 223–24). However, the first to declare Jesus to be the "Son of God" is God himself (Matt 3:17; cf. also 1:22–23; 2:15). This is no coincidence, for Matthew intends to present Jesus' divine sonship as divine revelation (Pesch 1967, 416; cf. Matt 16:16–17). This divine declaration is followed by the account of Satan challenging it (4:3, 6; but cf. 8:29). In his temptation, Jesus demonstrated filial loyalty.

In Matthew's Gospel, people confess Jesus' divine sonship in key passages. In the *first* incidence, Jesus appears to his disciples on the sea during a storm (14:22–33). This scene conveys several theophanic elements, such as the disciples' fear when seeing Jesus, Jesus' call to his disciples to fear not, and Jesus' words egō eimi ("I am"; cf. the discussion in Leim 2015, 140–43; cf. Nolland 2005, 603). After Jesus calms the storm, his disciples worship him and confess his divine sonship (14:33). In this context, the worship is religious worship (cf. Nolland 2005, 603).

In the *second* instance (viz. 16:16), Peter confesses Jesus to be "the Messiah, the son of the living God." While Peter's confession is also found in Mark 8:29 and Luke 9:29, only Matthew has the addition of "the son of the living God." Matthew including these words in this central confession demonstrates their importance for Matthew's message—they link Jesus' messiahship to his divine sonship. Jesus affirms that this knowledge came only through divine revelation (cf. v. 17).

In the *third* instance, the centurion and his soldiers confess Jesus to be truly the son of God (27:54). This confession contrasts the *blasphemy* (27:39; cf. Nolland 2005, 1196) of the passersby, trying him concerning his divine sonship (cf. v. 40, echoing Satan's challenge in 4:3, 6), and the mocking of the people's leadership, again, regarding his divine sonship (vv. 41–43).

Thus Matthew links Jesus' messiahship to two titles: "Son of David" and "Son of God." This connection clarifies that the awaited royal Messiah was actually the divine son of God—revealed to his disciples and vehemently rejected by his people and their leadership. As the Son of God, he is truly Immanuel (i.e., "God with us"; cf. 1:23 with 28:20).

Jesus as the Messiah in Mark

Of the four Gospel accounts, Mark's Gospel uses the term *christos* ("Christ" or the "anointed one") least frequently. However, this should not be misunderstood as if Mark has little to say about Jesus' messiahship. The depiction of Jesus' messiahship is not limited to the occurrences of this title. Rather, the entire book of Mark is about "Jesus the Messiah, the son of God" (cf. 1:1).

Mark's Gospel consists of two main parts: 1:1–8:26, describing Jesus' power; and 8:27–16:8, describing his suffering (cf. Williams 2006, 510–12). Seeing and understanding the development from the Gospel's first part to its second part enables a better understanding of Mark's christological message. Thus this will be the focus of the following paragraphs.

The Gospel's *first* half emphasizes Jesus' many and various miracles and his authoritative teaching. It is only after witnessing all of this that Peter confesses Jesus to be the promised Messiah (viz. 8:27–30). However, the following interaction with Jesus in vv. 31–33 demonstrates that Peter was not thinking of a suffering Messiah. Instead, his confession seems to be based on the events reported in the Gospel's first half.

As noted above, the Gospel's *second* half concentrates on Jesus' sufferings. Indeed, the emphasis of this section on Jesus' suffering has led scholars to address prominence of Jesus' passion within the book's overall structure. For example, Carson and Moo note: "Mark wants his readers to understand that Jesus is the Son of God, but especially the *suffering* Son of God" (2005, 186; italics in original). And, somewhat unsurprisingly, Kähler's description of the Gospels as "passion narratives with extended introductions" (1964, 80) has been attributed by various scholars specifically to Mark's Gospel (cf. e.g., Carson and Moo 2005, 185; Telford 1999, 125). Indeed, the great attention that Mark devotes to Christ's passion is noteworthy.

Looking deeper into the structure of the second part of Mark's Gospel (viz. 8:27–16:8) affirms that Jesus' passion is a central topic. For, as Williams observes, this part consists of three sections. The *first* section (8:28–10:52) describes Jesus' ministry on the way to Jerusalem. It contains three passion predictions (8:31; 9:31; 10:32–34), each followed by the disciples' misunderstanding (8:32; 9:33–34; 10:35–41), and teaching about true discipleship (8:34–38; 9:35–50; 10:42–45). The *second* section (11:1–13) describes events occurring on the way to the temple, in the temple and on the way out of the temple. Here, the conflict with the religious leadership grows stronger and becomes more visible. The *third* section (14:1–16:8) concentrates on Jesus' death (cf. Williams 2006, 518–19).

While Jesus' messiahship was confessed by Peter in 8:29, he was, after he died on the cross, confessed to be "the Son of God" (Mark 15:39) by the centurion. The centurion's confession is juxtaposed to the blasphemy of the passersby (cf. *blasphēmeō* in 15:29) and the religious authorities' mocking (v. 31).

Since Wrede's study *The Messianic Secret*, much attention has been given to the mysteries in Mark; namely, the silencing commands regarding Jesus' identity as pronounced to the disciples (8:30; 9:9) and to the demons (1:25, 34; 3:12), the disciples' lack of understanding (4:13; 7:18; 8:32–33; 9:5–6, 32), the incomprehensible teaching (4:11–12), the motif of secret healings (1:44; 5:43; 7:36), and his secret journey to the Galilee (9:30). It would go too far to present all the conclusions that have been made on this topic. However, surrounded by so much secrecy and incomprehensible, these confessions of Peter and the centurion appear highlighted.

Jesus as the Messiah in Luke

Many of the theological themes Luke presents in his Gospel are further developed in the book of Acts. Some have even argued that Luke wrote his Gospel from the outset with the intention of continuing the story in a second volume (cf. Bock 2012, 55–57). Thus when looking into Luke's presentation of Jesus as the Messiah, one must include the book of Acts.

In the Gospels, the verb *chriō* (i.e., "to anoint") is found only in Luke's report of Jesus' teaching in the synagogue of Nazareth (cf. 4:16–30); specifically, in the passage that Jesus quotes there from the scroll of the prophet Isaiah (61:1–2 and 58:6). This reference to the anointing points the reader to the descent of the Holy Spirit on Jesus after his baptism (cf. 3:21–22 with Acts 10:38; cf. Bock 1994, 407). By applying this passage to himself, Jesus confirms that he is the anointed one—that is, the Messiah.

The wording in 4:17 suggests that Jesus himself opened this passage (cf. Bock 1994, 404). Thus when describing that Jesus *found* this passage, Luke implies that Jesus intentionally searched for Isa 61:1–2. After all, this passage is not part of the synagogal Haftara reading. With this description, Luke "emphasized Jesus' messianic consciousness as he began his ministry" (Stein 1992, 155).

By positioning this report at the beginning of Jesus' activity, Luke ascribes to the Isaiah passage a programmatic function for Jesus' ministry, describing Christ's entire earthly activity (cf. Rusam 2003, 200). According to 4:18–19, Jesus was anointed, *first*, to proclaim good news to the poor (Luke 4:18). Consequently, Luke describes how Jesus' ministry fulfills this task: Jesus calls the poor "blessed," for theirs is the kingdom (6:20); he describes them as the ones "invited" into the kingdom (14:16–24); and, answering John the Baptist's question, Jesus confirms that he preaches the good news to the poor (7:22). The poor (just as the captives, the blind, and the oppressed; cf. below) are not merely financially disadvantaged; rather, they represent the group of people who are in need and lack esteem. This group has "special need of dependence on God" (Liefeld 1984, ad loc.)

Second, Jesus was anointed to set captives free. The use of *kēryssō* (i.e., "proclaim") and *aphesis* (i.e., "forgiveness, release") is paralleled in 3:3 and 24:47. Thus within the Gospel of Luke, it seems most appropriate to understand these words as referring to the proclamation of the forgiveness of sins (cf. Rusam 2003, 185). The imagery of captivity fits this theme, for "since the judgment of captivity is tied to sin, such an association is natural" (Bock 1994, 409).

Third, Jesus was anointed to proclaim recovery of the sight to the blind. Indeed, 7:21 reports of the healing of many blind people. Thus in his answer to John the Baptist, Jesus confirms that he is the one to come (7:19) by pointing to his activity of recovering the sight of the blind (v. 22). However, it seems that one should not read 4:18 as referring merely to physical blindness but to also include spiritual blindness. After all, in Luke-Acts, blindness and sight serve as metaphors for spiritual conditions (cf. especially Acts 26:18; but also Luke 1:79; 2:30–32; 3:6; cf. Hamm 1986, 457–77). In light of this, the last healing report in Luke (viz., 18:35–43) is especially interesting: while the crowd speaks of Jesus as "Jesus of Nazareth," the blind man's faith drives him to call out to him using the messianic epithet "Son of David" (cf. vv. 38 and 39). In Luke, this is the only person to address Jesus with this epithet—and he does so repeatedly. Thus this passage is not merely a report about the recovery of a blind man's sight, but also about the movement from darkness to light; namely, recognizing Jesus as the Messiah (vv. 28–39), believing in him (v. 42), and following him (v. 43).

Fourth, Jesus was anointed to set the oppressed free. Though these words are not part of Isa 61:1–2 but are inserted from 58:6, they fit the chiastic structure (cf. Bailey 1976, 68) and support the message. This description may refer in Luke-Acts to physical illnesses; however, a "connection with exorcism is . . . near at hand" (Nolland 1989, 197). The reports of exorcisms that follow this passage describe multiple exorcisms (cf. vv. 31–37, 41). Furthermore, in 13:10–17, Jesus sets a woman free who was bound by Satan for eighteen years.

Fifth, Jesus was anointed to proclaim the year of the Lord's favor. As Bock notes, the language "clearly ties the passage to the Jubilee theme" (Bock 1994, 410). As the year of Jubilee was a time of the release of debts and slavery, so Christ is anointed to free people from sin and its effects. Indeed, this is a time of good news.

Strikingly, Second Temple Judaism does not seem to have regarded Isa 61:1–2 as a typical messianic passage. This enables Jesus to define his messianic ministry based on Scripture, instead of being defined by widespread expectations. Indeed, Luke's account demonstrates how Isa 61:1–2 is fulfilled in Jesus' entire ministry. Furthermore, when John the Baptist asked Jesus if he is "the coming one" (7:19–20), Jesus answered him by pointing at his ministry (v. 22). As the list in v. 22 opens with the healing of the blind and concludes with the poor being preached the good news, the reader is reminded of 4:18–19. Thus Jesus confirms that his activity should be considered as the fulfillment of Isa 61:1–2.

The Use of the Old Testament

One more aspect must be addressed: the use of Scripture; that is, the Old Testament. The Gospels unanimously point to messianic prophecies in the Old Testament to apply them to Jesus. The evangelists explain from Scripture that as the Messiah, Jesus had to be born of a virgin (Matt 1:23) in Bethlehem (2:6), be called a Nazarene (2:23), be proclaimed by John the Baptist (Matt 3:1; 11:10; Mark 1:2; Luke 3:4; 7:27), preach in the Galilee and its surroundings (Matt 4:14–16), heal the sick (Matt 8:16), enter Jerusalem as a king (21:4), be forsaken by his followers (Matt 26:31; Mark

14:27), and die according to Scripture (Mark 9:12; 14:21; Luke 24:25). Thus they confirm that Jesus is indeed the *promised* Messiah.

The evangelists' use of the Old Testament demonstrates how they answered the discrepancy between prevailing messianic expectations and Jesus' ministry. However, it is noteworthy that the Gospels do not debate or attack existing messianic expectations, for some of them are expected to be fulfilled in the future (see, e.g., Acts 1:6–7).

Conclusion

It seems that all the Synoptic Gospels set out to detach (at least to some degree) Jesus' messiahship from the common expectations and demonstrate the superiority of his being and ministry over all of the prevailing messianic expectations. The four Gospels emphasize that Jesus is indeed the long-awaited Son of David—that is, the Messiah. However, they equally emphasize that this Messiah is actually the Son of God who came to search for sinners and give his life for them.

Works Cited

Bailey, Kenneth E. 1976. *Poet & Peasant and Through Peasant Eyes: A Literary-Cultural Approach to the Parables of Luke.* Combined ed. Grand Rapids: Eerdmans.

Baldwin, Joyce G. 1988. *1 and 2 Samuel: An Introduction and Commentary.* TOTC 8. Downers Grove, IL: InterVarsity Press.

Bock, Darrell L.1994. *Luke.* Vol. 1. BECNT 3a. Grand Rapids: Baker Academic.

———. 2012. *A Theology of the Luke and Acts.* BTNT. Edited by Andreas J. Köstenberger. Grand Rapids: Zondervan.

Bovon, François. 1989. *Das Evangelium nach Lukas.* Vol. 1. EKKNT 3. Zurich: Benziger.

Carson, D. A., and Douglas J. Moo. 2005. *An Introduction to the New Testament.* 2nd ed. Grand Rapids: Zondervan.

France, R. T. 1985. *Matthew: An Introduction and Commentary.* TNTC 1. Downers Grove, IL: InterVarsity Press.

Hamm, Dennis. 1986. "Sight to the Blind: Vision as Metaphor in Luke." *Bib* 67: 457–77.

Kähler, Martin. 1964. *The So-Called Historical Jesus and the Historic Biblical Christ.* Translated by Carl E. Braaten. Philadelphia: Fortress.

Kingsbury, Jack Dean. 1976. "The Title 'Son of David' in Matthew's Gospel." *JBL* 95: 591–602.

Leim, Joshua E. 2015. *Matthew's Theological Grammar: The Father and the Son.* WUNT. 2nd ser. 402. Tübingen: Mohr Siebeck.

Liefeld, Walter L. 1984. *Luke.* EBC 8. Grand Rapids: Zondervan.

Nolan, Brian M. 1979. *The Royal Son of God: The Christology of Matthew 1–2 in the Setting of the Gospel.* OBO 23. Göttingen: Vandenhoeck & Rupprecht.

Nolland, John. 2005. *The Gospel of Matthew.* NIGTC. Grand Rapids: Eerdmans.

———. 1989. *Luke 1–9:20.* WBC 35A. Dallas: Word Books.

Novakovic, Lidija. 1997. "Jesus as the Davidic Messiah in Matthew." *HBT* 19:148–91.

Oswalt, John N. 1998. *The Book of Isaiah: Chapters 40–66.* NICOT. Grand Rapids: Eerdmans.

———. 1997. "מֹשֶׁה." Pages 1123–27 in vol. 2 of *NIDOTTE.* Grand Rapids: Zondervan.

Pesch, Rudolf. 1967. "Der Gottessohn im matthäischen Evangelienprolog (Mt 1–2): Beobachtungen zu den Zitationsformeln der Reflexionzitate." *Bib* 48: 395–420.

Rusam, Dietrich. 2003. *Das Alte Testament bei Lukas.* Berlin: de Gruyter.

Stein, Robert H. 1992. *Luke.* NAC 24. Nashville: Broadman & Holman.

Stuhlmacher, Peter. 2018. *Biblical Theology of the New Testament.* Edited by J. Ådna. Translated by D. P. Bailey. Grand Rapids: Eerdmans.

Telford, W. R. 1999. *The Theology of the Gospel of Mark.* Cambridge: Cambridge University Press.

Williams, Joel. 2006. "Does Mark's Gospel Have an Outline?" *JETS* 49: 505–25.

Wrede, William. 1971. *The Messianic Secret.* Translated by J. C. G. Greig. London: James Clarke.

3.5 The Feasts of Israel in John's Gospel

Carsten Claussen

The Fourth Gospel is a text of Jewish feasts and festivals (cf. Claussen 2008, 200–3). Already the witness of John the Baptist very likely relates Jesus to Passover when he refers to him as "the Lamb of God" (1:29; cf. 1:36). The first sign of Jesus appears at a Jewish wedding at Cana. Directly following this episode, John 2:13, 23 marks the first Passover and also the first of Jesus' three journeys to Jerusalem to attend Jewish festivals (cf. 5:1; 7:10). Altogether, the Gospel of John mentions three Passovers (2:13; 6:4; 11:55; cf. 12:1). In the introduction of the healing of a man at the pool of Bethesda, an unnamed "festival of the Jews" (5:1) on a Sabbath (5:9) is mentioned. In the next chapter, a second Passover (6:4) sets the scene for the feeding of the multitude (6:1–14). Some controversies in John's Gospel between Jesus and his adversaries relate to the Sabbath—that is, the healing of the man at the pool of Bethesda (5:9, 10, 16, 18), again referred to in another dispute on circumcision (7:23), and the healing of a blind man (9:14, 16). The Jewish Festival of Booths or Shelters, also called Sukkot, the Feast of Tabernacles (7:2, 10) or the Feast of Ingathering, provides the background for Jesus claiming to be the source of "living water" (7:37–39) and the "light of the world" (8:12). The scene of Jesus teaching in the temple (10:22–42) takes place at Hanukkah, the Festival of Dedication (10:22). The third Passover (11:55; 12:1) draws near when Jesus' public ministry gradually comes to a close. He then dies on the cross at the same time as the Passover lambs were being slaughtered in the Jerusalem temple (18:28; 19:14, 31). Thus Jesus' ministry in the Fourth Gospel spanned at least more than two years. In the Synoptics, his ministry is related to only one Passover and a timespan of maybe only one year. In the Johannine narrative, these Jewish feasts seem to be related to certain aspects of Jesus' words and deeds.

A Jewish Wedding Feast (2:1–12)

Only the Fourth Gospel contains the story of Jesus being invited to a wedding in Cana of Galilee (2:1–12). There he performed his first miracle, turning water into wine. The wedding is marked as Jewish by the mention of water used for cleansing (2:6). A small detail of this story is often overlooked. When the chief steward observed that suddenly good wine appeared, he holds the bridegroom accountable and complains about the breach of the usual practice: "Everyone serves the good wine first, and then the inferior wine after the guests have become drunk. But you have kept the good wine until now" (2:10 NRSV). Why was it the case that the bridegroom should have been in charge of providing the wine and not the chief steward? Later on, Jesus is characterized by John the Baptist not only as the Messiah but also as the bridegroom (3:28–29; cf. Mark 2:19–20 par.; Matt 25:1–13). Thus there are suddenly two bridegrooms at the wedding: one earthly, who is held responsible for a shortage of wine; and another one, who supplies an enormous amount of wine. Ruben Zimmermann (2018, 367–73) provides good evidence for possible messianic overtones of "bride" and "bridegroom" metaphors in ancient Jewish sources (cf. 4Q171 frag. 4; T. Jud. 24:1; 4 Ezra 7:26) and also unambiguous references in later rabbinic literature (Pesiq. Rab. 37). So, when John portrays Jesus as stepping in for an earthly bridegroom at a wedding by providing more and even better wine, it may be the case that he sees Jesus subtly revealing himself as the messianic bridegroom and also as the fulfillment of Israel's hopes for a bountiful amount of wine at the eschatological banquet (Isa 25:6; cf. water and wine imagery in Isa 55:1). The witness of John the Baptist confirms such identification of Jesus as the messianic bridegroom (John 3:29 NRSV): "He who has the bride is the bridegroom. The friend of the bridegroom, who stands and hears him, rejoices greatly at the bridegroom's voice. For this reason, my joy has been fulfilled." Thus in the combination of John 2–3, "the bridegroom metaphor is an example of Johannine distinction yet part of the milieu of Jewish messianism" (Zimmermann 2018, 381; cf. Wheaton 2015, 54–59), and at the same time part of John's attempt to present Jesus as the true fulfillment of expectations raised by a Jewish feast.

Sabbath (5:1–47; 7:14–24; 9:1–41)

The Sabbath was already a central identity and boundary marker (cf. Dunn 1988, lxix, lxxi) in ancient Judaism. However, and especially in the Fourth Gospel, the episodes relating to the weekly Sabbath feast (Yee 1989, 39–47) also articulate Christology (esp. 5:17–18; cf. 5:9, 10, 16; 7:23; 9:14, 16). As Jesus heals on a Sabbath, his opponents accuse him that he is violating or even destroying the Sabbath (see *elyen* in 5:18), and they "started persecuting" him (5:16). In his answer, Jesus does not comment on Sabbath observance as such, but he talks about his special relationship with his Father. This increases the debate with his opponents: "For this reason the Jews were seeking all the more to kill him, because he was not only breaking the Sabbath but was also calling God his own Father, thereby making himself equal to God" (5:18

NRSV). How are the issues of Sabbath observance and of Jesus' relationship to God related? For Jesus' opponents, there must have been a clear conviction that according to Gen 2:2–3 (NRSV), "God rested on the seventh day from all the work he had done. So, God blessed the seventh day and hallowed it, because on it God rested from all the work that he had done in creation." However, as Philo already points out, this only means that God's activity on the seventh day required no labor. Nevertheless, since all creation continues to depend on him, he never ceases from his activity (Philo, *Alleg. Interp.* 1.5, 18; *Cher.* 87). Therefore, when Jesus performs a sign on the Sabbath, he is subtly claiming that due to his special relationship with God, such activity is allowed for him. What his opponents see as a breach of Sabbath observance is indeed an implicit proclamation of his unique relationship with God, whom he calls "*my* Father" (5:17). Jesus' way of celebrating the feast of Sabbath includes performing a sign that reveals his christological identity.

Passover (John 1:29; 2:13–25; 6; 13–19)

Unlike the Synoptics, the Gospel of John reports three festivals of Passover in Jerusalem (2:13; 6:4; 11:55; cf. 12:1; 13:1; 18:28, 39; 19:14). Passover commemorates the exodus from Egypt (cf. Exod 12:21–23, 27). The origin as an apotropaic rite is illustrated by the blood sprinkled at the entrances of the Israelites' dwelling places. This rite was meant to avert the deadly punishment the Egyptians were about to execute (Exod 12:12–13, 23). By the time of Jesus, large numbers of pilgrims went up to Jerusalem for Passover (Josephus *J.W.* 6.422–423; cf. Luke 2:41–42). For the celebration of the feast, which was originally celebrated in the family home, an unblemished lamb was slaughtered in the temple. This happened on the "Day of Preparation" (i.e., the fourteenth of Nisan). Then, when the fifteenth of Nisan began just after sunset, the lamb would be eaten.

In the Fourth Gospel, the interpretation of Jesus' death is linked to imagery from Passover. When John the Baptist sees Jesus, he declares: "Here is the Lamb of God who takes away the sin of the world!" (1:29; cf. 1:36). It is not so clear why Jesus is called "the Lamb." The Passover lamb is not a sacrifice for sin. Thus, it is quite likely that multiple streams of tradition flow together in this verse. The reference may partly be to the servant lamb of Isa 53:7. However, the later Johannine presentation of Jesus as the Passover lamb may shed some light on this verse.

The earliest undisputed mention of Passover in the Fourth Gospel occurs in the story of Jesus' protest against money changing in the temple precincts (2:13–25). The pericope begins with a reference to Jesus' first journey and pilgrimage to Jerusalem when "the Passover of the Jews was near" (2:13). Unlike the Synoptics, the Fourth Gospel presents the story of the cleansing of the temple and thus the beginning of the confrontation with the Jewish authorities and opponents very early in the narrative. In this context, one finds the first references to Jesus being lifted up on the cross (2:19–22) and to his resurrection (2:22). Although Passover is mentioned explicitly, there are no specific references to this festival in the whole scene. However, it is noteworthy that the text connects Passover to Jesus' passion, a connection that will gradually unfold, and that travel to Jerusalem is linked to controversy.

When the second Passover is reported as being near (6:4), there is surprisingly no mention of a pilgrimage of Jesus up to Jerusalem. Here, it becomes clear that the references to Passover also serve as a literary device and a signal for the upcoming final travel of Jesus to Jerusalem. The opposition between Jesus and his adversaries is also emphasized in another way: "While crowds of pilgrims are making their way to Jerusalem, another crowd is thronging around Jesus in Galilee" (Culpepper 1998, 154). However, this impression is only short lived. By the end of the chapter, not only the crowds but also "many of his disciples" (6:60, 66) will have left Jesus. Two metaphors in particular that are linked to Passover stand out in this story. First, the central motif of Jesus' speech is "bread." Already, the feeding of the multitude is reminiscent of God providing the exodus people with manna (Exod 16). The reference to Moses makes this explicit: "Very truly, I tell you, it was not Moses who gave you the bread from heaven, but it is my Father who gives you the true bread from heaven. For the bread of God is that which comes down from heaven and gives life to the world" (6:32–33). The Passover tradition also includes the manna tradition. However, while the feeding of the multitude as well as the feeding of the Israelites in the desert only provided food with a short-lasting effect, Jesus proclaims himself as the bread that brings eternal life (6:40, 51). Second, "blood" is also linked to Passover. The blood of the Passover lamb served an apotropaic purpose to save the Israelites' lives in Egypt (Exod 12:7, 13). The references to eating Jesus' flesh and blood (6:51c–58) are clearly related to the Passover tradition, and they also point to the interpretation of Jesus as the eschatological Passover lamb.

For a third time, the formula "the Passover of the Jews was near" appears in John 11:55 (cf. 2:13; 6:4); it is mentioned just after the narrative reveals the plot to kill Jesus (11:45–53). So far, Passover has always been "near," but now it finally comes. Moreover, the connection is even clearer: the chronology of Passover provides the framework for the passion narrative. Finally, readers are informed about the preparations for the feast. These have not been mentioned before, but now people are traveling to Jerusalem. They purify themselves. Furthermore, they wonder whether Jesus may turn up at the festival. His opponents were looking for information about his whereabouts and started to plan his arrest (11:55–57). The date and place of Jesus' abode are mentioned at the beginning of the following episode of Mary anointing Jesus: "Six days before the Passover Jesus came to Bethany, the home of Lazarus, whom he had raised from the dead" (12:1 NRSV). However, even a chapter later, Passover had still not come (13:1). The next indication of the chronology follows just before Jesus is brought before Pilate: "Then they took Jesus from Caiaphas to Pilate's headquarters. It was early in the morning. They themselves did not enter the headquarters, so as to avoid ritual defilement and to be able to eat the Passover" (18:28 NRSV). Thus the readers are informed that the Seder evening, the fifteenth of Nisan, had not yet begun. In contrast to the Synoptic Gospels, where Jesus celebrated the Seder together with his disciples (Mark 14:12–26 parr.) and was then crucified on the first day of Passover (i.e., the fifteenth of Nisan), this is different here. In John's Gospel, Jesus was arrested on the "Day of Preparation" (i.e., the fourteenth of Nisan). This dating is confirmed in John 19:14, "Now it was the day of Preparation for the Passover; and it was about noon," and repeated in John 19:31, 42. The crucifixion then takes place at precisely the same time that the Passover lambs are slaughtered in the temple—i.e., during the afternoon of the fourteenth of Nisan (cf. Philo *Spec.* 2.145; Josephus, *J.W.* 6.423; Jub. 49:10–12).

More aspects of Passover imagery appear in the nearer context of the crucifixion. In order to provide Jesus with a drink of sour wine as he hangs on the cross, they "put a sponge full of the wine on a branch of hyssop and held it to his mouth." The mention of hyssop is reminiscent of the exodus narrative. At the first Passover in Egypt, the Israelites were supposed to "take a bunch of hyssop, dip it in the blood that is in the basin, and touch the lintel and the two doorposts with the blood in the basin" (Exod 12:22). By mentioning hyssop, the Fourth Evangelist recalls the role of the blood, which saved the Israelites' lives long ago, and links it to Jesus' blood, which leads to eternal life (6:54). Another even more striking indication for the identification of Jesus with the Passover lamb is provided by the renunciation of the crurifragium. Often, the legs of a crucified person were broken with an iron club to speed up the execution process and to hasten the death. To find out whether Jesus had already died, the soldiers pierced his side with a spear (19:34). The Fourth Gospel sees both of these actions as fulfillment of Old Testament traditions and quotes the following verses: "None of his bones shall be broken" (19:36), and "They will look on the one whom they have pierced" (19:37). The first verse is seen as a possible reference to Exod 12:46 ("and you shall not break any of its bones") and Num 9:12 ("They shall leave none of it until morning, nor break a bone of it; according to all the statutes for the Passover they shall keep it"). Both verses give instructions for the preparation of the Passover lamb. The bones of the lamb shall not be broken. Some influence, especially for the verbal form *syntribēsetai* (John 19:36), may also come from the fate of the righteous as described in LXX Ps 33:21: "The Lord will guard all their bones; not one of them will be crushed" (NETS). However, the identification of Jesus as the Passover lamb obviously provides a closer connection. The second verse (19:37) does not reflect a quote from the Old Testament. However, a close parallel may be found in Zech 12:10, where God talks about himself as "the one whom they have pierced."

Thus the usage of the Passover chronology, the reference to hyssop, and the non-breaking of the bones support the Johannine identification of Jesus as the new Passover lamb and signifies the protection from death, not just temporarily but eternally. In light of this, John 1:29 may then be seen as pointing to the atonement that the new Passover lamb brings on the cross.

An Unnamed Festival (John 5:1)

Little can be known about the unnamed festival, which sets the timeframe for the healing of a man at the pool of Bethesda (5:1–18). Both the identities of the feast and of the man are among the enigmas of the Fourth Gospel. The festival is set in Jerusalem on a Sabbath (5:9b). A manuscript from the fourteenth century, minuscule 131, identifies the feast as Tabernacles (*skēnopēgia*). This identification is supported among other manuscripts by the Codex Sinaiticus, which adds a definite article. Then this could either refer to Tabernacles, which is customarily called "the feast" (Daise 2007, 12; Felsch 2011, 51). Or the articular use could also anticipate the following the Passover (6:4). Textual criticism, however, points in the direction of the article being added by later copyists. Thus, in the end, the identification of the feast remains a matter of speculation.

Jesus took a pilgrimage to Jerusalem in order to attend this feast. His healing on a Sabbath provoked protest (5:10–16), and he was accused of Sabbath violation (5:16) and blasphemy (5:18). He responded with a long speech, emphasizing that his authority came from his Father (5:19, 30). The wording "a festival of the Jews" may also indicate the distance of the Johannine author from this feast. While Jesus had celebrated it, this was most likely not the case for the Johannine author or his audience.

Tabernacles (John 7:2–52; 8:12)

The Feast of Tabernacles is mentioned in John 7:2 and in John 7:10, 14, 37. The celebration of this festival covers at least John 7:2–52, but it may also relate to John 8:12. Compared to John 5, the controversies between Jesus and his adversaries now increase dramatically. While they see themselves as "descendants of Abraham" (8:33, 37, cf. 8:39), he accuses them of being children of the devil, who "was a murderer from the beginning and does not stand in the truth" (8:44).

The Feast of Tabernacles is also referred to as the Feast of Booths, Sukkoth, or simply the "Feast of the Lord" (Lev 23:39; Judg 21:19). The earliest OT festal calendars refer to it as a "festival of ingathering at the end of the year" (Exod 23:16; 34:22)—i.e., a "Harvest Festival." It later became a commemoration of the Israelites' forty years of wandering in the desert and living in temporary shelters (Lev 23:33–36, 39–43; Deut 16:13–15). During the Second Temple period and thus in Jesus' time, the three most outstanding features of this feast had become the camping out in huts, the ceremonial drawing of water from the pool of Siloam each morning, and the light provided each night by large lamps in the Court of the Women of the temple. The Feast of Tabernacles lasts for a whole week, beginning on the fifteenth of the month of Tishri.

How does Sukkot relate to Jesus' ministry and self-definition? Precisely "on the last day of the festival, the great day" of Tabernacles, Jesus cried out: "Let anyone who is thirsty come to me and let the one who believes in me drink" (7:37–38). Thus Jesus claims and indeed proclaims that he is the source of living water. This water is then identified as the Spirit, which reminds the readers of Jesus' role as the one who baptizes not only with water (3:22, 26) but also with the Holy Spirit (1:33; 3:5). Later on, Jesus identifies himself as "the light of the world" (8:12). Essentially, Jesus draws on the imagery of water and light, which is significant for the Feast of Tabernacles. He reveals himself as the fulfillment of what thirsty people and those in darkness were hoping for. While the pilgrims celebrated a joyous feast involving water and light for a few days, Jesus drives the fulfillment to the top: through him, thirst and darkness will be overcome (7:37; 8:12).

Dedication (John 10:22–39)

The Feast of Dedication, or Feast of Lights, also called Hanukkah, sets the scene for an appearance of Jesus in the temple, more precisely in the portico of Solomon

(10:22–39). As this feast was celebrated in winter (10:22), it was not as popular for travel to Jerusalem, especially from the diaspora, as it was for the three pilgrimage festivals of Tabernacles, Passover, or Shavuot. As a result, there is no mention of Jesus going up to Jerusalem, especially to celebrate the Feast of Dedication. He was already there and, probably due to cold weather, dwelled in the colonnaded area of the temple.

In 167 BCE, the Seleucid ruler Antiochus IV Epiphanes (ca. 215–164 BCE) had desecrated the Jerusalem temple. Three years later, in 164 BCE, a revolt of the Maccabees was successful and made the cleansing and rededication of the temple possible (1 Macc 4:36–59; 2 Macc 10:1–8; Josephus *Ant.* 12.316–322). This event was then celebrated each year as a feast of gladness and joy. It begins on the twenty-fifth day of Chislev and lasts for eight days, "in the manner of the festival of booths" (2 Macc 10:6). However, unlike Tabernacles, the Feast of Dedication could be celebrated at home. Among other rituals, this feast is celebrated with the lighting of lamps (2 Macc 1:8, 18–36; cf. 1 Macc 4:50), in particular with a lampstand with eight lamps.

It is meaningful that the controversies and the rejection of Jesus by his adversaries in John 10:22–39 happen in the Jerusalem temple at the time of the Festival of Dedication, as Hanukkah celebrates the rededication of the temple. This feast draws peoples' minds back to the blasphemous deeds of Antiochus IV, who pretended to be a god. In the time of Jesus, people expected a Messiah to overthrow the Roman rule and restore Israel as it had been under David and Solomon (cf. the reference to Solomon's portico in 10:23). When the Jews gathering around Jesus ask him, "How long will you keep us in suspense? If you are the Messiah, tell us plainly" (10:24 NRSV), they show their longing for a Messiah who shall free them from the pagan rulership of the Romans. However, the reaction of Jesus points in another direction. He tells the surrounding people: "The Father and I are one" (10:30). Thus in the temple where the Holy of Holies stands for the presence of God among Israel, Jesus expresses the highest christological claim in the Fourth Gospel. However, this may have reminded the listeners more of the blasphemous claims of Antiochus IV than of the Messiah they were hoping for. Consequently, they "took up stones again to stone him" (10:31).

Conclusion

The connection between the words and deeds of Jesus and the Jewish feasts mentioned in the Fourth Gospel is obvious. R. Alan Culpepper rightly notes: "What Jesus does or says here (i.e., at the Jewish festival) will point to the way in which he is the fulfillment of what the festival celebrated" (1998, 182). Thus John makes use of the Sabbath feast, a wedding feast, and the feasts of Passover, Tabernacles, and Dedication to illustrate his Christology. The Fourth Evangelist portrays Jesus as the one who is allowed to be active on the Sabbath. He is the real bridegroom who is able to provide abundant wine of excellent quality. Jesus is the new Passover lamb who brings eternal life and thus overcomes death. He helps those who are thirsty and those in darkness and thus fulfills expectations, which relate to the festivals of Tabernacles and Dedication. In conclusion, therefore, one may summarize that John is, among other things, writing a Jewish festival Christology.

Works Cited

Chilton, Bruce D. 2000. "Festivals and Holy Days: Jewish." Pages 371–77 in *DNTB*.

Claussen, Carsten. 2008. "Festivals and Feasts, Jewish." Pages 200–3 in *Encyclopedia of the Historical Jesus*. Edited by Craig A. Evans. London: Routledge.

Culpepper, R. Alan. 1998. *The Gospel and Letters of John*. Nashville: Abingdon Press.

Daise, Michael A. 2007. *Feasts in John: Jewish Festivals and Jesus' 'Hour' in the Fourth Gospel*. Tübingen: Mohr Siebeck.

Dunn, James D. G. 1988. *Romans 1–8*. Dallas: Word.

Felsch, Dorit. 2011. *Die Feste im Johannesevangelium: Jüdische Tradition und christologische Deutung*. Tübingen: Mohr Siebeck.

Guilding, Aileen. 1960. *The Fourth Gospel and Jewish Worship: A Study of the Relation of St. John's Gospel to the Ancient Jewish Lectionary System*. Oxford: Clarendon Press.

Wheaton, Gerry. 2015. *The Role of Jewish Feasts in John's Gospel*. Cambridge: Cambridge University Press.

Yee, Gale A. 1989. *Jewish Feasts and the Gospel of John*. Wilmington, DE: Glazier.

Zimmerman, Ruben. 2018. "Jesus—the Divine Bridegroom? John 2–4 and Its Christological Implications." Pages 358–86 in *Reading the Gospel of John's Christology as Jewish Messianism: Royal, Prophetic, and Divine Messiahs*. AJEC 106. Edited by Benjamin E. Reynolds and Gabriele Boccaccini. Leiden: Brill.

3.6 Jesus as Prophet in the Gospel Narratives

Jeffrey A. Gibbs

This essay takes up the question of how and to what extent the Gospels present Jesus of Nazareth in terms of the Jewish category of a "prophet." I shall begin with a brief discussion of reading strategies that have been employed, also indicating the strategy employed in this essay. Then I will summarize aspects of the Jewish background that relate to "prophets" in the Hebrew Scriptures and in early Judaism, as well as suggest how narrative readings direct *how one sorts through the data* as various voices perceive (or do not perceive) Jesus as a prophet. The essay will then comment on how "Jesus as prophet" functions in Matthew, Luke, and John.

Recent Reading Strategies

One common reading strategy arises from "Historical Jesus research," which has been prominent over the last several hundred years. Concluding that the four Gospels do not always provide credible historical information, the materials in the Gospels are assessed according to a variety of criteria to determine whether events reported or words recorded are authentic to the historical Jesus in general, or to the specific question of his identity as a prophet. This approach does not play a role in this essay.

The scholarly consensus holds that of the three Synoptic Gospels, Mark was written first and that Matthew and Luke used Mark (and probably Q) as a major source. On this basis, it is valid to *compare* a Gospel to its source(s), focusing especially on material that Luke, for instance, has added to Mark. Emphasizing texts that evoke or imply the view that Jesus is a Jewish prophet, this strategy holds that "Jesus as prophet" is an important part of Luke's Christology (McWhirter 2013, 11–12). In the case of John's Gospel, scholarship perceives earlier sources reflected in the final form of the Gospel. At least some of the data regarding Jesus as a prophet in the present form of John, then, is attributed to earlier strands of tradition that portray Jesus positively as a prophet, even if the Gospel itself in its final form prefers other christological emphases (Williams 2019, 105–7). This essay will not be an exercise in such redaction-critical readings.

The Gospels as Ancient Narratives

In recent decades, Gospel scholarship has—through more literary, holistic readings—focused on "the Gospels as they stand." This has resulted in a variety of reading strategies that might be termed "narrative" readings. This field of Gospel scholarship can't be quickly summarized. Common to this overall approach, however, are (1) a strong emphasis on the Gospels in their final form (as opposed to earlier strata or sources), and (2) an attention to how narratives in general aim to communicate and to persuade their readers, especially with regard to a "protagonist" and how that central figure of the narrative is characterized.

This brief essay will offer a reading of the Gospels as "ancient narratives," searching for how and to what extent *the narratives* positively portray Jesus as a prophet. Reading the Gospels as *ancient* rightly emphasizes their background rooted in the Scriptures of Israel and in the context of early Judaism. Reading the Gospels as *narratives* raises important questions of how to assess the portrait of Jesus as prophet as various characters within the narrative respond to Jesus.

The Gospels all presume that their readers (originally, of course, hearers) will be familiar with the Hebrew Scriptures—in some ways, exceedingly familiar. Moreover, they all also presume familiarity with the sorts of thinking common in the early Judaism in which the characters, events, and settings of the narratives take place. It is appropriate to ask, then, how the Hebrew Bible describes prophetic figures as well as how early Judaism reflected on the existence of prophets and prophecy, and to what extent future prophets were expected to arrive on the scene to minister to God's people Israel.

In early Judaism, it was the prophets in Israel's Scriptures who provided the template for how people thought about prophets and prophecy—past, present, and future. At times, scholars have claimed that early Judaism believed that prophecy had ceased in Israel during the postexilic period; this is almost certainly an overstatement

(Aune 1983, 103–6; Wright 1996, 151–52). Prophecy had continued, albeit in different forms and with different themes and formal characteristics (Aune 1983, 106–21). Despite the view that prophecy was continuing in Israel, it does seem to be the case that the very idea of a "prophet" or even a particular "eschatological prophet" took its definition and description from the accounts of Israel's prophets as found in the Hebrew Bible, as well as from other scriptural texts. Cho has argued that both Philo and Josephus are reluctant to refer positively to "modern" figures as "prophets" at all (2006, 80–83). Summarizing the overall portrait in the Scriptures of early Judaism, he offers six characteristics of a prophet: they (1) spoke for God, (2) had an intimate relationship with God, (3) could predict future events, (4) used symbolic actions to communicate their message, (5) performed miracles, and (6) interceded for Israel (2006, 93). In general, manifesting these characteristics would place a figure (such as Jesus of Nazareth) somewhere on the grid of "prophet" in the Jewish context in which the Gospels narrate his ministry.

More specifically, in the Jewish context of the Gospels there were expectations that an "eschatological prophet/prophets" would come (Aune 1983, 124). This expectation was part of a larger phenomenon; some (and perhaps many) in early Judaism longed for God to "sunder the heavens and come down" (Isa 64:1) to intervene decisively in the world. Such eschatological expectation, however, was anything but monolithic and the Gospels themselves reflect this diversity (Matt 16:13–14; Luke 9:7–9; John 7:40–43). Perhaps the most widely attested stream of eschatological expectation did not draw directly upon the prophetic pattern found in Israel's Scriptures, but rather clung to the promise originally articulated (canonically speaking) in 2 Sam 7:12–16. This royal, Davidic hope is widely attested in the Hebrew Scriptures, as well as in the extant literature of early Judaism. The Gospels repeatedly reflect this Jewish way of thinking (e.g., Matt 1:1; Mark 11:10; Luke 1:32–33; John 7:42). This is not, however, the hope that a *prophet* would appear, but rather a triumphant kingly figure in line with the original promise in 2 Sam 7.

Even when focused on an eschatological *prophet*, the available data remain somewhat elusive and incomplete. Collins rightly begins a discussion of these matters thus: "The eschatological prophet is a shadowy figure, not only in the Scrolls but generally in the Judaism of the time" (1995, 116). Based on Mal 3:1–6; 4:5–6, at times a prophet like Elijah of old was the focus; Teeple calls this view "fairly common" (1957, 3). This Jewish hope is explicitly reflected in some of the documents of early Judaism (Collins 1995, 116; Sir 48:10; cf. 4 Ezra 6:26; Sib. Or. 2:34–37).

Much the same can be said about "the prophet like Moses." Rooted in Deut 18:15–22, this hope was "in the air" in early Judaism; in the New Testament, Acts 3:22 and 7:37 reflect this. The Samaritans looked for such a prophet as part of the renewal of all things, although it may have been Moses himself who was expected (Cho 2006, 87; Meeks 1967, 223; Teeple 1957, 63–64). The clearest Jewish evidence for the prophet like Moses occurs at Qumran; two passages are commonly cited: 4Q175 I, 5–8 and 1QS IX, 11. The former places Deut 18:18–19 along with other passages in the Hebrew Bible in a context of God's judgment and deliverance. The latter contains the famous line, "They should not depart from any counsel of the law . . . until the prophet comes, and the Messiahs of Aaron and Israel" (García Martínez 1996, 13–14). The "prophet" in the latter citation, most scholars have argued, depends on the use of Deut 18:15–22 in the former. Williams, however, reasonably reminds us that the evidence that *clearly* refers to a prophet who fulfills Deut 18:15–22 is "quite limited in late Second Temple Jewish literature and later rabbinic traditions" (2019, 94). The expectation of "a prophet like Moses" is part of the mix in early Judaism, but extant sources do not show it to be widespread. There is no reason to think of it as the dominant way of thinking about "an eschatological prophet"; the data are simply too sparse.

One final aspect of the Gospels' Jewishness pertains to the category of the persecuted or rejected prophets. Aune avers that the expectation that true prophets are rejected by Israel and/or its leaders was "widespread in early Judaism" (1983, 157). Turner surveys the Hebrew Bible as well as the literature of the Second Temple period, concluding that "the rejected prophet motif recurs frequently" (2015, 53). This theme may the most consistent "prophetic" way that the Gospels want their readers to view Jesus, namely, as one who stands in solidarity with earlier persecuted prophets.

Now a brief but important discussion on narratives and how one sorts through the different voices and points of view regarding Jesus as a prophet in the Gospels. The consensus view is that each of the Gospels in its own way presents an overall "point of view" by which readers are to judge and evaluate events, characters, and what they say and do in the narrative. The voice of the narrator is the arbiter in this regard; what the narrator says about God, about Jesus, about everything is determinative. Other characters and their points of view are more or less reliable, for they may or may not align themselves with the overall point of view of the narrative (Powell 1990, 23–25). If a character in one of the Gospels makes a claim about Jesus (or about anything), the narrative is not necessarily endorsing that point of view. To pick an obvious example, when some Pharisees attribute Jesus' exorcisms to the power of Beelzebul (Matt 12:24), any discerning reader knows this does not align with the values of the narrative.

Alter offers a taxonomy for how characters are presented and assessed in reliable, third-person narratives (e.g., 1 Sam 18:14–30). His comments apply also to the Gospels. In ascending order of reliability are character portrayals by means of: (1) reported actions and nonverbal signifiers such as gestures or dress, (2) one character's comment about another, (3) direct speech by a character, (4) the report of a character's interior monologue/thoughts, and (5) assertions or explanations about a character provided by the narrator (2011, 146). Reports of action are inherently ambiguous (e.g., Jesus' healing on the Sabbath in John 5), and so are lowest on Alter's scale. One character's comment about another may or may not conform to the narrative's point of view. A character's own speech reveals clearly his/her point of view (assuming sincerity), as does the reliable narrator's report of internal thoughts or emotions (e.g., Matt 26:37). In addition to the narrator's own reliable statements about any character, certain persons in the Gospels can always be trusted in their speech: God (speaking either directly or through the citation of the Hebrew Scriptures) and Jesus (Karakolis 2017, 122). This taxonomy will guide the remainder of this discussion as we turn to how and to what extent the Gospels' narratives present Jesus as a prophet. Owing to space limitation, I shall take up in turn Matthew, Luke, and John.

Jesus as Rejected Prophet in Matthew

On the one hand, Foster rightly describes Matthew's emphasis on the general concept of prophecy and references to prophets past, present, and future as a "major interest in prophets and the theme of prophetism in his gospel" (Foster 2010, 117). On the other hand, the First Gospel evinces limited interest in presenting Jesus as a prophet. (The extent to which Jesus is portrayed in Matthew as a "New Moses" is a topic beyond the scope of this essay.) The pertinent references are in order of the discussion below: (1) 16:14; 21:11, 46; (2) 12:39; 13:57; 23:37; and (3) 17:5.

First, when Jesus asks "Who do people say that the Son of Man is?," the disciples respond, "Some [say] John the Baptist, and others [say] Elijah, and others [say] Jeremiah or one of the prophets" (16:13–14). In two ways, their answer reflects the Jewish background of the narrative. First, the disciples report a variety of speculations about Jesus' identity among the people; this matches the varied expectations current in early Judaism. Second, people are thinking of Jesus, a powerful and controversial figure, as in some sense a prophet, especially as a prophet after patterns established in the Scriptures of Israel. If people were looking for an eschatological prophet, it likely would have been like "one of the prophets" in the Bible. In one sense, then, the people have "positive" views of Jesus in that they regard him favorably.

The narrative, however, immediately assesses these "positive" views as inadequate. Jesus repeats his question, sharpening it with the personal pronouns: "But *you*—who do you say that *I* am?" (Matt 16:15). Peter answers, naming Jesus the Christ, the Living God's Son (16:16). Attributing Peter's answer to God-given revelation, Jesus validates the disciple's response. Moreover, the narrator has already named Jesus both "Christ" (1:1, 16–18; 11:2) and "God's Son" (2:15), with God himself declaring Jesus' divine sonship on two occasions (3:17; 17:5). The view of the "people" that Jesus is a prophetic figure shows that they view him favorably, but the view itself is inadequate.

This evaluation also carries over to 21:11, 46, where the narrator reports what "the crowds" think of Jesus. In 21:11, the crowds answer the question of the personified city "Who is this?" with the words, "This is the prophet Jesus, from Nazareth of Galilee" (21:11). Despite the attempt to perceive an allusion to Deut 18:15 in the bare phrase "the prophet," neither the varied and disparate expectations in early Judaism nor the larger strokes of Matthew's narrative support such an attempt (Cousland 2002, 208–13). After initially expressing a royal view of Jesus as "the Son of David" (21:9), the crowd's answer here disappoints. They view him only as the prophet from Galilee. This is then carried forward as the narrator reports that the crowds' view of Jesus has not changed, despite the teaching he has been doing in Jerusalem. Still, the crowds hold Jesus to be a prophet (21:46).

Second, in one very Jewish sense, Jesus is a prophet: he is a prophet who, like many before him, will be rejected by those to whom he was sent. Even here, of course, Jesus is much more than a prophet, as the parable of the wicked tenants explicitly states: "But last, he sent to them his son" (Matt 21:37). At several places, however, Jesus locates himself within this trajectory of Israel's "rejected prophets." His proverbial words in 13:57, as the people of Nazareth are being caused to stumble because of him, tragically join him in solidarity with earlier Jewish prophets rejected by their own people. In 12:39, Jesus compares himself to the prophet Jonah as he is being opposed by "an evil and adulterous generation"; of course, however, one greater than Jonah is here (Matt 12:41). In his lament over Jerusalem in 23:37–39, Jesus addresses the city that kills the prophets; the leaders in that city will work to hand Jesus over to Pilate, who will deliver Jesus over to death by crucifixion. Jesus becomes "the ultimate rejected prophet" (Turner 2015, 154).

Third, at times Matt 17:1–5 is brought into the mix by scholars. When the Father's voice says, "This is my beloved son, in whom I am well pleased; listen to him" (17:5, *akouete autou*), it is suggested that the last short clause alludes to LXX Deut 18:15, "You shall listen to him according to everything" (*autou akousesthe kata panta*). Scholars conclude that Jesus is likely portrayed in this text in part as the "prophet like Moses" (France 2007, 650). Several things make this unlikely. First, if Matthew intended a verbal link with LXX Deut 18:15, it would have been remarkably easy to align his wording more closely to the passage from LXX Deuteronomy. Second, the scene on the mountain portrays Jesus as incomparably superior to Moses and Elijah; when the scene is over, the two worthies are gone and Jesus himself alone remains. It is unlikely that such a sequence advances the view that Jesus is a prophet "like" Moses. Third and most obviously, Jesus' identity is definitively marked out by the voice from heaven: he is the Son of God.

Jesus Is a Prophet—and Much More than a Prophet—in Luke

Luke's presentation might be summarized thus: "Yes, Jesus is a prophet, but so much more than a prophet." Consider first how Luke 1–2 portrays Jesus, especially in relation to John the Baptist. On the one hand, John and Jesus are closely paralleled through *reliable* speech by various characters (angels, humans filled with the Spirit, or humans trusting in God). For both John and Jesus, the angel Gabriel announces the unexpected pregnancy, provides a name, and describes the significance of each. On the other hand, the narrative even more strongly contrasts the two figures: conception by aged parents pales before a virginal conception, pregnant Elizabeth names Mary's child as "my Lord," and friends and family celebrate one birth while an angelic army rejoices in the other. Note especially that John will be "great before the Lord" (1:15), and he will be called "the prophet of the Most High" (1:76). By contrast, Jesus will be "great and he will be called son of the Most High" and will reign on David's throne over the house of Jacob forever (1:32–33).

Jesus' identity further emerges via acclamations of both angelic and human spokespersons. To shepherds, the angel declares the birth of one who is Savior, Christ, and Lord (2:11). Simeon experiences the Holy Spirit's promise that he would see the Lord's Christ. Nowhere in any of this is Jesus named as prophet; in fact, he is immeasurably greater than John, who is great precisely because he is the Most High's prophet. In Luke 1–2, Jesus' identity as greater than John—as Son of God, Christ, and Lord—has been emphatically established.

Scholars point to Luke 4:16–30 as a key text wherein the narrative reliably sets forth Jesus as a prophet. Jesus reads and then claims to be fulfilling Isa 61:1–2a in his own growing ministry in Galilee (4:14–15). The people in the synagogue ask about Jesus' identity, but oddly all they say is, "This is Joseph's son, isn't it?" (4:22). Jesus' proverb about no prophet being acceptable in his hometown leads into his comparison of how Elijah's and Elisha's ministries took them to Gentiles and into Gentile territory to perform miracles (4:24–27). While this unit also introduces the theme of "Jesus as rejected prophet," for the moment note that Jesus compares his own ministry to that of two prophets in the Scriptures of Israel (Bock 2012, 162). If, as many conclude, the speaker in Isa 61:1–2a is also a prophetic figure, then here Jesus is aligning himself with the prophets of old.

In Luke 7:11–17, Jesus is reliably acclaimed as a great prophet, even as there is more. Luke is paralleling the miracle at Nain with Elijah's raising of the widow's son at Zarephath. To be sure, Jesus' miracle is much greater; where Elijah prays twice and stretches himself three times on the dead boy's body (1 Kgs 17:17–24), Jesus simply speaks to the dead young man and immediately he sits up and begins to speak (Luke 7:14–15). Seized by fear and glorifying God, the onlookers say, "A great prophet is risen among us" and "God has visited his people" (Luke 7:16). Their assessments likely are reliable. Jesus is a great prophet, greater than Elijah of old. That in Jesus, God is visiting his people is already announced in Luke 1:68 (cf. 1:78). The Nain scene indicates that not only has a great prophet arisen, but it is even more: God himself has chosen to visit his people through the one whom the narrator names there at the side of the dead man, "the Lord" (7:13).

The theme that Jesus is "a great prophet, but even more" is implicit in 7:11–17; it is also on display in the rest of Luke 7. First, Luke 7:18–35 narrates John's question about Jesus' identity (7:19). In his teaching, Jesus says that John is not only a prophet but "more than a prophet"—indeed, the greatest born of women before the coming of the kingdom (7:26, 28). And yet, Jesus has been emphatically declared by Luke's story as immeasurably greater than John! Second, in the home of Simon the Pharisee (Luke 7:36–50), Jesus' identity again is front and center. Simon thinks that Jesus cannot be a prophet because he does not know who the sinful woman from the city is (7:39). Jesus knows, of course, both who she is as well as what Simon is thinking, thus showing himself to be a prophet. He goes on, however, to lay claim to being much more. Both the woman and Simon are spiritually indebted *to Jesus himself*, and the woman's great love for Jesus is evidence of the great forgiveness he has granted her. The question of Jesus' identity arises again: "Who is this who even forgives sins?" The strong links with the healing of the paralytic (5:21) underscore the message. Jesus is much more a prophet who knows who people are and who reads thoughts. "On a completely different level and category," Jesus is the one in whom God has visited his people, exercising divine authority to forgive sins (Verheyden 2010, 199).

One final Lukan passage (at the least!) exemplifies the theme of "a prophet and much more than a prophet." Luke 24:13–35 is a complex unit. For our purposes, notice that in reply to the query of the unrecognized Jesus, the two disciples relate how they had thought Jesus was a mighty prophet, and they had hoped he was going to redeem Israel. Now, later on the third day, they have heard the women's eyewitness report of an empty tomb and angelic proclamation, but they do not believe it. Jesus calls them, "Foolish and slow of heart to believe all that the *prophets* have written" (Luke 24:25). Then he shows them from Moses and the Prophets—the Scriptures of Israel—all the things that had to happen to the *Christ*: that is, to himself. Jesus was a prophet mighty in word and deed. He was, however, much more than that, and the Emmaus disciples do not yet believe about Jesus what they need to believe; namely, that he was the Christ foretold and that now he has redeemed Israel (cf. 1:68).

Luke also puts on display the variety of views about Jesus, and this reflects early Judaism's variegated eschatological thinking (Bock 2012, 190). In Luke 9:7–9, Herod Antipas is confused after hearing about Jesus and the activities of the Twelve because "some" have been claiming various things: John the Baptist has been raised, or Elijah had come, or one of the prophets of old had arisen. When Jesus asks the disciples who the crowd say that he is, they reply in identical terms (9:18–19).

Finally, Luke also presents the theme of Jesus as "rejected prophet." This widespread Jewish view about "true prophets" is featured especially in Luke 13:33–34. There, Jesus' determination to finish his course in Jerusalem is couched in terms of necessity, "for it cannot be that a prophet should perish away from Jerusalem." Jesus' lament over Jerusalem's unwillingness for him to gather its children adds a tragic note to the theme, as it also does in Matt 23:37–39. On the way to his crucifixion, Jesus says, "Daughters of Jerusalem, do not weep for me, but weep for yourselves and for your children" (Luke 23:28).

Jesus Is a/the Prophet in John—but also the Holy One of God

John's Gospel narrative offers a somewhat different approach to the topic of Jesus as prophet. There are, to be sure, some similarities with Matthew and Luke. John 4:44 is the narrator's reliable commentary that Jesus knew he would be rejected in his own hometown (cf. John 1:11); here is the "rejected prophet" motif. In addition, early Judaism's diversity is reflected in John 7. After Jesus speaks of living water, a division occurs among the people: Is he a/the prophet, or is he the Christ (7:40–44)? The first question is left hanging for the moment, but some deny that he is the Christ because he is from Galilee, not Bethlehem. This indirectly attests to the presence of a royal Davidic expectation ("Bethlehem"), widespread in early Judaism. A few verses later, the query about Jesus as a prophet receives an answer from fellow Pharisees who respond to Nicodemus's objection that Jesus is already being judged: "Are you from Galilee too? Search and see that no prophet arises from Galilee" (7:50–52).

Scholarly study of the Gospel of John has emphasized the early Jewish expectation of "the prophet like Moses" (Deut 18:15, 18), and a few comments on that topic will conclude this section. In a way, however, what characters are referring to when they term Jesus as "prophet" in John often does not materially affect the chief motif this narrative offers. That chief motif is this: Viewing Jesus as a prophet can be a right step along a path, but the path must be travelled until faith reaches a more profound understanding of Jesus. This motif occurs in John 4, 6, and 9. Therein, Jesus' supernatural power (knowledge, feeding, healing) reveals that, yes, he is a prophet. What is not sufficient, however, is for one's view of Jesus to *remain* there.

The account in John 4 proceeds fairly quickly to the crucial moment when Jesus reveals that he knows the past and present relationships of the woman at the well (4:18). In response, the woman says, "Sir, I perceive that you are a prophet"

(4:19; grammatically the translation could also be definite, "the Prophet"). Interestingly, she continues to address Jesus as a Samaritan speaking to a Jewish prophet (Williams 2019, 97). The conversation, however, proceeds to the place where she acknowledges that the Messiah, who is called Christ, is coming to answer all of her questions. Jesus emphatically declares himself to be that Christ. This climactic moment in their interaction leads her to go and speak to fellow Samaritans and to wonder, not whether Jesus is a (or the) prophet, but the Christ. Jesus' words about reaping and harvesting indicate that the woman (and her fellow Samaritans) has arrived at the faith that this narrative prioritizes. Jesus is the Christ (John 1:17, 41; 11:27; 17:3; 20:31). Her faith in Jesus as a prophet continued to grow, and it became what it needed to become.

John 9 follows a similar pattern, again in response to Jesus' miraculous power. On the one hand, the Pharisees' view of Jesus does not progress. They name Jesus as "not from God": that is, a sinner (9:16). They repeat the view that Jesus is a sinner (9:24), averring that they do not even know where he is from (9:29). At the end they remain blind, opposed to Jesus. Contrariwise, the man born blind begins by merely knowing the name of the man who healed him (9:11, "the man called Jesus"). Next, he declares that Jesus is a prophet who, like the prophets in Israel's Scriptures, worked wonders (9:17). Criticized, the healed man refuses to back down, even contradicting the Pharisees' earlier assessment (9:16): "If this man were not from God, he could do nothing" (9:33). His faith progresses, and then Jesus finds him and brings him the rest of the way: that is, to see and believe in the Son of Man. He believes and worships Jesus, the Son of Man. As with the Samaritan woman, this is faith in the fullest sense in John's Gospel (1:51; 3:13–14; 6:27; 8:28; 12:23, 31).

John 6 exemplifies the failure of faith to progress. Given the textual associations with Moses and the manna, it is likely that in response to Jesus' miracle, the people conclude that Jesus is the eschatological prophet promised in Deut 18; as such, they regard him as one who should be king (6:14–15). Jesus, however, rejects this assessment—likely because they misunderstand what it means for Jesus to be that prophet, as well what it means for him to be a king (cf. John 19:33–38). When the interaction resumes, Jesus presses the crowds to a deeper understanding of himself as the Bread of Life, as far greater than even Moses himself (Harstine 2002, 64; Williams 2019, 99). They repeatedly question Jesus, naming him merely Joseph's son (6:42). Their faith does not progress; it withers and dies. Peter continues in faith, however, confessing Jesus not as the prophet but as "the Holy One of God" (John 6:69). Barrett suggests this refers to Jesus as the one who "comes from God and goes to God" (1978, 307). Were the crowds right in thinking that Jesus was the eschatological prophet? They were, in a sense. But such knowledge cannot be the last word; it is only a "stepping stone" (Karakolis 2017, 139), and faith must progress until it confesses the Son as the emissary of the Father.

How clearly is the Jewish expectation of an eschatological prophet like Moses (Deut 18:15–22) displayed in the background of John's Gospel? Caution seems appropriate in answering. On the one hand, the evidence for this focused expectation is limited in scope, and not every reference to a coming prophet refers to the figure in Deut 18 (Williams 2019, 94–95). (This may, of course, only speak to the paucity of ancient source material.) On the other hand, this expectation was in the air in early Judaism. In a text like John 6, where the figure of Moses looms large or in John 4 set in Samaria, one should conclude that this expectation is in the background. The mere mention of Jesus (or John the Baptist; see 1:21, 23) as a prophet, however, does not indicate that the figure of Deut 18 is in view.

Works Cited

Alter, Robert. 2011. *The Art of Biblical Narrative*. New York: Basic Books.

Aune, David E. 1983. *Prophecy in Early Christianity and the Ancient Mediterranean World*. Grand Rapids: Eerdmans.

Barrett, C. K. 1978. *The Gospel According to St. John: An Introduction with Commentary and Notes on the Greek Text*. Philadelphia: Westminster.

Bock, Darrell L. 2012. *A Theology of Luke and Acts*. Grand Rapids: Zondervan.

Cho, Sukmin. 2006. *Jesus as Prophet in the Fourth Gospel*. NTM 15. London: Sheffield.

Cousland, J. R. C. 2002. *The Crowds in the Gospel of Matthew*. NovTSup 102. Leiden: Brill.

Foster, Paul. 2010. "Prophets and Prophetism in Matthew." Pages 117–38 in *Prophets and Prophecy in Jewish and Early Christian Literature*. Edited by Joseph Verheyden, Korinna Zamfir, and Tobias Nicklas. WUNT 2 Reihe 286. Tübingen: Mohr Siebeck.

France, R. T. *The Gospel of Matthew*. 2007. NICNT. Grand Rapids: Eerdmans.

García Martínez, Florentino. 1996. *The Dead Sea Scrolls Translated: The Qumran Texts in English*. 2nd ed. Translated by Wilfred G. E. Watson. Grand Rapids: Eerdmans.

Harstine, Stan. 2002. *Moses as a Character in the Fourth Gospel*. JSNTSup 229. London: Sheffield.

Karakolis, Christos. 2017. "Is Jesus a Prophet According to the Witness of the Fourth Gospel?: A Narrative-Critical Perspective." Pages 119–39 in *Christ of the Sacred Stories*. Edited by Pedrag Dragutinović, Tobias Nicklas, Kelsie G. Rodenbiker, and Vladan Tatalović. WUNT 453.2. Tübingen: Mohr Siebeck.

McWhirter, Jocelyn. 2013. *Rejected Prophets: Jesus and His Witnesses in Luke-Acts*. Minneapolis, MN: Fortress Press.

Meeks, Wayne A. 1967. *The Prophet-King: Moses Traditions and the Johannine Christology*. NovTSup 14. Leiden: Brill.

Powell, Mark Allan. 1990. *What is Narrative Criticism?* Minneapolis, MN: Fortress Press.

Teeple, Howard M. 1957. *The Mosaic Eschatological Prophet*. JBLMS 10. Philadelphia: Society of Biblical Literature.

Turner, David L. 2015. *Israel's Last Prophet: Jesus and the Jewish Leaders in Matthew 23*. Minneapolis, MN: Fortress Press.

Williams, Catrin H. 1991. "Jesus the Prophet: Crossing the Boundaries of Prophetic Beliefs and Expectations in the Gospel of John." Pages 91–108 in *Portraits of Jesus in the Gospel of John: A Christological Spectrum*. Edited by Craig R. Koester. LNTS 589. London: T&T Clark.

Wright, N. T. 1996. *Jesus and the Victory of God*. Minneapolis, MN: Fortress Press.

3.7 Jesus and Women in the Gospels

Sisi Soref

The four canonical Gospels portray the life and ministry of Jesus as offering a unique place to women, and an honored one at that. The exact role of women in the world of Second Temple Judaism, and the extent to which Jesus' interactions were unique, has certainly been debated (Levine 1991; Kitzberger 2000). But Jesus' relationship to women is noteworthy first of all because of the volume and diversity of examples. From start to finish, the evangelists include women in the story. At the beginning, there is Anna, who is described as among the righteous remnant waiting for the Messiah and who is specifically described as a prophetess (Luke 2:36–38). At the end, all four Gospels record that the Jesus movement began with the proclamation by women that his tomb was empty (Matt 28:5–8; Mark 16:1–6; Luke 24:1–11; John 20:1–17). He had female disciples (Matt 27:55, Luke 8:3). This in itself may not be unprecedented in the ancient world (Ilan 2017), but the prominence of women mentioned in connection to this one particular rabbi is in fact unique. As a healer, he transformed the lives of women who were suffering from evil spirits (Matt 15:22–28; Luke 8:2; 13:11), physical infirmities (Mark 5:27–34; Luke 4:38), and spiritual dilemmas (John 4:4–26; 8:3–11). He praised women for their faith (Mark 12:43–44 // Luke 21:1–4), included women as examples in his parables (Matt 25:1–13; Luke 15:8–10; 18:1–8), and pronounced their sins forgiven (Luke 7:48; John 8:11). These encounters are not incidental to the narrative, they are a foundational part of the life and message of Jesus.

It is also interesting to note that the Gospels do not include examples of Jesus speaking negatively or derogatively against women. One possible exception is how he spoke to his mother in John 2:4: "Woman, what concern is that to you and me? My hour has not yet come" (NRSV). But when the language in this verse (specifically the use of the word *woman*, which sounds odd in English) is compared with the use of the same word in John 19:26–27 (when Jesus was on the cross and yet making plans to care for her), it becomes difficult to accuse him of misogyny. Likewise, Matt 10:34–37 and Luke 12:51–53 should be seen as hyperbolic warnings of the potential consequences of a radical commitment to following Jesus as Messiah and not as negative statements. His teachings on divorce (Matt 19:3–10; Mark 10:2–12) are more complicated and go beyond the discussion here, but modern commentators need to take into account both the historical and legal factors of the day (see Instone-Brewer 2002; Satlow 2017), as well as the way in which Jesus is presented throughout the Gospels.

In this article, I will argue that the specific places where women are mentioned bear a specific meaning that the author intends to communicate. Further, I will attempt to demonstrate that understanding this context is paramount to understanding the value Jesus placed on women, which leads to lessons that are applicable to all. I will highlight this through observing some of the stories of the unnamed women mentioned in the Gospels (see also Bauckham 2002).

I will focus on five accounts of women paired with accounts of men in the Gospels: the Samaritan woman in comparison with Nicodemus; the sinful woman from the city contrasted with Simon the Pharisee; the bleeding woman in comparison with Jairus, the head of the synagogue; the Syrophoenician woman contrasted with the disciples; and lastly, the bent-over woman in comparison with Zacchaeus. I believe these examples provide deep and rich insight into how Jesus related to people regardless of gender.

The Samaritan Woman at the Well

John presents the encounter of Jesus with the Samaritan woman at the well as an intentional meeting by stating that "he needed to go through Samaria" (John 4:4). Immediately prior to this narrative, we read in John 3:29 that John the Baptist gave Jesus the title of "bridegroom." Jesus' meeting with the woman at the well in chapter 4 will show the connection to his bridegroom title, when he chooses a most unlikely bride, restoring her dignity and worth and giving her a new identity and mission.

The story of a Jewish man meeting his bride by a well is seen in the Torah (Gen 24; 29:1–20; Exod 2:15–21). Several parallels are found in these encounters. For example: (1) the men are in a foreign land—Jacob in Haran, Moses in the land of Midian, and Jesus in Samaria; (2) the encounter is divinely appointed; (3) the well is a meeting point; (4) and the women coming toward the well to draw water. There are also some striking contrasts that highlight important truths in this story. A familiarity with the Torah creates anticipation that Jesus will be meeting a special woman. But then the unexpected happens. A woman from a despised ethnicity with a broken life appears to meet her bridegroom. This encounter of Jesus with the Samaritan woman highlights a striking contrast to first-century Judaism. A famous passage in the Mishnah illustrates:

> Yose ben Yochanan [a man] of Jerusalem used to say: Engage not in too much conversation with women. They said this with regard to one's own wife, how much more [does the rule apply] with regard to another man's wife. From here the Sages said: as long as a man engages in too much conversation with women, he causes evil to himself, he neglects the study of the Torah, and in the end, he will inherit *gehinnom*. (m. 'Abot 1:5; all English translations of rabbinic literature are from sefaria.org.il.)

A later passage in the Talmud continues the conversation, where Rabbi Yehuda makes a similar statement, yet Yalta (the wife of Rabbi Nachman) disagrees and offers an alternate opinion. Since Yalta herself was the daughter of a noted rabbi, she could not be easily silenced and ultimately challenged the decision in the Mishnah (m. 'Abot, quoted immediately above).

> One may not send greetings to a woman even with a messenger, as this may cause the messenger and the woman to relate to each other inappropriately. Rav Nachman countered by suggesting that he send his greetings with her husband, which would remove all concerns. Rav Yehudah said to him: This is what Shmuel says: One may not send greetings to a woman at all. Yalta, his wife, who overheard that Rav Yehudah was getting the better of the exchange,

sent a message to him: Release him and conclude your business with him, so
that he not equate you with another ignoramus. (b. Qidd. 70b)

Jesus was clearly challenging the social norms of his day by speaking with the woman
at the well, and he was also breaking boundaries by speaking with a Samaritan.
This, too, was radical. The Mishnah records the following: "Hence (the sages) said:
Everyone who eats the bread of the Cutheans [Samaritans] is as though he had
eaten of the flesh of swine. Let no man make a proselyte in Israel from among the
Cutheans" (Midr. Pirqe R. El. 38.25; for earlier tradition, see Sir 50:25–26, where
Samaritans are called fools, and Jub. 30:5–6, 23, where we are told that Samaritans
can be killed with divine approval). In contrast to this, Jesus asks the woman to give
him water. This rabbi was not afraid to be "contaminated" by an "unclean woman"
or to drink water from her "contaminated hands." Jesus is no ordinary Jewish man.
He does not reject her, nor is he repulsed by her. He lets her draw near to him by
drawing near to her. Even his request for water ("give me a drink," 4:7) was a way
of showing honor to the woman. In modern Western culture, it is usually assumed
that it is an honor to be the one who is served. But in many cultures, as here, it is
an honor to do the serving. The seemingly simple request for water was a way of
beginning the conversation by showing honor and respect to this "outcast."

When we read this account in light of the previous chapter (ch. 3), we see that
the author intends us to read those two accounts together. Nicodemus, a highly
respected rabbi, seeks Jesus at night, while Jesus seeks this unnamed, unclean,
Samaritan woman with the worst reputation in broad daylight at the well. John
Johnson notes that "one of the first observations is that John has positioned this
conversation right after the conversation with Nicodemus to create an antithesis"
(2017, 75). He goes on to say: "The two conversations are juxtaposed to show irony.
In John 3, a religious leader goes out of his way to protect his reputation; in John 4,
the Messiah goes out of His way to ruin his reputation" (76).

In each encounter, Jesus talks about spiritual truth. But it is only to the Samaritan woman that he explicitly reveals his messianic identity, saying "I am he" (v. 26).
The most unlikely person to receive salvation and acceptance into God's kingdom
(a woman; specifically, a woman with a highly questionable history with multiple
husbands, and a Samaritan as well) is welcomed by Jesus the Messiah and is invited
to share the high privilege of entering his kingdom and blessings.

The spiritual revival of the whole village is connected directly to the testimony
of this woman, which in those days would have been extraordinary since the testimony of such a woman was not usually considered valuable. When the disciples
arrive, they are amazed to see him speaking to a woman. Jesus tells them the parable
of the harvest. The Samaritan woman was part of the harvest and became both a
sower and a reaper in God's kingdom (John 4:34–42).

The Sinner in Simon's House

The woman in Simon's house is contrasted by Luke with "Simon the Pharisee"
("There was a woman in the city who was a sinner," Luke 7:37). There is a noticeable

difference in the way pharisaic Judaism viewed sin, sinners, and repentance, and the way in which the Gospels present these issues. One of the major differences is that Jesus dealt directly with both the sin and the sinner as the one who came to take sin upon himself. The prevailing attitude of teachers of the day was quite different. Arnold Fruchtenbaum sums up this contrast:

> Pharisees must neither buy nor sell to a publican or a sinner anything that is in a dry or fluid state. A Pharisee was not to eat at a sinner's table and thus partake of something that might not have been tithed first. He was not to admit a publican or sinner to his table unless they put on the clothes of a Pharisee, meaning they converted to Pharisaism. The Pharisee must never perform anything in the presence of a sinner that related to the laws of purification, lest the sinner himself should be convicted and want to be purified. . . . The Pharisees taught that there was joy in heaven when those who provoked God perished from the earth. (2017, 116–17)

By contrast, Jesus looked to associate with sinners and minister to them (Luke 15:1–2). Jesus spoke directly to shame attached to sinners by associating with them, touching them, and allowing them to minister to him. This was indeed an unusual rabbi.

When Jesus enters Simon's house by invitation, he is dishonored by his host, who withholds from him the customary hospitality that was expected in those times, such as the washing of feet, greeting one's guest with a kiss, and anointing one's head with oil (Fruchtenbaum 2016, 361). In contrast to Simon, this unnamed woman is willing to express her love for Jesus in a most extraordinary way. She has no reservations about her outpouring of emotion. Her name is already connected to something shameful and dirty. She takes hold of this opportunity and falls at his feet. She cries for her sins while Simon is cold and unmoved by his. Her tears wet Jesus' feet and her hair wipes his feet. With her lips she kisses his feet, which is a humble act of honor for Jesus, and with her hands she anoints his feet with oil. Everything that the respected, righteous man did not give the Messiah, this "dirty sinner" did. Indeed, "whosoever loves much is forgiven much" (Luke 7:47). With these words, Jesus emphasized the love of God as seen by his abundant forgiveness. Ben Witherington comments that "kissing the feet is usually the act of someone, such as a criminal, who has just been freed or whose debt was remitted, and in some sense, this was the condition of this woman" (1987, 164). Jesus shows his acceptance of this women's love and pronounces her salvation in contrast to Simon's outright rejection of her. She receives words of life and forgiveness while he receives a rebuke. There is great irony in Jesus' rebuke, which contrasts everything the woman did with what Simon failed to do. Witherington adds, "Here we see a reversal—a sinful woman is praised at the expense of and by comparison to a 'good' Jewish man" (1987, 56).

The Bleeding Woman

The Gospel of Mark has heroes, but his heroes are unlikely ones. One of them is identified by her sickness as "a woman who was bleeding for twelve years." In the account of this woman, Mark compares and contrasts two daughters and two fathers. The bleeding woman's story is written in light of Jairus, "the head of the Synagogue." Everything about Jairus is visible, while she is invisible. This noble man—respected, loved, and "worthy"—comes forward and falls at Jesus' feet, begging him to heal his daughter (Mark 5:22–23). This unnamed woman is unclean and unwelcomed. She is part of a large crowd pressing Jesus on their way to see him heal Jairus's daughter. He approaches Jesus from the front, while she approaches Jesus from the back, hidden from the crowd. Jairus expresses his desire out loud, while her desires do not have a voice. It seems he is the main character of this event, but as we read further, we see that she is the focus of the author. He is loved and respected and therefore considered deserving of Jesus' attention. She is unclean and does not deserve to be approached by a "holy rabbi." Her faith and touch are hidden from all, yet she is healed immediately. The words she hears in her ears strike deeply: "Daughter" and "your faith has made you whole" (v. 34).

Mark records that many sick people touched Jesus' garment (Mark 6:56), but only this woman's touch receives attention. Jesus stops, turns around, and asks, "Who touched me?" (Mark 5:30). He desires for her to come forward, and he will show everyone that not only did her unclean state not defile him but rather she was made whole by her faith. Further, he will show those around him that this daughter of his is welcomed and loved by him. He will speak straight into her fears and bless her with peace.

Instead of an unknown "bleeding woman" (a title that emphasizes how others speak of her), Jesus gives her a new name: "daughter." In all three Synoptic Gospels, this word is repeated (Matt 9:22; Mark 5:34; Luke 8:48). Jesus wants to show who God's daughters are: those who receive him in faith. In the same way Jairus pleads for his beloved and only daughter of twelve years, so Jesus pleads for this "daughter" who has been sick for twelve years. Jesus reserves this title just for her. I believe this teaches us that Jesus welcomes each woman—no matter how dark her circumstances are or how defiled she is—into his presence and embrace. Just as the crowd hurries to see Jesus heal the daughter of this important man Jairus, Jesus hurries to minister to this important, unnoticed daughter. Both daughters will be raised to new life.

The Syrophoenician Woman

The Syrophoenician (or Canaanite) woman is one of the most extraordinary women recorded in the Gospels. This very unlikely person receives praise from Jesus for her "great faith," and she is the only woman in the Gospels to hear those words (Matt 15:28). She is coupled with the centurion of great faith, the only man in the Gospels who receives such praise (Matt 8:10). Both are Gentiles and both are praised for their great faith.

In Mark's Gospel, the Canaanite woman's story is placed between two different crowds being fed by Jesus (6:30–42; 8:1–10). After the miracle of feeding the multitude of five thousand, Jesus commands his disciples to collect the leftovers so that nothing will be lost (John 6:12). In Mark 6:42, we read that his disciples collected twelve baskets filled with leftovers after everyone ate and was satisfied. In his book

I Am He, John Seiden says that the fact that this is recorded in all four Gospels is significant. Even the leftovers serve a purpose to teach the disciples a spiritual lesson: God does not waste any of it (Matt 15:27; see Seiden 2015, 25). Immediately after this incident, Matthew uses those words again when Jesus feeds a multitude of four thousand Gentiles: "And they ate and were satisfied" (Matt 15:37; Mark 8:1–8).

In between the two feedings of the two crowds who ate and were physically satisfied, we read this woman's words through which the reader is taught about spiritual food: "Sir, even the dogs under the table eat the children's crumbs" (Mark 7:28). She stands in contrast to the disciples, who saw the miracle of the bread and gathered leftovers but did not understand (Mark 6:52; 7:18; 8:17–18). This is evident when, right after they gathered the leftovers, Jesus commands the disciples to get into the boat and wait on the other side of the lake. Matthew, Mark, and John all mention the storm that hits the boat in which the disciples have the leftovers gathered at their feet. Mark points out that the disciples were terrified and that their hearts were hardened (Mark 6:50–52).

The fact that this woman is positioned in between the feeding of these two multitudes is significant for understanding the profound lesson Mark wants us to see: Here is a woman and a Gentile whose spiritual perception is greater than that of Jesus' own disciples. Rather than being offended by Jesus' comment, she shows great theological perception, greater than that of the men most close to Jesus. For them, she was a nuisance to get rid of (Matt 15:23), but she is here an example of faith.

Mark points out another contrast: What was considered unclean and unworthy by his contemporaries, Jesus considered worthy and valuable. It is no surprise that after Jesus' argument with the leaders in regard to what makes a person unclean (Mark 7:1–22), he goes against tradition and enters the vicinity of the "unclean" Gentiles, relates to an "unclean Gentile" woman (vv. 27–29), and casts out an unclean spirit (vv. 15, 30). It seems like Jesus is purposefully going in the direction of unclean people to teach his disciples an important lesson. This amazing woman becomes the mediator to the Gentiles. Both Mark and Mathew present her as a hero, and so does Jesus.

A Woman with the Spirit of Infirmity

Jesus' healing of the woman with the spirit of infirmity also presents a challenge as he enters the synagogue on the Sabbath day, touches her, and declares her "loosed" from her infirmity (Luke 13:10–17). Jesus specifically uses those words to highlight the fact that the devil had "bound" her for eighteen years (v. 16). The head of the synagogue should have recognized this healing as God visiting his people in the way Luke describes it: "And he laid his hands on her: and immediately she was made straight and glorified God." This echoes the words of the psalmist, "The LORD raises up those who are bowed down" (Ps 146:8; cf. 145:14).

Jesus demonstrates his authority by loosening this woman from Satan's power and healing her. The fact that he chose to do this on the Sabbath day has a special meaning, for it points to the power Satan gained over humanity in Eden through sin, thus disrupting an eternal Sabbath rest for God's people. By loosening her on the Sabbath day, Jesus highlights the fact that he came to undo the works of evil and usher them into the true meaning of Sabbath rest.

Jesus shows how the contemporary rules and regulations were far from God's heart by rebuking the head of the synagogue (Luke 13:15). He contrasts his own special care and concern for this "daughter of Abraham" (v. 16) with their special care for their animals on the Sabbath, and he argues that they give greater honor to their animals than they do to a daughter of Abraham. By calling her a "daughter of Abraham" (the only place in the Gospels where this title is used), he highlights the honor and value he has for this woman, thus demonstrating that God's kingdom is accessible for all.

This woman is contrasted with Zacchaeus, who receives the title "son of Abraham" (Luke 19:9). There are interesting parallels between these two passages. Zacchaeus is short and unable to see Jesus, whereas this woman is so bent over she also cannot see Jesus. Both do not expect Jesus to call them, yet Zacchaeus is called to come down from his perch in a tree to fellowship with Jesus, and the woman is called to come to him and is raised up. Both need Jesus to see them and act on their behalf. Both are children of Abraham, and both need to be "loosed" by the Savior.

People with disabilities of all sorts were considered sinners from their mother's womb, and the deaf were considered without rights and without demands. The rabbinical term for this was *Chashu*, which stands for a deaf-mute, an imbecile, or a minor (m. B. Qam. 8.4). Jesus, however, showed respect to people with disabilities. He even said that the blind may see while those who are physically able to see, yet claim to see spiritual truths, may in fact be the ones who are blind (John 9:41).

Conclusion

Through both his words and actions toward women, Jesus demonstrates what God has intended for them since the beginning of creation—namely, to be coheirs and co-rulers in his kingdom (Gen 1:28). He also teaches men how they should value and treat women as equal image-bearers, reorienting men's common perception of women at the time (and today). They needed to learn to see women as he sees them.

Jesus' treatment of women exhibits the value he places on them, proving that God sees women as honored, equal, and valued, just as much as men. This *was* radical in light of the cultural norms of the ancient world. He accepted women into his kingdom just as he accepted men. He praised great faith in a Canaanite woman in contrast to his own disciples' lack of it. He deliberately showed that the most unlikely woman understood kingdom realities better than his own disciples. Jesus valued and showed deep care to *daughters* of Abraham just as much as to sons of Abraham. Jesus' harshest rebukes were kept for the highly respected religious leaders, in contrast to his acceptance and welcoming words to the outcasts—those who were rejected and considered unworthy of society. By this, he turned customs of his day upside down and showed that his kingdom was "not of this world" (John 18:36).

Jesus never treated women according to what they could give men or what they accomplished. He desired women to enjoy an equal status and purpose in his kingdom. Jesus talked to women about deep spiritual issues and allowed them places of discipleship. He was not repulsed by women who were considered unclean, polluted, or of low means. He restored and redeemed women to their place of great worth and lifted them up to their intended position: sowers and reapers in his kingdom, honored daughters among the family of God, coheirs in the kingdom, the bride to their heavenly bridegroom.

Works Cited

Bauckham, Richard. 2002. *Gospel Women: Studies of the Named Women in the Gospel*. Grand Rapids: Eerdmans.
Fruchtenbaum, Arnold G. 2016. *Yeshua: The Life of Messiah from a Messianic Jewish Perspective*. Vol. 2. San Antonio: Ariel.
———. 2017. *Yeshua: The Life of Messiah from a Messianic Jewish Perspective*. Vol. 3. San Antonio: Ariel.
Ilan, Tal. 2017. "Gender." Pages 611–14 in *The Jewish Annotated New Testament*. Edited by Amy-Jill Levine and Marc Brettler. New York: Oxford University Press.
Instone-Brewer, David. 2002. *Divorce and Remarriage in the Bible: The Social and Literary Context*. Grand Rapids: Eerdmans.
Johnson, John E. 2017. *Under an Open Heaven: A New Way of Life Revealed in John's Gospel*. Grand Rapids: Kregel Publications.
Kitzberger, Ingrid Rosa. 2000. *Transformative Encounters: Jesus and Women Re-Viewed*. BibInt 43. Leiden: Brill.
Levine, Amy-Jill. 1991. *Women like This: New Perspectives on Women in the Greco-Roman World (Early Judaism and Its Literature)*. Atlanta: SBL Press.
Satlow. Michael L. 2017. "Marriage and Divorce." Pages 608–11 in *The Jewish Annotated New Testament*. 2nd ed. Edited by Amy-Jill Levine and Marc Brettler. New York: Oxford University Press.
Seiden, John. 2015. *I Am He*. Jerusalem: Keren Ahava Meshihit.
Witherington, Ben III. 1987. *Women in the Ministry of Jesus: A Study of Jesus' Attitudes to Women and Their Roles as Reflected in His Earthly Life*. Cambridge: Cambridge University Press.

3.8 The Resurrection of the Saints and the Guard at the Tomb in Matthew

Charles L. Quarles

Although most of Matthew's account of Jesus' crucifixion and resurrection has close parallels with the accounts in the other Gospels, it also contains important and unique material. Matthew's accounts of the resurrection of the saints (27:51–53) and the guard at the tomb (27:62–66; 28:2–4, 11–15) are unparalleled. These accounts are crucial to Matthew's theological emphases and his apologetic purpose.

The Resurrection of the Saints

Comparison with Other Gospels

All three of the Synoptic Gospels mention the rending of the veil at the time of Jesus' death (Matt 27:51; Mark 15:38; Luke 23:45). Matthew's description of the event most closely resembles Mark's. Mark 15:38 states that at the moment of Jesus' death, "the veil of the temple was split in two from the top to the bottom." Matthew 27:51 agrees verbatim with Mark's wording except that Matthew places the phrase "in two" at the end of the clause. However, after this initial close agreement with Mark, the rest of the passage is completely unique to Matthew. Of our four Gospels, only Matthew (27:51–53) mentions the earthquake that shatters the rocks, the opening of the tombs, the resurrection of the saints, and their entrance into the holy city. The spectacular nature of these phenomena combined with the absence of any mention of them in the other Gospels has stirred the suspicion of many scholars that these events did not occur historically.

Scholars often use the criterion of multiple independent attestation to confirm that a tradition preserved in the Gospels is early and, probably, authentic. However, the criterion functions positively, not negatively. Although multiple independent attestation supports the antiquity and authenticity of accounts, the *lack* of multiple independent attestation does not *preclude* or render improbable their antiquity and authenticity. Scholars often accept the authenticity of material that lacks multiple independent attestation. Many scholars affirm the authenticity of material that is unique to a single Gospel, even when this material describes supernatural phenomena (e.g., Mark 8:22–26; Luke 1:5–25, 57–80; 7:11–17; 17:11–19; John 2:1–11; 5:2–47; 9:1–41; 11:1–44). Thus, unless one holds a worldview that precludes the possibility of the events described in Matt 27:51–53, the lack of multiple independent attestation is not sufficient grounds for rejecting the historicity of the account.

Interpretation of Matthew 27:51–53

The resurrection of the saints is the climax in a series of related phenomena that occurred at the time of Jesus' death. Most of the phenomena are presented in what appears to be a natural, chronological order. The earthquake described in 27:51b was the direct force that shattered the rocks and opened the tombs so that the resurrected saints could exit. Initially, 27:51a seems to be out of place in this sequence. One would expect that the earthquake would also be the direct force that shakes the temple and causes the veil to tear. However, the unexpected order is probably intentional and significant. Matthew portrays the entire sequence of events as an act of God in which his power descends, first splitting the veil from the top to the bottom and then hammering the earth and splitting the bedrock beneath the city of Jerusalem, with the force spreading until it reaches beyond the city walls to the cemeteries on the outskirts of the city. The expression "from the top to the bottom" indicates that this is an act of God. This suggests that the passive verbs in this text are to be seen as "divine passives" in which God is the unnamed agent who is performing the action. Thus God ripped the veil, shook the earth, split the rocks, opened the tombs, and raised the saints.

The "veil of the temple" (*to katapetasma tou naou*) is probably one of the two veils in the inner sanctum of the temple complex (Josephus, *Ant.* 8.3.3 §72; *J.W.* 5.5.4 §212; 5.5.5 §219), since Matthew generally uses the term *hieron* to refer to the larger temple precincts and reserves *naos* to refer either to the Holy Place or to the holy of holies. One veil covered the entrance to the Holy Place and served to separate it from the outer court ('Ed. 8.6). Another veil separated the Holy Place from the holy of holies (Exod 26:33; Yoma 5.1). The Mishnah claims that this latter curtain was a handbreadth thick and that its weight was so great, it took three hundred priests to immerse it in water for cleansing (Šeqal. 8.4). Matthew likely intends to refer to this inner veil (Gurtner 2007, 46).

Scholars still debate the significance of the rending of the veil. Although many interpreters have argued that the tearing of the curtain indicates that God has reconciled sinners to himself and given them full access to his presence, this view usually appeals to a mistaken interpretation of Heb 10:19–22 (Morris 1992, 724; Hagner 1995, 849). Other scholars suggest that the event invites Gentiles to enter the temple and worship God, and thereby demonstrates the inclusion of the Gentiles in the people of God (Blomberg 1992, 421). Others regard the event as a sign of the coming destruction of the temple (Jerome, *Epist.* 18a; *Epist.* 46; *Epist.* 120; *Comm. Matt.* 4; *Comm. Isa.* 3; Tertullian, *Adv. Jud.*13.15; de Jonge 1986; Brown 2010; Quarles 2016). The most detailed study argues that the torn veil depicts the apocalyptic opening of the heavens. which enables one to behold the vision of the fulfillment of Ezek 37 accomplished in heaven through the death of Christ (Gurtner 2007, 169).

Although some translations suggest that the "earth" was shaken, Matthew describes the shaking of the "land"; that is, the land of Israel (cf. 2:6, 20, 21; 24:30). In the OT, earthquakes often serve as a sign of God's wrath and coming destruction (2 Sam 22:8 LXX; Joel 2:10; 3:16; Isa 13:13; 24:18, 20; Jer 8:16; 27:46 LXX; and Dan 2:40 LXX; cf. Josephus, *J.W.* 4.4.5 §286–287). The earthquake that hit the region ruptured the massive boulders of the area. The term translated "rocks" here is the same term used in 7:24–25 to describe the bedrock on which the wise builder constructed his house. The trembling of the earth cracked open the limestone tombs that contained the remains of deceased saints. These saints are probably those mentioned in 23:29—righteous people whose tombs were venerated by the people, even though their own ancestors had martyred some of these saints (cf. Somov 2021b). The definite article modifying "tombs" in the Greek text suggests an allusion to 23:29. Although the definite article with "saints" is needed to demonstrate that the adjective is functioning as a substantive, the definite article with "tombs" is best explained as anaphoric (i.e., the article of previous reference). Thus the construction points back to the tombs of important saints mentioned in 23:29. Ignatius (*Ign. Magn.* 9.2) identified these saints as OT prophets. Later traditions claimed that a total of five hundred saints were raised and among them were figures such as Abel, Noah, the patriarchs, Joseph, Baruch, John the Baptist, Hezekiah, and Daniel and the three youths (Somov 2021a). These saints were raised from the dead and left their tombs. Some scholars have misread the text as if it implied that the resurrected saints sat in their tombs for the next three days and only abandoned their tombs after Jesus' resurrection. However, Matthew's normal grammar and style indicate that the phrase "after his resurrection" modifies the verbs "entered" and "appeared" rather than the participle meaning "exited" (Brown 1994, 1130–31). The implication is that the resurrected saints left their tombs immediately after their resurrection but did not enter the Holy City, Jerusalem, until after Jesus' resurrection. The resurrected saints appeared to many people. Matthew 27:54 may imply that these saints were seen by the Roman centurion and his soldiers who were supervising the crucifixion. They witnessed the earthquake and the (other) things (pl.) that happened. The additional things they witnessed likely included at least the splitting of the rocks and the opening of the tombs. Matthew may intend to imply that they witnessed the saints exit the tombs as well. He clearly intends to communicate that the saints later appeared to the inhabitants of Jerusalem.

Matthew does not state how the Jerusalemites reacted to the appearance of these saints. We may assume that the sight frightened them, especially if some of these saints were those that their ancestors had murdered. Matthew also does not indicate what happened to these saints after their appearance in Jerusalem. Did they live to die again? Did they ascend to heaven with Jesus? Matthew simply does not say. However, this is not surprising since he also does not record what happened to the resurrected Jesus after he issues the Great Commission (Matt 28:18–20).

Text of Matthew 27:51–53

Several German and Dutch scholars of the eighteenth and nineteenth centuries argued that Matt 27:52–53 is an early scribal interpolation. This intriguing theory has been revived in recent scholarship (Evans 2012, 466), and the arguments for it are initially persuasive. However, the external and internal evidence weighs strongly in favor of the conclusion that the text is an original part of the Gospel of Matthew (Quarles 2017). All ancient witnesses for which this portion of Matthew is extant contain these verses. Unlike early interpolations, such as Mark 16:9–20, Matt 27:52–53 was enumerated in the Eusebian sections. Although ancient scribes often used asterisks or obeli to mark texts that were suspected of being interpolations, no such indications of suspicion mark Matt 27:52–53 in the ancient witnesses.

Early Christian literature clearly alludes to and even directly quotes these verses as well (Quarles 2017). Allusions are found in Ignatius's *Epistle to the Magnesians* 9.2, the Akhmîm Gospel fragment, T. Levi 4, Tertullian (*Adv. Jud.* 13), and Julius Africanus (*Chron.*, frag. 93). Direct quotations appear in P. Egerton 3 (early third century) by Clement of Alexandria (*Strom.* 6.6 §47–48 which quotes Matt 27:53 and ascribes the quotation to "the Gospel"). Origen made several references to Matt 27:51–53, including a complete and almost verbatim quotation in his *Commentary on John* (19.16 §103).

The internal evidence also supports the view that this text is an original part of Matthew's Gospel. The text contains vocabulary and expressions that are distinctively Matthean. Although some *hapax legomena* appear in this passage, their frequency is not unusual for Matthew's Gospel. Subtle features of Matthean grammar and style appear that few ancient scribes would have had the skill to mimic in an interpolation. Overall, this text appears to bear the literary fingerprint of the author of the First Gospel.

Since the very early twentieth century, several scholars have argued that the phrase "after his resurrection" is a scribal interpolation. This view has been widely supported by Matthean scholars (e.g., Davies and Allison 1997, 634–45; Schnackenburg 2002, 290; Luz 2007, 568–69). However, this view is based on a misreading of the evidence (Quarles 2015, 1–15). Although scholars have recently claimed that P. Egerton 3, the Diatessaron, minuscule 243, and the Palestinian Syriac Gospel lectionaries are witnesses to the omission of the phrase "after his resurrection," these claims are largely mistaken. Only the Palestinian Syriac Gospel lectionaries stand as witnesses to the absence of the phrase. However, their late date (eleventh century) and their other textual corruptions make it unlikely that they preserve a text superior to that found in the major majuscules of the fourth and fifth centuries.

Genre of Matthew 27:51–53

Many modern scholars have suggested that Matt 27:51–53 is poetic symbolism, apocalyptic imagery, an apocalyptic vision, or narrative "special effects" that are not intended to be interpreted as literal earthly historical events (e.g., Licona 2010, 548–53; Gurtner 2007, 138–98). Space does not permit a thorough response to each of these suggestions. The claim that the text is poetic is undermined by the several disruptions to the symmetry of the text (Quarles 2016, 276–77).

Matthew's description of the rending of the veil is almost identical to the description in Mark. Few would dispute that Mark intends to present the event as literal history. If Matthew likewise presents 27:51a as literal historical narrative and then shifts to apocalyptic in 27:51b, we have a major genre shift in a single sentence followed by a shift back to historical narrative in the very next sentence. It is difficult to imagine that Matthew would have expected his readers to understand these shifts.

If Matthew were suddenly shifting his genre from historical narrative to apocalyptic imagery, then one would have expected him to alert his readers to that shift in order to prevent them from misunderstanding these verses and interpreting them literally (Quarles 2012, 71–98). The only conceivable notification of the genre shift could be the *idou* at the beginning of verse 51. However, Matthew uses the particle sixty-two times to call attention to a detail or to emphasize a point, but never to signal a change in genre. Furthermore, if Matthew, like Mark, views the rending of the veil as a historical event, then the placement of the *idou* could not mark a shift to the apocalyptic genre—a shift that supposedly would not begin until 51b (Quarles 2012, 75–76).

Furthermore, the claims that the Roman centurion and other bystanders saw the earthquake and at least two of the other phenomena (27:54) and that the resurrected saints were seen by many in the Holy City seem to describe a literal historical event. As we will soon see, early Christian interpreters unanimously interpreted the phenomena as portents that really occurred.

Allusions to the OT in Matthew 27:51–53

Various scholars have suggested that this passage contains allusions to several OT texts (Isa 2:19; 1 Kgs 19:11–13; Zech 14:4; Nah 1:5–6; Ezek 37:12–13). Some have suggested dependency on extrabiblical texts such as Testament of Levi 4:1. However, the verbal and even thematic connections with these texts are so weak that any Matthean allusion to them is doubtful except for Ezek 37:12–13. Several features of Matthew's description seem intended to parallel Ezek 37, Ezekiel's vision of the Valley of Dry Bones (Quarles 2016, 278–282). Ezekiel 37:7 (LXX) contains the expression, "Behold, an earthquake." Matthew 27:51 contains the interjection "Behold" and refers to an earthquake. Ezekiel 37:12 and Matt 27:52 both contain references to God opening up tombs. Matthew's insistence that Jesus' resurrection preceded the resurrected saints' entrance into the city implies a scenario like the one described in Ezek 37:12–14. Even Matthew's unusual expression, "he released the Spirit/breath," may imply that Jesus imparted the Spirit to the dead saints to raise them from the dead just as the Lord's Spirit raised the dead in Ezek 37:5, 9–10, 14. The use of the *nomen sacrum* form of "Spirit" in Codex Vaticanus suggests that the fourth-century scribe who copied this important manuscript (or the scribe of one of its ancestors) viewed the spirit/breath in Matthew 27:50 as a reference to the Holy Spirit.

Early Interpretation of Matthew 27:51–53

A dozen early Christian texts quote or allude to Matt 27:51–53. These include Ign. *Magn.* 10; T. Levi 4; P. Egerton 3; Tertullian, *Adv. Jud.* 13; Pseudo-Clement, *Recognitions* 1.41; Clement of Alexandria, *Strom.* 6.6; Julius Africanus, *Chronology* 18; several works by Origen including *Cels.* 2.33; *Comm. Matt.* 12.43; *Comm. Cant.* 3.13; *Comm. Jo.* 19.16 §103; and the Syriac document described in Eusebius, *Hist. eccl.* 1.13. These early interpreters generally identified the resurrection saints as OT figures such as Moses, Elijah, and other prophets. Most indicated that the resurrection of the saints occurred at the time of Jesus' crucifixion, not his resurrection. They interpreted the text as referring to literal, historical events, although Origen identified the "Holy City," which the resurrected saints entered, as heaven rather than Jerusalem.

Significance of Matthew 27:51–53 for Matthean Theology

The account of the resurrection of the saints resonates with important themes of Matthean theology. By this act, Jesus fulfills OT prophecy and initiates the restoration of creation (Quarles 2013; Turner 2008, 670). Since the resurrection of the dead in Ezek 37 illustrates the fulfillment of the new covenant (37:14, 26; cf. Ezek 36:25–27) and Matthew's account clearly alludes to Ezekiel's text, the event confirms Jesus' statement that his death serves as the sacrifice that will enact the new covenant (Matt 26:28). The sending of the resurrected saints, who had been martyred by the people of Jerusalem, serves as an indictment of the people of the city and thus reminds the reader of the divine judgment that will befall the city (Matt 23:37–39; 24:1–2; 27:25; Luz, 467–68; Schwindt 2007).

The Guard at the Tomb

Matthew also contains behind-the-scenes details about Jesus' resurrection that do not appear in the other Gospels. These details provide compelling evidence for Jesus' bodily resurrection that counteract the false narrative that circulated among some of Matthew's Jewish contemporaries.

The Request for the Guard

Several of the chief priests and Pharisees approached the residence of the Roman prefect, Pontius Pilate, seeking to present him a request. This is not an official meeting involving the entire Sanhedrin Council, since Matthew does not mention the "elders of the people" (cf. Matt 27:1). After Jesus' crucifixion and burial, these leaders recalled Jesus' promise that he would rise again after three days. This is a reference to the statement Jesus made in the presence of the scribes and Pharisees (Matt 12:38): "The Son of Man will be in the earth three days and three nights" (12:40). The group claims that they wish to place a guard at Jesus' tomb to prevent his disciples from stealing his corpse and then claiming that he had risen from the dead. This probably was the motivation for the request as far as the chief priests were concerned, since the chief priests were Sadducees who did not believe in resurrection. However, the Pharisees, who did believe in resurrection, may have had another motivation. The phenomena that accompanied Jesus' crucifixion may have struck them with the realization that Jesus' prophecy of his resurrection could be fulfilled. Perhaps they thought that a guard at the tomb might serve to prevent the fulfillment of Jesus' promise. The soldiers would probably attempt to kill the condemned man again if he somehow exited the tomb.

The group's description of Jesus as "that deceiver" (Matt 27:63) and their concern that "the last deception will be worse than the first" (27:64) are ironic. These men had prosecuted Jesus using false witnesses (26:59–61). Their knowledge of Jesus' prophecy about his resurrection after three days (27:63) suggests that they knew that the statement of the false witnesses in 26:61 was a distortion of what Jesus really said (cf. John 2:19). After Jesus' resurrection, the group would bribe the guards to lie about what had occurred to hide the fact that they had crucified the Messiah whose claims had been confirmed by his resurrection. They were the true deceivers whose "last deception" (lie denying the resurrection) would be even worse than the first (false accusations during Jesus' trial).

The Nature of the Guard

Pilate's reply "You have a guard" (Matt 27:65) may be understood in two different ways. This may be a declaration that the group already had their own guard of soldiers (the temple police) so that they should use this force to guard the tomb. However, the statement may grant permission for the Jewish leaders to use a Roman guard under Pilate's direct authority to secure the tomb. Several features of the account better support the latter view that the guard is a Roman guard: (1) Pilate uses the

Latin loan-word *custodia* to refer to the guard; (2) Matt 28:12 says that the *custodia* consisted of "soldiers," a description more apt for the Roman troops (27:27) than for the temple police; (3) the Jewish leaders must later bribe the guard to ensure that they share the false report the leaders crafted; and (4) the Jewish leaders offer to protect the guard from Pilate if he hears that the guard fell asleep (Davies and Allison 2004, 655; Gundry 1994, 584; Nolland 2005, 1238–39; Turner 2008, 677; cf. France 2007, 1094–95). These last two features of the account suggest that the guard is under the direct authority of the Roman prefect rather than the Jewish leaders. Furthermore, the earliest extant document that retells Matthew's account that appears in the Akhmîm fragment (late-second century) describes the guard as Roman (Quarles 2005).

Matthew does not specify the number of soldiers in the assigned detachment. A Roman *custodia* would probably have been large enough to fend off at least eleven armed disciples. It would also probably have consisted of a number large enough to guard the tomb in rotating watches. The Akhmîm fragment claims that the guard consisted of an entire Roman century, which consisted of about eighty well-armed and trained soldiers.

The Sealing of the Tomb

Pilate's command "Go and make it as secure as you know how" (27:65) seems to imply that securing the tomb will be more difficult than the Jewish leaders assume, even with their Roman guard. Pilate may merely be insulting the Jewish leaders by implying that they are completely inept and will only bungle the effort to secure the tomb. On the other hand, the details of his wife's dream (27:19) had been power-fully confirmed by the phenomena that occurred during Jesus' resurrection (27:45, 51–53). Pilate himself would have witnessed some of these phenomena, and others were likely reported to him by the centurion assigned to supervise the crucifixion (27:54). Pilate would naturally wonder if Jesus' prophecy will be fulfilled and if the Jewish leaders would be unable to prevent that fulfillment (Bruner 1990, 776).

The Jewish leaders probably supervised the Roman guard while they secured and sealed the tomb. The Mishnah warned that the stone that sealed a tomb conveyed uncleanness by direct contact and even by overshadowing ('Ohal. 2.4). If the Jewish leaders were close enough to the tomb that they cast shadows that touched the stone or the shadow of the stone, or even if their shadows blended with the shadow of the stone or the shadows of the soldiers as they milled about the tomb, they would have contracted ritual defilement that would last seven days. Thus they probably kept their distance while the Roman soldiers stretched a cord across the stone that sealed the tomb and attached the rope to the sides of the entrance with a lump of clay or wax impressed with the Roman seal (cf. Dan 6:17). Breaking into the tomb would require breaking the Roman seal, an act of defiance against the authority of the Roman Em-pire. Any person guilty of such an act would be quickly seized and severely punished.

The Overwhelming of the Guard

If Pilate had a premonition that the Jewish leaders' efforts to secure the tomb were futile, then the premonition was accurate. When Jesus rose from the dead, an angel descended from the sky, approached the tomb, and rolled away the heavy, round slab of stone that covered the tomb entrance, and then sat on the stone. The angel's movements caused an earthquake just as powerful as the one that occurred when Jesus died. The angel's appearance is reminiscent of the angel in Dan 10:6 since his face shone as bright as a flash of lightning. His garments even resembled Yahweh's appearance since they were as white as snow gleaming in the sunlight (cf. Dan 7:9). Even the seasoned soldiers who guarded the tomb were terrified at the sight of the angel. They fell to the ground comatose as if they had been struck dead. This is similar to Daniel's reaction to the appearance of an angel in Dan 10:8–9.

The Report and Bribery of the Guard

After the angel left, the guards regained consciousness, and a group of them returned to Jerusalem to report to the chief priests what had happened. Some scholars argue that if the guard consisted of Roman soldiers, they would have first reported to Pilate. However, if Matt 27:65 grants a Roman *custodia* to the chief priests, then Pilate placed the guard under the authority of the Jewish leaders for this specific mission. Thus the chief priests are the direct authorities over the soldier in this temporary chain of command.

Matthew's description of the soldiers' report assists in calculating the minimum number of soldiers in the custodia. Matthew reports that "some" of the guard reported to the chief priests. This definitely included several soldiers, probably including the superiors of the group—a number large enough that the soldiers hoped would convince the chief priests of the truthfulness of their testimony, even though they realized their account would sound incredible. The adjective "some" (*tines*) with the partitive genitive normally refers to the minority of a group. This suggests that the guard included no fewer than seven soldiers and probably more.

The guard reported everything that happened. The report probably included details about the angel's appearance, the opening of the tomb, and, most importantly, that the tomb, which was occupied when they sealed it, was now empty. Although the chief priests and a few representatives of the Pharisees had acted independently in securing the tomb, they now felt the need to seek the counsel of the entire Sanhedrin. After their deliberation, the Sanhedrin arrived at a simple solution to their dilemma. They paid a handsome bribe to the guard to report that they had fallen asleep at their posts and that Jesus' disciples came and stole the body while they slept. The story included an obvious presumption. If the soldiers were truly asleep when the body had disappeared, they could not know what had actually happened to it. The claim that it was stolen by Jesus' disciples would have been nothing more than a mere guess based on the Jewish leaders' prior suspicion (27:64). The story also entailed a serious risk for the soldiers. A soldier who fell asleep at his post would face brutal punishment such as scourging (Euripides, *Rhes.* 812–19) or being buried alive (*Rhes.* 825–27). A soldier who allowed a corpse to be stolen faced such severe punishment that he preferred suicide (Petronius, *Sat.* 112). Similarly, if a Levite who was at watch fell asleep at his post in the temple, he would be beaten with a staff by the captain in charge of the Temple Mount, and his garment would be

188 A Handbook on the Jewish Roots of the Gospels

burned, evidently in hopes that the chill of the air would prevent him from falling asleep again (m. Mid. 1.2). The Jewish leaders assured the soldiers that if reports of their falling asleep at their post reached the Roman prefect, they would personally persuade the prefect to excuse their offense. The soldiers took the bribe and began to circulate the story the Jewish leaders had rehearsed with them.

At the time that Matthew composed his Gospel, this story still circulated among the Jews, and Justin Martyr reported that the story was still circulating in the second century (Justin, *Dial.* 108). By specifying that the fabricated report circulated "among the Jews," Matthew may be implying that the truth about the soldiers' experience circulated even among some of the Romans.

Conclusion

Matthew's unique account of the resurrection of the saints highlights some of the most important theological themes of his Gospel. The account shows that Jesus is the Son of God who enacted the new covenant, began the miracle of new creation, and who will judge Jerusalem, its temple, and its leaders.

Matthew's unique account of the guard at the tomb displays his skill as an apologist. He reveals the plot put forth by the leaders to hide his resurrection. He also demonstrates the implausibility of their narrative and provides his readers with the necessary details to recognize that the story about the theft of Jesus' body was obviously contrived.

Works Cited

Akin, Daniel L., Craig L. Blomberg, Paul Copan, Michael Kruger, Michael Licona, and Charles Quarles. 2012. "A Roundtable Discussion with Michael Licona on *The Resurrection of Jesus: A New Historiographical Approach*." STR 3:71–98.

Blomberg, Craig L. 1992. *Matthew*. Nashville: Broadman & Holman.

Brown, Raymond. 2010. *The Death of the Messiah: From Gethsemane to the Grave*. 2 vols. New Haven: Yale University Press.

Bruner, Frederick D. 1990. *The Churchbook: Matthew 13–28*. Grand Rapids: Eerdmans.

Davies, W. D., and Dale C. Allison, Jr. 2004. *Matthew 19–28*. Vol. 3. *A Critical and Exegetical Commentary on the Gospel According to Saint Matthew*. 3rd ed. London: T&T Clark.

De Jonge, M. 1986. "Matthew 27:51 in Early Christian Exegesis." HTR 79:67–79.

Evans, Craig A. 2012. *Matthew*. New Cambridge Bible Commentary. New York: Cambridge University Press.

France, R. T. 2007. *The Gospel of Matthew*. NICNT. Grand Rapids: Eerdmans.

Gundry, Robert H. 1994. *Matthew: A Commentary on His Handbook for a Mixed Church under Persecution*. Grand Rapids: Eerdmans.

Gurtner, Daniel. 2007. *The Torn Veil: Matthew's Exposition of the Death of Jesus*. Cambridge: Cambridge University Press.

Hagner, Donald. 1995. *Matthew 14–28*. WBC 33B. Nashville: Nelson.

Licona, Michael. 2010. *The Resurrection of Jesus: A New Historiographical Approach.* Downers Grove, IL: IVP Academic.

Luz, Ulrich. 2007. *Matthew 21–28.* CC. Minneapolis: Augsburg Fortress.

Monasterio, R. A. 1980. *Exegesis de Mateo, 27, 51b-53: para una teologia de la muerte de Jesus en el Evangelio de Mateo.* Vitoria: Eset.

Morris, Leon. 1992. *Matthew.* Pillar New Testament Commentary. Grand Rapids: Eerdmans.

Nolland, John. 2005. *Matthew.* NIGTC. Grand Rapids: Eerdmans.

Quarles, Charles L. 2006. "The Gospel of Peter: Does It Contain a Precanonical Resurrection Narrative?" Pages 106–20 in *The Resurrection of Jesus: John Dominic Crossan and N. T. Wright in Dialogue.* Minneapolis, MN: Fortress Press.

———. 2016. "Matthew 27:51-53: Meaning, Genre, Intertextuality, Theology, and Reception History." *JETS* 59: 271–86.

———. 2017. "Matthew 27:52-53 as a Scribal Interpolation: Testing a Recent Proposal." *BBR* 27: 207–26.

———. 2015. "ΜΕΤΑ ΤΗΝ ΕΓΕΡΣΙΝ ΑΥΤΟΥ: A Scribal Interpolation in Matthew 27:53?" *TC* 20: 1–15.

———. 2013. *A Theology of Matthew.* Philipsburg, NJ: P&R.

Schnackenburg, Rudolph. 2002. *The Gospel of Matthew.* Grand Rapids: Eerdmans.

Schweizer, Eduard. 1975. *The Good News According to Matthew.* Translated by David E. Green. Atlanta: John Knox.

Schwindt, R. 2007. "Kein Heil ohne Gericht: Die Antwort Gottes auf Jesu Tod nach Mt 27, 51-54." *BN* 132:87–104.

Somov, Alexey. 2021. "The Martyrdom of Daniel and the Three Youths: The Legend about Their Death and Resurrection in Eastern Church Hagiography." *JSP* 30.4:198–227.

———. 2021. "Resurrection of the Righteous Sufferers in the New Testament." Pages 365–80 in *The Gospel of Matthew in Its Historical and Theological Context.* Edited by Mikhail Seleznev, William R. G. Loader, and Karl-Wilhelm Niebuhr. WUNT 459. Tübingen: Mohr Siebeck.

Turner, David. 2008. *Matthew.* BECNT. Grand Rapids: Baker Academic.

CHAPTER 4

Theological Roots

4.1 The Son of Man in the Gospel of Mark

Eckhard J. Schnabel

The expression "Son of Man" is *the* self-designation of Jesus of Nazareth. Jesus is never addressed by disciples, sympathizers, or opponents as Son of Man, and neither the earliest believers in the church in Jerusalem nor the apostle Paul confessed or worshiped Jesus as the Son of Man. And yet the authors of the four Gospels regarded the expression as significant when they wrote their reports of the ministry of Jesus. They seem to have been convinced that the "Son of Man" expression used by Jesus had continued significance for the Jesus followers and congregations who would read their texts.

Terminology

In Mark's Gospel, the expression "the son of (the) man" (*ho huios tou anthrōpou*) is found fourteen times (compare thirty uses in Matthew, twenty-five in Luke, and thirteen in John). The expression sounds as odd in English as it sounded in ancient Greek—and also in Biblical Hebrew and in the Aramaic of Jesus' time (Hurtado 2011, 167). Its meaning has to be established on the basis of similar underlying Aramaic and Hebrew phrases that are idiomatic in both Semitic languages. The phrase *huios anthrōpou* in the LXX is a wooden Greek translation of the Hebrew (nonarticular) phrase *ben 'adam* (singular form, without the article; e.g., Num 23:19; Ps 8:4), and the Aramaic phrase *bar 'enash* (Dan 7:13). The phrase describes "a single man within the species or race" (H. Haag, *TDOT* 2:159), "a single individual in a group" (*HALOT* s.v. *ben* 4). It occurs most often in Ezekiel (93x). The articular (determinative) form *ben ha-'adam* occurs only as a scribal addition in a Qumran manuscript (1QS XI, 20). The LXX has about one hundred twelve instances of the singular form for "(a) son of man" as a consistent translation of the corresponding singular Hebrew or Aramaic form, refraining from adding the article, even when this would be grammatically appropriate. The expression also occurs in the plural to denote single men in the plural of the human race, mankind (Hebrew *bene 'adam*, e.g., Deut 32:8; Ps 11:4; *bene ha'adam*, Ps 33:13; Aramaic *bene 'anasha,'* e.g., Dan 2:38; 5:21), translated in the LXX as *hoi huioi tōn anthrōpōn* (articular) or *huioi anthrōpōn*. The singular form refers to an individual human being (e.g., Isa 51:12;

Ezek 2:1), often highlighting the frailty and weakness of the person (e.g., Job 25:6; Ps 8:4). Sometimes the phrase designates a person who represents others (e.g., Ps 80:18 [Eng. 80:17]; Dan 7:13). In Dan 7:13–14, the figure of "one like a son of man" coming with the clouds of heaven is a heavenly figure.

The discussion about the meaning of the term has been varied and intense (cf. Burkett 1999; Yarbro Collins and Collins 2008, 149–74; Müller 2008; Hurtado and Owen 2011; Reynolds 2018). The expression "the son of man" has been understood as a circumlocution for "I" (Vermes 1998); as particularizing the more general or indefinite sense of the expression with the meaning "that son of man" (Casey 1977, 11–22); "a man in my position" (Lindars 1983, 23–24); as a phrase "deliberately fashioned to carry the nuance of a title" (Fitzmyer 1997, 154); "a human being" in general, the speaker identifying himself "only as a particular example of the general rule" (Collins 2011, 1566); and "a man like me" (Dunn 2003, 739). The articular "*the* son of (the) man" was not a familiar expression and probably would have been regarded as peculiar. It has now been demonstrated that there is no evidence for a common use definite-singular (emphatic) expression *bar 'enasha'* in Aramaic Palestinian texts of the Second Temple period, and that it is dubious to claim that the Aramaic phrase(s) translated as "son of man," whatever the form, represented the characteristic manner of referring to human individuals (Owen and Shepherd 2001, 121–22; Hurtado and Owen 2011, 28–60). The phrase should thus most plausibly be understood as meaning "a human figure of particular significance" (Hurtado 2003, 304).

In the New Testament texts, we find the articular-singular expression "the son of (the) man" (*ho huios tou anthrōpou*), which is surprising both in terms of the frequency of the phrase and the preference for this grammatical form (seventy-nine instances in the Gospels, once in Acts 7:56). The few cases of the non-articular singular form (*huios anthrōpou*) is found in Heb 2:6 (quotation of Ps 8:4), and in Rev 1:13; 14:14 (probably alluding to Dan 7:13). It is obvious in some passages that *ho huios tou anthrōpou* could be understood as a circumlocution for "I": in Jesus' question concerning what people say about him, Matt 16:13 has "the Son of Man" while Mark 8:27 and Luke 9:18 use the first-person pronoun. This fact, and the diversity of contexts in which the phrase is used, shows that it did not have a precise fixed meaning. The authors of the Gospels knew the phrase "as the distinctive way that Jesus typically referred to himself, and so deployed it accordingly when they sought to represent Jesus uttering sayings that included a self-reference. . . . [It is] Jesus' unique self-referential device reflecting some sort of emphasis on him as a particular human being . . . reflecting Jesus' sense that he had a particular, even unique, vocation in God's redemptive purposes" (Hurtado 2011, 167–68, 175).

Narrative Context in the Gospel of Mark

We will now analyze the fourteen references to the Son of Man in the Gospel of Mark in their narrative contexts.

Mark 2:10

Amid the popular excitement provoked by Jesus' exorcisms and healings, Jesus returns to Capernaum where he encounters a paralyzed man in the synagogue. He responds to the faith of the man and his friends, who believe that Jesus can and will cure the paralysis, by pronouncing the man's sins forgiven. When Jesus senses the opposition of the teachers of the law who are present and who believe he has uttered a blasphemy, he brings into the open the question whether he has the authority to forgive sins, a privilege that in Scripture and in Jewish thought only God has. After asserting that physically healing the paralyzed man is more difficult to accomplish than to verbally declare that his sins are forgiven, since the former cannot be falsified, Jesus states:

> But so that you may know that the *Son of Man* has authority on earth to forgive sins—he said to the paralytic—I say to you, stand up, take your mat, and go to your home. (Mark 2:10–11 NRSV; emphasis mine)

The term "Son of Man" is used, for the first time in the Gospel of Mark, in the context of the authority of Jesus. The emphatic phrase "I say to you" rules out a collective understanding of the Son of Man. Since the authority to forgive sins is divine authority, Mark depicts Jesus as referring to himself at least in the sense of being uniquely significant, since only an extraordinary human being ("on earth") could have the authority to forgive sins and to heal a paralyzed person instantaneously. Jesus might be interpreted to allude to Ezekiel's "son of man" who enacts God's plan. He might allude to Daniel's "son of man," implying that he has been given authority from heaven, in the present, on earth (rather than in heaven and in the future), with the result that he can forgive sins and heal illnesses no human being can heal (France 2002, 128). If Ps 8 was understood as a messianic psalm in the first century, then Jesus' audience could see an allusion to the messianic son of man whom God granted rule over the works of creation (Yarbro Collins 2007, 186): "What is man that You take thought of him, and the son of man that You care for him? Yet You have made him a little lower than God, and You crown him with glory and majesty! You make him to rule over the works of Your hands; You have put all things under his feet" (Ps 8:4–6 NASB). The reference to Jesus' authority "on earth" can be compared with the authority of the Son of God in 4Q246, while the emphasis on the judgment of sinners by the son of man in the context of the establishment of God's rule in the Similitudes and 4 Ezra is replaced by Jesus forgiving the sin of sinners. One can see here the ambiguity regarding "whether Jesus himself is acting or whether God is acting through him" (Marcus 2000, 224).

Mark 2:28

After discussions about eating with sinners and fasting, Jesus ends a dispute about the Sabbath with the statement, "The sabbath was made for humankind, and not humankind for the sabbath; so the *Son of Man* is lord even of the sabbath" (Mark 2:27–28 NRSV; emphasis mine). The reference to humankind in verse 27 (*ho anthrōpos*, in the generic sense of "human beings" or "people") may suggest a generic sense of the expression "son of man": the Sabbath is not the lord of people, but humanity is the lord over the Sabbath (Neirynck 1975). However, since the Sabbath was instituted by Yahweh, it is not very plausible that Jesus, or the teachers of the law, would have argued that human beings have authority over the Sabbath. Since the context is a debate about what Jesus allows his disciples to do on the Sabbath, the reference to the Son of Man being "lord" (*kyrios*) points to the sovereignty of Jesus as *the* Son of Man. Jesus asserts that he is the unique man who has the authority to override the traditions of the Sabbath laws. Jesus claims a unique authority that affects the Sabbath—one of the foundational institutions of the Jewish people. Since Jesus argues in vv. 25–26 with the precedent of David's behavior, his claim that he has the authority of the Lord of the Sabbath alludes, at least for Mark, to the authority of the son of man in Dan 7:13–14, understood in the Jewish tradition as endowed with the authority of God's Messiah (cf. Marcus 2000, 246, who also refers to the Sabbath given as a divine gift for the benefit of Adam in Gen 2:2–3, which is now under the sovereignty of Adam's eschatological counterpart). The close relationship there between the divine figure of the Son of Man and Yahweh is reflected in Jesus' statement: It was Yahweh who decreed the Sabbath, to whom the Sabbath belonged, and in whose honor the Sabbath was celebrated (note the expressions "my Sabbaths" in Exod 31:13; Lev 19:3; Ezek 20:12–13, and "a Sabbath of/to Yahweh" in Exod 16:25; 20:10; Deut 5:14; France 2002, 148). Now it is Jesus who is the Lord of the Sabbath.

Mark 8:31

Immediately following Peter's confession that Jesus is not simply a prophet but indeed the Messiah, Jesus admonishes the disciples not to publicly proclaim the truth of his messianic identity. Mark continues, "Then he began to teach them that the *son of man* must undergo great suffering, and be rejected by the elders, the chief priests, and the scribes, and be killed, and after three days rise again" (Mark 8:31 NRSV; emphasis mine).

In Jesus' statement, the expression "Son of Man" replaces the term "Messiah" in Peter's statement. "Son of Man" was a much more ambiguous expression than the title "Messiah," who was generally understood to be a political leader (king) from the line of David, fulfilling the prophecy of 2 Sam 7:12–16 (see Pss Sol. 17–18, where the author anticipates a messiah who will establish David's throne, destroy sinners, purge Jerusalem of Gentiles, gather the twelve tribes of Israel, and inaugurate a period of holiness and righteousness). Apart from the connection between the son of man and divine authority in heaven and/or on earth in Dan 7:13–14, and the understanding of the son of man as preexistent and exercising God's judgment of sinners, there was no blueprint for the mission of the son of man on earth. This is what Jesus describes here: the earthly mission of the Son of Man. His divine mission (note the term *dei*, "must," which here describes divine purpose) as the Son of Man is characterized in terms of four events. (1) He will suffer (i.e., experience ill treatment and bodily harm). (2) He will be rejected (i.e., declared useless, regarded as unworthy, his message dismissed, and his actions opposed by members of the lay aristocracy [*presbyteroi*, "elders"], the priestly aristocracy [*archiereis*, "chief priests"], and the experts of the Mosaic law [*grammateis*, "scribes"]. (3) He will be killed (i.e., executed). (4) He will rise again (i.e., return from the dead). The reason for the necessity of Jesus' suffering is made explicit in Mark 9:12: The Son of Man has to suffer because "it is written" (i.e., because of God's purposes revealed in the Scriptures). The scriptural references implied in the term "must" are seen in passages describing the righteous sufferer persecuted by Israel's leaders (Pss 22; 69; 118); the suffering servant whose death is linked with the restoration of the people of God (Isa 53); the savior figure who is rejected by his people, pierced, and tormented (Zech 11:4–14; 12:10–14; 13:7–9); and God bringing about a resurrection on the third day (Hos 6:2).

Daniel's "son of man" appears in the context of suffering (Dan 7:15–27; Evans 2001, 16). However, Daniel's "son of man" represents the weary "holy ones" (Dan 7:25) not in their suffering but in their victory (Dan 7:14). Jesus' statement that the Son of Man must suffer is more plausibly linked with Ezekiel's "son of man." Against the background of human frailty implied in the phrase *ben 'adam*, Ezekiel, the son of man, is commissioned to speak to a nation of rebels and, as Yahweh's agent, experiences suffering, conflict, rejection, and vindication (Mitchell 2019, 82). Jesus' reference to the rising of the Son of Man after three days can be taken to allude to the exaltation of Daniel's "son of man" to heavenly glory (Hooker 1967, 189–98; Marcus 2000, 613).

Mark 8:38

Since the disciples need to see Jesus' mission in the new light of his passion prediction, they, and indeed the crowds of people who come to listen to Jesus, need to see their own lives in a new light as well. Jesus teaches them that they must transform human values that promote self and ambition in the light of the logic of the mission of Jesus whose triumph leads through death, challenging them to be willing to take up their cross and follow him. Jesus then declares, "Those who are ashamed of me and of my words in this adulterous and sinful generation, of them the *Son of Man* will also be ashamed when he comes in the glory of his Father with the holy angels" (Mark 8:38 NRSV; emphasis mine).

Since Jesus will be rejected by the elders, the chief priests, and the scribes (v. 38), there is indeed a good reason why some people might be "ashamed" of Jesus, thinking that following Jesus might cause them to suffer a loss of status, and thus prompting them to conceal their allegiance to him. The link between people being ashamed of Jesus and of the Son of Man being ashamed of these people establishes, for the first time in Mark's Gospel, that Jesus speaks of himself as the "Son" of God who is "his Father." Jesus' self-designation as "Son" should be understood in the context of the tradition that the messianic savior would have a unique relationship, as Son, to God the Father (2 Sam 7:14; Ps 2:7; 89:26; 4Q174 I, 11; 4Q246), and in the context of Jesus' acceptance of Peter's confession that he, Jesus, was the Messiah (Mark 8:29). The assertion that he shares the Father's divine attribute of glory can be understood in the context of Daniel's "son of man," who is presented before God's throne in the presence of the angels and given sovereignty over the nations. In contrast to Daniel's "son of man" who enters the presence of God's glory and later brings judgment, here the Son of Man, who is Jesus, comes from God's presence "with the holy angels" (cf. the "holy ones" of Dan 7:22, 25, 27), judging those who rejected him when he lived on earth. Note that Enoch's "son of man" brings judgment over the sinners so that the faces of the wicked will be covered with shame (1 En. 46:4–6) because they have "denied the Lord of the Spirits and his messiah" who is the son of man (1 En. 48:2, 10).

Mark 9:9

Jesus' consultation of Elijah and Moses on the mountain concludes with the heavenly voice of God who acknowledges Jesus as his unique Son, for the benefit of Peter, James, and John who are commanded to listen to him. Mark then continues, "As they were coming down the mountain, he ordered them to tell no one about what they had seen, until after the *Son of Man* had risen from the dead" (Mark 9:9 NRSV; emphasis mine).

Jesus' reference to the Son of Man's resurrection from the dead, understood in the context of the previous reference to the execution of the Son of Man in Mark 8:31 and his identification with the Son of Man in Mark 8:38, must be understood as a reference to his own resurrection. The otherworldly splendor of Jesus' appearance on the mountain can be properly understood only after his death, which is a core element of his mission on earth. The implied reference to the divine glory of the Son of Man, who is Jesus, can be understood to allude to Daniel's "son of man" who enters the presence of God's glory; and the implied reference to the killing of the Son of Man requiring resurrection can be understood to allude to the vindication of the "son of man" who is Ezekiel.

Mark 9:12

Peter, James, and John do not understand Jesus' reference to the Son of Man rising from the dead. They wonder about the relationship between Elijah's presence on the mountain, his prophesied coming before the day of judgment with a mission to bring healing to human relationships (Mal 4:5–6), and the ministry of Jesus. Jesus responds to their query, "Elijah is indeed coming first to restore all things. How then is it written about the *Son of Man*, that he is to go through many sufferings and be treated with contempt?" (Mark 9:12 NRSV; emphasis mine).

Jesus affirms that the scribes' interpretation of Malachi is correct when they say that Elijah will come before the day of judgment to bring peace to families and restore the tribes of Israel: "He will turn the hearts of parents to their children and the hearts of children to their parents" (Mal 4:6); cf. Sir 48:10: "At the appointed time, it is written, you [Elijah] are destined to calm the wrath of God before it breaks out in fury, to turn the hearts of parents to their children, and to restore the tribes of Jacob." The conundrum of the connection between the coming of Elijah and the coming of the Son of Man (i.e., Jesus) is resolved by the statement in Mark 9:13: "But I tell you that Elijah has come, and they did to him whatever they pleased, as it is written about him." Jesus challenges the three disciples with a rhetorical question to understand Elijah's coming in the light of the coming of the son of man, who was preceded by the coming of John the Baptist. Jesus does not explicitly mention John (but see the version of the dialogue in Matt 11:14), although he can expect they would recognize the allusion since he, Jesus, had been linked by many both with Elijah and with John the Baptist (Mark 6:14–15; 8:28). The suffering of both Elijah and John the Baptist foreshadows the suffering of the Son of Man: Elijah's potentially fatal conflict with Ahab and Jezebel (1 Kgs 19:2–3, 10, 14) typologically foreshadowed the suffering and death of John the Baptist caused by his conflict with Antipas and Herodias (Mark 6:17–28). Both the suffering of Elijah and the suffering (and death) of John the Baptist foreshadow the suffering of Jesus, the Son of Man who has just appeared in divine splendor on the mountain. Malachi's prophecy of the coming of Elijah was fulfilled in the coming of John the Baptist, whereas the appearance of Elijah on the mountain, which happened after John's ministry had ended, signals that it is not Elijah/John, but Jesus who is the fulfillment of the hopes prophesied in the Scriptures. Jesus is the Son of Man who has to suffer before the disciples can tell others about his divine glory (France 2002, 358–60).

Mark 9:31

As Jesus continues to instruct the disciples who need to learn that his suffering, death, and resurrection are an integral part of his mission, he states, "The *Son of Man* is going to be delivered into the hands of men. They will kill him, and after three days he will rise" (Mark NIV; emphasis mine). The prediction that Jesus will be "delivered" (*paradidotai*, "hand over") into the hands of human beings (*anthrōpoi*), formulated with a passive verb form, refers to the actions of Judas Iscariot who collaborated with the Jewish authorities in Jerusalem, and to the actions of the latter who turned Jesus over to the Roman prefect, as Mark will report later (Mark 14:10, 43–53; 15:1, 10). The passive of the verb can also be understood as divine passive, referring to the action of God in the process of Jesus' suffering, death, and resurrection. Jesus' teaching (*didaskein*) may have included the explanation of the scriptural background of the prophecy. Two passages have been suggested. According to Isa 53:6, 12 LXX, God will hand over the suffering servant to death for our sins. Since the Hebrew text of Isaiah does not have clear echoes of this language, Dan 7:25 is the more plausible context of Jesus' prophecy: the "holy ones" of the Most High who include the "one like a son of man" (Dan 7:13–14) are delivered into the hands of the evil kingdom, but only for a short time until the sovereignty of all kingdoms under heaven are handed over to the people of the holy ones whose kingdom shall be an everlasting kingdom. In other words, Jesus describes himself to be the Son of Man—that is, the individual to whom God has given authority "and who, together with the saints, will contend against the kingdom of evil, which will prevail for a brief season, but the kingdom of God will suddenly and surely overcome it" (Evans 2001, 57). The Son of Man will be executed but vindicated after three days in the resurrection.

Mark 10:33–34

Jesus' third explicit passion prediction, uttered as he and the disciples were approaching Jerusalem, is the most explicit.

> "See, we are going up to Jerusalem, and the *son of man* will be handed over to the chief priests and the scribes, and they will condemn him to death; then they will hand him over to the Gentiles; they will mock him, and spit upon him, and flog him, and kill him; and after three days he will rise again."
>
> (Mark 10:33–34 NRSV; emphasis mine)

The geographical marker at the beginning of the statement, which is emphasized ("see"), identifies Jerusalem, the religious capital of Judea and the location of the Sanhedrin, the highest Jewish court, as the place where Jesus will suffer a violent death. Jesus again speaks of himself as the Son of Man who will be handed over to members of the priestly aristocracy and the experts of the law who will impose a death sentence. The elders (Mark 8:31) are not mentioned, which is not significant since it was the chief priests who controlled the Sanhedrin. Experts of the law may be specifically mentioned here since scribes from Jerusalem had traveled to Galilee and rendered an expert opinion that Jesus performs exorcisms with the power of Satan (Mark 3:22; 7:1). The passive verb "(he) will be handed over" refers, again, to the actions of Judas, the Jewish authorities, and God himself who has commissioned the Son of Man to suffer and be killed. The language of "handing over" the Son of Man may again allude to Daniel's vision. Jesus implies that there will be a Jewish trial before the Jewish court in which he will be convicted on a death penalty charge, and he asserts that there will be a Roman trial that will also issue a death sentence. Two actions of the Jewish leaders in Jerusalem are mentioned: they will condemn him to death, meaning they will pronounce a sentence after determination of guilt (*katakrinein*), specifically a death sentence (*thanatos*); and then they will hand him over to the Gentiles, since it was the only the Roman prefect of Roman Judea who had the authority to indict suspects in death penalty cases and carry out a death sentence (on the jurisdiction of the Sanhedrin and the transfer of court cases from local courts to the Roman provincial administration; cf. Schnabel 2019, 15–31, 142–51). The Roman trial is described with four verbs: they will mock him (i.e., subject him to ridicule as a pathetic would-be king; cf. Mark 15:16–20); they will spit on him (i.e., treat him with utter contempt; cf. Mark 15:19); they will flog him (i.e., beat him with a whip; cf. Mark 15:15); and they will kill him (i.e., he will be executed by crucifixion; cf. Mark 15:15, 24). Each of these four elements (although not the verbs) is mentioned in Isaiah's description of the suffering servant (Isa 53:3, 5, 8–9, 12; cf. Watts 1998). The prediction of Jesus' resurrection is formulated with the same words as in Mark 8:31; 9:31.

Mark 10:45

Following the third explicit passion prediction, Jesus teaches the disciples that true greatness comes with self-sacrificial service. He responds to the request of

James and John to be given positions of honor in the kingdom of God, presumably taking Jesus' use of the expression "son of man" and his message of the kingdom of God to mean that the people closest to him, who surely belong to the holy ones of the Most High, will participate in the enthronement and judicial authority of Jesus; i.e., the son of man of Dan 7:9, 13–14, 27. Jesus illustrates the reversal of values that he has been teaching the disciples with his own mission. "For the *Son of Man* came not to be served but to serve, and to give his life a ransom for many" (Mark 10:45 NRSV; emphasis mine).

The mission of Jesus involves serving the people by giving his life as a ransom. The term "ransom" (*lytron*) is used for the expiation of a life that was forfeited (Exod 21:30; 30:12); e.g., for the redemption of the firstborn son (Num 8:15). The term is sometimes connected with atonement, understood in the sense of a ransom being paid for a life that is forfeited (Exod 21:30; 30:12; Num 35:31). The ransom payment is Jesus' own life, the life of the unique man. Jesus gives his own life as "payment" so that the many who are unable to pay the ransom themselves can be released and thus saved. The mission of Jesus therefore resembles the actions of Isaiah's suffering servant who serves God (Isa 52:13; 53:11), who makes the life of the servant an "offering for sin" for others, pouring out his life to death, the one suffering for the many (Isa 53:10; cf. 53:4, 5, 6, 11–12; Watts 2000, 349–65; Evans 2001, 120–24). The assertion that the Son of Man "came not to be served" qualifies the vision of Dan 7:13–14 where the son of man comes with the clouds of heaven before God who gives him authority, glory, and power, who is worshiped by all nations, and who receives an eternal kingdom. Jesus is the Son of Man, but now, as the climax of his earthly mission, he serves as Isaiah's suffering servant as he dies as a sin offering for the benefit of sinners.

Mark 13:26–27

After Jesus' symbolic action on the Temple Mount in Jerusalem, which announced the destruction of the temple and the conversion of the Gentiles (by alluding to Jer 7:11 and Isa 56:7) and the subsequent debates with the Jewish authorities about political and theological questions, he teaches the disciples privately about the coming destruction of the temple and the distress of the last days. He asserts at one point that the sun and the moon will darken, the stars will fall from heaven, and the order of the universe will dissolve, and then states,

> "Then they will see 'the *Son of Man* coming in clouds' with great power and glory. Then he will send out the angels, and gather his elect from the four winds, from the ends of the earth to the ends of heaven." (Mark 13:26–27 NRSV; emphasis mine)

The description of the coming of the Son of Man after the distress of the last days and in the context of the dissolution of the universe resembles images from Dan 7:13–14 (and other texts), although the direction of movement is reversed. The description has five elements. First, the Son of Man will come in a visible manner, seen by his enemies (cf. Mark 14:62; cf. Evans 2001, 329), the celestial powers (Marcus

2009, 908), or people in general. Second, he will come "in clouds" (cf. Dan 7:13), a divine mode of transport (Mark 9:7; 14:62; cf. Exod 34:5; Ps 18:12–13). Third, he will come "with great power and glory" (cf. Dan 7:14), establishing the kingdom of God in power (Mark 9:1), sharing the glory of God (Mark 8:38; 10:37; cf. Ps 8:6). Fourth, he will "send out the angels" (cf. Dan 7:14, 18, 22, 27; cf. Mark 8:38), demonstrating his divine sovereignty. And fifth, he will "gather his elect" (cf. 1 En. 62:13–14), who are the followers of Jesus who live at the ends of the earth (cf. Acts 1:8; the elect at the "ends of heaven" may be Jesus' followers who have died when he returns; so Marcus 2009, 905, with reference to 1 En. 39:3–7; cf. Evans 2001, 329, who sees an allusion to Zech 2:6 that prophesies the gathering of the exiles of God's people). Jesus, the Son of Man and thus God's unique messianic agent, assures his disciples—whom he had taught to expect union with him in his self-sacrificial suffering—that he will make a sudden appearance after his death and resurrection, which he had predicted several times. The coming of the Son of Man in power and glory who gathers the elect constitutes the culmination of the disciples' "being with him" (Mark 3:14; Marcus 2009, 909).

Mark 14:21

During his last supper with his disciples, Jesus predicts that one of them will betray him, stating,

> "For the *Son of Man* goes as it is written of him, but woe to that one by whom the *Son of Man* is betrayed! It would have been better for that one not to have been born." (Mark 14:21 NRSV; emphasis mine)

Jesus describes the consequences of the act of betrayal committed by one of the Twelve for himself and for his betrayer. Jesus will "go" to experience the rejection by the Jewish leaders, the trial on a death penalty charge, and the execution, as he had predicted several times (Mark 8:31; 9:31; 10:33–34) and as is necessary for the mission of the Son of Man (Mark 8:31; 9:9, 12). If "go" alludes to the betrayal, then the reference to what "is written about him" would refer to several scriptural passages (Ps 41:9; Zech 13:7; Isa 53:11; Dan 9:26). The consequences for the disciple who will betray him are severe, introduced by a woe formula that underlines the disaster that will fall on the betrayer.

Mark 14:41

When Jesus had prayed three times in Gethsemane and then finds Peter, James, and John sleeping, again, he says, "Are you still sleeping and taking your rest? Enough! The hour has come; the *Son of Man* is betrayed into the hands of sinners" (Mark 14:41 NRSV; emphasis mine). The first part of the statement is plausibly understood as an ironic comment ("You can sleep on now and have your rest. It is all over." NJB) or an indignant question ("Are you still sleeping and taking your rest? Enough!" NRSV; cf. NIV, GNB). Jesus rebukes the disciples a third time. The statement "the hour has come" refers back to 14:35: the time has come when Jesus' predictions of betrayal, arrest, trial, and execution (Mark 8:31; 9:31; 10:33–34) will be fulfilled. The first event in this sequence of events is his betrayal. This is the paradox of Jesus' mission: he is the Son of Man of Daniel's vision who is given dominion, glory, and kingship (Dan 7:13–14) and who will come with great power and glory (Mark 13:26–27). But now, as he approaches the climactic end of his earthly mission, he is given over into the hands of sinners.

Mark 14:62

After the high priest Caiaphas had failed to secure reliable witness testimony during the Sanhedrin trial that would be sufficient evidence to issue a death penalty, he directly addresses Jesus, who had been silent throughout the legal proceedings. Caiaphas attempts to initiate a cross-examination during which Jesus could be enticed to make a statement about his identity, which might lead to a conviction (Schnabel 2018, 256–66). Caiaphas puts Jesus under oath in order to truthfully answer the question: "Are you the Messiah, the Son of the Blessed One?" (Mark 14:61). The term "messiah" means "the Anointed One," and the phrase "the Son of the Blessed One" means "the Son of God." The expression "Son of God" was used for the royal descendent of the house of David (2 Sam 7:12–14; 1 Chr 17:13; Ps 2:2, 7). In Jewish tradition, it was only the royal descendant of the house of David who is referred to as being in some sense the Son of God (1Q28b; 4Q174; 4Q246). Caiaphas wanted to establish whether Jesus of Nazareth claimed to be the Messiah, the expected eschatological king of Israel (the Son of David), with the special relationship to God as the Son of God. Jesus had never publicly claimed to be the Messiah, nor had he explicitly claimed to be the Son of God. However, his teaching and his actions raised the question whether Jesus claimed to have divine authority—e.g., his claim to have the authority to forgive sins, his healings on the Sabbath when work was prohibited, his public demonstrations of sovereign power over demons, and his triumphal approach to Jerusalem accompanied by messianic celebrations. Jesus broke his silence and answered Caiaphas: "I am; and you will see the *Son of Man* seated at the right hand of the Power, and coming with the clouds of heaven" (Mark 14:62 NRSV; emphasis mine).

Jesus answered Caiaphas in the affirmative: "I am," meaning "I am the Messiah, the Son of God." Then he proceeded to qualify the titles of "Messiah" and "Son of God" by describing his status and his mission. He is the Messiah as the Son of Man in Daniel's vision ("you will see the Son of Man . . . coming with the clouds of heaven;" cf. Dan 7:13) and as the divine Son of God in Ps 110:1 (cited by Jesus in Mark 12:36 to demonstrate that the Messiah, who is David's Lord, must be more than a royal son of David). Jesus asserts that he is indeed the Messiah—not in the political sense of a national deliverer, but as Daniel's "son of man" who shares God's authority. He is presently rejected just as Ezekiel, the son of man commissioned by God to bring the word of Yahweh to the Jewish people, was rejected by the leaders of the people. But he will be vindicated when he returns as the Son of Man who will judge those now sitting in judgment over him. The high priest and the Jewish leaders in the Sanhedrin responded to Jesus' declaration with a charge of blasphemy warranting the death sentence (Mark 14:63–64).

Synthesis

Jesus' use of the phrase "the Son of Man" for himself in the context of statements about his mission evidently did not provoke surprise or indignation among his listeners. This suggests that the expression should most plausibly be regarded as a unique, if ambiguous, self-reference. It appears that Jesus used the expression particularly in situations in which he wanted to be ambiguous about his identity and his mission. "Son of Man" was an ambivalent phrase that, depending on the presumed scriptural origins, could imply variegated claims: to have divine status and authority (Dan 7:13–14), to be the messianic king who accomplishes the rule of God as Son of God and as the representative of the true people of God (Dan 7:13–14, and Isaiah's servant), to possess divine dignity involving preexistence (1 En. 48:2–3, 6; 4 Ezra 12:11), and to be the judge of the world (1 En. 61:8–9; 62:2).

It has been customary to divide the Son of Man passages in the Gospels into three groups: (1) sayings about the present ministry of the Son of Man, (2) the suffering of the Son of Man, and (3) the future coming of the Son of Man (e.g., Stuhlmacher 2018, 137–43). More helpful seems Volker Hampel's analysis in terms of four groups: (1) sayings about the present lowliness of the Son of Man (Mark 9:12; 10:45); (2) the present majesty, or authority, of the Son of Man (e.g., Mark 2:10, 28); (3) the suffering, death, and resurrection of the Son of Man (Mark 8:31; 9:12; 9:31; 10:45); and (4) the future majesty of the Son of Man (Mark 8:38; 14:62; Hampel 1990, adapted by Hengel and Schwemer 2019, 561–62). Jesus uses the "Son of Man" expression to point to the reality of his human existence; to signal that he is God's agent, commissioned and empowered to speak for God and enact his will; to highlight the cost his mission has for himself, seen in the conflict with the Jewish leaders and in his suffering and rejection; to qualify the contemporary (nationalistic) messianic expectations in terms of his mission that includes suffering, rejection, and death as a ransom for sinners; to signal his dignity and his authority, which is divine authority, hidden throughout his ministry but revealed shortly before his death, which is part of his mission to establish the kingdom of God;and to convey his assurance of his ultimate vindication after his death, in his resurrection, and in his triumphant return.

Works Cited

Burkett, Delbert R. 1999. *The Son of Man Debate: A History and Evaluation*. SNTSMS 107. Cambridge: Cambridge University Press.

Caragounis, Chrys C. 1986 *The Son of Man: Vision and Interpretation*. WUNT 38. Tübingen: Mohr Siebeck.

Casey, Maurice. 1977. *The Origin of Christology*. Cambridge: Cambridge University Press.

Collins, John J. 2016. *The Apocalyptic Imagination: An Introduction to Jewish Apocalyptic Literature*. 3rd ed. Grand Rapids: Eerdmans.

———. 1994. *Daniel*. Hermeneia. Philadelphia: Fortress.

————. 2010. *The Scepter and the Star: Messianism in Light of the Dead Sea Scrolls.* 2nd ed. Grand Rapids: Eerdmans.

————. 2011. "The Son of Man in Ancient Judaism." Pages 1545–68 in vol. 2 of *Handbook for the Study of the Historical Jesus.* Edited by T. Holmén and Stanley E. Porter. Leiden: Brill.

Dunn, James D. G. 2003. *Jesus Remembered.* Christianity in the Making 1. Grand Rapids: Eerdmans.

Evans, Craig A. 2001. *Mark 8:27–16:20.* WBC 34B. Nashville: Nelson.

Fitzmyer, Joseph A. 1997 [1971]. *Essays on the Semitic Background of the New Testament.* London: Chapman.

France, R. T. 2002. *The Gospel of Mark.* NIGTC. Eerdmans: Grand Rapids.

Hampel, Volker 1990. *Menschensohn und historischer Jesus. Ein Rätselwort als Schlüssel zum messanischen Selbstverständnis Jesu.* Neukirchen-Vluyn: Neukirchener Verlag.

Hengel, Martin, and Anna Maria Schwemer. 2019. *Jesus and Judaism.* Translated by W. Coppins. Waco, TX: Baylor University Press; Tübingen: Mohr Siebeck.

Hooker, Morna D. 1967. *The Son of Man in Mark: A Study of the Background of the Term "Son of Man" and Its Use in St. Mark's Gospel.* London: SPCK.

Hurtado, Larry W. 2011. "Summary and Concluding Remarks." Pages 159–77 in *"Who is this Son of Man?": The Latest Scholarship on a Puzzling Expression of the Historical Jesus.* LNTS 390. London: T&T Clark.

Hurtado, Larry W., and Paul Owen, eds. 2011. *"Who Is This Son of Man?" The Latest Scholarship on a Puzzling Expression of the Historical Jesus.* LNTS 390. London: T&T Clark.

Lindars, Barnabas. 1983. *Jesus Son of Man: A Fresh Examination of the Son of Man Sayings in the Gospels.* London: SPCK.

Marcus, Joel. 2000, 2009. *Mark.* 2 vols. AYB 27, 28. New Haven: Yale University Press.

Mitchell, David F. 2019. *The Son of Man in Mark's Gospel: Exploring its Possible Connections with the Book of Ezekiel.* Australian College of Theology Monograph Series. Eugene, OR: Wipf & Stock.

Müller, Mogens. 2008. *The Expression 'Son of Man' and the Development of Christology: A History of Interpretation.* London: Equinox.

Müller, Ulrich B. 1972. *Messias und Menschensohn in jüdischien Apokalypsen und in der Offenbarung des Johannes.* SNT 6. Gütersloh: Mohn.

Neirynck, Frans. 1975. "Jesus and the Sabbath: Some Observations on Mark II, 27." Pages 227–70 in *Jésus aux origines de la christologie.* Edited by J. Dupont. BETL 40. Leuven: Leuven University Press.

Owen, Paul, and David Shepherd. 2001. "Speaking Up for Qumran, Dalman, and the Son of Man: Was *Bar Enasha* a Common Term for 'Man' in the Time of Jesus?" *JSNT* 81 (2001): 81–122.

Reynolds, Benjamin E., ed. 2018. *The Son of Man Problem: Critical Readings.* London: T&T Clark.

Schnabel, Eckhard J. 2018. *Jesus in Jerusalem: The Last Days.* Grand Rapids: Eerdmans.

————. 2019. "The Jewish Trial before the Sanhedrin." Pages 1–151 in *The Trial and Crucifixion of Jesus: Texts and Commentary.* Rev. ed. Edited by D. W. Chapman and Eckhard J. Schnabel. Peabody, MA: Hendrickson.

Stuhlmacher, Peter. 2018. *Biblical Theology of the New Testament*. Translated by Daniel P. Bailey. Grand Rapids: Eerdmans.

Vermes, Geza. 1998. "The Use of *bar nash/bar nasha* in Jewish Aramaic [1946]." Pages 310–28 in *An Aramaic Approach to the Gospels and Acts*, by Matthew Black. 3rd ed. Peabody, MA: Hendrickson.

Watts, Rikki E. 2000. *Isaiah's New Exodus and Mark*. Reprint. Grand Rapids: Baker Academic.

———. 1998. "Jesus' Death, Isaiah 53, and Mark 10:45: A Crux Revisited." Pages 125–51 in *Jesus and the Suffering Servant: Isaiah 53 and Christian Origins*. Edited by W. H. Bellinger and W. R. Farmer. Harrisburg: Trinity Press.

Yarbro Collins, Adela. 2007. *Mark: A Commentary*. Hermeneia. Minneapolis, MN: Fortress Press.

Yarbro Collins, Adela, and John J. Collins. 2008. *King and Messiah as Son of God: Divine, Human, and Angelic Messianic Figures in Biblical and Related Literature*. Grand Rapids: Eerdmans.

4.2 The Triune God in the Gospels

Cristian S. Ile

The doctrine of the Trinity is fundamental to Christianity, the only religion that believes in the Trinity of God as Father, Son, and Holy Spirit. However, modern theologians tend to gravitate to one of two viewpoints in regard to the Trinity. The first group claims that the doctrine of the Trinity is not present in the New Testament texts but is only a later development of the church fathers (Bruner 1943, 122; Chafer 1940, 5; Ferguson 1987, 22; Fortman 1972, 14–30; Kaye 1980, 23; Franks 1953, 3; Guthrie 1981, 113; O'Donnell 1983, 182; McDougall 2003, 182; Moltmann 1989, 60). The second group of scholars employs a systematic theology method to demonstrate the Trinitarian dogma within the New Testament (Bickersteth 1984; Wainwright 1962). While the conclusions of the first group are unsatisfactory, the methodology of the second is unpersuasive. Therefore, this article employs Bauckham's divine identity method (1999; 2008), further developed and applied by my PhD research in pneumatology (Ile 2016), to discuss what the Gospels actually reveal about God as Trinity.

The divine identity model comes to the text by asking: how does God reveal himself? In addition, and as a result of this approach, it functions within the confines of a firm monotheism (according to the *Shema*, Deut 6:4) that reveals the one God of Israel as distinct from all creation (Bauckham 1999, 45–48). Within this theological frame, God reveals his unique "personal identity" (Vanhoozer 1999, 47; Ricoeur 1988, 246; Ile 2016, 44–50) in his character (Exod 34:6), in relation to the whole universe as sole creator and ruler, as well as in relation to Israel by revealing his unique name YHWH, and as Israel's redeemer and teacher (Bauckham 2008, 6–11; Ile 2016, 44–49). With this methodology in mind, and provided that the Gospel writers present Jesus and the Spirit in divine identity terms, I set out to challenge the Trinitarian status quo and, hopefully, to contribute to our understanding of God as Trinity already within the four Gospels.

Divine Identity Christology in the Synoptic Gospels

The Synoptics appear to portray Jesus in divine identity terminology. While not assuming an exhaustive list of instances in which this is the case in the Gospels, I point out how the Synoptic Gospels describe Jesus through the main elements of God's unique identity.

Jesus as Ruler over the Universe

While the first three Gospels do not emphasize Jesus as creator of the cosmos, they do present him as having dominion over creation in several ways. First, he is "Lord of the Sabbath" (Matt 12:8; Mark 2:28; Luke 6:5; ESV). The Sabbath was established by God as early as the creation account as part of the uninterrupted cycle of life on the earth: man, following God's example, is directed to work for six days and to rest on the seventh. God alone created the universe, designed it to function on space and time coordinates, and only he could impose a time limit on the work-rest routine in the cosmos. Ever since the beginning of creation, the order set by God follows the lunar, biblical calendar, based on a twenty-eight-day month and a seven-day week pattern (Gen 2:2–3; Lev 23). This pattern of working for six days and resting on the seventh could rightfully be altered only by the creator God. Hence, the shock of Jesus' audience when he dares to perform "work" on the Sabbath (Luke 13:14; John 5:17). Only God could and should bypass that order, which points precisely to the divine authority that Jesus claims here.

A second way in which Jesus' dominion over the created world is shown is by his power to challenge and change the laws the created world must follow to remain in balance. Specifically, Jesus commands the wind and the sea to stop, essentially calming a storm (Mark 4:35–39). In a different situation, Jesus literally goes for a walk on the waters of the Kinneret Lake (Matt 14:25–27; Mark 6:48–50; John 6:19–21). This supernatural action represents a direct defiance and overruling of the law of gravity. Under Jesus' feet and at his command, space and matter behave differently than designed by God himself to function.

Third, upon his resurrection, Jesus defies space barriers as he simply appears (Mark 16:14; Luke 24:36) in the locked upper room, and as he "disappears" from before the eyes of his two followers in Emmaus (Luke 24:31). Both transpositions are physical impossibilities for the natural way in which the universe was created to function. Only the creator himself could change the natural order in which space and time function.

A fourth and final way in which Jesus' dominion over the universe is manifested is in the supernatural signs and wonders he performs. Jesus is often seen casting demons out of the demon possessed (Matt 8:16, 28–34; 12:22; Mark 5:1–15; Luke 8:26–39), healing the sick (Matt 4:23–24; 9:35), and even raising the dead (Mark

5:22–43; Luke 7:11–17; 8:40–56; John 11). The miracles of Jesus point out his power both over the created order and over the angelic realm, which is something only the ruler of the universe can do.

Jesus as Redeemer and Teacher of Israel

The God who brought Israel out of Egyptian captivity, the God who continued to liberate Israel in the time of the judges and of the kings from various empires that had conquered it, is also the God who promised a future redemption under the ultimate savior of Israel, the Messiah. Could it be that Jesus is the redeemer Israel has been expecting? Much has been written on the topic of messianic prophecies already (Rydelnik 2019; Lockyer 1988), and so it is not my intent here to present an exhaustive list of all the messianic prophecies Jesus fulfilled. However, it is worth pointing out three important sets of prophecies that are tied into Israel's eschatological redemption hopes. First, the initial promise of redemption in the protoevangelium (Gen 3:15) is matched at least twice in Jesus' life: in the temptation event and in the resurrection event. In the temptation event (Matt 4:1–11; Mark 1:12–13; Luke 4:1–13), the devil himself attempts repeatedly to discredit Jesus' identity. Nevertheless, Jesus proves his divine identity in the temptation event, not only by his amazing display of self-control, defeating hunger and a desire for world dominion, but also in that he has the power and authority to command Lucifer to leave. In the entire universe, only the God who created the whole world, angels included, has the power to demand submission from the angel of darkness (a point also made by Job's story). The other event that emphasizes Jesus' superiority over the demonic world is his resurrection. The entire narrative is predicted by King David (Pss 2 and 16) and is attested to by more than five hundred eyewitnesses who have seen and experienced the resurrected redeemer, Jesus the Messiah (Acts 2; 1 Cor 15). David prophesied that the Messiah would not see putrefaction and the eyewitnesses testified that Jesus rose again three days after his death, before his body could begin to decompose. In his resurrection and defeat of the devil's temptations, Jesus proves that he is indeed the one whom the Scriptures foresaw, the Lord's anointed Messiah, the ultimate redeemer promised to Adam and Eve.

The redemptive nature of the divinely anointed Messiah is also described in terms of the unparalleled presence of the Spirit upon him (Isa 11:2–5). The Spirit of YHWH (Isa 11:2) will rest (נוּחַ) on the "shoot from the stump of Jesse." The seven aspects of the Spirit, like the seven Spirits of God (Rev 5:6), represent the fullness of the Spirit of God. In addition, Jesus' conception as well as his miracle-peppered ministry are both attributed to the intervention of the Spirit (Matt 1:20; Luke 1:35). The coming of the Spirit upon Jesus immediately after his baptism precedes his public ministry and is described in unique ways. In the Synoptic Gospels (Matt 3:16; Mark 1:10; Luke 3:22; cf. John 1:33–34), the Baptizer's account relates that John saw "the heavens open" and the Spirit of God descending from heaven like a dove and remaining upon Jesus. No other prophet of God experienced the Spirit coming upon him or her in such a manner or remaining upon them indefinitely (and "without measure," as John adds in 3:34).

Isaiah's prophecy (11:2–4) distinguishes the Messiah by his just judging and by his unmatched teaching ministry. It is not surprising then that the Synoptics frequently refer to Jesus as teacher or rabbi (Matt 8:19; 9:11; 10:24–25; Mark 4:38; 5:35; Luke 3:12; 6:40). In fact, based on the dating of the New Testament manuscripts, it may be that the first historical reference to a person being called "rabbi" carrying the meaning of "teacher" is in connection to Jesus. The title "rabbi" begins to be used only "in the generation after Hillel . . . employed as a title for the sages. The passage in the New Testament (Matt 23:7) in which the Scribes and the Pharisees are criticized because they 'love . . . to be called . . . Rabbi' probably reflects the fact of its recent introduction" (Klatzkin 1972, 1445). More specifically, the term "rabbi" becomes commonly used after 70 CE, in connection with the leaders of the Pharisaic sect that was evolving into Rabbinic Judaism (Freedman 1992, 600–1).

Jesus as Participant in the Divine Name

One of the primary ways God makes himself known in the Old Testament is by his unique names. God's names reveal his character and make him recognizable (Exod 3:13–15; 5:2; 6:3; 7:5, 17; 8:6; 9:29; 10:2; 14:4). Therefore, God prohibits the misuse of his name and warns of severe punishment for anyone who fails to uphold this command (Exod 20:7; Lev 24:11, 16; Payne 1962, 144). God reveals his names and extends an intimate relationship to his covenantal people. There are three reasons God reveals his names to Israel: to reveal his majesty and love, to reflect intervention in the nation's life, and to highlight his relationship with Israel (Dyrness 1977, 45).

Jesus' revelation of the divine name as "the name of the Father and of the Son and of the Holy Spirit" (Matt 28:19) is one of the most revolutionary theological developments in Jewish monotheism. In one statement, paralleling Moses' significant revelation of the divine name to Israel (Exod 3:14), Matthew presents Jesus (and the Spirit) as partaking in the divine name. Notably, the Greek text uses the idiom *to onoma* ("the name") in the singular form in Matt 28:19. The writer could have easily used the plural "names," thereby avoiding the possibility of a divine plurality within the Godhead. The use of a single name in the baptism formula reveals a unity of "the name" concept and a plurality of distinct "persons." In more simple terms, the concept of "name" here could be parallel to the concept of "family." While there are five members in my family, we are yet one and the same family. We are not one member with a fluid identity or a personality disorder; that would be a conversation to be had in psychology. We are five unique individuals who share the same last name and DNA. Circling back to Matthew, Gathercole points out two other texts that further emphasize Jesus' inclusion in the divine name by substituting the divine name of God, YHWH, with the name of Jesus (7:22; 18:20; 2011, 4–5). In these three significant Matthean texts, the writer masterfully includes Jesus in the divine identity of the one God of Israel while maintaining Jewish monotheism.

Examining the Synoptics' Christology through the lens of divine identity proves to be a rewarding study. The Synoptic Gospel writers present Jesus as having dominion over the created world, as well as Israel's Spirit-filled redeemer, Messiah, and teacher. Matthew's depiction of Jesus' identity culminates with naming him within God's own name.

Divine Identity Pneumatology in the Synoptic Gospels

Thus far we have looked at how the Synoptic Gospels describe Jesus in divine identity terminology. Let us turn our attention to the divine identity markers in relation to the Spirit.

The Spirit's Role in Creation and Life Giving

Creating and giving life are abilities that belong exclusively to God. The Synoptics do not focus on the Spirit's participation in creation, much like their treatment of Jesus' role as creator. Nevertheless, Jesus' miraculous conception is one way in which the Spirit's ability to create and give life is evident. When Mary is told she will give birth to the Son of God, the angel informs her that the pregnancy will be a supernatural intervention attributed to the Holy Spirit (Matt 1:18, 20; Luke 1:35). Consistent with the Old Testament narrative (Ps 104:24–30; Ezek 37:1–14; Isa 7:14), as well as with the Gospel of John (John 6:63), Mary's miraculous pregnancy in the Synoptics shows the Spirit's participation in creating new life.

The Spirit and Redemption

The Spirit's role in Israel's redemption is reflected in the Synoptics in his participation in the conception of the Messiah (Luke 1:34–35), and in his descent upon Jesus at Jesus' baptism. Moreover, the Spirit remains upon Jesus the Messiah throughout his ministry (Matt 3:12–4:1; 12:28; Mark 1:9–13; Luke 3:21–22). The Spirit's involvement in Jesus' conception, as well as his coming and remaining upon Jesus, reflect the Old Testament narratives in which the Spirit came upon Israel's past kings and prophets. Thus the Gospel writers portray the Spirit's role in redeeming Israel through the Messiah.

The Spirit as the Disciples' Teacher

Another indicator of the Spirit's divine identity is noticeable in his role as teacher of Israel. This characterization applies to the Spirit in the Synoptics, particularly in the disciples' highest time of need during their persecution: "When they bring you before the synagogues and the rulers and the authorities, do not be anxious . . . for the Holy Spirit will teach you in that very hour what you ought to say" (Luke 12:11–12). The Greek verb used here *didaskō* (to teach) leaves no doubt that the Spirit will instruct Jesus' followers how to respond when faced with persecution. However, the Spirit's teaching is enjoyed only by those who have believed in Jesus as God's Messiah.

The Spirit and the Name of God

By including the Spirit in the divine name alongside the Father and the Son, Matthew reveals the Spirit's unique identity in a way that both reinforces

Old Testament theology (Isa 48:12–16) and revolutionizes our understanding of the Spirit of God (Matt 28:19). As in Jesus' case, the Spirit is here revealed in terms of equality in identity with the one God of Israel. Additionally, the Spirit's descending upon Jesus in the baptism event (Matt 3:16; Luke 3:22; John 1:32), while the Father remains and declares from heaven that Jesus "is my beloved Son," highlights the Spirit's personal distinction from Jesus as well as from the Father. For a time, the Spirit is with neither of them; the Father is in heaven and Jesus on earth while the person of the Spirit is in between heaven and earth, coming from one realm to the other. Evidently, the Spirit cannot simply be one and the same spirit with the Father or with the Son, for that would mean that either the Father also descended from heaven upon Jesus or that Jesus did not have a spirit up to this moment. Thus the Spirit is not only the third divine being that the Synoptics reveal; he is also an entirely distinct person from the other two members of the Godhead. Although his name is enumerated alongside the Father and the Son, the Spirit's mission shows that he is distinct from the other two persons who co-share in the divine name.

In conclusion thus far, the Synoptic Gospels identify the Spirit by unique identity markers. He is portrayed as one who can give life, who empowers Israel's Messiah and thus participates in Israel's redemption, who teaches the disciples during persecution, and who shares in the one name of God alongside the Father and the Son. At the same time, the Spirit remains distinct from the other two divine beings. In the Synoptics, therefore, the Spirit is included in God's unique identity.

Divine Identity Christology in John's Gospel

My purpose in this section is to point out the effectiveness of examining Johannine Christology through the lenses of divine identity markers and in the context of strict Jewish monotheism. In this, I seek to add my voice to the informative divine identity christological studies that have influenced my understanding of Johannine Christology (Bauckham 2007; 2015; Köstenberger and Swain 2008).

Jesus as Creator of the Cosmos

One of the distinctives of divine identity is God's ability to create. John's Gospel spells out already in the Prologue that Jesus was involved in the creation of the entire universe: "All things were made through him, and without him was not any thing made that was made" (1:3). The text points Jesus out as creator and co-creator of the entire universe with God the Father, with whom Jesus was from the beginning.

The Fourth Gospel also reveals Jesus as giver of life, physical and spiritual, which ties directly into the creative power of the one God of Israel (Gen 2:7). It is God alone who is sovereign "over life and death (Deut 32:39). God is the only living one, that is, the only one to whom life belongs eternally and intrinsically" (Bauckham 2007, 242). As creator and as "the life" (John 11:25; 14:6), Jesus heals the royal official's son, who was about to die (John 4:46–54). He also resurrects Lazarus, who had been already dead for four days (John 11:14, 17, 43–44).

Perhaps the strongest presentation of Jesus' ability to give life and to resurrect the dead is made in John 5. Here, Jesus initially emphasizes that "as the Father raises the dead and gives them life, so also the Son gives life to whom he will" (5:21, 25–26). In typical Johannine fashion, Jesus switches the conversation from the physical realm to the spiritual one. On one hand, the Father and Jesus have the power to give life and to resurrect the dead; on the other, by hearing the words of Jesus and believing in his Father, one is guaranteed "eternal life" (5:24). This eternal life starts by being born from above into God's kingdom (John 3:15–16, 36), is made possible by eating "the bread of life" (John 6:48–51) and by taking "the way" into the kingdom of God (John 14:6). Evidently, these are metaphors for believing in Jesus, the one who came down from heaven (John 3:13, 31).

John's Gospel therefore portrays Jesus as creator of the physical cosmos. It also describes him as possessing divine abilities, which are manifested in his power to resurrect the dead and, especially, to give not only physical but also eternal life to those who hear his words and believe in God.

Jesus as Ruler over the Universe

Unlike the Synoptic Gospels, in which Jesus teaches on judgment (Matt 5:25; 7:1; Luke 6:37; 12:57–58) but is not necessarily mentioned in the role of judge (Luke 12:13–14), John does not shy away from portraying Jesus as the sovereign judge of the world (5:22, 27, 30; 8:15–16, 26). In ancient Jewish tradition, God alone is "the judge of the earth" (Gen 18:25; Judg 11:27; 1 Chr 16:33; Ps 94:2). Therefore, by judging the world according to the Father's guidance, the author identifies Jesus as participant alongside the Father in God's unique role as judge of the universe.

Jesus as Redeemer of Israel

The Old Testament foretells of a time when the Messiah would come and bring ultimate redemption to God's people Israel (Gen 3:15; Ps 2; Isa 9:1–7). The Fourth Evangelist makes it clear that Jesus is that Messiah (1:41; 4:25). In fact, Jesus himself admits that he is indeed the Messiah (4:26). In addition, in John's Gospel, Jesus is repeatedly called "Christ," the Greek term for "Messiah" (1:17; 4:29; 7:41; 11:27; 20:31). Whether in the confession of Andrew or in that of the Samaritan woman, and of Jesus himself, the author highlights that Jesus is indeed Israel's Messiah and long-awaited redeemer.

Jesus as Teacher of Israel

God's role as teacher of Israel is another unique way in which the divine identity of Jesus is revealed by John. Granted, when compared to Matthew and Luke, John focuses less on Jesus' role as a teacher and mentions the twelve disciples later and less. Thus it could easily be perceived that Jesus' role as teacher is downplayed by the Fourth Gospel (Bauckham 2015, 189–90). Nevertheless, the writer refers frequently to Jesus as a rabbi or a teacher (1:38; 6:25; 8:4–5; 9:2; 11:28; 20:16), even a teacher who came "from God" (3:2). While it is claimed that John does not have a major sermon given by Jesus, like Matthew's Sermon on the Mount or Luke's Sermon on the Plain, I submit that Jesus' teaching in the upper room (John 13–17), the Farewell Discourse, constitutes a teaching session of no lesser importance than the Synoptic sermons. The upper room teaching gives the theological framework for the transition of Jesus' disciples from being taught by God through the ministry of Jesus to being taught by the Father and the Son through the promised Spirit (Ile 2008, 4).

God's role as teacher of Israel is portrayed by the Fourth Gospel in reference to Jesus and to the Spirit. In a dispute between Jesus and other Jews (6:41–59), Jesus claims his divinity by pointing to the prophets' promise of a time when God would teach all of Israel. Jesus reminds his audience, "It is written in the Prophets, 'And they will be all taught by God'" (6:45; cf. Isa 54:13). In the famous new covenant prophecy (31:31–37), Jeremiah describes a time when God will "put [his] law within them, and . . . write it on their hearts" (31:33). That putting and writing God's law in the hearts of his people is done through a teaching activity is probably the case, since the very next verse (Jer 31:34) claims that there will no longer be a need for the Israelites to teach one other. Since they will be taught by God himself, the Jewish people no longer have a need for other teachers. Consequently, John is probably alluding here to the fulfillment of Isaiah's prophecy: God is now teaching Israel through Jesus. Jesus' subsequent claim that he speaks only what he hears from the Father (8:26, 28) probably refers to Jesus' teaching ministry, which John describes as taking place both at the temple (7:14; 8:2) and in synagogues (18:20; Bauckham 2015, 189–90). The teaching attribute of God then becomes an important way in which John's Gospel reveals Jesus' inclusion in the identity of the one God of Israel. Jesus' reference to the prophecies of a future time when God himself will instruct his people and his allusion to their fulfillment in his ministry is remarkable; not only does it give authority to Jesus' own teaching and ministry but also to his unique identity as the focus of YHWH's instruction.

Jesus as Participant in the Divine Name

The names by which Jesus refers to the one God of the Old Testament in John's Gospel are *ho theos* ("God") and *ho patēr* ("the Father"; Ile 2016, 161). The inclusion of Jesus in the divine names and his connection to the Johannine divine titles for "God" and "the Father" are remarkable (1:18). The Prologue itself suffices to point out that not only before creation but also in the creation event, Jesus is named alongside God and linked to the Father in a masterful way that leaves no doubt as to Jesus' inclusion in the divine identity. Jesus, as *ho logos* ("the Word"), is with God and is himself God (1:1). In addition, Jesus is the only one begotten from God (1:4), while being "the only God, who is at the Father's side" (1:18).

Although far more could be said about John's Christology, I want to point out a few major theological points. First, Jesus' identity revolves around the Father-Son relationship. As such, the author makes it obvious from the beginning that Jesus, like the Father, is God. This is apparent from his inclusion in the divine name (1:1, 18) and in the act of creation (1:3). Second, the oneness of the Father-Son bond reveals their strong unity and co-shared divine identity: "I and the Father are one"

(10:29). Therefore, they judge as one, they create as one, and they co-send the Spirit (14:16) to the disciples. Third, and just as important as the Father-Son unity, is their distinctiveness. Although God the Father and Jesus share the same the divine identity, they are nonetheless two different persons with two different roles within the Godhead. This distinction is noticeable in the fact that Jesus came to earth, leaving the Father, so as to declare his words and to do his works, and Jesus returns to the Father (1:14; 3:13; 16:28) once his earthly mission is complete.

In conclusion, the Fourth Gospel's depiction of Jesus reveals his inclusion in the divine identity. All creation comes into being through Jesus' creative act, the Father gives all judgment to the Son, and the author uses different characters to point out again and again that Jesus is the promised redeemer, the Messiah himself. Without compromising Jewish monotheism, already in the Prologue, John reveals Jesus' divine identity. Last but not least, John portrays Jesus as the ultimate teacher of Israel, the one foreseen by Isaiah (54:13).

Divine Identity Pneumatology in John's Gospel

The Greek word for "spirit," *pneuma*, as well as the uniquely Johannine term *paraklētos* ("Paraclete") used to describe the Spirit, appear frequently in the Fourth Gospel: in fourteen out of the twenty-four occurrences, *pneuma* refers to the Spirit, while *Paraclete* appears four times (14:16, 26; 15:26; 16:7). Although there have been many insightful studies in John's pneumatology in general (Swete 1919; Berg 1988; Breck 1991; Brown 2003), with some focused on the Paraclete (Carson 1979; Matthews 1992) in modern scholarship, the attempt to examine the Spirit from a divine identity standpoint is novel (Ile 2016, 134–64).

The Spirit's Role in Creation and the New Creation and in Life Giving

The Old Testament describes the Spirit of God as participating in God's divine identity by co-creating alongside God (Gen 1:1–2) and by giving life (Ps 104:24–30; Ezek 37:1–14). However, the Spirit's involvement in creation is mentioned neither in John's Prologue nor anywhere else in John's Gospel. Perhaps this is because "in the New Testament the work of the Spirit is seen in the closest association with the work of Christ and the new life that he brings, rather than in the context of creation" (Smail 1988, 167; cf. also Moule 1978, 19–20). Nevertheless, the Spirit's ability to give life to all creatures is clearly reflected in the Fourth Gospel (3:4–8; 6:63; 7:37–39).

The discussion Jesus has with Nicodemus (3:1–21) emphasizes the cruciality of the Spirit's work to the new birth (3:3–6). In fact, a person's entrance into the kingdom of God is conditioned on their birth by the Spirit. That the Spirit is the agent of the new birth is also supported by John 7:37–39: those who believe in Jesus will become sources of "rivers of living water." The text itself (7:39) interprets these rivers of living water to refer to the Spirit. Since "living water" is used by John elsewhere (4:14) in connection to eternal life, it seems reasonable to conclude that this passage also attributes spiritual lifegiving power to the Spirit. The third Johannine text (6:63) describes the Spirit as the one who gives life, without providing any further explanation of whether this life is meant in a physical or in a spiritual sense. Since the Old Testament literature describes the Spirit as giving physical life to creation (Ps 104:24–30; Ezek 37:1–14), it seems reasonable to interpret this Johannine reference to the Spirit as physical life-giver (6:63). Consequently, the Fourth Gospel reveals the Holy Spirit as the agent of the new birth and as giver of life, physical and spiritual.

The Spirit's Role in Redemption: The Spirit and Jesus the Messiah

An important aspect of ancient Jewish eschatology is the coming of the Spirit-filled Messiah (Isa 11:1–2; 42:1; 61:1–2). The Fourth Gospel underlines the special relationship between the Spirit and Jesus the Messiah (1:18; 4:26; 6:69). The coming and remaining of the Spirit upon Jesus identifies him as the promised Messiah (1:32–34). Unlike Saul, from whom the Spirit departed (1 Sam 16:14), and David, who asked God not to take the Spirit from him (Ps 51:13), Jesus enjoys the abounding and abiding presence of the Spirit (1:32), even "without measure" (3:34–35). This is a possible allusion to Isa 11:2 (see also Lev. Rab. 15.2), where the Messiah is described as endowed with the Spirit in unprecedented ways.

The Farewell Discourse (John 14–16, esp.14:15–18, 25–26; 15:26; 16:7–15) further highlights the unique relation between the Spirit and Jesus. During his final evening before his crucifixion, Jesus tells his followers that after his ascension he will ask God the Father for another *Paraclete* to be with them forever (John 14:16). The term *paraklētos* "yields the clear picture of a legal adviser or helper or advocate in the relevant court" (Behm 1964, 157–58; Ile 2016, 157–58), and includes the idea of an active speaker on behalf of someone and before someone (Bultmann 1950, 438; Mowinckel 1933, 118). The Spirit's role as a Paraclete will be that of a vital, advocating *helper* and *guide* for the disciples. Jesus' reference to the Spirit as *allon paraklēton* ("another Paraclete," 14:16) "is carefully chosen. It indicates 'another of the same kind,' to preserve the continuity of divine exchange" (Harm 1987, 120). This equation between the Spirit and Jesus is a remarkable revelation concerning the identity of the Spirit: "As *another Paraclete*, the Paraclete is, as it were, another [person like] Jesus" (Brown 1967, 128). The main purpose of John is to demonstrate that Jesus is the Messiah (20:31), God's own Son (1:18; 6:69). Therefore, by presenting the Son and the Spirit as equal, John makes it clear that the Spirit, like the Son, participates in God's redemptive identity as well.

The Spirit as the Disciples' Teacher

The prophet Joel anticipates a time when God's Spirit will be poured out upon the entire nation (2:28–29). John (14:16) pinpoints that time to the moment when Jesus returns to heaven and asks the Father to send the Spirit. The outpouring of the Spirit upon the followers of Jesus, only ten days after Jesus' ascension (Acts 1–2), marks the initial fulfillment of Israel's eschatological expectations. In addition, Jesus promises that when the Spirit of truth (14:17; 15:26) comes, he will remain with the disciples forever (14:16). The abiding presence of the Holy Spirit (14:26) with the disciples not only resembles his permanent indwelling of Jesus, but it also contrasts the Spirit's sporadic presence with Israel's past leaders (Ps 51:13). The coming of the Holy Spirit upon the first disciples is a foretaste of what is to come for the entire nation of Israel. While in the past, the nation benefitted from temporarily Spirit-filled leaders, it will now benefit from leaders who are called to reveal God's will (15:26–27) and upon whom the Spirit will remain permanently.

John's Gospel describes the Spirit's role among the disciples in several ways: he is to endow and equip them (7:37–39; 14:16, 26; 15:26; 16:7–15; 20:22); as Paraclete, he will comfort, encourage, and advocate on their behalf (most likely before the Father; Rom 8:26; 1 John 2:1); and as the "another Paraclete," the Spirit will teach, help, and guide the believers. Thus the Spirit will teach them "all things" (14:26), will remind them of "all" Jesus taught them (14:26), will "guide them in all truth" (16:13), and will proclaim the revelations of Jesus to them (16:14). Moreover, the Spirit's teaching is two-dimensional: he bases his instruction on Jesus' past teachings, and he will also reveal to them things that will take place in the future. Therefore, the Spirit's own instruction is in harmony with Jesus' words and yet brings fresh revelation to the disciples.

In his role as teacher of the Messiah's disciples, the Spirit is fulfilling another divine identity attribute. God continues to be Israel's teacher as the teaching baton is passed on from Jesus the Messiah to the Spirit of truth. Isaiah's prophecy (54:13) is fulfilled, and Israel is finally being taught by God himself directly and on an ongoing basis, through the Messiah and subsequently through the Spirit.

The relationship between the Spirit and the disciples also reveals the individuality of the Spirit's identity. The Spirit will descend by himself to abide with the disciples, while Jesus and the Father remain in the heavenly realm. Thus John distinguished the Spirit as a separate individual from the Father and from the Son in that he alone will dwell in the future body of believers.

As conclusion to our divine identity incursion into the Fourth Gospel, we can affirm that John describes both Jesus and the Spirit in terms of divine identity, while maintaining a strict monotheism. Jesus shares in the divine name, in the creation and judgment of the world alongside the Father, and in giving life. Also, Jesus is the redeeming Messiah and Israel's ultimate teacher. Not only Jesus but also the Spirit appears in the Gospel of John as giving life, physical and spiritual, thus making the new creation possible, as being involved in Israel's redemption by virtue of his empowerment of Jesus and his disciples, and as the disciples' future teacher. While the Spirit does not appear as intimately connected to God's name as Jesus is, as "another Paraclete" the Spirit functions nonetheless as an equivalent, divine substitute for Jesus. Therefore, the Holy Spirit is included in the divine activities reserved for God alone. While Jesus and the Spirit equally share in God's unique identity, John also describes them as distinct individuals from each other and from God, the Father.

Theological Implications for God as Trinity in the Gospels

The application of the divine identity methodology to Jesus and to the Spirit in all four Gospels has direct implications on understanding God as Trinity. In relation to the universe, each of the three—the Spirit, Jesus, and the Father—give life, physical and spiritual, and participate in the new creation. Although there are only undertones pertaining to the Spirit's involvement in creation, there is no doubt that Jesus co-creates the cosmos with the Father.

John describes Jesus as judge of the universe, co-judging with the Father. While the Spirit is not referenced in this role of judge and ruler of the universe by the Gospel writers, both Isaiah and the Gospels emphasize that the Messiah can judge only with supernatural insight because the Spirit comes upon him without measure and remains upon him forever.

God's role as Israel's redeemer points to a time when God will intervene miraculously in Israel's affairs by sending both the Messiah and the Spirit (Isa 48:12–16). These divine interventions have the mark of a God who reveals himself in three distinct beings—yet is one God—as revealed by his name: Father, Son, and Holy Spirit (Matt 28:19).

The prophet Isaiah depicts God as Israel's eschatological teacher (54:13). In fulfillment of that prophecy, the Gospels portray Jesus and subsequently the Spirit as the ultimate teachers of the Messiah's disciples. The Gospels therefore reveal the Son, the Spirit, and the Father in divine identity terminology by showing their involvement in life-giving and the new creation, in Israel's eschatological redemption, in teaching the nation through the followers of Jesus, and in the revelation of God's name in such a way as to include the Father, the Son, and the Spirit while preserving monotheism. To this astounding revelation the Gospels instruct us what our appropriate response must be: reverence and worship of the one true God (Bauckham 2007, 243; Gathercole 2011, 6; Mark 1:40; Matt 4:10; 28:17; John 5:23).

Conclusion

The application of divine identity methodology to Christology and pneumatology in the four Gospels reflects some variations from the Synoptics to John. These foundational New Testament texts describe God as a unity of three persons who share the same divine identity and yet maintain their own individuality. In 325 CE, the Council of Nicaea defined the Godhead in the Greek and Latin philosophical categories of "essence" and "person." Nevertheless, the Triune God is revealed in biblical and Jewish terminology, defined in the ways God reveals his identity to Israel in the Old Testament as well as in the person and teachings of Jesus.

Works Cited

Bauckham, Richard. 2015. *Gospel of Glory: Major Themes in Johannine Theology.* Grand Rapids: Baker Academic.

———. 2008. *Jesus and the God of Israel: God Crucified and Other Studies on the New Testament's Christology of Divine Identity.* Carlisle: Paternoster.

———. 2007. *The Testimony of the Beloved Disciple.* Grand Rapids: Baker Academic.

————. 1999. "The Throne of God and the Worship of Jesus." Pages 43–69 in *Jewish Roots of Christological Monotheism: Papers from the St. Andrews Conference on the Historical Origins of the Worship of Jesus.* Edited by Carey C. Newman, J. R. Davila, and Gladys S. Lewis. Leiden: Brill.

Behm, Johannes. 1964. "παράκλητος." Pages 800–14 in vol. 5 of *TDNT*. Grand Rapids: Eerdmans.

Berg, Robert Alan. 1988. "Pneumatology and the History of the Johannine Community: Insights from the Farewell Discourse and the First Epistle." PhD diss., Drew University.

Bickersteth, Edward Henry. 1984. *The Trinity*. Grand Rapids: Kregel Publications.

Breck, John. 1991. *Spirit of Truth: The Holy Spirit in Johannine Tradition*. Crestwood: St. Vladimir's Seminary Press.

Brown, Francis. 1967. "The Paraclete in the Fourth Gospel." *NTS* 13.2: 113–32.

Brown, Tricia Gates. 2003. *The Spirit in the Writings of John: Johannine Pneumatology in Social scientific Perspective*. London: T&T Clark.

Bruner, Emil. 1943. *The Divine-Human Encounter*. Translated by Amandus W. Loos. Philadelphia: Westminster.

Bultmann, Rudolf. 1950. *Das Evangelium des Johannes*. Göttingen: Vandenhoeck & Ruprecht.

Burge, Gary. 1987. *The Anointed Community: The Holy Spirit in the Johannine Tradition*. Grand Rapids: Eerdmans.

Carson, D. A. 1979. "The Function of the Paraclete in John 16:7–11." *JBL* 98.4:547–66.

Chafer, Lewis Sperry. 1940. "Trinitarianism." *BSac* 97.385: 5–26.

Dyrness, William. 1977. *Themes in Old Testament Theology*. Downers Grove: InterVarsity Press; Carlisle: Paternoster.

Ferguson, Everett. 1987. *Early Christians Speak: Faith and Life in the First Three Centuries*. Rev. ed. Abilene, TX: Abilene Christian University Press.

Fortman, Edmund J. 1972. *The Triune God: A Historical Study of the Doctrine of the Trinity*. Grand Rapids: Baker.

Franks, R. S. 1953. *The Doctrine of the Trinity*. London: Duckworth.

Freedman, David Noel, et al., eds. 1992. "Rabbi." Pages 600–601 in vol. 5 of *ABD*. New York: Doubleday.

Gathercole, Simon J. 2011. "The Trinity in the Synoptic Gospels and Acts." Pages 55–68 in *The Oxford Handbook of the Trinity*. Edited by Gilles Emery and Matthew Levering. Oxford: Oxford University Press.

Guthrie, Donald. 1981. *New Testament Theology*. Downers Grove: InterVarsity Press.

Harm, Frederick R. 1987. "Distinctive Titles of the Holy Spirit in the Writings of John." *Concordia Journal* 13.2: 119–35.

Ile, Cristian S. 2008. "Discipleship from Jesus to Paul." MTh diss., Queen's University Belfast.

————. 2016. "The Trinity in the New Testament: The Application of Unique Identity Methodology to the Spirit of God." PhD diss., Queen's University Belfast.

Kaye, Bruce N. 1980. "The New Testament." Pages 11–26 in *One God in Trinity*. Edited by Peter Toon and James D. Spiceland. London: Samuel Bagster & Sons.

Klatzkin, Jacob. 1972. "Rabbi." Pages 1445–46 in vol. 13 of *Encyclopaedia Judaica*. Jerusalem: Keter.

Köstenberger, Andreas J., and Scott R. Swain. 2008. *Father, Son and Spirit: The Trinity and John's Gospel*. Downers Grove: InterVarsity; Nottingham: Apollos.

Lockyer, Herbert. 1988. *All the Messianic Prophecies of the Bible*. Grand Rapids: Zondervan.

Matthews, Revi J. 1992. "The Spirit-Paraclete in the Testament of Jesus According to Saint John's Gospel." PhD diss., Fordham University.

McDougall, Joy Ann. 2003. "The Return of Trinitarian Praxis? Moltmann on the Trinity and the Christian Life." *JR* 83.2:177–203.

Moltmann, Jürgen. 1989. *The Trinity and the Kingdom of God: The Doctrine of God*. Translated by Margaret Kohl. London: SCM Press.

Moule, Charles F. D. 1978. *The Holy Spirit*. London: Mowbrays.

Mowinckel, Sigmund. 1934. "'The Spirit' and 'the Word' in the Pre-exilic Reforming Prophets." *JBL* 53: 199–227.

O'Donnell, John J. 1983. *Trinity and Temporality: The Christian Doctrine of God in the Light of Progress Theology and the Theology of Hope*. Oxford: Oxford University Press.

Payne, J. Barton. 1962. *The Theology of the Older Testament*. Grand Rapids: Zondervan.

Ricoeur, Paul. 1988. *Time and Narrative*. Vol. 3. Edited by Kathleen Blamey and David Pellauer. Chicago: University of Chicago Press.

Rydelnik, Michael, and Edwin Bloom, eds. 2019. *The Moody Handbook of Messianic Prophecy: Studies and Expositions of the Messiah in the Old Testament*. Chicago: Moody.

Smail, Thomas A. 1988. *The Giving Gift*. London: Hodder & Stoughton.

Swete, Henry Barclay. 1909; 1919. *The Holy Spirit in the New Testament: A Study of Primitive Christian Teaching*. London: Macmillan.

Vanhoozer, Kevin J. 1997. "Does the Trinity Belong to a Theology of Religions? On Angling in the Rubicon and the 'Identity' of God." Pages 41–71 in *The Trinity in a Pluralistic Age*. Edited by Kevin J. Vanhoozer. Grand Rapids: Eerdmans.

Wainwright, Arthur W. 1962. *The Trinity in the New Testament*. London: SPCK.

4.3 The Kingdom of God in the Gospels

Noam Hendren

The kingdom of God is the central theme of Jesus' teaching and ministry according to the Gospels (Bright 1953, 17; Jeremias 1971, 96; Evans 2019, 152; Hengel and Schwemer 2019, 427). From the beginning of his ministry (Mark 1:15) and through the Last Supper (Mark 14:25), the "kingdom of God" was on his lips. According to Matthew, Jesus taught his disciples to pray:

> "Our Father who is in heaven
> May your name be revered as holy,
> May your kingdom come,
> May your will be done on earth even as it is in heaven."
>   (Matt 6:9–10, author's translation; cf. Luke 11:2–4)

This prayer assumes several facts: First of all, that the "kingdom" being prayed for had not yet "come" when Jesus taught his disciples this prayer (and one may assume the same to be true for Matthew's—and Luke's—readers decades later). Second, the coming of the kingdom would involve God's rule ("your will") being perfectly realized "on earth," as a realm parallel to "in heaven" where the Father dwells and reigns absolutely (Pennington 2007, 281–99, 318). Finally, the "name" of the Father—his person—would be recognized and honored as holy by all when this prayer would be answered. No such reality was realized during Jesus' earthly ministry, according to the Gospels.

What, then, was the nature of the "kingdom of God" that Jesus proclaimed and for which his followers were to pray? And how was the announcement "the kingdom of God has come near" understood and received by those who heard it proclaimed and witnessed the ministry of those who proclaimed it?

The phrase "kingdom of God" and its parallels—"kingdom of heaven" (in Matthew), or simply "the Father's/your/the kingdom"—appear in all four Gospels (over eighty times total). The single passage in John that uses the phrase (John 3:3, 5) establishes a clear connection between "the kingdom of God" and "eternal life" (Frey 2016; Ladd 1993, 295), a connection that also appears in the Synoptics (Matt 19:12–17, 21–29; 25:34–46; Mark 9:43–47; 10:14–30; Luke 18:16–18, 22–30; cf. 10:25–28, "inherit eternal life"). The latter concept becomes the dominant theme in John's Gospel (John 1:4; 20:31), which highlights "having life" now through faith in Jesus by the indwelling Spirit of God (John 3:3–8, 15–16, 36; 6:63; 7:39; 20:31) in anticipation of the kingdom's future realization on earth (Goldsworthy et al. 2000, 127, 616; Keener 2003, 322–23).

The Kingdom of God in the Tanakh and Intertestamental Literature

Although the precise term "kingdom of God" is not found in the Hebrew Bible ("Kingdom of YHWH" appears in 1 Chr 28:5 and references to "your/his/my [in context, God's] kingdom" are found in Pss 103:19; 145:11–13; 1 Chr 17:14), nevertheless, the kingship of God and his rule are fundamental to OT theology. The kingdom of God in the Tanakh has two distinct but closely related referents: on the one hand, it refers to the universal and timeless rule of God; but there is also an expectation of the concrete realization of God's rule on earth in the eschatological future (Jeremias 1971, 98–99; Hengel and Schwemer 2019, 430–31).

God's universal rule stems from his role as creator with the absolute right to impose his will as sovereign lord and judge (Gen 1:1–3; 18:25; Exod 15:1–18; Isa 33:22; Pss 74:12–17; 95:3–5; 135:6; Patrick 1987, 73; Evans and Johnston 2018). The "enthronement psalms" (Pss 47, 95–99) extol the timeless reality of God's kingship ("YHWH rules!") and Psalm 145 declares, "Your kingdom is an everlasting kingdom, and your dominion endures throughout all generations" (145:13; cf. Dan 4:2–3; 6:26).

God's rule is exercised throughout the entire universe but with the earth as the focus of his purposes (Michaels 1987, 114; Saucy 1997, 311). "The earth is the LORD's and all that is in it, the world and those who live in it" (Ps 24:1–2). The subjects of God's rule include all living beings (Pss 103:20; 95:3; 24:8; Merrill 2016, 321), but particularly his covenant people, Israel ("King of Israel," Isa 44:6; 33:22; Ross 2011, 156).

According to Gen 1, God sovereignly determined not to rule the earth directly, but through humankind created to reflect his character (his "image") and execute his will (Ross 1988, 112–113; Merrill 2016, 334).

> Then God said, "Let us make humankind in our image, according to our likeness" . . . and God said to them, "Be fruitful and multiply, and fill the earth and subdue it; and have dominion." (Gen 1:26, 28; cf. Ps 8)

God authorized his image-bearers to extend his sovereignty worldwide as his representative rulers. This mediated ("theocratic") rule was briefly realized in the undisturbed *shalom*—physical, relational, and spiritual wholeness, and well-being—of Eden (Gen 2:8–25), "a prototype of the kingdom of God" (Goldsworthy et al. 2000, 618; Merrill 1987, 298).

The first couple's rebellion created a dissonance between God's universal rule and his mediated rule on earth (Jeremias 1971, 99; Bock 2017, 567). God's purpose in the election of Israel was to create a "kingdom of priests and a holy nation" that would be his instrument to restore Edenic blessing of the "kingdom of God" to the world (Gen 12:1–3; 17:1–2; Exod 19:4–6; Lev 11:44–45; 26:11–12; Eichrodt 1961, 476; Hendren 2019; Hahn 2012, 75–77). Israel's own rebellion brought severe punishments designed to restore them to God: "In your distress, . . . you will return to the LORD your God and heed him" (Deut 4:30; 28:15–30:2; Lev 26:14–45). Only then would God regather Israel's exiles and "circumcise your hearts," that he might bless them and "walk among" them, as in the Garden (Deut 30:3–9; Lev 26:11–12).

God's covenant with David (2 Sam 7:11–16; Pss 132:11–18; cf. 89:3–4, 19–37) promised him an everlasting dynasty in which the Davidic king would be YHWH's adopted son, to "shepherd" Israel and the world into submission to God (Ps 78:70–72; Ps 2, interpreted messianically at Qumran, 4Q174; Stuhlmacher 2005, 329). Israel's prophets predicted that a future son of David, empowered by the Spirit of God, would judge the wicked, rescue the oppressed, and establish God's kingdom of universal righteousness and peace (Isa 11:1–10; 9:1–7; Jer 23:5–6; Ezek 34:23–30; 37:24). This "servant of the Lord" would heal the curse of sin (Isa 42:1–7; 61:1–2; cf. 53:4–5) and restore Israel to God, pouring out his Spirit on the repentant nation that they might fulfill their calling, "that my salvation may reach to the end of the earth" (Isa 49:1–6; 59:20–61:7; 2:2–4; Zech 12:10–13:1; 2:10–12; Jeremias 1971, 99); in short, restoring the kingdom of God on earth (1 Chr 17:13–14; Hahn 2012, 70; Eichrodt 1961, 473, 479–80).

The book of Daniel became the model of intertestamental expectation in this period (Evans 2001, 502–507). It reasserted God's universal and absolute kingship, despite Israel's oppressed condition (Dan 4:32, 34; cf. 2:37–38; 4:2–3, 25; 6:26), and anticipated the day when "the God of heaven will set up a kingdom that . . . shall crush all these [human] kingdoms and bring them to an end, and it shall stand forever" (Dan 2:44–45; cf. 2:35; Evans 2005, 55). God's agent and co-regent, according to Daniel, would be the heavenly "Son of Man" (7:13) to whom God would give dominion over his kingdom on behalf of "the people of the holy ones of the Most High" (7:14, 18, 22, 26–27; cf. 2:37–38, 44–45; Evans 2001, 498–501; Wenham 1987, 132–33). These themes, as vividly reframed in Daniel, are broadly reflected throughout intertestamental literature, especially in last two centuries prior to the ministry of Jesus (Collins 1987, 85–91; Viviano 1987, 104–6; Lattke 1984, 81).

The Similitudes of Enoch (1 En. 37–71) speak of God's "Elect one," identified as "the Son of Man" (1 En. 46:1–5) and as "Messiah" (48:10; 52:4; Evans 2005, 58; Collins 1987, 89), who "shall sit on the seat of glory" and judge (1 En. 45:3; Sim 1996, 119–21); who "shall depose the kings from their thrones and kingdoms," destroy the wicked, and dwell in a "paradisical state" (Collins 1987, 88) along with the "righteous ones" of Israel (1 En. 45:5–7; 51:1–5; cf. Dan 12:2–3; see also 1 En. 22 and 25:3, 6). "Glory and honor shall be given back" to Israel, because they will "repent and forsake the deeds of their hands" (1 En. 50:1–4; Evans 2002, 10).

The book of Daniel was "intensively interpreted" at Qumran (Hengel and Schwemer 2019, 175) and "seems to have encouraged, perhaps even guided" them in their biblical interpretation" (Evans 2001, 502). According to Atkinson, the "Son of God" text (4Q246 II, 8–9) presents the Davidic Messiah as a warrior who would "cast down his enemies before assuming the throne for an everlasting reign," establishing "the kingdom of God" (Atkinson 2000, 120). The Midrash on Eschatology (4Q174) "brings together . . . eschatological temple, realization of the kingdom of God, Davidic and priestly-prophetic Messiah" (Hengel and Schwemer 2019, 173).

The Psalms of Solomon 17 and 18 (late first century BCE) distill the longings of the Jewish people under the boot of Rome at the time of Jesus' birth:

> "See, Lord, and raise up for them their king, the son of David, to rule over your servant Israel . . . to purge Jerusalem from gentiles who trample her to destruction. . . . He will gather a holy people whom he will lead in righteousness; . . . And he will purge Jerusalem (and make it) holy as it was even from the beginning, (for) nations to come from the ends of the earth to see his glory, . . . there will be no unrighteousness among them in these days, for all shall be holy, and their king shall be the Lord Messiah. . . . The Lord himself is his [i.e., Messiah's] king." (Pss. Sol. 17:21, 26, 30–32, 34, trans. Charlesworth 1985; cf. Luke 1:68–75)

In other words, Messiah the son of David would be God's representative ruler on a restored earth, a renewal of the original creation mandate (Gen 1:26–28).

The Prophetic Preview to the Kingdom of God in the Gospels

The Synoptic Gospels—particularly Matthew and Luke—show a close affinity with Jewish expectations for the kingdom of God in their prophetic previews to the life of Jesus and the ministry of John the Baptist (Matt 1–2; Luke 1–2).

The Gospel of Matthew opens with a terse declaration of Jesus' identity: "an account of the genealogy of Jesus the Messiah, the son of David, the son of Abraham" (Matt 1:1), with an emphasis on Jesus' descent from "*King* David" (Matt 1:6, 16–20). The magi were told to seek "the King of the Jews" in Bethlehem, from which "shall come a *ruler* who is to *shepherd my people Israel*" (Matt 2:6, quoting Mic 5:2; cf. Isa 40:10–11; Ezek 34:23). This promise was understood as the establishment of the rule of the Lord himself on earth by the Messiah (Pss. Sol. 17:40–42).

The angel's promise that Jesus would "save his people from their sins" (Matt 1:21) emphasized Messiah's servant-priestly function: dealing with sin as the source of Israel's suffering—political, physical, and spiritual (Deut 28:47–52, 59–68; Pss. Sol. 17:5–20). Matthew would identify Jesus' exorcism and healing ministry with Isaiah's suffering servant: "He took our infirmities and bore our diseases" (Matt 8:16–17, quoting Isa 53:4; cf. Isa 42:1–7; 61:1–2; Ps 130:7–8; Pss. Sol. 18:3–8).

The Gospel of Luke opens with a series of angelic visitations and prophetic encounters that portray the kingdom of God that John and Jesus would proclaim as a national, earthly, political, and yet spiritual kingdom (Ridderbos 1962, 28; Michaels 1987, 114). Angelic visitations announced the coming of "Messiah the Lord" (Luke 2:11; Pss. Sol. 18:0, 7), the ultimate son of David and literal son of God (Luke 1:35; cf. Ps 2:7; 1 Chr 17:13–14), who would rule Israel from David's throne in an everlasting kingdom, as the prophets had predicted (Luke 1:32–35; 2:11; cf. Isa 9:6–7; 11:1–10; Jer 23:5–6; Ezek 37:24–25; Dan 7:14). Zechariah's son, "in the spirit of Elijah," would summon Israel to national repentance in preparation for the coming of "the Lord" as both eschatological judge and savior (Luke 1:8–17; cf. Mal 3:1–3; 4:1–6; Zeph 2:1–3; Pss. Sol. 18:5–9).

Prophetic revelations to Zechariah and to Mary and Joseph contain multiple allusions to the prophetic hope for the "consolation of Israel" and the "redemption of Jerusalem" (Luke 1:67–79; 2:25–38). Zechariah, "filled with the Holy Spirit," announced the divine "visitation" (*epeskepsato*) of Israel in the person of the Davidic Messiah, who would save Israel from its enemies and bring the blessing promised to Abraham, liberating Israel to worship the Lord "in holiness and righteousness . . . all our days" (Luke 1:67–75; cf. Gen 12:1–3; Isa 11:1–9; Zeph 3:12–20; cf. Pss. Sol. 17:21–27, 32; Hahn 2012, 190; Ladd 1974, 48).

Zechariah's son, John, would prepare Israel to share in the messianic redemption: "to give knowledge of salvation to his people and the forgiveness of their sins . . . to give light to those who sit in darkness . . . to guide our feet into the way of peace" (Luke 1:76–79). According to the Psalms of Solomon, the Messiah "will thrust out sinners from (the) inheritance. . . . And he will gather together a holy people, whom he will lead in righteousness" (Pss. Sol. 17:23, 26, translated by Evans and Zacharias 2014). Israel's national repentance and cleansing from sin would be a vital precondition for participation in the coming kingdom of God.

John's Proclamation of the Coming Kingdom

Each of the Gospels introduces the ministry of Jesus with the preaching of John the Baptizer (Matt 3:1–17; Mark 1:1–11; Luke 3:2–22; John 1:15, 19–37), but only the Synoptics give details of John's "baptism of repentance for the forgiveness of sins," linking him with the prophesied herald "of Israel's anticipated restoration" (Evans 2002, 6; Isa 40:3–11; with Mal 3:1 in Mark), which Luke calls "the salvation of God" (Luke 3:4–6, quoting LXX Isa 40:3–5; cf. Luke 1:69–77).

Matthew summarizes John's message as, "Repent, for the kingdom of heaven has come near" (3:2), using an expression ("kingdom *of heaven*") unique to his Gospel. This terminology emphasizes both the divine origin and nature of God's kingdom ("heavenly" vs. "earthly"), as well as its spatial aspects as the blessed realm that will replace all human kingdoms on earth (Pennington 2007, 281–99, based on Dan 2–7; for Daniel's influence on the NT, see Evans 2001, 498–521).

John declared that God was about to impose his rule on the world ("the kingdom . . . has come near"). The verb translated "come near" was used in the Tanakh to express "the imminent approach of the Day of Yahweh" (*NIDNTT* s.v. ἐγγίζω [*engizō*]), and the language of imminence called for an immediate choice, as judgment or redemption depended on the hearers' response (Isa 13:6; 24:1–3; Joel 2:1–2, 12–14; cf. Jon 3:4–5, 10; Deut 30:15–20). Thus John's announcement reminded his hearers of the cataclysmic judgments that would purge the wicked from Israel *prior* to the kingdom's arrival (Isa 10:22–23; Joel 1:15; 2:30–3:2; Amos 5:18–20; 9:8–15; Zeph 1:14–18; 2:1–3; Sim 1996, 114–15). Only those who turn to the Lord in sincere repentance, demonstrated by sincere obedience to his Torah, could hope to survive God's wrath and enter his kingdom on earth (Matt 3:7–12; Luke 3:7–14, 17; cf. Isa 4:2–4; 59:15b–21; 66:24; Ezek 20:33–38). That Israel's national repentance was required for its national restoration was commonly understood at the time (Tob. 13:6; Jub. 23:18–31; T. Jud. 23:5; Pss. Sol. 9:6–7; Evans 1999, 90; cf. Deut 30:1–6; Jer 24:7).

The "good news" in this terrifying scenario was that the day of repentance and forgiveness had also "come near" and that John was its prophet (Mark 1:4; Luke 3:18).

Jesus thoroughly identified himself with John's proclamation of God's kingdom (Evans 2002, 7, 9–10): first, by accepting baptism at his hands (Matt 3:13–15; Allison 2010, 53–54); then after John's arrest, taking up John's call to repentance as his own (Matt 4:12, 17; Mark 1:15; Evans 2012, 90); and finally, sending out the Twelve with the same message (Matt 10:2–4). Later, Jesus would praise John's role as the ultimate prophet and his forerunner as Messiah (Matt 11:7–19; Luke 7:24–35), and he would affirm John's baptism as being "from heaven" (Matt 21:23–32; Mark 11:27–33; Luke 20:1–8; cf. Allison 2010, 213–20).

The Nature of the Kingdom in the Preaching of Jesus

Jesus' descriptions of the kingdom of God are consistent with common Jewish expectations and imagery. In the beatitudes, those who are heirs of the kingdom ("theirs is the kingdom of heaven") are those who will enjoy the future blessings of a restored world (*Tikkun Olam*) in the presence of God (Matt 3:3–10; Luke 6:20–26; cf. Isa 61:1–11; Pss 37:9, 11, 18, 22, 27, 29, 34, 37; Pennington 2007, 93; Evans 2012, 102). All who respond to the summons of the kingdom would share equally in its blessings, which are graciously given without distinctions (Matt 20:1–16). The present "blessedness" of the heirs of the kingdom is their certitude of this glorious future inheritance, despite their bleak daily experience in a corrupt and oppressive world (Matt 5:3–10; Luke 6:20–22; parallel to 4Q171, cited by Evans 2012, 105–6; cf. Luke 6:23, "for surely your reward is great *in heaven*"; cf. Pss. Sol. 9:5).

Jesus describes the joys of the kingdom experience as a "'messianic banquet,' probably the most important metaphor of Jesus for the description of the future time of salvation" (Hengel and Schwemer 2019, 435–36; cf. Isa 24:23–25:9; 2 Bar. 29:3–8; 1 En. 62:14; 1Q28a II, 17–22; Evans 2012, 204–05) in which the righteous—including Gentiles of faith—will feast together with the resurrected saints of old (Matt 8:10–12; Luke 13:23–30; cf. Matt 22:2–13; 25:1–12; Luke 14:15–24). At the final Passover meal, Jesus told his disciples, "I will never again drink of this fruit of the vine until that day when I drink it new with you in my Father's Kingdom" (Matt 26:29; cf. Mark 14:25; Luke 22:18: "until the kingdom of God comes"; Luke 22:29–30: "at my table in my kingdom"; Hagner 1993, 744).

The kingdom of God will come with the coming of "the Son of Man . . . in his kingdom" "at the renewal of all things" to sit on his glorious throne and judge at "the end of the age" (Matt 19:28; 16:27–28; 24:3; 25:31–46; Mark 8:38; Luke 21:27; Sim 1996, 114–16). His coming is described as an eschatological "harvest" in which the angels will remove all evildoers and gather his elect into his kingdom where they will "shine like the sun in the kingdom of their Father" (Matt 13:37–43; cf. Dan 12:3; Matt 24:30–31, 37–42; Mark 13:26–27; cf. Matt 3:12; Luke 3:17; Hengel and Schwemer 2019, 392; Sim 1996, 115, 230–31).

Who Are the Heirs of the Kingdom?

Jesus' call to repentance (Matt 4:17), as explicated in the Sermon on the Mount, warned that "unless your righteousness exceeds that of the scribes and Pharisees, you will never enter the kingdom of heaven" (Matt 5:20) and setting as the standard of righteousness, "Be perfect, therefore, as your heavenly Father and is perfect" (Matt 5:48; 7:21; cf. Lev 11:44–45; Farmer 1987, 127). Throughout the sermon, Jesus pointed to himself as the "gatekeeper" of the kingdom, so that one's relationship to him and obedience to his teaching (equivalent to "the will of my Father") would determine who would enter the kingdom and who would be judged (Matt 5:11–12, 20–45; 7:21–27; cf. Mark 9:42–48, where to "enter life" means "enter the kingdom of God" in contrast to going "to hell, to the unquenchable fire"; cf. Isa 66:24).

In Mark 10:14–15, Jesus told his disciples, "Let the little children *come to me*; do not stop them; for it is *to such as these* that the kingdom of God *belongs*. Truly I tell you, whoever does not *receive the kingdom of God* as a little child *will never enter it*" (emphasis mine). Here, Jesus identified "come to me" with "receive the kingdom," which in turn "belongs . . . to such as these" (in 9:42, those "who believe in me"). Nevertheless, actual entry into the kingdom is still spoken of as a future event, rather than a present reality or experience (cf. Matt 19:13–15; Luke 18:15–17). Thus one can "enter" and be "in" the kingdom as its heir ("child of the kingdom," Matt 13:38; cf. Luke 10:20, "your names are written in heaven"; cf. Phil 3:21); while possession of the inheritance will take place only "in the age to come" (Mark 10:30; cf. Paul's analogy of the heir in Gal 4:1–2).

In contrast to the children, the man who wished "*to inherit eternal life*" but refused Jesus' call to give up his wealth and follow him demonstrated "how hard it *will be* for those who have wealth *to enter the Kingdom of God!*" (Mark 10:17–25, emphasis mine; cf. Matt 19:16–23; Luke 18:18–25). Whereas for the disciples, who gave up all to follow Jesus, being "saved," inheriting "eternal life . . . in the age to come," and participating in the Son of Man's glorious kingdom were assured (Mark 10:26–30; Matt 19:25–29; Luke 18:26–30; cf. Matt 25:31–34).

The Presence of the Kingdom in the Person of the King

Jesus went beyond merely proclaiming John's message, "Repent, for the kingdom of heaven has come near" (Matt 4:17; Mark 1:15). According to the Synoptics, he also manifested the kingdom's presence in his person through the miracles of healing and exorcism he performed (Matt 4:23–24; Nolland 1993, 725). These miracles constituted irrefutable evidence that he was the promised Messiah with the power to redeem the world and "set the captives free" (detailed in Matt 8:1–9:35, an expansion of 4:23–25; Isa 61:1–2; 35:4–6; Luke 13:16; cf. Luke 4:18–21; Farmer 1987, 128; Evans 2012, 234). Like Fleming's penicillium mold, everywhere Jesus went there was a ring of corruption-free space about him: a microcosm of the kingdom of God in his own person driving back demons, disease, and death. In line with Luke's characterization of the messianic kingdom in Zechariah's prophecy (Luke 1:67–75), the astounded witnesses of Jesus' miraculous works exclaimed, "God has visited [*epeskepsato*] his people!" (Luke 7:16 NASB).

In the exorcism of demons, the Gospels, and especially Mark, highlight the war of the kingdom of God—in the person of Jesus—against the kingdom of Satan (Kelber 1974, 15–16). Satan's attack on Jesus, tempting him with "all the kingdoms of the world" (Matt 4:8–9; Luke 4:5–7; in contrast to Dan 7:13–14), was followed by Jesus' counterattack on Satan's kingdom (Mark 1:13, 21–27; Evans 2005, 66–68). The demonic reaction, "What have you to do with us, Son of God? Have you come here to torment us *before the time*?" (Matt 8:29; cf. Mark 1:24; Luke 4:34), points to the authority of Jesus to carry out the final judgment of Satan and his hordes, a key component of the realization of the kingdom of God on earth in Jewish thought of the time (see the War Scroll [1QM] from Qumran; T. Levi 3:3; 18:12; Jub. 23:29; Evans 2005, 56–63; Evans and Johnston 2018; Sim 1996, 36–39). Those commissioned and sent out by Jesus as "fellow campaigners" received the same authority (Matt 10:1; Mark 6:7; Luke 9:1; cf. 10:1; Hengel and Schwemer 2019, 391–93) and saw the same results: "Lord, in your name even the demons submit to us!" (Luke 10:17–20).

Jesus asserted the presence of the kingdom in his person only in controversies with his opponents. When the scribes and Pharisees attributed Jesus' exorcisms to sorcery, claiming that he was in league with Satan (Matt 12:22–45; Luke 11:14–32; Mark 3:22–35; Evans 2012, 255), Jesus refuted their claims logically and then presented the only reasonable alternative: "But if it is by the Spirit of God that I cast out demons, then the kingdom of God has come to you" (Matt 12:28; Luke 11:20, "by the finger of God"). Rather than reasserting that the kingdom had merely "come near" (*ēngiken*), Jesus declared that the kingdom had actually arrived ("has come to you" [*ephthasen eph' hymas*], or even "come upon you," as if overtaking them suddenly, BDAG, s.v. φθάνω [*phthanō*]; Berkey 1963; Evans 2005, 72). In another dialogue with the Pharisees, found in Luke, Jesus declared, "The kingdom of God is not coming with things that can be observed; nor will they say, 'Look, here it is!' or 'There it is!' For, in fact, the kingdom of God is among you" (Luke 17:20–21).

In both instances, Jesus used shocking language as a rebuke to his opponents for denying what was right before their eyes. In Matthew, Jesus told his accusers that the kingdom of God had already "caught you by surprise"; that Jesus' healings and especially his exorcisms were proof positive that the power of the kingdom—the Spirit of God—was present and at work in his person. In Luke, he told them that while searching for "signs" of the kingdom's soon appearance (Nolland 1993, 852), they had failed to recognize that the kingdom of God in the person of the king was standing right before them (Green 2013, 478). "Jesus does not merely teach about the kingdom of God . . . or even bring it; he is the embodiment of the kingdom" (Edwards 2015, 627–28).

Jesus so closely linked the kingdom of God with himself, the "Son of Man," that acceptance or rejection of Jesus in the present would be tantamount to accepting or rejecting the kingdom itself (Luke 10:16; 7:28–30, see below; 9:26; Mark 8:38; and note Luke 21:27–31, below; Hooker 2000, 88). Thus the leadership's blasphemous accusation against Jesus would "not be forgiven," but "on the day of judgment" they would "be condemned" (Matt 12:24, 32, 34–37) along with the "evil and adulterous generation" they represented and whom their accusation was intended to mislead (Matt 12:38–45; cf. 12:23–24; 23:13, 15, 36–39; Hagner 1993, 353–54; France 1985, 216–17).

The presence of the kingdom in Jesus was briefly unveiled to his three closest disciples when they received the promised foretaste of "the Son of Man coming in his kingdom" (Matt 16:28), "the kingdom of God . . . come with power" (Mark 8:34), or simply "the kingdom of God" (Luke 9:27; Nolland 1993, 497). All three Gospels indicate that this promise was fulfilled when they saw Jesus as the Son of Man "in glory," overshadowed by a cloud and acclaimed "my son" by the heavenly voice (Matt 17:1–5; Mark 9:2–7; Luke 9:28–35; cf. Dan 7:13–14; Evans 1989, 35–36; Hagner 1993, 494). Although Jesus was on his way to rejection and death (Matt 16:21; Mark 8:31; Luke 9:22), this revelation reassured the disciples that he would yet return as the glorious Son of Man to establish his kingdom (cf. Luke 21:27; Nolland 1993, 502–3; Evans 1989, 35).

The Rejection of the King and the Delay of the Kingdom

Both Matthew and Luke present the rejection of Jesus by the religious leadership and "this evil generation" as a game changer that would result in the delay of the establishment of the promised kingdom of God on earth. This corresponds with the Old Testament demand for national repentance as a necessary precondition for Israel's national redemption (Deut 4:27–30; 30:1–5, 10; Isa 10:20–23), as reflected in the Second Temple literature (Evans 1999, 93) and in Peter's sermon in Acts 3:19–21.

Luke builds this theme around the promised divine "visitation" in the person of Jesus to bring in the kingdom (Luke 1:67–79; Nolland 1993, 91–92). While God's visitation was recognized by many through Jesus' miraculous works (Luke 7:16), the religious leadership "rejected God's purpose for themselves" by rejecting the Messiah's forerunner, and they would mislead "this generation" into rejecting of Jesus as well (Luke 7:28–31; cf. 9:22, 41; 17:25; 18:31–33; 20:17). As a result, the time would come when even Jesus' disciples would not see "one of the days of the Son of Man" (Luke 17:22) and the "bridegroom [would] be taken away from them and then they will fast" (Luke 5:33–35, in contrast to the joys of the messianic banquet).

Despite his followers' expectation that, upon his arrival in Jerusalem "the kingdom of God was to appear immediately" (Luke 19:11, 37–38), Jesus told a parable to reveal a delay in its establishment, which would be realized only upon his return (19:12, 15–27). Instead, Jesus focused on how the king's future subjects should serve him in his absence (Green 1997, 674–74; cf. Matt 25:14–30). Jesus explained the reason for this delay in a prophetic dirge over Jerusalem (Luke 19:41–44; cf. 13:34–35; Matt 23:37–39), in which the failure to recognize "the things that make for peace" (19:42; cf. 1:79)—that is, "the time of your visitation from God" in Jesus (19:44; cf. 1:68; Green 1997, 689–90)—would bring "desolation," "days of vengeance," and "wrath against this people" (Luke 21:20–24; for the linkage of Luke 19 with 21, see Nolland 1993, 917). Instead, only after "the times of the Gentiles" could they hope to "see the Son of Man coming in a cloud with power and great glory" and know that their "redemption" and "the kingdom of God is near" (Luke 21:27–28, 31; cf. 17:22–37).

For Matthew, the religious leadership's blasphemous and unforgiveable accusation (12:24; Mark 3:29–30)—a decisive rejection of the "kingdom of God" that "has come to you" in the person and works of Jesus (Matt 12:28, 31–32)—becomes a turning point in the narrative and a harbinger of "that generation's" unrepentance and subsequent bitter fate (Matt 12:36–37, 39–42, 45; Hagner 1993, 298; Nolland 2005, 533n35). From that point on, God would withhold "the secrets of the kingdom" from those identified with "this evil generation" (Matt 13:11; Hagner 1993, 372) who had hardened their hearts, preventing them from understanding, repenting ("turn"), and being healed (Matt 13:11–15; Mark 4:11–12, "be forgiven;" cf. Isa 6:9–12; Oswalt 1986, 189).

In Matthew, Jesus connected the future suffering of the nation with the corruption of the religious leadership (Matt 23:1–36), who "lock people out of the kingdom of heaven" (23:13) by rejecting the testimony concerning Jesus (23:34), and who thus would bring upon themselves and "this generation" the guilt of all the martyrs of Israel (23:35–36). The result would be the desolation of Jerusalem and the temple (23:37–24:2; cf. Luke 13:34–35) and ultimately, "great suffering" threatening the nation's very existence (Matt 24:21–22; cf. Luke 21, above; cf. Dan 12:1; Jer 30:4–7; cf. intertestamental expectations in Evans 1999, 87; Green 1997, 738–39). Only a reversal of the nation's rejection of Jesus would bring about his return as the Son of Man to judge the wicked, regather Israel's exiles, and rule as king over all the nations (Matt 23:39; 24:29–31; 25:31–46; cf. Zech 12:1–3, 9–10; 14:1–4, 9, 16).

The Parables of the Kingdom: Between Rejection and Redemption

According to Matthew, on the very day of the Pharisees' "blasphemous accusation" (13:1), Jesus taught a series of parables to equip his disciples as scribes "trained for the kingdom of heaven" (Matt 13:52; Nolland 2005, 370–71; cf. 23:34, "I send you . . . scribes"; 28:19, to "make disciples"). From the beginning, Jesus had promised his disciples that they would "fish for people" (Matt 4:19), and he prepared them "to be sent out to proclaim the message" (Mark 3:14; Matt 10). Having learned "the secrets of the kingdom" from the king himself throughout his ministry (Matt 13:11), they were soon to continue their proclamation of the "word of the kingdom" without him, in the face of human and satanic opposition (13:19, 38–39).

These parables anticipate the mixed results that the disciples should expect in gathering new "children of the kingdom" (13:19–23, 38) and at the same time highlight the long-term promise of their seemingly inconspicuous efforts (13:31–33, "smallest seed"; yeast "hidden" [enekrypsen] in dough), culminating in the discriminating judgment "at the end of the age" (13:40–42, 49–50; cf. 24:3, 14) and the blessedness of the kingdom to come (13:43–46). The clear eschatological elements in these parables are consistent with Jesus' presentation of the kingdom to this point and are therefore not themselves "mysteries." What is surprising is that "the end of the age," once thought to be imminent, retreats to an uncertain future (Matt 23:37; Luke 13:33–34); and the disciples, who had looked forward eagerly to a "triumphal entry," still have a long and challenging ministry ahead of them (cf. Matt 23:34; 24:9–14; Hengel and Schwemer 2019, 444).

Kingdom Life Now in the Gospel of John

In contrast with the Synoptics, the Gospel of John mentions the kingdom of God only twice, in the night dialogue with Nicodemus (John 3:3–5). In both cases, the kingdom is presented, in line with current Jewish thinking, as a future blessed realm one may "see" and "enter," but only if "born from above . . . of the Spirit" (3:6–8; Keener 2003, 323). This is consistent with the Old Testament expectation of the last days' outpouring of the Spirit of God on the nation of Israel, purifying and transforming it to enter into the blessings of God's kingdom (Ezek 36:25–30; 39:25–29; Joel 2:28–3:1; Isa 32:15–20; 44:3; 59:20–60:3; Zech 12:10–13:1; cf. John 3:10; 1QS IV, 20–22).

As in the Synoptics, John connects entering the kingdom with receiving "eternal life" through faith in Jesus, the Son of Man (3:14–16). He who "has eternal life" is contrasted with the one who "will not see life, but must endure God's wrath" (3:36), which again casts seeing or entering life (i.e., the kingdom of God) as an eschatological event like the judgment (cf. Matt 3:9, "the wrath to come"). Later, Jesus would identify himself with the Son of Man who will raise the dead and consign them to "life" or to "condemnation," both last-day events in John (John 5:25–29; cf. 6:39–40, 44, 54). These passages may be considered parallel to the Synoptic concept that one can "enter" and "be in" the kingdom now, as a present heir of a future reality, without asserting the kingdom's present realization, or even "inauguration," in the world.

But John's unique emphasis is on the believer's present experience of "eternal life" through the indwelling Spirit of God, whom "the Son of Man" gives "without measure" (3:34). The indwelling Spirit, compared to "rivers of living water," whom believers were to receive after Jesus' glorification, would be the conduit of that divine life (John 7:37–39; 6:63; cf. John 5:26; 6:57) that the Son gives (5:21; 4:14). Thus, according to John, the believer in Jesus can experience the life of the future kingdom now with total confidence for the future, knowing they will "not come under judgment" but have already "passed from death to life" (John 5:24; Köstenberger 2009, 297).

Works Cited

Allison, Dale C., Jr. 2010. *Constructing Jesus: Memory, Imagination, and History*. Grand Rapids: Baker Academic.

———. 1999. "Jesus and the Victory of Apocalyptic." Pages 126–41 in *Jesus and the Restoration of Israel: A Critical Assessment of N.T. Wright's Jesus and the Victory of God*. Edited by Carey C. Newman. Downers Grove, IL: InterVarsity Press.

Atkinson, Kenneth R. 2000. "On the Use of Scripture in the Development of Militant Davidic Messianism at Qumran: New Light from *Psalms of Solomon* 17." Pages 106–23 in *The Interpretation of Scripture in Early Judaism and Christianity: Studies in Language and Tradition*. Edited by Craig A. Evans. JSPSup 33. SSEJC 7. Sheffield: Sheffield Academic Press.

Berkey, Robert F. 1963. "ΕΓΓΙΖΕΙΝ, ΦΘΑΝΕΙΝ, and Realized Eschatology." *JBL* 82.2: 177–87.

Bock, Darrell L. 2017. *Jesus According to Scripture: Restoring the Portrait from the Gospels*. 2nd ed. Grand Rapids: Baker Academic.

Bright, John. 1953. *The Kingdom of God*. Nashville: Abingdon.

Charlesworth, James H., ed. 1985. *The Old Testament Pseudepigrapha*. Vols 1 and 2. New Haven: Yale University Press.

Collins, John J. 1987. "The Kingdom of God in the Apocrypha and Pseudepigrapha." Pages 81–95 in *The Kingdom of God in 20th-Century Interpretation*. Edited by Wendell Willis. Peabody, MA: Hendrickson.

Edwards, James R. 2015. *The Gospel According to Luke*. Pillar New Testament Commentary. Grand Rapids: Eerdmans.

Eichrodt, Walther. 1961. *Theology of the Old Testament*. Vol. 1. Philadelphia: Westminster.

Evans Craig A. 2002. "Authenticating the Activities of Jesus." Pages 3–29 in *Authenticating the Activities of Jesus*. Edited by Bruce Chilton and Craig A. Evans. Boston: Brill.

———. "Daniel in the New Testament: Visions of God's Kingdom." Pages 490–527 in vol. 2 of *The Book of Daniel: Composition and Reception*. Edited by John J. Collins and Peter W. Flint. Leiden: Brill.

———. "Inaugurating the Kingdom of God and Defeating the Kingdom of Satan." *BBR* 15.1: 49–75.

———. 1999. "Jesus and the Continuing Exile of Israel." Pages 77–100 in *Jesus and the Restoration of Israel: A Critical Assessment of N. T. Wright's Jesus and the Victory of God*. Edited by Carey C. Newman. Downers Grove, IL: InterVarsity Press.

———. 2019. "The Life and Ministry of Jesus." Pages 151–57 in *A Handbook on the Jewish Roots of the Christian Faith*. Edited by Craig A. Evans and David Mishkin. Peabody, MA: Hendrickson.

———. 1988. *Mark 8:27–16:20*. WBC 34B. Nashville: Thomas Nelson.

———. 2012. *Matthew*. New Cambridge Bible Commentary. New York: Cambridge University Press.

Evans, Craig A., and J. J. Johnston. 2018. "Kingdom of God" in *Brill Encyclopedia of Early Christianity Online*. Edited by David G. Hunter, Paul J. J. van

Geest, and Bert Jan Lietaert Peerbolte. Accessed March 31, 2021. http://dx.doi
.org/10.1163/2589–7993_EECO_SIM_00001867.

Evans, Craig A., and H. Daniel Zacharias. 2014. *Old Testament Pseudepigrapha:
Greek & English*. Grand Rapids: Eerdmans.

Farmer, Ron. 1987. "The Kingdom of God in the Gospel of Matthew." Pages 119–30
in *The Kingdom of God in 20th-Century Interpretation*. Edited by Wendell Willis.
Peabody, MA: Hendrickson.

France, R. T. 1985. *Matthew: An Introduction and Commentary*. TNTC 1. Downers
Grove, IL: InterVarsity Press.

Frey, Jörg. 2016. "From the 'Kingdom of God' to 'Eternal Life': The Transforma-
tion of Theological Language in the Fourth Gospel." Pages 439–58 in vol. 3 of
John, Jesus, and History. Edited by Paul N. Anderson, Felix Just, S.J., and Tom
Thatcher. Atlanta: SBL Press.

Goldsworthy, G., T. Desmond Alexander, and Brian S. Rosner, eds. 2000. *New Dictionary of Biblical Theology*. Downers Grove, IL: InterVarsity Press.

Green, J. B. 2013. "Kingdom of God/Heaven." Pages 468–81 in *DJG*. Edited by Joel
B. Green, Jeannine K. Brown, and Nicholas Perrin. 2nd ed. Downers Grove,
IL: InterVarsity Press.

Green, Joel B. 1997. *The Gospel of Luke*. NICNT. Grand Rapids: Eerdmans.

Hagner, Donald A. 1993. *Matthew 1–13*. WBC 33A. Grand Rapids: Zondervan.

Hahn, Scott W. 2012. *The Kingdom of God as Liturgical Empire: A Theological Commentary on 1–2 Chronicles*. Grand Rapids: Baker Academic.

Hendren, Noam. 2019. "The Kingdom and the Covenants." Pages 9–12 in *A Handbook on the Jewish Roots of the Christian Faith*. Edited by Craig A. Evans and
David Mishkin. Peabody, MA: Hendrickson.

Hengel, Martin, and Anna Maria Schwemer. 2019. *Jesus and Judaism*. Translated
by Wayne Coppins. Waco, TX: Baylor University Press.

Hooker, Morna D. 2000. "Mark's Parables of the Kingdom (Mark 4:1–34)." Pages
79–101 in *The Challenge of Jesus' Parables*. Edited By Richard N. Longenecker.
Grand Rapids: Eerdmans.

Jeremias, Joachim. 1971. *New Testament Theology: The Proclamation of Jesus*. New
York: Scribner's Sons.

Keener, Craig S. 2003. *The Gospel of John: A Commentary*. 2 vols. Grand Rapids:
Baker Academic.

Kelber, Werner H. 1974. *The Kingdom in Mark: A New Place and a New Time*.
Philadelphia: Fortress.

Köstenberger, Andreas. 2009. *A Theology of John's Gospel and Letters: Biblical Theology of the New Testament*. Grand Rapids: Zondervan.

Ladd, George Eldon. 1974. *The Presence of the Future: The Eschatology of Biblical
Realism*. Grand Rapids: Eerdmans.

———. 1993. *A Theology of the New Testament*. Rev. ed. Edited by Donald A. Hagner.
Grand Rapids: Eerdmans.

Lattke, Michael. 1984. "On the Jewish Background of the Synoptic Concept 'The
Kingdom of God.'" Pages 72–90 in *The Kingdom of God in the Teaching of Jesus*.
Edited by Bruce Chilton. Philadelphia: Fortress.

Merrill, Eugene H. 1987. "Covenant and the Kingdom: Genesis 1–3 as Foundation for Biblical Theology." *CTR* 1.2:295–308.

———. 2016. *Everlasting Dominion: A Theology of the Old Testament*. Nashville: Broadman and Holman.

Michaels, Ramsey. 1987. "The Kingdom of God and the Historical Jesus." Pages 109–18 in *The Kingdom of God in 20th-Century Interpretation*. Edited by Wendell Willis. Peabody, MA: Hendrickson.

Nolland, John. 2005. *The Gospel of Matthew*. NIGTC. Grand Rapids: Eerdmans.

———. 1993. *Luke 9:21–18:34*. WBC 35B. Grand Rapids: Zondervan.

Oswalt, John N. 1986. *The Book of Isaiah: Chapters 1–39*. NICOT. Grand Rapids: Eerdmans.

Patrick, Dale. 1987. "The Kingdom of God in the Old Testament." Pages 67–79 in *The Kingdom of God in 20th-Century Interpretation*. Edited by Wendell Willis. Peabody, MA: Hendrickson.

Pennington, Jonathan T. 2007. *Heaven and Earth in the Gospel of Matthew*. NovTSup 126. Leiden: Brill.

Ridderbos, Herman. 1962. *The Coming of the Kingdom*. Phillipsburg, NJ: P&R.

Ross, Allen P. 1988. *Creation and Blessing: A Guide to the Study and Exposition of Genesis*. Grand Rapids: Baker.

———. 2011. *A Commentary on the Psalms*. Vol. 1. Kregel Exegetical Library. Accordance electronic ed., version 1.0. Grand Rapids: Kregel.

Saucy, Mark R. 1997. *The Kingdom of God in the Teaching of Jesus: In 20th Century Theology*. Dallas: Word.

Sim, David C. 1996. *Apocalyptic Eschatology in the Gospel of Matthew*. New York: Cambridge University Press.

Stuhlmacher, Peter. 2005. "The Messianic Son of Man: Jesus' Claim to Deity." Pages 325–44 in *The Historical Jesus in Recent Research*. Edited by James D. G. Dunn and Scot McKnight. Winona Lake, IN: Eisenbrauns.

Viviano, B. T. 1987. "The Kingdom of God in the Qumran Literature." Pages 97–107 in *The Kingdom of God in 20th-Century Interpretation*. Edited by Wendell Willis. Peabody, MA: Hendrickson.

Wenham, David. 1987. "The Kingdom of God and Daniel." *ExpTim* 98: 132–34.

4.4 The Theology of the Land in the Gospels

Michael J. Wilkins

When considering the Jewish roots of the Gospels, a theme that regularly surfaces is "fulfillment." Indeed, Craig Blomberg, in his recent development of NT theology, suggests that fulfillment is a central integrating theme that describes the relationship of the OT with the NT. He speaks of the theme of fulfillment as the shift of the ages, or salvation history, which in his mind is "the history of God's redemptive acts for humanity as highlighted in Scripture, narrated progressively, and tied to his covenants and the various stages of the arrival of his kingdom and the fulfillment of his promises" (2018, 12). Tracing the fulfillment of God's promises—which harken back as far as Eden, through the patriarchs, the Davidic line, the Prophets, and into the NT and the arrival of Jesus Messiah—is a key concentration of the NT authors. In this section, our task is to focus on just one of those promises: the promise of the "land" and its relationship to God's other promises.

Land in the Old Testament

The most common word for "land" in the OT is *eretz*, which occurs some 2,190 times. It can indicate the "ground" or "soil" beneath our feet (Gen 18:2; Judg 6:37), a piece of "property" as one's personal acreage (Gen 23:15), a "territory" such as the country of Egypt (Gen 47:13), and the totality of the "earth" that God created (Gen 1:1) (Holladay 1988, 28; all English translations are from the ESV unless otherwise noted). Land may indicate arable "ground" or the "field" on which plants can grow, in distinction from the "sea," or it may indicate the entire "earth" in distinction from "heaven."

In addition to being a physical entity, land is also a significant symbol with a range of meanings reflected in the biblical texts. Norman Habel points to a number of symbolic and ideological meanings of "land" in the OT. It may indicate family lots that point to ancestral households (e.g., Lev 25–27; Josh 15:1; 16:1; 17:1). "Land" may also indicate a royal domain, such as Solomon's empire (cf. 1 Kgs 3–10). "Land" especially points to God's heritage (*naḥalah*) to own and to bestow, significantly upon Israel (Jer 2:7; 17:4) (Habel 1995).

Walter Brueggemann maintains that it is important to recognize that in biblical usage and in contemporary usage as well, land continually moves back and forth between literal and symbolic intentions. A symbolic sense of the term affirms that "land" is not simply physical dirt but is freighted with social, political, and theological meanings derived from historical experience. A literal understanding of the term will protect us from excessive spiritualization, so that we recognize that "land" is always a serious historical enterprise (2002, Kindle loc. 305–8).

God's Creation of the Heavens and the Earth

The first verse of the Bible indicates that the story of creation is a "landed" enterprise: God's creation included the "heavens" and the "earth" (*'eretz*, Gen 1:1). The first humans were created in the image of God so that they might rule over the earth and all created beings for God (Gen 1:26–28). This indicates the beginning of God's cosmological goal to establish his kingdom on earth. However, Adam and Eve, those first humans, soon violated their covenant with God and were ejected from their Edenic paradise and were forced out into an earth that was now under God's curse (Gen 1:17–19).

The accomplishment of God's goal was radically mutilated but not demolished, for God makes a promise to Eve of a seed (Gen 3:15). The seed ("offspring" ESV) promised to Eve is foundational to all of the covenants in establishing God's kingdom (Waltke 2007, 148). Numerous covenants are introduced at crucial times in salvation history, "which serve to reverse the curses of Eden and bring about the escalated re-establishment of the universal expansion of God's kingdom" (Martin 2015, 42). This is illustrated in the covenant God made with Noah after the flood "that never again shall all flesh be cut off by the waters of the flood, and never again shall there be a flood to destroy the earth" (*'eretz*, Gen 9:11).

Abraham and the Land

With Abraham, a new development in divine revelation to humans commences that focuses on God's word of blessing and promise—God promises that Abraham would be a blessing to the world (see Gen 12:1–3; 13:14–16; 15:4–12; 17:4–16). Walter Kaiser suggests that the core of the covenant between God and Abraham consisted of a promise that was basically threefold: (1) a "seed" (*zera'*), (2) a "land" (*'eretz*), and (3) a "blessing (*berakah*) to all of the nations of the earth" (Kaiser 2008, 54). First, through Abraham's seed/descendants, God promises to make a great nation (*goy*), which would become the nation of Israel. And through this nation, the third aspect of God's promise to Abraham was that his seed would be a blessing for all nations.

Our focus in this section is on the second aspect of God's promise to Abraham: the land. The promise of the land to Abraham, Isaac, and Jacob and their seed runs through the narratives related to the patriarchs (Gen 12:1, 7; 13:15, 17; 15:7–8, 18; 17:8; 24:7; 26:3–5; etc.). The borders of this promised land are specified: "On that day the Lord made a covenant with Abram, saying, 'To your offspring I give this land [*'eretz*], from the river of Egypt to the great river, the river Euphrates'" (Gen 15:18). The land promise and the promise of a seed are binding aspects of God's message to the patriarchs as an "everlasting covenant" (17:7, 13, 19) and an "everlasting possession" (17:8; 48:4) (Kaiser 2008, 54–64). These promises were fulfilled in the later settlement of the land under Joshua, and this was the signal that the people of Israel would inhabit the land so that they would be an everlasting instrument of God's blessing to all of the nations. The promise of the land of Israel (*'erets Yisrael*) operated "as a formative, dynamic, seminal force in the history of Israel" (Davies 1974, 18).

David and the Throne in Jerusalem

This promise of the land is reiterated in the covenant God made with David, with a set of promises that Bruce Waltke argues also pertain to the remote future: (1) David's house (i.e., his dynasty) will endure forever, (2) his kingdom will endure forever, and (3) his throne will be established forever (2 Sam 7:16) (Waltke 2007, 661). As seen in 2 Sam 7 and Ps 89, God makes a commitment to maintain the Davidic dynasty forever, but he preserves the divine freedom to punish individual members of the dynasty who rebel against God's sovereign rule (Roberts 2005, 210). Kaiser comments: "Rascals there may be, but the blessing would never be revoked from the family; thus it was an 'everlasting covenant'" (2008, 122). Consequently, the throne of David in Jerusalem is secured by an everlasting covenant.

The promised new covenant (Jer 31:31–34; Ezek 36:25–35) also involves the land of Israel, and the descendant of David functions as the mediator of the new covenant. This includes the repossession of the promised land (Jer 24:6; 31:28; 32:41; Amos 9:15), the reuniting of Israel in one kingdom ruled by one king (Jer 50:4; Ezek 34:23; 37:22), and a rebuilt sanctuary in Jerusalem (Ezek 34:23–28; 37:22–27) (Alexander 1998, 169–206; Kaiser 2008, 199–203, 209–11).

God's Own Land Granted to Israel

In the Torah, Yahweh speaks of the land of Canaan as his own land: "The land shall not be sold in perpetuity, for *the land is mine*" (Lev 25:23; emphasis mine). But throughout the Hebrew Bible, Yahweh makes clear that "Canaan is YHWH's land grant to Israel" (Habel 1995, Kindle loc. 533).

The land of Israel was a basic component of Jewish belief and religious practice as found in the OT. Brueggemann argues that "land is a central, if not *the central theme* of biblical faith. Biblical faith is a pursuit of historical belonging that includes a sense of destiny derived from such belonging" (2002, Kindle loc. 313; emphasis original). From this land, God will use Israel as an instrument of blessing to the whole earth. Even after the sinfulness of the people caused them to lose the land for a period of time in the catastrophes of the fall of Samaria in 722 BCE and in the fall of Jerusalem in 586 BCE, this land, *'erets Yisrael*, continued to be the geographical platform on which the story of the Bible is staged. Ronald Allen states emphatically, "No other land on the planet is as important in terms of God's work of salvation as the little land of Israel" (1998, 18–19). God granted this one area of land to Israel to be a base of blessing to all of God's created earth.

Land in the Gospels

The milieu in which the NT began and its authors wrote was steeped in the OT concept of the *land* as the "earth" that God created and as a specific "territory" God granted to Israel in its role as an instrument of blessing to the earth. The land of Israel is where the temple and throne of David are located: Israel is the holy land. "The Holy Land is a central category in Judaism; it is where Israel, the people, belong, and it is owned uniquely by Israel, the people, in partnership God" (Neusner and Green 1996, 323). As we transition to the NT, we will attempt to see how the authors of the Gospels understood the "land" in the light of God's salvific-historical plan as it developed with the arrival of Jesus Messiah and his gospel message to establish the kingdom of God throughout the earth.

The primary terms for "land" in the Gospels are *gē*, *chōra*, and *xēros*. *Gē* is by far the most frequently occurring term, found some one hundred times in the Gospels, with Matthew using the term the most (Matt 43x; Mark 19x; Luke 25x; John 13x). *Chōra* occurs twenty times (Matt 4x; Mark 4x; Luke 9x; John 3x), while *xēros* occurs eight times (Matt 2x; Mark 1x; Luke 4x; John 1x). Similar to usage of terms for land in the OT, these terms for land in the Gospels identify physical and symbolic entities.

Land in the Gospel of Mark

The Gospel of Mark has two primary terms that refer to "land": *chōra* (4x) and *gē* (19x). The term *chōra* refers to the *"region* of Judea" as the inhabitants of Judea who, with "all Jerusalem," were going out to be baptized by John the Baptist (1:5). In the other three uses of the term, it refers generally to the *regions* of the Gerasenes (5:1, 10) and the *region* surrounding Gennesaret (6:53–55).

Of the nineteen times Mark uses *gē*, none have an explicit, symbolic reference to Israel and its land. Four times he uses *gē* to refer to the entire *world* (2:10; 4:31; 9:3: 13:27), once to refer to *earth* in contrast to heaven (13:31), once as the darkness over the whole *land* at Jesus' crucifixion (15:33), three times the *shore* in distinction from the sea (4:1; 6:47, 53), and three times as simply the *ground* beneath one's feet (8:6; 9:20; 14:35). Most frequently (7x), Mark uses *gē* to refer to agricultural *soil* (4:5 2x; 4:8, 20; 4:26, 28, 31).

The traditional understanding of the Second Gospel is that it was written by John Mark from Rome under the influence of the apostle Peter toward the end of Peter's life (Schnabel 2017, 7–17). Mark's intention appears to center on giving a brief exposition of the arrival of Jesus Messiah to establish the kingdom of God through his sacrificial death and resurrection as the basis for the expansion of the gospel in the Roman world (for discussion, see Gundry 1993, 1022–45). While Mark was apparently raised under and influenced by the religious and cultural milieu of the OT's focus on the "land of Israel," his purposes did not include an explicit intention to reflect upon the land in which he was raised. He appears to have in mind persecuted Christians in the broader Roman world (Lux 2010, 51). We will have to look elsewhere for an explicit focus on the "land of Israel."

Land in the Gospel of Luke

The Gospel of Luke also has two primary terms to refer to "land": *chōra* and *gē*. Luke uses *chōra* nine times to denote geographical spheres—the *local area* where shepherds are out in the field (Luke 2:8), the sociopolitical *district* of the Gerasenes (8:26), and the larger political *region* of Ituraea and Trachonitis (3:1). Luke records parables where Jesus alludes to the *land* of a rich man (12:16) and a far *country* (15:13–15; 19:12). Luke also makes a prophetic reference contrasting the *countryside* and the city of Jerusalem (21:21). While this is simply a geographical notation, it contains an important prophetic element, to which we will return below.

As with all of the Gospels, Luke uses the term *gē* most often to refer to various aspects of "land" (25x). A significant eleven times, Luke uses *gē* to refer to the entire *world* (2:14; 5:24; 11:31; 12:49, 51, 56; 18:8; 21:23, 25, 33, 35), also to refer to *earth* in contrast to heaven (10:21; 16:17), to designate the entire *land* of a great famine (4:25) or the darkness at Jesus' crucifixion (23:44), the *shore* in distinction from the sea (5:3, 11; 8:27), simply the *ground* beneath one's feet (6:49; 22:44; 24:5), and four times to refer to agricultural *soil* (8:8, 15; 13:7; 14:35).

As noted above, Luke's Gospel also includes records of Jesus' prophetic statements that have bearing on our study of the "land of Israel." Richard Bauckham provides a helpful argument for the general theme of Israel's restoration to the land (2010, 325–70), but space here limits us to two primary texts. Since Matthew's Gospel has versions of these texts, we will primarily raise their significance for Luke's emphases.

In the first text, 13:33–35, Jesus has revealed himself to be a prophet (v. 33) and speaks of both present judgment and future activity related to Jerusalem. Israel's house, a metaphor for the nation (Bock 1996, 1250), is said to be "forsaken" (ESV) or "desolate" (NASB) (*aphiēmi*), because it is rejecting its Messiah. Then Jesus says prophetically, "And I tell you, you will not see me until you say, 'Blessed is he who comes in the name of the Lord!'" (13:35). Jesus has in view here the parousia and Israel's response to his coming. A significant number of interpreters understand this to be a negative statement: Israel will call Jesus blessed at the parousia, something they failed to do in the present, but then it will be too late (e.g., Wolter 2017, 206). "They will recognize him, but as their Judge rather than as their Savior" (Osborne 2018, 357). However, another significant number of interpreters understand Jesus' statement to be a positive note of prophecy regarding Israel (e.g., Bock 1996, 1251; Nolland 1993, 742). François Bovon comments on Jesus' statement to Israel: "from being enemies, 'you' will become friends at the time of his return. Once favorable to his elimination, 'you' will be happy about his return" (2013, 332). In my view, this is a more consistent interpretation with Luke's emphases: Luke accentuates that Israel and the city of Jerusalem in the land of Israel will receive Jesus joyfully at the parousia.

In the second text, 21:21–24, Luke provides a record of Jesus' eschatological discourse. It is my conviction that Jesus speaks here of events both in the lifetime of his audience as well as events in the distant future. There is comprehensive theological cohesion in the discourse between Jesus' treatment of the fall of Jerusalem in 70 CE and events at the parousia, but there is no clear dividing point between historical and eschatological fulfillment. The resolution is that the two are purposely intertwined under what may be called a "double reference" prophecy or "prophetic foreshortening," where the near event serves as a partial fulfillment and symbol for the fulfillment of far events (for discussion, see Wilkins 2004, 788–91). In this view, the events of 21:8–19 are a general description of the life of the church during this age, perhaps with some increase of activity in 24:16–19. But at 21:20 begins a double reference to events that will be partially fulfilled at 70 CE with the destruction of the temple and Jerusalem, culminating in the future fulfillment of the complex of events surrounding the return of Jesus—the abomination that causes desolation, the end of the age, and the parousia.

In the middle of this description of eschatological events, Jesus makes an important prophecy: "Jerusalem will be trampled underfoot by the Gentiles, until the times of the Gentiles are fulfilled" (21:24). The important prophetic element to be noted is the emphasis on the future of the city of Jerusalem and the land of Israel. Bock indicates that this verse points toward a turnabout in Israel's fate: Jerusalem is trampled down *until* the times of the Gentiles are fulfilled. "It refers to a period of Gentile domination (Dan 2:44; 8:13–14; 12:5–13), while alluding to a subsequent hope for Israel" (2014, 109). There is a time of judgment for Israel, but there is hope for a time of vindication in the future, which is similar to what Paul argues in Rom 11:25–26. Israel has a future in God's plan, where Israel is once again seen back in the land and in the city of Jerusalem (Bock 1996, 1681; cf. Nolland 1993, 1002–4).

Land in the Gospel of John

Like the Gospels of Mark and Luke, John's Gospel has two primary terms that refer to "land": *chōra* and *gē*. John uses *chōra* three times: to refer metaphorically to the *fields* of people that are ready for harvest (4:35), to refer to the geographical *region* near the wilderness (11:54), and to refer to the *country* generally in distinction from the city of Jerusalem (11:55). John uses *gē* a total of thirteen times, the least of any of the Gospels. These include an emphasis on the *earth* in contrast to heaven (3:31 [3x]; 12:32; 17:4), the *shore* in distinction from the sea (6:21; 21:8, 9, 11), the *ground* beneath one's feet (8:6, 8), agricultural *soil* (12:24), and the Judean *countryside* (3:22). John makes two allusions to the land of Judea, but these are simply geographical notations in contrast to Galilee and Samaria (cf. 3:22 with 4:3–4). Therefore, it appears that John's Gospel has no explicit symbolical use of the land as the holy land of Israel.

This lack of explicit symbolical reference to the land of Israel is interpreted differently by Johannine scholars. Some suggest that there is an anti-Jewish tendency in John because of some Jewish leaders' rejection of Jesus and because in John's day they were persecuting Jesus' disciples. The church has replaced Israel, and the promises made to Israel are now the inheritance of the church (Schnackenburg 1990, 159–60, 165–67). While not claiming that John's Gospel is anti-Jewish, others likewise suggest that Israel, although acknowledged as Jesus' own people by race, have shown by their rejection of him to belong totally to the world. They have no other claim to make, and thus the church has replaced Israel and its promises now belong to the church (Pryor 1990, 218).

Following this line of thought leads other scholars to the conclusion that in the Fourth Gospel the land is subsumed within John's theology of christological replacement/fulfillment. One explains:

> What Judaism sought in its festivals and institutions, it can now find in Christ. What it sought in its Temple is now fulfilled in Christ. And the energies Judaism directed to the land must now be redirected to the One Vine of the vineyard who encompassed in his life the very promises life in the land had to offer. (Burge 2010, 1141)

But a mediating position is offered by other Johannine scholars whereby Israel as an ethnic group has not ceased to be a factor in God's salvific purposes. Paul's argument in Rom 9–11 makes clear that God still has a purpose for ethnic Israel. At the present time, his focus has shifted to bringing in the Gentiles, but at the end of salvation history his attention will once again be directed to the Jewish nation. At last, at Christ's return, the Jews will recognize their Messiah and "in this way all Israel will be saved" (Rom 11:26). It is faith that constitutes the grounds for salvation, not human merit or ethnicity (Köstenberger 2013, location 3925–45).

I would thus emphasize "fulfillment" more than "replacement." "Fulfill" indicates the way in which the value of the law and the temple continues but is brought to its intended full meaning in Jesus. Each of these still hold a valuable place in salvation history and God's dealings with humanity. The Torah is fulfilled in Jesus but not done away with (Matt 5:17–20). The Torah still has value as God's word, but it now needs to be understood in the light of Jesus' fulfillment of it. We are to be "Torah readers" to understand salvation history.

We could say that the "land of Israel" as God's holy place found its fulfillment in Jesus, so that he is now our holy place as we are now "in Christ" and that wherever we are as Christians there is a holy place. However, that does not eliminate a future where God will use Israel and the land in his plans. Thus the land promises to Israel will still be a factor in God's salvific-historical plans (cf. Blaising 2016, 84–85).

Land in the Gospel of Matthew

Matthew's Gospel has three primary terms that refer to "land": *chōra*, *xēros*, and *gē*. Matthew uses *chōra* four times to refer to various geographical locations: the magi's own home *country* (2:12), the *region* and shadow of death (4:16), the *country* of the Gadarenes (8:28), and the *region* of Gennesaret (14:35). Matthew uses *xēros* two times to refer to "dryness": a *withered* hand (12:10) and the *land* in distinction from the sea (23:15).

As with the other Gospels, *gē* is used in Matthew most frequently and the most of any Gospel: forty-three times to refer to various aspects of *land*. *Gē* refers four times simply to the *ground* beneath one's feet (10:29; 15:35; 25:18; 25:25; 27:51), four times to refer to agricultural *soil* (13:5 [2x], 8, 23), two times to refer to the *shore* in distinction from the sea (14:24; 14:34) and to refer to the *land* over which darkness came at Jesus' crucifixion (27:45). A large majority of these times, Matthew uses *gē* to refer to the *earth* in distinction from heaven (13x: 5:18, 35; 6:10, 19; 11:25; 16:19 [2x]; 18:18 [2x], 19; 23:9; 24:35; 28:18) and similarly to refer to the entire *world* (9x: 5:5, 13; 9:6; 10:34; 12:40, 42; 17:25; 23:35; 24:30). Matthew also makes reference to the general geographical *district* in which Jesus was ministering (9:26–31) as well as the *land* of Sodom and Gomorrah (10:15; 11:24).

An intriguing use of *gē* occurs in Jesus' statement in the Sermon on the Mount: "Blessed are the meek, for they shall inherit the earth" (5:5). Some interpret this as a fulfillment of the land promise to Israel (Hsieh 2017, 41–75) and a promise that the land promise extends throughout the whole earth. This interpretation confuses the wider sense of *gē* as the whole *earth* with the normal more restricted sense when referring to the *land* of Israel. In the broader context of the sermon and the use of *gē* generally, most commentators understand the reference to the "meek" to refer to Jesus' disciples (cf. 5:1–2) and ultimately the establishment of the kingdom of heaven and the reign of Christ upon the whole earth (25:35) (e.g., Weaver 2015, 6–29).

A very interesting use of *gē* in Matthew's Gospel is to make reference to various geographical *lands* belonging to the tribes of Israel: the *land of Judah* (2:6), and the *land of Zebulun* and the *land of Naphtali* (4:15). Also interesting and unique to Matthew's gospel is the use of *gē* to make reference to the *land of Israel*: while in Egypt, Joseph is directed by an angel in a dream to take the infant Jesus and his mother and go to the "land of Israel," which they did (2:20–21). This paves the way for *gē* to be used to refer to the land of Israel elsewhere in Matthew's Gospel, as we will see below.

Matthew's Gospel has long been noted for having complex perspectives of the nation of Israel—e.g., particularistic and universal, positive and negative. Matthew has recorded quite positive accounts of responses to Jesus within Israel: individuals such as the prophet John the Baptist, the twelve diverse disciples, tax collectors and "sinners," women, and religious leaders such as Joseph of Arimathea. On the other hand, a quick survey of Matthew's Gospel reveals negative responses to Jesus' offer of the kingdom of heaven, which resulted in significant bleak consequences for Israel. But in spite of these bleak consequences, Matthew clearly demonstrates that there is a future for ethnic Israel in God's plan of salvation. There is no mistaking the prominent place the people of Israel play in Matthew's Gospel, and there is also a striking emphasis on the land and future of Israel (see also Wilkins 2014, 87–101; Wilkins forthcoming 2021). Five points stand out.

(1) There is a continuing mission to Israel in the land during this age until the coming of the Son of Man at the parousia (10:23). Israel will have a presence in the cities/land of Israel and will experience the preaching of the gospel until the parousia. As Jesus offers comfort to the mission disciples about their ultimate salvation unto the end (10:22), he warns them not to abandon Israel. When persecuted in one city, they should flee to the next, because the mission to Israel will not conclude before the Son of Man returns. This verse "reflects Matthew's concern that the mission to God's people Israel not be abandoned" (Davies and Allison 1991, 189–90).

This is a powerful apologetic to the Jews in Jesus' ministry, and to those within hearing of Matthew's Gospel in the first century, as well as today: God has not abandoned his covenantal promises to Israel in the land. While it is the church today that bears a position of leadership as the agent proclaiming the gospel of the kingdom of God, it is a challenging and sober call to the mission disciples to endure to the end with the message of the gospel to all peoples—both Jew and Gentile in the whole earth, and Jews in the land of Israel (Konradt 2014, 82–87).

(2) The twelve apostles will sit on twelve thrones "judging" the twelve tribes of Israel (19:28). Although "judging" can indicate condemnation of Israel for rejecting Jesus as national Messiah, the idea of the Twelve ruling or governing with Jesus as the Son of Man is paramount (cf. Rev 3:21; 20:6). Condemning Israel would bring no pleasure to the disciples but reward would, which was the point of Peter's request (19:27) (Konradt 2014, 259–63).

This apparently speaks to the political reconstitution of a twelve-tribe nation state. "Matthew assumes, it appears, that in the future in the restored Davidic kingdom, the twelve disciples will govern over *restored* tribal territories" (Willitts 2016, 138; emphasis original). This is a potent expectation of the future restoration of Israel.

(3) Israel will be in Jerusalem in the land of Israel until they bless the Coming One (23:37–39). Jesus gives what appears to be a prophetic announcement that when he returns, remorseful Israel will utter in sincere repentance the words, "Blessed is he who comes in the name of the Lord" (23:39). This is God's merciful offer of hope to his people who will receive the blessing of the land. Israel will be in the land, in the city of Jerusalem, when Messiah returns. and will receive the eschatological blessings that they had previously rejected (Turner 2015, 328).

(4) A future desolation of sacrilege in the Holy Place, and emphasis on the land of Judea, indicates a future role of Israel in the *land* (24:14–16). Some contend that

at this point Jesus focuses exclusively on the destruction of the temple in 70 CE (e.g., France 2007, 910–28), while a wide spectrum of scholars contend that these events also presage a future time of eschatological defilement and destruction (e.g., Davies and Allison 1997, 344). Jesus anticipates the fulfillment of the covenantal promises to Israel to be restored to the land, with an apparently (and seemingly implausible) rebuilt temple and attendant desecration, which will usher in the messianic kingdom (24:15).

(5) The imperative of the Great Commission to "make disciples of all the nations" includes a continuing mission to Israel (28:19–20). Although ethnic Israel is not at present functionally the instrument and witness of the outworking of the kingdom of God (21:43), individual Jews are invited to participate in the salvation brought by Jesus with the arrival of the kingdom, to be incorporated in discipleship to Jesus that includes Jews/Gentiles, men/women, and commoner/elite, and to become participants in the missional outreach to all the nations.

Conclusion

In spite of Matthew's recounting of bleak consequences for Israel's rejection of Jesus, he has a vision of a future for ethnic Israel. Israel is not removed from its place as God's elect people, but it shares in God's salvation through the unique and necessary death and resurrection of Jesus (see Konradt 2014, 379; contra Kim 2002, 280–90).

Jesus' disciples are the church, which is the fulfillment in part of the promises to Israel, especially the spiritual aspects of that messianic kingdom, including the blessings of the new covenant (e.g., regeneration, forgiveness of sins, the indwelling Spirit, fruit of the Spirit, etc.). Jesus' disciples—whether Gentile or Jew—experience the blessings of the new covenant. And Jesus' disciples have the privilege to announce the presence and means of entrance to the kingdom.

But Jesus' disciples as the church do not replace Israel nor become Israel. Israel is still kept in view as receiving in the future the eschatological fulfillment of the promises of the kingdom, including both the mediation of the kingdom and the land of Israel (cf. Rom 11:25–32; 15:7–13; Rev 7:1–8).

Works Cited

Alexander, Ralph H. 1998. "A New Covenant—An Eternal People (Jeremiah 31)." Pages 169–206 in *Israel, The Land and the People: An Evangelical Affirmation of God's Promises.* Edited by H. Wayne House. Grand Rapids: Kregel.

Allen, Ronald B. 1998. "The Land of Israel." Pages 18–33 in *Israel, The Land and the People: An Evangelical Affirmation of God's Promises.* Edited by H. Wayne House. Grand Rapids: Kregel.

Bauckham, Richard. 2010. "The Restoration of Israel in Luke-Acts." Pages 325–70 in *The Jewish World around the New Testament.* Grand Rapids: Baker [Tübingen: Mohr Siebeck, 2008]. Reprinted from pages 435–87 in *Restoration: Old*

Testament, Jewish and Christian Perspectives. JSJSup 72. Edited by James M. Scott. Leiden: Brill, 2001.

Blaising, Craig. 2016. "Biblical Hermeneutics: How Are We to Interpret the Relation between the Tanakh and the New Testament on This Question?" Pages 79–105 in *The New Christian Zionism: Fresh Perspectives on Israel and the Land*. Downers Grove, IL: InterVarsity Press.

Blomberg, Craig L. 2018. *A New Testament Theology*. Waco, TX: Baylor University Press.

Bock, Darrell L. 2014. "Israel in Luke–Acts." Pages 103–15 in *The People, The Land, and the Future of Israel: Israel and the Jewish People in the Plan of God*. Edited by Darrell L. Bock and Mitch Glaser. Grand Rapids: Kregel.

———. 1996. *Luke 9:51–24:53*. BECNT. Grand Rapids: Baker.

Bovon, François. 2013. *Luke 2: A Commentary on the Gospel of Luke 9:51–19:27*. Translated by Donald S. Deer. Hermeneia. Minneapolis, MN: Fortress.

Brueggemann, Walter. 2002. *The Land: Place As Gift, Promise, and Challenge in Biblical Faith*. Rev. ed. OBT. Minneapolis, MN: Fortress.

Burge, Gary M. 2010. *Jesus and the Land: The New Testament Challenge to "Holy Land" Theology*. Grand Rapids: Baker. Kindle edition.

Davies, W. D. 1974. *The Gospel and the Land: Early Christianity and Jewish Territorial Doctrine*. Berkeley: University of California Press.

Davies, W. D., and Dale C. Allison, Jr. 1991. *Matthew 8–18*. Vol. 2 of *A Critical and Exegetical Commentary on the Gospel According to Saint Matthew*. ICC. Edinburgh: T&T Clark.

Davies, W. D., and Dale C. Allison, Jr. 1997. *Matthew 19–28*. Vol. 3 of *A Critical and Exegetical Commentary on the Gospel According to Saint Matthew*. ICC. Edinburgh: T&T Clark.

France, R. T. 2007. *The Gospel of Matthew*. NICNT. Grand Rapids: Eerdmans.

Gundry, Robert H. 1993. *Mark: A Commentary on His Apology for the Cross*. Grand Rapids: Eerdmans.

Habel, Norman C. 1995. *The Land Is Mine: Six Biblical Land Ideologies*. OBT. Minneapolis, MN: Fortress Press.

Holladay, William L. 1988. *A Concise Hebrew and Aramaic Lexicon of the Old Testament*. 15th impression. Leiden: Brill.

Hsieh, Nelson S. 2017. "Matthew 5:5 and the Old Testament Land Promises: An Inheritance of the Earth, or the Land of Israel?" *MSJ* 28.1:41–75.

Kaiser, Walter C., Jr. 2008. *The Promise-Plan of God: A Biblical Theology of the Old and New Testaments*. Grand Rapids: Zondervan.

Kim, Joon-Sik. 2002. "'Your Kingdom Come on Earth': The Promise of the Land and the Kingdom of Heaven in the Gospel of Matthew." PhD diss., Princeton Theological Seminary.

Konradt, Matthias. 2014. *Israel, Church, and the Gentiles in the Gospel of Matthew*. Translated by Kathleen Ess. Baylor-Mohr Siebeck Studies in Early Christianity. Waco, TX: Baylor University Press.

Köstenberger, Andreas J. 2013. *Encountering John: The Gospel In Historical, Literary, and Theological Perspective*. Encountering Biblical Studies. 2nd ed. Grand Rapids: Baker. Kindle edition.

Lux, Richard C. 2010. *The Jewish People, the Holy Land, and the State of Israel: A Catholic View*. Studies in Judaism and Christianity. Mahwah, NJ: Paulist.

Martin, Oren R. 2015. *Bound for the Promised Land: The Land Promise in God's Redemptive Plan*. NSBT 34. Downers Grove, IL: InterVarsity Press. Kindle ed.

Neusner, Jacob, and William Scott Green, eds. 1996. *Dictionary of Judaism in the Biblical Period: 450 B.C.E. to 600 C.E.* Peabody, MA: Hendrickson.

Nolland, John. 1993. *Luke 9:21–18:34*. WBC 35B. Dallas: Word.

Osborne, Grant R. 2018. *Luke: Verse by Verse*. Osborne New Testament Commentaries. Bellingham, WA: Lexham.

Pryor, John W. 1990. "Jesus and Israel in the Fourth Gospel—John 1:11." *NovT* 32.3: 201–18.

Roberts, J. J. M. 2005. "Davidic Covenant." Pages 206–211 in *DOTHB*. Downers Grove, IL: InterVarsity Press.

Schnabel, Eckhard J. 2017. *Mark: An Introduction and Commentary*. TNTC 2. Downers Grove, IL: InterVarsity Press.

Schnackenburg, Rudolf. 1990. *The Gospel According to St. John: Volume One: Introduction and Commentary on Chapters 1–4*. New York: Crossroad.

Turner, David L. 2015. *Israel's Last Prophet: Jesus and the Jewish Leaders in Matthew 23*. Minneapolis, MN: Fortress Press.

Waltke, Bruce K., with Charles Yu. 2007. *An Old Testament Theology: An Exegetical, Canonical, and Thematic Approach*. Grand Rapids: Zondervan.

Weaver, Dorothy Jean. 2015. "Inheriting the Earth: Towards a Geotheology of Matthew's Narrative." *JIBS* 2.1: 6–29. Asbury Theological Seminary. DOI: 10.7252/JOURNAL.02.2015S.02.

Wilkins, Michael J. Forthcoming 2021. "The Consideration of a Future for Israel in the Light of the Apparently Bleak Consequences for Negative Responses to Jesus' Ministry in the Gospel of Matthew." In *The Future Restoration of Israel*. Edited by Stanley E. Porter and Alan E. Kurschner. Hamilton, ON: McMaster Divinity College Press; Eugene, OR: Wipf & Stock.

———. 2014. "Israel According to the Gospels." Pages 87–101 in *The People, the Land, and the Future of Israel: Israel and the Jewish People in the Plan of God*. Edited by Darrell L. Bock and Mitch Glaser. Grand Rapids: Kregel.

———. 2004. *Matthew*. NIVAC. Grand Rapids: Zondervan.

Willitts, Joel. 2016. "Zionism in the Gospel of Matthew." Pages 107–40 in *The New Christian Zionism: Fresh Perspectives on Israel and the Land*. Edited by Gerald R. McDermott. Downers Grove: InterVarsity Press.

Wolter, Michael. 2017. *The Gospel According to Luke: Volume II (Luke 9:51–24)*. Translated by Wayne Coppins and Christoph Heilig. Baylor–Mohr Siebeck Studies in Early Christianity. Waco, TX: Baylor University Press.

4.5 Satan and Demons in the Gospels

Ryan E. Stokes

To read the New Testament Gospels is to encounter a world that is populated not only by human beings but also by numerous personal superhuman entities. Some of these superhuman beings are benevolent angels who obediently carry out God's work on earth. Others are of a more sinister variety; they are demonic or even satanic. What is more, these malevolent spiritual beings figure prominently in the theological perspective of the Gospels. They pose a physical threat to humans. They lead humans into moral error. And, most significantly in the narratives of the Gospels, these evil forces oppose and are opposed by Jesus Christ, the Son of God.

While such a depiction of the world and the "spiritual" entities who inhabit it may be familiar to many readers who have been exposed to this through Christian teaching or popular theology, readers of the Gospels may not be aware of how such beliefs arose and developed or how the teachings of the Gospels compare with other early Jewish teachings about the superhuman realm. What the Gospels say about demons and Satan is not simply what the Jews had been saying about them since the beginning of their faith but is the product of centuries of theological reflection and creativity. Nor is what the Gospels say about evil superhuman forces simply what all the Jews of the New Testament era were saying. Jewish literature from the centuries just prior to the rise of Christianity attests a variety of perspectives on evil and its superhuman proponents. It contains differing views of how these beings impinge on humankind, some of which are contrary to the claims of the Gospels. By situating the teachings of the Gospels within the historical development of Jewish beliefs and among the variety of teachings of early Judaism, one is able better to comprehend their significance.

Demons, Evil Spirits, and the Satan in the Old Testament

A consideration of Jewish views of the superhuman realm must begin with the Old Testament. These writings provide us with our earliest examples of beliefs that would eventually be featured in the literature of early Judaism and the New Testament. The OT texts also are those to which the NT authors and other Jews of their day would look for much, though certainly not all, of their information about the superhuman realm.

Readers who are more accustomed to thinking in the terms of NT theology, however, are often surprised by what the OT says (or rather how little it says) about Satan, demons, and related figures. Given the prominence of the devil, demons, and evil spirits in NT writings, the OT contains surprisingly few references to these figures. For instance, of the thirty-nine books in the OT, only two mention Satan (Zechariah and Job). If one includes the debatable reference in 1 Chr 21, then this brings the total number of OT references to Satan to three. In contrast, of the twenty-seven NT books, nineteen clearly refer to Satan. All four Gospels mention Satan multiple times. The OT also contrasts with the NT in that the few OT passages that actually refer to Satan or demons depict these figures differently from the better-known NT teachings.

A figure referred to as "the Satan" appears in Zech 3 and Job 1–2. Although the Satan is at odds with God in both of these works, neither Zechariah nor Job depicts him as morally evil, much less as God's enemy. Instead, they assume he is an officer in God's heavenly government, an agent of punishment who harms or kills humans whose wicked behavior warrants this treatment. Although he harms a righteous man in the book of Job, the narrative presumes that this sort of activity on the part of the Satan is exceptional. One should probably compare the Satan to the destroying angel mentioned elsewhere in the OT (cf. Exod 12:23; 2 Sam 24:15–17). He is not named "Satan" but is referred to by the title "the Satan," which probably means something like "the Attacker" or "the Executioner" (Stokes 2014). The Satan in these passages is not presumed to be a tempter, nor is he said to be in league with demons or evil spirits. It would be a few more centuries more before these sorts of claims would be made about the Satan.

A small number of OT passages mention "spirits" who create problems for humans. One of these is the "evil" or "harmful" spirit whom God sends to afflict a disobedient King Saul (1 Sam 16:14–23; 18:10; 19:9). God sends another spirit to mislead the prophets of the wicked Israelite King Ahab, so that the king would go to war and be killed. As with the Satan, neither of these spirits is said to be morally "evil." Rather, they are harmful and, like the Satan, are emissaries of God to punish sinners.

Two OT passages refer to "demons": Deut 32:16–17 and Ps 106:37. Both identify demons as the false or illicit gods worshiped by the nations. They reveal no more about the precise nature of these "demons." Interestingly, the OT does not identify "demons" as "spirits"; this differs considerably from popular conceptions in which the labels "demon" and "evil spirit" are largely synonymous. In other words, in the OT, a demon does not appear to be the same thing as an evil spirit. Spirits are sent by God to punish humans, and demons are the so-called gods worshiped by the nations.

In sum, in the OT, information about Satan, evil spirits, and demons is relatively sparse, and what it does say differs from what later literature will claim about these beings. Although we should be careful not to overstate the difference between the Old and New Testaments, if we mistakenly read NT theology back into the OT, then we compromise our understanding of the NT's theological context and run the risk of misunderstanding the teachings of both testaments.

Demons, Evil Spirits, and the Satan in Early Jewish Literature

The literature of early Judaism bridges much of the historical and theological gaps between the Old and New Testaments. In this literature, one observes that speculation about evil superhuman beings rose to prominence in the theologies of many writers. This literature also develops many of the ideas that are absent from the OT but that would come to characterize NT theology, including that of the four Gospels. The writings of early Judaism also contain some ideas that would be rejected by the earliest Christians.

Categories of and Relationships among Evil Superhuman Beings

One important theological development during the centuries just prior to the rise of Christianity is that notions of demons, harmful spirits, and Satan (which in the OT are disparate concepts) are combined into systematic explanations of superhuman evil. The third-century BCE Book of the Watchers (1 En. 1–36) claims that a group of angels, called "watchers," rebelled against God by marrying human women and having children. These sinful angels, whom God imprisoned in the earth for their transgressions, are the "demons" worshiped erroneously by the nations as if they were gods (1 En. 19:1). The hybrid offspring of these angels/demons' intermingling with human women, on the other hand, became evil spirits who serve their demonic fathers (1 En. 15:8–16:1; 19:1). While the Book of the Watchers goes beyond OT literature in that it associates "demons" with "evil spirits," this work does not claim that the two categories are identical. The second-century BCE book Jubilees, however, uses the designations "spirit" and "demon" interchangeably as synonymous labels (Jub. 10:1–6). These two categories of beings, which were distinct in the OT and the Book of the Watchers, are combined in the vocabulary of Jubilees much as they would be in several passages in the Gospels. Still other texts, rather than consolidating categories for speaking of superhuman evil, multiply them in comparison with the OT. One Dead Sea text, Song of the Maskil, lists "spirits of the destroying angels, spirits of the bastards, demons, Lilith, howlers," among other harmful beings (4Q511 I, 6–7). There were many ways for categorizing and relating evil superhuman figures in early Judaism.

Another development in this period first attested in the book of Jubilees is the united thinking about the Satan with demons/spirits in a common explanation of superhuman evil. Jubilees explains that evil spirits (a.k.a., demons in this work) all serve the Prince of Hostility (= Satan), assisting him in his work of misleading and harming humankind (Jub. 10:7–14). The relationship between the Satan and his malevolent minions, which is taken for granted in several NT texts, is a notion that does not appear in the OT but that arose in early Judaism. The theology of early Jewish literature was not uniform, however, and other Jewish texts would continue to speak of the Satan and evil spirits/demons operating independently of one another.

The Activity of Evil Superhuman Beings

The sorts of activities attributed to these dangerous beings also underwent considerable expansion in the era just prior to the composition of the NT. In a similar way to the OT, early Jewish texts speak of the Satan and evil spirits harming human beings, especially sinners (e.g., Jub. 10:7–9). In addition, writings from this period go beyond OT claims, asserting that the Satan and superhuman spirits are responsible not only for harming humans physically but also for leading humankind into moral error. These invisible beings tempt, deceive, and otherwise lead humans to commit various kinds of sin. Some texts blame these beings for leading the Gentiles to worship idols (1 En. 19:1; Jub. 11:5). The deceptive work of Satan and his minions comes to the fore especially in several of the Dead Sea Scrolls. These writings typically refer to the Satan by the name "Belial," which means something like "worthlessness" or "wickedness." The Damascus Document blames Belial for leading astray even the people of Israel (CD IV, 12–13). The Treatise on the Two Spirits (1QS III, 13 – IV, 26) divides humankind into two groups: the sons of light, who are under the dominion of the Prince of Lights/Angel of Truth; and the sons of darkness, who are under the dominion of the "Angel of Darkness/Spirit of Deceit." This latter being is responsible for leading all humankind, even the sons of light, into various sins.

Although many Jewish writers found the idea that the Satan and other spiritual forces were to blame for human sin compelling, others were dissatisfied with this explanation of moral evil. These Jews were apparently concerned that some people might use such beliefs to excuse human sin or perhaps even to blame God for it. For these Jews, neither God nor any other superhuman being sent lawlessness among humankind, but humans themselves created sin and are justly condemned for it (1 En. 98:4; cf. Sir 15:11–20). Evil spirits do not lead humans to worship demons; idolaters' own corrupt hearts do this (1 En. 99:6–9). These Jews contended that those who looking for someone to blame for their problems needed only to look to humankind's own propensity for evil. Nevertheless, the belief that the Satan and the spirits who served him were responsible for human sin grew in popularity in early Judaism.

As the Satan and his evil hosts received credit for more of humankind's woes, they also came to be regarded less as God's servants—carrying out the just and necessary work of punishing sinners—and increasingly as the enemies of God and opponents of God's people. Relatedly, the Satan also came to be regarded as the invisible power behind the Gentile nations, who were a perennial source of troubles for Israel. During the Exodus era, Jubilees 48 explains, the Satan attempted to thwart God's plan to bless Israel by stirring up the Egyptians to attack them. In a Dead Sea text called the War Rule, the sons of light are pitted in eschatological battle against the sons of darkness. Michael and other angels fight alongside the sons of light, and Belial fights on the side of the sons of darkness. In fact, the War Rule also calls the sons of light "the lot of God" and the sons of darkness "the lot of Belial" (1QM I, 5; XIII, 4–5). For his opposition to God and Israel, Belial is destined to receive God's wrath (1QM IV, 1–2; XVIII, 1).

Numerous Jewish writings from before the turn of the era exhibit the tendency to attribute greater and greater responsibility for human sin to superhuman powers, external to humans. Nevertheless, this was not the only explanation of moral evil available, and some Jews argued that humans alone were to blame for their misdeeds.

Means of Protection from Evil Superhuman Beings

Those who perceived the superhuman realm to be a threat, however, devised various ways for defending themselves. For the sake of convenience here, these defenses against invisible malevolent forces may be divided into two categories: (1) apotropaism topreempt a spiritual attack, and (2) exorcism to relieve someone from an existing spiritual affliction (Morris 2017). Both kinds of defense against the spiritual realm are reflected in early Jewish texts. Apocryphal Psalms (11Q11) contains several psalms to assist an afflicted person in exorcisms. Numerous texts from this period also contain apotropaic prayers asking God to protect the supplicant from the activity of a harmful superhuman entity. The DSS text Prayer for Deliverance, for example, contains the request: "Let no satan rule over me, nor an unclean spirit" (11Q5 XIX, 15). In other texts, an important person from the history of Israel prays that no evil spirit will mislead the people (e.g., Moses in Jub. 1:20).

Additionally, some Jewish texts claimed that by being faithful to Mosaic law, one acquires protection from malicious spiritual forces. The Damascus Document, for instance, states that when a person promises to return to the law of Moses, the angel of hostility will leave them, provided they actually follow through with their commitment (CD XVI, 1–5). The book of Jubilees exemplifies the idea that following the law of Moses affords one protection from evil spiritual entities. In this work, Noah asks God to protect his children from harmful spirits, and God responds by having an angel of the presence reveal heavenly literature to him, which Noah bequeaths to his son Shem (Jub. 10:1–14). Later, when Abram asks for protection from these spirits, God has an angel of the presence teach him Hebrew so he can read the literature revealed to his ancestors (Jub. 12:16–27). The book of Jubilees presents itself as the most recent edition of divinely revealed instruction that provides protection, for those who heed it, from superhuman evil. In the book's introductory section, Moses prays that God will not allow a spirit of belial (= wickedness) to rule over Israel, and God responds to this request by instructing an angel of the presence to dictate words from a heavenly tablet to Moses, which Moses records in the book of Jubilees (Jub. 1:19–28). According to this work, by heeding the instructions of the law of Moses, especially as it is contained in Jubilees, one acquires protection from the harmful forces that threaten to destroy humankind (Stokes 2020).

Satan and Demons in the Gospels

Both the explicit teachings and the theological presuppositions of the NT Gospels pertaining to the superhuman realm have a great deal in common with the literature of early Judaism. One also finds in the Gospels the writings of early Christian thinkers who reoriented their understanding of the Satan and his demons in light of their belief that Jesus Christ was God's Son who dealt a decisive blow to the forces of evil.

Categories and Relationships among Evil Superhuman Beings in the Gospels

Early Jewish literature categorizes superhuman evil and relates various entities to one another in differing ways. Some of these writings maintain categories found in OT literature (or even multiply them), whereas others bring disparate categories into conversation with one another or even combine them. While none of the Gospels (nor any other NT book) addresses the origin of these beings or offers a systematic explanation of the relationships among them, one may infer much about their conceptions of superhuman evil beings. The Synoptic Gospels, in particular, reflect the combination of traditions regarding the superhuman realm that we observe in the book of Jubilees and some of the Dead Sea Scrolls.

The Synoptic Gospels are full of references to "demons" and harmful "spirits," which attests to the importance of such beings in their theology. These Gospels seem to employ these two designations interchangeably, using "demon" and "spirit" (in some instances unambiguously) to refer to the same type of beings (e.g., Matt 8:16; Mark 7:25–30; Luke 9:39–42). Interestingly, other NT texts preserve the distinction between "demons," who are worshiped by idolaters, and spirits, who harm and mislead (1 Cor 10:20; 1 Tim 4:1; cf. 1 En. 19:1). One should not assume that first-century Christianity was uniform in its conception of these evil beings or that these Gospels reflect the common vocabulary of early Christians. Further, while the authors of the Synoptics did not distinguish a "demon" from a "spirit," this does not imply that these authors did not differentiate subcategories of these beings. For example, it is plausible that Luke regarded a "spirit of an unclean demon" (Luke 4:33–41) as a different sort of spirit from a "spirit of divination" (Acts 16:16).

Satan/the Satan also makes numerous appearances in the Synoptic Gospels, as well as in the Gospel of John. He goes by various names and titles in these works, corresponding to the various activities the Gospel authors attribute to this antagonist. He is called the "tempter" (Matt 4:3), the "evil one" (John 17:15), the "ruler of this world" (John 12:31), and "Beelzebul" (Mark 3:22). The Gospels also borrow from the Hebrew of the OT, referring to this figure as "the Satan" or perhaps "Satan." An ambiguity of Greek grammar makes it difficult to determine whether "Satan" is a name or a title in these various NT passages. It is likely that some passages preserve the OT title "the Satan," whereas others employ "Satan" as a name for this figure (e.g., Luke 22:3). (Out of deference to tradition, and since "Satan" is likely used as a name in at least some Gospel passages, this article will refer to this figure in the Gospels simply as "Satan" from this point forward.) Last, but certainly not least, the Gospels refer to Satan as "the devil" (e.g., Matt 4:1), which is simply a Greek translation of the Hebrew "the Satan" and denotes this figure's adversarial nature. With respect to his relationship to other evil beings, Satan is presumed to be the leader of harmful spirits/demons (Mark 3:22–30; Luke 13:10–17) or evil angels (Matt 25:41), though none of the Gospels ever specifies whether the Satan is himself one of these beings or is of yet another class of harmful being.

The Activity of Satan and Demons in the Gospels

Demons occupy a relatively prominent place in the Synoptics due to their role in numerous exorcism accounts, which feature malevolent spirits as personal entities who afflict humans with various physical maladies. In these stories, Jesus is cast in the role of exorcist or healer. A small number of Gospel passages also implicate Satan as the leader of the harmful spirits in their activity of afflicting humans (e.g., Luke 13:10–17). Intriguingly, the Gospel of John is unique among the Gospels in that it contains no exorcism accounts. John mentions demons only in the context of false accusations by Jesus' detractors that Jesus has a demon.

Although Satan is presumed to be the leader of harmful spirits who inflict illness on humankind, the Gospels have more to say about Satan's activity in other capacities. Probably best known of these is Satan's work as a tempter and deceiver. All three Synoptics recount Jesus' temptation by Satan in the wilderness (Matt 4:1–11; Mark 1:12–13; Luke 4:1–13). In the more elaborate accounts of Jesus' encounter with Satan in Matthew and Luke, Jesus rebuffs the devil by quoting from the law of Moses, which is consistent with early Jewish teachings that this literature affords one protection from Satan (e.g., Jub. 10:13; CD XVI, 1–5). Other instances in the Gospels of Satan leading people into sin include Satan's role in Judas's betrayal of Jesus (Luke 22:3; John 13:2). According to Jesus' parable of the soils, Satan is the one who prevents some people from receiving Jesus' message (Mark 4:15 and parallels). According to Matthew, Jesus taught that people should pray that God will not lead them into temptation or testing but will deliver them from the evil one (Matt 6:12). While some early Jewish texts oppose the idea that Satan or other spiritual forces might lead humans into sin, the Gospels are unanimous that Satan poses not merely a physical threat but also a moral threat to humankind.

Relatedly, some Gospel passages assume that Satan is also the invisible being who wields control over the nations of the world. In both Matthew and Luke, Satan promises to give Jesus all of the kingdoms of the world if Jesus would simply bow down and worship him (Matt 4:8–10; Luke 4:5–8). In Luke's version of Jesus' temptation, the devil explains that authority over these kingdoms has been given to him and that he can give it to whomever he wishes (Luke 4:6). Certain Gospel texts assert, moreover, that even certain Jews—namely, Jesus' Jewish opponents—are under the dominion of Satan. In the Gospel of John, in particular, Jesus tells those Jews who wish to kill him that they are neither children of Abraham nor children of God, but that they are children of the devil (John 8:44). The teaching that Satan has authority over the nations and even over some Jews has antecedents in numerous early Jewish texts (e.g., CD IV, 12–13; 1QS III, 13 – IV, 26; 1QM I, 1).

Less prominent in the Gospels is the notion of Satan as the punisher of sinners. Perhaps Satan's role as "the tempter" presumes that Satan was also authorized by God to chastise a person who succumbed to temptation, but this is never stated explicitly. While the common Jewish belief that Satan would bring physical harm on those who merit it is found elsewhere in the NT (e.g., 1 Cor 5:5; 1 Tim 1:20; Heb 2:14), the Gospels speak only implicitly, at best, on this matter.

Protection from Satan and Demons in the Gospels

The Gospel authors were certainly familiar with contemporary Jewish apotropaic and exorcistic practices. Matthew and Luke even mention such Jewish exorcists (Matt 12:27 // Luke 11:19; cf. Acts 19:11–20). The Synoptics, however, contrast Jesus' ability to exorcise demons with that of other exorcists. It is not clear precisely how Jesus' practice of exorcism resembled and/or differed from that of his contemporaries, though scholars have offered differing hypotheses (see recently, e.g., Elder 2021, who argues that Jesus speaks directly to the demons, rather than read or write texts in order to exorcise them, that distinguishes his exorcistic practices from those of other Jews). Most importantly, according to the Gospels, what distinguished Jesus' work from others was not a peculiar methodology, but the efficacy of his exorcisms. "What is this? A new teaching—with authority! He commands even the unclean spirits, and they obey him" (Mark 1:27). It is especially Jesus' unique authority, in fact, that many of the Synoptic exorcism stories are intended to demonstrate.

To be sure, while the Gospel exorcism stories are more about who Jesus is and what he accomplishes than they are a guide to Christian exorcism, the Gospels also assume that early Christian communities would engage in similar practices. Mark 9 tells of an instance in which Jesus' followers were unable to cast a spirit from a boy. After Jesus makes short work of this spirit, his disciples ask him why they had not been successful at exorcising the spirit. Jesus explains, "This kind can come out only through prayer" (Mark 9:29). This conversation between Jesus and his disciples presumes a context in which readers of Mark's Gospel would need to know that different sorts of spirits required different approaches to exorcism (cf. Mark 16:17, though this passage is very probably a somewhat later addition to the Gospel). For some spirits, a standard exorcism will suffice while others require prayer. Luke 10:17–20 also suggests that Jesus' followers would cast out demons, taking part in Jesus' victory over Satan.

Strategies for defense against invisible, harmful entities in the Gospels, as in other early Jewish texts, also included apotropaic prayers. These prayers ask for God's protection from Satan. In John 17, as one of his final acts before his arrest and crucifixion, Jesus asks God to protect his followers from the evil one (John 17:15). In this respect, Jesus resembles Noah, Abraham, and Moses, all of whom prayed that God would protect Israel from the harmful influence of the Satan and the spirits in his service (e.g., Jub. 1:20; 10:3–6; 12:20; Stuckenbruck 2014). In Matthew's version of the Lord's Prayer, Jesus directs his followers when they pray to similarly ask God to deliver them from the evil one (Matt 6:13).

Jesus Versus Satan and Demons in the Gospels

Although much could be written about the place of Satan and demons in the theology of the Gospels, the most significant claim the Gospels make is that Jesus was engaged in a conflict with these spiritual forces and that he, along with his faithful followers, would be the victor in this conflict. This is also what is most Christian about the Gospels' teaching. While much that the Gospels say about Satan and demons have analogues in early Jewish texts outside of the NT, the Gospel authors reoriented their thinking so that Jesus Christ was at the center of it. As a result, they present Jesus as the solution to the problems posed by Satan and demons.

The conflict between Satan and Jesus includes Satan's efforts to have Jesus killed (Luke 22:3; John 13:2). Such efforts resemble those of the Prince of Hostility to kill Moses and Isaac and to stir up the Egyptians to attack Israel (Jub. 17:15–18:13; 48:1–4, 9–19). In the case of Jesus, however, God is not only delivering Jesus from Satan's attack, but he is also ushering in the kingdom of God through Jesus. Demons recognize that Jesus is able to torment and destroy them (Mark 1:24; 5:7), and his exorcisms of these spirits demonstrate that God's kingdom has come (Matt 12:28 // Luke 11:20). Likewise, in Luke, Jesus gives his disciples authority to perform exorcisms, allowing them to take part as well in Satan's eschatological defeat and fall from heaven (Luke 10:17–18). According to the Gospel of John, which contains no exorcism stories, Jesus is driving out Satan, "the ruler of this world," particularly by his death and exaltation (John 12:31). Ultimately, Jesus teaches that Satan and those associated with him are destined for judgment (Matt 25:41). In all four Gospels, the work of Jesus Christ accomplishes and/or anticipates Satan's defeat.

Why Was Jesus Accused of Having a Demon?

All four Gospels relate a seemingly bizarre allegation on the part of Jesus' opponents that Jesus himself was empowered, misled, or afflicted by a demon. Interestingly, different Gospel passages explain this accusation in different ways.

In Mark, which scholars generally regard as the earliest of the Gospels, Jesus was initially accused of being afflicted by a demon because he neglected to eat. In ancient Near Eastern thought, including that of early Judaism, one of the symptoms of a spiritual affliction was a loss of appetite (e.g., 1 En. 15:11). Mark 3:20–30 mentions a time when Jesus' ministry was so demanding that he had no opportunity to eat. As a result, his family became concerned that he was in poor mental health. Certain scribes, however, seized on Jesus' neglect to eat as an opportunity to allege that he had an unclean spirit. Although this accusation was based on some genuine concern about Jesus' mental well-being, the accusation itself was less than genuine and primarily served as a convenient excuse for these scribes to discredit his work. This allowed Jesus' opponents to claim that his ability to cast out demons did not demonstrate that the kingdom of God had arrived, as Jesus claimed, but was merely due to his affiliation with Beelzebul, the ruler of demons. Jesus refuted their accusation, explaining that such thinking was illogical. It would be nonsensical for Satan's kingdom to make war against itself. Perhaps Jesus' response was additionally effective in that his ability to articulate such a reasoned defense indicated that he was indeed of sound mind and unlikely to be afflicted by a spirit.

In the other three Gospels, the basis for the accusation that Jesus was under the influence of a demon differ. Both Matthew and Luke dispense with the context of Jesus' inability to eat and present the accusation that he was in league with Beelzebul purely as an attempt to discredit Jesus' impressive accomplishments as an exorcist (Matt 12:22–32; Luke 11:14–23). The Gospel of John tells of three occasions in which Jesus was accused of having a demon (John 7:20; 8:48–52; 10:20–21). As is typical in John, those who hear Jesus' words are baffled by them. In these passages, failing to make sense his teachings, Jesus' listeners conclude he is out of his mind and under the influence of a demon.

The Gospel of Mark relates an occasion in which there was some genuine confusion about Jesus' mental well-being and his opponents took advantage of the opportunity to claim that he was afflicted by a demon. Matthew and Luke focus on the latter component of the scenario, presenting the allegation of demonic affliction as no more than a false attack on Jesus' credibility. John, on the other hand, focuses on the former: what is perhaps a genuine, albeit unsympathetic, confusion about Jesus' mental state.

As stated at the beginning of this chapter, there is much about the Gospels' perspectives on Satan and demons that is familiar to modern readers. Situating these texts within their early Jewish context, however, highlights several elements of their theology that are less familiar. Attention to the context of the Gospels also allows us to discern what aspects of their theology, though seemingly unremarkable to modern readers, would have been significant or controversial in their ancient context. The apparent familiarity of the Gospels' theology can lure one into taking for granted that their theology corresponds to one's own preconceived understanding more so than it actually does. Examining these works in their early Jewish setting challenges the assumptions with which we mistakenly approach these ancient texts and positions us to be more astute interpreters of them.

Works Cited

Brand, Miryam T. 2013. *Evil Within and Without: The Source of Sin and Its Nature as Portrayed in Second Temple Literature*. Göttingen: Vandenhoeck & Ruprecht.

Dochhorn, Jan. 2013. "The Devil in the Gospel of Mark." Pages 98–107 in *Evil and the Devil*. Edited by Ida Frölich and Erkki Koskenniemi. LNTS 481. London: Bloomsbury.

Elder, Nicholas A. 2021. "Scribes and Demons: Literacy and Authority in a Capernaum Synagogue (Mark 1:21–28)." *CBQ* 83:75–94.

Garrett, Susan R. *Demise of the Devil*. Minneapolis, MN: Fortress Press, 1990.

Morris, Michael J. 2017. *Warding off Evil: Apotropaic Traditions in the Dead Sea Scrolls and Synoptic Gospels*. WUNT 451.2. Tübingen: Mohr Siebeck.

Pagels, Elaine. 1995. *The Origin of Satan: How Christians Demonized Jews, Pagans, and Heretics*. New York: Random House.

Stokes, Ryan E. 2020. "Mosaic Torah and Defense against Demons in the Book of Jubilees." Pages 185–96 in *The Early Reception of the Torah*. DCLS 39. Edited by Kristin De Troyer et al. Berlin: de Gruyter, 2020.

———. 2019. *The Satan: How God's Executioner Became the Enemy*. Grand Rapids: Eerdmans.

———. 2014. "Satan, YHWH's Executioner." *JBL* 133: 251–70.

Stuckenbruck, Loren T. 2014. "The Need for Protection from the Evil One and John's Gospel." Pages 187–215 in *The Myth of Rebellious Angels: Studies in Second Temple Judaism and New Testament Texts*. WUNT 335. Edited by Loren T. Stuckenbruck. Tübingen: Mohr Siebeck.

Twelftree, Graham H. 2011. *Jesus the Exorcist: A Contribution to the Study of the Historical Jesus*. Eugene, OR: Wipf & Stock.

Wright, Archie T. "The Demonology of 1 Enoch and the New Testament Gospels." Pages 215–43 in *Enoch and the Synoptic Gospels: Reminiscences, Allusions, Intertextuality*. EJL 44. Edited by Loren T. Stuckenbruck and Gabriele Boccaccini. Atlanta: SBL Press, 2016.

4.6 "Innocent Blood" in the Gospel of Matthew

Catherine Sider Hamilton

Matthew's Gospel frames Jesus' trial with two scenes that echo each other. At the climax of Jesus' trial, Pilate takes water and washes his hands, saying, "I am innocent (*athōos*) of this man's blood [*haimatos*]." The whole people respond: "His blood be upon us and upon our children" (27:24–25). Pilate's words echo, and reverse, Judas's words at the beginning of the same chapter. "I have sinned," Judas says, "in handing over innocent blood" (*haima athōon*, 27:4). Judas confesses responsibility for shedding innocent blood, and Pilate seeks to refuse responsibility. Matthew draws the two scenes together by means of narrative congruities: it is when the chief priests and elders of the people determine to hand Jesus over to Pilate to be put to death that Judas makes his confession of "innocent blood"; it is when Pilate determines to hand Jesus over to be put to death that he claims he is innocent of his blood. When Judas confesses to "handing over innocent blood," the priests say, "See to it yourself" (*sy opsē*). When Pilate seeks to wash his hands, he says to the people, "See to it yourselves" (*humeis opsesthe*). In thus drawing together the two scenes, Matthew presents Jesus' death as a matter of "innocent blood." In this, Matthew is unique among the Gospels.

The term "innocent blood" is opaque to us, yet it has rich Jewish roots. "Innocent blood" is found in the Prophets and in the Psalms, in the Deuteronomistic history and in the Chronicler; it is found also in a variety of (now) extracanonical Second Temple literature and in rabbinic literature (cf. Davies and Allison 2004, 563). It appears often in reflection on the great crises of Israel's history: the destruction of the temple and the exile. It is, that is, a Jewish term. Its appearance in Matthew, at a critical juncture in the narrative, locates Jesus' death—and Matthew's Gospel—within a Jewish conversation to which, as we will see, questions of pollution and purgation and the fate of the people in the land are central. In what follows, I will trace the idea of "innocent blood" in Israel's scriptures and (briefly) in the Pseudepigrapha and rabbinic literature and show points of contact with Matthew. I will then ask how innocent blood and the logic of pollution and purgation illuminate the death of Jesus in Matthew.

Innocent Blood in the Scriptures of Israel

Jeremiah

When Judas sees that Jesus is condemned to death, he says, "I have sinned in handing over innocent blood [*haima athōon*]" (Matt 27:4). "Know that if you put me to death," Jeremiah says, "you bring innocent blood [*haima athōon*; *dam naqi*] upon yourselves and upon this city and upon those who dwell in it" (LXX Jer 26:15; 33:15; translations of MT follow the NRSV; where they differ, they are my own).

"Innocent blood" (*dam naqi* in Hebrew; in Greek *haima athōon*) as the same term in Jeremiah and Matthew. The context, too, is similar: Jeremiah invokes "innocent blood" after the priests, prophets, and people seize Jeremiah and demand the death sentence for him from their rulers (Jer 26:8–11; [LXX 33:8–11]); likewise, Judas invokes "innocent blood" after the chief priests and elders of the people bind Jesus and take him to the governor to demand the death sentence (Matt 27:1–3).

Further points of contact with Jeremiah are evident in Matt 27:24–25. Innocent blood, Jeremiah says, will come "upon yourselves and upon this city and upon those who dwell in it." In Matt 27:25, the people call for Jesus' blood to be "upon us and upon our children." In Jeremiah, it is the priests, prophets, and "the whole people" (*pas ho laos*, Jer 26:8–9, 11–12 [LXX 33:8–9, 11–12]) who demand Jeremiah's death. In Matthew, it is the priests, elders, and "the whole people" (*pas ho laos*, Matt 27:25, cf. 27:1, 20) who demand Jesus' death. In the background is the desolation of the city and the temple: Jeremiah is charged with announcing their desolation (26/33:9 *erēmōthēsetai*), andJesus is charged with saying he will destroy the temple (Matt 26:61; cf. 23:38 *erēmos*). Only the outcome is different: in Jeremiah, at the words "innocent blood," the people hastily change their minds. "We are about to bring disaster upon ourselves!" some of the elders say (Jer 26:16, 19 [LXX 33:16, 19]).

There is here not only a verbal echo but also a shared thought world: (1) unjust execution, (2) at the hands of priests and rulers, (3) in which the whole city is involved, (4) the consequences—expressed as "blood"—coming upon the people, (5) the prophecy of the temple's destruction in the background, and (6) all this correlated with the charge of "innocent blood." Several other occurrences of innocent blood in Jeremiah share elements of the same thought world.

Jer 2: "Also on your skirts," Jeremiah says in 2:34, "is found the lifeblood of the innocent poor"—literally, "the blood of the innocent" (*haimata . . . athōon; dam . . . neqiyyim*). This is the conclusion of Jeremiah's opening salvo against Israel: the charge of innocent blood caps the list of Israel's offenses. As in Jer 26, it describes an unjust charge leading to death ("though you did not catch them breaking in" [1 above]), an act all the more heinous because the victims are the vulnerable poor. In Jerusalem, Jeremiah speaks to "all the families of the house of Israel": all the people are involved (2:2, 4; cf. 2:9 "you and your children's children" [3 above]). He warns in the wake of these sins of desolation coming upon the people: the city's destruction and exile. "You will come away with your hands on your head" (2:37 [4–5]). All this is correlated with the charge of the "blood of the innocent" (6 above).

Jer 7 and 22: At Jer 7:6 and at 22:3, the charge of innocent blood appears again. Here it is part of the call to justice. Act justly, the prophet says; do not go after other gods, and "do not oppress the alien, the orphan and the widow or shed innocent blood [*haima athōon, dam naqi* (6)]) in this place" (22:3; cf. 7:6). Again, innocent blood is correlated with injustice (1). In Jer 7, the prophet speaks to the people of Judah: all the people are involved (3). In Jer 22, he speaks to Judah's king (2). The charge is oppression and injustice: "But your eyes and heart are only on your dishonest gain, for shedding innocent blood [*to haima to athōon; dam-hannaqi* (6)], and for practicing oppression and violence" (22:17 [1]). The consequence is devastation not just for the king but for the temple and city: "this house shall become a desolation" (22:5 *erēmōsin*, cf. 7:14–15 [4–5]). So, too, in Jer 7: the consequence of Israel's iniquity, of which innocent blood is part, is destruction and exile (7:14–15 [4–5]).

Jer 19: In 19:4, innocent blood appears again. Jeremiah says to the kings of Judah and people of Jerusalem, "Because the people have forsaken me and have profaned this place . . . and because they have filled this place with the blood of the innocent [*haimatōn athōon, dam neqiyyim* (6)]," therefore the days are coming when they will call this place "the valley of Slaughter" (19:4–6 [5]). Innocent blood serves as graphic capstone of a litany of sins in which all the people and the rulers are involved (2–3), leading the whole city to desolation (4–5).

Jeremiah 19, like Jer 26, has significant points of contact with Matt 27:4–10: "a potter (Jer 18:2–6, 19:1 [cf. Matt 27:7]), a purchase (Jer 19:1, [Matt 27:7]), the Valley of Hinnom (where the Field of Blood is traditionally located, Jer 19:2 [Matt 27:8]), 'innocent blood' (Jer 19:4 [Matt 27:4]), and the renaming of a place for burial (Jer 19:6, 11 [Matt 27:7–8])" (Davies and Allison 2004: 569, cf. Gundry 1975, 125; and the extensive discussion in Hamilton 2017, 188–91). Further, in both passages, innocent blood—sign and part of the people's abandonment of God—ends in desolation: "And I will make this city a horror" (19:8), "And throwing the silver into the temple he went out and hanged himself" (27:5), "Wherefore that field is called the Field of Blood to this day" (27:7). Against the background of Jeremiah, the heft of Judas's cry—"I have sinned; I have handed over innocent blood!"—begins to be felt. This is a term that has a long backstory in the history of the people and their God, pointing to the sins of ruler and people—injustice and idolatry, the abandonment of God—and a consequent desolation.

Isaiah

Jeremiah stands out among the prophets for his climactic use of *dam naqi*, innocent blood, in the narrative of the prophet's life. Nevertheless, the problem of innocent blood appears also in Isaiah, much as Jeremiah conceives it. In Isa 59, innocent blood describes the sins of the people and leads into desolation. "Their feet run to evil and they rush to shed innocent blood" (59:7 *dam naqi*, here rendered by the LXX *haima*). As in Jer 2, innocent blood is linked to injustice: "No one brings suit justly. . . . [T]hey speak lies . . . and deeds of violence are in their hands" (59:4–6). Blood, indeed, begins and ends the litany of sins: "For your hands are defiled with blood. . . . [T]hey rush to shed innocent blood" (Isa 59:3, 7). The consequence for the whole people is desolation: Therefore, the people walk in darkness, "among the vigorous as though we were dead" (Isa 59:7, 9–10).

It is the image of bloodshed, not the term "innocent blood," that opens the book of Isaiah. "Your country lies desolate," Isaiah begins (1:7). The people's sins—forsaking the Lord, acts of injustice and bloodshed—stain their hands like blood (1:15: "though your sins are like scarlet . . . red like crimson"), and so God turns away: "When you stretch out your hands, I will hide my eyes from you. . . . [Y]our hands are full of blood" (1:15). In Isa 1 as in Isa 59 and in Jeremiah, there is a direct line from hands full of blood (metonymy for injustice and idolatry) to the land's desolation.

Minor Prophets, Proverbs

Innocent blood appears again in Joel—where *Egypt* will become a desolation because they shed innocent blood in Judah's land (4:19, Eng. 3:19 *dam naqi*, rendered by the LXX *haima dikaion*)—and in Jonah, where the sailors fear to shed innocent blood lest they perish (1:14, *dam naqi, haima dikaion*). It is also used as an image for injustice and oppression in Proverbs (6:17, *dam naqi, haima dikaiou*).

Innocent Blood and the Problem of Pollution

Psalm 106 succinctly states the problem described by innocent blood and in so doing articulates its logic. The long history of Israel's disobedience, from Egypt to the promised land, culminates in innocent blood: "They served [the nations'] idols, . . . they poured out innocent blood [*dam naqi, haima athōon*], the blood of their sons and daughters, . . . and the land was polluted with blood" (106:38; LXX 105:38). The consequence is exile. "Then the anger of the LORD was kindled against his people, and he abhorred his heritage; he gave them into the hands of the nations" (106:40–41). Innocent blood—the sign and fruit of idolatry and injustice, the capstone in Jeremiah, Isaiah, and Ps 106 of the sins of Israel—pollutes the land. So, God abhors his heritage, and the people are cast out.

The logic that moves from innocent blood (and the sin it sums up) to pollution and thence to exile is the logic of Num 35: "You shall not defile [*ṭāmē'*] the land in which you live, in which I also dwell," God says to the Israelites through Moses as they prepare to enter the land (35:34). Blood, Numbers says—murder, the blood of an innocent person unjustly shed—defiles the land: "You shall not pollute [*khanaph*] the land in which you live; for blood pollutes the land, and no expiation can be made for the land, for the blood that is shed in it, except by the blood of the one who shed it" (Num 35:33). Here, (moral) pollution and (ritual) defilement are brought together. Though, Barton notes, "the behaviour that causes the sanctuary, or still more the whole land, to become impure . . . is still referred to with the root *tm,'* it can also be described as pollution [*khanaph*]" (2014: 198; cf. 197: while [*khanaph*] only describes moral impurity, both ritual and moral impurity in Israel's scriptures "are described using the same term [*tame'*]"). The problem of moral "pollution" is also one of defilement: it renders the land unclean, and land that is defiled "will vomit you out for defiling it" (Lev 18:28, Milgrom 1990, 295; cf. Wright 2020 on the Holiness school's [H] development, in Numbers, of P's sin-offering legislation to incorporate the life of the people in the land). So, a murderer must be put to death (Num 35:16–21, 30–32; cf. Gen 9:6), and when a body is found lying on the land whose killer is unidentified, there is the ceremony of handwashing over an unworked heifer:

> All the elders of that town nearest the body shall wash their hands over the heifer whose neck was broken in the wadi, and they shall declare, "Our hands did not shed this blood, nor were we witnesses to it. Absolve, O Lord, your people Israel, whom you redeemed; do not let the guilt of innocent blood remain in the midst of your people Israel." (Deut 21:6–8 *dam naqi, haima anaition*)

The purpose of the ceremony was to purge the land: "so you shall purge the guilt of innocent blood from your midst" (Deut 21:9; cf. Tigay 1996; Patai 1939).

For the land that is defiled vomits out its inhabitants (Lev 18:25, 28; *tame'*). It is the land "in which I also dwell" (Num 35:34), and the holy God "will not tolerate the pollution of his home" (Frymer-Kensky 1983, 406). Israel "thus considered the non-pollution of the land a matter of national survival" (Frymer-Kensky 1983, 408; Hamilton 2008, 89–95; 2017: 59–63). Innocent blood—murder or unjust execution or even, as in Jer 2:34 and Prov 6:17, the life-destroying oppression of the poor—is by no means the only iniquity that pollutes the land, as Frymer-Kensky notes. "These three classes of pollutants—murder, sexual abominations, and idolatry—pollute both the people and the land" (1983, 408; cf. Milgrom 1991, 295, 1054; Barton 2014, 198: "To defile the whole land of Israel seems to require repeated and blatant acts of idolatry, sexual immorality, and murder by the entire community"). But innocent blood stands as graphic instance and summation of the land's defilement: "your hands are full of blood" (Isa 1:15).

When Judas cries "innocent blood" as Jesus is handed over to Pilate to be put to death, and when Pilate washes his hands as he condemns Jesus to death, saying, "I am innocent of this man's blood" (an echo of Deut 21:6–7, but an ironic echo, as Pilate is both witness and perpetrator in the shedding of Jesus' blood; see further below), a whole scriptural history sounds. In framing the death of Jesus as a matter of innocent blood, Matthew sets it within the narrative of the Prophets and Psalms, of the people and the land in which God dwells. In Jeremiah, Isaiah, and Ps 106, innocent blood serves as an image for the sins of the people; it is climactic because it clearly points to defilement and its consequence of the people being cast out of the land.

Innocent Blood and Pollution in Matthew's Narrative of Jesus' Death

The Jewish background of innocent blood illuminates Matthew's narrative. In Jeremiah, the city's destruction consequent upon idolatry and innocent blood is described in images of defilement: in the Valley of Slaughter, the dead lie unburied, and the birds eat them (19:7), "and I will make them eat the flesh of their sons and the flesh of their daughters" (19:9). "And the houses of Jerusalem and the houses of the kings of Judah shall be defiled like the place of Topheth" (19:13). So in Matthew, Judas's cry—"I have betrayed innocent blood"—is accompanied by images of defilement. When his repentance is refused, Judas throws the silver, the price of Jesus' innocent blood, into the temple. This is pollution, innocent blood on the hands of the priests of Israel reaching even into the holy place. Judas hangs himself: the hanged man is cursed and defiles the land (Deut 21:23, cf. 27:25, "Cursed be the one who takes a bribe to shed innocent blood," *dam naqi, haimatos athōou*). With the blood money, the priests buy a burial ground for foreigners as tombs, of course, are unclean (Matt 23:37; cf. 1QM IX, 7 for impurity of Gentile corpses; Hamilton 2008, 97). So, the price of innocent blood wends its way through the narrative, leaving its defiling mark on temple and land alike, ending in the "Field of Blood" (Matt 27:8; see further Hamilton 2018, 423–27). Numbers sounds in the background: "You shall not pollute the land in which you live"—in which God also dwells—"for blood pollutes the land."

The consequence of innocent blood, a sign and part of Israel's sins and the defilement of the land, is the city's desolation. At the climax of Jesus' woes against the Pharisees, he invokes innocent blood: You "kill and crucify" the prophets, he says, so that "all the innocent blood [*haima dikaion*] that has been poured out upon the land may come upon you. . . . Truly I tell you, all this will come upon this generation" (23:35–36; *haima dikaion* in the LXX renders the MT's *dam naqi*, innocent blood, in Joel 4:19, Jon 1:14, and Prov 6:17). Jesus moves directly from innocent blood poured out on the land to the desolation of Jerusalem: "Jerusalem, Jerusalem, city that kills the prophets and stones those sent to her . . . behold, your house is left to you, desolate" (23:37–38). This is the logic of Jeremiah, Isaiah, Numbers, and the Deuteronomist. "Know for certain," Jeremiah says, "that if you put me to death you bring innocent blood upon yourselves and upon this city and upon those who dwell in it" (26:15; cf. 19:3–6). The Deuteronomist articulates the logic at the end of his history: "Moreover, Manasseh shed very much innocent blood [*dam naqi, haima athōon*], until he had filled Jerusalem from one end to another, besides the sin that he caused Judah to sin" (2 Kgs 21:16; cf. 2 Chr 36:5 LXX). Therefore, God says, "I will . . . give them into the hand of their enemies" (21:14). So, Nebuchadnezzar and then the Moabites and Ammonites come against Judah "to destroy it . . . for the sins of Manasseh, for all that he had committed, and also for the innocent blood that he had shed; for he filled Jerusalem with innocent blood, and the LORD was not willing to pardon" (*dam-hannaqi, haima athōon*, 2 Kgs 24:2–4). Matthew's description of Jesus' death as a matter of innocent blood follows the logic of Jeremiah, the Deuteronomist, Numbers, and the problem of the land's defilement: in the wake of innocent blood, the temple's desolation sounds. When at the death of Jesus the temple veil is torn, it is—in the Jewish paradigm of innocent blood—the story's logical end. In the Pseudepigrapha, the tearing of the temple veil signifies the Shekinah's departure and presages the temple's destruction and the exile (Liv. Pro. 12:12; 2 Bar. 6:8; Josephus, *J. W.* 6.288–309; Davies and Allison 2004, 630–31; Keener 2009, 686).

In thus linking Jesus' innocent blood to the desolation of Jerusalem and the tearing of the temple veil, Matthew joins the prophets and the Deuteronomist. "Gilead is a city of evildoers, tracked with blood," Hosea cries. "[The priests] murder on the road to Shechem" (Hos 6:8–9). "Ah city of bloodshed, utterly deceitful. . . . I am against you, says the LORD of hosts . . . and I will let nations look on your nakedness" (Nah 3:1, 5). "The princes of Israel in you . . . have been bent on shedding blood," Ezekiel says. "See, I strike my hands together at the dishonest gain you have made, and at the blood that has been shed within you. . . . I will scatter you among the nations" (Ezek 22:6, 13, 15; cf. 7:23–24; 9:9; 36:18–19 MT). "It was for the sins of her prophets and the iniquities of her priests, who shed the blood of the righteous [*dam tsaddiqim, haima dikaiōn*] in the midst of her," Lamentations says in reflection on Jerusalem's destruction and the exile. Prophet and priest were "defiled with blood," and so the people were scattered. "'Away! Unclean! [*tame'*]' people shouted at them. . . . So they became fugitives and wanderers" (Lam 4:13–15).

The book of Lamentations here illuminates Matthew: "They became fugitives and wanderers." Commentators suggest that Lamentation's reflection on the destruction of Jerusalem echoes Gen 4 and the story of Cain's bloodshed and consequent wandering (Berlin 2002, 110; Lee 1999). In the same way, Matthew recalls Cain's bloodshed as Jesus weeps for the desolation of "your house" (23:38). You kill and crucify the prophets and sages and scribes, Jesus says to the Pharisees, so that "all the innocent blood that has been poured out upon the land may come upon you, from the blood of righteous Abel to the blood of Zechariah" (23:35). In this passage, Matthew deliberately ties Abel's blood to the death of Jesus. Only Matthew adds "crucify" to "kill" (contrast Luke 11:49, "kill and persecute"), thus including Jesus in 23:35 among those whose innocent blood is shed. Further, in Matthew alone the blood that comes upon the Pharisees and this generation (*eph' hymas . . . haima* 23:35) finds an echo at the moment Jesus is condemned to death, as this generation says, "His blood be upon us" (27:25 *haima . . . eph' hēmas*; with 23:35 contrast Luke 11:50 *ekzētēthē to haima*). In Matthew as in Lamentations, Jesus' death, like the death of Abel, is a matter of innocent blood and its consequences. Matthew's logic is the logic of the Jewish Scriptures, from Hosea to Lamentations, Numbers to Deuteronomy, and Jeremiah to Ps 106.

Innocent Blood in Second Temple Literature and the Rabbis: Abel and Zechariah

It is also the logic of Jewish literature beyond the Old Testament. Jesus cites the innocent blood of Abel and of Zechariah as outstanding instances of innocent blood poured out upon the earth and "coming" ominously upon the people. Abel and Zechariah each feature in Jewish literature before, contemporaneous with, and after Mathew's Gospel, precisely in regard to their shed blood and the consequences for the land. In a variety of Second Temple Jewish texts, the blood of Abel cries out from the earth that has swallowed it and brings cataclysm upon the land. In 1 Enoch's Book of the Watchers, the blood of the innocent murdered cries out from the ground to the gates of heaven with a voice like Abel's (1 En. 9:2; 22:7; 85:3–4). In response, God sends the cataclysm—not only to destroy the Giants for the blood they have shed, but also to purge and cleanse the land (1 En. 10–11, 85–90; Hamilton 2017, 47–69). In 1 Enoch's logic, the end that follows the blood of the innocent poured out upon the land like Abel's blood is, in the first place, destruction: the archangels cry to God that the earth is filled with blood and oppression (1 En. 9:9), and God sends Gabriel to Noah: "the whole earth will perish; and tell him that a deluge is about to come on the whole earth" (1 En. 10:2; Nickelsburg 2001). But the cataclysm also points to cleansing and restoration, a new life for the people in the renewed land. After the destroying flood, after the punishment of the rebel angels, "the earth shall be cleansed from all pollution, and from all sin, and from all plague and from all suffering," and all the people will live long lives in peace, "and all the trees of the earth will be glad" (1 En. 10:22; 17–19). This vision of the blood of Abel polluting the land and calling down upon it the cataclysm—a cataclysm, however, that is cleansing as well as destroying, leading to restoration—can be traced in a variety of renditions through Second Temple texts from Jubilees and the Damascus Document to Sibylline Oracles 3, from Susanna to Pseudo-Philo, and even Jude (Hamilton 2017, 71–129).

If Matthew shares with Lamentations and Second Temple literature an interest in the blood of Abel, then he shares with the rabbis an interest in Zechariah's blood. In a legend attributed to "an old man from Jerusalem" (b. Giṭ. 57b), Zechariah's blood, poured out in the temple court in the time of King Joash (2 Chr 24:20–22), boils in the streets of Jerusalem and will not be quieted; it is to appease the blood that Nebu-zaradan comes down upon Jerusalem. "Seven sins did the Israelites commit on that day," the rabbis say in reference to the stoning of Zechariah in the court of the house of the Lord in 2 Chr 24:21:

> They killed priest, prophet, and judge.
> They spilled innocent blood [*dam naqi*].
> They contaminated the courtyard.
>
> And it was a Sabbath that coincided with the Day of Atonement as well.
>
> (y. Taʿan. 69ab trans. Neusner; cf. Lam. Rab. 2.2.4; 4.13.16; Eccl. Rab. 3.16.1, 10.4.1; Pesiq. Rab. Kah. 15.7)

For the rabbis—in Mekilta de Rabbi Ishmael, Palestinian and Babylonian Talmud, midrash Rabbah on Lamentations and Ecclesiastes, Pesiqta de Rab Kahana, even the Targum on Esther—the murder of Zechariah explicates the fate of Jerusalem in the day of Babylon and again in the day of Rome. The rabbis quote Hos 4:2 ("bloodshed follows bloodshed"), Ezek 24:7–9 ("Woe to the bloody city!"), and Isa 1:21 ("the city that was full of justice, righteousness lodged in her—but now murderers!"; cf. 1:15, 18 with 1:7): the innocent blood of Zechariah staining the temple stones, unexpiated and seething, brings down disaster upon the city. As in the Prophets, as in the Deuteronomist, and in keeping with reflection on the pollution of the land in Numbers and Leviticus, innocent blood sums up the sins of the city and requires purgation. As Jesus moves from the blood of Abel and Zechariah to the desolation of Jerusalem (Matt 23:35–38), so the rabbis move from Zechariah's blood to the city's destruction. It is a sequence that appeared in connection with Zechariah's blood already in Lives of the Prophets 23 (see further Hamilton 2017, 130–80).

Yet, though the story of innocent blood in rabbinic reflection leads to desolation, the temple torn down, and Babylon at the gates, it does not end there. While it is true that Nebu-zaradan exacts a terrible toll on the city seething with blood, he cannot purge it. With respect to Zechariah's murder and Abel's, the rabbis note that the Hebrew text is plural: the "bloods" of Abel and of Zechariah is their blood and the blood of all their unborn descendants crying out from the earth on which it has been shed for all time (Gen 4:10; 2 Chr 24:25; 1 En. 9:2–3; 22:5–7; Sanh. 4.5; Gen. Rab. 22.9). Even Nebu-zaradan's slaughter cannot cover the blood. It depends, they conclude (with Jeremiah and Ezekiel); on the mercy of God. "Forthwith the Holy One, Blessed be He, was filled with mercy, and gave a hint to the blood, which was swallowed up in the same spot" (Lam. Rab. 4.13.16;

Freedman and Simon; cf. Taʻan. 69ab; Pesiq. Rab. Kah. 15.7). The boiling blood stops not at Nebu-zaradan's slaughter but at God's word. Nor is this the end in the story of Zechariah's blood. Nebu-zaradan, seeing such a mighty retribution for the blood of one man, is stricken. "What will happen to me, who have killed so many?" he asks in the Talmudic versions, and he flees away and becomes a convert. Thus in the mercy of God, the blood of Zechariah ends in the triumph of the Torah, even over the pagan conqueror. The Holy One (the Talmud says) purposed to lead them all in this way "under the wings of the Shekinah" (Giṭ. 57b; Sanh. 96b). In both the blood of Abel traditions and the blood of Zechariah traditions, the blood that pollutes the land brings down disaster upon it. But that is not all: the cataclysm is cleansing in 1 Enoch, and Nebu-zaradan's bloodbath ends in the mercy of God and the ascendancy of the Torah.

"Innocent Blood" and the "Blood Poured out for Many": The Meaning of Jesus' Death in Matthew

What of Matthew? If Matthew shares an interest in Abel's blood and its polluting effect and in Zechariah's blood and its consequence for Jerusalem, and if he sees in the wake of innocent blood the cataclysm, then does he share the rabbis' hope? Does he share 1 Enoch's conviction that the cataclysm is cleansing? Matthew raises the problem of pollution in the death of Jesus and sees the temple veil torn and a shattered land. But like 1 Enoch and the rabbis—like Jeremiah and the Prophets too—Matthew does not end there. Into the cataclysm at Jesus' death, Matthew inserts this scene: As the temple veil is torn, as the earth shakes and the rocks are split, "the tombs also were opened," and "many bodies of the holy ones who had fallen asleep were raised, and coming out of their tombs after his resurrection they went into the holy city" (27:52–53). The narrative is awkward in its separation of the tombs' opening from the saints' coming out of the tombs and going into the holy city, as commentators universally note. But Matthew achieves in it an echo of Ezekiel: "I am going to open your tombs," God says to Israel in the Valley of Dry Bones, "and bring you forth out of your tombs, O my people, and I will bring you back into the land of Israel" (Ezek 37:12). Now at Jesus' death and proleptic resurrection, as the tombs are opened, and the people are brought out and go into Jerusalem, Ezekiel's prophecy sounds (cf. Gundry 1994, 576; Senior 1975, 320; France 2007, 1081–82). This is the ancient hope of Israel for restoration, realized at the heart of Israel.

This scene of hope at the cross of Jesus—Israel's dry bones raised, its people walking again into the holy city, just as Ezekiel said they would—is peculiar to Matthew. It is not only death that follows from Jesus' innocent blood, Matthew's proleptic resurrection seems to say. There is also death—and it is real, measured in blood and bones—in the temple's torn walls. Like Jeremiah and the rabbis, Matthew does not skate over the real suffering of Jerusalem at the hands of Babylon and again of Rome. But there is also and finally life: life for the dry bones of Israel and restoration, a return to the city called "holy" again.

Further, it is a restoration described as purification: those who rise are holy (*sōmata . . . hagiōn*), and they go into the city called "holy" (*hagian*) again. There is one final point to be made about Matthew's use of the language of blood in relation to the death of Jesus. Together with the term "innocent blood," Matthew has another word to say about the blood of Jesus, and it is a word that addresses the problem of innocent blood and pollution. In 26:28, Matthew deliberately links Jesus' innocent blood poured out in crucifixion to Jesus' blood poured out for many. "This is my blood of the covenant, poured out for many for the forgiveness of sins," Jesus says at the Last Supper with his disciples. "Blood poured out" (*haima ekchunnomenon*): These are precisely the words Jesus uses in 23:35 to describe "all the innocent blood poured out" upon the earth, bringing devastation (*haima ekchunnomenon*), although Luke's Gospel says it differently (11:50). The repetition in Matthew draws together the two passages, as does Matthew's addition of "crucify" in 23:34. The blood poured out upon the earth in 23:35—Jesus' innocent blood—is also Jesus' blood "poured out for many."

"For many": *peri pollōn*. This is the language of sacrifice. Matthew makes the reference clear by changing Mark's *hyper* (Mark 14:24) to *peri* and adding "for the forgiveness of sins." In Lev 4, the priest slaughters the bull of the sin offering, puts some of the blood on the horns of the altar, and then pours out (*ekcheō*) at the foot of the altar "all [the rest of] its blood." In this way, Leviticus says, "the priest shall make atonement *for* [*peri*] them" (4:20; cf. 4:26, 35; cf. 16:6, 11, 15). Their sin, Lev 4 concludes, "will be forgiven them" (*aphethēsetai autois hē hamartia*, Lev 4:20, 26, 35). "This is my blood poured out [*ekcheō*]," Jesus says in Matthew, "for [*peri*] many, for the forgiveness of sins" (*eis aphesin hamartiōn*). Matthew's word *forgiveness* is the noun form of the verb "forgive" in LXX Leviticus. "Blood poured out," "for many," "for forgiveness": the language is the same in Matthew and in Leviticus. Quite precisely, Matthew is using the language of Levitical sacrifice, the blood of the sin offering poured out for the people—the blood, in Leviticus, that atones (4:20, 26, 31, 35; 16:6, 11, 16–18, 20).

Why is atonement necessary? Because, Milgrom says, the sanctuary and the land are polluted by Israel's sins, the accidental and the brazen. The blood is for purgation (1991, 1033–39; Eberhart 2020, 20; Wright 2020, 46). Long before the prophets, "the Priestly legislators have constructed a system based on the postulate that severe impurity pollutes the sanctuary (P) and the land (H)" (Milgrom 1991, 1005). Ezekiel sees in Israel's sins the contamination of the temple and therefore its destruction (5:11; 8:6; 22:1–15; 23:37–39, 47). The restoration for which he longs is a purification: a cleansed people who will return to a holy temple (36:23–25, 33–35; 37:23, 28; Milgrom 1991, 982). In Matthew, at Jesus' death, as his innocent blood is poured out, the earth is shattered. But at the same time, the tombs are opened; and in Jesus' resurrection—brought together in Matthew with Jesus' death—the holy ones come out and return to the holy city.

Matthew raises the problem of pollution in the death of Jesus and sees the temple veil torn and a shattered land. But like Ezekiel, Jeremiah, 1 Enoch, and also the rabbis, Matthew does not end there. As in the rabbis, in 1 Enoch, and indeed in Jer 31:15–17, back-to-back with the devastation that is the price of innocent blood, hope rises. In Jesus, innocent blood—the blood that is the sign of sin, the blood poured out for the pollution of the land—meets the blood of the sin offering, the blood poured out for many for the forgiveness of sin.

Conclusion

Matthew frames Jesus' death as a matter of innocent blood. It is a figure with deep Jewish roots, in the Prophets and histories, in the Pseudepigrapha and the rabbis. Although it is just one figure in the rich world of Matthew's Passion Narrative, it offers a fruitful and largely unplumbed lens through which to hear the familiar story. It is a Jewish lens, reflecting on the great crises of Israel's history, exile, and the destruction of the temple in the time of Babylon and again in the time of Rome. Its logic is the logic of the people whose God is holy, whose God dwells among a people called to be holy in the holy land. Innocent blood takes sin seriously, for blood in graphic metonymy for the sins of the people pollutes the land, and "you shall not defile the land in which you live, in which I also dwell" (Num 35:33–34). Matthew's Gospel follows this logic, with Jeremiah and Ezekiel and the rabbis, to its end in the place of devastation. Yet there, with the Prophets and the rabbis, it finds hope. Unlike the rabbis, it finds this hope in Jesus' blood—blood rendered by the people as "innocent blood," and rendered by Jesus as the blood poured out for many. The scope of innocent blood is enormous, and it brings devastation in its wake. Like Jeremiah and the rabbis, Matthew does not skate over Jerusalem's desolation, the people's real suffering. But that devastation is not in isolation from the mercy of God (cf. Barton 2014, 207). In Jeremiah and the rabbis, weeping and mercy stand back-to-back. So, too, in Matthew. Matthew's resurrection is proleptic: hope is here at the cross, in the ruins, and it is for cleansing. The holy ones will come out of the tombs, and they will go into the holy city.

Works Cited

Barton, John. 2014. *Ethics in Ancient Israel*. Oxford: Oxford University Press.

Berlin, Adele. 2002. *Lamentations: A Commentary*. Louisville: Westminster John Knox.

Black, Matthew, and Albert-Marie Denis, eds. 1970. *Apocalypsis Henochi Graece. Fragmenta Pseudepigraphorum Quae Supersunt Graeca*. Leiden: Brill.

Davies, W. D., and Dale C. Allison, Jr. 2004. *Matthew 19–28*. Vol. 3 of *A Critical and Exegetical Commentary on the Gospel according to Matthew*. ICC. London: T&T Clark.

Eberhart, Christian A. 2020. "Atonement amid Alexandria, Alamo, and Avatar." Pages 17–30 in *Atonement: Jewish and Christian Origins*. Edited by Max Botner, Justin Harrison Duff, and Simon Dürr. Grand Rapids: Eerdmans.

France, R. T. 2007. *The Gospel of Matthew*. NICNT. Grand Rapids: Eerdmans.

Freedman, H., and Maurice Simon, eds. *Midrash Rabbah*. 10 vols. London: Soncino, 1939.

Frymer-Kensky, Tikva. 1983. "Pollution, Purification, and Purgation in Biblical Israel." Pages 398–414 in *The Word of the Lord Shall Go Forth: Essays in Honor of David Noel Freedman in Celebration of His Sixtieth Birthday*. Edited by Carol L. Meyers and M. O'Connor. American Schools of Oriental Research Special Volume Series 1. Winona Lake, IN: Eisenbrauns.

Gundry, Robert H. 1994. *Matthew: A Commentary on His Handbook for a Mixed Church under Persecution*. 2nd ed. Grand Rapids: Eerdmans.

————. 1975. *The Use of the Old Testament in Matthew's Gospel: With Special Reference to the Messianic Hope*. Leiden: Brill.

Hamilton, Catherine Sider. 2017. *The Death of Jesus in Matthew: Innocent Blood and the End of Exile*. SNTSMS 167. Cambridge: Cambridge University Press.

————. 2018. "The Death of Judas in Matthew: Matt 27:9 Reconsidered." *JBL* 137.2: 419–37.

————. 2008. " 'His Blood Be upon Us': Innocent Blood and the Death of Jesus in Matthew." *CBQ* 70: 82–100.

Keener, Craig S. 2009. *The Gospel of Matthew: A Socio-Rhetorical Commentary*. Grand Rapids: Eerdmans.

Lee, Nancy C. "Exposing a Buried Subtext in Jeremiah and Lamentations: Going after Baal and . . . Abel." Pages 87–128 in *Troubling Jeremiah*. Edited by A. R. Pete Diamond, Kathleen O'Connor, and Louis Stulman. JSOTSup 260. Sheffield: Sheffield Academic Press, 1999.

Malinowitz, Chaim, Yisroel Simcha Schorr, and Mordecai Marcus, eds. 2007. *Talmud Yerushalmi*. Schottenstein edition. 12 vols. New York: Mezorah Publications.

Milgrom, Jacob. 1991. *Leviticus 1–16: A New Translation with Introduction and Commentary*. AB 3. New York: Doubleday.

————. 1990. *Numbers*. JPS Torah Commentary. Philadelphia: Jewish Publication Society.

Neusner, Jacob. 1988. *The Mishnah: A New Translation*. New Haven: Yale University Press.

————. 1987. *The Talmud of the Land of Israel: A Preliminary Translation and Explanation: Volume 18: Besah and Taanit*. Chicago: University of Chicago Press.

Nickelsburg, George. W. E. 2001. *1 Enoch*. Hermeneia. Minneapolis, MN: Fortress Press.

Patai, Raphael. 1939. "The 'Egla 'Arufa or the Expiation of the Polluted Land." *JQR* 30: 59–69.

Senior, Donald. 1975. *The Passion Narrative according to Matthew: A Redactional Study*. BETL 39. Leuven: Leuven University Press.

Tigay, Jeffrey H. 1996. *Deuteronomy*. JPS Torah Commentary. Philadelphia: Jewish Publication Society.

Wright, David P. 2020. "Atonement beyond Israel: The Holiness School's Amendment to Priestly Legislation on the Sin Sacrifice (*ḥaṭṭā't*)." Pages 45–62 in *Atonement: Jewish and Christian Origins*. Edited by Max Botner, Justin Harrison Duff, and Simon Dürr. Grand Rapids: Eerdmans.

(Translations of ancient sources are my own unless otherwise noted.)

4.7 The Jewish Roots of the Gospels' Soteriology

Oliver Marjot

Broadly speaking, "soteriology" refers to the "what, when, who, and how" of salvation, from the Greek terms *sōzō* ("to save, heal, make well"), *sōtēria* ("salvation, healing"), and *sōtēr* ("savior"). The question of how the soteriology of New Testament texts relate to their Jewish heritage and context is a fraught one; this has particularly been the case in Pauline studies since the publication of E. P. Sanders' *Paul and Palestinian Judaism* in 1977. Part of the problem is that as a doctrinal category native to systematic theology, "soteriology" is a problematic term to apply to non-systematic texts, a category that includes the four Gospels and most, if not all, of ancient Jewish literature. The brief overview here intentionally tries to avoid approaching the question with reference to doctrinal or systematic terminology; and in order to be fair to what the Gospels are actually saying, I have particularly made a point of avoiding the terms and categories that have become native to the Pauline debate ("covenant nomism," "legalism," "merit theology," "indicative and imperative"), though the interested student would also do well to acquaint themselves with those terms (see, for an overview, Westerholm 2004). As with many of the topics in this volume, in the space allotted to this article we can only scratch the surface of the Jewish roots of the Gospels' soteriology. The following is therefore intended primarily as food for thought and as a starting place for the interested student of the Gospels.

The Jewish Roots of Mark's Soteriology

George Nickelsburg has written that "eschatology was the air that early Christianity breathed" (2003, 88). This is true of the soteriology of the Synoptic Gospels (Matthew, Mark, and Luke), and particularly true of Mark's. The basic Markan view of salvation—one that the Second Gospel bequeaths to both Matthew and Luke—is firmly rooted in Jewish convictions about a definitive, future eschatological judgment, particularly as those expectations are developed in Second Temple apocalyptic literature. Prominent (though not universally attested) features of this tradition include the futurity of salvation, the limitation of salvation to an "elect" community, the soteriological importance of revelation and alertness, and the presence (in some but not all sources) of a supernatural or semi-divine agent to enact the eschatological judgment. All of these are found in Mark.

Jesus' apocalyptic discourse in Mark 13 sets out a roadmap for the Second Gospel's variation on this quintessentially Jewish theme. The events outlined in this chapter—including preliminary, geopolitical turmoil (13:8), cosmic upheaval (13:24–25), the arrival of the messianic Son of Man (13:26), and the ingathering of the elect (13:27)—closely parallel Second Temple Jewish apocalyptic texts (see for example 1 En. 69:29; cf. 4 Ezra 12:34; cf. Jub. 5:10; T. Levi 4:1; As. Moses 10); these are themselves rooted in the biblical prophetic expectation of the "Day of the

Lord" (cf. e.g., Zeph 2:3; also Joel 2:31; Amos 5:18), and the Markan Jesus explicitly highlights this indebtedness in his quotation of Isa 13:10 at Mark 13:24. This strong eschatological orientation means that in Mark, as in Second Temple Jewish apocalyptic texts, salvation is predominantly understood as a one-time event situated in the authorial future; rather than primarily associated with the death of Jesus (in the past) or individual conversion (in the present). Although Jesus' message firmly proclaims the beginning of the eschaton ("the time is fulfilled"; Mark 1:15a), it is nonetheless important for the Gospel's soteriological conception that the kingdom of God has only "come near" (Mark 1:15b) and is not yet fully present.

In Mark, salvation is explicitly limited to membership of "the elect, whom [the Lord] chose" (13:20); it is at no point assured to all (or any) of the recipients of Jesus' earthly ministry. Membership of the elect rests mainly on inscrutable divine choice and preservation (13:20), coupled with correct understanding (4:12), perseverance (13:13), and alertness (13:33, 35–37) on the part of the elect. All of these features are strikingly similar to ideas found in the thought of 4 Ezra, Jubilees, the Enochic literature, and the Qumran sectarians (see, e.g., 1 En. 1:1; 93:2; 1QpHab V, 4; 1Q14 frag. 10, lines 5–6; 4Q169 frag. 1–2, II, 8; Jub. 1:29). Although the collective election of Israel to salvation is an important theme in Jewish thought (see below on Matthew and Luke), a characteristic feature of Jewish apocalyptic and eschatological thought is the invocation (whether explicit or implicit) of the biblical "remnant" motif, and accordingly the limitation of salvation to a sub-set of Israel (e.g., Isa 10:21–22; Jer 50:20; Zech 9:7; and in the postbiblical literature, 1QS II, 5–10; CD III, 13; 4 Ezra 9:21–22). The same pattern of thought is clear in Mark's unwillingness to offer assurances of salvation to his readers in advance of the divine judgement in the eschaton. Mark's general warning against complacency in the face of the final judgment mirrors similar warnings found in both biblical and noncanonical Second Temple Jewish texts (see especially 1 En. 82:1–3 for the motif of alertness with regard to revealed, saving knowledge). The Markan Jesus lays great emphasis on the importance of understanding the significance of his message (Mark 4:10–13); and as in the Enochic literature, the soteriological value of this understanding seems to lie largely in that it defines the community of the elect (e.g., 1 En. 93:10; see Nickelsburg 2011 for comments on revelation-as-salvation). In this respect, the Markan emphasis differs from the Qumran sectarians and from the writers of 4 Ezra and 2 Baruch, whose respective revelations were intended to prompt a specific, salvific standard of obedience to the Torah (see e.g., 2 Bar. 51:7; 57:6).

The invocation of a supernatural figure who mediates divine salvation and judgment is an important feature of many (though importantly, not all) strands of Second Temple Jewish soteriological thought: a figure variously referred to in both Mark and Jewish sources as "messiah," "son of man," and "son of God" (Yarbro Collins 2007, 53–59; cf. Mark 8:38; 1 En. 52:1–9; 4 Ezra 7:26–29; 12:31–34). For Mark, the soteriological importance of the title "Son of Man" (Mark 2:10, 28; 8:31, 38; 9:9, 12, 31; 10:33, 45, 48; 13:24, 26; 14:21, 62) cannot be unrelated to the centrality of the Son of Man in the world of thought represented by 1 Enoch, which can in turn be linked to the vision of "one like a son of man" in Dan 7:13. Importantly, for Mark, as for the other Gospel writers, the advent of this divine mediator is no longer situated wholly in the future; instead, he is identified with the earthly, historical figure of Jesus of Nazareth. One result of this identification is that for Mark, although salvation is located at the eschaton, favorable judgment at the Son of Man's return is closely associated with his readers' individual and collective response to the person and ministry of the earthly Jesus (8:34–35, 38). Thus, although at Qumran and in the Enochic literature positive response to the content of the revelation in question is associated with favorable judgment and salvation (e.g., 4Q174 I, 10–12; 1 En. 50:1–3; 81:5–6; 82:1–3), in Mark—and the other Gospels—this motif is transposed into a positive response to the *person* in and through whom the saving revelation is made.

The notion of vicarious atonement on the part of the eschatological judge is not generally part of the apocalyptic repertoire; it is Mark's identification of the crucified Jesus of Nazareth with the eschatological Son of Man (Mark 8:31; 9:9) that makes soteriological reflection on Jesus' death a significant feature of the Gospel, a feature that distances it from the soteriology of its Jewish apocalyptic cousins. There is, nonetheless, an important conversation in the scholarship about the extent to which the Markan idea of the Son of Man's suffering and death as a ransom for many (Mark 10:45, an undeniably soteriological notion) should be understood as drawing on authentically Jewish roots. Many argue that the Markan imagery is grounded in the Isaianic language of the vicarious death of the servant of the Lord, especially with reference to Isa 53. Although Mark does not cite Isaiah explicitly to this effect, and although the language of "ransom" (Greek *lytron*) does not appear in this part of Isaiah, both the Greek and Hebrew of Isa 53:11–12 feature the idea of an obedient servant dying for the benefit of others, and *lytron* is used elsewhere in the LXX in connection with expiation or redemption (e.g., Exod 30:11–16; Num 3:11–13 LXX; the verbal form *lytroō* is closely associated with God's salvation or redemption of Israel; see below). In addition to the relationship with Isa 53, Simon Gathercole has argued that Mark's idea of the vicariously suffering Son of Man can in fact also be traced back to the Son of Man's identification with the suffering saints of the Most High in Daniel (2004).

Thus it is possible to view the idea of Jesus' obedient death effecting a vicarious salvation or redemption as drawing on authentically Jewish roots (see Yarbro Collins 2007, 81–82, 499–504 for an excellent overview). On the other hand, Mark is far from explicit about the precise nature and extent of the soteriological efficacy of Jesus' death. On the whole, the idea of Jesus' saving death, while clearly an important element in the Gospel's overall soteriological schema, seems to be poorly integrated into other elements of Mark's soteriological conception: for example, no saving effect of the cross is invoked in Jesus' description of the role of the Son of Man in the preservation and salvation of the elect in the last days in Mark 13. Either way, the broad eschatological and messianic shape of Mark's soteriological conception arguably remains primarily indebted to apocalyptic and eschatologically oriented Jewish models, both biblical and noncanonical.

The Jewish Roots of Matthew's Soteriology

Matthew and Luke inherit Mark's basically Jewish apocalyptic soteriology: both expect an eschatological judgment during which salvation will be definitively enacted, and both identify Jesus of Nazareth with the coming Son of Man who will act as God's agent for judgment and salvation. Each, however, also has his own soteriological emphases in addition to this apocalyptic orientation.

From the very beginning of Matthew's Gospel, the mission of Jesus is explicitly associated with salvation ("He will save his people from their sins," Matt 1:21). There is debate among scholars as to both the "who" and the "how" of this salvation, with a significant bearing on Matthew's relationship with Judaism. As far as the "who" is concerned, an important question is whether and to what extent Matthew means ethnic Israel when he refers to "his people" in 1:21. Most scholars would not dispute that a dominant idea in Jewish soteriology is God's redemption of Israel on the basis of the covenant promises made first with Abraham and then with the whole people of Israel at Sinai (cf. e.g., Ps 105:8–10; Rom 11:26–27; Jub. 15:30–32). Does Matthew preserve this central Jewish notion, or does he deconstruct it? In other words, does "his people" in Matt 1:21 refer to ethnic Israel (or a remnant thereof), as one would automatically assume in the case of an undisputedly Jewish text, or does it refer in a supersessionist, transposed sense to the Christian community? Some contemporary Matthean scholars would argue the former (see Sim 1998; Willitts 2007), while others have argued the latter (e.g., Luz 1995, who sees in Matthew's narrative an implicit but definitive turning away from ethnic Israel on the part of the Matthean community). An important *media via* on this count is represented by Matthias Konradt, who has argued recently that the saved community in Matthew includes ethnic Israel as a theologically significant category, but it also transcends the bounds of ethnicity to include Gentiles in a wider *ekklēsia* ("gathering" or "community" of followers of Jesus; Konradt 2014). From this last point of view, Matthew's conception of the intended recipients of salvation has roots both in the quintessentially Jewish idea of God's specific promises to save ethnic Israel (cf. e.g., Isa 45:17; Jer 33:14) as well as the equally biblical motif of the extension of that salvation to the nations (that is, non-Israelites or Gentiles, cf. Isa 49:6; see more below).

As to the "how" of salvation in Matt 1:21, many commentators have assumed the primary reference is to Jesus' saving death on the cross, pointing to the fact that Matthew removes the Markan reference to forgiveness of sins in the context of John's baptismal ministry at Mark 1:4, and he associates it instead with Jesus' death (Matt 26:28). Nathan Eubank has argued for a thoroughly Jewish Matthean theology of vicarious atonement rooted in Second Temple Jewish conceptions of sin as debt and heavenly treasure as "wages" for righteousness; according to this reading, Matthew interprets the early belief in the vicariously atoning death of Christ through a profoundly Jewish conception of the relationship between salvation and righteousness (Eubank 2013). However, many readers of Matthew have suggested that, as in Mark, the saving function of Jesus' *death* specifically, while certainly present, is not well integrated into the bulk of the Gospel's soteriological material. For some, Jesus' primary saving function is as a teacher of the Torah, or at the very least as a teacher of the kind of righteous life required for salvation: functions that perhaps fit more comfortably into Jewish soteriological categories (see Loader 2017 for an overview of both sides of the argument).

It is undeniable that for Matthew the righteousness taught by Jesus is a crucial soteriological theme. In a key passage near the beginning of the Sermon on the

Mount, the Matthean Jesus tells his audience that unless their righteousness exceeds that of the scribes and Pharisees, they will never enter the kingdom of heaven (Matt 5:20). This "exceeding righteousness" is described as "perfection" (5:48) and characterized as an intensification of the moral standards demanded by the Jewish law (5:17–19, 21–47), which Matthew understands as still having authority for at least his Jewish readers (5:17, though see France 1989 for an opposing view). The language of righteousness is far too pervasive in the Hebrew Bible to give an effective account of its use here; but see as an example Ps 7, which speaks about the righteousness of both human beings (7:8–9) and God himself (7:11) (for the close connection between righteousness and salvation, see also Isa 45:8 and 65:10). Matthew expands on Mark's general soteriological admonitions to readiness and alertness by emphasizing the moral and ethical criteria for salvation (see especially Matt 18:23–35 and 25:31–46). Although Matthew may exhibit a particularly christological conception of what it means to observe the law and therefore live righteously (Matt 25:40), in general terms the Gospel participates in a distinctively Jewish soteriological discourse in its clear concern with the relationship between human righteousness and God's salvation.

Scholars have long been divided over the extent to which a specifically Jewish concept of righteousness is central to Matthew's soteriological conception. Some interpreters argue that Matthew takes the Jewish category of righteousness and *contrasts* it with the superior mode of being defined as "perfection," which is possible only for disciples of Christ (see especially Przybylski 1981). Others argue that Matthew's notion of righteousness, while particularly strict, is just one variation among first-century sectarian Jewish interpretations (e.g., Sim 1998; Kampen 2019). When read in isolation, some of the more uncompromising Matthean statements about human righteousness do echo the demands for strict law observance as a condition for salvation found in 4 Ezra and the Dead Sea Scrolls (cf. CD VI, 14; 4 Ezra 7:45–47). Many contemporary interpreters of Matthew are therefore keen to read Matthew "within Judaism" (that is, as a Jewish text, albeit a "Jewish-Christian" one; see Runesson and Gurtner 2020); and some have reconstructed a hypothetical "Matthean community" that, very similarly to the Qumran community, saw itself as the faithful remnant of Israel, enforcing strict ethical and moral standards in accordance with its interpretation of the Torah, and viewing salvation as limited to its own members (Sim 1998; White 2014).

An alternative to this approach is to read Matthew as earnestly engaged in the more mainstream Jewish enterprise of interpreting the law and its relationship to salvation in a nuanced way. The era of characterizing Jewish soteriology in blanket terms as "works righteousness" is fortunately long gone in NT scholarship (see Sanders 1977), and most scholars today recognize that the soteriological perspective of ancient Judaism is best understood as a "variegated nomism" ("nomism" from the Greek *nomos*, meaning "law")—that is, as exhibiting a rich variety of different stances on the relationship between Torah observance and salvation (Carson et al. 2001). Balancing Matthew's apparently uncompromising standards with regard to personal and sexual ethics is the Gospel's emphasis on prioritizing the "weightier matters of the law" (justice, mercy and faith; 23:23) and the twofold love commandment (22:34–40) over the "less weighty" commandments (though Matthew is clear that this priority does not annul or abrogate the latter; 23:23d). Both concepts—the idea of weightier and less weighty matters of the law and the priority of the twofold love command—are evidenced in rabbinic sources (see e.g., Sipra Qod. 4.12) and have their roots in the Hebrew Bible (Lev 19:18; Deut 6:4–5; Mic 6:8). Although not explicitly related to salvation, these passages are part of the Matthean debate over ethics and law observance, which is in turn closely related to judgment (25:31–46), receipt of eternal life (19:17), and entry into the kingdom of heaven (5:20)—all of which are undeniably soteriological categories.

Finally, the Matthean Beatitudes (5:2–11), shared in part with Luke, exhibit the quintessentially Jewish theme of God's concern for the weak, the vulnerable, and the marginalized (e.g., Deut 10:18; Isa 1:7; Mic 2:2; also e.g., 4Q434 frag. 1). Although Matthew's ethical standards are undeniably high, there is a significant tension at the heart of the Gospel's soteriology between, on the one hand, the conviction that "exceeding righteousness" is necessary for entry into the kingdom of heaven (5:20) and, on the other hand, the belief that salvation is ultimately a divine prerogative, extended mercifully to those who cannot earn it (5:2–11; 19:26; 18:23–35). This same tension characterizes Jewish soteriological reflection across the range of extant ancient sources. E. P. Sanders tried to resolve it in his influential, sweeping characterization of Jewish soteriology as "covenant nomism," but it is probably fairest to recognize that the two impulses are simply in tension with each other (Loader 2017), both in the Jewish sources and in Matthew.

The Jewish Roots of Luke's Soteriology

The opening chapters of Luke's Gospel—composed of material for the most part not shared with Matthew or Mark—contain a wealth of unique soteriological material that systematically draws on Jewish scriptural traditions, making Luke's language about salvation arguably the most explicitly Jewish of all the Gospels. The Lukan Mary praises the God of Israel because in the conception of Jesus and John, "He has helped his servant Israel . . . according to the promise made to Abraham" (Luke 1:54–55). This reference to the founding of God's covenant with the Jewish people in the promises made to the patriarch Abraham (cf. Gen 15; 17) not only draws on Jewish scriptural themes but it also, crucially, puts Israel center stage in the unfolding of God's salvation in the Gospel's narrative present. If God's salvation of Israel on the basis of his covenant promises is understood as a *sine qua non* of Jewish soteriology (Sanders 1977), then Luke appears to put his Gospel squarely in this category.

The Lukan Mary understands God's salvation of Israel in terms of relief for the oppressed and vulnerable (1:52–53). This is closely paralleled in the central concerns of the pre-exilic prophets (e.g., Amos 5:11–15) as well as the Psalms (Pss 35:10; 72:13; 82:3–4) and Second Temple texts (Sir 35:22–25). Luke uses the song of Zechariah (1:68–79) to ground this conception of salvation in the literary genre of Israelite prophecy, describing Zechariah's hymn of praise as a prophecy spoken through the inspiration of the Holy Spirit (1:67). The Lukan Zechariah expresses God's salvation of Israel as redemption (1:68; Gk. *lytrōsis*; cf. Exod 15:13;

Isa 44:23 LXX and elsewhere)—a redemption associated with the raising up of a Davidic messianic figure (Luke 1:69; cf. Zech 10:8 in connection with the promise of a royal Messiah figure in Zech 9:9–10). Salvation is thus associated with Israel's rescue from its enemies (1:71, 74), remaining very much within the range of expectations exhibited in the Hebrew Bible (Foerster 2000). Luke also associates salvation explicitly with forgiveness of sins (1:77), making it proleptically clear that in his conception salvation has to do with individual standing before God, as well as (perhaps instead of) the geopolitical restoration of Israel (Steyn 2005; cf. Luke 24:27), but a focus on forgiveness of sins as an eschatological act of salvation is also very much in line with biblical and first-century Jewish expectation (e.g., Ps 79:9; 11Q13 II, 4–8, 13; Sir 2:11).

Zechariah compounds the Israel- and covenant-centric soteriology articulated by Mary with his references to the oath that God swore to Abraham (1:73) and the "holy covenant" between God and Israel (1:72)—it is hard to imagine a more explicitly Jewish set of soteriological ideas! Chapter 2 of Luke's Gospel continues the Israel-centric soteriological theme. Appearing to the shepherds to announce Jesus' birth, the angel describes him in quintessential Davidic-messianic terms as "a Savior who is the Messiah, the Lord" and who is "born this day in the city of David" (Luke 2:11; cf. Mic 5:2). Likewise, Jesus is described in Simeon's psalm as "your salvation, which you have prepared in the sight of all people, a light . . . for the glory of your people Israel" (Luke 2:29–32). Significantly, however, Simeon describes Jesus in the same breath as "a light for revelation to the Gentiles," a sentiment echoed in the authorial citation of Isa 40:5 in the next chapter, "and all flesh shall see the salvation of God" (Luke 3:6). Luke thus introduces the important and no less Jewish notion of the extension of Israel's salvation to the Gentile nations. Although many biblical and Second Temple sources are ambivalent about the ultimate fate of the Gentiles (and some emphatically reject it as a possibility; e.g., Jub. 15:26), positive soteriological attitudes to non-Jews are also to be found throughout the Hebrew Bible, particularly in the postexilic prophetic books (e.g., Isa 49:6; 42:1–4; Zech 2:11; 8:23), and they feature particularly strikingly in the Enochic literature (see, e.g., 1 En. 10:21; 50:1–3; 90:37–38; 91:14; 93:14; 104:12–105:2); they should thus be understood as very much native to Jewish thought (see Donaldson 2007 for an excellent general overview of "patterns of universalism" in Second Temple Jewish soteriologies).

Subsequent to the special Lukan material in chapters 1 and 2, Luke's basic soteriological schema is similar to Matthew's: a combination of Mark's apocalyptic admonition to readiness and understanding on the one hand, and the greater ethical emphasis of the double tradition (or "Q") material on the other. A significant, consistent soteriological emphasis in Luke is the importance of charity and humility, the latter of which is epitomized at Luke 18:13–14: "Everyone who exalts himself will be humbled, and he who humbles himself will be exalted." Needless to say, ideas of God's concern for (and ultimate vindication of) the needy are found throughout the Jewish scriptural tradition, as highlighted above (cf. also, from Qumran, 4Q258 frag. 7; 4Q434 frag. 1; CD VI, 20–21). This prominent scriptural motif is the basis of the equally Jewish emphasis on almsgiving. See Tob 12:9 for an extreme example of the soteriological value of charitable giving (though perhaps no less extreme than Luke's story of the rich man and Lazarus; Luke 16; cf. 6:24–26).

Many commentators have argued that a characteristic feature of Luke's soteriology is a certain emphasis on the *present reality* of salvation (see, e.g., Steyn 2005).
The Lukan Jesus can say that "*today*, salvation has come" to the house of Zacchaeus
(Luke 19:9; emphasis mine), and he characterizes the eschatological signs of salvation
in Isa 61:1–2 (good news for the poor, sight to the blind, freedom to prisoners) as
"having been fulfilled *today*" (Luke 4:21; emphasis mine). Nickelsburg characterizes
the present salvation represented in the story of Zacchaeus as being "transferred
from God's disfavor to the realm of divine blessing . . . and [being] rescued from the
divine wrath that will be executed at the final judgment," and he at least sees this
explicitly in terms of the Deuteronomic covenantal paradigm (2003, 81; cf. Deut
30:11–20). Here perhaps, Luke begins to move away from the emphatic futurity
associated with salvation in Jewish apocalyptic thought as well as in Mark and
Matthew: the eschatological salvation anticipated as a future event from the point of
view of the biblical prophets and the apocalyptic literature is precisely the salvation
that Luke sees as "having now come" in and through the historical person of Jesus.
Nonetheless, it remains the case that there is also a clear focus in Luke on salvation
as a future event (cf. 9:24; 13:23), in line with dominant strains in both biblical and
postbiblical Judaism (see above, on Mark).

The Jewish Roots of John's Soteriology

In John, this future soteriological horizon so urgently present in Mark, Matthew,
and Luke is less in focus, and the question of present salvation is correspondingly
sharpened. This is not to say that John does not envisage a future day of eschatological
judgment and salvation; simply that his conception of it is (perhaps intentionally)
rather vague. While Jesus speaks of his authority as Son of Man to judge at John
5:22 and 27, recalling a lynchpin of Synoptic soteriology, he seems to reject this very
role for himself at 12:47, though here he does mention "the last day," on which "the
word that I have spoken will serve as judge" (John 12:48). In addition, the idea of a
"last day" is referenced by Jesus at 6:39–54, and by Martha the sister of Lazarus at
11:24. In both contexts, however, the emphasis is on the resurrection to eternal life
of those who have already been saved. In neither instance is the last day associated
with the judgment and damnation of the wicked—only with the raising of those
who "see the Son, believe in him, and [therefore] have eternal life" (John 6:40).
"Life" and "eternal life" are John's soteriological watchwords, ubiquitously present
throughout the Gospel, and shared with early Jewish sources (cf. e.g., 1QS IV, 8–9,
Wis 5:15–16, Jub. 23:29–30; 2 Macc 12:43–44).

Where Matthew and Luke (and to a much lesser extent Mark) retain a clear
impression of the importance of human ethical and moral behaviors in their respective soteriological strata, for John it is *belief* (or perhaps "trust") in Jesus that is
the paramount soteriological category: "This is the work of God, that you believe
in him whom he has sent" (John 6:29). Differently from Mark and Matthew, in the
Johannine conception, salvation occurs not at the eschatological judgment but has
already occurred when an individual believes and trusts in the revelation of God
in Jesus (John 3:17). For John, the eschatological revelation that recognized and

shared within the elect community generates faith, which in turn grants the gift of eternal life *here and now* (Nickelsburg 2003, 84). Nickelsburg sees this paradigm of salvation-through-revelation as paralleled in 1 Enoch and other Jewish revelatory and apocalyptic literature (e.g., 1QS V, 8–9; CD II, 14; 1 En. 62:7). This is perhaps particularly a point of contact between John, Mark, and Second Temple Jewish apocalyptic literature, although no Jewish text emphasizes the present reality of salvation in the life of the believer so clearly as John does.

If John explicitly emphasizes belief as the grounds for receiving salvation rather than condemnation, this is in no way to suggest that the Fourth Gospel rejects the importance of right moral and personal conduct that is so central to the biblical and postbiblical conception of Israel's collective and individual relationship with God: Jesus speaks quite clearly of the evil deeds of those in darkness in contrast to the deeds "done in God" by those who have come into the light (John 3:19–21; cf. Deut 28; 29:11–30). It is, however, important to note that for John, right actions are the *result* of being "in the light"—that is, of having welcomed the revelation of God in Jesus, who is himself "the light of the world" (1:9; 8:12). Good deeds are not therefore grounds for favorable judgment in John's soteriological conception; rather, they are symptomatic of the salvation that has already taken place at the moment of belief (cf. perhaps Jas 2:14–26). In some ways, this theological nexus of revelation, light, dark, election, and salvation is paralleled by the stark eschatological, metaphysical dualism of the Qumran literature (Thatcher 2017; cf. 1QS I, 8–9; III, 3, 15–16; T. Ash. 6:4–6); though John lacks the Qumranic emphasis on rigorous observance of the Mosaic law and its purity regulations, because for him it is belief in Jesus, above and beyond Torah observance, that is the primary expression of faithfulness to God and therefore the principal ground for salvation.

As in the Synoptics and throughout the Jewish tradition, John's soteriology exhibits a somewhat uneasy tension between human responsibility and divine choice in the matter of who is to be saved (Tuppurainen 2012). Although the language of believing or not believing is generally relatively neutral, implying an element of human agency, Jesus does also speak about his having "chosen" his disciples (John 15:16–19) rather than their having chosen him, and elsewhere he speaks of the Son giving life "to whom he is pleased to give it" (John 5:21). Additionally, John explains the lack of belief among some of the Jewish authorities in terms of a divine hardening of their hearts (12:39–40, quoting Isa 6:10). This explicit link with Isaiah in particular demonstrates that John's soteriology is, as far as he is concerned, rooted in Israel's scriptures (Thatcher 2017, 7). This theme of divine election as the prerequisite for salvation, which is emphasized by Andreas Köstenberger in his reading of the Johannine literature, can also be seen as closely parallel to similar soteriological convictions among Jews both at Qumran and elsewhere (Köstenberger 2009; cf. 1QS III, 11–12; CD II, 7–10).

John exhibits other continuities and discontinuities with early Judaism. Both Jesus and his Jewish adversaries, despite their opposing views, are rooted in the same basic soteriological presupposition that the source of salvation is the God of Israel's scriptures, particularly the universal God of the later exilic and postexilic literature (cf. John 4:22; van der Watt 2005, 103). However, although John insists on a certain continuity between the Jewish tradition and God's work of salvation in Jesus

(John 4:22), in general his soteriology is much less closely tied to the Israel-centric soteriological worldview of the Hebrew Bible than either Matthew or Luke. It is true that some individual (Jewish) characters in the Gospel interpret Jesus' salvific role in specifically Israel-centric terms: at 1:31, John the Baptist refers to Jesus' being "revealed to Israel"; at 1:49, Nathaniel addresses Jesus as "the Messiah, the king of Israel," and at 12:13, the crowds acclaim him as "the one who comes in the name of the Lord—the king of Israel." Jesus himself, however, explicitly disassociates his kingship from any earthly conception of Israel (John 18:36), and the soteriological value of Abrahamic descent (that is, ethnic membership of Israel) is firmly problematized in John 8:39–59 (as it also is in Matt 3:9 and Luke 3:8). Similarly, John's narrative voice firmly emphasizes the extension of salvation beyond the bounds of ethnic Israel, referring to Jesus' death as "not only for that [Jewish] nation, but also for the scattered children of God, to bring them together and make them one" (John 11:51–52).

William Loader concludes that the best way to understand John's relationship with Jewish soteriology is in terms of a "transposed Jewish spirituality"—that is, John does not radically reject or depart from basic Jewish soteriological convictions about revelation from and relationship with God; rather, he disassociates them from their anchors in the Jewish matrix (namely, temple, land, and Torah) and applies them instead to Jesus. Thus Jesus takes on the saving significance associated with those symbols of God's saving work among and for his people. In John 6 and John 4, Jesus, not the Torah, is the bread of life and the living water, respectively (cf. CD VI, 4; VIII, 21–22 for references to the law and the covenant community as a "well" and "living water"). Likewise, in John 8, Jesus, not the temple, is the locus of God's saving light in the world (cf. 2 Chr 7:1) (Loader 2017). Accordingly, although John may be seen as engaged in a deeper reformulation of Jewish soteriological categories than the Synoptics, the Fourth Gospel should not be seen as any less rooted in authentically Jewish soteriological soil than are Matthew, Mark, and Luke.

Conclusion: Jewish Roots or Jewish Gospels?

An important question to ask in conclusion is whether or not this rootedness in Jewish soil is enough to justify reading the Gospels' soteriologies as authentically *Jewish* soteriologies. Almost two thousand years of characterizing the New Testament documents as "Christian" texts and defining "Christian soteriology" largely in terms of opposition to "Jewish soteriology" has made it difficult for many readers of the Gospels, whether Jewish or Christian, to think of the Gospels as espousing authentically Jewish views about salvation. In contemporary New Testament scholarship, however, an increasing number of scholars are attempting to reread the Gospels as being in various respects (including soteriologically) "within Judaism," though the student of the Gospels should be aware that ultimately the answer to the question must always depend on how "Judaism" and "Jewishness" are defined. What is clear is that when some of the historic overemphases of the Christian interpretive and polemical tradition are redressed and reassessed, much common soteriological ground between the Gospel writers and their Jewish contemporaries is revealed.

Works Cited

Carson, D. A., Peter Thomas O'Brien, and Mark A. Seifrid, eds. 2001. *Justification and Variegated Nomism*. Tübingen: Mohr Siebeck.

Donaldson, Terence L. 2007. *Judaism and the Gentiles: Jewish Patterns of Universalism (to 135 CE)*. Waco, TX: Baylor University Press.

Foerster, W., and Fohrer, G. 1964. "σῴζω, σωτηρία, σωτήρ, σωτήριος." Pages 964–1024 in vol. 7 of *TDNT*. Grand Rapids: Eerdmans.

France, R. T. 1989. *Matthew: Evangelist and Teacher*. Exeter; Milton Keynes: Paternoster.

Gathercole, Simon. 2004. "The Son of Man in Mark's Gospel." *ExpTim* 115.11: 366–72.

Kampen, John. 2019. *Matthew with Sectarian Judaism*. New Haven: Yale University Press.

Konradt, Matthias. 2014. *Israel, Church and the Gentiles in the Gospel of Matthew*. Translated by Kathleen Ess. Waco, TX: Baylor University Press.

Köstenberg, Andreas J. 2009. *A Theology of John's Gospel and Letters*. Grand Rapids: Zondervan.

Loader, William. 2017. "Tensions in Matthean and Johannine Soteriology Viewed in Their Jewish Context." Pages 175–88 in *John and Judaism: A Contested Relationship in Context*. Edited by R. Alan Culpepper and Paul N. Anderson. Atlanta: SBL Press.

Luz, Ulrich. 1995. *The Theology of the Gospel of Matthew*. Cambridge: Cambridge University Press.

Nickelsburg, George. 2011. "Salvation among the Jews: Some Comments and Observations." Pages 299–314 in *This World and the World to Come: Soteriology in Early Judaism*. Edited by Daniel Gurtner. London: T&T Clark.

Przybylski, Benno. 1981. *Righteousness in Matthew and his World of Thought*. Cambridge: Cambridge University Press.

Runesson, Anders, and Daniel M. Gurtner, eds. 2020. *Matthew within Judaism: Israel and the Nations in the First Gospel*. ECL 27. Atlanta: SBL Press.

Sanders, E. P. 1977. *Paul and Palestinian Judaism: A Comparison of Patterns of Religion*. London: SCM Press.

Sim, David. 1998. *The Gospel of Matthew and Christian Judaism: The History and Social Setting of the Matthean Community*. Edinburgh: T&T Clark.

Steyn, Gert J. 2005. "Soteriological Perspectives in Luke's Gospel." Pages 67–100 in *Salvation in the New Testament*. Edited by J. G. Van der Watt. Leiden: Brill.

Thatcher, Tom. 2017. "John and the Jews: Recent Research and Future Questions." Pages 3–38 in *John and Judaism: A Contested Relationship in Context*. Edited by R. Alan Culpepper and Paul N. Anderson. Atlanta: SBL Press.

Tuppurainen, Riku. 2012. "Divine Sovereignty and Human Responsibility in the Gospel of John." *JEPTA* 32.1:28–40.

Van der Watt, Jan G. 2005. "Salvation in the Gospel according to John." Pages 101–32 in *Salvation in the New Testament*. Edited by J. G. Van der Watt. Leiden: Brill.

Westerholm, Stephen. 2004. *Perspectives Old and New on Paul: The "Lutheran" Paul and his Critics*. Grand Rapids: Eerdmans.

White, Benjamin. 2014. "The Eschatological Conversion of 'All the Nations' in Matthew 28.19–20: (Mis)reading Matthew through Paul." *JSNT* 36.4: 353–82.

Willitts, Joel. 2007. *Matthew's Messianic Shepherd-King: In Search of "The Lost Sheep of the House of Israel."* Berlin: de Gruyter.

Yarbro Collins, Adela. 2007. *Mark: A Commentary.* Hermeneia. Minneapolis, MN: Fortress Press.

4.8 Ecclesiology: Jews and Gentiles in the Gospels

Jim R. Sibley

According to Acts 2, the church began on the Feast of Shavuot (Pentecost), probably on May 24, 33 CE, at 9:00 a.m. ("the third hour of the day," Acts 2:15). Within the temple enclosure in Jerusalem, the church was birthed in Solomon's Portico on the site now occupied by the Al-Aqsa Mosque. Two centuries later, to emphasize that the church's origin was not from Gentile paganism, Tertullian insisted that "our principles come from the Porch of Solomon" (*Praescr.* 7.10; Greenslade 1956, 7). The church was born at the very center of Jewish life, the temple in Jerusalem. To be sure, although the timing and the location are certainly not insignificant, the emphasis of Luke is primarily on what occurred at that significant time and place.

Since the church began following the events recorded in the Gospels, we will examine the Gospels to discover their prospective ecclesiology. In this study, we also will treat the Gospels as the product of divine inspiration and as having been written with apostolic sanction. This is in contrast with scholars such as J. C. O'Neill, Gene R. Smillie, Daniel N. Gullotta, and others who attribute the Gospels to redactional activity reflecting the perspectives of specific Christian communities in the latter half of the first century (O'Neill 1997; Smillie 2002; Gullotta 2014). In other words, we want to deal with the text as we have it, rather than with the speculative history of how the text evolved or the ethnic issues in these early communities. To do otherwise is to be set adrift on a sea of speculation. Such speculations might assist on the journey from unwarranted assumptions to foregone conclusions, but that is a dangerous journey to undertake.

This study will examine the status and condition of Israel and the Gentiles in the Gospels. It will then turn attention to the function and message of Jesus. After then dealing with the topics of the kingdom and the apostles, it will survey key passages and conclude with summary truths for a prospective ecclesiology of the Gospels.

Israel's Status in the Gospels

What was Israel's status in the days of Jesus' earthly ministry? The evangelists focus on Jesus rather than Israel, but Israel is viewed favorably. Later, Paul sees a continuing place for Israel in the purposes of God (e.g., cf. Rom 3:2; 9:4–5; 11:29). Is the picture of Jesus and his disciples as portrayed in the Gospels congruent with the teaching of Paul? Matthias Konradt says of Matthew, he "purposefully presents Jesus as Israel's Messiah" (2014, 52). This is reflected in the genealogy of Jesus recorded in Matthew (1:1–17) and Luke (3:23–38). Jesus is explicitly referred to as the "Son of David" seventeen times in the Gospels, with another seven references to him as the heir of the Davidic throne (Mark 11:10; Luke 1:32, 69; 2:4, 11; 20:41; John 7:42).

Regarding the Gospel of Matthew, Donald Senior writes, "Virtually all modern interpreters concede that Matthew was concerned to demonstrate the essentially Jewish character of Jesus and his mission" (1999, 18). Regarding his birth, Mary said, "He has given help to Israel his servant, in remembrance of his mercy, as he spoke to our fathers, to Abraham and his offspring forever" (Luke 1:54–55). Zechariah said that his son, John, the forerunner of the Messiah, was "to give to his people the knowledge of salvation by the forgiveness of their sins, because of the tender mercy of our God" (Luke 1:77–78a).

It can be argued that from the perspective of the evangelists, Jesus is the heart and soul of Jewish history and faith. He is the epitome of all Israel was to be, the one who perfectly fulfilled the law, the one who embodied the hope of Israel (compare Jer 17:13 with John 4:14), and the one who was sent by the God of Israel (mentioned forty-one times in the Gospel of John alone; e.g., see 9:4, 16, 18, 26, 29, 42).

Not only was Jesus inextricably connected to Israel, but so also were his disciples. Surely, Nicodemus (John 3:1) and Joseph of Arimathea (Matt 27:57) were notable leaders in Jerusalem. Israel is never denounced in the Gospels, though its leadership (Matt 23) and specific cities are (Matt 11:21–24).

Despite the evidence, which should be compelling, the influence of earlier scholars who have attempted to de-Judaize the Bible and new covenant faith still remains. Historically, this was the motivation for those associated with the German Christian movement during the Nazi era, such as Gerhard Kittel, Emanuel Hirsch, Walter Bauer, Ethelbert Stauffer, and others in Germany, and Arthur Headlam in England.

David Seccombe says, "There is not the slightest indication that [Luke] sees it [i.e., the church] as a replacement of Israel, or 'the new Israel' as it is termed in much present-day theology" (1997, 57). Should we look for Gentile disciples of Jesus in the Gospels? He answers, "The Gentile line is not crossed until the incident of Cornelius" (i.e., Acts 10; 58).

How is Israel related to the church? The tension between Jesus and the religious leaders in the Gospels should not be understood as a contest between Jews and Gentiles, or between the synagogue and the church. The real struggle in the Gospels is an intramural struggle between Jesus and his disciples on the one hand and the religious leadership of the nation on the other. Yet some seize on any hint of a Gentile emphasis as a turning away from the Jewish people. Others see a Jewish emphasis in the Gospels as an excuse to heap condemnation on Israel for the nation's refusal to accept Jesus.

Israel's Condition in the Gospels

What was Israel's condition in the days of Jesus' earthly ministry as recorded in the Gospels? The majority was supernaturally blinded to spiritual truth. The *locus classicus* on the blindness of Israel, Isa 6:9–10, is quoted at least partially in each of the

Gospels, Acts, and Romans (Matt 13:14–15; Mark 4:12; Luke 8:10; John 12:39–40; Acts 28:26; and Rom 11:8). God told Isaiah that this judgment would render the majority of Israel unable to "see with their eyes, hear with their ears, understand with their hearts, and return and be healed" (Isa 6:10).

Even more significant than the number of direct quotations is the important role this theme plays in the Gospels. Jesus used this passage to explain his reason for teaching in parables. In Luke 19:42, Jesus wept over Jerusalem and said, "If you had known in this day, even you, the things which make for peace! But now *they have been hidden from your eyes*" (emphasis mine).

Craig A. Evans suggests that the two major sections of the Gospel of John, the Book of the Signs (John 2–11) and the Book of the Passion (John 13–20), implicitly raise questions for the reader (1982). The question raised by the first is this: "How did the people of Israel fail to recognize their Messiah, in spite of all of these supernatural signs that he performed in their sight?" The implied question in the Book of the Passion is: "How was it possible for them not only to reject their own Messiah, but to deliver him up for crucifixion?"

According to Evans, the answer to both questions is found in the "hinge"— chapter 12. In 12:37–50, John first says that "though he had performed so many signs before them, *yet they were not* believing in him; that the word of Isaiah the prophet might be fulfilled." He then quotes Isa 53:1 and says, "for this cause *they could not believe*" (John 12:39; emphasis mine), followed by Isa 6:10 to explain why they could not believe. In other words, the majority of the people did not recognize him as the Messiah and also delivered him up for crucifixion because of their spiritual blindness. Paul will explain later in Rom 11:11–12 that God used this blindness in opening salvation to the Gentiles.

John does note that "nevertheless, many even of the rulers believed in him" (12:42a). This speaks of the remnant, who *does* see, hear, and believe. The remainder of the chapter may be seen as Jesus' invitation to those who have ears to hear, and multitudes did. Regarding Luke, Jervell says, "Luke never had any conception of the church as the new or true Israel. Luke is rather concerned to show that when the gospel was preached, the one people of God, Israel, was split in two" (1972, 15; see also 41–74).

The repentant are the Jewish disciples of Jesus who constitute the remnant of Israel. Jervell continues, "'Israel' does not refer to a church that is made up of Jews and Gentiles, but to the repentant portion of the 'empirical' Israel; they are Jews who have accepted the gospel, to whom and for whom the promises have been fulfilled" (43). The ministry of Jesus then was calling out from the nation those who had "ears to hear" (Matt 11:15; Mark 4:9, 23; Luke 8:8; 14:35; see also Matt 7:24–27).

Thus any discussion of the prospective ecclesiology of the Gospels must give full weight both to the blindness of the majority and to the vigorous vitality of the remnant of Israel, composed of the disciples of Jesus. Israel was not rejected but divided by Jesus (Jervell 1972). In Matt 10:34, he says, "Do not think that I came to bring peace on the earth. I did not come to bring peace, but a sword." Acts would argue that thousands of Jews were becoming disciples of Jesus following the resurrection (Acts 2:41, 47; 4:4; 5:14; 21:20); and in Romans, Paul speaks of the significance and duration of the remnant of Israel (11:1–5, 11–12, 15). There would always be a remnant of Jewish believers in Jesus, and their existence would serve as a guarantee that God would bring the nation to salvation at the parousia (Rom 11:26).

Gentiles' Status in the Gospels

Jesus told his disciples not to go to the Gentiles but to "the lost sheep of the house of Israel" (Matt 10:5–6). In response to their faith, some Gentiles received physical healing, the expulsion of demons, or blessing, but these were considered the "crumbs" from the table of Israel (Matt 15:27).

A Gentile mission was envisioned (Matt 12:21; 24:14; 26:13; Mark 13:10; 14:9; John 3:16), but this was for the future. The promise of the fathers (e.g., Gen 12:1–3) not only included blessings for Israel, but a blessing that would extend to "all the families of the earth."

Nevertheless, prior to the institution of the new covenant (Matt 26:28), Gentiles had no option other than to become a part of the people of Israel and adhere, by faith, to the God of Israel, for the previous covenants of Israel were restrictive. Paul says to Gentile Christians, "Remember that you were at that time [i.e., prior to the new covenant] separate from Christ, excluded from the commonwealth of Israel, and strangers to the covenants of promise, having no hope and without God in the world" (Eph 2:12). Later, of course, much is made of Cornelius as the first Gentile who found salvation through faith in Jesus (Acts 10:34–48).

The Function and Message of Jesus in the Gospels

Jesus came as a prophet, a priest, and a king. These were to be his identities, but how did he function in the days of his earthly ministry as recorded in the Gospels? His function was that of the prophet like Moses (Deut 18:15–19). The only character in the Old Testament who truly fulfills this prophecy is the servant of the Lord as prophesied in Isaiah (Sibley 2019, 333–34). In the Gospels, Jesus functions as both the prophet like Moses and as the servant of the Lord. Dale Allison says, "In more than one recent work the new Moses theme has in fact, for whatever reason, suffered interment. But the burial is premature" (1993, 267).

What did this role entail? As the prophet like Moses, he taught with God's direct authority, he worked authenticating miracles by God's power, and he endured rejection, suffering, and death on behalf of others. These functions all contributed to the making of disciples, for his mission was "to seek and save the lost" (Luke 19:10; Matt 18:11).

For most of his public ministry, he was calling out the remnant of Israel to become his disciples and thereby to gain citizenship in his future kingdom. His message was the same as that of John the Baptist who had preceded him, and it was the same message he gave to his disciples: "Repent, for the kingdom of heaven is at hand" (Matt 3:2; 4:17; 10:7). This has been interpreted in a variety of ways, but since it is synonymous with "the gospel" (Luke 9:2, 6; Matt 4:23; 11:5), it seems most natural to understand it to have been a call to follow him. After his resurrection, he taught his disciples, preparing them for his departure and for their disciple-making under the new covenant. In all of this, the ministry of Jesus was to Israel that it might eventually be for all.

The Kingdom and the Apostles

The Kingdom

The kingdom is not to be equated with the church. "Kingdom" usually refers either to God's universal kingdom or to the messianic kingdom. Paul says that God "works all things after the counsel of his will" (Eph 1:11). This is reflected in the Gospels. During his earthly ministry, Jesus claimed not to speak or do anything apart from the plan of God (John 5:19; 12:49–50). He also bore witness to the sovereignty of God in the care of even the sparrows and the grass in the field (Matt 10:29–31; 6:30; Luke 12:28). These bear witness to God's sovereignty over his universal kingdom.

Since God has always exercised sovereign control of the universe, as soon as the Scriptures speak of a coming messianic king, we are to understand that there will be another kingdom: one that is to be distinguished from God's universal kingdom, although the two are related. This new kingdom may be referred to as the messianic kingdom, for God's authority will be mediated through the Messiah.

Jesus intended for there to be a community of his Jewish disciples, to whom would be granted citizenship in the messianic kingdom on the basis of faith in him as "the Messiah, the Son of the living God" (Matt 16:16). This community would be a nation within the nation. These disciples would have a distinct communal identity. Eckhard Schnabel helps reset the question: "The scholarly discussion of the last 150 years often focused on the question of whether the kingdom of God should be regarded as a purely future entity or as a present reality, ignoring the fact that a more important question for Jesus was that of *who belongs* to the kingdom of God" (2004, 210–11; emphasis original).

Most either see this kingdom as already inaugurated or as postponed, following Israel's supposed rejection of the kingdom (e.g., Saucy 1994). However, more probably, the majority of Israel did not reject the kingdom but the gospel of the kingdom; that is, the message of salvation that, if accepted, would have yielded citizenship in the future kingdom. If so, then this kingdom has neither been inaugurated nor has it been postponed (Matt 6:9–10; Luke 19:11–15).

The Apostles

How are the apostles related to the church? Some may think of the apostles only in relationship to the church—they are Christians. However, in the Gospels they are primarily portrayed in relationship to a restored, eschatological Israel—they are Jews. In the Gospels, apostles were the authorized leaders of the remnant of Israel (Matt 21:43–45). They stood as representatives of the twelve tribes of Israel. Jesus told them, "Truly I say to you, that you who have followed me, in the regeneration when the Son of Man will sit on his glorious throne, you also shall sit upon twelve thrones, judging the twelve tribes of Israel" (Matt 19:28; cf. Luke 22:30). That they were twelve is specifically referenced thirty-two times in the Gospels.

The canonical Gospels are their legacy, as they convey the message of Jesus, and as they call others to become his disciples and provide training for them as well. In Acts, this remnant, led by the apostles, also forms the foundation for the initial Jewish church and becomes the core to which Gentile disciples are later joined.

The phrase "the keys of the kingdom" is used in both passages in which the word *ekklēsia* is used (Matt 16:17–19; 18:15–18). The first of these passages follows Peter's confession and conveys three emphases based on faith in Jesus as the Messiah: Jesus' intention to build a distinct community, his assurance that this community will survive death, and his gift to them of spiritual authority for this community. These keys are to be used to bind and loose; that is, to determine what is permitted and what is forbidden. What is permitted is the proclamation of the truth regarding citizenship in the coming kingdom (it is only open to true disciples of Jesus the Messiah, the Son of the living God) and the acceptance of true disciples into the community. What is forbidden is false teaching, false believers, and the unrepentant.

This spiritual authority of binding and loosing seems to be related to Jesus' teaching in Matt 21. In Matt 21:43, Jesus says to the religious leadership, "Therefore I say to you, the kingdom of God will be taken away from you, and be given to a nation producing the fruit of it." Here, Jesus uses "kingdom of God" for the spiritual authority to direct others to the kingdom. By way of contrast, in Matt 23:13 Jesus would later condemn the religious leaders, "because [they] shut off the kingdom of heaven from men; for [they] do not enter in [themselves], nor do [they] allow those who are entering to go in." They "shut off the kingdom of heaven from men" by their failure to tell them how to enter. They misused the keys of the kingdom, so this authority was taken from them and given to the apostles.

This authority is now resident in the New Testament Scriptures, written under their authority. They are to be used by the church to determine the gospel message, true doctrine, true believers, and the walk of a true disciple. The apostles are the leaders of the remnant of Israel and also serve as the foundation of the church.

Key Passages in the Gospels

Matthew

David Turner points out, "The Gospel of Matthew, though often and truly described as the most Jewish of the Gospels, is also the only Gospel to use the word 'church'" (2008, 46). Since the Gospel of Matthew seems to be most relevant to any discussion of ecclesiology, it has given rise to perhaps the most vigorous debate between those who argue for the Jewishness of the message and mission of this Gospel and those who argue for an emphasis on Gentiles and the presence of a Gentile mission.

Many point to the first four women in Matthew's genealogy as Gentiles, who foreshadow a Gentile mission or Gentile faith (e.g., Hutchison 2001); but the ethnicity of Tamar and Bathsheba is uncertain, and Ruth and Rahab are examples of Gentiles who were integrated into the people of Israel (Senior 1999, 8). Furthermore, these women are linked to Mary, who is clearly Jewish, making it difficult to discern a deliberate Gentile emphasis. It may well be that the common denominator is that they were all women who played crucial roles in the eventual birth of the seed of a woman (Gen 3:15). According to Matthew, the Old Testament does anticipate a mission to the Gentiles, but it does not appear that the genealogy played a part in such a strategy.

The magi (2:1–12) are often thought to be harbingers of a largely Gentile church. However, they may instead highlight the blindness of the majority of Israel and point to the more distant future when the nations will bring their treasure to Jerusalem (Isa 60:5; 66:20; Matt 25:32). Likewise, when Jesus refers to the repentance of the men of Nineveh at the preaching of Jonah and to the interest of the Queen of the South in Wis 12:41–42, some see hints of a Gentile mission, while others see a condemnation of the majority of his own people for their failure to repent and to become his disciples (see Senior 1999, 12).

Although Bradley Trout may overemphasize the discontinuity of the church with Israel, he has argued persuasively "that Matthew 5:17–19 is not primarily about demonstrating law-observance, but fulfillment." He says, "More prominent than Jesus' view of the law is the law's (and the prophets') view of Jesus" (2016). In any case, Jesus radically redefined Torah observance.

In Matt 12:41–42, Jesus rebuked the majority of the people of his day ("this generation") with comparisons to the men of Nineveh and the Queen of the South. Some see in this a general condemnation of Israel, but it is a rebuke of the majority who are not repenting (as the Ninevites) or seeking him (as the Queen of the South sought Solomon) due to their spiritual blindness.

Following the episode of the feeding of the five thousand men (Matt 14:14–21), Jesus also miraculously fed four thousand (15:29–39). There has been a major discussion regarding the ethnic composition of the four thousand, with some claiming that Jesus ventured deep into the Decapolis so that he could have a broader ministry among the Gentiles. They see this as a harbinger of the great Gentile influx later. Scholarship is divided on the issue. J. Benjamin Hussung argues that the four thousand were Gentiles, based on Matthew's literary context. He sees a "Gentile trajectory of the literary context of this section of Matthew's Gospel" (2020, 481). It seems this "Gentile trajectory" is in the eye of the beholder. It was not Jewish "traditions that removed them from Gentiles" (Hussung 2020, 486) but the Mosaic covenant.

After following several lines of inquiry that proved inconclusive, J. R. C. Cousland demonstrated

> that "God of Israel" [Matt 15:31] was not an expression in any way typical of non-Jewish usage, but one highly characteristic of it. . . . It follows, therefore, that the multitudes in the first gospel were Jewish and not gentile. . . . Matthew takes what Jesus says very seriously. Thus, when he has Jesus say he was "sent only to the lost sheep of the house of Israel" (15:24), he has Jesus act in a manner that accords with Jesus' utterance. (1999, 23).

In the parallel passage in Mark 7:31, we find that Jesus was in the midst of the *horion* of the Decapolis. The standard reference lexicon of New Testament Greek says that this word may mean "region" but most often means a "marker of division between two areas, boundary" (BDAG, s.v. ὅριον [*horion*]). Most likely, Jesus was on the northeastern quadrant of the shoreline of the Sea of Galilee near the border of the Decapolis. Cousland concludes, "Thus Jesus engages in a particularist mission to the Jewish people, and his disciples do the same" (1999, 23).

In Matthew, it is clear to contemporary Christians that Jesus envisioned a future mission to the nations. In 24:9, he says that his disciples will be "hated by all nations," and this will be because "this gospel of the kingdom shall be preached in the whole world for a witness to all nations" (24:14). Furthermore, there is to be an eschatological judgment of the nations (Matt 25:32).

Finally, the Great Commission carries the imperative to "make disciples of all the nations" (Matt 28:19–20). It is of interest that it was approximately ten years after Pentecost before the first Gentile became a disciple of Jesus (Acts 10). This came about due only to dramatic supernatural revelation (Acts 10:3–22). If it was so surprising to Peter that the gospel was to go to the Gentiles, then how had he understood the Great Commission? Perhaps he and his companions understood it as a commission to Diaspora Jews. Rather than attribute this delay to a failure of the apostles, it may be better to ascribe it to God's intention to firmly establish the church in Israel prior to the Gentile mission.

Along this line, the disciples were given a mission in Matt 10, specifically "to the lost sheep of the house of Israel" (10:6). There are indications in this passage that more is intended than a limited outing, but these have often been ignored. Jesus tells them, "You shall not finish going through the cities of Israel until the Son of Man comes" (10:23). Perhaps the commission in Matthew consists of a commission to Israel in chapter 10 and a universal commission in chapter 28.

Mark

Even if Mark does not directly mention the church, some can find nothing positive to say about Israel's treatment in Mark. They seem not to notice those in the synagogue who "were amazed at his teaching" (1:22) or those who came to him for healing (1:32–34, 40; 2:3; etc.), or those who "were glorifying God, saying, 'We have never seen anything like this'" (2:12). Instead, there is nothing but blanket condemnation. For example, George Eldon Ladd says, "Israel as a whole rejected both Jesus and his message about the Kingdom. . . . Mark pictures conflict and rejection from the beginning" (1993, 105).

Regarding the incident of the Syrophoenician woman, when Jesus says, "Let the children first be fed" in Mark 7:27a, Stephen G. Wilson says that the word *first* (*prōton*) "probably reflects the notion 'Jew first and then Greek' as it is found in Rom 1:16. . . . Israel's priority becomes a passing right of only temporary significance, for as a result of her refusal the Gospel goes to the Gentiles" (1973, 30–31). He is apparently not aware that the dependent clauses in Rom 1:16 cannot be treated separately. Paul says that the gospel is (1) "the power of God for salvation," (2) "to everyone who believes," and (3) "to the Jew first." If it is not still "to the Jew first," neither is it "the power of God unto salvation."

In contrast to these views, Mark should be seen as emphasizing Jesus' focus on making disciples in Israel. Konradt rightly concludes, "The focus on Israel positively indicates the significance of Israel's special position in the theological thought of the first evangelist" (2014, 264). Morna Hooker says, "It is clear enough that the ministry of Jesus and his disciples is confined to Israel during his lifetime. Gentiles who appear in the story are an anomaly; most notably the Syro-Phoenician woman [7:24–30], whose faith wins her a 'crumb' from the children's table" (1997, 36). The emphasis is on that which has priority for the time and attention of Jesus, the "children" of Israel. Nevertheless, Jesus spoke of a future mission to the nations (*ethnoi*) in Mark 13:10, and there may also be an allusion in 14:9.

The Jewish disciples of Jesus in the earthly ministry of Jesus, then, provide the template or model for the church. Disciples should be characterized by humility and compassion. Hooker summarizes,

> Mark's vision for the Church, then, is quite simple. It is a vision of a community that is all that God intended Israel to be—a community that accepts his reign, as it was proclaimed in the ministry of Jesus, and is obedient to the divine command to love God and to love others. The community that believes in Jesus as Messiah and Son of God will do these things, and so follow faithfully in the footsteps of its Lord. (42–43)

Luke

Many of the passages that could be emphasized in Luke have already appeared in Matthew and Mark, but each of the Gospels portrays the opposition Jesus encountered. As we have seen, the condition pronounced by Isaiah and described by later prophets fits exactly with the opposition of the Messiah that they foresaw. Seccombe, for example, says, "Jesus follows a similar description of Jewish hardness, which he too explains from Isa 6:9, with the appeal, 'Take heed then how you hear' (Luke 8:10, 18)" (1997, 61).

Regarding the Gospel of Luke, George Goldman makes an important point when he says, "Some may mistakenly assume that Luke's vision for the church of his day is more fully reflected in Acts than in his Gospel. . . . However, such an approach wrongly minimizes something Luke assumes—the significance of the example and teaching of Jesus for the church" (2012, 41). He continues by commenting that in Acts, "Luke describes the church as a community of believers in Jesus who continue what Jesus 'began' to do and to teach" (2012, 57).

As we have seen, the mission of Jesus was universal, without destroying the continuing priority of the Jewish mission. Some may point to Luke 19:10, where Jesus says, "For the Son of Man has come to seek and to save that which was lost." But the context was the salvation of Zacchaeus, in a thoroughly Jewish setting.

John

The Jewish disciples prior to Pentecost (*Shavuot*) anticipate the church but do not yet constitute the church. As Thomas H. Olbricht says, "The footings for the church were poured in the call of the disciples. . . . The disciples play as prominent a role in John" (2012, 69).

In the Gospel of John, the emphasis is on persuading people to become disciples of Jesus, "and that believing [they] may have life in his name" (20:30b). This is the theme from beginning to end. In John 1:12, we read, "But as many as received him, to them he gave the right to become children of God, even to those who believe in his name." The programmatic statement in John 3:16 is certainly relevant here as well. Becoming a disciple of Jesus through faith brought redemption, the new birth, eternal life, and a new standing with God.

Likewise, the kingdom is seen as a future reality, but citizenship in that kingdom can be gained only by becoming a disciple of Jesus. Olbricht comments:

> In the Synoptic Gospels the church is often anticipated when referring to either the kingdom of God or the kingdom of heaven. . . . His statements likely envision entering both into the church and the eternal kingdom. "Jesus answered him, 'Very truly, I tell you, no one can see the kingdom of God without being born from above'" (John 3:3). Then again, in John 3 we read, "Jesus answered, 'Very truly, I tell you, no one can enter the kingdom of God without being born of water and Spirit.'" (2012, 16)

It is not that the kingdom enters them, but that they enter the kingdom, in the sense that they have standing or citizenship in the kingdom. Apart from the new birth, no one can "see" or "enter" the kingdom.

In addition, the Jewish disciples of Jesus encountered in the Gospel of John constitute the remnant of Israel. As such, descriptions of this remnant and its relationship to the Lord are certainly appropriate to apply to the church, which later was formed initially with this remnant. Again, there is only one way into the sheepfold (John 10:7–15), but perhaps the clearest anticipation of the church comes with the next verse: "And I have other sheep, which are not of this fold; I must bring them also, and they shall hear my voice; and they shall become one flock with one shepherd" (John 10:16).

Truths for Prospective Ecclesiology

Regarding the source for a study of the ecclesiology of the Gospels, we should learn from the inspired text, not from speculations regarding the ethnic and social context of the church in the time of the composition of the texts. Regarding the substance of our study, we should examine the biblical teachings of Jesus for his disciples that inform our ecclesiology.

The teachings given to the apostles regarding discipleship were to characterize relations within their communities and should inform all discipleship in the church. These would include loving God supremely, loving neighbors sacrificially, living by faith, love, unity, forgiveness, holiness, discipline, and concern for the lost.

An important component that seems to be neglected today is a genuine concern for the Jewish people. Jesus modeled such concern and taught the priority of the Jewish people in God's economy. Seccombe says, "Luke's vision through all this is for a truly multiracial Church, which is Jewish in foundation and Jewish in its foundational membership, but which welcomes people of all nations" (1997, 61). He asks, "How shall a vision like this be honoured in what are now in many parts of the world exclusively Gentile churches?" (1997, 62). One way would be "by extending fellowship to Jewish people in a way that does not imply that they need to abandon their Jewishness and adopt Gentile Christian customs" (62). Another would be to pray for the salvation of Israel.

Works Cited

Allison, Dale C., Jr. 1993. *The New Moses: A Matthean Typology*. Minneapolis, MN: Fortress Press.

Cousland, J. R. C. 1999. "The Feeding of the Four Thousand *Gentiles* in Matthew? Matthew 15:29–39 as a Test Case." *NovT* 41.1: 1–23.

Evans, Craig A. 1982. "The Function of Isaiah 6:9–10 in Mark and John." *NovT* 24.2: 124–38.

Goldman, George II. 2012. "The Church in Luke-Acts." Pages 41–60 in *The New Testament Church: The Challenge of Developing Ecclesiologies*. Edited by John P. Harrison and James D. Dvorak. Eugene, OR: Pickwick.

Goulder, Michael T. 1997. "Matthew's Vision for the Church." Pages 19–32 in *A Vision for the Church: Studies in Early Christian Ecclesiology in Honour of J. P. M. Sweet*. Edited by Markus Bockmuehl and Michael B. Thompson. Edinburgh: T&T Clark.

Greenslade, S. L. 1956. "Tertullian, Prescription against Heretics." Pages 31–64 in *Early Latin Theology: Selections from Tertullian, Cyprian, Ambrose and Jerome*. LCC. Edited and translated by S. L. Greenslade. Philadelphia: Westminster.

Gullotta, Daniel N. 2014. "Among Dogs and Disciples: An Examination of the Story of the Canaanite Woman (Matthew 15:21–28) and the Question of the Gentile Mission within the Matthean Community." *Neot* 48.2: 325–40.

Hooker, Morna D. 1997. "Mark's Vision for the Church. Pages 33–43 in *A Vision for the Church: Studies in Early Christian Ecclesiology in Honour of J. P. M. Sweet*. Edited by Markus Bockmuehl and Michael B. Thompson. Edinburgh: T&T Clark.

Hussung, J. Benjamin. 2020. "Jesus's Feeding of the Gentiles in Matt 15:29–39: How the Literary Context Supports a Gentile Four Thousand." *JETS* 63.3: 473–89.

Hutchison, John C. 2001. "Women, Gentiles, and the Messianic Mission in Matthew's Genealogy." *BSac* 158: 152–64.

Jervell, Jacob. 1972. "The Divided People of God." Pages 41–74 in his *Luke and the People of God: A New Look at Luke-Acts*. Minneapolis, MN: Augsburg.

Konradt, Matthias. 2014. *Israel, Church, and the Gentiles in the Gospel of Matthew*. Translated by Kathleen Ess. Waco, TX: Baylor University Press and Tübingen: Mohr Siebeck.

Ladd, George Eldon. 1993. *A Theology of the New Testament*. Rev. ed. Edited by Donald A. Hagner. Grand Rapids: Eerdmans.

Olbricht, Thomas H. 2012. "The Church in the Gospel and Epistles of John." Pages 61–84 in *The New Testament Church: The Challenge of Developing Ecclesiologies*. Edited by John P. Harrison and James D. Dvorak. Eugene, OR: Pickwick.

O'Neill, J. C. 1997. "A Vision for the Church: John's Gospel." Pages 79–93 in *A Vision for the Church: Studies in Early Christian Ecclesiology in Honour of J. P. M. Sweet.* Edited by Markus Bockmuehl and Michael B. Thompson. Edinburgh: T&T Clark.

Saucy, Mark. 1994. "The Kingdom-of-God Sayings in Matthew." *BSac* 151:175–97.

Schnabel, Eckhard J. 2004. *Early Christian Mission: Jesus and the Twelve.* Downers Grove, IL: InterVarsity Press.

Seccombe, David. 1997. "A Vision for the Church: John's Gospel." Pages 45–63 in *A Vision for the Church: Studies in Early Christian Ecclesiology in Honour of J. P. M. Sweet.* Edited by Markus Bockmuehl and Michael B. Thompson. Edinburgh: T&T Clark.

Senior, Donald. 1999. "Between Two Worlds: Gentiles and Jewish Christians in Matthew's Gospel." *CBQ* 61.1: 1–23.

Sibley, Jim R. 2019. "Deuteronomy 18:15–19: The Prophet Like Moses." Pages 325–41 in *The Moody Handbook of Messianic Prophecy: Studies and Expositions of the Messiah in the Old Testament.* Edited by Michael Rydelnik and Edwin Blum. Chicago: Moody.

Smillie, Gene R. 2002. "'Even the Dogs': Gentiles in the Gospel of Matthew." *JETS* 45.1:73–97.

Trout, Bradley. 2016. "Matthew 5:17 and Matthew's Community." *HvTSt* 72.3. a3201. Https://dx.doi.org/10.4102/hts.v72i3.3201.

Turner, David L. 2008. *Matthew.* BECNT. Grand Rapids: Baker Academic.

Wilson, Stephen G. 1973. *The Gentiles and the Gentile Mission in Luke-Acts.* SNTSMS 23. Cambridge: Cambridge University Press.

CHAPTER 5

Intercultural Roots

5.1 Matthew 27:25 and Jewish-Christian Relations

David Mishkin

The history of Jewish-Christian relations is complex, sad, and often misunderstood. Two groups that began (literally) on the same soil would, in the coming centuries, evolve into mutually exclusive entities. After the destruction of the temple, Rabbinic Judaism began to develop. It was based on the Pharisaic system and incorporated most of the remaining factions of Judaism. The other Jewish group, the followers of Jesus, continued to grow and included Gentiles into the fold. The Gentile arm of the movement would become dominant and eventually (until the modern period) the only expression of faith in Jesus. Each group claimed to represent the continuation of the Tanakh.

What began as a sectarian Jewish dispute soon became a bitter conflict (Gregerman 2016). The role of the NT in this debate has often presented a challenge. To what extent was it the *cause* of the inflamed rhetoric that would follow and/or to what extent was it merely used to that end by the early church that was attempting to silence its main rival? The answer will usually depend on one's view of the dating, authorship, original audience, and historicity of the individual NT books. One of the most challenging passages is Matt 27:25.

In Matt 27, Pontius Pilate had the opportunity to release either Jesus or Barabbas. The "chief priests and elders" persuaded the crowd to request the release of Barabbas in place of Jesus. Pilate washed his hands and said, "I am innocent of this man's blood" (27:24). Then comes verse 25: "And all the people said, 'His blood shall be on us and our children.'" This verse has raised a number of questions: *What was Pilate's motive? Who exactly were meant to be the recipients of this curse? all Jews for all time? the Jews who were physically present at that moment? the leaders? What did the curse entail—the destruction of the temple or an ongoing punishment throughout history? Did these people have the authority to speak for the entire Jewish community?* This article will survey the impact this verse has had on Jewish-Christian relations. Of special interest will be the context in which interpretations have appeared.

Views in Christendom throughout History

The rivalry between the two burgeoning groups that were to become Judaism and Christianity played a major role in early Christian interpretations of the NT. Matthew

27:25 was read with the assumption that God was finished with the Jews. Origen, for example, wrote the following in his commentary on Matthew:

> [The Jews] were not only unwilling to clean themselves from the blood of Christ but even incurred it upon themselves. . . . [T]herefore they are accused not only of the blood of the prophets but, filling up the measure of their fathers, they are accused also of the blood of Christ, so that they hear God saying to them, "When you stretch out your hands to me, I will hide my eyes from you; for your hands are full of blood" (Isa 1:15). Therefore the blood of Jesus came not only on those who lived at those times but also on all subsequent generations of Jews until the consummation (of the world). Therefore until now their house is desolate (Matt 23:38). (cited in Meiser 2018, 225).

By the early Middle Ages, the practical outgrowth of such polemical views against the Jewish people would leave a permanent stain on Jewish-Christian relations. Several factors contributed to this. The first was the charge of *deicide*, the belief that the Jewish people are (exclusively) responsible for killing Jesus (Cohen 2007). This claim is usually traced back to a second-century homily by Melito of Sardis called "On the Pascha." This, of course, is the complete opposite of what the Gospel of Matthew (and the entire New Testament) actually teaches. The crucifixion was not an accident; it was God's plan all along (Matt 26:39–42; Acts 2:23). Nevertheless, this lie would take on a life of its own and lead to further absurdities.

One such absurdity was the "Blood libel." Beginning in 1144 in England, various stories were spread about Jews slaughtering Christians and using their blood to make matzah for Passover. An offshoot of this was the "Host desecration." Here, the story was that Jews stole the wafer of the Communion service (which was considered by the Catholic Church to be the actual body of Jesus) and attempted to kill it again by stabbing and other means. The point was that the "Christ killers" are still determined to kill him. These events may at first seem too silly and too distant for modern readers to take seriously. But the retaliation against the Jews for these and other alleged crimes resulted in thousands upon thousands of Jews being slaughtered throughout history, and remnants of this theology continue today (Teter 2020). Apart from the theological problems, the attitude that characterized much of the church in regard to the Jewish people was equally abhorrent. Indeed, it is in the Gospel of Matthew—the source often used to justify the blood libel—where Jesus said, "Love your enemies and pray for those who persecute you" (Matt 5:44).

Another outgrowth of the "Christ killer" charge was the Passion Play. This was a mix of Catholic mass, theater, and an opportunity to remind the church that Jews killed Jesus. Most famously, the town of Oberammergau in Germany produced a version of the play (starting in the early seventeenth century), which is presented approximately every ten years and continues to this day. In 1934, Adolf Hitler saw the play and said that "never has the menace of Jewry been so convincingly portrayed as in this presentation" (cited in Cohen 2007, 215). By the later part of the century, changes were made to some of the content of the play in response to Jewish-Catholic dialogue. This long history was also the reason why the 2004 Mel Gibson film *The Passion of the Christ* was so controversial.

The Protestant Reformation and the cry of *sola scriptura* was a step in the right direction, but it was certainly not without its anti-Jewish rhetoric (most obvious is Martin Luther's book, *On the Jews and Their Lies*). Over the next few centuries, some streams of Christendom would recognize that God's plan for the Jewish people includes a future restoration in their homeland. The twentieth century would see major changes in the Christian understanding and approach to the Jewish people. The horrors of the Holocaust, in particular, called for a new examination. A reckoning was needed. In the early 1960s, the Catholic Church held Vatican II. One result was the document *Nostra Aetate* ("In Our Time"), which described the Catholic Church's relationship with other world religions and specifically focused on the Jewish people. In 2011, Pope Benedict wrote a book in which he formally announced that the Jews are not responsible for the death of Jesus (Ratzinger 2011).

New Testament scholarship has also undergone a revolution in the last century, with a new appreciation for the Jewish background of the life of Jesus. This would influence interpretations of Matt 27:25. A survey of the commentaries over the last one hundred years—or even the last twenty years—would require a separate essay. But one clear trend is that the Gospel of Matthew is increasingly being approached as a Jewish text (see Nolland 2008; Runesson and Gurtner 2020; the article above by Hamilton). Three examples will suffice.

Matthean scholar David Turner addressed Matt 27:25 in light of the question of anti-Semitism. He rejects the national guilt interpretation, since all the founders of the church were Jews and there have been Jewish followers of Jesus throughout history. Likewise, it does not fit that Israel lost their national relationship with God, as this is both an idea developed much later in history, and it does not take into account the Deuteronomic structure of the Gospel of Matthew. It must also be remembered that the words of this text were made in "the heat of the moment" and should not be seen as a carefully reasoned theological position. These words form "an ironic double entendre," given that Matthew's use of "blood" throughout his Gospel refers to those who are righteous and innocent. And despite the people's limited understanding at this point, God will indeed save "his people" from their sins through Jesus (Matt 1:21). Turner concludes: "Finally, the most severe criticism in Matthew's Gospel is leveled against the leadership, and they are the ones who bear the brunt of the blame for the crowd's unfortunate statement in 27:25, and for Pilate's unprincipled acquiescence to the crowd's inflamed request" (2015, 263–64).

Matthias Konradt begins his discussion with a comparison of the "crowd" of verse 24 and "all the people" in verse 25. Does the phrase "all of the people" simply refer to those who are present at the time (i.e., "the crowd"), or does it include the entirety of the Jewish people who are guilty of calling for the death of Jesus? Based on the usage of this phrase throughout the NT (and in Josephus), as well as in the immediate context, he argues that it refers to the specific people gathered at that time and place. But more importantly, he noticed the theme of the people of Jerusalem being against Jesus and/or God's prophets throughout the Gospel of Matthew (2:3; 16:21; 21:10–11; 23:37). These verses anticipate the words of Matt 27:25. The group that is accepting responsibility for the death of Jesus, and therefore bringing "innocent blood" upon themselves, is ultimately setting the stage for the destruction of Jerusalem. Since Jerusalem does not represent Israel in Matthew's understanding, the destruction of the city "cannot be understood as a prefiguration of the eschatological judgment of Israel" (Konradt 2014, 164). Konradt summarizes this as follows: "A crowd of inhabitants of Jerusalem is seduced by the authorities and, together with their seducers takes on the responsibility and thus the guilt for Jesus' death, as well as the consequence that is manifested in the destruction of Jerusalem" (2014, 165).

One final comment on this verse is relevant as much for its scholarship as for the context in which it appears. Bruce Longenecker wrote a book about Rolf Gompertz, a Jewish man who survived the Holocaust and later in life wrote a quite positive book about the life of Jesus. An appendix in the book focuses on Matt 27:25. Longenecker begins by placing the Gospel in a Jewish context and by drawing a distinction between Matthew's view of the Jewish people as a whole as opposed to Jewish leaders. The latter are seen as leading the former astray. As for Pilate, his acts were cowardly and self-serving.

> Narratively speaking, the situation is virtually Shakespearean in its dripping irony and tragic outcome. And narratively speaking, it is a variation on the theme established toward the beginning of the narrative, when Herod, jealous that another might usurp his power, acted in self-interest and slaughtered the innocents. . . . In its context, then, the cry of Matt 27:25 is anything but anti-Semitic, and nothing if it is not anti-elite. The Matthean evangelist does not intend his audience to brutalize the Jewish people on the basis of that verse; they have already been brutalized by their leaders. Therein lies their national calamity, in the eyes of the Matthean evangelist. (2014, 175)

Traditional Jewish Views

As with the Christian world, comments on Matt 27:25 from the Jewish community have ranged from the polemical to the scholarly. The historic charge of deicide and the question of guilt for the death of Jesus have made this verse particularly relevant. The changing scholarship over the last century regarding the Jewish Jesus has significantly challenged interpretations of this verse.

In 1967, Israeli Supreme court justice Haim Cohen wrote a book about the trial of Jesus. It was the question of historic Jewish guilt, rather than an interest in the historical Jesus, that inspired this undertaking. Cohen noticed that Paul and Luke offered hope and forgiveness to any Jewish sin involved in the crucifixion. By contrast, he believed Matthew's words in 27:25 present something quite different, as it was the "Jewish self-arraignment invented by Matthew that became the theological, or pseudo-theological, basis of never-ending persecution and tyranny" (1967, 275). This verse was again a point of controversy when Mel Gibson produced the movie *The Passion of the Christ* in 2004. Jewish scholars were quick to comment both before and after its release to explain the historic implications and the potential dangers in the present (Greenberg 2004; Segal 2004; Reinhartz 2004; Sandmel 2006; Garber 2006). The movie was released with Matt 27:25 spoken in Aramaic but without a translation on the screen, which was given for the remainder of the dialogue.

Jeremy Cohen addressed this topic in his book *Christ Killers: The Jews and The Passion from the Bible to the Big Screen*. He begins with a brief overview of the New Testament. Regarding Matt 27:25, he says that the passage does not mean, as interpreters a century later would argue, that all Jews for all time are condemned. Nevertheless, he says this passage did "sow the seed" for such an understanding (2007, 32). Similarly, in a discussion on the Gospel of John (and just as relevant for our Matthew passage), he says that once the Gospel was circulated, "the evangelist surrendered control over its meaning to his readers, and they, interpreting the gospel as they did over the course of many centuries, only sharpened its anti-Jewish implications" (35).

In the middle of the twentieth century, a new trend was developing. Previously, Jewish studies of the New Testament were undertaken by authors who were outsiders to both the faith and the formal study of the New Testament. Samuel Sandmel was the first major Jewish author to approach the subject as a trained New Testament scholar. For him, the question of whether or not the New Testament has an anti-Jewish tone depends largely on whether or not the events are historical (1978, xvii; cf. Sandmel 1956). He believed that much of the narrative in the Gospels represented the creativity of the evangelistsand therefore concluded that the New Testament is a "repository for hostility toward Jews and Judaism" (1978, 160). The Gospel of Matthew specifically is a mix of "sublimity and astonishing animosity" (Sandmel 1978, 68). Matthew 27:25, he wrote without further comment, is "the most glaring" example of anti-Jewish sentiment in Matthew's Gospel (1978, 66).

A student of Sandmel's, Michael J. Cook, continued in this same vein. One of his earlier articles discussed the four Gospels and argued that later anti-Jewish sentiments in church history are the direct result of the tone set by the New Testament (1983, 127). Cook has taught New Testament at Hebrew Union College Jewish Institute of Religion for many years. In a more recent book (2008), he addresses the Jewish community to help them approach the New Testament and help them understand its construction. There are a few random references to Matt 27:25. For example, he writes, "This is Matthew's theological justification, in the 80s, for the Temple's fall in 70" (2008, 51). Cook also devotes a whole chapter to Matthew, where he takes Sandmel's thesis a step or two further. He argues that even the passages that traditionally have been understood as "pro-Jewish" (as Matthew has often been called the "most Jewish" Gospel) are actually themselves "anti-Jewish." He concludes this chapter by saying that "the final editor was writing for a church that was reeling from destabilizing turbulence transpiring in Syria and the land of Israel during the 60s and 70s. This turbulence dramatically altered this church's demographics" (2008, 208). In other words, the anti-Jewish tone of Matthew is because the "final editor" was not Jewish and was hostile to Jews.

Toward the end of the twentieth century, and certainly by the early part of this century, Jewish NT scholarship began to grow exponentially to the point that it is no longer a novelty. Amy-Jill Levine was one of the first prominent voices. In 1988, she wrote a book that, among other things, challenged the prevailing attitude that Matthew was anti-Jewish. She argued that "the crowd" and "all the people" of Matt 27:24–55 must be juxtaposed with other Jewish characters mentioned in the same chapter; this includes the women from Galilee (Matt 27:55), Joseph of Arimathea (27:57), and probably Simon the Cyrene (27:32). She concludes:

According to Matthew, the church is formed on a Jewish base, the Great Commission is pronounced by a Jew, addressed to a group of Jews, and includes Jews in its scope. Further, Matthew highlights the church's retention not only of the written Torah but also of many Pharisaic interpretations. Finally, according to the gospel's soteriological perspective, God has not rejected the Jews as a corporate community nor have the Jews rejected God. Rather, the evangelist has condemned the elite of both Jewish and gentile religious and political organizations who exploit or ignore others on the social, economic, and spatial peripheries. (1988, 271)

Other Jewish scholars have commented on this verse briefly. Samuel Tobias Lachs, in a book comparing New Testament verses to rabbinic writings, wrote succinctly on Matt 27:25: "This has a hebraic ring" (1987, 428). Aaron M. Gale's comment in the Jewish Annotated New Testament is equally brief: "Matthew's first readers likely related the verse to the Jerusalem population, killed or enslaved by the Romans as a result of the First Revolt against Rome in 66–70 CE. Early followers of Jesus may have viewed the devastation as punishment for condemning Jesus" (2017, 64).

Finally, Claudia Setzer recently wrote a full-length article on this passage. She argues that the use of the phrase "all the people" in Matt 27:25 can be traced to two main sources. First, "all the people" of Israel are considered God's covenant partners in the book of Exodus (see Exod 19:4; 24:3, 8), which of course includes such elements as the appearance of the ultimate prophet, Moses, and "the blood of the covenant." The second antecedent is Matthew's own "anti-Pharisaic polemic" in chapter 23. Here, the Pharisees are described as killing and persecuting the prophets, and specifically spilling innocent blood (Matt 23:35). Both of these themes meet in Matt 27:25, which she describes as "the culmination of the innocent blood narrative, where the people's prophet meets his inevitable death at the hands of the people" (2018, 179). She also argues, following Runesson, that Matthew and his community were once closely related to the Pharisees. This explains the harsh words against them. In the end, "Matthew casts blame for the death of Jesus on his proximate opponents, situating it as an event within the grand history of Israel" (183).

Views of Jewish Followers of Jesus

This last category represents a relatively new edition to NT scholarship, although ironically the verse in question was itself written, most would agree, by a Jewish follower of Jesus. Whether referred to as Hebrew Christians, Jewish Christians, or messianic Jews, they have been steadily contributing to the conversation in recent decades (and earlier; see Edersheim 1983). The Gospel of Matthew has been of particular interest (Kasdan 2011; Cohen 2016).

Michael Rydelnik has taught at Moody Bible Institute for several decades, although he was raised in an Orthodox Jewish family. His interest in Matt 27:25 is both academic and personal (2005). In one article (1987), he responded to interpretations that either promote an anti-Jewish reading and/or challenge the historicity of the narrative. Regarding the latter critique (that the account is fictional), there are three specific charges: this passage appears in Matthew alone; handwashing was a Jewish gesture and would have been foreign to Pilate; and it is a theological polemic against Jews. Rydelnik responds: The fact that it appears in only one Gospel is not evidence of it being ahistorical. In fact, Matthew may have understood the significance more than the other evangelists and recognized its value in communicating the narrative. As for the handwashing, it needs to be remembered that Pilate was in Judea for at least four years and perhaps longer. It would not be surprising that he learned customs that were significant for the local population, especially as they would come before him when cases were being tried. This gesture would have also spoken more loudly to the crowd than his words (which would have been in Greek and not fully understood by all). Regarding the claim that this scene was merely a polemical invention, the argument does not stand up. The passage, Rydelnik continues, needs first to be exegeted to determine its meaning and whether or not it is polemical (and against whom it is being polemical), before dismissing it as ahistorical. He concludes:

> Thus the rejection of Jesus by the leaders brought judgment on the people of Israel and their children. Yet the cry of the crowd came from a small body who, under the direction of their leaders, accepted responsibility for the death of Jesus. Their act, infamous as it was, did not constitute Israel a nation of Christ-Killers; it merely confirmed the judgment to come. (6)

Matthew 27:25 remains a challenging verse, and the variety of interpretations attest to its complexity. But much of the modern scholarship has been agreeing that it is not ultimately anti-Jewish (and most certainly does not warrant the reactions seen throughout much of church history). The verse remains difficult because that very history will not go away, nor should it ever be forgotten. At the same time, an undue focus on the death of Jesus (and the damage that has been caused by false accusations of blame) must not shift the focus away from the narrative and the event that happened three days after the crucifixion. This brings us to the final author in this section.

On Good Friday in 1995 (the year of the fiftieth anniversary of the end of World War Two), Joel Marcus preached a series of sermons about the relationship between the crucifixion and the Holocaust. He is uniquely qualified to address this topic as he is, in his words, "a Jew by birth, a Christian by choice." He is also a noted New Testament scholar. Commenting on the Jewish view of Jesus, he mentioned several twentieth-century artists and writers who began to embrace Jesus as a fellow Jew in spite of the long history of persecution. He sees this as a "testimony to the amazing power of Jesus to break through human misunderstanding and to present himself anew, unshackled from human preconceptions, to each generation" (2017, 15). The crucifixion, Marcus argues, must be seen together with the resurrection and all of the healing that entails, as mentioned in both the Tanakh and the New Testament. He concludes his book with the following words:

It is the central intuition of this book that these two forms of communion—with the tragedies of Jewish history, culminating in the Holocaust, and with Jesus' death on the cross—are inextricably bound up with each other. A corollary is that the *tikkun* of the world, its repair, restoration, and redemption—including the redemption of

Israel—has already been decisively inaugurated in Jesus' resurrection from the dead. But that corollary belongs essentially to the preaching of Easter rather than to that of Good Friday. (1997, 118; emphasis original).

Works Cited

Basser, Herbert, and Marsha B. Cohen. 2015. *The Gospel of Matthew and Judaic Traditions: A Relevance-Based Commentary*. Leiden: Brill.

Cohen, Akiva. 2016. *Matthew and the Mishnah: Redefining Identity and Ethos in the Shadow of the Second Temple's Destruction*. WUNT 2 Reihe 418. Tübingen: Mohr Siebeck.

Cohen, Haim. 1967. *The Trial of Jesus of Nazareth*. London: Weidenfeld and Nicolson.

Cohen, Jeremy. 2007. *Christ Killers: The Jews and the Passion from the Bible to the Big Screen*. Oxford: Oxford University Press.

Cook, Michael J. 1983. "Anti-Judaism in the New Testament." *USQR* 38.2:125–37.

———. 2008. *Modern Jews Engage the New Testament, Enhancing Jewish Well-Being in a Christian Environment*. Woodstock, VT: Jewish Lights.

Edersheim, Alfred. 1983. *The Life and Times of Jesus the Messiah*. Peabody, MA: Hendrickson.

Gale, Aaron M. 2017. "Matthew, Introduction and Annotation." Pages 9–66 in *The Jewish Annotated New Testament*. 2nd ed. Edited by Amy-Jill Levine and Marc Zvi Brettler. New York: Oxford University Press.

Garber, Zev. 2006. *Mel Gibson's Passion: The Film, the Controversy, and its Implications*. Shofar Supplements in Jewish Studies. West Lafayette: Purdue University Press.

Gregerman, Adam. 2016. *Building on the Ruins of the Temple: Apologetics and Polemics in Early Christianity and Rabbinic Judaism*. TSAJ 165. Tübingen: Mohr Siebeck.

Greenberg, Irving. 2004. "Anti-Semitism in 'The Passion.'" *Commonwealth* 131.9: 10–13.

Kasdan, Barney. 2011. *Matthew Presents Yeshua King Messiah: A Messianic Commentary*. Clarksville, MD: Messianic Jewish Publishers.

Konradt, Matthias. 2014. *Israel, Church, and the Gentiles in the Gospel of Matthew*. Tübingen: Mohr Siebeck.

Lachs, Samuel Tobias. 1987. *A Rabbinic Commentary on the New Testament: The Gospels of Matthew, Mark and Luke*. NY: Ktav.

Levine, Amy-Jill. 1988. *The Social and Ethnic Dimensions of Matthean Social History*. SBEC 14. Lewiston, NY: Mellen.

Longenecker, Bruce. 2014. *Hitler, Jesus, and Our Common Humanity: A Jewish Survivor Interprets Life, History, and the Gospels*. Eugene, OR: Cascade.

Marcus, Joel. 1997. *Jesus and the Holocaust: Reflections on Suffering and Hope*. Grand Rapids: Eerdmans.

Meiser, Martin. 2018. "Matt 27:25 in Ancient Christian Writings." Pages 221–40 in *The New Testament as a Polemical Tool: Studies in Ancient Christian Anti-Jewish Rhetoric and Beliefs*. Edited by Reimer Roukema and Hagit Amirav. Göttingen: Vandenhoeck & Ruprecht.

Nolland, John. 2008. "The Gospel of Matthew and Anti-Semitism." Pages 154–69 in *Built upon this Rock: Studies in the Gospel of Matthew*. Edited by Daniel M. Gurtner and John Nolland. Grand Rapids: Eerdmans.

Ratzinger, Joseph. 2011. *Jesus of Nazareth: From the Entrance into Jerusalem to the Resurrection*. Vatican: Ignatius Press.

Reinhartz, Adele. 2004. "Reflections on Gibson's *The Passion of Christ*." *AJS* Spring/Summer: 12–13.

Runesson, Andrew, and Daniel M. Gurtner. 2020. *Matthew within Judaism*. ECL 27. Atlanta: SBL Press.

Rydelnik, Michael. 1987. "His Blood Be upon Us: An Examination of the Deicide Charge in Matthew 27:25." *Mishkan* 6: 1–9.

Rydelnik, Michael. 2005. *They Called Me Christ Killer* (Discovery Series, *A Personal Perspective on Who Killed Jesus*). Grand Rapids: RBC Ministries.

Sandmel, David Fox, 2006. "Jews, Christians, and Gibson's *The Passion of the Christ*." *Judaism* 7: 12–20.

Sandmel, Samuel. 1978. *Anti-Semitism in the New Testament?* Philadelphia: Fortress.

———. 1956. *A Jewish Understanding of the New Testament*. Cincinnati: Hebrew Union College Press.

Segal, Alan F. 2004. "How I Stopped Worrying about Mel Gibson and Learned to Love the Historical Jesus: A Review of Mel Gibson's *The Passion of the Christ*." *JSHJ* 2: 190–208.

Setzer, Claudia. 2018. "Sinai, Covenant, and Innocent Blood Traditions in Matthew's Blood Cry (Matt 27:25)." Pages 169–85 in *The Ways That Often Parted: Essays in Honor of Joel Marcus*. Edited by Lori Baron, Jill Hicks-Keeton, and Matthew Thiessen. Atlanta: SBL Press.

Teter, Magda. 2020. *Blood Libel: On the Trail of an Anti-Semitic Myth*. Cambridge: Harvard University Press.

Turner, David. 2015. *Israel's Last Prophet, Jesus and the Jewish Leaders in Matthew 23*. Minneapolis, MN: Fortress Press.

5.2 The Gospel of Luke and Jewish-Christian Relations

Michael L. Brown

When discussing the question of alleged anti-Semitism in the New Testament, it is common to point to John's Gospel and its use of "the Jews," or to Matthew's treatment of "the Pharisees," or to a number of select passages, including Matt 27:25; John 8:44; Phil 3:2–3; 1 Thess 2:14–16 (see the summary in Brown 2000, 145–75). Scholars will also point to Luke's use of "the Jews" in Acts as reflecting anti-Semitic or at the least anti-Judaic tendencies (see Wills 1991). Luke's Gospel, however, is not as often cited for alleged anti-Semitic attitudes. (Hereafter, unless the context indicates a reference to the person of Luke, all references to "Luke" refer to his

Gospel. For the minority suggestion that Luke himself might have been Jewish, see Lizorkin-Eyzenberg 2018).

After all, Luke only mentions "the Jews" four times in his Gospel, with three of those times occurring in one chapter (see 7:3; 23:3, 37–38, all in the phrase "King of the Jews"; the adjective "Jewish" occurs in 23:50). Contrast this with references to "the Jews" in Acts (almost 80x; see Wills 1991). On the other hand, when it comes to "the Pharisees," Luke's Gospel does mention them frequently, almost always in negative contexts (especially in Luke 11), containing a parallel passage to Matt 23 with its series of "woes" pronounced over the Pharisees. (The Pharisees are mentioned in Luke 5:17, 21, 30; 6:2, 7, 11; 7:30, 36, 39; 11:37, 39, 42–43, 53; 12:1; 13:31; 14:1, 3; 15:2; 16:14; 17:20; 18:10–11; 19:39). And while it is true that Jesus is a guest at the home of several Pharisees for meals, in each case, Pharisees (either individually or corporately) are then targeted for correction and even rebuke (see Luke 7:36–50; 11:37–54; 14:1–24). The sole, potentially positive reference to the Pharisees is found in 13:31, where they warn Jesus that Herod wants to kill him. Still, the passage ends with a prophecy of the coming judgment on sinful Jerusalem (Luke 13:34–35). In response to these passages, the *Jewish Annotated New Testament* states, "The Gospel's presentation of Pharisees is puzzling, inconsistent, and complex" (Levine and Brettler 2017, 122).

In addition to Luke's negative depiction of the Pharisees, some scholars also point to the passion narrative in Luke (claiming it transfers all responsibility from the Romans to the Jews; see, quite strongly Nicholls 1993, 164–65), along with specific passages in the Gospel. These include the parable of the good Samaritan (10:25–27), in which the Samaritan is portrayed in compassionate terms, in contrast with the selfish and legalistic priest and Levite; and the healing of the ten lepers (17:11–19), only one of whom returns to give thanks to Jesus—namely, the Samaritan, called "that foreigner" in 17:19 (see below). Some would also point to Jesus' inaugural sermon in Nazareth (4:16–30), where he states that "no prophet is accepted in his hometown" (4:24), noting that God sent Elijah to sustain a Sidonian widow during the famine and used Elisha to heal a Syrian leper (4:25–27).

It is, therefore, no surprise that Samuel Sandmel devotes a chapter to Luke and Acts in his *Anti-Semitism in the New Testament?* (1978, 71–100), that Lillian C. Freudmann addresses Luke in her *Anti-Semitism in the New Testament* (1994), that Daryl D. Schmidt contributes a chapter on "Anti-Judaism and the Gospel of Luke" in *Anti-Judaism and the Gospels* (1999, 63–120, including responses), that Lloyd Gaston writes on "Anti-Judaism and the Passion Narrative in Luke and Acts" in *Anti-Judaism in Early Christianity* (1986, 127–53), or that David L. Tiede devotes a chapter to discussing "'Fighting Against God': Luke's Interpretation of Jewish Rejection of the Messiah Jesus" in *Anti-Semitism and Early Christianity: Issues of Polemic and Faith* (1993, 102–12).

According to Sandmel,

With this concern to win Jews and still portray their recurrent malevolence, there is to be found in Luke frequent subtle, genteel anti-Semitism. We shall find such subtlety primarily in the Gospel; in part the subtlety persists in Acts, but there it recedes, and the anti-Semitism becomes overt and direct. (1978, 73)

Freudmann opines, "Luke had no sympathy for, and even less knowledge of, Jews or Judea" (1994, 227). In the view of Schmidt, the texts in Luke-Acts are "potentially anti-Jewish" (1999, 96).

More pointedly, with reference to the passion narrative, Nicholls claims:

> While the intention of the writer is certainly to transfer the guilt for the death of Jesus from the Romans to the Jews, an aim accomplished with singular thoroughness, it is not clear which is his primary objective, to exculpate the Romans or to incriminate the Jews. Probably, as in Matthew's case, it is the latter.

He continues, "Like Matthew, Luke involves the whole people in the guilt for Jesus' death." And "Luke so plays down the role of the Romans that the natural way to read the narrative is to think that the Jews were the ones who actually carried out the crucifixion of Jesus" (1993, 164–65). How should we evaluate these claims?

Luke, the Pharisees, and the Samaritans

On three occasions, Jesus eats at the home of a Pharisee, which at least shows that some civility existed between him and them. But in each instance, as stated, the meal setting provides the occasion for the rebuke. See Luke 7:36–48 where Jesus contrasts the treatment he received from a sinful woman with the treatment he received from Simon the Pharisee; 11:37–54 where Jesus is invited to the home of a Pharisee who heard him speak, only to be soundly rebuked, with the final verse reading, "When Jesus went outside, the Pharisees and the teachers of the law began to oppose him fiercely and to besiege him with questions, waiting to catch him in something he might say"; and 14:1–23 where Jesus dines with a Pharisee on the Sabbath; there, he proceeds to heal a man, leaving them speechless when he challenges their views, then teaches them about humility and tacitly rebukes them with a parable. One had better think twice before inviting Jesus home for a meal.

But these narratives are in keeping with virtually every other reference to the Pharisees in Luke; except for 13:31, mentioned above, where some Pharisees warn him that Herod wants to kill him. Otherwise, the remaining references break down as follows:

- 5:17–26. Jesus heals a man in the presence of the Pharisees and Torah teachers after pronouncing the man's sins forgiven, about which they grumble.
- 5:27–38. The Pharisees question Jesus choosing Levi, a tax collector; his parable about new wineskins is meant as a rebuke to their mindset.
- 6:1–11. The Pharisees are upset with Jesus for healing on the Sabbath; verse 11 reads, "But the Pharisees and the teachers of the law were furious and began to discuss with one another what they might do to Jesus."
- 7:30. While all the people, including the sinful ones, acknowledged John's baptism, "the Pharisees and the experts in the law rejected God's purpose for themselves, because they had not been baptized by John."

- 12:1–3. As a crowd of many thousands gathers, Jesus first says to his disciples, "Be on your guard against the yeast of the Pharisees, which is hypocrisy. There is nothing concealed that will not be disclosed, or hidden that will not be made known" (12:1–2).

- 15:1–2. As a crowd of sinners gathered around Jesus, the Pharisees mutter, "This man welcomes sinners and eats with them." This led to Jesus telling the threefold parable of the lost sheep, the lost coin, and the lost son, where some claim that the latter's older, judgmental brother represented the Pharisees.

- 16:14–15. After Jesus taught that you cannot serve both God and mammon, Luke writes, "The Pharisees, who loved money, heard all this and were sneering at Jesus. He said to them, 'You are the ones who justify yourselves in the eyes of others, but God knows your hearts. What people value highly is detestable in God's sight.'"

- 17:20–21. The Pharisees question Jesus about the kingdom of God, to which he explains that it is in their midst.

- 18:9–14. "To some who were confident of their own righteousness and looked down on everyone else"—meaning the Pharisees, among others—Jesus told the parable of the Pharisee and the tax collector.

- 19:28–40. As Jesus made his triumphal entry into Jerusalem and the crowds hailed him as the Messiah, the Pharisees urged Jesus to rebuke his disciples; in reply, he said that if they kept quiet then the stones would cry out.

Strikingly, then, with hardly any exception (specifically, Luke 13:31), *every single reference to the Pharisees in Luke paints them in a negative light.* They are hypocrites, they are legalists, they are spiritually blind, they are judgmental, they are greedy, and they have "rejected God's purpose for themselves." Thus, speaking of the witness of the Gospels and Acts together, Freudmann writes, "Pharisees, Sadducees, scribes, priests, and teachers of the law are the villains. Despite disparate loyalties and beliefs among these Jewish parties, they are lumped together under one pejorative heading called 'the Jews'" (1994, 225; contrast Tomson [2008, 112] who, with reference to Luke-Acts, states that with rare exception, "the Pharisees do not have a negative role in these Luke and Acts"). That would appear to be a far too positive assessment. But is Luke actually guilty of anti-Semitism? Or can he rightly be accused of anti-Judaism?

Interestingly, as the time of Jesus' death draws near, the Pharisees are not mentioned at all. Instead, as the Lord teaches daily at the temple, "the chief priests, the teachers of the law and the leaders among the people were trying to kill him" (Luke 19:47). It is these same players who are portrayed negatively throughout Luke 20, with the Sadducees singled out in 20:27–34. In 22:47–71, where Jesus is arrested and subjected to a mock trial, it is the high priests and elders who are the main culprits; while in 23:1–35, it is these same players, along with a crowd of the people, who insist to Pilate that Jesus be crucified, with "the rulers" mocking him as he hangs on the cross.

But in all these accounts, the Pharisees are not mentioned once and, contra Nicholls, Luke's goal in the passion narrative is hardly to transfer the full blame for the crucifixion to the Jewish people as a whole. To the contrary, the three references to "the Jews" in Luke 23 are found in verses 3 and 37 (2x), all in the phrase, "King of the Jews." Yes, the man who is being crucified, by the order of Pilate, is king of the Jews. How can this be perceived as either anti-Semitic or anti-Jewish? As for the one person specifically mentioned with the referent "Jewish," it is none other than Joseph "from the Jewish town of Arimathea. He was a member of the council, a good and righteous man" (Luke 23:50). Only Luke speaks of Arimathea as "Jewish," which is hardly the work of a writer out to demonize the Jews as a people. Luke also gives us insight into the friendship that was forged between Pilate and Herod in their joint mistreatment of Jesus (Luke 23:12; only Luke records this).

As for passages such as Luke 18, the story of the Pharisee and the tax collector, the *Jewish Annotated New Testament* explains,

> Some readers dismiss the Pharisee as hypocritical, sanctimonious, and legalistic, and in turn identify with the tax collector, the repentant, humble, and justified sinner. This approach is not surprising, given that Luke has presented numerous maleficent Pharisees as well as several admirable tax collectors. However, once readers choose to identify with the tax collector and reject the Pharisee, the parable traps them: to conclude in effect (following 18:11), "God, I thank you that I am not like this Pharisee" places readers in the very position they condemn. Moreover, this interpretation overlooks the Pharisee's numerous excellent qualities: tithing, fasting, giving thanks without asking for something in return. (Levine and Brettler, 152)

It is also important to remember that both the Pharisee and the tax collector pray in the temple, so this is a contrast between *two Jews*, not between a Jew and a Gentile. As for the parable of the good Samaritan where it is the Samaritan who cares for a beaten and wounded man (presumably a Jew) rather than the priest or the Levite who simply pass by, or the healing of the ten lepers where the only non-Jew (the Samaritan) returns to give him praise, it is wrong to read these passages as anti-Semitic. With regard to the good Samaritan, Jesus is rebuking the self-righteous attitude of an "expert in religious law" (10:25 NET), a man who wanted to limit the definition of "neighbor" in the Torah injunction to "love your neighbor as yourself" (10:25–29) by asking, "And who is my neighbor?" (10:29). To expose this wrongful mindset, Jesus points to the sacrificial, godly actions of the Samaritan, in contrast with the fastidiously religious attitude of the priest, ending with this exchange: "'Which of these three, do you think, proved to be a neighbor to the man who fell among the robbers?' [The religious expert] said, 'The one who showed him mercy.' And Jesus said to him, 'You go, and do likewise.'" (10:36–37) Fitzmyer asks:

> Is this Lucan parable anti-Semitic? It can, of course, be read that way, as if Luke were suggesting a Samaritan as a paradigm for Christian conduct in contrast to the two Jews. . . . To read the parable in this way, however, is just another subtle way of allegorizing it. The emphasis in this Lucan passage lies

in the last injunction, "Go and do the same yourself," and if it has an interest in the Samaritan, it is simply the Lucan stress on universalism which makes him seek out those in Palestinian society who were not the most important. Even H. Conzelmann (*Theology*, 146) refused to see in "the extreme sharpness of polemic" that Luke manifests at times between Christians and Jews any espousal of "Christian anti-Semitism," a "development" that he describes to early Catholicism. In the long run, to read the Lucan Gospel in this way is to import into it anachronistic issues that were not really looks concerned. (1985, 885; for a different perspective, see Levine and Brettler 2017, 136)

Note also that in the chapter preceding the parable of the good Samaritan, these very people—the Samaritans—are painted in a negative light (see 9:51–56). There, as Jesus makes his way to Jerusalem, a Samaritan village will not receive him; and although the Lord rebukes the vengeful attitude of his disciples, this certainly does not lessen Samaritan guilt. They were hardly heroes of virtue themselves, and this in turn helps underscore the point Luke was making when, on two occasions, he painted a Samaritan as the hero of the story.

Note that in Luke 17:18 in the story of the ten lepers, Jesus calls the grateful Samaritan a "foreigner" (*allogenēs*), a word found only here in the NT and hardly a compliment, given the Jewish view that the Samaritans were half-breeds. In fact, it was this very word that was used in the Greek inscription in the temple, forbidding foreigners from entering. Thus a messianic Jewish teaching site explains,

> The intended ironic punch-line to the story works only if both the Gospel writer and his readers reckon Samaritans to be outside the pale and of a lower spiritual dignity than the Jewish people. That's how Jewish people in the first century regarded Samaritans, and the Gospels assume that worldview. For example, the Parable of the Good Samaritan employs the same reversal of expectation. In that parable, we would have expected the man who showed mercy to be Jewish. When it turns out to be a Samaritan, it's a real shocker that forces us to open our eyes to the dignity and goodness of all human beings, even when they come from outside of our religious circle. (Firstfruits of Zion)

Not dissimilar to this is God's word to Ezekiel at the time of his calling, when the Lord said to him, "If I was sending you to foreigners, to people whose language you do not understand, they would listen to you. But your own people—my people—will not listen. They are stiff-necked and hardhearted" (my paraphrase of Ezek 3:4–7). See also Isa 2:1–4, which follows on the heels of an oracle of judgment on Jerusalem and Judah at the end of chapter 1, describing a glorious scene in which the nations of the world would come streaming to Jerusalem to learn God's teaching (*torah*). Based on this and with powerful alliteration in the Hebrew, Isaiah then turns to his own people, at that time disobedient, urging them as Yahweh's chosen nation to also walk in his ways as these Gentile nations will do in the future. As with these Lukan parables, the prophets also contrasted the faith of the outsider with the faithlessness of Israel (Luke's inclusion of women is also quite striking and certainly relevant here; see the list in "The Prominence of Women").

These considerations lead to two important questions: First, as much as Luke consistently paints the Pharisees in a negative light, is it possible that later readers have read anti-Semitic overtones into his perspective (on this, cf. esp. Tiede 1993)? Second, is it anti-Semitic or anti-Judaic to paint a particular group of Jews (namely, the Pharisees) in a negative light if, in fact, they were perceived to be guilty of legalism or religious hypocrisy or, more fundamentally, of rejecting Israel's Messiah? And should all such descriptions in the Gospels be attributed to the later conflict between Jesus' followers and different Jewish groups decades after his crucifixion and resurrection, allegedly projected back into the Gospel accounts? Could these accounts not reflect historical reality? We could point to the attacks on messianic Jews in Israel today by ultra-Orthodox Jews, sometimes leading to harassment and even physical violence. Is it anti-Semitic to report this?

And is there not substantial evidence of fierce sectarian rivalries and critiques among Jewish groups in the first century BCE and the first century CE, as recorded in the Dead Sea Scrolls and Josephus? Craig Evans, after comparing the language and tone of the Dead Sea Scrolls with that of the New Testament, notes:

> The polemic found in the writings of Qumran surpasses in intensity that of the New Testament. In contrast to Qumran's esoteric and exclusive posture, the early church proclaimed its message and invited all believers to join its fellowship. Never does the New Testament enjoin Christians to curse unbelievers or opponents. Never does the New Testament petition God to damn the enemies of the church. But Qumran did. If this group had survived and had its membership gradually become gentile over the centuries and had its distinctive writings become the group's Bible, I suspect that most of the passages cited above would be viewed as expressions of anti-Semitism. But the group did not survive, nor did it become a gentile religion, and so its criticisms have never been thought of as anti-Semitic. There is no subsequent history of the Qumran community to muddy the waters. We interpret Qumran as we should. We interpret it in its Jewish context, for it never existed in any other context, and thus no one ever describes its polemic as anti-Semitic. (1993, 8; cf. Johnson 1989)

This is exactly how Luke's Gospel should be interpreted.

Evans also notes that "Josephus's polemic against fellow Jews outstrips anything found in the New Testament" (1993, 8). Speaking of the Zealots, Josephus wrote, "In rapine and murder you vie with one another. . . . [T]he Temple has become the sink of all, and native hands have polluted these divine precincts" (*J. W.* 5.402). And of the Sicarii he stated, they are "imposters and brigands . . . slaves, the dregs of society, and the bastard scum of the nation" (2.264; 5.443–444; see further Johnson 1989).

Such quotes could be easily multiplied, yet no one would ever accuse Josephus of anti-Semitism or the authors of the Dead Sea Scrolls of anti-Judaism. Why should Luke be thus accused? Rather, Scot McKnight's summary of Matthew's polemic against the Pharisees can be applied equally to Luke's: "Matthew's polemic is with a particular form of Judaism, namely nonMessianic Judaism, especially as led by the scribes and Pharisees, and that polemic is motivated religiously and socially, but not racially" (1993, 61).

Ironically, Jews through the ages have affirmed that it was right for their forefathers to reject Jesus as Messiah, agreeing that he did not in fact fulfill the messianic prophecies. Why, then, should Luke be faulted for describing their rejection of Jesus on the one hand, and the Lord's polemic against them on the other? Don't these differences lie at the very foundation of the breach between Judaism and Christianity or, more apropos to a first-century setting, Pharisaic Jewish faith and messianic Jewish faith? Traditional Jews have no problem rejecting the messianic claims of Rabbi Yeshua, with rabbinic literature even polemicizing against him (see Schäfer 2009; for the abuse of such material by contemporary anti-Semites, see Brown 2021). Conversely, traditional Christians have no problem accepting Yeshua's polemics against the religious Jewish leaders who came against him. And that is the crux of the issue, as opposed to asking if Luke is anti-Semitic. Instead, the relevant question is, "Is Jesus really the king of the Jews?"

Godly Jews in Luke and the Focus on Israel's Redemption

In this light, it is important to emphasize how pro-Jewish and pro-Israel Luke's Gospel actually is. There are other, godly Jews who are mentioned in Luke (along with Joseph of Arimathea), including Simeon and Anna, who recognized Jesus as the Messiah when he was brought to the temple by his parents (Luke 2:22–36), meaning that toward the beginning and end of Luke, godly Jews are mentioned by name and singled out for praise. And note that Simeon "was waiting for the consolation of Israel" (Luke 2:25–26) and that he prophesied that Jesus would be "a light for revelation to the Gentiles, and the glory of your people Israel" (Luke 2:32), as well as someone "destined to cause the falling and rising of many in Israel" (Luke 2:34). As for Anna, upon seeing Jesus, "she gave thanks to God and spoke about the child to all who were looking forward to the redemption of Jerusalem" (Luke 2:38).

Even more fundamentally, the first chapter of Luke is as Jewish as could be, even hailing Zechariah and Elizabeth, the aged parents of John the Immerser, as "righteous in the sight of God, observing all the Lord's commands and decrees blamelessly" (Luke 1:6). Later, after Joseph and Miriam (Mary) brought Jesus to the temple as a baby, Luke records that they did "everything required by the law of the Lord" (2:39). For her part, Miriam (Mary), herself pregnant with the Messiah, speaks these words of praise after meeting with her cousin Elizabeth: "He has helped his servant Israel, remembering to be merciful to Abraham and his descendants forever, just as he promised our ancestors" (1:54–55). Would an anti-Jewish or anti-Semitic author pen such words, thereby connecting Jesus the Messiah to God's mercy to Israel and his promises to the patriarchs?

Even more powerfully, after the baby John is circumcised, his father Zechariah, who had been struck dumb in the previous months because of his doubting the angel Gabriel (1:11–20), begins his paean of praise with these words:

> "Praise be to the Lord, the God of Israel, because he has come to his people and redeemed them. He has raised up a horn of salvation for us in the house of his servant David (as he said through his holy prophets of long ago), salvation from

our enemies and from the hand of all who hate us—to show mercy to our ancestors and to remember his holy covenant, the oath he swore to our father Abraham: to rescue us from the hand of our enemies, and to enable us to serve him without fear in holiness and righteousness before him all our days." (Luke 1:68–75)

Nowhere in Luke are these sentiments contradicted or dismissed in the least; and it is on this quite pro-Israel, pro-Jewish foundation that the rest of Luke is built. In fact, Sandmel observes "how consistently Luke portrays Christians as undeviatingly faithful to Judaism" (1978, 73). Obviously, it would have been felicitous to substitute something like "Jewish followers of Jesus" rather than "Christians," while David Balch writes, "With Josephus, Luke-Acts honors the antiquity of the Jews. . . . Luke honors Moses as founder and lawgiver throughout the work" (1999, 108–9). Tomson even states, "With regard to the Sabbath, the author has a frankly positive attitude toward Jews and Judaism. . . . The author has a remarkably positive view of Judaism" (2008, 111–12).

In Luke 2, we read that Jesus went with his family to Jerusalem in the annual Passover pilgrimage to engage in sophisticated dialogue with the religious leaders; and in that context, those leaders are not painted in a negative light (2:41–50). Once Jesus began his ministry, he frequented the local synagogues (Luke 4:15–16, 20, 28, 33, 38, 44; 6:6; 13:10; note also 7:5; 8:41, 49; and see 21:12, where he warns his disciples that they will be handed over to the synagogues because of their preaching, once again grounding their mission in a Jewish context as fellow Jews). He even reads from the scroll of Isaiah in his hometown synagogue on the Sabbath, proceeding to ground his own calling in the text he recites from Isa 61 (Luke 4:16–21; note that, according to Levine and Brettler 2017, 118: "The rejection of Jesus is not prompted by xenophobia; it is prompted instead by Jesus' refusal to provide his hometown with messianic blessings").

There are other important citations of the Tanakh (along with allusions to the Tanakh) in Luke (see 1:17, 46–50, 68, 76, 79; 2:23–24; 3:4–6; 4:4, 8, 10–12, 18–19; 7:15, 22, 27; 8:10; 9:54; 10:15, 27, 29, 36; 11:20; 12:53; 13:35; 17:32; 18:20; 19:38, 46; 20:17, 28, 37, 43; 21:26–27; 22:37, 69; 23:30, 34–36, 46), with Jesus himself pointing back to the Hebrew Scriptures after his resurrection as further confirmation of his pre-ordained, already-foretold messianic mission (24:25–27, 44–45; note especially 24:44: "This is what I told you while I was still with you: Everything must be fulfilled that is written about me in the law of Moses, the Prophets and the Psalms"). To ask again: Would an anti-Judaic or anti-Semitic author write this? Why go out of your way to ground the mission of the Messiah in the Jewish Scriptures unless those Scriptures were considered sacred rather than obsolete, outmoded, and outdated?

There are also thirty-three references to Jerusalem in Luke including passages where Jesus, in keeping with the prophets of old, weeps over the city as he foretells its destruction (19:41–44; see also 23:27–31, where he calls on the "daughters of Jerusalem" to weep for the terrible calamities coming on them and their children; see also Giblin 1985). Not only so, but Luke's presentation of the Great Commission reads, "This is what is written: The Messiah will suffer and rise from the dead on the third day, and repentance for the forgiveness of sins will be preached in his name to all nations, *beginning at Jerusalem*" (24:46–47; emphasis mine). And what are the closing verses of Luke? "When he had led them out to the vicinity of Bethany, he lifted up his hands and blessed them. While he was blessing them, he left them and was taken up into heaven. Then they worshiped him and returned to Jerusalem with great joy. And they stayed continually at the temple, praising God" (24:50–53). Does an anti-Semite end a book like that? Does an anti-Jewish author allow for such positive associations with both Jerusalem and the temple? Would not such an author end his book with either a subtle or overt indication that God was finished with Jerusalem and that the temple was passé? As noted by Mark Kinzer:

> According to Luke–Acts, Jerusalem possesses a unique status not only because "the kingdom of Christ" is "historically anchored" there but even more because that kingdom will achieve its eschatological consummation within its walls. This means that the land of Israel also retains its unique status for Luke–Acts, for the city of Jerusalem functioned from the time of the postexilic prophets as a symbol for the land as a whole, as well as for the people destined to inherit it. (2016, 141–42)

He adds,

> Luke underlines the thematic centrality of Jerusalem for his two-volume work by structuring his narrative geographically, with Jerusalem as its pivot. No other book in the New Testament adheres to such a defined geographical pattern as a primary principle of organization. This author also gives more attention to the destiny of Jerusalem than does any other New Testament writer.

Additionally,

> Among the four Gospels, only Luke begins in Jerusalem—and not merely in Jerusalem but at the heart of the city, the holy Temple, where the future father of John the Baptist offers incense and receives an angelic visitation (Luke 1:5–23). [Thus] among the canonical Gospels only Luke begins in Jerusalem, ends in Jerusalem and orients its central narrative around a journey *to* Jerusalem [referring to 9:51]. This geographical structure underlines Luke's unique concern for the holy city and its enduring theological significance. (143–44; emphasis original)

Indeed, Kinzer states, "Luke is unique in his portrait of Jesus' sympathy for the suffering that Jerusalem will undergo" (147); and when Jesus prophesies that Jerusalem will be trampled on by the Gentiles until the times of the Gentiles is fulfilled, he is prophesying Jerusalem's future restoration (cf. Tannehill 1996, 305–6). To quote Kinzer again: "Luke is thus unique among the Gospels not only in its emphasis on Jerusalem's coming destruction but also in its anticipation of the city's future restoration" (151). To ask once more: Are these the words of an anti-Judaic or anti-Semitic author? Do such authors portray a Messiah who weeps over the destruction of the holy city and then prophesies its restoration?

We should also draw attention to Luke's emphasis on the importance of Abraham, mentioned in 1:55, 73; 3:8 (2x); 3:34; 13:16, 28; 16:22–25, 29–30; 19:9; 20:37. On the one hand, in Luke, Jesus rebukes the religious leaders for trusting in their lineage for righteousness, noting that "God is able from these stones to raise up children for Abraham" (3:8b); while in 13:28, he warns the (presumably Jewish) crowd that "there will be weeping and gnashing of teeth, when you see Abraham and Isaac and Jacob and all the prophets in the kingdom of God but you yourselves cast out." But in both these cases, Abraham is presented in a positive way, as is connection to him and the other patriarchs by means of a living faith. What is rebuked is religious formalism and legalistic righteousness.

On the other hand, and with a more explicitly positive emphasis, the afflicted woman who has been crippled by Satan for eighteen long years should be healed on the Sabbath since she is a daughter of Abraham (13:16), while the repentant Zacchaeus should be forgiven "since he also is a son of Abraham" (19:9). Note that poor and afflicted Lazarus goes to Abraham's bosom after his death, while the selfish rich man goes to a place of torment (16:19–31) despite appealing to "Father Abraham" (16:24, 30). In fact, a closer reading of Luke points in particular to Abraham's role as father (see 1:55, 73; the rebuke in 3:8; 3:34; 13:16, daughter of Abraham; 16:24, 30; 19:9, son of Abraham). For Siker, Abraham is the "father of the outcast" (1991, 104–118). Note, however, that Siker's overall emphasis is different from mine. Luke thus grounds the redemptive work of Jesus in the promises to Abraham and the patriarchs—not as a guarantee to salvation for all of his descendants, but rather as a sacred heritage that benefits the afflicted, the lowly, and the repentant. Those are the children of Abraham in both body and spirit. Is there anything anti-Semitic or anti-Jewish in such sentiments, especially when being a son or daughter of Abraham makes one a special candidate for healing and forgiveness?

Works Cited

Balch, David L. 1999. "Response to Daryl L. Schmidt: Luke-Acts is Catechesis to Christians, Not Kerygma to Jews." Pages 97–110 in *Anti-Judaism and the Gospels*. Edited by William R. Farmer. Harrisburg, PA: Trinity Press International.

Brown, Michael L. 2000. *Answering Jewish Objections to Jesus: Vol. 1, General and Historical Objections*. Grand Rapids: Baker Books.

———. 2021. *Christian Anti-Semitism: Confronting the Lies in Today's Church*. Lake Mary, FL: Charisma House.

Evans, Craig A. 1993. "The New Testament and First-century Judaism." Pages 1–17 in *Anti-Semitism in Early Christianity: Issues of Polemic and Faith*. Edited by Craig A. Evans and Donald Hagner. Minneapolis, MN: Fortress Press.

Firstfruits of Zion. "Nine Ungrateful Lepers." https://torahportions.ffoz.org/disciples/luke/nine-ungrateful-lepers.html.

Fitzmyer, Joseph A. 1985. *The Gospel According to Luke X–XXIV: Introduction, Translation, and Notes*. AB 28A. Garden City, NY: Doubleday.

Freudmann, Lillian C. 1994. *Anti-Semitism in the New Testament*. Lanham, MD: University Press of America.

Gaston, Lloyd. 1986. "Anti-Judaism and the Passion Narrative in Luke and Acts." Pages 127–53 in *Anti-Judaism in Early Christianity: Vol. 1, Paul and the Gospels*.

Edited by Peter Richardson with David Granskou. Waterloo, ON: Wilfred Laurier University Press.

Giblin, Charles Homer. 1985. *The Destruction of Jerusalem according to Luke's Gospel: A Historical-Typological Moral.* Rome: Biblical Institute Press.

Grace Communion International. "The Prominence of Women in the Gospel of Luke." https://www.gci.org/articles/the-prominence-of-women-in-the-gospel -of-luke.

Johnson, Luke T. 1989. "The New Testament's Anti-Jewish Slander and the Conventions of Ancient Polemic." *JBL* 108.3: 419–41.

Levine, Amy Jill, and Marc Zvi Brettler. 2017. *The Jewish Annotated New Testament.* 2nd ed. New York: Oxford University Press.

Lizorkin-Eyzenberg, Eli. "Could Luke Be Jewish?" *Israel Bible Weekly*, June 25, 2018. https://weekly.israelbiblecenter.com/luke-jewish-possibly-part-1.

Kinzer, Mark S. 2016. "Zionism in Luke-Acts: Do the People of Israel and the Land of Israel Persist as Abiding Concerns in Luke's Two Volumes?" Pages 141–66 in *The New Christian Zionism: Fresh Perspectives on Israel and the Land.* Downers Grove, IL: InterVarsity Press.

McKnight, Scot. 1993. "A Loyal Critic: Matthew's Polemic with Judaism in Theological Perspective." Pages 55–79 in *Anti-Semitism in Early Christianity: Issues of Polemic and Faith.* Edited by Craig A. Evans and Donald Hagner. Minneapolis, MN: Fortress Press.

Nicholls, William. 1993. *Christian Anti-Semitism: A History of Hate.* Northvale, NJ: Jason Aronson.

Sandmel, Samuel. 1978. *Anti-Semitism in the New Testament.* Philadelphia: Fortress.

Schäfer, Peter. 2009. *Jesus in the Talmud.* Princeton: Princeton University Press.

Schmidt, Daryl D. 1999. "Anti-Judaism and the Gospel of Luke." Pages 63–96 in *Anti-Judaism and the Gospels.* Edited by William R. Farmer. Harrisburg, PA: Trinity Press International.

Siker, Jeffrey S. 1991. *Disinheriting the Jews: Abraham in Early Christian Controversy.* Louisville: Westminster John Knox.

Tannehill, Robert C. 1996. *Luke.* ANTC. Nashville: Abingdon.

Tiede, David L. 1993. " 'Fighting Against God': Luke's Interpretation of Jewish Rejection of the Messiah Jesus." Pages 102–12 in *Anti-Semitism in Early Christianity: Issues of Polemic and Faith.* Edited by Craig A. Evans and Donald Hagner. Minneapolis, MN: Fortress Press.

Tomson, Peter J. 2008. *Presumed Guilty.* Minneapolis, MN: Fortress Press.

Wills, Lawrence M. 1991. "The Depiction of the Jews in Acts." *JBL* 110.4: 631–54.

5.3 The Gospel of John and Jewish-Christian Relations

Mitch Glaser

The Gospel of John is viewed as the "bad boy Gospel" by the Jewish community because of its alleged anti-Semitic character. Well-known and respected Jewish scholar of the New Testament Samuel Sandmel remarked years ago that John is "the most overtly anti-Semitic of the gospels" (1978, 101). The bases for these accusations are described in many books and articles and by New Testament scholars—Jewish, Evangelical, Catholic, and Protestant—and cover a wide array of textual, historical, and theological concerns, ranging from dating to the authorship of the Gospel of John. (For a recent and impressive collection of studies, see Culpepper and Anderson 2017; Reinhartz et al. 2018. For an insightful engage treatment of the Gospel of John from a Jewish perspective, see Reinhartz 2001.)

Of first concern to many Christian scholars and members of the Jewish community is the ways John uses the term *Ioudaioi*, historically translated as "the Jews." There is considerable debate as to the precise community of Jewish people John is referring to when the term is used. There are many different ways to approach this question (Miller 2010). Commentators recognize that in John, *Ioudaioi* usually refers to the "Judeans" (John 1:19; 4:22), as opposed to Galileans (4:45), Samaritans (4:9, 39; 8:48), and, perhaps, Hellenists (7:35; 12:20). A few times, *Ioudaioi* may refer to Jews in general, but even then the point may be the Jewish faith as taught by the Jews of Jerusalem and Judea.

When the traditional dating (90–100 CE) and authorship of John are accepted, identifying the Jewish people John portrayed as adversarial toward Jesus becomes primarily a contextual and exegetical issue. If the Gospel is deemed to be written later, then the alleged negativism toward the Jews may be the voice of a growing Gentile church, separating from and competitive with a post-temple diaspora Judaism.

As Craig Keener notes in his excellent and Jewish-sensitive introduction to his massive two-volume commentary on the Gospel of John,

> The authorship of the fourth Gospel has been vigorously debated although the traditional consensus from early Christian centuries that the apostle John wrote it has now given way to a majority scholarly skepticism toward that claim. But this consensus has been challenged by some recent conservative commentators, most notably Leon Morris, D. A. Carson and Craig Blomberg, and it has been challenged with good reason. (2003, 83–84)

A second concern takes the more immediate date of authorship into consideration. If the Gospel of John was written in approximately 90 CE, then the *Birkat ha Minim*—the synagogue prayer against the apostates (including messianic Jews) allegedly penned in 80 CE by Rabbi Samuel the Small—may be viewed as creating the context for the negative attitude toward the Jewish people found in the Gospel.

The revised twelfth benediction reads in part: "May the Nazarenes and the heretics be destroyed in a moment and may they be blotted out of the book of life" (Marcus 2009, 524). Such a revision of the Amidah would have made it very difficult for Christians to participate in synagogue liturgy. This proposed background, however, is much debated (criticized in Reinhartz 2001, 113–15; defended in Marcus 2009). We must determine if John was recording his firsthand rehearsal of events transpiring sixty years earlier during the actual three years of Jesus' ministry (as Bernier 2013 argues), or if the conflicts between Jesus and the Jewish leaders reflect the *Birkat haMinim* penned decades later. John's alleged negativism toward the Jews would reflect the growing acrimonious relationship between the Jewish Jesus followers and Jewish leaders of post-temple Judaism (Kysar 1993).

Some scholars date the writing of the Gospel later than the first century and presume the author wrote it when the chasm between Judaism and Christianity had grown even wider and harsher. An unintended result of modern criticism facilitates laying the blame for anti-Jewish sentiments at the feet of the growing Gentile church.

Throughout the centuries, anti-Semitism in the writings of the ante- and post-Nicene fathers, the medieval church, and the Catholic Church until *Nostrae Aetate* and Vatican II were thought to be influenced by the Gospel of John, which became the fountainhead of ecclesial anti-Semitism. In his classic work *The Anguish of the Jews*, Father Edward Flannery affirms and confesses that the traditional Jewish accusations about the Gospel of John are true and apologizes on behalf of the church. He believed this was the way forward to create a better and more fruitful dialogue with the Jewish community.

The difficult question to address is whether there is something for which the church should apologize. By the church saying "I'm sorry" for the alleged inherent anti-Judaism in the Gospel of John, there is an admission that the writing of the New Testament was later than traditionally accepted and that the "apparent" acrimony against the Jewish people within the Fourth Gospel was primarily Gentile Christian in origin. This perspective, therefore, demands that someone other than John, the disciple, wrote the Gospel in the first few centuries CE and reflected the anti-Jewish attitudes of a growing Christianity, which became *religio licita* under Constantine. This is not an admission that I or many other Evangelicals are willing to make.

A better explanation might be that the Gospel of John, and even the remainder of the New Testament, expressed familial tensions between Jewish people, some of whom believed in Jesus as the Messiah and others who did not. The polemic of the New Testament writings reflects an intramural debate, not unlike we find in other bodies of Jewish literature, such the scrolls recovered from Qumran (Evans 1993).

D. Moody Smith, late professor of New Testament at Duke and the mentor of Craig Keener of Asbury Seminary, writes,

> It is fair to say that in John the Jews stand over against Jesus and his disciples, who are distinguished from them. Yet the Evangelist obviously knows that Jesus is a Jew (4:9) from Nazareth, the son of Joseph (1:45). His disciples, some of whom were followers of John the Baptist (1:35), were Jews as well (cf. 18:15). Despite his knowledge of the historical facts, John insists on characterizing the Jews as somehow dearly different and distinguishable from the band of

Jesus and his disciples. . . . By and large, "the Jews" in John are the opponents of Jesus. (1990, 1)

Smith and others may also have in mind the warnings of the Jewish leaders to the parents of the man born blind whom Jesus healed in John 9. If they admitted that Jesus healed their son, the synagogue would cast them out, which ultimately happened to the formerly blind man himself. Some argue that this is one possible historical linkage to the *Birkat haMinim*, which was possibly designed to alienate the messianic Jews from the quickly evolving post-temple Jewish community.

However, regardless of any connection to synagogue liturgy, it is apparent from the original historical context—sixty years before John, if his authorship is accepted—that strained relations already existed between Jewish Jesus followers and some first-century Jewish leaders. These tensions existed before the crucifixion and the later events surrounding the destruction of the temple, which included the messianic Jews fleeing from Jerusalem (Luke 21:20–25).

Countering the alleged anti-Jewish sentiments found in the Gospel of John is of issue as these arguments have emboldened devastating anti-Jewish views, which became the basis for the mistreatment of the Jewish people by the church for millennia. (One thinks of the unfortunate influence of passions plays, such as the Oberammergau Passion Play, first performed in 1634.) Charges such as deicide were also leveled against the Jewish people by the early church (Eastern and Western), increasing the speed and ferocity of anti-Judaism throughout the medieval period, powering its way into the Holocaust and post-Holocaust era, and wreaking massive destruction and the loss of Jewish lives.

After the Holocaust, many Christians in Europe were apt to ask, "What is left to be said to the Jewish people?" How can we communicate the love of Jesus to the Savior's kinsman according to the flesh in light of a monumental tragedy that so obviously grew from the seeds planted by the early church and—in some instances, as redaction critics might even suggest—the New Testament itself?

The Gospel of John was written by John the Jewish apostle, reflecting his experience of walking with Jesus during his ministry. John would have celebrated Passover with Yeshua and other Jewish holidays with the Messiah. Also, without qualification, the Jesus of John tells the Samaritan woman, "Salvation is from the Jews" (John 4:22). A statement like this is hard to square with the notion that John's Gospel is anti-Jewish. Additionally, John stood at the foot of the cross as the Savior died. If this is true, then the use of the Gospel of John in Christian history to fuel anti-Semitism requires a different type of apology that does not impugn the New Testaments or the Gospel of John to be inherently anti-Semitic. In fact, an apology in light of the bloody history between Christians and Jews would indeed be a good step forward irrespective of one's views on the Gospel of John.

Assuming that the traditional view of the dating and authorship is accepted, then how do we explain some of the alleged anti-Jewish statements and sentiments that are hard to ignore in the Gospel of John? We would suggest that the tensions between Jewish followers of Jesus and the leaders who opposed him may be viewed as an internal Jewish family battle and not a series of attacks by post-Second-Temple Gentile Christians against first-century Jews in general. The apostle John spoke to the Jewish leaders who were opposed to Jesus in a way that evoked the language and themes of the great Jewish prophets, who when necessary were critical of the Jewish establishment. Reading anti-Semitism into the Gospel of John is anachronistic. We wholeheartedly reject the idea that the Gospel of John was inherently anti-Jewish or anti-Semitic.

Works Cited

Ahr, Peter G. April 20, 2020 (7:57 pm), comment on " 'The Jews' in the Gospel of John" by Lawrence E. Frizzell. https://blogs.shu.edu/lawrencefrizzell/the -jews-in-the-gospel-of-john/.

Berger, David. 2008. *The Jewish-Christian Debate in the High Middle Ages: A Critical Edition of the Nizzahon Vetus*. n.p.: ACLS Humanities e-book.

Bernier, Jonathan. 2013. *Aposynagōgos and the Historical Jesus in John: Rethinking the Historicity of the Johannine Expulsion Passages*. BibInt 122. Leiden: Brill.

Chazan, Robert. 1992. *Barcelona and Beyond: The Disputation of 1263 and Its Aftermath*. Oakland: University of California Press.

Culpepper, R. Alan, and Paul N. Anderson, eds. 2017. *John and Judaism: A Contested Relationship in Context*. SBLRBS 87. Atlanta: SBL Press.

Evans, Craig A. "Faith and Polemic: The New Testament and First-century Judaism." Pages 1–17 in *Anti-Semitism and Early Christianity: Issues of Polemic and Faith*. Edited by Craig A. Evans and Donald A. Hagner. Minneapolis, MN: Fortress Press.

Garroway, Joshua D. 2017. "*Ioudaios*." Pages 596–98 in *The Jewish Annotated New Testament*. 2nd ed. Edited by Amy-Jill Levine and Marc Zvi Brettler. New York: Oxford University Press.

Keener, Craig. 2003. *The Gospel of John*. 2 vols. Grand Rapids: Baker Academic.

Kysar, Robert. 1993. "Anti-Semitism and the Gospel of John." Pages 113–27 in *Anti-Semitism and Early Christianity: Issues of Polemic and Faith*. Edited by Craig A. Evans and Donald A. Hagner. Minneapolis, MN: Fortress Press.

Levine, Amy-Jill, and Marc Zvi Brettler, eds. 2017. *The Jewish Annotated New Testament*. 2nd ed. New York: Oxford University Press.

Marcus, Joel. "*Birkat ha-Minim* Revisited." NTS 55 (2009): 523–51.

Miller, David M. 2010. "The Meaning of *Ioudaios* and Its Relationship to Other Group Labels in Ancient 'Judaism.' " CurBR 9: 98–126.

Novikoff, Alex J. 2013. *The Medieval Culture of Disputation: Pedagogy, Practice, and Performance*. The Middle Ages Series. Philadelphia: University of Pennsylvania Press.

Patterson, Paige. 1989. Private letters between Dr. Paige Patterson and members of the Jewish Federation.

Reinhartz, Adele. 2001. *Befriending the Beloved Disciple: A Jewish Reading of the Gospel of John*. London: Continuum.

———. 2017. "Introduction and Annotations to the Gospel According to John." Pages 168–218 in *The Jewish Annotated New Testament*. 2nd ed. Edited by Amy-Jill Levine and Marc Zvi Brettler. New York: Oxford University Press.

————. 2017. "Story and History: John, Judaism, and the Historical Imagination."
    Pages 113–26 in *John and Judaism: A Contested Relationship in Context*. Edited
    by R. Alan Culpepper and Paul N. Anderson. SBLRBS 87. Atlanta: SBL Press.
————, ed. 2018. *The Gospel of John and Jewish Christian Relations*. Minneapolis,
    MN: Fortress Press.
Ruether, Rosemary Radford. 2001 [1989]. *To Change the World: Christology and
    Cultural Criticism*. Eugene, OR: Wipf & Stock.
Sandmel, Samuel. 1978. *Anti-Semitism in the New Testament?* Philadelphia: Fortress.
Smith, D. Moody. 1990. "Judaism and the Gospel of John." Pages 76–96 in *Jews
    and Christians: Exploring the Past, Present, and Future*. Edited by James H.
    Charlesworth. New York: Crossroad.
Toalston, Ari. 1999. "SBC's Patterson Invites Dialogue with 6 Jewish Leaders
    Charging 'Deception.'" *Baptist Press*. November 10, 1999. https://www
    .baptistpress.com/resource-library/news/sbcs-patterson-invites-dialogue
    -with-6-jewish-leaders-charging-deception/.

5.4 Matthew 5:17–19 and the Law of Moses Today

Michael Rydelnik

When I first became a leader of a messianic congregation some thirty years ago, I was surprised to find a significant dispute in that small community. People repeatedly asked me, "Are you Torah positive or Torah negative?" Others framed their question as "Should we continue to keep the Torah, or have we been freed from its obligations?" These questions persist in messianic circles even today.

What I've discovered is that whatever position a person takes on this issue, they have favorite proof texts to cite. For example, those who hold that believers in Yeshua are not required to keep the Torah of Moses will cite multiple verses from the Pauline corpus, indicating that the Torah has been rendered inoperative (e.g., Rom 7:1–6; 1 Cor 9:20–21; Gal 3:23–25; Eph 2:15). On the other hand, those who hold that believers in Yeshua remain obligated to keep the Torah will cite Matt 5:17–20, maintaining that Yeshua said he did not come to abolish the law.

So which is it? Are we to maintain adherence to the Torah, which Yeshua did not abolish, or have we been freed from the Torah of Moses and been placed under a new messianic Torah? When asked these questions, I default to the answer Tevye gave when a dispute came up in his presence. Upon hearing both sides of a particular argument, Tevye affirmed both positions as correct. When challenged that both sides can't be right, he responded, "You're also right." My point is that I believe Yeshua's words and that, yes, we are under the authority of the Torah. Further, I believe the New Testament teachings about the law and that, no, we are no longer bound by the Torah of Moses. How can both positions be right? That's what this chapter will attempt to explain.

First, this chapter will provide a careful exposition of Yeshua's teaching about the Torah found in Matt 5:17–20. Then it will examine some key passages from the New Testament epistles regarding the law of Moses. Afterwards, it will briefly address the idea of a messianic Torah in rabbinic thought. Finally, it will present the ways the law of Moses continues to be authoritative today.

The Exposition of Matthew 5:17–20

The Context of Matthew 5:17–20

The passage under discussion is found in the Sermon on the Mount (Matt 5:1–7:29), the first major teaching section in the Gospel of Matthew. The Sermon on the Mount can be understood as Yeshua's messianic manifesto, describing how kingdom citizens are to live as they await the arrival of the messianic kingdom on earth. The prologue (5:1–16) serves to identify true kingdom citizens by their character (5:3–12) and their influence (5:14–16). They are to be characterized by a distinctive spiritual joy ("blessed") and to influence society by preventing decay ("salt") and promoting righteousness ("light").

Having established the identity of kingdom citizens, Yeshua transitions to the main body of his sermon (5:17–7:12). The mention of the law and the prophets in both Matt 5:17 and 7:12 serves as an *inclusio*, bracketing the beginning and end of the main section of the sermon. This section of Yeshua's message clarifies the deeper and more demanding standards that he requires of kingdom citizens. These requirements insist that true kingdom citizens have (1) genuine obedience to the Scriptures (obedience that includes their motives and not merely formal adherence, 5:17–48); (2) honest motives in worship (devotion that is sincere before God and not a show for other people, 6:1–18); and (3) full integration into everyday life (so that eternal perspectives transform temporal behavior, 6:19–7:12). The sermon concludes with Yeshua calling his listeners to choose the way of the king and to become kingdom citizens (7:13–34).

The opening section of the main body of the sermon (5:17–20) addresses the issue of the Bible's indestructibility. In essence, Yeshua is responding to the Pharisaic charge that he was lessening God's righteous demands. He answers by reaffirming the Hebrew Bible's indestructible nature as being the eternal and inviolable word of God. Having done so, he continues by showing that the messianic standard of obedience "surpasses that of the scribes and Pharisees" (5:21–48).

The Details of Matthew 5:17–20

Yeshua taught that the Hebrew Bible is indestructible because it is eternal (5:17–18)

Matthew records Yeshua's explanation of the indestructibility of the Scriptures. Yeshua spoke not of the law alone but of "the law or the prophets" (v. 17), an expression used to describe the entire Bible. The Bible is indestructible, because Yeshua's purpose was to fulfill its teaching and God intended the Bible to last forever.

The Hebrew Bible is indestructible because Yeshua's purpose was not to destroy but to fulfill (5:17)

The opening prohibition ("Do not think") alludes to a view in circulation that Yeshua was somehow opposed to the Torah of Moses and was seeking to destroy it. This may have been the result of Yeshua's healing on the Sabbath or opposing Pharisaic traditions. Whatever the cause, Yeshua explains that the purpose of his coming was not to overthrow the Bible's validity or authority but to fulfill it ("not to destroy . . . but to fulfill" are both infinitives of purpose; Burton 1978, 368). The meaning of "fulfill" is to establish completely (Cremer 1895, 500). The term is elastic enough to include at least two ways in which Yeshua established the Scriptures. First, Hill explains that Yeshua "establishes the Law and the Prophets by realizing (or actualizing) them completely in his teaching and his life" (1972, 117). Thus the Messiah's perfect explanation and obedience to the Scriptures establishes them. Second, Yeshua established the messianic predictions of the Law and the Prophets with his life and ministry. Just as the entire Hebrew Bible prophesied a coming Messiah, so Yeshua fulfilled those predictions (Luke 24:27, 44).

The Hebrew Bible is indestructible until heaven and earth pass away, even in its minutest details (5:18)

The conjunction "for" is explanatory and points to the reason Yeshua did not come to destroy. The phrase "I say to you" is a formula used only by Yeshua (here for the first of thirty-one times in Matthew) and indicates an authoritative pronouncement. This is in contrast to the rabbinic pattern wherein they spoke only "in the name" of another authoritative teacher. Thus with an authoritative pronouncement, Yeshua gives the reason that the law and the prophets will not be destroyed.

The Hebrew Bible is indestructible until the end of the world (5:18a)

After beginning by assuring that he came to fulfill "the law or the prophets" as a reference to the Scriptures as a whole (5:17), throughout the rest of the paragraph, Yeshua uses the term "law" without the word *prophets*. In doing this, he is not shifting to speak of the Torah of Moses alone. Instead, the context indicates that he means the entire Hebrew Bible. It was common in Judaism to use the word *law* (or Torah) of all the Hebrew Scriptures not the Torah of Moses alone (Heller 1967, 243). Yeshua now likely emphasized the word *law* because it was his teaching and observance of the law of Moses that was the source of so much controversy with the Pharisees.

The messianic argument about the indestructibility of the Torah begins with a statement about its eternal nature. Yeshua says the law will never be destroyed because it will abide "until" (indicating time) heaven and earth pass away. It is understood that there will come a time when the heaven and earth will perish (Ps 102:26). This is at the end of the world and before the creation of the new heavens and earth (Isa 65:17). Besides explaining how long the Torah will last, Yeshua next explains to what extent the Torah is indestructible. He moves from the duration of the Torah to its details.

The Hebrew Bible is indestructible in its minutest detail (5:18b)

Yeshua affirms the Hebrew Bible's indestructibility by saying that "not the smallest letter [Greek *iota*] or stroke" will pass away. The *iota* is the smallest Greek letter and represents the *yod*, the smallest Hebrew letter. The word *stroke* can mean "hook" and may refer to the Hebrew letter *vav*, which copyists often omitted (as they also did the *yod*); or it could mean a stroke such as distinguished between various similar Hebrew letters (e.g., *hey*, *khet*, *NIDNTT* 3:182). It could also refer to the decorative horns found on Hebrew letters themselves.

After describing the extent of the Hebrew Bible's abiding nature, Yeshua returns once again to Bible's duration. It will be "until all is accomplished." Although this may refer to Messiah Yeshua's own death, it is better to see it eschatologically because of the previous mention of the passing away of the heaven and the earth. Thus the Bible's authority will abide in detail to the end of the age.

Yeshua taught that the Hebrew Bible affirmed its own indestructibility because it is inviolable (5:19–20)

There are two aspects to Yeshua's teaching on the Hebrew Bible's indestructibility with regard to its inviolability. First, the Torah's authority is such that its demands cannot be relaxed but must be obeyed completely (5:19). Second, the Torah's authority is so great that its demands are intensified to include internal motives not merely superficial obedience (5:20).

The indestructible Hebrew Bible is inviolable in that it must be fully obeyed (5:19)

The conjunction "therefore" (HCSB, Greek *oun*) indicates the conclusion to be drawn from the Bible's indestructibility. As such, it is fully authoritative, so every command must be obeyed. By the New Testament era, the rabbinic traditions had graded the commandments from what was considered most important to the least (cf. Matt 22:36). Moreover, they had relaxed the demands of the Torah by ingenious and legalistic easing of its commands. An example of this was Hillel's *prosbul*, a legal formulation he innovated so that creditors could still collect debts during the sabbatical year (see m. Šeb. 10). The *prosbul* was considered a benefit to the rich and the poor—to the rich because it secured their loans, and to the poor because it made it possible for them to borrow (Gi̧t. 37a). Nevertheless, it loosened the authority of the command by allowing lenders to collect debts in the sabbatical year, clearly a "work around" for the commandment. There were many of these contrivances to loosen the demands of the Torah. Therefore, Yeshua instructed that true obedience encompassed complete observance of the Torah, from the least command to the greatest, as the lawgiver had intended them to be observed.

The word *law* as used here refers to the whole Bible but emphasizes the commandments of the Torah. While some have argued that it refers to a revised law as given by Yeshua, the entire tenor of the passage indicates that Yeshua is speaking of the Mosaic Torah.

The verb "annuls" (*lyo*) can be translated "to relax or to loose" and refers to the common rabbinic practice of "loosing" or finding loopholes in the law (as shown above with the *prosbul*). The Sermon on the Mount proceeds to show how commandments have been relaxed (*NIDNTT* 3:183). In contrast to rabbinic loosing, Yeshua's teaching allows for no relaxation of God's righteous requirement, but he rather intensifies the Torah in relation to personal motives as well as the letter of law (see Matt 5:21–48).

Thus Yeshua gives a stern rebuke to the Pharisaic approach to the Torah: those who adapt it and relax its requirements (as the Pharisees did; see Matt 15:1–9) will be considered small in God's kingdom. "But" (an adversative designed to show contrast with the Pharisaic teachings) those who teach and practice the true meaning of the Torah and the entire Bible will be considered great. In this statement, Yeshua is turning the tables on the Pharisees. They accused Yeshua of not keeping the Torah by not following their traditional explanations of the Torah. But Yeshua states (and will show in 5:21–48) that it was the Pharisees who failed to keep the Torah by emphasizing the letter of the law and ignoring the intentions of the heart.

The indestructible Hebrew Bible is inviolable in that its demands surpass mere superficial obedience (5:20)

The word *for* (Greek *gar*, v. 20) is explanatory, indicating how the Torah is the standard of righteousness and therefore the requirement for entrance into the kingdom of heaven. The righteousness God requires must surpass even Pharisaic righteousness. The Pharisaic self-perception was that they kept the Torah perfectly. Hence, Paul could speak of himself as a Pharisee, saying that "as to the righteousness which is found in the law, [I was] found blameless" (Phil 3:6). The Pharisees had attained this perspective of obedience to the Torah in two ways: first, by legalistic adherence and additional fences around the Torah; and second, by ingenious ways of loosening the Torah's demands.

The use of the word *surpasses* with the untranslated adverb "*pleion*" is emphatic ("greatly surpasses") and heightens the genitive of comparison ("of the scribes and Pharisees") that follows (BDF §246). Yeshua's words indicate that the righteousness of kingdom citizens must *greatly surpass* that of the scribes and the Pharisees. This was difficult for Yeshua's hearers to comprehend, because the Pharisees were looked upon as the most scrupulous keepers of the Torah (cf. Phil 3:5, 6). The scribes were included in this statement, because they were the experts on the laws that established the teachings and practices of the Pharisees. As Hill states, Yeshua's "criticism of the Pharisees . . . is not that they were not good, but that they were not good enough!" (1972, 119). The reason they were not good enough is that they had only superficial obedience, whereas God looked at the internal motive. So in the section that follows (5:21–48), Yeshua gives the proper interpretation of the Torah, showing that superior righteousness is necessary. This is righteousness derived from the spirit as well as the letter.

Yeshua is not teaching works-salvation. Rather, he is demonstrating that absolute righteousness is necessary to enter God's kingdom. In other words, he is saying that entrance into God's kingdom by right is derived solely from perfect obedience to the spirit and letter of the Torah. Since this is unattainable by any person, even a Pharisee, one must be justified by faith, as was the sinner in the parable of the Pharisee and the tax gatherer (Luke 18:9–14). It was the sinful tax gatherer who begged for mercy and then was declared righteous by God.

The Summary of Matthew 5:17–20

Yeshua has affirmed the indestructible nature of the Bible generally and the law specifically. The Bible, as God's righteous requirement, is indestructible because it will last forever and because Yeshua's interpretation intensified its scope to cover motive as well as action. In sum, in this passage, Yeshua affirms that the whole Hebrew Bible, including the Torah, remains authoritative until the eschaton. This would fit with my answer mentioned at the outset of this chapter that, yes, we remain under the authority of the Torah. But, of course, there was also my negative response: that we are not under the Torah. This comes from the New Testament epistles and also needs to be examined.

The New Testament Epistles and the Law of Moses

The New Testament epistles, primarily Paul's letters, indicate that there has been some change in the law of Moses since the arrival of Yeshua the Messiah. What follows will be observations on this biblical data regarding the Torah.

Romans 7:7–13

It is frequently maintained that the apostle Paul held to a negative view of the Torah. But Rom 7:7–13 makes it abundantly clear that in Paul's view, there was no problem with the Torah. Rather, the trouble lay in the Jewish people's ability to obey it. In this passage, Paul asks, "Is the law sin?" and responds to his own question with a resounding "*mē genoito*" (Rom 7:7), the strongest and most intense way of saying "NO!" in New Testament Greek. He affirms that "the law is holy, and the commandment is holy and righteous and good" (Rom 7:12). According to Paul, the holy and good Torah serves to prove the sinfulness of people. Using himself as an example, he states that the command not to covet caused his own sinful nature to produce in him "coveting of every kind" (Rom 7:8–9). Paul's point is similar to Carl Sandburg's insight:

> Why did the children
> put beans in their ears
> when the one thing we told the children
> they must not do
> was put beans in their ears?

The effect of God's holy commandments was to prove the utter sinfulness of humanity (Rom 7:13).

Galatians 3:19–25

In Gal 3:19–25, a passage related to Rom 7, Paul asks why God gave the Torah. His answer is that it was "added because of transgressions" (Gal 3:19). This likely refers to the restraining aspect of the commandments. John H. Sailhamer has noted that in the Pentateuch, every time Israel committed a significant sin, another collection of laws (the covenant code, the priestly code, and the holiness code) were added, in order to restrain Israel from sin (1998, 7–51). So, when Paul asks his question, he is clearly speaking of the commandments God gave Israel, not the Pentateuch as a whole. Herein lies an important distinction in the way the word *law* is used. It can refer to the book of the Law, the entire Pentateuch, including the narratives, oracles, poems, and commandments, from Genesis to Deuteronomy. This is the way Yeshua spoke of the Torah in Matt 5:17–19. Or it can be used as Paul did in Gal 3:19 to refer only to the commandments—the laws placed in the Pentateuch.

Paul also maintains that these laws were added "until the seed would come" (Gal 3:19). He has already identified that the Messiah is "the seed" of whom he speaks. Therefore, Paul's point is that these laws will be the authority for Israel only until the promised Messiah comes. Since Yeshua has arrived, the Mosaic commandments are no longer the constitution for Israel. Paul goes on to argue that the Torah's commandments functioned as a pedagogue, a term much like a babysitter who was no longer needed when a child became an adult (see BDAG 748). The commandments functioned as Israel's babysitter until Messiah would come (Gal 3:24). Clearly, the preposition *eis* should be taken temporally (as in the CSB, "our guardian *until* Christ," Gal 3:24), because of all the temporal expressions in the paragraph and its association with the parallel thought in Gal 3:19 (Schreiner 1993, 127–28). Plainly, Paul sees the restraining nature of the commandments as fulfilled with the arrival of the Messiah Yeshua.

Ephesians 2:15

Yet another verse in the Pauline corpus, Eph 2:15, indicates that the law of commandments is no longer the rule of life for any follower of Yeshua. Referring to the death of Yeshua, Paul declares that it has "nullified" (NET) or abolished (NASB) the law of commandments. The Greek word *katargeō* is better translated "rendered inoperative" (Thayer §5373), since the commandments still exist but are no longer the operative force for the believer's lifestyle. It is similar to the DOS computer operating system: it still exists but it has been rendered inoperative by a later version of Windows. In much the same way, the Torah clearly exists but it is no longer the operating system for followers of Yeshua.

2 Corinthians 3:7–11

In 2 Cor 3:7–11, Paul once again addresses the issue of the commandments being rendered inoperative. In a comparison of the laws with the new covenant, Paul calls the Ten Commandments "a ministry of death, in letters engraved on stones" (2 Cor 3:7). Although it was glorious, the Torah was surpassed by the even more glorious new covenant (2 Cor. 3:8–10). Once again (as in Eph 2:15), Paul uses the term *katargeō* (render inoperative), saying "that which *fades away* [*katargeō*] was with glory, much more that remains is in glory" (2 Cor 3:11). Although most versions translate it here as "fading away" to link it with the fading of the glory of Moses' face, it is better viewed as the commandments, even the Ten Commandments, as being rendered inoperative for the follower of Yeshua.

Hebrews 7:11–12, 18–19

The author of Hebrews makes clear the need for a change in the operative law, marking the change from the failing Levitical priesthood of the Mosaic Torah to the perfect Melchizedekian priesthood of Messiah of the new covenant (Heb 7:11–12). There are two reasons a change was required. First, for Yeshua to be our high priest, not being from the Levitical priesthood, demanded a change in operating system. His point is that "when the priesthood is changed, of necessity there takes place a change of law also (Heb 7:12). Second, since the law could not perfect anyone (in fact, it could only show human inability to keep it), it was considered weak and unprofitable (often translated "useless") in providing a transformed life. Therefore, there needed to be a change from the Mosaic covenant to the new covenant (Heb 7:18–19).

Other Passages

In 1 Cor 9:20–21, Paul declares he is not under the law of Moses but now under the law of the Messiah (another term for the new covenant). In Romans 6:12–14, he states that followers of Messiah are not under law but under grace. In Romans 10:4, Paul says that the Messiah Yeshua "is the end of the law for righteousness to everyone who believes." Although C. E. B. Cranfield has made the case that the word *end* (*telos*) should be understood as "goal" rather than end (2:515–20), this does not diminish the significance of this verse. Even when translated "goal," the word implies that when the goal has been reached, the end has arrived (see Strickland 1993, 267). For a Jewish person who has *not* been justified by faith, absolute obedience to the law of Moses is God's righteous requirement. This standard is impossible for any person except the Messiah Yeshua, who fulfilled the law perfectly. Paul agrees and says the law is rendered inoperative only for believers. For believers, God's standard is still righteous behavior, but that demand for righteousness is now expressed in the law of Messiah (1 Cor 9:20–21).

The view of the Pauline Epistles and Hebrews seems to anticipate changes in law. It would be helpful to see how similar this New Testament perspective is to rabbinic thought.

Rabbinic Thought and the Messianic Torah

Some might be surprised to learn that rabbinic literature, with its highly elevated view of the Torah, still anticipates significant changes in the Torah when the Messiah comes (see Davies 1952, esp. 50–83). Although this subject is worthy of a chapter itself, following is just a brief summary of the ways rabbinic thought expected the Torah to change in the messianic age.

First, there was an expectation that the Messiah would bring change to the Torah.

According to Sifre Deut. §160 (on Deut 17:18), "[the Mishnah Torah] (Deuteronomy) is destined to be changed" in the messianic age. In other words, it was believed that the coming of the Messiah would somehow modify the Torah. But what sort of changes? According to some, one anticipated alteration is that in the messianic times, the commandments of the Torah would be annulled: "the commandments will be abolished in the age to come" (Nid. 61b).

Others believe that only some of the commandments will cease. According to Lev. Rab. 9.7, "In the age to come, all sacrifices will be annulled but that of thanksgiving." Yet others maintain that "all festivals will cease but not Purim" (Yal. Prov. 9:2). Another view is that the laws of kosher will be altered, as in Midr. Pss. 146.4 (on Ps 146:7), "Some say that of every animal whose flesh it is forbidden to eat in this world, the Holy One, blessed be He, will declare in the time-to-come that the eating of its flesh is permitted." This view is seemingly rejected by the limiting phrase "some say." Nevertheless, it appears that some rabbis considered the possibility of changes to the dietary laws. A further view is that there will be a reduction of commandments in the messianic age: "When the Messiah comes, he will give [the exiles] thirty precepts" (Gen. Rab. 98.9).

Second, there was an expectation that there would be a Torah of Messiah in the messianic age, one different from the Torah of Moses. According to Eccl. Rab. 11.8, "The Torah which a man learns in this world is but vanity compared to the Torah of Messiah." The expression "Torah of Messiah" is identical to the New Testament expression "law of Messiah" (1 Cor 9:21; Gal 6:2). Although the written rabbinical documents about changes in the Torah and their inclusion of the expression "Torah of Moses" antedate the New Testament, they are certainly based on earlier oral traditions.

The New Testament epistles' view of the law of Messiah and their recognition of some sort of alteration in the commandments certainly reflect a stream of first-century Jewish thought. Thus Paul and the author of Hebrews echo the same ideas found in rabbinic thought, since they believed that Yeshua had inaugurated the messianic age (although certainly not yet consummated it).

Clearly, the New Testament epistles view the commandments of the Torah as having been rendered inoperative for the follower of the Messiah Yeshua. This is the "no" part of my position on the Torah as still binding. On the other hand, Yeshua clearly embraced the eternal inviolability of the Torah, as part of "the Law or the Prophets" (Matt 5:17–20; see above). This is the source of my affirmative response to the continued authority of the Torah. Can these two positions be harmonized? That's what I hope to do in this next section.

The Torah and the Believer's Life Today

When Yeshua spoke of the continuing authority of the Torah, he did so by linking it to the Prophets. His assertion was plain: "I did not come to destroy *the Law or the Prophets*," shorthand for the entire Hebrew Bible. The Torah, as part of the Scriptures, remains inspired and authoritative. This is exactly what Paul meant when he wrote that "all Scripture is God-breathed and profitable for teaching, for reproof, for correction, for training in righteousness" (2 Tim 3:16). Clearly, Paul's affirmation of the authority of Scripture included the Torah.

So what did Paul and the author of Hebrews mean when stating that believers are no longer under the law of Moses? Likely, they referred to the Sinai covenant, the commandments given to Israel and contained in the literary work called the Torah or the Pentateuch. Although these commandments were included in the Pentateuch and therefore in God's inspired word, they were now surpassed by the new covenant or the law of Messiah. Therefore, these laws are no longer the individual rules of life for the believer, but they certainly remain part of Scripture. As such, there are several ways the Torah should continue to have an authoritative function in the lives of believers.

The Holiness of God

First, the Torah remains a revelation of God's holiness. All the precise requirements of the Torah reveal a God who cares about how we are to approach him. Thus, at the conclusion of the dietary commandments, there is a reminder that these are to be obeyed not to lose weight or for a healthier lifestyle but out of obedience to God. He declares: "You shall be holy, for I am holy" (Lev 11:45). Drawing on this principle revealed in the Torah, Peter calls Jewish followers of Yeshua to leave the lusts of their pre-faith lives and practice holy behavior. The authority for his command is that Torah says, "You shall be holy, for I am holy" (1 Pet 1:14–16).

The Revelation of the Messiah

Second, the Torah remains the authoritative revelation of the Messiah. Yeshua made this point to those who opposed his ministry, challenging them by saying, "You search the Scriptures because you think that in them you have eternal life; it is these that testify about me" (John 5:39). Further in this interaction, Yeshua declared that the Torah itself revealed he was the Messiah: "If you believed Moses, you would believe me, for he wrote of me" (John 5:46). Some of the significant messianic passages in the Torah include Gen 3:15; 22:17b-18; 49:8–12; Num 24:5–9, 17–19; Deut 18:15–19; 34:10. In the view of the Messiah Yeshua, the Torah was an authoritative revelation of his messianic office, designed to lead people to faith in him.

The Examples of Behavior

Third, the Torah remains an authoritative revelation by providing examples for its readers. Too often, the Torah is viewed as a book of law when in reality it is a book about the laws given to Moses. As such, it contains numerous examples of both faithless and faithful behavior. We are to learn from both, rejecting the examples of disobedient behavior and embracing the examples of faithful obedience.

In 1 Cor 10:6–13, Paul cites the ungodly examples of Israel in the wilderness, repudiating those who had greedy desires, or practiced idolatry, or behaved immorally, or grumbled incessantly. His point was that "these things happened to them as an example, and they were written for our instruction" (1 Cor 10:11). Clearly, these negative examples were revealed in the Torah so followers of Messiah would learn not to behave similarly.

In Heb 11:1–29, the author recounts the faithfulness of godly men and women, as found in the Hebrew Bible, from Abel in Genesis to the Prophets. Although the roll call of faith cited there continues to mention examples from the later books of the Bible, clearly the author included the Torah, seeing it as an authoritative guide to faithful living. He calls these good examples a "great cloud of witnesses," referring to their role as those who testify to the value of faith. As such, they remind us to lay aside sin and "run with endurance the race that is set before us" (Heb 12:1). Obviously, the Torah remains an authoritative revelation for us, guiding our behavior, teaching us to reject disobedience and, instead, to embrace faithfulness.

A Book of Theology

Fourth, the Torah remains authoritative in teaching theology. In fact, one would be hard-pressed to find a new covenant doctrine not taught in the Torah. For example, in Rom 3:31, Paul asks, "Do we nullify the Law through faith? May it never be! On the contrary, we establish the Law." His point is that justification by faith is not contrary to the Torah but is actually taught in the Torah. He is establishing the law's teaching. He goes on to show that the Torah itself teaches justification by faith by citing Gen 15:6: "Abraham believed God and it was credited to him as righteousness" (Rom 4:3).

The Torah teaches that Israel would not be able to keep the Torah (Deut 31:29), just as Paul teaches (Rom 7:7–12). The law reveals Israel's restoration "at the end of Days" (Deut 4:30), just as Paul does (Rom 11:26). It points Israel to its only hope—the new covenant with its ability to change the heart (Deut 30:6)—just as the New Testament does (Heb 8:7–13). The Torah's theology is essential to understanding the New Testament's teaching.

The Wisdom of God

Fifth, the Torah remains the authoritative guide for wise behavior. This is an important aspect of understanding the ongoing aspect of the Torah's commandments. Israel's obedience would "show your wisdom and understanding in the eyes of the peoples," causing others to say, "surely this great nation is a wise and understanding people" (Deut 4:6). Just as other ancient Near Eastern law codes were thought of as collections of a king's wise judgments, so the Torah was viewed as Israel's source of wisdom. Therefore, by reading the Torah commands as reflecting divine wisdom (much as we read the book of Proverbs), we can discern the wisdom principle in the commandments and apply them in contemporary circumstances (Sailhamer 2009, 558–62).

For example, the New Testament does not repeat the Sabbath command of the Torah (in fact, it is the only one of the Ten Commandments not repeated there). Moreover, Rom 14:5 indicates that choosing which day to worship is a matter of conscience. This does not mean that a new covenant believer should be a workaholic. It is a wise principle to take one day a week for spiritual renewal and physical rest.

Another example, as found in the New Testament, is Paul's justification for paying salary to those in vocational ministry (1 Cor 9:8–14). Citing the commandment "You shall not muzzle the ox while he is threshing" (1 Cor 9:9 // Deut 25:4) and the provision of sacrificial food for priests (1 Cor 9; Lev 6:16, 26; 7:6, 31–36), Paul derives a wisdom principle from the Torah. In fact, he says of the commandment regarding the ox that it was written "for our sake" so we could learn its wisdom. Reading the commandments as wisdom and obeying the underlying wisdom principle recognizes the eternal authority of God's Torah, including its commandments.

Conclusion

So, is the modern follower of Yeshua the Messiah still under the authority of the Torah? I remain certain that the answer is both "yes" and "no." Yes, because Yeshua considered it part of God's eternal word, and therefore authoritative in every aspect of our lives. No, because the commandments contained in the Torah have been changed and now followers of Yeshua are under the authority of the Torah of Messiah. With this understanding of the Torah, we can declare with the psalmist, "I will never forget your precepts, for by them you have revived me" (Ps 119:93).

Works Cited

Burton, Ernest DeWitt. 1978 [1900]. *Syntax of the Moods and Tenses in New Testament Greek*. Grand Rapids: Kregel.

Cranfield, C. E. B. 1975–79. *A Critical and Exegetical Commentary on the Epistle to the Romans*. 2 vols. Edinburgh: T&T Clark.

Cremer, Hermann. 1895. *Biblico-Theological Lexicon of New Testament Greek*. 4th Eng. ed. Translated by William Urwick. Edinburgh: T&T Clark.

Davies, W. D. 1952. *The Torah in the Messianic Age and/or the Age to Come*. JBL Monograph Series 7. Philadelphia: Society of Biblical Literature.

Heller, Abraham Mayer. 1967. *The Vocabulary of Jewish Life*. Rev. ed. New York: Hebrew Publishing.

Hill, David. 1972. *The Gospel of Matthew*. NCBC. Grand Rapids: Eerdmans.

Sailhamer, John H. 2009. *The Meaning of the Pentateuch*. Downers Grove, IL: InterVarsity Press.

———. 1992. *The Pentateuch as Narrative*. Grand Rapids: Zondervan.

Sandburg, Carl. 1936. "Why did the children put beans in their ears?" *The People, Yes*. New York: Harcourt, Brace & Company.

Schreiner, Thomas. 1993. *The Law and Its Fulfillment: A Pauline Theology of Law.* Grand Rapids: Baker Books.

Strickland, Wayne G. 1993. "The Inauguration of the Law of Christ with the Gospel of Christ: A Dispensational View." Pages 229–318 in *The Law, the Gospel, and the Modern Christian: Five Views.* Edited by Wayne G. Strickland. Grand Rapids: Zondervan.

Thayer, Joseph H. 1977. *Thayer's Greek-English Lexicon of the New Testament.* Grand Rapids: Baker.

5.5 Jesus, the Pharisees, and the Conversion of the Jewish World

Golan Broshi

The main purpose of this article is to demonstrate how an internal Jewish debate, between the messianic movement and the rabbinic movement as it is portrayed in the Gospels, brought about—and literally created—two artificially distinct religions; namely, "Judaism" and "Christianity." In doing so, this chapter will focus on the "traditions" of the Pharisaic sect (Matt 15; Mark 7) and mainly on their missionary efforts to make converts (to proselytize), both of Jews and of Gentiles (Matt 23). As I seek to prove, this "conversion" was, and still is, the key for understanding how the rabbis became the gatekeepers of both the Jewish world and of Jewish identity (Shapira 2012).

The Two Judaisms

On the verge of the Second Temple's destruction, two relatively new Jewish movements were going to survive the inevitable calamities and revive the Jewish faith afresh (see Flusser 1980, 9–12). Judaism has not been "invented" yet, and many forms of "Judaisms" existed (Boyarin 2012, 4–5). With the destruction of the temple, most other sects were destined to disappear, leaving only two to remain standing. In place of the Sinai covenant that had its base in the priests, in the temple and in the sacrifices therein, a new covenant of some sort had to come about. These two Jewish movements came each with its own idea of a new covenant; and due to the absolute contrast between them, only one would keep its "Jewish" identity.

There are perhaps no other documents that portray the unadulterated power struggle and dichotomy between these two Jewish movements better than the writings of the New Testament (especially, the Gospels and Acts). On one corner of this spiritual rivalry stood the Pharisaic (soon to be rabbinic) tradition; on the other stood the messianic faith, with Rabbi Yeshua (Jesus) of Nazareth at its center. These two movements—or "sister theologies" and "two competing redemptive narratives," as Prof. Yuval (1996) referred to them—developed side-by-side in the first century in an attempt to continue the biblical faith and give religious hope amid the Roman occupation and the destruction of the temple (for a discussion on the Mishnah's studies being "as equivalent to performing temple-related rituals," see Cohen 2016, 330–31).

No wonder, then, that most of Jesus' disputes recorded in the Gospels are with the scribes and Pharisees. One of the harshest exhortations between the two parties is depicted in Mark 7:5–9, 13, where it is written:

> So the Pharisees and teachers of the law asked Jesus, "Why don't your disciples live according to the tradition of the elders instead of eating their food with defiled hands?" He replied, "Isaiah was right when he prophesied about you hypocrites; as it is written: 'These people honor me with their lips but their hearts are far from me. They worship me in vain; their teachings are merely human rules.' You have let go of the commands of God and are holding on to human traditions. . . . Thus you nullify the word of God by your tradition that you have handed down. And you do many things like that." (NIV)

Here, Jesus is drawing a complete and utter opposition between the traditions of the Pharisees and his teachings (i.e., the word of God). In describing the rabbis' traditions, Mark uses the Greek term *paradosin*, which literally means a handing down or over, an instruction—a tradition. Jesus' argument is particularly interesting compared with R. Akiva's saying: "Tradition is the fence of the Torah" (m. Abot 3:13) and especially against the backdrop of Abot 1.1:

> Moses received the Torah [i.e., the Oral Law] at Sinai and transmitted it to Joshua, Joshua to the elders, and the elders to the prophets, and the prophets to the Men of the Great Assembly.

Here, in this short but extremely bold statement, lies the heart of the debate between the two parties: the Pharisees claim their way is rooted way back, in Moses and the Torah (see, b. Ber. 34b); while the opposition—the disciples of Jesus—were in fact pressing the same claim (Matt 5:17; Luke 16:29–31; 24:27, 44; John 1:46; 5:46). In other words, both Jewish movements saw their spiritual mandate rooted in the Hebrew Bible; both acted as if they fulfill the natural (or supernatural) continuum of the Old Testament (Tanakh).

Both claims beg the question: which faith therefore truly continues the Tanakh? Hence, with a simple textual investigation, we can experiment and check which writings—the Mishnah or the Gospels—make a better extension to the Tanakh. Bible scholars (see Brin 2002, 260) believe that the Hebrew Scriptures end with the hope reflected in Malachi's prophecy:

> I will send my messenger, who will prepare the way before me. . . . See, I will send the prophet Elijah to you before that great and dreadful day of the Lord comes. He will turn the hearts of the parents to their children, and the hearts of the children to their parents; or else I will come and strike the land with total destruction. (Mal 1:1; 4:5–6)

The Tanakh ends with this hope. Therefore, we now need to compare the earliest literature of both Jewish movements and see which one continues this narrative. The most ancient piece of writings we possess from the rabbinic tradition is the Mishnah, dated between the second and third century CE (Bat-Em and Sharon 2011, 11). The Mishnah starts with tractate Berakot, so let us then examine whether it continues the biblical narrative that ended with Malachi:

> From when, that is, from what time, does one recite Shema in the evening? From the time when the priests enter to partake of their *teruma*. Until when does the time for the recitation of the evening Shema extend? Until the end of the first watch. The term used in the Torah (Deuteronomy 6:7) to indicate the time for the recitation of the evening Shema is *beshokhbekha*, when you lie down, which refers to the time in which individuals go to sleep. Therefore, the time for the recitation of Shema is the first portion of the night, when individuals typically prepare for sleep. That is the statement of Rabbi Eliezer. The Rabbis say: The time for the recitation of the evening Shema is until midnight. Rabban Gamliel says: One may recite Shema until dawn, indicating that *beshokhbekha* is to be understood as a reference to the entire time people sleep in their beds, the whole night. (m. Ber. 1.1)

This is how the earliest rabbinic writings start! Obviously, there is no contextual way to connect this passage to Malachi's prophecy. The Mishnah appears as a pure legal document that portraits discussions and debates among the rabbis concerning the right way to implement their traditions (Yuval 2011). Moreover, not only does the content have nothing to do with Malachi's narrative, but the entire genre (literary style) of the Mishnah is utterly foreign to the Bible (Neusner 1971). While the Mishnah is merely a legal document, the Tanakh is mainly a narrative (Chavel 2011, 227–28). Hence, when scholars compare the Mishnah to the Tanakh and to other contemporary Jewish writings, they are rightfully referring to it as an unprecedented revolutionary literature (Rosen-Tzvi 2018, 64; see also Henshke 1977).

Now let us move to the NT and see whether its writings attempt to continue Malachi's hope. Scholars believe that the Gospel of Mark was the first of the four to be written (Boyarin 2012, 105). In Mark 1:1–5 we read:

> The beginning of the gospel of Jesus Christ, the Son of God; As it is written in the prophets: "Behold, I send my messenger before thy face, which shall prepare thy way before thee. The voice of one crying in the wilderness, prepare ye the way of the Lord, make his paths straight." John did baptize in the wilderness, and preach the baptism of repentance for the remission of sins. And there went out unto him all the land of Judaea, and they of Jerusalem, and were all baptized of him in the river of Jordan, confessing their sins. (KJV)

Mark's attempt to continue the narrative of Malachi and present its fulfilment in the coming of the Messiah seems much more compelling than its counter religion: i.e., the Mishnah. Thus even from the start, we can already establish that considering the content and literary style, the New Testament provided by the messianic side is closer to Biblical Judaism than the rabbinic tradition. But even if the Pharisees were lacking biblical ground, they still had enough political and religious power to keep their momentum going strong, in their efforts to become the gatekeepers of the Jewish world (Levin 1996, 136–38).

Mission to Convert

It is important to note that both Judaisms (i.e., messianic and Pharisaic) attracted to their movements not only Jews but also God-fearing Gentiles. Although a few scholars claim that the rabbinic religion never had missionary ambitions (Brinker 2007, 11), in reality, Second Temple historians note that the Pharisees were devoted missionaries who made extreme efforts to proselytize and make countless converts from among the nations (see Bird 2010, 140–49; Feldman 1996, 344–46; Herr 1985, 15; see also the final chapter of the present book). In fact, ancient Roman historians also testify to this phenomenon (Isaac 2001; Rokah 1995). But perhaps the earliest Jewish mention of massive conversions appears in the Gospel of Mathew 23:15:

> "Woe to you, teachers of the law and Pharisees, you hypocrites! You travel over land and sea to win a single convert, and when you have succeeded, you make them twice as much a child of hell as you are."

Due to the Greek word used for "convert" (*prosēlyton*) and the historical context, some scholars have suggested that this verse refers to the rabbinic efforts to make new converts to their movement, not necessarily from the pagan world but from among the Jewish people themselves (Rokah 1995). Others (Bird 2010, 67–68; Vromen 2019, 76–77) describe the vast missionary efforts of the rabbis as a two-edged sword:

1. An in-house attempt, aimed at joining as many Jews as possible to their religious camp, by means of repentance (so called *Hazarah BiTshuva* in Hebrew).

2. An outer attempt to make converts, targeted at the Gentile world, by means of proselytization (so called *Giur* in Hebrew).

We can understand the Pharisees' effort to persuade as many Jews as they could to join their party and respect their authority, but why would they also go to the Gentiles—especially to the "God-fearers"—in an effort to "turn" them into Jews? Actually, this effort served two goals: first, as we mentioned earlier, the Jewish world at that time had several competing "Judaisms" (or sects) that had a political-religious desire to recruit as many members as possible to their ranks, and the Pharisees were by no means an exception. Second, the rabbis knew only too well that even though formal conversion (*Giur*) did not exist in the Bible (see Picard 2012, 115; Levin 1984, 238), by now this institution had become the gate by which one entered the Jewish world (Shapira 2012). Hence, if the rabbis governed the conversion institution, then they would possess control over Jewish identity; their tradition would detriment who is "Jewish" and who is not; who's in and who's out.

Now, we have reached the heart of the matter. Remember, after the destruction of the Second Temple, that mainly two Jewish movements remained standing:

Messianic Judaism and Rabbinic Judaism. Both had no need for a physical temple, for priests from the house of Levi, or for the sacrificial system. Both movements were based on faith—either faith in the teaching of the rabbi of the Gospels (Yeshua), or faith in the teachings of the rabbis of the Mishnah (the Tannaim). Each faith had a unique Jewish theology of its own, and each came with a different substitution for the temple sacrifices: according to Messianic Judaism, atonement and redemption come through the works of Messiah Jesus (Mark 10:45; John 3:15–18); according to Rabbinic Judaism, atonement comes through the works of the rabbis themselves, especially the "wise-disciples" among them who constantly study the Talmud (Midr. S. Eli. Zut. §1). These similarities between the two Judaisms, together with many others, made some scholars see them as "sister" religions, which developed side-by-side and bore obvious resemblances one to the other (Yuval 2011; Boyarin 2004).

One of the most vital parallels between the two movements—at least concerning this article—was the mandate to make disciples: Jesus encouraged his Jewish followers to become true disciples (John 8:31) and make disciples of all nations (Matt 28:19). The rabbis of the Mishnah did the same, elevating the status of the wise disciples ("Torah Scholars") above kings and the priests of Israel (Hor. 3.8) and commending their followers to "raise many disciples" (Abot 1.1). Making new disciples—or converts—to their own faith was therefore the hallmark of these to Judaism. But (and that is an important "but," for it contains the seed that brought forth "Judaism" and "Christianity" as we know them today) they differed on one important decision or question: What to do with "God-fearing" Gentiles who wish to join the faith? We can read about this dilemma in Acts 15:1–2:

> Certain people came down from Judea to Antioch and were teaching the believers: "Unless you are circumcised, according to the custom taught by Moses, you cannot be saved." This brought Paul and Barnabas into sharp dispute and debate with them. So Paul and Barnabas were appointed, along with some other believers, to go up to Jerusalem to see the apostles and elders about this question.

In other words, some messianic Jews from a Pharisaic background argued that the Gentiles who had embraced the messianic faith must "convert" through circumcision and become Jewish, thus keeping the law of Moses (i.e., the Torah). In accordance with their rabbis' saying (in Matt 23:15), the apostles in Jerusalem ruled against "converting" the Gentiles, meaning that people from othernations need not become Jewish when grafted into the faith (Acts 15:19–29). This resolution was no less than groundbreaking, considering the rabbinic position that mandated that anyone—Jew or Gentile—who joined their idea of Judaism must be circumcised and follow the Oral Torah (see Wechsler 2017). In fact, according to rabbinic law, a Gentile is forbidden to keep the Torah and could even face death if he does (see b. Sanh. 58b; Mishneh Torah, Kings and Wars 10.9).

Thus, on one hand, Messianic Judaism gave the foreigners who flocked to its gates the opportunity to remain Gentiles; on the other hand, Rabbinic Judaism demanded that Gentiles who joined to convert and "become" Jewish. Add to this the fact that messianic Jews suffered excommunication by the hands of the rabbis due to their loyalty to Jesus rather than supporting Bar-Kokhba (Siegal 2019, 5–16; Oppenheimer 2007, 47–48) and the end result was quite clear: inevitably, the messianic community grew more and more "Gentile," while the rabbinic movement grew rapidly but remained purely Jewish, thanks to intensive inner-proselytization of Jewish people and outer-missionary conversions of Gentiles (Malach 2019, 169). By the late second century CE, and moreover, after "Christianity" had become the official religion of Rome (see Zakai 2008, 54–55), there were already two distinct and opposing religions: "Judaism" (i.e., rabbinic tradition) and "Christianity" (i.e., messianic tradition) (Yuval 2003, 25–28). Indeed, it is hard to imagine all of this came about due to a "minor" decision not to convert the God-fearing Gentiles who came to faith in Messiah Jesus. One can only speculate how both of these first-century Judaisms might look if the apostles (in Acts 15) had decided differently (see Alexander 1999, 25). It is vital to remember that the rabbinic conversion of Gentiles was not merely theoretical, nor was it bound to the first century alone. On the contrary, it had significant religious, theological, and socially practical implications on the Jewish world for the next two millennia.

The Bible reveals a clear distinction between the ethnic people of Israel and their religion, so that even if Israel fails to keep the commandments of the Torah, they nevertheless remain "Jewish" (a particular people chosen by God). But with the idea of the rabbinic conversion came an astonishing reformation, according to which one can no longer separate his ethnicity from his religion. Furthermore, religion—or theology—can even determine a person's ethnic identity. The two are now interlinked in such a manner that if Israel fails to submit to the Oral traditions, their Jewish identity might be at risk. Rabbi Saadia Gaon's (tenth century CE) saying "Our nation is not a nation, but through the Torah" reflects the revolutionary shift from "ethnos"-based identity to "ethos"-based identity of Israel (as described by S. Cohen, 2001). This approach, which sees Judaism mainly as dependent on one specific theology or dogma, paved the way for the sages to gain religious and political control over the Jewish people (A. Cohen 2006, 130–38).

Rabbinic conversion, therefore, did not deal merely with proselytizing Gentiles; it literally converted the entire Jewish world. Yirmiahu Yovel (2007, 110) claims that these conversions, done by the sages toward Biblical Judaism, was so radical that one can see both religions as two completely distinct faiths. Yovel mentions some of the reformations done by the Pharisees:

- Unlike Biblical Judaism, which centered on the sacrificial system in the temple, the rabbinic religion is centered on learning the Talmud and praying from the Siddur.
- The temple was replaced by Beit-HaMidrash (the Yeshivah).
- The priests were replaced by the rabbis.
- The Written Torah was replaced by the Oral Torah.
- The authority to mediate the will of God to the masses and explain the Torah was taken from the priests and the prophets and put into the hands of the sages.

Prof. Amnon Shapira adds to these reforms the fact that the rabbis abolished the use of a "Voice from heaven" (*Bat Qol*), in favor of the use of the mind. They brought about a pluralistic and organic legal system, which can keep on developing according to the ever-changing circumstances. Also, they presented a totally new worldview of governing: unlike the priesthood or the royal system, which were transmitted from father to son, the rabbis adopted the Greek-philosophical model, according to which one can make one'sway up the social ladder by one's own merit—if one diligently studied the Talmud (Shapira 2015, 89). This model was nothing short of a complete and total revision, compared with the biblical norm; under the banner of Rabbinic Judaism, there were but two conditions for advancing up the ladder of hierarchy:

1. Being a man (not necessarily a Jew), for women were not allowed to study Talmud (Valler 2001, 14–15).

2. Studying in a recognized and authorized Yeshiva under ordained rabbis (Boyarin 2004, 301, 310–11).

These were the main keys to obtain honor, power, and wealth under the reformed system introduced to the Jewish world by the Pharisees. Of course, nepotism did not hurt either (e.g., b. B. Meṣ. 85a). As mentioned above, even a male Gentile could become a "Jewish" rabbi after undergoing conversion. In fact, many of the sages did not come from a Jewish background; they converted (or were sons of converts), like Shmaya and Avtalyon, Onkelos, R. Meir, and R. Akiva, to name a few. The rabbinic conversion was, therefore, a real and legal transformation to Judaism; so much so, that the Talmud describes the convert as a child who is born again—into Judaism (b. Yebam. 22a). His old ethnic background has passed, and he is no longer a foreigner but now possesses "Jewish" blood. As a matter of fact, once someone converts, rabbinic tradition claims that his soul was present at Mount Sinai when Moses gave the Torah; in other words, a Gentile who converts had a Jewish soul all along (Marx 2010, 289).

The Talmudic rabbis took their conversion so seriously, they actually believed that the former life of the convert was legally abolished once he completed the ceremony of *Giur*. Here are a few examples:

- If the firstborn is in a family converts, he is no longer entitled to inherit from his father because he is now Jewish and therefore not considered his father's son any longer (b. Yebam. 62a).

- Once a man with children has converted, it is considered to him as if he did not have children at all (b. Bek. 47a: "If a man had children when he was a gentile and he subsequently converted, . . . Rabbi Shimon ben Lakish says he has not fulfilled the mitzva to be fruitful and multiply. . . . [I]t is considered as though he did not have children").

- Maimonides ruled that a convert may even marry his own biological sister or mother (!) if they convert as well (Mishneh Torah, Forbidden Intercourse 14.12).

Indeed, the rabbinic conversion was real and held legal and practical implications. Thus when Jesus rebuked the rabbis for their conversion efforts, he did not merely attack this particular issue; rather, he undermined the bases upon which all of their tradition stood. The issue, therefore, did not only involve the "conversion" of Gentiles, but also—and more importantly—the conversion of Biblical Judaism into Rabbinic Judaism. Notice that both messianic and Rabbinic Judaisms were "missionary" movements, which had a goal to fill the void made by destruction of the temple with holy substance (Rokah 1995). They both used the Tanakh as their basis but differed on the right interpretation and purpose thereof. Perhaps there is no other issue clearer than the Sabbath, which demonstrates and highlights the gap between Yeshua and the Pharisees, concerning the true meaning of the Torah.

Breaking the Sabbath

It is not a mere happenstance, therefore, that many of Jesus' miraculous healings took place on the seventh day (Matt 12:10; Mark 3:2; Luke 6:6; 13:14; 14:1–4; John 5:16). It seems this was no coincidence but rather a setup. John 9 depicts such a case, where a man born blind was healed by Yeshua on the Sabbath, much to the detriment of the Pharisees:

> After saying this, he [Jesus] spit on the ground, made some mud with the saliva, and put it on the man's eyes. "Go," he told him, "wash in the Pool of Siloam" (this word means "Sent"). So the man went and washed, and came home seeing. . . . Now the day on which Jesus had made the mud and opened the man's eyes was a Sabbath. Therefore the Pharisees also asked him how he had received his sight. "He put mud on my eyes," the man replied, "and I washed, and now I see." Some of the Pharisees said, "This man is not from God, for he does not keep the Sabbath." But others asked, "How can a sinner perform such signs?" So they were divided. (John 9:6–7, 14–16)

This is not the only incident where Yeshua healed someone using spitting (see Mark 7:33; 8:22–25); in fact, healing this way was known throughout the ancient Jewish world. Some rabbinic midrashim document similar stories performed by rabbis, such as R. Meir (Lev. Rab. 9.9; see Weiss and Stav 2018, 26). But the Pharisees did not accuse Yeshua for breaking the Sabbath due to the act of spitting. That was not the case. Even in rabbinic tradition, spitting is not considered one of the thirty-nine works forbidden on the Sabbath (m. Šabb. 7.2). There is, however, a Talmudic debate whether healing should be considered as breaking the Sabbath. Surprisingly enough, Prof. Zeʿev Safrai concludes that by healing on the Sabbath, Jesus did not break rabbinic tradition (2020, 21–23). Instead, the problem concerned a couple of instances considered forbidden on the Sabbath:

1. Carrying "out an object from domain to domain" (m. Šabb. 7.2), as described in John 5:8–10:

Then Jesus said to him, "Get up! Pick up your mat and walk." At once the man was cured; he picked up his mat and walked. The day on which this took place was a Sabbath, and so the Jewish leaders said to the man who had been healed, "It is the Sabbath; the law forbids you to carry your mat."

2. Kneading water and sand together to make mud (Mishneh Torah, Sabbath 8.16[17]), as described in John 9:6:

[Jesus] spit on the ground, made some mud with the saliva, and put it on the man's eyes.

Assuming Jesus was familiar with this rabbinic tradition, why then did he deliberately choose to break it? David Brezis (2015, 368) argues that the answer involves the right religious priorities. Jesus valued *Pikuach-Nefesh* ("saving lives") more than he cared for keeping the traditions of men, or as he himself said, quoting Isa 29:13, "They worship me in vain; their teachings are merely human rules" (Mark 7:7). Brezis continues, saying that because this miracle took place on the Sabbath, "saving lives" and healing the blind man was the greater good and therefore overruled the traditions concerning keeping the Sabbath.

Moreover, the miracle happened on the feast of tabernacles (Sukkot), so opening the blind eyes (*'ayin*, in Hebrew) is connected to washing of the eyes in the Pool of Siloam. "Pool" and "eye" bear the same root in Hebrew. Thus when Jesus sends the blind man to wash his eye at that pool, he presents himself as the source of living water of the last days (John 7:37–38). Brezis ends his argument by pointing out that Jesus' approach to the Sabbath is not entirely different from some of the sages. After all, both Jesus and the Talmud say that "the Sabbath was made for man, not man for the Sabbath" (Mark 2:27; see b. Yoma 85b). And yet we see again that Brezis agrees with Safrai: when taken in the context of first-century Jewry, Jesus' actions and sayings are in accordance with at least some voices in the rabbinic camp. This means some of the Mishnah's sages themselves did not completely agree with certain parts of the rabbinic tradition (Sorek 2015, 215–23; Boyarin 2004, 307–9; Rosen-Zvi 2018, 63–64).

Conclusion

The confrontation documented in the Gospels between Jesus and the Pharisees was not merely a debate among two competing sects concerning the right applications of the law; rather, it demonstrated an ultimate collision between a claim for the uncompromised authority of the word of God against the traditional wisdom of men, or as Leo Strauss defined it, a dichotomy between two colliding worldviews: "Jerusalem" and "Athens"; between the "fear of God" and the "fear of men" (Rechnitzer 2012, 179–84). When Yeshua rebuked the rabbis for their practices, it was not just another heated discussion among colleagues in the yeshiva; this was a prophetic calling for repentance that would echo for centuries to come. The traditions of the Oral Law—and especially that of "conversion"—opened the door for a revision the kind of which the Jewish world had never before witnessed. Not only was Biblical Judaism about to face a total and extreme makeover, but the Jewish people as a whole were now coming under the authority of a rather small sect of six thousand men (see Flusser 1985, 1) for the next two millennia (Gafni 1997).

In Mark 7, Matt 23, and in fact all through the Gospels (see Luke 11; John 5, etc.), we witness reflections for the birthpains of both movements, especially when confronted by each other. Interestingly enough, under the unique circumstances of the first century, Messianic Judaism and Rabbinic Judaism were born as sister religions, baring parallel properties. Both had no need for a physical temple, priest, or animal sacrifice; their followers could worship anywhere in a congregational setting (i.e., synagogue/church). Both were missionary religions that focused on making disciples. Both had the Logos at their core: for messianic Jews, the Logos is the Messiah; for rabbinic Jews, the Logos is the Oral Torah (Boyarin 2011, 210–11). Both movements made communal teachings and written liturgy the focus of their religious expression. And both had a substitutional form of atonement in place of the temple sacrifices: messianic Jews claimed Jesus himself embodies their redemptive atonement; while rabbinic tradition argued that the "Wise-Disciples" themselves function as the atonement for Israel (S. Eli. Zut. §2). So clear were the resemblances and the interaction between the two faiths that Prof. Yuval dares to say that there would not have been Rabbinic Judaism if it wasn't for Messianic Judaism. In other words, he sees much of the Talmudic religion's aspects rooted deep in Messianic Judaism, or early "Christianity" as he refers to it (2011).

As was pointed out, though, there was one pivotal issue upon which the two movements took utterly different position: the way by which Gentiles were to join their faith. We have seen that both parties appeal to other Jews and non-Jews, especially "God-fearers." Nevertheless, while Jesus and his disciples were against the idea of "conversion" (Matt 23:15; Acts 15), the rabbis left no other option for Gentiles to join except through their own version of ordained conversion (Shapira 2012). Through the advent of "conversion," the rabbis could finally operate as the official gatekeepers of the new Jewish world, determining who can come in and who might be cast out (Kelner 2016, 37, 53). History teaches that this move, perhaps more than any other, contributed not merely to the total distinction and inevitable separation between the two religions, but to the reason why for almost two thousand years, Rabbinic Judaism has been considered "Jewish" while Messianic Judaism has been depicted as "Christian"—i.e., Gentile (see Yuval, 2003, 26–34).

Works Cited

All quotes from Rabbinic Literature (i.e., Oral Law) are taken from sefaria.org

Alexander, Philip S. 1999. "The Parting of the Ways." Pages 1–25 in *Jews and Christians*. Edited by James D. G. Dunn. Grand Rapids: Eerdmans.

Bat-Em, Ester, and Yehuda Sharon. 2011. *One Foot: The Development of the Oral Law* (Hebrew). Jerusalem: Ministry of Education.

Bird, Michael F. 2010. *Crossing over Sea and Land*. Peabody, MA: Hendrickson.

Boyarin, Daniel. 2011. *Intertextuality and Reading of Midrash* (Hebrew). New York: Shalom Hartman Institute.

————. 2012. *The Jewish Gospels: The Story of the Jewish Christ*. New York: The New Press.

————. 2004. In *Jews and Judaism in Israel at the Byzantine Era* (Hebrew). Edited by I. L. Levin. Tel-Aviv: Yad Itzhak Ben-Zvi.

Brezis, David. 2015. *Between Zealotry and Grace: Anti-Zealotic Trends in Rabbinic Thought* (Hebrew). Ramat Gan: Bar-Ilan University Press.

Brin, Gershon. 2002. In *Olam Ha-Tanach Encyclopedia: 12 Prophets* (Hebrew). Edited by Zeev Weisman. Tel-Aviv: Divrey HaYamim

Brinker, Menahem. 2007. *Israelis' Thoughts* (Hebrew). Tel-Aviv: Carmel.

Chavel, Simcha. 2011. In Vol. 1 of *Literature of the Hebrew Bible: Introductions and Studies* (Hebrew). Edited by Zipora Talshir. Israel: Yad Izhak Ben-Zvi Press.

Cohen, Akiva. 2016. *Mathew and the Mishnah*. WUNT 2 Reihe 418. Tübingen: Mohr Siebeck.

Cohen, Asher. 2006. *Jews and Non-Jews: Israeli Jewish Identity* (Hebrew). Jerusalem: Heartman Institution.

Cohen, Shaye J. D. 1999. *The Beginnings of Jewishness: Boundaries, Varieties, and Uncertainties*. Berkeley: University of California Press. See ch. 4.

Feldman, Louis Harry. 1996. *Israel in the Second Temple Period* (Hebrew). Tel-Aviv: Merkaz Zalman Shazar.

Flusser, David. 1985. *The Dead Sea Scrolls and the Essenes* (Hebrew). Jerusalem: Ministry of Defense Publications.

————. 1980. *Jewish Sources of Early Christianity* (Hebrew). Jerusalem: Ministry of Defense Publications.

Gafni, Isaiah. 1997. "Israel, Babel and Everything Between." Pages 213–42 in Vol. 3, 62 of *Zion*.

Henshke, David. 1977. *No Scripture Is Understood as a Pshat* (Hebrew). Pages 7–19 in Vol. 3, 17 of *HaMayan*.

Herr, Moshe David. 1985. *History of Israel in the Time of the Mishnah* (Hebrew). Jerusalem: Keter.

Isaac, Benjamin. 2001. "How the Romans Treated Jews and Judaism" (Hebrew). Pages 41–72 in Vol. 1 of *Zion*.

Kelner, Menachem. 2016. *Must a Jew Believe Anything?* (Hebrew). Jerusalem: Shalem.

Levin, Israel. 1984. *History of Israel at the Time of Rome* (Hebrew). Jerusalem: Keter.

————. 1996. "Jerusalem in Its Glory" (Hebrew). Pages 138–36 in *Ariel: A Magazine for the Knowledge the Land of Israel*.

Malach, Assaf. 2019. *From the Bible to the Jewish State* (Hebrew). Tel Aviv: Miskal.

Marx, Dalia. 2010. *When I Sleep and When I Wake*. Tel Aviv: Miskal.

Neusner, Jacob. 1971. "The Rabbinic Traditions about the Pharisees before A.D. 70: The Problem of Oral Transmission." *JJS* 22: 1–18.

Oppenheimer, Aharon. 2007. *The Bar-Kokhva Revolt* (Hebrew). Jerusalem: The Zalman Shazar Center.

Picard, Ariel. 2012. *Halacha in a New World* (Hebrew). New York: Shalom Hartman Institute.

Rechnitzer, Haim O. 2012. *Prophecy and the Perfect Political Order: The Political Theology of Leo Strauss*. Jerusalem: Bialik Institute.

Rokah, David. 1995. "Conversion in Antiquity" (Hebrew). Pages 135–52 in Vol. 2 of *HaMikra Veolamo: A Magazine for Research of the Bible and Its World*.

Rosen-Zvi, Ishai. 2018. *The Literature of the Sages in Israel* (Hebrew). Jerusalem: Yad Itzhak ben-Zvi.

Safrai, Ze'ev. 2020. *Mishnat Eretz Israel: Tractate Shabbat, with Historical and Sociological Commentary*. Mishnat Eretz Israel Project.

Shapira, Amnon. 2015. *Jewish Religious Anarchism* (Hebrew). Ariel: Ariel University Press.

Shapira, Jacob. 2012. The conversion in Israel and in Babel (Hebrew). Pages 267–301 in Vol. 27 of *Shnaton HaMispat HaIvri*.

Siegal, Michal bar-Asher. 2019. *Jewish-Christian Dialogues on Scripture in Late Antiquity: Heretic Narratives of the Babylonian Talmud*. Cambridge: Cambridge University Press.

Sorek, Yoav. 2015. *The Israeli Covenant* (Hebrew). Tel Aviv: Miskal.

Valler, Shulamit. 2001. *Women and Womanhood in the Stories of the Babylonian Talmud*. Israel: Hakibbutz Hameuchad.

Vromen, Ram. 2019. *The Secular Road* (Hebrew). Tel Aviv: Miskal.

Wechsler, Yoav. 2017. Rabbi Eliyahu Ben Amozag: The Universal Religion" (Hebrew). Pages 283–300 in *Daat: A Magazine for Jewish Philosophy and Kabbalah*.

Weiss, Haim, and Shira Stav. 2018. *The Return of the Missing Father: A New Reading of a Chain of Stories from the Babylonian Talmud* (Hebrew). Jerusalem: Bialik Institute.

Yovel, Yirmiahu. 2007. *New Jewish Times* (Hebrew). Tarbut Yehudit BeIdan Chiloni, Jerusalem: Lamda.

Yuval, Israel Jacob. 2011. "The Orality of Jewish Oral Law: From Pedagogy to Ideology." Pages 237–60 in *Judaism, Christianity, and Islam in the Course of History: Exchange and Conflicts*. Edited by Lothar Gall and Dietmar Willoweit. Munich: de Gruyter Oldenbourg.

———. 1996. *The Passover Haggadah and the Christian Easter* (Hebrew). Pages 5–28 in Vol. 1, 65 of *Tarbitz*.

———. 2006. *Two Nations in Your Womb: Perceptions of Jews and Christians in Late Antiquity and the Middle Ages*. Translated from the Hebrew by Barbara Harshav and Jonathan Chipman. (Originally published by Am Oved, 2003) Berkeley: University of California Press.

Zakai, Avihu. 2008. *History and Apocalypse: Religion and Historical Consciousness in Early Modern History in Europe and America*. Jerusalem: Bialik Institute.

5.6 Mission and Evangelism in the Gospels

Mark L. Strauss

At its heart, Christianity is a missionary religion, and the history of the church is the story of its growth and expansion in the world. Jesus' public ministry begins with the announcement, "The kingdom of God has come near. Repent and believe the good news!" (Mark 1:15). It ends with his commission to make disciples of all nations (Matt 28:18–20) and to take this message of salvation to the ends of the earth (Acts 1:8). In this article, we will briefly examine the question of the Jewish background to this missionary movement and how the theme of "mission" is developed in the theological and narrative purposes of the four Gospels and Acts.

Mission and Evangelism in Second Temple Judaism

The most significant and debated question with reference to the Jewish background of the church's mission is to what extent first-century Judaism was a missionary religion. Certain statements in the New Testament suggest that it was. In his pronouncement of "woes" against the scribes and Pharisees, Jesus says, "Woe to you, teachers of the law and Pharisees, you hypocrites! You travel over land and sea to win a single convert, and when you have succeeded, you make them twice as much a child of hell as you are" (Matt 23:15). Similarly, in Romans, Paul addresses his imaginary Jewish interlocutor as one who is "convinced that you are a guide for the blind, a light for those who are in the dark, an instructor of the foolish, a teacher of little children, because you have in the law the embodiment of knowledge and truth" (Rom 2:19–20). From a Jewish perspective, the Gentiles are blind and in darkness, foolish children for whom Jewish missionaries are bringing sight, light, wisdom, and maturity (Moo 1996, 162).

The older scholarly consensus was that Judaism was indeed a missionary religion in Jesus' day, and this set the stage for the missionary expansion of Christianity. This was the nearly unanimous claim of nineteenth- and early twentieth-century Protestant German scholarship. In 1926, Wilhelm Bousset wrote, "One cannot overrate the significance of the missionary activity of Judaism. It valiantly prepared the way for Christianity" (Schnabel 2004, 92). Similarly, the first sentence of Joachim Jeremias's classic little volume *Jesus' Promise to the Nations* reads "At the time of Jesus' appearance, an unparalleled period of missionary activity was in progress in Israel" (1982, 11). Jeremias claims that, although during its early history Israel was not actively engaged in mission, in the postexilic period and especially in the time of the Maccabees, an age of missions was launched. This movement was closely connected to the rise and development of the diaspora. When Jewish monotheism encountered the deep spiritual longing and void of the pagan world, it created intense interest among the Gentiles. Judaism's unique divinely revealed Scriptures, aniconic worship, and rigid intolerance of syncretism had special appeal to Gentiles searching for something greater than vacuous idolatry. "In short, it offered a form of divine worship towering far above all contemporary cults and systems of religion" (Jeremias 1982, 15). Proof of this flourishing of Jewish missions is the large number of proselytes and God-fearers connected with the synagogue found in literary, demographic, and inscriptional evidence (Feldman 1993, 288–341).

Yet, according to Jeremias, this missionary period was relatively short-lived in the larger context of Jewish history. Following the destruction of the temple in 70 CE and the sack of Jerusalem following the Bar-Kokhba revolt (132–135 CE), Jewish missionary activity declined. Competition with Christianity, which affirmed the same sacred Scriptures and monotheism but did not require the onerous practice of circumcision, rendered Jewish evangelism less appealing and less effective. The recognition of Christianity as the state religion and the enactment of laws forbidding conversion to Judaism further dampened Jewish evangelistic zeal, an attitude that continued through the rabbinic period and into the modern era. "Jesus thus came upon the scene in the midst of what was *par excellence* the missionary age of Jewish history" (Jeremias 1982, 12).

The roots of this missionary zeal were often traced to the prophetic vision of God's salvation for all nations, especially as found in Isaiah. G. F. Moore claimed that it was this theme of universal salvation of the nations that "led to efforts to convert the Gentiles to the worship of the one true God and to faith and obedience according to the revelation he had given, and made Judaism the first great missionary religion of the Mediterranean world" (1927, 1:323–24).

While this perspective of a flourishing Jewish mission in Jesus' time held the day for most of the twentieth century, much recent scholarship has challenged this notion, denying that Second Temple Judaism had a strong missionary vision. In his 1991 volume *A Light among the Gentiles: Jewish Missionary Activity in the Second Temple Period*, Scot McKnight concludes that, although Second Temple Jews often had friendly relations with Gentiles and accepted proselytes, it was never a missionary religion per se. While many Jews no doubt saw themselves as a "light to the Gentiles" and were pleased that Gentiles were attracted to that light, they did not set out to evangelize the Gentile world. McKnight claims that no firm conclusions can be drawn based on the large numbers of Jews spread throughout the world or from lists of significant proselytes. Population estimates are notoriously subjective, and we don't know the circumstances around the conversion of most proselytes. McKnight concludes that Jewish missionary zeal did not in any significant way set the stage for Christian missionary practice.

Other scholars have reached similar conclusions. Edouard Will and Claude Orrieux (1992) note that Matt 23:15, which has had a profound yet unwarranted impact on scholarship, is the only ancient statement to explicitly attribute a missionary impulse to (some) Jews. While it is undeniable that some Gentiles were attracted to Judaism, the existence of proselytes does not necessarily indicate *proselytism*. There are many factors that attracted Gentiles to Judaism. While some Jewish theology envisioned the eventual incorporation of Gentiles who submitted to the law, this universalism does not constitute a missionary movement (Will and Orrieux 1992, 60–80). Furthermore, the theme of universal salvation in writers like Philo is more apologetic than evangelistic, intended for an internal audience to affirm Jewish self-identity rather than to win converts (Will and Orrieux 1992, 81–89).

Martin Goodman's 1994 study, *Mission and Conversion: Proselytizing in the Religious History of the Roman Empire*, casts a wider net to include proselytizing in paganism and in early Christianity. His primary interest, however, is whether Judaism was a missionary religion. His conclusion is "no." While in the first century there were certainly attempts to gain Gentile sympathizers and an expectation that Gentiles would recognize the one true God in the eschatological age, there was no widespread impulse to draw Gentiles into the Jewish people in the present. Eckhard Schnabel (2004) reaches similar results. After a discussion of Jewish, Greco-Roman, and Christian sources, he concludes that in the century before and in the first centuries after Jesus, there was "no organized Jewish attempts to convert Gentiles to faith in Yahweh" (1:172).

All in all, there seems to be a growing consensus on several points: (1) There was great diversity in attitudes and actions in Second Temple Judaism concerning proselytes and proselytizing. (2) Many Gentiles were attracted to Judaism, resulting in large numbers of "God-fearers" and a lesser, though significant, number of proselytes. (3) Yet there was no widespread vision for evangelizing the world nor a significant movement to convert Gentiles to faith in Yahweh.

If early Christianity did not receive its missionary zeal from Second Temple Judaism, from where did it come? The most likely answer is from Jesus himself, who found motivation not primarily from his Jewish contemporaries but rather from his own sense of calling and from the Hebrew Scriptures. The evidence suggests that Jesus viewed himself as God's agent of eschatological salvation and that he instilled in his followers a vision to take this message of salvation to the people of Israel and to the ends of the earth.

Mission and Evangelism in Jesus' Ministry

Everything we know about the historical Jesus suggests he was a man on a mission (Schnabel 2004, 1:207–262) and that this mission concerned the restoration of Israel, the renewal of creation and salvation for the nations. The following characteristics can be attributed to the historical Jesus with a high degree of confidence.

1. Jesus' central message is universally recognized as the kingdom of God (Ladd 1993, 54). In the context of Second Temple Judaism, the coming kingdom/reign/dominion of God would be understood most commonly as the restoration of Israel and the concomitant renewal of creation predicted in the OT prophets and in apocalyptic Judaism (Wright 1992, 145–338).

2. Jesus described his message as the "good news" (*euangelion*) of the kingdom of God (Mark 1:14–15), a description with strong echoes of Isaiah's prophecies of eschatological renewal (Isa 2:2–5; 11:1–16; 40:1–11; 52:7; 61:1–11).

3. Jesus' ministry of preaching good news to the poor, healing the lame, giving sight to the blind, and making the deaf hear (Luke 7:22; Matt 11:4–5) clearly point to the Isaianic signs of eschatological salvation (Isa 29:18–19; 35:5–6; 61:1–2). The fact that Jesus called, trained, and then sent out a group of twelve disciples to replicate this ministry (Matt 10:7–8; Mark 6:7, 13; Luke 9:1–2) suggests that he viewed his mission as the restoration of the twelve tribes of Israel and a renewal of Israel's role as a light to the Gentiles (Isa 42:6; 49:6).

4. Jesus' favorite self-designation, "Son of Man," was almost certainly intended to evoke the eschatological vision of Dan 7:13–14, where "one like a son of man/human being" is given authority, glory, sovereign power, and an ever-

lasting kingdom, and "all nations and peoples of every language worship him" (cf. Mark 8:38; 13:26; 14:62).

5. Although Jesus focused his public ministry almost exclusively on the people of Israel, he affirmed implicitly and explicitly that God's intention was for this salvation to go to the Gentiles as well (Matt 8:11; 10:18; 21:43; 22:9; 24:14; Mark 13:10; Luke 14:15–24).

6. Jesus' repeated claims in the Synoptic Gospels that "I have come to" (Matt 5:17; 8:29; 10:35; Mark 1:24, 38; 2:17; Luke 12:49, 51) and that he was "sent" (Matt 10:40; 15:24; Mark 9:37; 12:6; Luke 4:18, 43; 10:16; cf. Mark 12:6; Luke 14:17) provides strong evidence *both* for Jesus' sense of mission and purpose as well as a claim to preexistence with the Father prior to his earthly ministry (Gathercole 2005, 113–89).

The New Testament documents reveal that Jesus' followers inherited his zeal for proclaiming the good news of salvation to all people everywhere. The letters of Paul certainly confirm that this "apostle to the Gentiles" (Rom 11:13) viewed his life's work as calling people to faith in Jesus and establishing evangelistic communities of faith. The New Testament narrative literature (the Gospels and Acts) demonstrate this same missionary purpose and goal.

While developing a detailed theology of mission for the four Gospels and Acts is well beyond the scope of this essay (see Bieder 1964; Hahn, 1981; Kertelge 1982; Larkin and Williams 1998; Köstenberger and O'Brien 2001; Schnabel 2013), in the discussion that follows we will suggest a primary missional focus for each of the four evangelists.

Mission and Evangelism in Matthew's Gospel

Pride of place in Gospel missional theology must go to the Great Commission in Matt 28:18–20, where Jesus commands his followers to make disciples of all nations. Yet, ironically, Matthew's Gospel also has the most exclusive-sounding statements from Jesus concerning the scope of his mission (Levine 1988; LaGrand 1995).

"I Was Sent Only to the Lost Sheep of Israel"

Only in Matthew's Gospel does Jesus explicitly focus his mission exclusively to the Jews. In the directives of Matt 10, Jesus instructs the Twelve:

"Do not go among the Gentiles or enter any town of the Samaritans. Go rather to the lost sheep of Israel. As you go, proclaim this message: 'The kingdom of heaven has come near.' Heal the sick, raise the dead, cleanse those who have leprosy, drive out demons." (Matt 10:5–8)

The features of this ministry—preaching the kingdom, healing the sick, and casting out demons—confirms that this is an extension of Jesus' own ministry, which was limited to the Jews. Though Mark (6:6–13, 30) and Luke (9:1–9) report the same mission of the Twelve, neither includes the injunction *not* to go to the Gentiles or to the Samaritans.

Matthew confirms this exclusion in the account of the Canaanite/Syrophoenician woman who begs Jesus to exorcise a demon from her daughter (Matt 15:21–28; Mark 7:24–30). While in both Matthew and Mark, Jesus insists that it is not right to take the bread of the "children" (= the Jews) and give it to the "dogs" (= the Gentiles), in Mark Jesus refuses the woman's request by saying, "*First* let the children eat all they want" (Mark 7:27), implying that the Gentiles may receive salvation blessings *after* the Jews. In Matthew, however, Jesus says more emphatically, "I was sent only to the lost sheep of Israel." It is of course significant that in both Gospels, Jesus ultimately grants the request to a Gentile. But Matthew's account—like his account of the mission of the Twelve—emphasizes the exclusion of the Gentiles, at least during the period of Jesus' public ministry.

"To the Jew First"

Of course, Matthew, like Mark and Luke, also has an inclusive vision of salvation. Although the Matthean Jesus does not command or initiate a mission to the Gentiles during his public ministry, he *anticipates* one in the future (Matt 8:11; 10:18; 21:43; 22:9; 24:14). But it is only *after* the resurrection that Jesus gives the Great Commission to make disciples "of all nations" (28:18–20).

Why is this? Some have accused Matthew of being a clumsy editor, who preserved contradictory traditions in 10:5 and 28:19. But this seems unlikely for a literary and theological artist of Matthew's abilities. More likely, Matthew, like Paul, sees an order of salvation (cf. Rom 1:16). It is to the Jew *first* and then to the Gentiles. There are a few likely reasons for this:

1. The salvation of the Jews confirms that God is faithful to his covenant promises to Israel. "The sending of the Messiah to the Jews, in fulfillment of the OT, is . . . a demonstration of God's love for his chosen people and proof that he is trustworthy: he fulfills his promises" (Davies and Allison 2004, 168).

2. The prophets consistently connect the salvation of the Gentiles with the dawn of the eschatological age (Isa 2:2, 4; 11:10; 42:1; 51:4–5; 56:7; 66:18, 20; Jer 3:17; Dan 7:14; Mic 4:2; Zeph 2:11; Zech 2:11; 8:22–23; Mal 1:11). It is not surprising, then, that the command to take the gospel to the nations begins only after the crucifixion and resurrection. These are eschatological events, which mark a key turning point in salvation history and the dawn of the new age (Meier 1976, 30–35).

3. As God's chosen people, Israel's role was to be a light to the Gentiles (Isa 42:6; 49:6; Luke 2:32; Acts 13:47). This means not just preserving the line of the Messiah but also being guardians and heralds of God's salvation (Rom 9:4). For this reason, the gospel must first be proclaimed to the covenant people Israel, *who would then take it* to the ends of the earth (cf. Rom 15:16).

Mission and Evangelism in Mark's Gospel

The Beginning of the Gospel

Mark's missionary interest surfaces in the first line of his Gospel: "The beginning of the good news about Jesus the Messiah, the Son of God" (1:1). The "good news" (*euangelion*) here refers not to a written volume or a literary genre, but rather to the oral proclamation of the message of the life, death, and resurrection of Jesus the Messiah that is spreading across the Roman world and giving birth to communities of faith like Mark's own. As Rudolf Pesch asserts, "The entire history of Jesus has become the content of the gospel. The entire book of Mark is a *missional book*" (Schnabel 2004, 2:1496).

This *euangelion* has its roots in the Hebrew Scriptures ("as it is written in Isaiah the prophet," 1:2), was testified to by the prophet John the Baptist (1:4–8), and concerns the arrival of "the kingdom of God" (1:15). The necessary response to join this community of faith is repentance from sin and belief in the good news that the kingdom has come near in the person of Jesus the Messiah (1:1, 9–15).

While Mark's Gospel has much in common literarily with the Greco-Roman *bioi* ("lives" = biographies) of his time (Burridge 2020), his purpose goes well beyond theirs of extolling the virtues and accomplishments of famous men. Mark draws from deep roots of Jewish prophetic and apocalyptic literature to present the coming of Jesus as the eschatological climax of human history, the turn of eras from the age of promise to the age of fulfillment (Yarbro Collins 2007, 42–44). His purpose is not just to entertain his readers and honor a great man of the past, but to call them to radical faith and allegiance to Jesus as the living Lord of the church.

The Mission of the Suffering Messiah

Mark's central theological purpose is christological and the whole Gospel stands under the shadow of the cross. How could anyone justify allegiance to a man who suffered the ignominious shame of Roman crucifixion? Mark's narrative response is twofold. The first half of the Gospel (1:1–8:30) demonstrates that Jesus is indeed the mighty Messiah and Son of God. Jesus heals the sick, casts out demons, raises the dead, and commands nature. When we get to the midpoint, Jesus asks the disciples who people say that he is and then, who *they* say he is. Peter answers for the rest: "You are the Messiah!" (8:29). Peter's answer is right, but Jesus then shockingly redefines the role of the Messiah: "He then began to teach them that the Son of Man must suffer many things and be rejected by the elders, the chief priests and the teachers of the law, and that he must be killed and after three days rise again" (8:31). This is the first of three "passion predictions" (9:31; 10:33–34) that mark out the second half of the Gospel, as Jesus begins his journey on the way to the cross (8:31–15:47) (Strauss 2014).

Robert Gundry has correctly identified Mark's Gospel as "an apology for the cross" (Gundry 1993, 3–4). Mark's whole Gospel is a narrative defense that the crucifixion did not negate the claim that Jesus is the Messiah and Son of God, but rather confirmed it. All along it was God's purpose for the Messiah to accomplish salvation by suffering as an atoning sacrifice for sins (10:45). The tearing of the temple curtain and acclamation of the centurion at the cross "Surely this man was the Son of God" (15:38–39)—sparked when he "saw how he died"—form an *inclusio* with the tearing open of the heavens at Jesus' baptism and the acclamation of the Father, "You are my Son, whom I love; with you I am well pleased" (1:10–11). The centurion's climactic cry confirms that *through his death* Jesus fulfills the role of the messianic Son of God.

Mission as Discipleship: "Follow Me"

If the mission of the Messiah is to call people to repentance and faith in the kingdom of God inaugurated through his life, death, and resurrection, then the method by which this mission is accomplished is discipleship. From the beginning, the disciples play a key role in Mark's narrative theology (Best 1981; Strauss 2019, 27–28). The first thing Jesus does is to call four fishermen to be his disciples (1:16–20). He then appoints the Twelve, "that they might be with him and that he might send them out to preach and to have authority to drive out demons" (3:14–15). These Twelve—representing the restored twelve tribes of Israel—are "apostles" or messengers whose mission replicates and expands Jesus' own. He commissions them and sends them out to do what he has been doing (6:12–13). To be his disciple, they must walk in his footsteps, denying themselves and taking up their cross and following him (8:34) through suffering and death to victory.

It is no surprise that the only explicit reference to the worldwide mission in Mark—"And the gospel must first be preached to all nations" (13:10)—is framed on either side by warnings about the persecution and suffering his disciples must endure (13:9, 11–13). The way of Jesus is the way of the cross, and the mission of the church will be accomplished through the faithful discipleship of the suffering people of God.

Mission and Evangelism in Luke-Acts

While the propagation of the gospel through the mission of the church is a key theme in all four Gospels, in Luke's writings it becomes *the* controlling narrative motif. This is obvious on the face of it, since only Luke produces a second volume that is meant to narrate the missionary expansion of the church following the ascension of Jesus. Here we will deal with two main sub-themes of Luke's theology of mission: (1) the worldwide scope of the gospel, and (2) the geographical and ethnic movement that characterizes its progress.

The Worldwide Scope of the Gospel

As we have seen, in Matthew's Gospel, Jesus' command to take the gospel to all nations does not come until after Jesus' resurrection. Prior to that, he explicitly limits his mission to the "lost sheep of his Israel." While Mark does not insist on this same exclusion, and in fact provides several positive encounters between Jesus and Gentiles, nevertheless there is no intentional or concerted ministry to Gentiles in Mark's Gospel. Only in the apostolic period will the gospel be preached to all nations (Mark 13:10). The same could be said of Luke's Gospel. It is not until the Cornelius episode in Acts 10–11 that the church comes to grips with the mandate that God's salvation available through Jesus the Messiah is to be offered to Gentiles. Yet while the mission itself is not launched until Acts, almost from the beginning the author makes it clear that God's *intention* is for the gospel to go to all nations. Here is some of the evidence for this:

1. Already in Luke's birth narrative, the author signals that the gospel will go to the Gentiles. The prophet Simeon meets Joseph and Mary in the Jerusalem temple and announces that Jesus will not only be "the glory of your people Israel," but also "a light for revelation to the Gentiles" (Luke 2:32, alluding to Isa 42:6; 49:6; cf. Acts 13:47).

2. In his quotation of the prophecy of Isa 40 about John the Baptist as the "voice of one calling in the wilderness," only Luke extends the quote from Isa 40 to verse 5. The purpose, no doubt, is to get to the crucial line, "And all people will see God's salvation" (Isa 40:5; Luke 3:6).

3. While Matthew's genealogy runs from Abraham to Jesus in order to stress the fulfillment of God's covenant promises to Israel, Luke's genealogy extends all the way back to Adam, the father of the human race, in order to stress the universal scope of Jesus' mission (Luke 3:23–38).

4. In Jesus' Nazareth Sermon (Luke 4:14–30), which Luke highlights by moving forward from a later place in Mark's Gospel (Mark 6:1–6), Jesus foreshadows both the rejection by his own people and the extension of salvation blessings to the Gentiles. Jesus reads the account of the eschatological year of Jubilee predicted in Isa 61:1–2 and announces, "Today this Scripture is fulfilled in your hearing" (Luke 4:21). The people respond favorably to this announcement but then turn violent when Jesus illustrates his message by citing examples from the Hebrew Scriptures of how God has blessed *Gentiles* (4:25–27). Jesus' message of good news to the outsiders and oppressed within Israel here expands to include the ultimate outsiders—the Gentiles.

5. Luke describes Jesus' healing of a Roman centurion's servant (7:1–10; cf. Matt 8:5–13). When the centurion expresses faith that Jesus can heal the man with a command even from a distance, Jesus pronounces, "I tell you, I have not found such great faith even in Israel" (Luke 7:9). Again, the mission to the Gentiles is foreshadowed.

6. Many of Jesus' parables in Luke concern the theme of reversal and God's love for the outsider (7:41–47; 10:25–37; 15:3–32; 16:19–31; 18:1–14). In the book of Acts, it become clear that the ultimate outsiders are the Gentiles. This is foreshadowed especially in the parable of the great banquet (Luke 14:15–24),

where the invitation first extended to "the poor, the crippled, the blind and the lame" (outsiders in Israel) is subsequently extended to "the roads and the country lanes" (14:23). In Luke's narrative design, this extension almost certainly points to the mission to the Gentiles in Acts.

Mission as Geographical and Ethnic Expansion

It is widely acknowledged that the book of Acts represents the progress of the gospel outward in concentric circles from its Jewish roots in Jerusalem, to Judea, to Samaria and to the ends of the earth (Acts 1:8). Despite many obstacles, the gospel advances relentlessly from Jerusalem to the ends of the earth, confirming that the Spirit-guided and Spirit-empowered church represents the true people of God in the present age (Acts 5:38–39). Beside this geographical movement is an ethnic one as the gospel is proclaimed to Jews, to Samaritans, and then to Gentiles.

This movement or journey motif is already present in Luke's Gospel. Luke greatly expands Jesus' brief journey to Jerusalem in Mark (10:32–52) into a "travel narrative," an entire phase of Jesus' ministry (Luke 9:51–19:27). After the transfiguration, Jesus "sets his face" toward Jerusalem (9:51) and for ten chapters travels with Jerusalem in his sights. While Jesus travels from place-to-place rather than in a linear fashion, Luke repeatedly notes his Jerusalem goal (9:51–56; 13:22, 33; 17:11; 18:31; 19:11, 28, 41; cf. 19:45). In short, while this is not a straight-line trip to Jerusalem, it is a theological journey to the cross, a period of heightened awareness and resolve by Jesus to fulfill his messianic mission.

When this journey motif *to Jerusalem* is combined with the missionary movement outward *from Jerusalem* in the book of Acts, a coherent ethno-geographic theology emerges:

> The whole of Luke-Acts can be viewed as a symbolic journey having Jerusalem as its center point. In the Gospel Jesus journeys toward Jerusalem, which represents the promise of salvation found in the old covenant. At the climax and center point, salvation is achieved through Jesus' life, death, resurrection, and ascension. The message of salvation now goes forth from Jerusalem to the ends of the earth (24:47; Acts 1:8). Luke's Gospel represents *salvation achieved*; the book of Acts, *salvation announced*. (Strauss 2018, 8)

Evangelism and Mission in John's Gospel

No book in the New Testament has a statement of purpose as expressly missional and evangelistic as the Gospel of John. The author concludes the main body of the book (before the epilogue) by noting that:

> Jesus performed many other signs in the presence of his disciples, which are not recorded in this book. But these are written that you may believe that Jesus is the Messiah, the Son of God, and that by believing you may have life in his name. (John 20:31)

Despite the apparent clarity of this statement, scholars debate its exact intent and whether the book is primarily written for the purpose of evangelism or for assurance to those who already believe. Many scholars assert the latter. Raymond Brown writes, "This is a Gospel designed to root the believer deeper in his faith. The stated purpose of the Gospel in 20:31 is probably not primarily missionary, and a good case can be made for understanding this verse in the sense of the reader's continuing to have faith that Jesus is the Messiah, the Son of God" (1974, lxxviii; cf. Schnackenburg 1982, 217; Conzelmann 1969, 332).

Others, however, assert an evangelistic purpose for the book; that is, calling unbelievers to faith. Some claim it was directed toward non-Christian readers in the Greco-Roman world (Dodd 1953, 9). Others claim a more specific audience of diaspora Jews and proselytes (Bornhäuser 1928). Still others suggest it is directed, at least in part, to a Samaritan audience (Bowman 1958; Freed 1970).

Whether the Gospel is primarily a missional or a community document is not an either/or option. The Gospel was likely written in and for a Christian community but with an eye on evangelism. As Schnabel writes, "The promotion of the faith of Christians through an exposition of the nature and the 'work' of Jesus always implies a missionary component. And the active propagation of faith in Jesus Christ among unbelievers always strengthens the faith of Christians" (2004, 2:1503; cf. Okure 1988)

Whatever the precise intent of John 20:31, there is no doubt that John's fundamental purpose is missional in the sense of a narrative expression of God's salvation purpose for the world: "John's entire gospel is pervaded by this divine mission: God, the Father, in love sending Jesus, his Son, to save all those who believe in him for eternal life" (Köstenberger 2009, 539).

Mission and Christology: The Sending of the Preexistent Son

When we think of "mission" in the Synoptics, our emphasis lies on Jesus' announcement of the kingdom of God and the inauguration of that kingdom through his life, death, and resurrection. The church's mission is to proclaim this message of salvation to the ends of the earth. For John, by contrast, the primary missional emphasis is on the *sending of the Son by the Father to bring eternal life to a lost world*.

John loves using synonyms for stylistic variation, and two Greek verbs for "send" occur with almost equal frequency in the Gospel, *pempō* (31x) and *apostellō* (27x). Jesus speaks of "the one who sent me/him" (*ho pempsōn me/auton*: 4:34; 5:24, 30; 6:38, 39; 7:16, 18, 28, 33; 8:26, 29; 9:4; 12:44, 45; 13:20; 15:21; 16:5), "the Father who sent me/him" (*ho pempsas me/auton patēr*: 5:23, 37; 6:44; 8:16, 18; 12:49; 14:24; *ho patēr me/him apestalken*: 5:36; 6:57; 10:36; 11:42; 20:21), and "God sent the Son/me" (*apesteilen ho theos ton huion/me*: 3:17, 34; 6:29; 8:42). The emphasis throughout is on the mission of the Father through the Son.

Jesus does speak of sending the disciples into the world. Following his Farewell Discourse (chs. 13–16), Jesus prays to the Father, "As you sent me into the world, I have sent them into the world" (17:18). Then, when he appears to the disciples after the resurrection, he commissions them, "As the Father has sent me, so I am sending you" (20:21). These references are important and confirm that the disciples will have a mission to the world following the resurrection, when the Father and the Son will send the Spirit to guide and teach them (14:26; 15:26; 16:7). At that time, is will be necessary for the disciples to "abide" in the Son so that they can bear good fruit (15:4–7).

But these references to the Son sending the disciples are dwarfed by the more than thirty references to the Father sending the Son. This is because John's central theme is *not* the mission of the church in the world. It is the self-revelation of the Father through the Son. God's mission to the world is achieved when the Son reveals the Father, provoking faith in him resulting in eternal life. Salvation in John's Gospel is not achieved by joining a religious movement or through religious rituals, but by coming to know the Father through the Son. "Now this is eternal life: that they know you, the only true God, and Jesus Christ, whom you have sent" (John 17:3).

Conclusion

The theme of mission in the Gospels reflects a balance of unity and diversity common to so many New Testament themes. In one sense, it is a unifying thread that runs throughout the New Testament. By its very nature, the gospel is the ultimate "good news" to be shared with all people.

At the same time, each evangelist provides a unique perspective on mission theology. For Matthew, the mission to the Gentiles is imperative because God's promises to Israel have been fulfilled. The righteous remnant of Israel must now fulfill its role as a light to the Gentiles by making disciples of all nations (Matt 28:18–20). For Mark, mission means especially Jesus' followers taking up their crosses and following the suffering role of Jesus, the Servant of the Lord, who gave his life as an atoning sacrifice for sins (Mark 8:34; 10:45). For Luke, the unstoppable progress of the gospel from Jerusalem to the ends of the earth is confirmation that Jesus is the Messiah and that the church made up of Jews and Gentiles represents the people of God in the present age (Luke 1:1–4; Acts 1:8). Finally, for John the central "mission" of the Bible is that God sent his Son as the incarnate Word, his self-revelation, so that those who believe in him might come into a relationship with the Father and receive eternal life. As the Father sent the Son, so now the Son sends his disciples empowered and directed by the Spirit to bring this message of salvation to the lost people of the world (John 3:16; 20:21).

Works Cited

Best, Ernest. 1981. *Following Jesus: Discipleship in the Gospel of Mark*. JSNTSup 4. Sheffield: JSOT Press.

Bieder, Werner. 1964. *Gottes Sendung und der missionarische Auftrag der Kirche nach Matthäus, Lukas, Paulus und Johannes*. ThSt 82. Zollikon-Zürich: Evangelischer Verlag.

Bornhäuser, Karl B. 1928. *Das Johannesevangelium, eine Missionsschrift für Israel*. BFCT 2.15. Gütersloh: Bertelsmann.

Bowman, John. 1958. "The Fourth Gospel and the Samaritans." *BJRL* 40: 298–308.

Brown, Raymond E. 1974. *The Gospel According to John I-XII.* AYB 29. New Haven: Yale University Press.

Burridge, Richard. 2020. *What Are the Gospels? A Comparison with Greco-Roman Biography. Twenty-fifth Anniversary Edition.* Waco, TX: Baylor University Press.

Conzelmann, Hans. 1969. *An Outline of the Theology of the New Testament.* London: SCM.

Davies, W. D., and Dale C. Allison, Jr. 2004. *Matthew 19–28.* Vol. 3 of *A Critical and Exegetical Commentary on the Gospel According to Saint Matthew.* ICC. London: T&T Clark.

Dodd, C. H. 1953. *The Interpretation of the Fourth Gospel.* Cambridge: Cambridge University Press.

Feldman, L. H. 1993. *Jew and Gentile in the Ancient World: Attitudes and Interactions from Alexander to Justinian.* Princeton: Princeton University Press.

Freed, Edwin D. 1970. "Did John Write His Gospel Partly to Win Samaritan Converts?" *NovT* 12: 141–46.

Goodman, Martin. 1994. *Mission and Conversion: Proselytizing in the Religious History of the Roman Empire.* Oxford: Clarendon Press.

Gundry Robert H. 1993. *Mark. A Commentary on His Apology for the Cross.* Grand Rapids: Eerdmans.

Hahn, Ferdinand. 1981. *Mission in the New Testament.* SBT 47. London: SCM.

Jeremias, Joachim. 1982. *Jesus' Promise to the Nations.* Philadelphia: Fortress.

Kertelge, Karl, ed. *Mission im Neuen Testament.* QD 93. Freiberg: Herder.

Köstenberger, Andreas J. 2009. *A Theology of John's Gospel and Letters.* Grand Rapids: Zondervan.

Köstenberger, Andreas J., and Peter T. O'Brien. 2001. *Salvation to the Ends of the Earth: A Biblical Theology of Mission.* NSBT 11. Downers Grove, IL: InterVarsity Press.

Ladd, George E. 1993. *A Theology of the New Testament.* Rev. ed. Grand Rapids: Eerdmans.

LaGrand, James. 1995. *The Earliest Christian Mission to "All Nations": In the Light of Matthew's Gospel.* Grand Rapids: Eerdmans.

Larkin, William J., and Joel F. Williams, eds. 1998. *Mission in the New Testament: An Evangelical Approach.* ASMS 27. New York: Orbis.

Levine, Amy-Jill. 1988. *The Social and Ethnic Dimensions of Matthean Salvation History: "Go Nowhere among the Gentiles."* Lewiston, NY: Mellen.

McKnight, Scot. 1991. *A Light among the Gentiles: Jewish Missionary Activity in the Second Temple Period.* Minneapolis, MN: Fortress Press.

———. 2000. "Proselytism and Godfearers." Pages 835–47 in *DNTB.*

Meier, John P. 1976. *Law and History in Matthew's Gospel.* AnBib 71. Rome.

Moo, Douglas J. 1996. *The Epistle to the Romans.* NICNT. Grand Rapids: Eerdmans.

Moore, G. F. 1927–30. *Judaism in the First Centuries of the Christian Era: The Age of the Tannaim.* 3 vols. Cambridge: Harvard University Press.

Okure, Teresa. 1988. *The Johannine Approach to Mission: A Contextual Study of John 4.1–42.* WUNT 2.31. Tübingen: Mohr-Siebeck.

Schnabel, Eckhard J. 2004. *Early Christian Mission. Volume One: Jesus and the Twelve: Volume Two: Jesus and the Twelve.* Downers Grove, IL: InterVarsity Press.

————. 2013. "Mission." Pages 604–10 in *DJG*.

Schnackenburg, Rudolf. 1982. *The Gospel According to St. John*. Vol. 3. London: Burns & Oates.

Strauss, Mark L. 2014. *Mark*. ZECNT. Grand Rapids: Zondervan.

————. 2019. "To Serve, Not to Be Served: Discipleship in Mark's Gospel." Pages 27–40 in *Following Jesus Christ: The New Testament Message of Discipleship for Today*. Edited by J. K. Goodrich and M. L. Strauss. Grand Rapids: Kregel.

————. 2018. "Typological Geography and the Progress of the Gospel in Acts (Acts 1:8, 27:1–28:16; 28:30–31)." Pages 1–18 in *Lexham Geographic Commentary on Acts through Revelation*. Edited by B. J. Beitzel, J. Parks, and D. Mangum. Bellingham, WA: Lexham Press.

Will, Edouard, and Claude Orrieux. 1992. *"Prosélytisme juif"? Histoire d'une erreur*. Paris: Les Belles Lettres.

Wright, N. T. 1992. *The New Testament People of God*. Minneapolis, MN: Fortress Press.

Yarbro Collins, Adela. 2007. *Mark: A Commentary*. Hermeneia. Minneapolis, MN: Fortress Press.

Index of Modern Authors

Index of Ancient Sources

8:15 198
9:12 159
10:33 90
13:17 121
13:29 121
15:40 45
19:11–13 140
23 106
23:18–24 107
23:19 190
23:22 107
23:24 107
24 106
24:5–9 319
24:8 106–8
24:9 107
24:17–19 319
24:17 107
27:16–17 78
27:17 88
28:9–10 60
30:2 54
35 254
35:16–21 254
35:30–32 254
35:31 198
35:33–34 260
35:33 254
35:34 254–55

Deuteronomy
1:7 121
1:19 121
2:37–38 218
3:27 87
4:2–3 218
4:6 320
4:25 218
4:27–30 224
4:30 218, 320
4:32 218
4:34 218
5:14 193
5:16–20 55
5:16 55
5:17 54
5:18 54
6:4–5 268
6:4 203
6:5 55
6:13 54
6:16 54, 87
6:26 218
8:3 54, 87
9:9 87
10:18 268
16:13–15 160
18 170
18:15–22 164–65, 170
18:15–19 319
18:15–18 141
18:15 61, 78, 166–67, 169
18:18–19 164, 277
18:18 61, 169

19:15 55
19:21 54
21:6–8 254
21:6–7 255
21:9 255
21:21–23 81
21:23 75, 255
22:6–7 50
24:1 44, 54–55
24:19 45
25:4 321
25:5 55
27:25 255
28 271
28:15–30:2 218
28:47–52 220
28:56–61 140
28:59–68 220
29 77–78
29:1–4 77–78
29:11–30 271
30:1–14 85
30:1–6 221
30:1–5 224
30:3–9 218
30:6 320
30:10 224
30:11–20 270
30:15–20 84, 221
31:1 84
31:16–21 85
31:23 61
31:24 84
31:29 85, 320
32:1–43 85
32:8 190
32:16–17 242
32:39 208
32:45 84
34:1–4 87
34:9 88, 90
34:10 319

Joshua
1:5–7 90
1:5 61
1:7 61
1:16–17 61
3:8 142
3:13 142
3:15–17 142
4:7 86
5:1 86
13:27 123
15:1 230
16:1 230
17:1 230
22:2 61

Judges
6:22 145
6:37 230
11:27 209
13:5–7 56–57

13:5 54
13:7 54
13:22 145
21:19 160

1 Samuel
2:1–10 134
2:1 134
15:27 140
16:14–23 242
16:14 212
18:10 242
18:14–30 165
19:9 242
21:1–6 60

2 Samuel
5:2 150
7 132, 164, 231
7:7 150
7:9 132
7:11–16 218
7:12–14 200
7:12–16 128, 164, 193
7:13 132
7:14 132, 194
7:16 107, 132, 231
22:8 181
24:15–17 242

1 Kings
2:27 56
3–10 230
4:25 143
8:15 56
10:8 87
13:4 141
17:17–24 140, 145, 168
17:18 145
17:23 145
19:2–3 196
19:10 196
19:11–13 184
19:14 196

2 Kings
4:32–37 140
4:42–44 141
4:44 142
5:10–13 146
11:40 106
15:29 118
18:31 143
21:14 256
21:16 256
24:2–4 256
25:25–26 106

1 Chronicles
16:22 148
16:33 209
17:13–14 218, 220
17:13 200
17:14 217

21 241
28:5 217
29:11–13 9
29:11 9

2 Chronicles
6:14–15 56
7:1 272
24:20–22 258
24:21 258
24:25 258
36:5 256
36:21 56

Job
1–2 242
9:8 142
25:6 191
28 96–97
38:8–11 139
42:5 145

Psalms
2 68, 205, 209
2:1–2 70
2:2 200
2:7 194, 200, 220
3:5 139
4:8 139
7 267
7:8–9 267
7:11 267
8 192, 218
8:2 60
8:3 55
8:4–6 192
8:4 190–92
11:4 190
16 205
16:8–11 68
18:12–13 199
22 194
22:1 56
22:15 80
22:18 76, 80
24:1–2 217
24:8 218
33:13 190
33:21 159
34:20 76, 80
35:10 268
35:19 76, 79–80
37:9 221
37:11 221
37:18 221
37:22 221
37:29 221
37:34 221
37:37 221
41:9 76, 79–80, 199
47 217
51:13 212–13
65:7 139
69 194

1 Clement
13:1–2 34
13:2 33
27:5 34
30:3 34
40:8 35
46:7–8 35

2 Clement
3:1–2 37
4:2 37

Clement of Alexandria

Paedagogus
1.2 11

Stromateis
6.6 39
6.6.47–48 182
6.14 11

Pseudo-Clement

Recognitions
1.41 184

Cyril of Jerusalem

Catechetical Lectures
14 10

Didache
1–7 31
1–6 35
1:2 31
1:5 31
3:7 31
6:2 31
8:2 31

Epiphanius

Panarion
30.3.7 10
76.5 7

Epistle of Barnabas
4.14 36
5.12 36
7.3 36
7.5 36

Eusebius

Historia ecclesiastica
3.25.1–7 7

3.29.17 116
3.39.16 10
4.28–29 33
5.8.2–8 7
5.25.3–14 7
6.25.3 82

Vita Constantini
iv.35–37 7

Gospel of Thomas
§3 14
§8 32
§14 14
§57 32

Ignatius

Ephesians
5.2 33
14.2 33
19.2–3 32

Magnesians
9.2 181–82

Philadelphians
3.1 33
5.2–9.2 32

Polycarp
2.2 32

Smyrnaeans
1.1 32

Trallians
11.1 33

Irenaeus

Haereses
1 37
1.28.1 33
3 38
3.1.1 10
3.9.1 38
3.9.3 38
3.11 38
3.11.8 38
3.14.3 11
3.21.1 38

Jerome

Commentariorum in Isaiam
3 181

Commentariorum in Mattheum
4 181
12:13 10

Epistulae
18 181
46 181
53 7
120 181

De viris illustribus
3 10

John Chrysostom

Homiliae in Matthaeum
86.2 39

Julius Africanus

Chronographia
Frag. 93 182

Justin Martyr

1 Apologia
15.1 36
15.2 36
15.3 36
15.12 36
15.13 36
33.1 37–38

Dialogus cum Tryphone
10.2 37
17.4 37
18.1 37
33.1 38
78.2 37
89.2 75
90.1 75
106.3 11
108 188

Martyrdom of Polycarp
1.1 33

Origen

Commentarii in evangelium Joannis
2.7 11
6.41 117
19.16 182

Contra Celsum
1.32 128
2.11–12 79
2.20 79

De principiis
3.1.7 11
3.1.16 11

Polycarp

Philippians
2.3 33
7.2 33

Shepherd of Hermas

Mandates
4.1.1 35
5.1–2 35
6.2 35
6.2.4 35
12.1–3 35

Similitudes
3.3 35
9.13.2 35
15.2 35

Visions
1.1.18 35

Tertullian

Adversus Judaeos
13 182
13.15 181

De praescriptione haereticorum
7.10 274

Theodoret

Haereticarum fabularum compendium
i.20 17

Theophilus

To Autolycus
3.14 34